THE ROAD FROM MONT PÈLERIN

The Making of the Neoliberal Thought Collective

EDITED BY

Philip Mirowski

Dieter Plehwe

HARVARD UNIVERSITY PRESS

Cambridge, Massachusetts

London, England

2009

Library of Congress Cataloging-in-Publication Data

The road from Mont Pèlerin : the making of the neoliberal thought collective /
edited by Philip Mirowski and Dieter Plehwe.

p.   cm.

Includes index.

ISBN 978-0-674-03318-4 (cloth: alk. paper)

1. Neoliberalism.   2. Neoliberalism—Case studies.   I. Mirowski, Philip,
1951–   II. Plehwe, Dieter.

JC574.R63   2009

320.51—dc22   2008039929

THE ROAD FROM MONT PÈLERIN

Contents

THE ROAD FROM MONT PÈLERIN

Introduction

DIETER PLEHWE

Neoliberalism is anything but a succinct, clearly defined political philosophy. Both friends and foes have done their share to simplify, if not popularize, neoliberal worldviews. Paradoxically, Margaret Thatcher's "TINA" (*there is no alternative*) corresponds with the left-wing critique, which posits that neoliberalism is best understood as an economic *pensée unique* (a concept popularized by Pierre Bourdieu). Growing self-confidence on the right coincided with an increasingly frustrated (old) left during the upheavals of the 1980s and 1990s, with both sides eventually converging on a perspective of a neoliberal one-dimensional man. In terms of academic disciplines, the neoliberal continues to be stereotypically imagined as a neoclassical economist (Harvey 2005, 20). This ignores the fact that interdisciplinary Austrian and ordoliberal (German/Swiss) reservoirs of neoliberal thought have been clearly at odds with neoclassical orthodoxy, as are more recent variations of (rational-choice–based) neo-institutionalism. It is curious to note how many pivotal historical contributions to neoliberalism are not recognized by subsequent generations. In Germany, for example, most scholars will raise their eyebrows if ordoliberal inspirations of the social market economy are vilified as neoliberal. But contrary to many who readily identify neoliberalism with Austrian economics, Foucault (2004, 112f.)

suggested that ordoliberalism has a legitimate claim to the neoliberal title because of its strong emphasis on the social character of economic relations. Although Foucault's juxtaposition of Austrian economics and German neoliberalism underestimates the Austrian contributions to the social construction of neoliberal thought (much of which has been crafted in exile in the UK and the United States), he pointed toward a better understanding of the early postwar varieties of neoliberalism in Germany and the United States. But let's pause for a moment: neoliberalism in the United States?

Social movements protesting against corporate globalization have blamed the United States for most, if not all, of the neoliberal misdeeds around the globe during recent decades. Nevertheless, one feels tempted to ask: "Why is there no neoliberalism in the United States?" invoking the analogy to Werner Sombart's famous question pointing to the absence of (European-style) socialism in the New World. Indeed, the term *neoliberalism* is hardly ever used to describe the U.S. configuration of "free market" forces, which mostly sail under the flags of libertarianism and neoconservatism. A prominent insider in U.S. neoconservative circles, Edwin J. Feulner of the Heritage Foundation, has felt compelled to clarify usage of the term in the United States. He maintains that the neoliberal intellectuals' Mont Pèlerin Society was founded "to uphold the principles of what Europeans call 'liberalism' (as opposed to 'statism') and what we Americans call 'conservatism' (as opposed to 'liberalism'): free markets, limited governments, and personal liberty under the rule of law" (Feulner 1999, 2).[1] Unlike socialism, neoliberalism flourished in the United States, even if it was more obscured here than elsewhere in the world.

In order to avoid superficial distinctions of neoliberalism and neoconservatism and the premature identification of one school of neoliberal thought with the whole, we need to recognize and closely examine the numerous and transnational linkages and dimensions of neoliberalism. Philip Czerny (2008) recently repeated calls to subject neoliberalism to comparative research (Overbeek 1993; Plehwe et al. 2006) and attempted to distinguish contemporary varieties of neoliberalism. Much like welfare state capitalism during the postwar era of Fordism, hegemonic neoliberalism[2] needs to be thought of as plural in terms of both political philosophy and political practice. The comparative research required to improve understanding of the historical and present pluralism within neoliberal confines clearly needs to go beyond isolated text and author. Rather, the need is to explore the numerous and sometimes confusing ways in which neoliberal ideas have been historically related to each other, to social classes, and to political and economic regimes. Although individual freedom served as a key value of neoliberalism in the effort to rally the opposition against the socialist regimes of Eastern Europe (Wainwright 1994), it continues to be difficult to reconcile the neoliberal message of individualism and freedom with the history of authoritarian neoliberal regimes in Latin America, for example.[3]

Because of the existing variety of neoliberalisms and their obscure history in different countries, disciplines, and discourses, the meaning of neoliberal scholarship and ideology needs to be clarified. Thus the purpose of this book is to examine closely what became one of the most important movements in political and economic thought in the second half of the twentieth century. A superficial acquaintance with the history of ideas and the social forces that nurtured those ideas does not suffice to obtain a clear perspective of either the scope and depth of neoliberalism or its rapid growth. Considering the expansion of neoliberalism over the last few decades, Perry Anderson (2000) speaks of a universal ideology. The extent to which neoliberal ideas have been widely accepted, even in nominally hostile environments of Social Democratic parties or formerly communist regimes such as China, requires closer scrutiny if the authority of neoliberal knowledge is not simply taken at face value.

In this volume, we revisit the historical origins of neoliberal knowledge in four countries—France, Germany, the UK, and the United States; we sample some of the key debates and conflicts among neoliberal scholars and their political and corporate allies during the 1950s and 1960s regarding trade unions, development economics, antitrust policies, and the influence of philanthropy; and then we explore the ways in which disagreement has been managed to bolster neoliberal claims to authoritative knowledge in structuring public and private affairs at national and international levels in Chile, Peru, and the United Nations. This book was written by a transnational and interdisciplinary slate of authors, covering a transnational but chronologically limited selection of topics in an effort to explain and better understand one of the most powerful bodies of political knowledge of the current era. Because the neoliberals were never parochial,[4] it would seem prudent for us to imitate their cosmopolitan stance. Diversity of nationalities and disciplines is necessary because neoliberalism remains a major ideology that is poorly understood but, curiously, draws some of its prodigious strength from that obscurity. There are ways, however, to shed light on crucial networks of people and organizations as well as channels of communication cutting across knowledge domains, social status groups, borders, and cultures that were crucial to the rise of neoliberalism to hegemony.

Identifying Self-Conscious Neoliberals in Time
and Space: Studying the Mont Pèlerin Society

Neoliberalism must be approached primarily as a historical "thought collective"[5] of increasingly global proportions. The following chapters focus on what we believe has been the central thought collective that has conscientiously developed the neoliberal identity for more than sixty years now. We will consider any person or group that bears any links to the Mont Pèlerin Society (MPS) since 1947 as falling within the purview of the neoliberal thought collective. Consequently, we will make use of the MPS network of organized neoliberal intellectuals (just over 1,000 members so far) and a closely related network of neoliberal partisan think tanks under the umbrella of the Atlas Economic Research Foundation[6] as a litmus test for identifying the relevant actors and their linkages to other organizations and institutions. This practice was first advocated in Plehwe and Walpen (2006) in their study of neoliberal hegemony in comparative perspective.

Depth studies of particular groups and issue areas within the range of the Mont Pèlerin Society networks like those presented in this volume are now possible owing to the rich material provided in Bernhard Walpen's (2004a) critical history of the MPS.[7] These studies also draw on Ronald M. Hartwell's (1995) "insider" history (he served as MPS president from 1992 to 1994). At least until the 1980s—when the advance of neoliberal ideas and thus the success of the original neoliberal networks led to a rapid multiplication of pretenders to the title of progenitors of neoliberalism—the MPS network can be safely used as a divining rod in order to define with sufficient precision the thought collective that has created and reproduced a distinctly neoliberal thought style in the era of its genesis. Although the influence of the MPS has arguably diminished over the last few decades, the society has nonetheless continued to perform an array of important functions, which continue to shape the further development of neoliberalism (as well as related think tank networks),[8] including the extension of neoliberal networks, the generation of survey data, the organization of academic conferences, the sounding of early warnings, and the campaign against perceived threats to the neoliberal cause. Occasionally, this network of individuals and organizations has attempted to authoritatively determine the broad outlines of MPS neoliberalism. James Buchanan made use of his 1986 presidential lecture at the general meeting in San Vincenzo, Italy, to explain the *neoliberal* understanding of the state, contrary to illusions spread by a growing number of anarchocapitalists[9] within the ranks of the MPS.

> Among our members, there are some who are able to imagine a viable society without a state. . . . For most of our members, however, social order without a state is not readily imagined, at least in any normatively preferred sense. . . . Of necessity, we must look at our relations with the state from several windows, to use the familiar Nietzschean metaphor. . . . Man is, and must remain, a slave to the state. But it is critically and vitally important to recognize that ten per cent slavery is different from fifty per cent slavery.[10]

The Mont Pèlerin Society and related networks of neoliberal partisan think tanks can serve as a directory of organized neoliberalism because it is part of a rather novel structure of intellectual discourse. It has been designed to advance and integrate various types of specialized knowledge within and across the confines of philosophy, academic research in economics, history, sociology, and applied policy knowledge in its various forms. A quick glance at the programs of MPS general conferences, originally held yearly (later biannually, alternating with world regional meetings), allows us to appreciate the wide range of fields and topics discussed at these conferences (Haegeman 2004; see also Plehwe and Walpen 2006). The neoliberal thought collective was structured along different lines from those pursued by the other "epistemic communities" that sought to change people's minds in the second half of the twentieth century.[11] The international academy Hayek sought was actually designed to create a space where like-minded people who shared philosophical ideas and political ideals could mingle and engage in a process of further education and collective learning dedicated to advancing a common neoliberal cause. The effort of the incipient neoliberal thought collective led to the creation of a *comprehensive* transnational discourse community.

The MPS community of neoliberal intellectuals was not restricted by a standard (pluralist, apolitical) understanding of a rigid separation of academic disciplines, or by the need to develop knowledge in a few restricted single-issue areas. Instead, the collective effort can be described as transdisciplinary (developing norms and principled beliefs guiding students in different disciplines), interdisciplinary (though mainly involving social scientists), and transacademic (though the endeavors to connect to particular audiences and the public at

large were in the main organized indirectly through think tanks and publishers). The various groups of neoliberals that joined the MPS from different
countries and professional backgrounds were driven by the desire to learn how
to effectively oppose what they summarily described as collectivism and socialism, and to develop an agenda diverging from classical liberalism. Scholars
from different disciplines shared their expertise and debated with a select group
of journalists, corporate leaders, and politicians, as well as a new breed of knowledge professionals (operating out of the rapidly proliferating neoliberal partisan think tanks). Each of these groups contributed its special resources and
competencies to the collective effort. The whole truly was more than the sum
of its parts, constituting complex and efficient knowledge machinery.

Though not necessarily running smoothly, over time the neoliberal networks
developed an increasingly fine-grained division of intellectual labor, which the
strategists of the Institute of Economic Affairs have sometimes described in military terms. According to Frost (2002), partisan think tanks that organize academic production of publications tailored to specific audiences constitute the
long-range artillery; both think tanks and journalists dedicated to marketing
neoliberal pamphlets (book reviews, interviews, dinner speeches, etc.) are considered the short-range artillery; whereas neoliberal politicians and other activist types are engaged in hand-to-hand combat. The perception of a need to
maintain a radical stance with regard to fundamental change in the long term,
rather than opportunistically subscribing to feasible change in the short term,
led neoliberals to combine elite scholarship with popular writing and intermit-
tent sophistication with populist simplification. Because many observers focus
solely on the marketing side of neoliberal operations, they fail to appreciate the
scholarly production network. Upon closer inspection, one can easily detect
the neoliberal technologies for the creation of international reputation, including academic honors provided by neoliberal universities such as Marroquin
University in Guatemala (Ayau 1990), the Milton Friedman Prize of the Cato
Institute, or the Antony Fisher Prize for think tanks. The international reputation of leading members of the neoliberal thought collective has worked wonders in local fund-raising efforts to establish or expand think tanks and other
organizations (Goodman and Marotz-Baden 1990; Frost 2002).

Even though neoliberal intellectuals depended on corporate funding, only
a few corporate leaders were admitted to the inner sanctum of the neoliberal
thought collective. Intellectuals were deeply suspicious of the opportunistic
pragmatism of postwar business leaders, many of whom had embraced corpo-

ratism and planning. Consequently, among the key tasks perceived by MPS leaders was a neoliberal reeducation of capitalists (cf. Cockett 1995; Yergin and Stanislaw 1998). Yet it is not enough to merely point at the political power of economic ideas, as did both John Maynard Keynes and Friedrich Hayek, nor is it sufficient to stress the variance of political power of economic ideas due to national institutional configurations as did Peter Hall (1989). The contributions to this book have been written to help us better understand the political and economic power of *neoliberal ideas* in philosophy, economics, law, political science, history, sociology, and many other disciplines. Contemporary neoliberalism copied, extended, and refined *elitist* efforts on the Fabian model to effectively organize the power of knowledge and ideas across borders.[12]

Historical Social Network Analysis: Detecting Layers of Knowledge

Perhaps an anecdote will help explain why it is necessary to accurately identify and recognize the historical importance of the MPS. The following recollections and reflections of John Williamson—the economist who coined the term *Washington Consensus* (WC)—constitutes proof that the Mont Pèlerin Society can be easily misunderstood, if not overlooked. While the structural dimensions of the historical sedimentation of knowledge in general and the occasionally powerful participation of strategic actors in authoritative deliberation and decision making have been the subject of discourse coalition research at the national level (cf. Wittrock, Wagner, and Wollman 1987; Hajer 1993), observing the Mont Pèlerin Society helps illuminate transnational discourse communities and coalitions.

John Williamson did not overlook the MPS. He has recently written some articles in which he acknowledges the role of the MPS in creating neoliberalism, but alas, not without adding tremendously to the existing confusion. Williamson (2003, 2004) has attempted to defend the Washington Consensus (WC) against popular and even professional vilification (Rodrik 1996; Stiglitz 1999). The WC combined a set of macroeconomic policies intended to restore economic stability and a set of liberalization policies aimed at structural reform. The WC's rallying cries were "structural adjustment" and "getting the prices right." Williamson's ten policy instruments included reduction of federal deficits, privatization of state-run enterprises, deregulation of key industries, and trade and financial sector liberalization. Critics outside of the economics profession had taken to equating Williamson's list with a roster of policies characteristic of neoliberalism.

Williamson rejected this characterization of the WC and has written in rebuttal: "I use the word 'neoliberalism' in its *original* sense, to refer to the doctrines espoused by the Mont Pèlerin Society. If there is another definition, I would love to hear what it is so that I can decide whether neoliberalism is more than an intellectual swear word" (Williamson 2004, 2; emphasis added). Instead of subjecting the aforementioned "MPS doctrines" to closer scrutiny, Williamson maintained that he himself was not an advocate the "policy innovations" of the Reagan and Thatcher administrations, *except for privatization.* "I thought all the other new ideas with which Reagan and Thatcher had entered office, notably monetarism, supply-side economics, and minimal government, had by then been discarded as impractical or undesirable fads, so *no trace of them can be found* in what I labelled the 'Washington Consensus' " (Williamson 2004, 2; emphasis added).

We may therefore deduce that Williamson believes that "monetarism, supply-side economics, and minimal government" provide an exhaustive census of MPS doctrines. These doctrines do indeed owe their contemporary existence to key contributions from influential MPS members such as Milton Friedman, Karl Brunner, and Sir Alan Walters, as well as Martin Feldstein, James Buchanan, and Gary Becker, to name just a few of the better known members. But within MPS, neoliberalism was elaborated and promoted by a total thought collective of more than one thousand scholars, journalists, (think tank) professionals, and corporate and political leaders around the globe for more than fifty years; their work can by no means be reduced to these three doctrines.

Leaving aside Williamson's hasty judgment on supply-side economics as a superseded fad,[13] privatization, deregulation, and financial and trade liberalization must assuredly be counted as key "MPS doctrines." For example, consider the theoretical contributions from MPS members such as George Stigler and Richard Posner with regard to regulatory reform ("capture theory"), property rights theorists Armen Alchian and Harold Demsetz with regard to privatization and efficient property rights, and trade theorists Gottfried Haberler and Herbert Giersch with regard to globalization, among many others. Reform is equated not with gross downsizing of the government as much as it is with removing government from those areas where a different sort of discipline is prescribed. What then are we to make of Williamson's fervent declaration that there is "no trace" of MPS doctrines in the Washington Consensus?

First, Williamson makes profound concessions to neoliberalism merely by subscribing to the privatization doctrine. "Visions" of comprehensive liberalization of financial markets were watchwords in the ranks of influential MPS members such as Fritz Machlup, Gottfried Haberler, and Milton Friedman, when the gold exchange standard collapsed in the early 1970s (Helleiner 1994). Williamson arguably felt that the WC had emerged as a promising strategy to fight poverty in the Third World and that, historically, those neoliberals did not really care about such issues (see Mitchell, Chapter 11 in this volume). However, it would be difficult to find dissenting voices to the WC within the neoliberal camp, especially when it comes to forging a link between liberalization and the creation of wealth advocated by MPS members such as Peter Bauer (compare Plehwe and Bair, Chapters 9 and 10, respectively, in this volume).

Perhaps most telling, Williamson seems oblivious to the extent to which MPS members actually participated in shaping and modifying the Washington Consensus. At least one MPS member has been actively involved in the process of clarifying the extent to which the WC was "complete" in the eyes of the contemporary economics profession. Williamson (2004, 4) reports that he invited Allan Meltzer of Carnegie Mellon University as a representative of the right wing of the political spectrum to respond to his original paper in 1989:

> Meltzer expressed his pleasure at finding how much the mainstream had learned (according to my account) about the futility of things like policy activism, exploiting the unemployment/inflation trade-off, and development planning. The two elements of my list on which he concentrated his criticism were once again the interest rate question (though here he focused more on my interim objective of a positive but moderate real interest rate than on the long run objective of interest rate liberalization) and a competitive exchange rate. The criticism of the interest rate objective I regard as merited. His alternative to a competitive exchange rate, namely a currency board, would certainly not be consensual, but the fact that he raised this issue was my first warning that on the exchange rate question I had misrepresented the degree of agreement in Washington.

Williamson appears to be unaware that Allan Meltzer has been a prominent member of the Mont Pèlerin Society (compare Weller and Singleton 2006). The extent of Williamson's own deference to Meltzer's positions should otherwise have signaled a convergence of doctrines between the WC and the

MPS. Elsewhere, Williamson (2003, 11) informed his readers that he owes much of his own economic thinking to his teacher Fritz Machlup, and in that regard he perhaps unwittingly names yet another prominent MPS member who seems to have had a formative influence on his own thinking.

The putatively nonpartisan WC, contrary to Williamson's own protesta-tions, displays many traces of the MPS neoliberalism in its very genes and has been forged with the help (and endorsement) of more than one influential MPS member, even according to Williamson's own account.[14] Clarifying MPS neoliberalism will in any case shed light on some of the largely forgotten origins of many occluded aspects of contemporary mainstream thinking.

The remainder of this introduction will provide a few preliminary notes on the (pre-) history of neoliberalism, and introduce some of the key features of the thought collective as rallied under the auspices of the Mont Pèlerin Soci-ety. United under the umbrella of the MPS since 1947, neoliberals mobilized for the first time a directed capacity for changing the world under peacetime conditions without the interruptions created by war and emigration. But it is important to recognize the earlier efforts made between World Wars I and II. During the 1930s, concerned liberals felt an increasingly urgent need to con-front the perceived evils of planning and the failures generated by the laissez-faire attitudes of fellow liberals.

How the "Neo" Got into Neoliberalism

Both the term and the concept of neoliberalism enjoyed a long prehistory in twentieth-century political and economic thought.[15] Probably the first foray into the twentieth-century reconsideration of the problems of how to secure a free market and to appropriately redefine the functions of the state in order to attain that goal—the key concern of MPS neoliberalism—can be found in the book *Old and New Economic Liberalism* by the well-known Swedish economist Eli F. Heckscher, written in 1921. While his student and collaborator in found-ing international trade theory, Bertil Ohlin (the Heckscher-Ohlin factor pro-portion model), served as head of the Liberal Party in Sweden from 1944 until 1967, Hekscher was among the second group of people invited to join the neo-liberal Mont Pèlerin Society in 1947. The term *neoliberalism,* in the modern sense,[16] probably appeared for the first time in 1925 in a book entitled *Trends of Economic Ideas,* written by the Swiss economist Hans Honegger. In his survey, Honegger identified "theoretical neoliberalism" as a concept based on the works of Alfred Marshall, Eugen von Böhm-Bawerk, Friedrich von Wieser, Karl Gustav Cassel, and others. Neoliberalism propagated doctrines of competition and entrepreneurship, and posited the rejection of advancing socialist ideas and bolshevism in particular (Walpen 2004a, 68). However, the functions of the state were understood in a negative way, and therefore the heritage of classical liberalism loomed large. In the mid-1920s, we also find the discussion of the dire condition of liberalism and the search for new approaches in the works of the Viennese sociologist Leopold von Wiese (1925) as well as in the booklet *Liberalism (Liberalismus)* by the Austrian economist Ludwig von Mises (1927, further discussed in Walpen 2004a, 69–70).

Interwar Vienna presaged certain neoliberal ideas and proto-MPS structures. In particular, it fostered the creation of a certain kind of extra-academic cosmopolitan intellectual formation. There Ludwig von Mises became a prominent opponent of socialist economics and planning as advocated by leading representatives of Austro-Marxism, such as Otto Bauer and Rudolf Hilferding, as well as a Logical Positivist brand of scientific Marxism represented by Otto Neurath. Mises, then secretary of the Vienna Chamber of Commerce and organizer of one of the most prominent *Privatseminars,* which included Friedrich Hayek and Fritz Machlup, initiated the "socialist calculation debate," eventually positioning neoliberal economics as the most important intellectual foe of scientific and technocratic socialism.[17] Mises's seminar attracted many foreign scholars (such as Lionel Robbins, Frank Knight, and John van Sickle), who would become key members of the Mont Pèlerin Society after World War II.[18] Discussions involved intellectuals who worked in academia cheek-by-jowl with intellectuals who could not attain traditional academic careers at the time for various reasons (including anti-Semitism). The Mises seminar encompassed "business" intellectuals such as Fritz Machlup (who had been forced to enter his father's family business for lack of academic opportunities) and officials of the Chamber of Commerce. At that time, Mises and Hayek earned their money at a private business cycle research institute funded by the Rockefeller Foundation to supply economic data to Austrian firms. Later characteristic features of organized neoliberalism can be discerned in the formative life experiences of leading neoliberals during the Viennese "golden" 1920s. Whereas the Mises *Privatseminar* provided fertile ground for the early attacks against the theoretical foundations of socialism, the critique of classical liberalism as the other face of neoliberalism was not yet apparent in the works of Ludwig von Mises and other Viennese colleagues; neoliberalism, therefore, truly was an offspring of the Great Depression.

Only in the 1930s did the term *neoliberalism* start to appear in multiple contexts, eventually to become established as the main designation of a new intellectual/political movement. The broadest discussion took place in France around 1935. A loose group of economists, philosophers, and sociologists[19] located in Paris organized the Colloque Walter Lippmann (CWL), which is often regarded as the precursor of the MPS. Yet another important country that simultaneously gave birth to neoliberalism was Germany, where Walter Eucken, Alexander Rüstow, and Wilhelm Röpke discussed the tasks of a "new liberalism" on the eve of the Nazis' rise to power. Significantly for later developments, Rüstow explicitly called for a "liberal interventionism" (see Ptak, Chapter 3 in this volume).

The incipient emergence of neoliberalism was not altogether free from ambiguity, however, since the term also began to pop up on the left. Frank Knight (1934) in Chicago rejected the mixing of ideologies he perceived in the new social liberalism, though research is needed to better understand the crisscrossing relationships between the left-leaning social liberalism and the right-leaning neoliberalism. How can it be explained that at the London School of Economics and Political Science, founded by Fabian Socialists Beatrice and Sidney Webb, the economics department developed a decidedly neoliberal orientation under the guidance of Edwin Cannan (Apel 1961, 9)? Cannan gathered together a group of young disciples who devoted themselves to a determined rethinking of market solutions to the challenges of the day in opposition to answers given by Keynes(ians) at Cambridge and elsewhere.[20] Foucault (2004, 130f.) focused on Karl Schiller to describe the process of Social Democratic approximation to a neoliberal understanding of economic policy making in Germany[21] before entering the federal government at the end of the 1960s. Both during the 1930s and the first decades after World War II, a certain amount of confusion persisted with regard to proper understanding of the political character of neoliberalism.

Another interwar institution that provided an organizational haven for concerned and committed liberals was established in Geneva, Switzerland. In 1927 the Institut Universitaire des Hautes Études Internationales (IUHEI) was launched by William E. Rappard and Paul Mantoux and provided a refuge for Frank D. Graham, Theodore Gregory, Ludwig von Mises, Wilhelm Röpke, Jacob Viner, and a host of others. The most famous representative of the Italian coterie of neoliberals, Luigi Einaudi, fled in 1943 from the fascists to Switzerland, where he was supported at the IUHEI by Rappard (Walpen 2000).

The publication of Walter Lippmann's *(An Inquiry into the Principles of) The Good Society* in 1937 marked the beginning of a new dawn in the history of neoliberalism. The book was enthusiastically welcomed by the liberal intellectuals in Europe, perhaps even more so than in America (Steel 1980). Lippmann's core message was the superiority of the market economy over state intervention, a principle that was (to say the least) leaning against the wind in the depths of the Great Depression. The book was brimming with insights that would later constitute the conventional wisdom in neoliberal circles, notably:

> In a free society the state does not administer the affairs of men. It administers justice among men who conduct their own affairs.

> [Statesmanship] is the ability to elucidate the confused and clamorous interests which converge upon the seat of government. It . . . consists in giving the people not what they want but what they will learn to want.[22]

Lippmann anticipated not only some principles, but also elements, of Friedrich Hayek's long-term strategy: Only steadfast, patient, and rigorous scientific work, as well as a revision of liberal theory, was regarded as a promising strategy to defeat "totalitarianism." Significantly, Lippmann's work discussed totalitarianism primarily with regard to the absence of private property, rather than the more commonplace reference to a lack of democracy or countervailing political power.[23]

Louis Rougier, the French philosopher, was quite taken with the book and organized a conference in Lippmann's honor, the eponymous Colloque Walter Lippmann, in Paris in 1938 (see Denord, Chapter 1 in this volume). Fifteen of those who were invited (including Raymond Aron, Louis Baudin, Friedrich August von Hayek, Ludwig von Mises, Michael Polanyi, Wilhelm Röpke, and Alexander Rüstow) would subsequently participate in the founding of the Mont Pèlerin Society nine years later (Walpen 2004a, 84f., 388, 391). Besides debates over the dangers of collectivism and the pitifully weak state of liberalism, they wrangled over the tenets as well as the designation of a renewed liberalism. The term *neoliberalism* triumphed against suggestions such as néo-capitalisme, libéralisme positif, libéralisme social, and even libéralisme de gauche (Walpen 2004a, 60). The colloquium defined the concept of neoliberalism as

- the priority of the price mechanism,
- the free enterprise,
- the system of competition, and
- a strong and impartial state.[24]

The participants launched the project agenda of neoliberalism, a journal *(Cahiers du Libéralisme)*, and a think tank, the Centre international d'études pour la rénovation du libéralisme (CIRL), with the head office in Paris (the first president was the entrepreneur Louis Marlio) and auxiliary offices in Geneva (Röpke), London (Hayek), and New York (Lippmann) (Walpen 2004a, 60–61).

As Richard Cockett (1995, 12) noted, however, "it was, of course, an inauspicious moment to start founding new international organizations of ambitious intentions." The outbreak of World War II abruptly halted this nascent attempt at organizing (neo)liberal forces. It scattered many of the participants, and of course, gave a tremendous boost to the socialists, thus recasting the enemy as a different species of totalitarian after the war.

To sum up the prehistory of MPS-neoliberalism, four points need to be emphasized:

1. Neoliberalism had a diverse number of places of origin (including, but not limited to, Chicago, Freiburg, Geneva, London, New York, and Paris). With regard to the important Austrian roots, and to a lesser extent German, Italian, and French, neoliberalism was a political philosophy developed by uprooted intellectuals in exile following the rise of Nazism, which may explain the intensity of the social bondage among people from different countries and cultures. Metaphors of "birth" are perhaps less apposite here than alternative metaphors of percolation and recombination.

2. Neoliberalism was anything but a "pensée unique" and at the outset drew on different theoretical approaches (e.g., the Austrian school, the incipient Chicago School of Economics, the Freiburg school of ordoliberalism, Lippmann's "realism"), which continue(d) to coexist, but also served to cross-fertilize these and other approaches (e.g., public choice, institutional design).

3. An understanding of neoliberalism needs to take into account its dynamic character in confronting both socialist planning philosophies

and classical laissez-faire liberalism, rather than searching for timeless (essentialist) content. It was primarily a quest for alternative intellectual resources to revive a moribund political project. It was flexible in its intellectual commitments, oriented primarily toward forging some new doctrines that might capture the imaginations of future generations. At various junctures, this might involve unexpected feints to the left as well as the right.

4. The Colloque Walter Lippmann helped spread the realization that honoring discrete academic disciplinary boundaries would probably hinder the project. The figures who gathered in 1938 saw the point of ranging widely over the traditional preserves of philosophy, politics, theology, and even the natural sciences. Neoliberals started to recognize the growing need "to organize individualism" in order to counter what was perceived as an unfortunate but irreversible politicization of economics and science (Zmirak 2001, 11). To achieve their goal of the "Good Society," neoliberal agents agreed on the need to develop long-term strategies projected over a horizon of several decades, possibly to involve several generations of neoliberal intellectuals. No single genius or "saviour" would deliver the neoliberals into their Promised Land.

Perpetual Mobilization: Mont Pèlerin

With the conclusion of the war, many forces conspired to bring the neoliberals together once more to try and organize the movement.[25] Under the leadership of Albert Hunold and Friedrich August von Hayek, a number of loosely connected neoliberal intellectuals in Europe and the United States assembled in Mont Pèlerin, a village close to Lake Geneva. From Tuesday, April 1, to Thursday, April 10, 1947, the first gathering took place at the Hôtel du Parc. The internationalist outlook and organizational effort were made possible through some timely corporate/institutional support. The Foundation for Economic Education in Irvington-on-Hudson, New York, which employed Ludwig von Mises, and the William Volker Fund based in Kansas City, provided subsidies. The Volker Fund was led by future MPS member Harold Luhnow, and it provided travel funds for the U.S. participants in the meeting. The Schweizerische Kreditanstalt (today known as Credit Swiss) paid 93 percent of the total conference costs—18,062.08 Swiss francs (Steiner 2007; Walpen 2004b).

What was the rationale for founding the Mont Pèlerin Society? There were at least two salient considerations. First, the (neo)liberals felt isolated and nearly alone: "The present position is one where we nearly despair."[26] Or, as George H. Nash (1976, 26) described it:

> The participants, high in the Swiss Alps, were only too conscious that they were outnumbered and without apparent influence on policymakers in the Western world. All across Europe, planning and socialism seemed ascendant.

Second, Hayek and others believed that classical liberalism had failed because of crippling conceptual flaws and that the only way to diagnose and rectify them was to withdraw into an intensive discussion group of similarly minded intellectuals. As Hayek stated in his opening address at the first meeting:

> Effective endeavors to elaborate the general principles of a liberal order are practicable only among a group of people who are in agreement on fundamentals, and among whom basic conceptions are not questioned at every step. . . . What we need are people who have faced the arguments from the other side, who have struggled with them and fought themselves through to a position from which they can both critically meet the objections against it and justify their own views . . . this should be regarded as a private meeting and all that is said here in discussion as "off the record." . . . it must remain a closed society, not open to all and sundry. (1967, 149, 151, 153, 158)

One can readily appreciate the trickiness of attempting to square the circle of remaining closed and relatively secretive while striving to be cosmopolitan and open to opposing currents, all the while scrutinizing a political doctrine (liberalism) that was at least nominally pitched in favor of diversity, broadmindedness, and open participation. The difficulties in building and managing a fairly diverse transnational network under the relatively adverse circumstances immediately following World War II can hardly be overestimated. One index of the MPS's balancing act can be gleaned from comparing the nationalities of the participants in the prewar Colloque Walter Lippmann to those in the society's early postwar conferences. The search to identify scattered intellectuals who could be trusted to advance the neoliberal cause originally concentrated on Western Europe but expanded rapidly to the United States, and eventually beyond the rising superpower. While U.S. participants in the Colloque Walter Lippmann had been a small minority (3 of 84), almost half of the participants in the MPS founding conference in 1947 came from the United States, although three Austrians (Machlup, Haberler, and Mises) reinforced the American numbers (17 of 39). By 1951, when the MPS had already grown to 172 members, 97 Europeans mingled with 62 individuals located in the United States. The remaining 13 members in 1951 came from various South American and Caribbean countries and from far away Australia, New Zealand, and Singapore (all figures from Walpen 2004a, 388 [CWL 1938], 381–382 [MPS 1947], 393–394 [MPS 1951]).

The MPS rapidly adjusted to the United States' postwar rise to economic hegemony in terms of membership,[27] though Europe arguably remained of equal, if not greater, importance as an epicenter of the neoliberal discourse community. Contrary to the conviction of many on the left that neoliberalism is an ideology "made in USA," fifteen of twenty-four MPS presidents have been European, and six have come from the United States (see Table I.1). Of the remaining three presidents, two were from Latin America and one from Japan.[28] So far only Europeans have served as secretaries of the MPS, though all of the five treasurers were citizens or permanent residents (Fritz Machlup) of the United States.[29] Twenty-seven general meetings between 1947 and 2004 took place in Europe compared to just four in the United States and one each in Canada, Chile, Hong Kong, and Japan (Walpen 2004a, 389). Regional meetings were more evenly distributed across Europe, the Americas, and Asia. Africa appeared late (2007) on the neoliberal map of conference locations (special meeting in Nairobi, Kenya).

A quantitative analysis of participation in MPS general meetings from 1947 until 1986[30] yields the following results (summarized in Figure I.1), making use of simple network theory algorithms: U.S. participants: ●, European: ○, other: ●. Ten of the most frequent participants identified in this analysis were originally from the United States, compared to twenty-one from Europe. An additional two of the U.S.-based "frequent MPS fliers" (Mises and Machlup) were from Austria, and one of the three individuals from elsewhere (Hutt) moved to South Africa from his native UK. Manuel Ayau from Guatemala and Chiaki Nishiyama from Japan were the only MPS members admitted into this core group of frequent participants, also serving as presidents, who were from neither Europe nor the United States.

The quantitative historical social network analysis helps to shed more light on the group of less well-known neoliberal activists, who all too frequently have remained hidden in the shadow of official leaders and prominent neoliberals like Friedrich August von Hayek and Milton Friedman. The Danish economist Christian Gandil, for example, was the only MPS member who attended all

Table I.1 Mont Pèlerin Society leaders

Presidents

Name	Period	Home country	Occupation
Friedrich A. von Hayek	1948–1960	Austria	Science (economics)
Wilhelm Röpke	1960–1961	Germany	Science (economics)
John Jewkes	1962–1964	UK	Science (economics)
Friedrich A. Lutz	1964–1967 1968–1970	Germany	Science (economics)
Daniel Villey	1967–1968	France	Science (economics)
Milton Friedman	1970–1972	USA	Science (economics)
Arthur A. Shenfield	1972–1974	UK	Think tank (economics)
Gaston Leduc	1974–1976	France	Science (economics)
George J. Stigler	1976–1978	USA	Science (economics)
Manuel Ayau	1978–1980	Guatemala	Business
Chiaki Nishiyama	1980–1982	Japan	Science (economics)
Ralph Harris	1982–1984	UK	Think tank
James M. Buchanan	1984–1986	USA	Science (economics)
Herbert H. Giersch	1986–1988	Germany	Science (economics)
Antonio Martino	1988–1990	Italy	Science (economics) / politics
Gary Becker	1990–1992	USA	Science (economics)
Max Hartwell	1992–1994	UK	Science (history)
Pascal Salin	1994–1996	France	Science (economics)
Dr. Edwin J. Feulner	1996–1998	USA	Think tank
Dr. Ramon P. Diaz	1998–2000	Uruguay	Science (economics)
Christian Watrin	2000–2002	Germany	Science (economics)
Leonard P. Liggio	2002–2004	USA	Science (law) / think tank
Victoria Curzon-Price	2004–2006	Switzerland	Science (economics)
Greg Lindsay	2006–	Australia	Think tank

Secretaries

Name	Period	Home country	Occupation
A. Hunold	1948–1960	Switzerland	Business
B. Leoni	1960–1967	Italy	Science (law)
R. Harris	1967–1976	UK	Think tank
M. Thurn	1976–1988	Austria	Politics

Secretary Treasurers

Name	Period	Home country	Occupation
Charles O. Hardy	1948	USA	Science (economics)
W. Allen Wallis	1948–1954	USA	Science (economics)
Fritz Machlup	1954–1959	Austria (then USA)	Science (economics)
Clarence E. Philbrook	1959–1969	USA	Science (economics)
Arthur Kemp	1969–1979	USA	Science (economics)
Edwin Feulner	1979–	USA	Think tank

Sources: Hartwell (1995); Walpen (2004); http://www.montpelerin.org/; data compiled by author.

twenty-four conferences between 1947 and 1986, closely followed by Hayek (twenty-three), a group of think tank officials (Leonard Read of the Foundation for Economic Education, Antony Fisher, Shenfield, and Seldon of the Institute of Economic Affairs), and two politicians (Max Thurn from Austria and Jean Pierre Hamilius from Luxemburg). However, two frequent participants (and key officials) of the early period—Albert Hunold and Wilhelm Röpke—do not appear in this picture only because they quit the MPS in the aftermath of the struggle over the future direction of the organization. The battle took place in the early 1960s and was lost by the Hunold-Röpke camp (cf. Walpen 2004a, 145f., on the Hunold-Hayek affair). A more detailed analysis than is possible here reveals additional groups of people who may have to be considered key actors during certain succinct periods of time (Plehwe and Walther 2008). Nevertheless, the core network identified in this introduction includes most of the key officials who formally served the MPS during the period 1947–1986, and shifts additional attention to a group of journalists and publishers (Davenport, Fertig, Fredborg, Hoff, Genin), corporate leaders (Fisher, Suenson-Taylor), think tank officials (Read, Seldon), and a politician (Hamilius). Marie-Thérèse Genin, a French publisher who helped to get major books by neoliberal authors translated and published, is the only woman among the regulars. She is among the few frequent conference attendants who never chaired a panel or gave a paper, a fate shared with the few other female fellows (Plehwe and Walther 2008).

The composition of MPS members mirrors the overall membership composition of the MPS (Plehwe and Walpen 2006), whereas the official positions

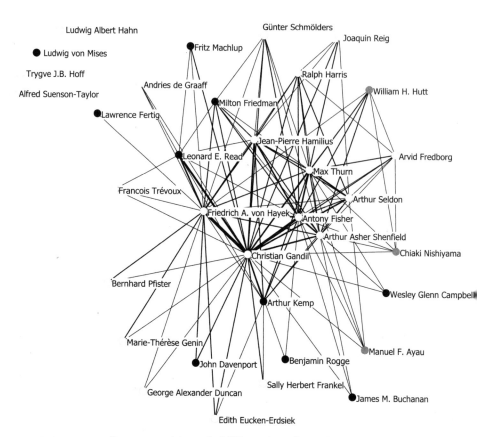

FIGURE I.I. Frequent participants in MPS meetings. *Source:* Participation lists, general MPS meetings 1947–1986 available at Liberaal Archief, Ghent, and Hoover Institution, Stanford. The individuals listed in the figure participated together with the individuals to which they are linked in at least 50 percent (13) of the 26 conferences. The four isolated participants (Mises, Hoff, Hahn, Suenson-Taylor) were also present 13 times, though not at least 13 times together with at least one other person. I am grateful to Katja Walther for data compilation on the basis of UCI-Net.

are almost exclusively held by the most numerous contingent of MPS members: academics. Very infrequently, corporate leaders (like Manuel Ayau) or think tank officials (like Edwin Feulner) served as MPS presidents. Many of the names in Figure I.1 will surface in the following chapters; however, the contributions of a few listed here to the neoliberal cause remains murky, calling for future research. Very little is known about the Japanese members and networks, for example. We do know that long-standing personal ties had been important with regard to the MPS's early recruiting effort: Hayek, Mises, Polanyi, Robbins, and Röpke were MPS founding members who had already participated in the 1938 Colloquium, and other CWL participants (including Raymond Aron, Louis Baudin, and Alexander Rüstow) were involved in the efforts to launch the MPS (Walpen 2004a, 84f., 388, 391). The "white emigrants" from Austria (Hayek, Mises, Machlup, Haberler, Popper) were key U.S or UK-based academic MPS members until the 1960s. Otherwise, two journalists (John Davenport and Henry Hazlitt) and one think tank official (Leonard Read of the Foundation for Economic Education [FEE]) formed the core of the U.S.-based neoliberal activists. Only during the 1960s did U.S. professors Milton Friedman, James Buchanan, and George Stigler ascend to leading positions, eventually being elected MPS presidents. According to Feichtinger (2001), already during World War II, Hayek (in London) and Haberler (in Boston) were indispensable with regard to the academic prospects of other emigrants who were MPS members. This is one reason, for example, for Popper's lasting gratitude to his benefactor, von Hayek (Nordmann 2005). Commenting on an early draft of Hartwell's MPS history, Christian Gandil (1986) named several friends he had made among U.S. MPS members and suggested: "the basis for a friendship is to be in agreement concerning outlook of life." The combination of sometimes even rather close personal ties among people of diverse professional backgrounds provided for a fertile mix of sympathy, respect, and competency prevailing among MPS members, notwithstanding occasional episodes suggesting the opposite.

The founding conference reflected the mix of academic and professional backgrounds that would come to characterize the Mont Pèlerin Society. A majority of university professors mingled with journalists (like *Fortune*'s John Davenport, Henry Hazlitt from *Newsweek,* and Cicely V. Wedgwood of *Time and Tide*), foundation/think tank executives (Floyd A. Harper and Vernon Watts of the Foundation for Economic Education, Herbert Corneulle from Volker), and business executives (Albert Hunold heading the Swiss watch manufacturing association) and publishing houses (George Révay from *Reader's Digest*). By 1951 several leading political figures, including Ludwig Erhard and Luigi Einaudi, were accepted, contradicting Hayek's claims of a rather draconian renunciation of political activism. The architects of the neoliberal thought collective have carefully connected and combined key spheres and institutions for the contest over hegemony—academia, the media, politics, and business. Both the networking capacity in terms of specialization and the organizing capacity of the new type of knowledge apparatus—the neoliberal partisan think tank—need to be better understood in order to explain the rise of neoliberal hegemony and the transformation of policy research. "Gone are the days when a think tank could operate with the motto 'research it, write it and they will find it.' Today, think tanks must be lean, mean, policy machines" (McGann 2007, 20). If think tank experts like McGann present the transformation of knowledge power structures at hand as driven by globalization, professionalization, and commercialization, the reasons for more than a hundred neoliberal think tanks coordinating their work within and across borders dating back to the 1950s[31] are easily overlooked. In addition to the central institutions in charge of think tank coordination created by the neoliberal thought collective (like the Atlas Economic Research Foundation or the European Stockholm Network), shared values and principled beliefs constitute decentralized guidance for MPS members setting up think tanks and for think tank professionals who belong to the neoliberal thought collective.[32] The development of a sort of smallest common denominator of MPS ideas was a key subject of the deliberations at the founding conference in Mont Pèlerin.

Even in the face of all the precautions over membership and participation, the early MPS members continued to experience difficulty in specifying precisely what held them together: this was a dilemma that would beset any group whose task lay more in prospective construction than in retrospective appreciation. The benighted band of brothers felt driven to draft a common creed, although Hayek himself warned, "I personally do not intend that any public manifesto should be issued" (Hartwell 1995, 33). A first pass at inscribing a communal Individualist creed was deputed to a committee consisting of Eucken, Hayek, Hazlitt, H. D. Gideonse, John Jewkes, and Carl Iverson and is reproduced here:

DRAFT STATEMENT OF AIMS, APRIL 7, 1947

1.   Individual freedom can be preserved only in a society in which an effective competitive market is the main agency for the direction

of economic activity. Only the decentralization of control through private property in the means of production can prevent those concentrations of power which threaten individual freedom.

2.   The freedom of the consumer in choosing what he shall buy, the freedom of the producer in choosing what he shall make, and the freedom of the worker in choosing his occupation and his place of employment, are essential not merely for the sake of freedom itself, but for efficiency in production. Such a system of freedom is essential if we are to maximize output in terms of individual satisfactions. Departure from these individual liberties leads to the production not only of fewer goods and services but of the wrong goods and services. We cannot enrich ourselves merely by consenting to be slaves.

3.   All rational men believe in planning for the future. But this involves the right of each individual to plan his own life. He is deprived of this right when he is forced to surrender his own initiative, will and liberty to the requirements of a central direction of the use of economic resources.

4.   The decline of competitive markets and the movement toward totalitarian control of society are not inevitable. They are the result mainly of mistaken beliefs about the appropriate means for securing a free and prosperous society and the policies based on these beliefs.

5.   The preservation of an effective competitive order depends upon a proper legal and institutional framework. The existing framework must be considerably modified to make the operation of competition more efficient and beneficial. The precise character of the legal and institutional framework within which competition will work most effectively and which will supplement the working of competition is an urgent problem on which continued exchange of views is required.

6.   As far as possible government activity should be limited by the rule of law. Government action can be made predictable only when it is bound by fixed rules. Tasks which require that authorities be given discretionary powers should therefore be reduced to the indispensable minimum. But it must be recognized that each extension of the power of the state gradually erodes the minimum basis for the maintenance of a free society. In general an automatic mechanism of adjustment, even where it functions imperfectly, is preferable to any which depends on "conscious" direction by government agencies.

7. The changes in current opinion which are responsible for the general trend toward totalitarianism are not confined to economic doctrines. They are part of a movement of ideas which find expression also in the field of morals and philosophy and in the interpretation of history. Those who wish to resist the encroachments on individual liberty must direct their attention to these wider ideas as well as to those in the strictly economic field.

8. Any free society presupposes, in particular, a widely accepted moral code. The principles of this moral code should govern collective no less than private action.

9. Among the most dangerous of intellectual errors which lead to the destruction of a free society is the historical fatalism which believes in out power to discover laws of historical development which we must obey, and the historical relativism which denies all absolute moral standards and tends to justify any political means by the purposes at which it aims.

10. Political pressures have brought new and serious threats to the freedom of thought and science. Complete intellectual freedom is so essential to the fulfillment of our aims that no consideration of social expediency must ever be allowed to impair it. (Hartwell 1995, 49–50)

Significantly enough, even this relatively nonspecific and anodyne set of neoliberal ten commandments proved too contentious to gain the assent of the individualists gathered at Mont Pèlerin, and so the oxymoronic Committee of Individualists deputed a redraft to Lionel Robbins, who complied and produced the "Statement of Aims" (reproduced below). All those gathered on April 8, 1947, except one (the French economist and Nobel laureate Maurice Allais)[33] fully accepted this rather less informative manifesto, which to this day remains the only "official" statement of the MPS. Thus, our readers should understand that they cannot look to any formal sanctioned publication of the MPS for a convenient definition of neoliberalism. Furthermore, this is precisely what we should expect even if the MPS had been convened in 1947 to *construct* a new version of liberalism, rather than simply codify what had been received hallowed wisdom.

STATEMENT OF AIMS OF THE MONT PÈLERIN SOCIETY

The central values of civilization are in danger. . . . The group holds that these developments have been fostered by the growth of a view of history

which denies all absolute moral standards and by the growth of theories
which question the desirability of the rule of law. It holds further that they
have been fostered by a decline of belief in private property and the competitive market; for without the diffused power and initiative associated
with these institutions it is difficult to imagine a society in which freedom
may be effectively preserved. Believing that what is essentially an ideological movement must be met by intellectual argument and the reassertion
of valid ideas, the group, having made a preliminary exploration of the
ground, is of the opinion that further study is desirable *inter alia* in regard
to the following matters:

1. The analysis and explanation of the nature of the present crisis so
   as to bring home to others its essential moral and economic origins.
2. The redefinition of the functions of the state so as to distinguish
   more clearly between the totalitarian and the liberal order.
3. Methods of reestablishing the rule of law and of assuring its
   development in such a manner that individuals and groups not in a
   position to encroach upon the freedom of others and private rights
   are not allowed to become a basis of predatory power.
4. The possibility of establishing minimum standards by means not
   inimical to initiative and the functioning of the market.
5. Methods of combating the misuse of history for the furtherance of
   creeds hostile to liberty.
6. The problem of the creation of an international order conducive
   to the safeguarding of peace and liberty and permitting the establishment of harmonious international economic relations . . .
   (Hartwell 1995, 41–42)

Comparison of these two sets of aims reveals a rather striking diminution
of more specific content in the MPS manifesto. After all, isn't the appeal to
the need for "further study" the last refuge of academic scoundrels? One can
interpret this not only as evidence of a fair amount of dissension within the
ranks of the MPS; but also as evidence that the transnational band of participants did not have a very clear idea of where the project was headed in 1947.
The only immutable truths to which they were eager to pledge their troth
were those of a more general philosophical and normative kind: the fundamental neoliberal values and principled beliefs we can discern in the short list
of six major tasks that have guided the neoliberal thought collective. These
tasks include economic freedom and individualism, the affirmation of moral

standards, and possibly surprising for many critiques: social minimum standards (acknowledging the limits of private charity). Among the principled beliefs were those in positive state functions, a system of law and order, and international trade. Notably absent are the range of human and political rights traditionally embraced by liberals (including the right to form coalitions and freedom of the press).

Shared values and principled beliefs constitute a crucial resource, empowering transnsational community groups. Looking at the neoliberal thought collective, we actually have the chance to observe the social construction of fundamental values and principled beliefs often neglected in the literature (Haas 1992; Keck and Sikkink 1998; Bislev et al. 2002). Stressing science and research rather than ideology and beliefs of course was the hallmark of the post–World War II ideological struggles. The neoliberal group paradoxically feared and appreciated the value of science as highlighted in their point number five: they recognized the paramount importance in political action of rewriting history, and in this recognition, the authors assembled here concur.

A Brief Overview

Part I examines important local/national roots of neoliberalism in the four most important homelands of the movement: France, Germany, the United Kingdom, and the United States. Yet, local analysis in these four countries has to take transnational dimensions of the neoliberal thought collective into account. By the time neoliberalism emerged—during the 1930s—nearly all the Austrian and several important German and French contributors had moved abroad (to Switzerland, the UK, and the United States, for example). The transnational dimension of the local/national history of neoliberalism has been particularly strong in the UK and the United States. Switzerland also deserves recognition as a particular transnational neoliberal space because of the hospitality of Swiss neoliberal intellectuals and institutions to Austrian, German, and Italian refugee neoliberals. It was certainly not mere coincidence that the Mont Pèlerin Society was founded in this country: only Switzerland provided neoliberal intellectuals the intellectual and institutional space and financial backing needed to organize an international conference of and for neoliberals right after World War II. Until the end of the 1950s, it remained easier for neoliberals to congregate in Switzerland than anywhere else: four of the ten Mont Pèlerin Society meetings between 1947 and 1960 took place in

Switzerland.[34] It took more than ten years after the war for a meeting to be held in the United States (see Phillips-Fein, Chapter 8 in this volume) or the UK (Oxford, in 1960). The focus on the four countries of neoliberalism's birth is therefore not meant to present a complete picture, but through their capture of the complex national and transnational origins of the movement will hopefully stimulate further discussion and research.

François Denord's treatment of the French roots of neoliberalism in Chapter 1 enumerates the different wings, intellectual factions, and political frictions of neoliberalism. The French MPS membership included moderately "left"-leaning neoliberals, who embraced certain aspects of social liberalism and planning, and very "right-wing" neoliberals, who in many ways were hardly distinguishable from pre-neoliberal laissez-faire advocates. These divisions seemed to coincide with the professional background and interest perspectives of the neoliberals in France: both neoliberal intellectuals who served policy advisory functions and neoliberal politicians helped build the French postwar state, whereas many French corporate sector neoliberals opposed the development toward modern state regulation and planning. However, other French business intellectuals embraced yet another perspective in an effort to align Catholic social and neoliberal economic doctrines. During the 1970s, a new French generation of radical MPS neoliberals eventually arose to attack the postwar compromises effected by French neoliberals. The more recent cohort of French neoliberals has begun to rewrite neoliberal history by mobilizing a French-Austrian combination of Bastiat, Say, Mises, and Hayek. Denord emphasizes the dialectical interplay of utopian and pragmatic aspects of French neoliberalism—the not always peaceful coexistence of moderate neoliberals and radical anticollectivists like Maurice Allais and Pierre Lhoste-Lachaume, respectively.

Whereas neoliberals in France were deeply divided over postwar issues of economic planning and social policy, German neoliberals were able to form a powerful alliance of intellectual, business, and political forces under the banner of ordoliberalism. Ordoliberals succeeded in developing an alternative third way to the Keynesian welfare and planning state right after World War II—the social market economy. In Chapter 3, Ralf Ptak explains that German neoliberals like Rüstow and Röpke quickly recognized the need for liberal interventionism during the years of the Great Depression, and that German neoliberals had a more compelling argument for a strong state that would secure competition and fortify a market society. Ptak tracks the evolution of German ordoliberalism during the Nazi era both in Germany (the Freiburg school) and in exile (Röpke in Switzerland, Rüstow in Turkey); this approach allows Ptak to closely observe the subtleties of a rather authoritarian version of neoliberalism. German (and Swiss) ordoliberals in exile were deeply suspicious of certain features of capitalism and democracy, namely, urbanization, large enterprise production, trade unions, and modern mass parties, all of which threatened their ideas about a traditional social order ruled by narrow elites and their romantic idea of individualism and merit-based mobility. German neoliberal economists shared an interdisciplinary perspective and sociological understanding of the interdependencies of political, economic, and social order. Although the resulting social theory was rigid and hardly adequate to handle the postwar tasks at hand, the social market economy concept provided the flexibility needed to apply neoliberal economic and social policy in government. The independent ordoliberal line of neoliberal thought has now nearly disappeared, but many of the more recent neoliberal "discoveries" (i.e., bounded rationality, institutions matter, law and economics) in the Anglo-Saxon world display more than a superficial affinity to what German and Swiss ordoliberals established in the past.

In contrast with France and Germany, the inversion of the relationship between economic and political freedom can be considered the key to the British contribution to neoliberalism. Paradoxically, the London School of Economics founded by Fabian socialists harbored the most important British originators of the neoliberal project. Lionel Robbins secured Hayek's presence in London to fortify the intellectual efforts against Keynes. In Chapter 2, Keith Tribe clarifies the ways in which Hayek's revisionist history of British liberalism has been accomplished, namely, by way of presenting the increasing weight of government in the British economy as a result of the intrusion of Germanic ideas (Hegel, Marx, List, etc.) rather than as a result of industrialization and imperialism. Whereas political freedom traditionally was regarded as a prerequisite of economic freedom in the British liberal tradition, economic freedom was now advocated as quintessential to preserve a new kind of political freedom of (limited) individual choice. The Austrian input strengthened the British tradition of principled market advocacy led by Robbins and Arnold Plant, which can be regarded as an early instance of the evolution of modern economics into a closed, self-referential system of thought. But although British neoliberals did indeed refuse to engage serious questions with regard to equilibrium theory addressed by Keynesian economics, they also started to develop a new literature on the disruptive impact of political and trade-union intervention, which ran

counter to the trend toward nationalization, stabilization, and planning. Attention was directed to the detrimental impact of the "rent-seeking behavior"
exhibited by trade-unionized white workers in South Africa or patent owners,
for example. Although British neoliberals convinced more people in terms of
advocating principles than substantiating their claims, and remained rather
marginal in the academic system for much of the post–World War II period,
the effective revival of neoliberal economics during the Thatcher era can be explained. Both the production of textbooks and the establishment of think
tanks like the Institute of Economic Affairs were crucial to maintaining and rebuilding neoliberal influence in the longer term.

Whereas postwar German neoliberalism emphasized a strong state, U.S.
neoliberals worked hard to narrowly define the areas in which a strong neoliberal state could ascertain its pro-capitalist power and roll back the New Deal
advance of social liberals and trade unionists. Chicago became the key staging
ground for forging a lasting alliance between neoliberal intellectuals and the
corporate opposition to the New Deal. Contrary to the widespread belief in a
continuous history of the Chicago School, Rob Van Horn and Phil Mirowski
in Chapter 4 document the central roles played by Henry Simons and
Friedrich von Hayek in founding the Chicago bastion of neoliberalism. The
combined effort of these two intellectuals succeeded in establishing the Free
Market Project in Chicago at the behest of the Volker Fund. Volker's president, Harold Luhnow, hoped to obtain an American version of Hayek's *Road
to Serfdom* and was willing to fund the academic positions of Aaron Director
and Hayek, as well as subsidize travel money for American participation in
Mont Pèlerin Society proceedings in Europe. But more importantly, a specific
Chicago version of young and radical neoliberalism emerged during the 1950s,
which differed markedly both from the liberalism of the older generation of
Chicago-based scholars like Simons and Knight, and from the Austrian economics and philosophy Hayek promoted. The chapter demonstrates that the
second Chicago School and the Mont Pèlerin Society were substantively parts
of one project rather than different parallel projects.

Following up on the pre- and early histories of neoliberalism, the four
chapters of Part II continue to observe neoliberal ambiguity, but also examine
the transformations of neoliberalism during the 1950s and 1960s. Contrary to
MPS neoliberalism understood as "preconceived gospel," the authors of these
four chapters closely observe debates and conflicts among neoliberals, focusing on controversies displayed at MPS meetings. These chapters help us gain

an appreciation of the hard work involved in developing neoliberal perspectives, as well as the variety of neoliberal perspectives innovated in response to differing political circumstances, which necessitated incongruous conclusions on specific questions in different locations.

In Chapter 5, Yves Steiner details the early effort to develop a neoliberal perspective on labor organizations. The trade-union question was perhaps the most important issue that had been tackled by the Mont Pèlerin group. A major conflict arose between U.S. neoliberals, including Austrian migrants like Hayek and Machlup (who were backed both financially and intellectually by U.S. corporate forces opposed to the New Deal), and European neoliberals. The U.S. neoliberals were radically opposed to trade unions and reflected on the best way to limit their power, whereas the European liberals were expressing a need to accommodate trade unions on the one hand and to support moderate trade unionists against radical trade unionists on the other. Accommodationist neoliberals advocated a social partnership to replace class struggle perspectives and attempted to convince business leaders of the merit of collective bargaining as a potential bulwark against welfare state planning. Still, the two camps agreed that trade-union power needed to be curbed in order to secure a free market economy.

Some of the early neoliberal traditions emphasizing competition have been turned upside down by a specific American current of neoliberal thought. In Chapter 6, Rob Van Horn contrasts German ordoliberal positions to U.S. positions to explain in great detail how the specific Chicago School variety of neoliberalism was developed as a clear departure from traditional liberal concerns about political and economic concentration of power. The Chicago Anti-Trust Project (1953–1957) led by Aaron Director effectively amounted to an apologetic "corporations can do no wrong" perspective, in stark contrast to the classical and the German variety of neoliberalism. At the same time, the neoliberal teamwork in Chicago benefited from the participation of European MPS members and from the communication processes within the transnational thought collective. The "as-if" reasoning developed by MPS member Leonard Miksch in Germany to implicate the state in organizing competition, for example, was further developed and applied by Milton Friedman in his dedicated effort to delimit state authority in antitrust politics. Ordoliberal studies stressing grave problems related to state ownership of railroads in Germany, in comparison with Chicago School research pointing to serious trouble with state regulation of private railroads, served to support one of the central and tenuous conclusions of Chicago School neoliberalism: unregulated private monopoly was a relatively benign phenomenon; the real danger instead emanated from the state and the courts' lack of economic understanding. While original Chicago School liberals like Simons insisted that the courts apply clear criteria—the rule of the law—rather than the vague rule of reason, the emerging neoliberal law and economics doctrine—developed by MPS member Henry G. Manne and financed by the Olin Foundation (compare Miller 2006)—demanded an entirely new approach. This new approach was at odds with the neoliberal emphasis on the rule of law: judges should instead be educated to apply a rule of (neoliberal) *economic* reason perspective.

Another subject fiercely debated by MPS members during the 1950s was the rise of the Third World. In Chapter 7, Dieter Plehwe observes how the heritage of colonial economics on the one hand and the overriding security concerns of the early Cold War on the other hampered the development of a neoliberal perspective on development. Early on, MPS analysts nurtured doubts both about the opportunity of independence and free markets in the developing world, and not just a few MPS members made a case for continued colonialism both explicitly and implicitly. But modernization theory and (state-led) industrialization strategies were soundly rejected, and it is possible to observe rudimentary forms of the export-oriented development paradigm neoliberals successfully advocated during the late 1970s. Only toward the end of the 1950s did Peter Bauer clarify a vision of a more complete neoliberal perspective on development: Bauer contradicted his fellow MPS members with regard to the existence of an entrepreneurial class in developing countries and planted seeds of doubt with regard to the effectiveness of providing state development aid in the fight against Soviet expansion. Based on such evidence, Chapter 7 concludes that the neoliberal revolution in development economics observed in the late 1970s and early 1980s had been conceived much earlier; perhaps as early as the late 1950s.

In her examination of the history of the MPS's first meeting in the United States (at Princeton in 1959), Kimberly Phillips-Fein in Chapter 8 shifts attention to the role of neoliberal philanthropy and business conservatives within the neoliberal thought collective. The key personality responsible for organizing the meeting and raising funds was Jasper Elliott Crane, a former vice president of DuPont who joined the MPS and eventually convinced business friends to finance the first U.S. meeting. Neoliberal intellectuals have always claimed to be independent because they are not financed by the state.

Phillips-Fein helps to establish more precisely the character and certain limits of business-financed freedom when she (unlike Hartwell 1995) observes the extent to which Crane attempted (and succeeded) in shaping the program of the Princeton MPS meeting. Crane and others, worried about the extent of MPS pluralism, insisted on prominently featuring the von Mises wing of neoliberalism. Hayek himself admitted the importance of leaders capable of financially backing their beliefs.

The three chapters of Part III are less concerned with detailing the internal conflicts and ambiguities of neoliberal theory than with tracing the mobilization and application of neoliberal knowledge originally generated by the neoliberal thought collective.

Although the links between General Pinochet and Milton Friedman are fairly well known, and the special relationship between Chicago and Santiago has been better researched than most other neoliberal forays, Karin Fischer in Chapter 9 fills important gaps in the literature by tracking and tracing local and foreign neoliberals in Chile before, during, and after the Pinochet dictatorship. Her examination of the *gremialista* pillar of the local neoliberal coalition and her account of the role of the economists Hayek and James Buchanan, in addition to the Chicago School neoliberals, demonstrates the extent to which neoliberal knowledge and capacity building extended well beyond the economic sphere. By carefully identifying transnational MPS circles, Fischer also reveals the flexible character of neoliberal cadres who were able to administer important policy shifts during the Pinochet era, and their survival after the end of Chile's military rule.

If Chile was an early arena of intensive experimentation with applied neoliberalism for prolonged periods of time, the United Nations remained an alien fortress in the eyes of many members of the neoliberal thought collective, at least until the collapse of the Soviet Union. Many previous political demands in favor of redistribution, foreign aid, and planning enjoyed strong support in diverse UN bodies, and the growing self-confidence of developing countries found expression during the 1970s in the demand for a New International Economic Order (NIEO). Jennifer Bair in Chapter 10 examines how MPS-related intellectuals and organizations had launched a coordinated attack against the NIEO in general and the effort to regulate multinational corporations in particular. The Heritage Foundation led by MPS member Ed Feulner should be singled out here because of its capacity to assemble and effectively market the neoliberal expertise that was crucial to undermine the

United Nations Center on Transnational Corporations (UNCTC). The UNCTC itself was eventually disbanded when it was unable to withstand the winds of change. The earlier emphasis of development experts and political leaders in both developed and developing countries on economic indepen- dence and sovereignty has been replaced by a neoliberal understanding of good governance and corporate citizenship expressed by the amicable rela- tions between corporate and political leaders in the UN Global Compact frame. The applied neoliberal policy knowledge unleashed by the Heritage Foundation was not created out of thin air, however, and the chapter demon- strates the original academic contribution to questions of international trade and foreign aid by four key MPS intellectuals in the background. Gottfried Haberler, Peter Bauer, Karl Brunner, and Deepak Lal were among the key international economics and development experts. While Haberler and Lal (during the 1980s) exerted some influence in the international organizations the General Agreement on Tariffs and Trade (GATT) and the World Bank, re- spectively, Bauer and Brunner primarily rallied corporate, civil society, and ac- ademic forces of opposition against the collectivist spirit of Third Worldism.

A new drive to identify liberalism in a positive way can finally be detected in the unlikely sphere of antipoverty politics. In Chapter 11, Tim Mitchell reexam- ines the expertise generated by Hernando de Soto's think tank in Peru in sup- port of titling programs, an alternative promoted by neoliberal forces instead of traditional welfare and antipoverty programs. The knowledge circuits unveiled in this chapter track the original academic production of property rights theory by MPS member Armen Alchian and his colleague Harold Demsetz to the pol- icy program applied in Peru, as well as its international promotion by the World Bank and subsequent export to a number of countries including Egypt. A key to explaining the opportunity created to succeed in the international sphere was the academic evaluation of the experiments on the ground. Upon closer inspec- tion, much of the evidence in support of the neoliberal scheme leading to a vir- tuous cycle of ownership and entrepreneurship collapses. Academic research re- veals the closed neoliberal circuits, including the branding of program and evaluation by neoliberal think tanks providing textbook material to teachers. Neoliberalism thus can be observed to be well and alive in the twenty-first cen- tury, despite such setbacks as the collapse of the Washington Consensus.

The Postface by Phil Mirowski discusses some of the reasons for the social construction of neoliberal obscurity as evidenced in ongoing Wikipedia dis- cussions that are nominally dedicated to clarifying the subject. Mirowski concludes this volume with a summary of the key content of neoliberalism emanating from the historical analysis of the neoliberal thought collective. Much like the group of scholars, writers, and managers who congregated at Mont Pèlerin more than sixty years ago, attempting to grapple with the core features of neoliberalism, we need to conduct further studies to fully appreciate the kinds of neoliberalism they eventually produced. In the absence of such studies, we are likely to underestimate the kinds of neoliberalism that will likely result from the future deliberations and projects of neoliberals, who are much better organized nowadays than they were half a century ago. Second- and third-generation neoliberals are already hard at work to overcome whatever midlife crisis the neoliberal thought collective may face.

Notes

1. Feulner, a professing Catholic, has served as president and secretary treasurer of the MPS. It is not possible to fully identify U.S. neoconservatism and neoliberalism, of course. Although neo-Straussian foreign policy neoconservatism should not be equated with neoliberalism, many authors fail to recognize the careful coalitions formed by the new right (including the religious right). It is important to note that Feulner's strong rhetoric of limited government refers to the welfare state but not to the police or the military. The neoliberal combination of limited government and strong state in defense of capitalism remains typically obscured behind the rhetoric of limited government, which is not identical to a weak state.

2. It is useful to maintain the broad distinction between "left" and "right" with regard to qualifying (neo)liberalism: namely, in order to distinguish between the new social liberalism and right-wing neoliberalism. The application of criteria suggested by Bobbio (1994) with regard to understanding equality in particular—the right holds inequality to be necessary and even beneficial, whereas the left has historically aimed to at least reduce inequality that is considered detrimental—helps to clarify whether (former) social liberals are turning toward neoliberalism. Neoliberals usually deny the existence of social Inequality rooted in the capitalist class structure and instead prefer to speak of the diversity of individuals or possibly groups. This is a perspective shared to a certain extent by postmodern philosophy (which stresses cultural diversity rather than social class).

3. Alejandro A. Chafuen of the Atlas Economic Research Foundation recently pointed out that "Latin Americans need to recognize they can confront this challenge [the "Bolivarian revolution"—D.P.] themselves" and that past "victories" in Latin America (Chile in particular) came at the expense of "weakening the institutions that had protected the rule of law and limited executive authorities" (Chafuen 2006a, 6). He still did not emphasize the weakening of individual freedoms of expression.

4. Max Thurn opened the 1964 Semmering (Austria) MPS meeting with the following words: "As the only Austrian member of the Society present at this meeting I
have the pleasure and privilege of welcoming you all to Austria. Many of you have been
to Austria before. There is little I can tell them about the country that they do not
know already. Others have come for the first time. They may like to get a general idea
of what this country was and what it is now before the meeting begins. What I can say
on this subject has of course nothing to do with the topics of the programme. As members of the Mt Pèlerin Society *we are not interested in the problems of individual nations*
or even groups of nations. What concerns us are general issues such as personal liberty
and private initiative" (Thurn, 1964 meeting records, MPS archive, Liberaal Archief,
Ghent, Belgium [henceforth cited as LAMP]; emphasis added).

5. According to Fleck (1980), knowledge/scientific development is characterized by
the contribution and relative power of competing professional/ideological groups, a
perspective that is at odds with standard models of linear accumulation of knowledge,
or models (following Kuhn) that identify revolutionary stages in scientific development
(compare Smith 2005). However, it is not possible to fully subscribe to Fleck's understanding of thought collectives because Fleck tends to overemphasize their coherence
(note: of collectives, not of individuals who can be members of different thought collectives, according to Fleck). Members of his thought collectives are held to fully share
the understanding of truth with regard to each and every statement, which seems to
preclude (productive) disagreement among members. It is difficult to see how, under
this condition, thought collectives can generate knowledge dynamics. It is also held
that members of Fleck's thought collectives do not communicate well to members of
other thought collectives; for example, physicists are suggested to be ill-prepared to talk
to theologians, as Steven Lukes reminded me. The members of the neoliberal thought
collective examined in this volume instead disagree on specific issues, and they try hard,
and certainly not without success, to convince both intellectuals and the general public
of the merits of neoliberal reasoning. Their capacity to jointly develop and widely dis-
tribute neoliberal knowledge is due to a set of shared values and principled beliefs,
which allow community members to effectively communicate across disciplines and
audiences in the pursuit of hegemonic strategies. See Stadler (1997, 481f.) for a general
usage of the term *thought collective* comparable to ours in capturing the Vienna circles
of logical empiricists. See Plehwe and Walpen (2007) for a full critique of Fleck's understanding of thought collectives. Bernhard Walpen contributed his original research
on the concept of thought collectives and styles to this chapter.

6. Most of the think tanks populating the Atlas Economic Research Foundation
network have been founded and are run with the help of at least one MPS member
(compare Cockett 1955; Frost 2002; Plehwe and Walpen 2006; and below).

7. Bernhard Walpen decided against participating in this volume after an irreconcilable conflict arose. This is deeply regrettable inasmuch as he was slated to be a co-
author of this introduction, which relies in part on his keynote lecture, "The Plan to

End Planning: A Short History of Neoliberalism," delivered at the New York University / International Center for Advanced Studies conference held April 28–30, 2005 (Walpen 2005). Nobody has contributed more than Bernhard Walpen to critical analysis of the Mont Pèlerin Society (including the development of databases of members and think tanks). Since Bernhard Walpen and I have co-authored at least nine book chapters and articles on the subject, I would like to ask readers to consult his work alongside this introduction so that they will gain clear recognition of his key role in developing many of the ideas presented in this volume. I do regard this introduction as being co-authored with Bernhard even if it does not formally carry his name.

8. In addition to the proliferation of think tanks within the Atlas Economic Research Foundation, innumerable think tank networks have been dedicated to world regions (e.g., the European Stockholm network founded in 1997), individual country (e.g., the U.S. State Policy network), and issue areas (e.g., the neoliberal sustainable development network founded in 2001; compare www.stockholm-network.org, www.spn.org, and www.sdnetwork.net, respectively).

9. To be sure, Buchanan also used the occasion to value radical libertarian perspectives when battling state ownership of means of production and state regulation.

10. James Buchanan, "Man and the State," MPS Presidential talk, August 31, 1986, p. 2, LAMP).

11. Although the partisan scientific character of the neoliberal thought collective may be unique, the apparent mix of political, ideological, and scientific work should not be misleadingly contrasted to real science (as recently done by Mooney 2005) since the political character of scientific knowledge needs to be generally recognized. On the (post-) World War II transformation of politicized (economics) science in contradistinction to the autonomy claims developed by philosophers of science during this period, see Mirowski (2002, 2004).

12. Accusations according to which a historical focus on elite networks amounts to conspiracy theory overlook the fact that corporate planning groups are forced to meet and coordinate in order to develop political strategies precisely because they do not control the world (van der Pijl 1995, 107; compare Mills 2000, 293).

13. "Feldstein's influence extends easily into the political realm. Much of President George W. Bush's economic team studied under, or was recommended by, Professor Feldstein. Among these are Lawrence Lindsey, R. Glen Hubbard, Richard Clarida, Assistant Secretary of the Treasury for Economic Policy, and Paul O'Neill, former Secretary of the Treasury. Indeed, Feldstein is generally credited as the father of 'supply-side' economics and helped to create President George W. Bush's 2001 tax cut plan" (Leonhardt 2002, quoted in Weller and Singleton 2006).

14. For a summary of the critique in the context of the Asian crisis, see Vestergaard (2006). For some other critics, see Soederberg, Menz, and Czerny (2005); Robison (2006). As economists have more recently begun to trumpet the emergence of a "post-Washington Consensus," it is interesting to observe the extent to which their position is moving even closer to a "constructivist" version of the relationship of the govern-

ment to the market, something argued below, is a hallmark of neoliberal political economy (compare Postface, in this volume).

15. The following section draws heavily on Walpen (2005); see also Walpen (2000).

16. References to Gide's (1898) use of the term tend to be misleading, since he uses it in regard to a "return" to the classical liberalism of Adam Smith, and not as a theoretical departure, as described herein. Thanks to Phil Mirowski for clarifying this point.

17. See Bohle and Neunhöffer (2006) and Hull (2006) for discussions of the socialist calculation debate with regard to the evolution of the neoliberal thought collective.

18. On the Vienna Circles, see Stadler (2001); Caldwell (2004); Nordmann (2005).

19. Raymond Aron, Marcel Bourgeois, Étienne Mantoux, Louis Marlio, Louis Rougier and Jacques Rueff all belonged to the French group. The story of the Colloque is covered in Denord (2003; 2007) and in Chapter 1 of this volume.

20. See Tribe, Chapter 2 in this volume. The most important members of the London School of Economics (LSE) contingent were Theodore E. Gregory, Lionel Robbins, Arnold Plant, Frederic Benham, William H. Hutt, and Frank W. Paish (Apel 1961; Dahrendorf 1995: 184–187). Gregory and Hutt, together with Ludwig Lachmann, made up the small neoliberal cadre in South Africa.

21. Karl Schiller first coined the phrase "planning as much as necessary, competition as much as possible" to reconfigure the traditional Social Democratic emphasis on planning (see Foucault 2004, 130–132).

22. It is important to highlight the seeming contradiction of treating the individual personality as inviolate, and yet eminently subject to manipulation through all sorts of technologies of "governmentality" and vigilant governance.

23. Several European neoliberals shared Lippmann's emphasis on the absence of economic rather than political freedom (e.g., Rappard and Rougier; compare Walpen 2004a, 56).

24. Neoliberalism's diversity, even at the moment of its creation, is illustrated by a set of principles best expressed in the final part of the proceedings of the Colloque Walter Lippmann, "Le compte-rendu des séances du Colloque Walter Lippmann," cited above as CWL, following Bernhard Walpen's keynote lecture (see note 7 above; compare Walpen 2004a, 60) and in the dispute over MPS's Statement of Aims, discussed below.

25. The four chapters of the first section detail the most important groups that eventually became closely linked across borders. Hartwell (1995, 101) calls the MPS a "two-man show" (i.e., Hayek and Hunold) prior to 1958, a perspective considerably at odds with the findings of the chapters in the second section of this volume. Walpen (2004a) and Plehwe and Walpen (2006) provide critical accounts of the processes leading up to the formation of the Mont Pèlerin Society.

26. Karl Popper, in Hartwell (1995, 35). Hayek's own attempts to refute socialism had not achieved much intellectual success by this juncture; for more on this, see Mirowski (2007), which is a meditation upon Caldwell (2004).

27. The total U.S. membership so far (until 2004) was 437, amounting to almost half of the MPS population (cf. Walpen 2004a, 395).

28. See www.montpelerin.org/mpsPresidents.cfm for details.

29. This may be due to the official registration of the MPS in the United States.

30. The years 1947–1986 mark the period for which information is fully available between the MPS archives in Ghent and Stanford. Unfortunately, the 1988 list of participants in the Tokyo meeting was available neither at the Liberaal Archief nor at the Hoover Institution. Information on participants in regional meetings available at the Hoover Institution is incomplete.

31. Christian Gandil (1970, 9) describes the almost yearly conferences of leaders of neoliberal organizations and associations from Denmark, Germany, and France.

32. A total of 136 MPS members have been identified who work for think tanks and foundations related to the MPS (Plehwe and Walpen 2006, 37).

33. Allais saw good reasons for public ownership of land, which led him to object (see Hartwell 1995, 42n.), though the alleged contradiction remains unclear in the written information available.

34. Readers curious for greater detail about the particular Swiss roots will have to turn to work published elsewhere in German and French (Walpen 2004b; Steiner 2007). Several other European countries, such as Sweden and Belgium, and non-European countries, for example, Mexico, South Africa, and Japan, also deserve closer scrutiny and recognition with regard to the roots of neoliberalism because they featured neoliberal activities at an early date. An account decidedly less focused on large countries and Europe remains to be researched and written.

References

Anderson, Perry. 2000. "Renewals." *New Left Review* 1 (January–February 2000): 5–25 (10).

Apel, Hans-Eberhard. 1961. *Edwin Cannan und seine Schüler. Die Neuliberalen an der London School of Economics.* Tübingen: J. C. B. Mohr.

Ayau, Manuel. 1990. "The War of Ideas in Guatemala." In John C. Goodman and Ramona Marotz-Baden, eds., *Fighting the War of Ideas in Latin America.* Dallas: National Center for Policy Analysis, 138–146.

Bislev, Sven, Dorte Salskov-Iversen, and Hans Krause Hansen. 2002. "The Global Diffusion of Managerialism: Transnational Discourse Communities at Work." *Global Society* 16(2): 199–212.

Bobbio, Norberto. 1994. *Rechts und Links. Gründe und Bedeutungen einer politischen Unterscheidung.* Berlin: Rotbuch.

Bohle, Dorothee, and Gisela Neunhöffer. 2006. "Why Is There No Third Way? The Role of Neoliberal Ideology, Networks and Think Tanks in Combating Market Socialism and Shaping Transformation in Poland." In Dieter Plehwe, Bernhard

Walpen, and Gisela Neunhöffer, eds., *Neoliberal Hegemony: A Global Critique.* London: Routledge, 89–104.

Caldwell, Bruce. 2004. *Hayek's Challenge.* Chicago: University of Chicago Press.

Chafuen, Alejandro A. 2006a. "Hope amid Turmoil in Latin America?" *Highlights (Quarterly Newsletter of the Atlas Economic Research Foundation)* (Spring): 1, 6, 7.

Cockett, Richard. 1995. *Thinking the Unthinkable: Think Tanks and the Economic Counter-revolution, 1931–83.* London: Fontana.

Czerny, Philip G. 2008. "Embedding Neoliberalism: The Evolution of a Hegemonic Paradigm." *Journal of International Trade and Diplomacy* 2(Spring): 1–46.

Dahrendorf, Ralf. 1995. *The LSE.* Oxford: Oxford University Press.

Denord, François. 2003. *Genèse et institutionnalisation du néo-libéralisme dans la France (années 1930–années 1950).* Paris.

Denord, François. 2007. *Néo-libéralisme version français.* Paris: Demopolis.

Feichtinger, Johannes. 2001. *Wissenschaft zwischen den Kulturen. Östereichische Hochschullehrer in der Emigration 1933–1945.* Frankfurt am Main: Campus.

Feulner, Edwin J. 1999. *Intellectual Pilgrims. The Fiftieth Anniversary of the Mont Pelerin Society.* Washington, DC: Heritage Foundation.

Fleck, Ludwik. 1980. *Entstehung und Entwicklung einer wissenschaftlichen Tatsache. Einführung in die Lehre vom Denkstil und Denkkollektiv.* Frankfurt am Main: Suhrkamp Verlag (reprint; orig. 1935).

Foucault, Michel. 2004. *Geschichte der Gouvernementalität II. Die Geburt der Biopolitik.* Frankfurt am Main: Suhrkamp Verlag.

Frost, Gerald. 2002. *Antony Fisher: Champion of Liberty.* London: Profile Books.

Gandil, Christian. 1970. "How to Improve the Image of the Entrepreneur." LAMP.

Gandil, Christian. 1986. "Comment on R. M. Hartwell: The History of the Mont Pelerin Society." LAMP.

Gide, Charles. 1898. "Has Co-operation Introduced a New Principle into Economics?" *Economic Journal* 8(32): 490–511.

Goodman, John C., and Ramona Marotz-Baden, eds. 1990. *Fighting the War of Ideas in Latin America.* Dallas: National Center for Policy Analysis.

Haas, Peter. 1992. "Introduction: Epistemic Communities and International Policy Coordination." *International Organization* 46(1): 1–36.

Haegeman, Marc. 2004. *Inventory of the General Meeting Files of the Mont Pèlerin Society (1947–1998).* Ghent: Liberaal Archief.

Hajer, Maarten A. 1993. "Discourse Coalitions and the Institutionalization of Practice: The Case of Acid Rain in Britain." In Frank Fischer and John Forrester, eds., *The Argumentative Turn in Policy Analysis and Planning.* Durham, NC: Duke University Press, 43–76.

Hall, Peter, ed. 1989. *The Political Power of Economic Ideas: Keynesianism across Nations.* Princeton, NJ: Princeton University Press.

Hartwell, Ronald M. 1995. *A History of the Mont Pelerin Society.* Indianapolis, IN: Liberty Fund.

Harvey, David. 2005. *A Brief History of Neoliberalism.* New York: Oxford University Press.

Hayek, Friedrich. 1967. *Studies in Philosophy, Politics and Economics.* New York: Simon & Schuster.

Helleiner, Eric. 1994. *States and the Re-emergence of Global Finance: From Bretton Woods to the 1990s.* Ithaca, NY: Cornell University Press.

Hull, Richard. 2006. "The Great Lie: Markets, Freedom and Knowledge." In Dieter Plehwe, Bernhard Walpen, and Gisela Neunhöffer, eds., *Neoliberal Hegemony: A Global Critique.* London: Routledge, 141–155.

Keck, Margaret, and Kathryn Sikkink. 1998. *Activists beyond Borders: Advocacy Networks in International Politics.* Ithaca, NY: Cornell University Press.

Knight, Frank. 1934. "Economic Theory and Nationalism." In Milton Friedman, Homer Jones, George Stigler, and Allen Wallis, eds., *Ethics of Competition.* London: Allen & Unwin.

Leonhardt, David. 2002. "Scholarly Mentor to Bush's Team." *New York Times,* December 1.

McGann, James G. 2007. The Global "Go-To Think Tanks." www.fpri.org/research/thinktanks/mcgann.globalgotothinktanks.pdf. Accessed June 1, 2007.

Miller, John J. 2006. *A Gift of Freedom: How the John M. Olin Foundation Changed America.* San Francisco: Encounter Books.

Mills, Charles W. 2000. *The Power Elite.* London: Oxford University Press.

Mirowski, Philip. 2002. *Machine Dreams.* New York: Cambridge University Press.

Mirowski, Philip. 2007. "Naturalizing the Market on the Road to Revisionism: Caldwell on Hayek's Challenge." *Journal of Institutional Economics* 3(3): 351–372.

Mises, Ludwig von. 1927. *Liberalismus.* Jena: Gustav Fischer Verlag.

Mooney, Chris. 2005. *The Republican War on Science.* New York: Basic Books.

Nash, George H. 1996 [1976]. *The Conservative Intellectual Movement in America since 1945.* Wilmington: Intercollegiate Studies Institute.

Nordmann, Jürgen. 2005. *Der lange Marsch zum Neoliberalismus.* Hamburg: VSA-Verlag.

Overbeek, Henk, ed. 1993. *Restructuring Hegemony in the Global Political Economy: The Rise of Transnational Neo-Liberalism in the 1980s.* London: Routledge.

Plehwe, Dieter, and Bernhard Walpen. 2007. "Neoliberale Denkkollektive und ihr Denkstil." In G. Arrighi et al., eds., *Kapitalismus Reloaded. Kontroversen zu Imperialismus, Empire und Hegemonie.* Hamburg: VSA-Verlag, 347–371.

Plehwe, Dieter, and Bernhard Walpen. 2006. "Between Network and Complex Organization: The Making of Neoliberal Knowledge and Hegemony." In Bernhard Walpen, Dieter Plehwe, and Gisela Nuenhöffer (eds.), *Neoliberal Hegemony: A Global Critique.* London: Routledge, 27–70.

Plehwe, Dieter, and Katja Walther. 2008. "Im Schatten von Hayek und Friedman: Die Vielflieger im Kreise der Mont Pèlerin Society. Quantitative Analyse als Explorationsinstrument der historisch-sozialen Netzwerkforschung." In

Berthold Unfried, Jürgen Mittag, and Marcel van der Linden, eds.,
  *Transnationale Netzwerke im 20. Jahrhundert. Historische Erkundungen zu Ideen
  und Praktiken, Individuen und Organisationen.* Vienna: Akademische
  Verlagsanstalt, 235–264.

Robison, Richard, ed. 2006. *The Neo-Liberal Revolution: Forging the Market State.*
  London: Palgrave.

Rodrik, Dani. 1996. "Understanding Economic Policy Reform." *Journal of Economic
  Literature* 34(1): 9–41.

Smith, Barbara Herrnstein. 2005. *Scandalous Knowledge: Science, Truth and the
  Human.* Durham, NC: Duke University Press.

Soederberg, Susan, George Menz, and Philip Czerny, eds. 2005. *Internalizing
  Globalization: The Rise of Neoliberalism.* London: Palgrave.

Sombart, Werner. 1976. *Why Is There No Socialism in the United States?* New York:
  Sharpe.

Stadler, Friedrich. 1997. *Studien zum Wiener Kreis. Ursprung, Entwicklung und
  Wirkung des Logischen Empirismus im Kontext.* Frankfurt am Main: Suhrkamp.

Stadler, Friedrich. 2001. *The Vienna Circle.* New York: Springer.

Steel, Ronald. 1980. *Walter Lippmann and the American Century.* Boston: Little, Brown.

Steiner, Yves. 2007. "Les riches amis suisses du néolibéralisme. De la débâcle de la revue
  Occident à la Conférence du Mont Pèlerin d'avril 1947." *Traverse* 14(1): 114–126.

Stiglitz, Joseph. 1999. "More Instruments and Broader Goals." In G. Kochendorfer-
  Lucius and B. Pleskovic, eds., *Development Issues in the 21st Century.* Berlin:
  German Foundation for International Development.

Van der Pijl, Kees. 1995. "The Second Glorious Revolution: Globalizing Elites and
  Historical Change." In Björn Hettne, ed., *International Political Economy:
  Understanding Global Disorder.* Halifax: Fernwood, 100–128.

Vestergaard, Jakob. 2006. *Discipline in the Global Economy.* Ph.D. thesis, University
  of Copenhagen.

Wainwright, Hilary. 1994. *Arguments for a New Left: Answering the Free-Market Right.*
  Oxford: Blackwell.

Walpen, Bernhard. 2000. "Von Igeln und Hasen oder: Ein Blick auf den
  Neoliberalismus." *UTOPIE kreativ*, No. 121/122 (November/December 2000):
  1066–1079.

Walpen, Bernhard. 2004a. *Die offenen Feinde und ihre Gesellschaft. Eine
  hegemonietheoretische Studie zur Mont Pèlerin Society.* Hamburg: VSA-Verlag.

Walpen, Bernhard. 2004b. "Die Schweiz—Kaderschmiede des Neoliberalismus. Zur
  Geschichte neoliberaler Institutionen und Vordenker." *Widerspruch* 24(46): 141–151.

Walpen, Bernhard. 2005. "The Plan to End Planning: A Short History of
  Neoliberalism." Keynote lecture delivered at the New York
  University / International Center for Advanced conference "How Neoliberalism
  Became a Transnational Movement," April 28–30.

Weller, Christian, and Laura Singleton. 2006. "Peddling Reform: The Role of Think Tanks in Shaping the Neoliberal Policy Agenda for the World Bank and International Monetary Fund." In Dieter Plehwe, Bernhard Walpen, and Gisela Neunhöffer, eds., *Neoliberal Hegemony: A Global Critique.* London: Routledge.

Wiese, Leopold von. 1925. "Gibt es noch Liberalismus?" In Moritz J. Bonn and Melchior Palyi, eds., *Die Wirtschaftswissenschaft nach dem Kriege. Festgabe für Lujo Bretano zum 80. Geburtstag, Bd. I: Wirtschaftspolitische Ideologien.* Munich–Leipzig.

Williamson, John. 2003. "From Reform Agenda to Damaged Brand Name: A Short History of the Washington Consensus and Suggestions for What to Do Next." *Finance & Development* (September 2003): 10–13.

Williamson, John. 2004. "A Short History of the Washington Consensus." Paper commissioned by Fundación CIDOB for the conference, "From the Washington Consensus towards a New Global Governance," Barcelona, September 24–25, 2004 (www.iie.com/publications/papers/williamson0904-2.pdf, download February 20, 2005).

Wittrock, Björn, Peter Wagner, and Hellmut Wollmann. 1987. *Social Science and the Modern State: Knowledge, Institutions, and Societal Transformations.* Berlin, WZB Discussion Paper P87-3.

Yergin, Daniel, and Joseph Stanislaw. 1998. *The Commanding Heights.* New York: Touchstone.

Zmirak, John. 2001. *William Röpke.* Wilmington, DE: ISI Books.

PART ONE

Origins of National Traditions

I

French Neoliberalism and Its Divisions

From the Colloque Walter Lippmann to the Fifth Republic

FRANÇOIS DENORD

The emergence of neoliberalism as an intellectual network is partly due to a French initiative. Organized by the philosopher Louis Rougier in 1938, the Colloque Walter Lippmann—an international congress held in Paris, consisting of twenty-six businessmen, top civil servants, and economists from several countries—contributed to the rise of this intellectual agenda. It also led to the creation of a nonprofit organization, the Centre international d'études pour la rénovation du libéralisme (CIRL), which attracted members of the ruling elite seeking an answer to "the crisis of capitalism." Established against advancing notions of the planned economy and collectivism, the CIRL disappeared when France entered World War II. Nevertheless, this institution provided the model for the Mont Pèlerin Society (MPS), which Friedrich Hayek and Wilhelm Röpke created in 1947.

Although a French neoliberal tradition has existed since the 1930s, its history is not very well known. This chapter compares the intellectual configurations of two eras (the 1930s and the 1950s–1960s) and emphasizes the transformations that affected economists and businessmen after World War II in order to explain the divisions of French neoliberalism. Whereas in the 1930s this set of ideas could find an audience beyond traditional liberal circles (attracting, for instance, trade-union leaders), this became impossible in the context of the Cold War. Neoliberalism was defended in the 1930s by some of the most renowned economists and businessmen, but its advocates formed only a minority within the intellectual field of the 1960s: French neoliberalism had become radicalized in opposition to the expansion of the welfare state. However, the conceptions traditionally associated with French neoliberalism subsequently spread into other groups. By the time French liberalism enjoyed a revival in the 1970s and 1980s, neoliberalism had already inspired governmental practice but was condemned by new neoliberals for its supposed collusion with social democracy.

The Legacy of the 1930s

Neoliberalism appeared in France at the end of the 1930s. Its development was facilitated by (1) the contestation of the liberal creed in the field of public policy (a consequence of World War I and of the Great Depression); and (2) the economic and political defeat of the Front Populaire, a left-wing government coalition that had failed to radically transform France's economic structures. At the beginning of 1938, in the view of the elites both classical liberalism and socialist planning had been discredited. In this context, a discourse seeking to reconcile not only opponents to the 1936 experiment but disillusioned socialists as well could find support. Faced with growing state intervention and the development of economic ideas that sought to enforce this tendency, neoliberalism seemed to offer an alternative. It promised the building of a liberal state protecting free enterprise and free competition and the retreat of the state away from the economy.

The preeminent advocate of a neoliberal solution to the crisis was Louis Rougier (1889–1982), a professor at the University of Besançon. As a philosopher, he occupied a marginal position in academia owing to his opposition to Bergsonism and rationalism.[1] As a political activist, he supported center-right leaders both against radicalism and communism, and against monarchism and fascism. As the promoter of an intellectual renewal of economic liberalism that would precede and sustain its political rebirth,[2] Rougier had developed contacts with businessmen and economists in France and in other countries (in particular in Austria and Switzerland). As a result of his involvement in different networks, he became associated with the foundation of a publishing house, La Librairie de Médicis (1937), and with convening an international conference around the French translation of Lippmann's *The Good Society*.[3]

The organization of the Colloque Walter Lippmann was relatively spontaneous. Learning of the imminent arrival of the eminent American journalist
in France, Louis Rougier initiated preparations at the end of May 1938. Initially, he only wanted to arrange a dinner to celebrate the author of the *Good
Society.* To some colleagues, like the Swiss William Rappard, however, it seemed
a curious dinner. Louis Rougier had promised a gathering of renowned intellectuals. Around Walter Lippmann were to be seated his French preface
writer, André Maurois, the economists Bernard Lavergne and Jacques Rueff,
one of the trustees of the Rockefeller Foundation, Tracy B. Kittredge, as well
as the French specialist in political science, André Siegfried.[4] Rougier did not
first propose the list of guests to Lippmann himself. Instead, Rougier simply
mentioned André Maurois and some "colleagues from the Law Faculty," but
added the names of Paul Baudouin, the director of the Banque d'Indochine,
and Marcel Bourgeois, "the sponsor of the Editions of Médicis."[5] Both Maurois and Baudouin had financed fascist movements such as the Parti Populaire
Français (PPF) of Jacques Doriot. Lippmann, who had met Louis Rougier
only once before—in Geneva with Ludwig von Mises, William Rappard, and
Wilhelm Röpke—became suspicious.[6] Although Friedrich Hayek had depicted his French interlocutor as "a distinguished philosopher," "very respected
for his work on the epistemological problems,"[7] Hayek understood that the
intellectual discussions could have been considered of secondary importance.
In a letter addressed to William Rappard, Louis Rougier did not hide its objective: to lead "an international crusade in favor of constructive liberalism."[8]
Perhaps because Friedrich Hayek and Ludwig von Mises took part in the Colloque, Walter Lippmann let himself be convinced to participate in "a restricted and closed conference, to discuss the main thesis of [his book]." This
conference was to be only a general rehearsal for "an international Congress in
1939 on the same subjects."[9] As it turned out, this congress never took place,
even if two conferences actually held around this time extended the efforts of
the summer of 1938: one devoted to the "economic, political and spiritual
status of tomorrow's Europe" in July 1939; and the other focused on "the economic conditions of a future federation of England and France" in April
1940.[10]

All the participants in the Colloque Lippmann were hand-picked. The
Marxist theorist Rudolf Hilferding and the former socialist minister Charles
Spinasse, who wished to attend the discussion, were nimbly excluded because
they "were [*sic*] politicians."[11] The international forum gathered some of the

most influential French corporate managers (Auguste Detoeuf, Louis Marlio, Ernest Mercier), senior civil servants (Jacques Rueff, Roger Auboin), and intellectuals (Raymond Aron) as well as members of a rising new generation of liberal economists (Friedrich Hayek, Ludwig von Mises, Wilhelm Röpke, etc.).[12] In retrospect, the participants in the Colloque Lippmann would appear to have constituted a prestigious conclave: its members would later become a Nobel Prize winner in economics (Friedrich Hayek), the general secretary of the Organization for European Economic Co-Operation (Robert Marjolin), the architects of the German social market economy (Wilhelm Röpke, Alexander Rüstow), the director of the Bank for International Settlements (Roger Auboin), the financial adviser of General Charles de Gaulle (Jacques Rueff), the power behind Ronald Reagan's Star Wars project (Stephan Possony), and so on.

The congress attendees disagreed on many points: Is freedom an end in itself (a position defended by Etienne Mantoux and Louis Rougier) or merely a means (espoused by Louis Baudin, Robert Marjolin)? Is liberalism only the rigorous application of the laws of economics (Louis Marlio) or an ideology (Robert Marjolin)? Does liberalism have to take into account the provision of social security (Louis Rougier, Walter Lippmann) or not (Jacques Rueff)? Clear oppositions surfaced several times. With regard to the question of industrial concentration, it was criticized by the economists, whereas the industrialists defended the trusts. Confronting the problem of money, Jacques Rueff or Louis Baudin did not want to see it "directed," whereas Walter Lippmann preached its management and condemned the legal statute of companies. Thus, the backers of the Colloque Lippmann were not of one mind along many dimensions.

Neoliberalism was not a unified phenomenon. Even the name of the doctrine was a problem: Louis Baudin preferred "individualism," Louis Rougier "positive liberalism," while Jacques Rueff favored "left-wing liberalism." The term *neoliberalism* became prevalent only after the Colloque for strategic reasons: "the words 'neo' and 'renovation,'" declared Louis Marlio, . . . "distinguish us from several authors of whom we did not accept all the practical theories and all objections [against] interventions which are accepted by most of us like perfectly normal things. For those who know it, . . . the word 'neo' is perhaps not essential, but for those who do not know it, it is totally useful."[13] To be "neoliberal" was supposed to imply the recognition that "laissez-faire" economics was not enough and that, in the name of liberalism, a modern economic policy was needed.

Consequently, several commentators could point to the existence of two groups within the Colloque. On one side were "those for which neoliberalism was fundamentally different, in its spirit and its program of traditional liberalism"[14] (these included Louis Rougier, Auguste Detoeuf, Louis Marlio, Wilhelm Röpke, and Alexandre Rüstow), and on the other side were defenders of the "old liberalism" headed by Louis Baudin, Jacques Rueff, and the Austrian School (Friedrich Hayek, Ludwig von Mises). Some of the participants directly grappled with this division. Alexander Rüstow went straight to the point: "it is undeniable that here, in our circle, two different points of view are represented. Those who do not find anything essential to be criticized or to change with traditional liberalism. . . . We, the others, who are seeking the responsibility for the decline of liberalism in liberalism itself; and consequently, are seeking the solution in a fundamental renewal of liberalism."[15] Publicly, Rüstow conformed to the rules of academic propriety, but privately, he confessed to Wilhelm Röpke what he thought of Friedrich Hayek and Ludwig von Mises: their place was in the museum, in the formalin, Rüstow said.[16] It was people of their ilk who were responsible for the great crisis of market legitimacy of the twentieth century. Some of the conflicts that were to mark the history of neoliberalism in the later years began to become manifest: at the Colloque between "German ordoliberalism" and radical libertarianism; between the acceptance of interventionism and its rejection; between the partisans of a voluntarist liberal policy and those nostalgic for laissez-faire.

Nevertheless, this international meeting became a landmark in the history of liberalism. For the first time, neoliberalism was defined by a set of postulates that constituted an agenda: the use of the price mechanism as the best way to obtain the maximal satisfaction of human expectations; the responsibility of the state for instituting a juridical framework adjusted to the order defined by the market; the possibility for the state to follow goals other than short-term expedients and to further them by levying taxes; the acceptance of state intervention if it does not favor any particular group and seeks to act upon the causes of the economic difficulties. "To be [neo]liberal, said Louis Rougier, doesn't mean to be a 'Manchesterian' who leaves the cars circulating in all directions, if such is their will, which can only result in traffic jams and incessant accidents; it doesn't mean to be a 'Planist' who gives every car its exit time and its route; it means to impose a highway code while admitting that it is not necessary to be the same at the time of the accelerated transports as at the time of diligences."[17] This metaphor, which Hayek also used in his *Road to*

Serfdom, has an enhanced significance: it supposes that in order to function properly, economic competition requires dedicated institutions. It therefore specifies the type of intervention that is compatible with a liberal economic policy: the state creates the framework within which competition is free. It begins to clarify what a neoliberal state must be: a regulator that punishes deviations from the "correct" legal framework.

In the context of an economic and political crisis, neoliberalism unexpectedly rallied together people who had previously seemed to be irreconcilable. Founded in 1939 after the Colloque Lippmann, the Centre international d'études pour la rénovation du libéralisme brought together classical liberals, neoliberals, corporatists, and disabused planning advocates. Two aspects distinguished the CIRL from other economic circles that had sprung up in the interwar period. First, it recruited equally among academic economists (Louis Baudin, Gaëtan Pirou, Charles Rist, etc.) and important corporate managers (Auguste Detoeuf, Louis Marlio, Ernest Mercier, etc.). These two groups had been competing throughout the 1930s to establish what should be sanctioned as the legitimate approach to economic problems. To the extent that it gave prominence to legal issues, neoliberalism could convince both economists, who at that time were trained and taught in law faculties, and managers, who promoted industrial rationalization and the building of a legal order in which reasonable planning would be possible. The second peculiarity of the CIRL was that leaders of the labor union Confédération Génerale du Travail (CGT) (René Belin, Robert Lacoste, Christian Pineau, Louis Vallon) also participated in the discussion of neoliberal ideas. Apparently, this rapprochement between neoliberals and trade unionists, which a member of the CGT found "odd," took place only in France. Although their attendance did not mean that these trade unionists had necessarily adopted a liberal point of view or that they had formally joined the CIRL, they still took part in the CIRL's workshops. These reformists doubted the future of economic planning and tried to counter the growing influence of the communists in their trade unions.

The mobilization of these individuals was partly due to their involvement in structured networks that established junctions between industrialists and trade unionists (associations such as X-Crise or Les Nouveaux Cahiers) and between businessmen and faculty members (societies such as the Société d'économie politique and l'Académie des sciences morales et politiques). At the end of the 1930s, neoliberalism appeared to offer a possible compromise between different factions of the ruling elite trying to safeguard the autonomy of the economic field. This success also had a political foundation: the Daladier government (1938–1940) adopted a liberal economic agenda in contrast with the policy of the Front Populaire. It reduced the public deficit, increased working time, and foiled the general strike organized by the trade unions in 1938.[18]

World War II put an abrupt end to these experiments. The war economy and the structural reforms planned by the Resistance, or Free French, and the Vichy regime helped marginalize neoliberalism.[19] Faced with the arbitrary nature of the governing authority, the original group of French neoliberals split. A minority joined the Resistance (Raymond Aron, René Courtin, Gaston Leduc, Robert Marjolin), some neoliberals played an important role in the Vichy regime (Joseph-Barthélemy, Emile Mireaux, Henri Moysset), while others preferred not to commit (Charles Rist) or left the country (Louis Marlio). The disintegration of the group was all the quicker because its existence depended on a few key individuals, particularly Louis Rougier. Initially hesitating between joining de Gaulle or Vichy, Rougier tried, unsuccessfully, to effect a secret agreement between Pétain and Churchill; subsequently, Rougier left France for the United States, where he soon found himself marginalized at the New York School for Social Research after he refused to recognize the legitimacy of France Libre.

After the Liberation and the reforms introduced by the republican government between 1944 and 1946 (consisting of nationalizations, social security, and planning), it seemed that neoliberalism had been definitely left in the lurch. Actually, the Liberation had two opposite effects: it marked the institutional defeat of neoliberalism within France, but it also led to a reconfiguration of the political field, which nurtured the rebirth of liberalism.

Neoliberalism and the Dynamic of the Cold War

Neoliberal criticisms of structural reforms found their way into the economic press and the daily newspapers (*Le Figaro* but also *Le Monde,* where René Courtin was initially one of the directors),[20] mobilizing a broad segment of the business community. Although right-wing parties were particularly concerned by the *épuration* (that is, the lustration trials following the fall of the Vichy regime) and although communists and socialists were in a dominant position, economic liberalism was still represented by a patchwork of formations, which were sometimes difficult to locate politically.[21] The postwar period caused divisions within parties and collective shifts between them, with some former left-wing movements, like the Radical Party, joining the center-right. Among the groups that explicitly claimed their liberalism in 1945–1947, the Parti Républicain de la Liberté (PRL) was the most active. It proudly sported the name of its program: neoliberalism.[22] Formed in December 1945 in opposition to the Social Catholics (Mouvement Républicain Populaire, or MRP) and the communists, the PRL recruited both among the Resistance and among the former Petainists. In the Parliament, it opposed any project inspired by "Marxism."

The borders between the political movements supporting economic liberalism were porous, and points of dissension were numerous but indistinct. In 1946, the Rassemblement des Gauches Républicaines (RGR) was founded. Hostile to state intervention and economic nationalization, it attracted movements emanating from both the left and the right. But it was not until the creation of the Centre national des indépendants (CNI) in 1948 that economic liberalism found genuine representation in the political field. The CNI promoted the union of the "moderates" and, from the beginning, benefited from the support of many notables and right-wing intellectuals like Jacques Rueff and other members of the Mont Pèlerin Society. Until the turning point of the 1950s, economic liberalism could hardly provide a counterweight against the left and against the Rassemblement du Peuple Français (RPF) formed by de Gaulle in 1947. The Cold War, however, progressively modified power relations within the political field. With the end of the three-party government in 1947, the Fourth Republic needed an alliance of the socialists, radicals, independents, and MRP in order to ensure stability. As a result, the economic policy of the years 1944–1946 was increasingly questioned, as demonstrated by the exclusion of the interventionists from the Ramadier government in October 1947 and the policies adopted by the successive ministers of finance, including René Mayer[23]— a former member of the CIRL—and Maurice Petsche.[24] Economic and social policy around 1950 was characterized by the search for a balanced budget and the fight against inflation. Neoliberalism as an alternative inspired Henri Queuille as well as Edgar Faure and Antoine Pinay—"moderates" who sought to re-create through state interventionism the conditions of a free competition.

This political resurgence of neoliberalism reflected first and foremost the strength of anticommunism in French political life. It brought together individuals who were otherwise far apart from each other politically. Thus, the Congress for Cultural Freedom, an instrument of American cultural diplomacy located in Paris in 1951, immediately obtained a measure of intellectual respectability. Its journal *Preuves* brought together representatives of the anti-

communist left (members of the Rassemblement Démocratique Révolution-
naire like David Rousset), conservatives (Thierry Maulnier, journalist at *Le
Figaro*), Gaullists, and liberals of the journal *Liberté de l'esprit* (Raymond
Aron).[25] In the context of the Cold War, anticommunism also offered the
vanquished of World War II the possibility of an acceptable political identity.
Atlanticism and neoliberalism often constituted the social philosophy around
which they rallied. Starting in May 1946, the *Revue des études américaines,* a
quarterly journal directed by Achille Dauphin-Meunier, was the rallying
ground of this reconfiguration of alliances with the United States and against
the Soviet Union. The ideological convergence between some former supporters of the Vichy regime, atlanticists, and neoliberals was also behind the creation of the *Nouvelle revue de l'économie contemporaine* in 1950. It numbered
among its editorial board several collaborators of *Les Ecrits de Paris,* a journal
that gathered intellectuals from the right wing and the extreme right wing
who criticized "resistantialism" (Jacques Chastenet, Bertrand de Jouvenel,
Claude-Joseph Gignoux, Louis Rougier). The authors included Vichy ministers, leaders of the CNI, old liberals of the Law Faculty, former supporters of
corporatism, engineer economists (Maurice Allais and his student Edmond
Malinvaud), and of course business leaders such as Georges Villiers. The *Nouvelle revue de l'économie contemporaine* was probably the first review in France
to publish an article about the Mont Pèlerin Society.[26]

Neoliberalism thus indirectly benefited from the impact of the Cold War
on French politics and from the revival of the right, with all the ambiguities it
involved. Obviously, neoliberalism found its main supporters among businessmen. They protested against the growth of the state since the Liberation
and against "modernization," whose methods they had been excluded from
defining. Neoliberalism constituted a common denominator for many businessmen, whatever their sectors of origin and their divergences of interest. It
was thus with the support of the leading authorities of the Centre national du
patronat français (CNPF) that the Association de la libre entreprise (ALE) was
created in 1947, an organization aiming at "defending and . . . recommending
freedom of enterprise from the economic and social point of view with all its
consequences."[27] Inspired by the Foundation for Economic Education and
maintaining relationships to a score of similar organizations disseminated in
Europe and in the United States,[28] the ALE distributed "educational" booklets on the market economy. The objective was simple: "to highlight the misdeeds of state intervention . . . and to denounce it as the cancer of France."[29]

The ALE was directed by Georges Villiers, the president of the CNPF, and led by Georges Morisot, an engineer at Michelin. Both were members of the Mont Pèlerin Society. The composition of the board of directors of the ALE gives an outline of the vast array of support available to the liberal cause in the mid-1950s: representatives of industrial large-scale employers, notables, an adviser of the Centre des Jeunes Patrons (Hyacinthe Dubreuil), and members of organizations for small companies.[30] Commitment to liberalism transcended ordinary divisions among businessmen. It did not mean, however, that liberalism bore the same meaning for each mobilized fraction. Like in the 1930s, a substantial share of liberal businessmen were recruited from the organizations related to trade and export industries.

The conferences organized by the Comité d'action économique et douanière (CAED) were the occasion to bring together academic neoliberals (Louis Baudin, Daniel Villey, etc.) and businessmen. The neoliberalism that was defended there, although it was placed "in the shade of the Colloque Lippmann,"[31] remained radically anti-interventionist and convergent with the immediate interests of big business: it primarily had to do with limiting economic regulation, reducing the bureaucracy, alleviating fiscal pressure, and so on. The neoliberalism of the Centre des Jeunes Patrons (CJP) was built on quite different foundations. It was inspired by Social Catholicism and by the ideal of a professional organization. The CJP advocated a "concrete liberalism," while at the same time praising free enterprise, "fair" competition, and scientific management.[32] Unlike trade employers, CJP members accepted nationalizations, if they related to real monopolies, and unlike the liberal Catholics, they supported the cooperation of workers and management via mixed committees. Nothing was more opposite to the policies embraced by an organization like the Association interprofessionnelle de l'entreprise à capital personnel (AIECP). The program of the AIECP, a group founded in Lyon in August 1940, focused on the faction contained in its name. The AIECP represented companies based on personal capital ("the company based on personal capital is, in all the professions, the one where the Chief, the "Owner" works at the same time with his money, with his brain and often, with its hands"), and as such its goal was to defend the owner-businessmen, heirs or founders of small and medium companies, against the intrusion of the state and the interference of trade unions. Property, profit, and freedom of trade were thus the catchwords for the liberalism of an organization clamoring for the return of nationalized companies to the private sector.[33] The liberalism defended by the leaders of the AIECP (Lucien Daffos,

René Berger-Perrin) was resonant with a base made up of independent small engineers and provincial owners. From a doctrinal point of view, it was largely nourished by the liberalism of another organization: the Point de Rencontre Libéral-Spiritualiste. Founded in March 1947 by Pierre Lhoste-Lachaume, this organization spread a radical liberalism associated with Christian doctrines.[34]

Although neoliberalism had enjoyed a modicum of support in both the political field and the business sector, its position was quite different in the university. Between the end of the 1940s and the end of the 1950s, the discipline of economics underwent major transformations: its central role in public policy and the large increase in the number of teaching and research sites helped widen the teaching cadre and diversify its cherished values. Neoliberalism now seemed largely outré. In law schools, it found advocates among the heirs of the older generation who opposed the conversion of economics into a science at the service of the state. They rejected the extension of economic models to all fields of human life, as well as the development of macroeconomics and mathematical formalization.[35] Almost everything set them against Maurice Allais, the great figure of academic neoliberalism in the 1950s. In the 1930s and the 1940s, this former student of the École Polytechnique was connected with the most representative leaders of the technocratic circles, such as Auguste Detoeuf, who exerted a decisive influence on him. In line with his activities as a civil servant, Allais tried to show that economics could be understood through use of mathematics. As a professor of theoretical economics at the Statistical institute of the University of Paris (November 1947) and as a director of research at the National Center for Scientific Research (October 1954), he sought to become the theorist of a "competitive planning" who would bring together a decentralized economic organization and a planned institutional framework.[36] Even though Maurice Allais had disciples, in particular among econometricians, neoliberalism found itself in a paradoxical situation. On the one side, because of its divisions, it had mounted only a small intellectual bulwark against Marxism, Social Catholicism and, to a lesser extent, Keynesianism. On the other side, neoliberal conceptions seeped into consciousness even if the term *neoliberalism* itself remained unpopular and even if the neoliberals themselves had become marginalized.

Two Opposing Neoliberalisms

Analysis of the Mont Pèlerin Society's recruitment during the 1950s and the 1960s seems to underscore the intellectual decline of this ideology in France.

The Frenchmen whom Friedrich Hayek and Wilhelm Röpke initially contacted—René Courtin and Charles Rist first, then Maurice Allais, Daniel Villey, and Jacques Rueff—unlike Louis Rougier, had exhibited irreproachable behavior during World War II. The Mont Pèlerin Society sought out intellectuals, but its recruitment extended gradually toward businessmen. Academics nominated those businessmen whom they thought were the most qualified, and the designated businessmen in turn recommended other managers, as well as academics. The French section of the Mont Pèlerin Society owed its development to some individuals who were able to transcend various social fields. Jacques Rueff was one of the more influential of these individuals, although he devoted the largest part of his efforts to international organizations such as the Inter-Allied Reparations Agency and the Court of Justice of the European Coal and Steel Community. The first years of MPS's French section were characterized by a certain dynamism. In 1951, eighteen Frenchmen belonged to the MPS, which placed France second in Europe in membership, just behind Great Britain. Initially, the French section's financial contribution was also important. The CNPF of Georges Villiers subsidized the MPS in Europe and sponsored its meetings. The fourth congress of the Society was thus held in France in September 1951. Organized in Beauvallon, on the French Riviera, and bringing together sixty-eight participants, it cost the CNPF nearly 2 million francs (the rough equivalent of 39,000 contemporary euros).[37] But in fact, the French section, whose president was Jacques Rueff and whose treasurer was Roger Truptil,[38] was headed up by individuals with little time or inclination for international meetings dedicated to theoretical discussions. Thus, the French section quickly became the victim of the ravages of time. It lost several of its members famous for their combat in the name of liberalism (Louis Marlio, Ernest Mercier, and Charles Rist died during the 1950s), and in addition, it had difficulties replacing them. Except for Edmond Giscard d'Estaing (the father of later French president Valéry Giscard d'Estaing) and Jacques Georges-Picot, the CEO of the Suez Company, the businessmen recruited by the MPS during the 1950s were members of the Association interprofessionnelle de l'entreprise à capital personnel or of the Point de Rencontre Libéral-Spiritualiste. In the same way, the only academics joining the MPS during this period were notably less famous than their predecessors: Gaston Leduc, from the Law Faculty of Paris, Henry Hornobstel, from Poitiers, and Louis Rougier. At the beginning of the 1960s, the resignation of Raymond Aron and Bertrand de Jouvenel, who no longer accepted the version of liberalism defended by the Mont Pèlerin Society, revealed how difficult it was to get the French neoliberals to work together.

In France, as within the MPS, social liberalism and libertarianism were in competition. From this point of view, Maurice Allais and Pierre Lhoste-Lachaume constituted the two extremes of French neoliberalism. While Maurice Allais was among the few Frenchmen attending the first meeting of the Mont Pèlerin Society, he was the only participant who refused to sign the organization's original Statement of Aims (see the Introduction to this volume). According to Allais, the institution of private property was only a historical contingency and in no case could it be an aim in itself.[39] Faithful to the model of the third way asserted by the neoliberals of the 1930s, Allais argued for an alliance between socialists and neoliberals against collectivism and laissez-faire. Thus, the Mouvement pour une Société Libre, a political organization he created in 1958, strongly divided French neoliberals. It was supported by radicals, independents (René Mayer and Antoine Pinay), and intellectuals (Luc Bourcier de Carbon, René Courtin, Gaston Leduc, Louis Rougier, and Jacques Rueff). Yet for Pierre Lhoste-Lachaume, the attempt to reconcile liberalism and socialism was illusory and portended a dishonest compromise with collectivism.[40] In fact, two opposing groups arose within the movement: on one side were politicians and intellectuals, who had maintained a certain academic legitimacy and believed there could be no liberalism without state intervention; on the other side were small businessmen and their spokesmen, who attempted to safeguard their social position and tended to avoid any questioning of traditional social structures.

This opposition reflected a more general phenomenon. At the end of the 1950s, French neoliberals were not united. Whereas the creation of the Centre international d'études pour la renovation du libéralisme in the 1930s helped bring together under the neoliberal label an array of individuals with clashing economic conceptions, no institution played a comparable role after 1945. Liberal organizations multiplied without coordinating their action or their proposals. The alignments forged during World War II and the transformations of the role of the state triggered subsequent divisions. French neoliberals often shared neither the same religious convictions nor the same political opinions, so that they would naturally have contradictory reactions to later major events in the country.[41] Under these circumstances, it is not surprising that it was impossible to create an organization like the Aktionsgemeinschaft Soziale Marktwirtschaft in Germany, which brought neoliberal politicians,

economists, and businessmen into one network. The French neoliberals discovered they could not even unanimously endorse the term *neoliberalism*.
Whereas Jacques Rueff, who opposed the term in the 1930s, finally ended up
accepting it, others refused, finding that the term was either "worn down,
compromised . . . by the unhappy destiny of neo-socialism,"[42] or that it was
synonymous with an interventionism that compromised the existence of a
competitive order. In his book *L'Aube d'un nouveau libéralisme,* when Louis
Baudin recalled the principles constituting the agenda adopted during the
Colloque Walter Lippmann, he omitted some of the principles justifying the
existence of an overall policy giving the state a leading role.[43] This disagreement over terms was not just a quarrel over words. When defined as a doctrine aiming to preserve the framework within which a market economy is
sustainable, neoliberalism could potentially inspire a form of planning.

The majority of French liberals were not ready to subscribe to a doctrine that
in any way resembled the tenets of the economic planners of the postwar period. After 1945 France adopted a hybrid model of development.[44] Following
the Liberation, the question was no longer one of choosing between liberalism
and state intervention: only the methods of interventionism remained to be determined. The structural reforms endowed the state with a powerful means of
intervention (nationalization of the credit system, energy, transportation);
moreover, trade unions now played a significant role, and regulations were pervasive. Nevertheless, the market economy was preserved. Economic recovery accompanied the building of new institutions: the Commissariat général du Plan
indicated the economic goals that were to be achieved; the Institut National de
la Statitisque et des Études Economiques (INSEE) provided economic information; and the Institut d'Études politiques de Paris (Sciences Po) and the Ecole
nationale d'Administration trained the top executives of the national economy.
These institutions produced a new generation of elite civil servants.

In 1946, François Perroux introduced his course on economic doctrines at Sciences Po with an analysis of the "significance of the Keynesian revolution."[45] Two
distinguished civil servants taught the future civil servants a conception of economic policy as distinct from political economy, personified by Jacques Rueff.[46]
In his courses, Rueff, the general secretary of the National Foundation of Political Sciences, treated neoliberalism without once mentioning its French advocates. He was ironical and disdainful about the Colloque Lippmann[47] and disparaged the point of view of the intransigent liberals (notably, Friedrich Hayek in
The Road to Serfdom): "According to them, any intervention of the state in the

economic life . . . would be likely to lead, and even would lead inevitably to a completely collectivist Society, Gestapo and gas chamber included."[48] But discrediting liberalism did not mean that socialism was to be defended. The activist policy pursued by the authorities and the search for growth and full employment were used as mandates: "production and productivity, therefore equipment and modernization."[49] Thus, the Plan Monnet (1947–1952) was the example to be followed because it "was not a bureaucratic work."[50] The goal was to substitute the old discredited liberalism with a rationalized capitalism: "French planning [was] the search for a middle way reconciling the attachment to freedom and individual initiative with a common orientation of development."[51] Therefore, this model was not incompatible with a form of neoliberalism, even if neoliberals, and in particular businessmen, denounced it.[52]

During the 1950s, neoliberal ideas thus spread beyond traditional liberal circles. France discovered (though not for the first time) English and American economics. The doctrines were circulated without their original context and therefore could be dissociated from their national promoters.[53] The Institut de Science Economique Appliquée (ISEA) led by François Perroux promoted the British version of neoliberalism.[54] Some economists supported the idea of a state that was not economically neutral but intervened in accordance "with the internal logic of . . . the market economy."[55] German neoliberalism was far less familiar. If it had untiring promoters among businessmen and in the person of Jacques Rueff,[56] it was little studied, but some followers did emerge: neoliberals like François Bilger[57] or Social Catholics like André Piettre,[58] who compared German neoliberalism and French planning. Unquestionably, the doctrines of foreign neoliberals circulated, and some economists tried to synthesize them with domestic themes. Such was the case of Raymond Barre. Translator of Hayek and close reader of Walter Eucken and Lionel Robbins, Barre claimed that one of the goals of economics was to define conditions under which intervention in a market economy was viable. He therefore proposed an economic policy combining "planning for competition" (Hayek) and an income-driven policy.[59] For the young economists who studied neoliberalism, this doctrine did not appear incompatible with either the French model of development or the "concerted economy" preached by some planners like François Bloch-Lainé.[60] In his Ph.D. dissertation about neoliberalism, Jacques Cros, who was to become a European civil servant, even established a link between the ideas discussed during the Colloque Lippmann, Keynesianism, and the proposals of the French Social Catholics.[61]

Neoliberal ideas made headway during the 1950s and the 1960s, even if only among a few economists or civil servants who later declared themselves to be neoliberals. This renewal was facilitated by the lack of a credible alternative in economic policy. Keynesianism was introduced in France only under the Occupation. After 1945, it was defended by some socialists, civil servants, and economists affiliated with Social Catholicism (in particular Henri Guitton and Alain Barrère),[62] but it was not generally considered legitimate from a left-wing perspective. For numerous French economists, the lesson of the *General Theory* was to consider "the growth harmonized by a deliberate policy"[63] as the main economic phenomenon. It explains why Keynesianism divided neoliberals, some of them adamantly criticizing this theory (Jacques Rueff)[64] and others accepting it as portending progress for economics (Raymond Aron or Daniel Villey).[65] In practice, Social Catholicism was more influential than Keynesianism in the economic debates of the postwar period. Alongside of Christian trade unionists and ecclesiastics, academic economists, civil servants, as well as directors of the nationalized sector and large private companies all took part in the conferences organized by the Catholic authorities. The Semaines Sociales de France thus constituted a sort of small-scale model of the world of the "modernisateurs" in the 1950s. Within this framework, the traditional Catholic rejection of liberalism and socialism took on a new significance: at the Semaines Sociales one faction tried "to reconcile planning and freedom" and to associate "economic realism with social progress";[66] another condemned the planned economy but greeted "the considerable and partially original effort of organization"[67] realized since the Liberation. The participants in the Semaines Sociales were delighted by the coexistence of capitalism and socialism in France, a position that offered the double advantage of being in conformity with the papal encyclicals and of providing a bulwark against communism. Whereas neoliberalism was officially criticized within Social Catholic circles,[68] this criticism should not obscure the fact that an intellectual proximity existed between the right wing of Social Catholicism and the left wing of neoliberalism. Intransigent liberals still rejected the role Social Catholics granted to the state.[69] André Piettre and Jacques Rueff attempted to find a common ground between neoliberals and Social Catholics, viewing them as "men of goodwill whom . . . vain doctrinal oppositions divided."[70] Some economists belonged to these two parallel universes; among these economists was Gaston Leduc, who became president of the Mont Pèlerin Society in 1974.

Subsequent structural events progressively modified the power relations between economic doctrines in France. At the end of the 1950s, France underwent a significant political and economic crisis that exposed the political system in all its brittleness and its incapacity to manage the decolonization process, while inflation remained high. In this context, neoliberalism exploited its opportunity to take its intellectual revenge. France had been through a period of interventionism between 1944 and 1946, and the Fourth Republic was characterized by a form of revanchism between governments, which tried to restore the free market gradually and to form administrative structures that did not evolve. Owing to the influence of the Communist Party, the trade unions, and other groups, the authorities found it politically impossible to reform the welfare state in-depth. With the birth of the Fifth Republic in 1958, France acquired a solid political regime and was able to end governmental instability. Its leaders regained control of the economic administration, while a new generation of civil servants took the helm.[71] First the Pinay-Rueff Plan (1958)[72] and then the Armand-Rueff Committee (1959–1962) bore witness to the revival of neoliberalism. European construction also played a significant role: national economic development was anchored in a wider space, that of the Common Market, which served as "an institutional market" (Jacques Rueff) within which a neoliberal policy was rendered possible. Neoliberalism gradually gained ground in the state and in the economic administration: "with the 5th Plan [1966–1970] and, even more the 6th Plan [1971–1975], the state gave up its economic stewardship, and restricted itself to acting as a facilitator for economic concentration, the respect of competition and the conquest of external markets."[73] Nevertheless, the compromises that the new power had to strike did not satisfy the most radical neoliberals. The presidencies of Georges Pompidou (1970–1974) and Valéry Giscard d'Estaing (1974–1981), who chose Raymond Barre as prime minister, did not modify the situation. Whereas the successive governments followed neoliberal policies, the heirs of neoliberalism were disappointed by the government's policies of liberalization, which they considered too partial. When, in the mid-1970s, the economic crisis put an end to the state's traditional interventionist policies, the mood of the time no longer favored traditional neoliberalism.[74]

The liberals' dashed hopes partially accounted for the creation of the Association pour la Liberté Economique et le Progrès Social (ALEPS) in 1966. This organization, initially formed by André Arnoux, an industrialist who wanted to be admitted into the Académie des Sciences Morales et Politiques, organized every year until the middle of the 1970s a "Week of Liberal Thought" in counterpoint to the "Week of Marxist Thought." The sessions gathered academics, essayists, and right-wing politicians, and among the participants were Maurice Allais, Raymond Aron, Michel Crozier, Yvon Gattaz, Thierry Maulnier, and Jacques Rueff. In spite of its limited resources and its relatively few members (around 400 at the end of the 1970s),[75] ALEPS played a significant role in spreading the arguments against the social democracy, which at the end of the 1970s was defended by the so-called New Economists (including Florin Aftalion, Jacques Garello, Henri Lepage, and Pascal Salin). The promoters of the New Economy were economists related to businessmen or economic journalists linked to political parties arrayed in opposition to the Socialist Party and its intellectual adherents. They helped popularize monetarism and stigmatize Keynesianism, particularly through the creation of think tanks such as the Institut Economique de Paris. If their political proposals were frequently pitched toward extremists, the New Economists participated in the elaboration of a new intellectual mode that progressively became dominant in the 1980s after the victory of the socialist François Mitterrand. Benefiting from a new international context, such as the elections of Margaret Thatcher and Ronald Reagan, this generation of neoliberals sought to distance themselves from the older French neoliberal tradition. Their goal was not to give the state an active role in defending free enterprise, but on the contrary, to produce a full-bore reinstatement of laissez-faire economics. Whereas during the 1930s, the French neoliberals rejected the works of the classical liberals such as Frédéric Bastiat or Gustave de Molinari, because for many they meant "laisser souffrir,"[76] these authors turned out to be central for the new generation, in conjunction with American libertarian spokesmen. The New Economists are still not devoted to the national roots of neoliberalism (except for Jacques Rueff's work),[77] and when we compare their agenda to Lippmann's manifesto, Lippmann could be said to have a socialist agenda.

This radicalization explains why neoliberalism is often presented in France as if it were a foreign extremist discourse, imported from Great Britain or the United States, and appearing *de novo* in the 1970–1980s. The New Economist doctrine is, however, the product of a longer history that is partly French and that shows a whole sequence of transformations: those concerning the role of the state and its structures, as well as those of the economic doctrines that took part in this evolution. By reinstalling the state in the liberal theory, neoliberalism offered to its advocates a pragmatist solution to the crisis, especially because its competitors (planning, corporatism) could appear utopian. World War II helped discredit the corporatist hypothesis. With the Liberation, the building of a planned economy, combined with preservation of the principle of the market economy, placed neoliberals in a difficult position. They were faced with a Hobson's choice: either to justify state interventionism or to preach a return to laissez-faire. This second solution was undoubtedly the most intellectually coherent, but just like the left-wing critical discourses of the 1930s, it had the drawback of possessing a certain utopian character. Thus neoliberalism could adopt two very different faces: an administrative face, accepting the compromises and conquering power between the mid-1950s and mid-1970s; and a more radical face, benefiting from the failures of the first version of neoliberalism to overcome the crises of the 1970s, but also from the political victory of the socialists in 1981, which produced a strong electric shock for the right wing. These two versions of neoliberalism supported each other. The durability of the bureaucratic structures inherited from the Liberation masked the progress of the liberal ideas in the area of power. The neoliberal extremism of the 1980s ushered in privatization and deregulation and permitted right-wing politicians to acknowledge their fundamental adherence to neoliberalism. As Jacques Chirac declared in front of members of the Mont Pèlerin Society in 1984: "we need today an absolute liberalism to encourage us to make the necessary liberalism."[78]

Notes

Abbreviations in the Notes

HIA = Hoover Institution Archive, Stanford, CA.

WLP = Walter Lippmann Papers. Manuscripts and Archives, Yale University Library

1. Mathieu Marion, "Investigating Rougier," *Cahiers d'épistémologie* (2004), 314.

2. Louis Rougier, *Les mystiques économiques* (Paris: Médicis, 1938).

3. Walter Lippmann, *La cité libre* (Paris: Médicis, 1938).

4. Bernhard Walpen, *Die offenen Feinde und ihre Gesellschaft. Eine hegemonietheoretische Studie zur Mont Pèlerin Society* (Hamburg: VSA-Verlag, 2004), 56.

5. Louis Rougier to Walter Lippmann, May 28, 1938, WLP, Box 100, Folder 1848.

6. Walter Lippmann to Louis Rougier, July 1, 1938, ibid.

7. Friedrich Hayek to Walter Lippmann, July 10, 1937, WLP, Box 77, Folder 1011.

8. Walpen, *Eine hegemonietheoretische Studie,* 56.

9. Ibid.

10. Louis Rougier to Walter Lippmann, April 25, 1940, WLP, Box 100, Folder 1848.

11. Ibid., August 11, 1938.

12. CIRL, *Compte rendu des séances du Colloque Walter Lippmann* (Paris: Médicis, 1939).

13. "Interventions de Jacques Rueff au cours de la première séance de travail du Centre international pour la rénovation du libéralisme," in Emil M. Classen (dir.), *Les fondements philosophiques des systèmes économiques. Textes de Jacques Rueff et essais rédigés en son honneur* (Paris: Payot, 1967), 463.

14. Gaëtan Pirou, *Néo-libéralisme. Néo-corporatisme. Néo-socialisme* (Paris: Gallimard, 1939), 62.

15. CIRL, *Compte rendu,* 91.

16. Walpen, *Eine hegemonietheoretische Studie,* 57.

17. CIRL, *Compte rendu,* 16.

18. Michel Margairaz, *L'Etat, les finances et l'économie. L'histoire d'une conversion 1932–1952* (Paris: CHEFF, 1991), 467–492.

19. Andrew Shennan, *Rethinking France: Plans for Renewal 1940–1946* (Oxford: Clarendon Press, 1989).

20. Jean-Noël Jeanneney and Jacques Julliard, *Le monde de Beuve-Méry ou le métier d'Alceste* (Paris: Editions du Seuil, 1979).

21. Richard Vinen, *Bourgeois Politics in France, 1945–1951* (Cambridge: Cambridge University Press, 1995), 5.

22. PRL, "Le programme du néo-libéralisme," Fonds Louis Rougier, Château de Lourmarin de Provence, R 14.

23. François Caron, "Le plan Mayer: un retour aux réalités," *Histoire, économie et société,* 3, 1982, 423–437.

24. Olivier Dard, "Maurice Petsche, itinéraire, réseaux, valeurs," in François Roth (ed.), *Les modérés dans la vie politique française de 1870 à 1965* (Nancy: Presses universitaires de Nancy, 2000), 397–455.

25. Pierre Grémion, *Intelligence de l'anticommunisme. Le Congrès pour la liberté de la culture à Paris 1950–1975* (Paris: Fayard, 1995).

26. Marie-Thérèse Génin, "La Société du Mont-Pèlerin," *Nouvelle revue de l'économie contemporaine,* no. 11, November 1950, 27.

27. Association declared at the *Journal officiel de la République française,* October 16, 1947, 10268.

28. The Association de la libre entreprise organized a conference that gathered all these organizations in Paris in October 1950 to compare their means of action (booklets, conferences) and their goals (HIA, MPS, Box 31, Folder 8). We can here find an illustration of the "Russian Doll" thesis explained in the Postface to this volume by Philip Mirowski.

29. "Aux abonnés," *Voici les faits,* 15, 1953.

30. Fondation nationale des sciences politiques/Hubert Beuve-Méry Papers/97.

31. Laurence Badel, *Un milieu libéral et européen. Le grand commerce français (1925–1948)* (Paris: CHEFF, 1999), 372.

32. Albert Pasquier, *Les doctrines sociales en France. Vingt ans d'évolution 1930–1950* (Paris: R. Pichon and R. Durand-Auzias), 1950, 283.

33. Gustave Prost, "Le patronat doit être un patronat d'idées," *L'Informateur de l'entreprise à capital personnel,* September–October 1949, 103, 104, 105.

34. Pierre Lhoste-Lachaume, *La clef de voûte de la liberté* (Paris: SEDIF, 1954).

35. Daniel Villey, "Examen de conscience de l'économie politique," *Revue d'économie politique,* November–December 1951, 858–859; Louis Baudin, "Le carnaval des mots," *Nouvelle revue de l'économie contemporaine,* 4, April 1950, 1–2.

36. Maurice Allais, "Au-delà du laisser-fairisme et du totalitarisme," *Nouvelle revue de l'économie contemporaine,* 5, May 1950, 28.

37. Pierre Anselme to Albert Hunold, August 24, 1951, HIA, MPS, Box 7, Folder 4.

38. Jacques Rueff to Albert Hunold, November 24, 1950, HIA, MPS, Box 31, Folder 9.

39. Maurice Allais to Friedrich Hayek, May 12, 1947, HIA, Friedrich Hayek Papers, Box 72, Folder 6.

40. Pierre Lhoste-Lachaume, *Où gît le désaccord entre libéraux et socialistes? L'illusoire compromis de nos démocraties occidentales* (Paris: SEDIF, 1960).

41. The case of the war in Algeria illustrates it. While Raymond Aron accepted the self-determination of the Algerian people, Daniel Villey hoped for the victory of the paramilitary groups (Organisation de l'Armée Secrète) that fought the policy of General de Gaulle (Daniel Villey to Raymond Aron, February 21, 1962, Fonds Raymond Aron, Centre d'études politiques Raymond Aron, EHESS).

42. Pierre Dieterlen, "Libéralisme dogmatique et libéralisme critique," in Centre Paul Hymans, *Travaux du colloque international du libéralisme économique* (Brussels: Editions du Centre Paul Hymans, 1958), 325.

43. Louis Baudin, *L'Aube d'un nouveau libéralisme* (Paris: Médicis, 1953).

44. Richard Kuisel, *L'Etat et le capitalisme en France* (Paris: Gallimard, 1984).

45. François Perroux, *Histoire des doctrines économiques contemporaines* (Paris: Centre de documentation universitaire, 1947), 2–54.

46. Roger Nathan and Paul Delouvrier, *Politique économique de la France* (Paris: Les Cours de droit, Fascicule I, 1949), 2.

47. Jean Meynaud, Pierre Besse, François Bloch-lainé, Claude Gruson, and Maurice Pérouse, *La vie économique* (Paris: Les Cours de droit, Fascicule I, 1953), 65.

48. Jean Meynaud, *Politique économique comparée* (Paris: Les Cours de droit, Fascicule 1, 1955), 305.

49. Roger Nathan and Paul Delouvrier, *Politique économique de la France,* 322.

50. Ibid., 321.

51. Pierre Massé, *Le Plan ou l'anti-hasard* (Paris: Gallimard, 1965), 144.

52. Blaise Richard [Lucien Daffos], "Plan d'équipement ou Plan politique?" *L'informateur de l'entreprise à capital personnel,* 88, January 10, 1949.

53. Pierre Bourdieu, "Les conditions sociales de la circulation internationale des idées," *Actes de la recherche en sciences sociales*, 145, December 2002, 3–8.

54. Georges Rottier, "Aspects d'un nouveau libéralisme," *Economie appliquée*, 2, April–June 1949, 247–274; Yves Mainguy, "Capitalisme, socialisme et . . . néo-libéralisme. Notes sur un événement, une doctrine et une politique," *Economie appliquée*, 2, April–June 1951, 211–243.

55. Ibid., 211.

56. He wrote thus: "The German miracle in its reality is only a rational product of the neo-liberal doctrines expressly formulated and systematically applied," in Jacques Rueff, "Une vérification a contrario: la résurrection de l'Allemagne," *Revue des deux mondes*, June 15, 1953, 607.

57. François Bilger, *La pensée économique libérale dans l'Allemagne contemporaine* (Paris: LGDJ, 1964).

58. André Piettre, "L'économie allemande est-elle vraiment libérale?" *Revue économique*, 3, May 1962, 339–354.

59. Raymond Barre, "L'analyse économique au service de la science et de la politique économiques," *Critique*, April 1952, 332–346.

60. Bilger, *La pensée économique libérale*, 289.

61. Jacques Cros, *Le néo-libéralisme et la révision du libéralisme* (Ph.D. diss., Toulouse University, 1950).

62. Olivier Dard, "Economie et économistes des années trente aux années cinquante: un tournant keynésien?" *Historiens et géographes*, 361, March 1998, 173–195.

63. François Perroux, *La généralisation de la General Theory* (Istanbul, 1950), p. 4.

64. Jacques Rueff, "Les erreurs de la *Théorie générale* de Lord Keynes," *Revue d'économie politique*, 1, 1947, 5–33.

65. Daniel Villey, "Economique et morale," in *Pour une économie libérée* (Paris: SPID, 1946), p. 30; Raymond Aron, "Les limites de la théorie économique classique," *Critique*, 6, November 1946, 510–519.

66. Charles Flory, "Le conflit de l'économique et du social," in Semaines sociales de France, *Réalisme économique et progrès social* (Lyon: Chronique sociale de France, 1949), 29–30.

67. André Piettre, "Développement et limite de l'économie dirigée," in Semaines sociales de France, *Le catholicisme social face aux grands courants contemporains* (Lyon: Chronique sociale de France, 1947), 91.

68. Alain Barrère, "Les aspects actuels du libéralisme," ibid., 155–178.

69. Daniel Villey, "A propos du catholicisme social," *Revue d'économie politique*, 2, March–April 1948, 305–306; Pierre Lhoste-Lachaume, *Réhabilitation du libéralisme* (Paris: Sedif, 1950).

70. André Piettre to Jacques Rueff, April 26, 1950, Jacques Rueff Papers, Archives Nationales/579 AP/193.

71. Henri Rousso (ed.), *La planification en crise 1965–1985* (Paris: Editions du CNRS, 1987).

72. Michel-Pierre Chelini, "Le plan de stabilisation Pinay-Rueff: 1958," *Revue d'histoire moderne et contemporaine*, 4, October–December 2001, 102–122.

73. Pierre Birnbaum, *Les sommets de l'Etat. Essai sur l'élite au pouvoir en France* (Paris: Seuil, 1977), 123.

74. Suzanne Berger, "Liberalism Reborn: The New Liberal Synthesis in France," *Contemporary France: A Review of Interdisciplinary Studies*, 1987, 84–108.

75. "Activités de l'ALEPS au cours de l'exercice 1977 et activités futures," 3, Jacques Rueff Papers, AN/579 AP/193.

76. CIRL, *Compte rendu*, 30.

77. François Bourricaud and Pascal Salin, *Présence de Jacques Rueff* (Paris: Plon, 1988).

78. Jacques Chirac, "Le libéralisme peut-il inspirer un projet politique?" *Liberté économique et progrès social*, 49, March 1984, 22.

2

Liberalism and Neoliberalism in Britain, 1930–1980

For over two hundred years English ideas had been spreading eastward. The rule of freedom which had been achieved in England seemed destined to spread throughout the world. By about 1870 the reign of these ideas had probably reached its easternmost expansion. From then onwards it began to retreat and a different set of ideas, not really new but very old began to advance from the East. England lost her intellectual leadership in the political and social sphere and became an importer of ideas. For the next sixty years Germany became the centre from which the ideas destined to govern the world in the twentieth century spread east and west. Whether it was Hegel or Marx, List or Schmoller, Sombart or Mannheim, whether it was socialism in its more radical form or merely "organisation" or "planning" of a less radical kind, German ideas were everywhere readily imported and German institutions imitated.

F. A. von Hayek[1]

Introduction

Hayek's *Road to Serfdom* (1944) is a work that has assumed a central intellectual and symbolic importance for British neoliberalism. It was written in Britain during the early 1940s while Hayek, then professor of economics at the London School of Economics, was teaching in the school's wartime home—Cambridge. All of these factors are of importance, positively or negatively; but most readers of the book have misread these polarities. Hayek's chief line of argument is that the classical liberalism on which the liberty and prosperity of nineteenth-century Britain was built was threatened by statist, German ideas that furthered increasingly deliberate regulation of all social life. But while invoking classical liberalism, Hayek signally failed to consider why, by the later nineteenth century, it had already been displaced in Britain by "new liberalism." By midcentury this was also a spent force, because the political forces that had converted "classical" into "new" liberalism—the extension of the franchise, the emergence of the Labour Party, and the political consequences of World War I—had in turn fatally undermined new liberalism by the later 1920s.

This chapter first sketches this somewhat complex history of British liberalism to midcentury, so that we might more clearly perceive where neoliberalism fits into this history. Central to this story are economists from the London School of Economics (LSE), which was not only a stronghold of economic liberalism during the interwar period but exerted great influence on the teaching of economics throughout Britain and the Empire via its external degrees in commerce and economics. Lionel Robbins, professor of economics at LSE from 1929 to 1961, was no simple doctrinaire liberal. During World War II he headed the Economic Section, the principal grouping of economists recruited to advise on the organization of the wartime economy. The policy framework that these economists devised was bequeathed to postwar governments and provided the template for "Keynesian" economic management.

A small number of important British economists were active in the MPS, and Robbins himself drafted its program. During the immediate postwar period, neoliberal academic criticism of welfarism and planning could be directed at the activities of the Labour government; but criticism of the government from the right became more difficult once Labour gave way to the Conservatives in 1951. Academic opinion instead embraced a muted Keynesian synthesis, broadly aligning itself with governments of the day through the ensuing three decades of Conservative and Labour rule. During this period the neoliberal agenda was instead developed and advanced from new, nonacademic organizations, of which the Institute of Economic Affairs was the first. Except for a brief period in the early 1970s, these institutions found themselves firmly on the fringe of policy and politics. This changed with the election of Thatcher's Conservative government in 1979: what had hitherto been peripheral now became mainstream. British "Keynesian" academics were locked out of policy formation by the new government. They looked on as the government shaped an economic policy inspired by the ideas of monetarist zealots, journalists, and free market ideologues who could broadly be considered "neoliberal" in orientation.

This story has to begin with that classical liberalism around which Hayek built his critique.

"Classical" Liberalism

British liberalism—from John Stuart Mill through Thomas Gladstone to Henry Sidgwick, Lloyd George, William Beveridge, and John Maynard Keynes—had already by the mid-twentieth century followed an apparently perverse trajectory. Mill had made the argument concerning the boundaries between individual and state in his essay "On Liberty," attacking state education as tending to establish "a despotism over the mind, leading by natural tendency to one over the body."[2] At the time he wrote this essay, Britain did not have a system of compulsory elementary education; but less than two decades later this absence was widely considered a serious deficiency in a world where Britain faced more "progressive" economic competitors.

Mill's "On Liberty" is a monument to a classical liberalism that barely outlasted the nineteenth century, and whose conception of the relation between state and individual could not survive the development of parliamentary democracy based on universal suffrage.[3] By the close of the nineteenth century, liberalism stood for progressive policies on social reform and Irish independence, and labor representatives sat in the House of Commons as Liberal MPs. This new liberalism of the party elected on a landslide in 1906 coupled free trade and social reform, but the Labour Party had been formed in the same year and returned its first MPs in that election. By 1922 British parliamentary politics had been decisively recast as a contest between Conservative and Labour parties, and the Liberal Party was reduced permanently to a rump. Its social liberal agenda had developed from new liberalism and had recast Mill's demarcation of individual from state responsibility. No longer was the extension of state control perceived as an encroachment on individual liberty; instead, each enlargement of the state's authority and activity was now to be judged in terms of its positive or negative impact on personal liberty. Furthermore, the liberties that it defended in this way were increasingly conceived in economic, rather than political, terms: free trade and hostility to the corporatism of both employers and trade unions. Through the twentieth century the transition from political to economic freedom became the signature of a neoliberal agenda.

The novelty of Friedrich Hayek's critique of modernity, *The Road to Serfdom*, lay in his argument that the demise of the liberal tradition was due to "foreign ideas"—extending and generalizing positions he had already advanced in the mid-1930s concerning the impact of centralized planning on economic life.[4] There he had argued against the view, associated with the writings of Otto Neurath, Emil Lederer, and Walter Rathenau, that "deliberate regulation of all social affairs" was either practicable or efficient, echoing points made by von Mises in the 1920s.[5] *The Road to Serfdom* was a political tract for the times, not a work of economic analysis; but as a political tract it was strangely silent on the contribution of democratic institutional developments to the demise of classical liberalism. On the first page of the book that quickly became the canonical work of neoliberalism he warned that Britain, the country of Adam Smith and John Stuart Mill, was in danger of treading the same path to totalitarianism that had begun in Germany and Austria during the later years of World War I.

This millenarian cast of *The Road to Serfdom* is often overlooked by disciples and dissenters alike. But it is important for an appreciation of the force of Hayek's arguments that we understand the narrative strategy he adopted in this work. The basic historical development is plainly laid out in the epigraph to this chapter. In the nineteenth century Britain had set forth liberalism in theory (Mill's "On Liberty") and in practice (free trade, limited government, parliamentary sovereignty). "German" developments—the supremacy of the state (Hegel), socialism (Marx), economic nationalism (List), German historicism (Schmoller), cultural criticism of capitalism (Sombart), and the new social sciences (Mannheim)—began to roll back the diffusion of liberalism in the later part of the nineteenth century, a process that was accelerated rather than halted by the defeat of Germany in 1918. Hayek's tract pointed up in general terms the dangers inherent in the consequent belief that government could provide for the welfare of their citizens more efficiently than the citizens themselves.

A great deal of the rhetorical force of Hayek's book in the English-speaking world derives from this ostensibly "European" cast. Hayek in *Road to Serfdom* appears to defend an essentially English model of classical liberalism against the corrosive influence of "German ideas." The road to serfdom, Hayek argues, is a German road, an idea simple to grasp during the early 1940s in more ways than one. Read from a German interwar perspective, however, the rhetorical force of this line of argument collapses. The general principles advanced by Hayek clearly derive from a body of continental interwar literature concerning parliamentary democracy and the state in the first German republic.[6] When placed in this context, the arguments advanced in *Road to Serfdom* no longer seem so compelling or cogent. The most prominent, and notorious, figure in these debates was Carl Schmitt, whose critique of parliamentary democracy was all the more devastating for his recognition that classical liberalism and its limited state were both gone for good.[7] Some of the reasons for this critique will be outlined shortly, but Schmitt's arguments have survived into the twenty-first century because he articulated a problem that remains unresolved: how can political order and liberty be secured if the state has no limit other than laws passed by whoever controls Parliament and government?

Hayek responds to this problem, but his solution is a purely rhetorical one. His appeal to a golden age of the English liberal state elaborated in terms of the distribution of knowledge does indeed possess clarity and simplicity, but amounts to no more than a wish that the world were other than it is:

> The state should confine itself to establishing rules applying to general types of situations, and should allow the individuals freedom in everything which depends on the circumstances of time and place, because only the individuals concerned in each instance can fully know these circumstances and adapt their actions to them. If the individuals are to be able to use their knowledge effectively in making plans, they must be able to predict actions of the state which may affect these plans.[8]

We can gain some perspective on these generalities by returning to John Stuart Mill. Much of "On Liberty" is taken up with the issues of interpersonal freedom, and it is only in the final chapter, "Applications," that Mill explicitly raises the nature of an individual's relationship to the state. Here, inter alia, he takes the view that the education of children is a parental duty, specifically that of the father; but that unfortunately no obligation is laid upon the father to provide it. Clearly, where such responsibility is breached, the state ought to see it fulfilled "at the charge, as far as possible, of the parent."[9] This robust, if not libertarian, perspective could of course be extended into all the areas of activity of the modern state. Universal education was generally perceived as a desirable, modernizing force in all nineteenth-century industrialized countries, with the development of formal educational structures in Britain lagging behind those of European neighbors. Not until the later 1930s was a clear distinction made between primary and secondary education; the school-leaving age was raised first to 15 in 1947 and then to 16 in 1972;[10] only in 1944 were statutory regulations drafted so that pupils would be instructed according to their age rather than their abilities.[11]

But however slowly state control of education developed in Britain, from a modern perspective state control of the type so vehemently opposed by Mill was but one, apparently inevitable, part of the development of industrial economies. True, in mid-nineteenth century Britain, liberals were closely associated with the movement for social reform—in health, housing, employment, and education. What gave effect to such efforts and rendered their execution a responsibility increasingly of central, rather than local, government, was a function of taxation and representation. Universal provision as a right generally meant centralized administration since there was a clear limit to local taxation such as the poor rate, and universal provision implied the standardized services that only central control could assure.

First, the demand side was driven by political reform. Pressure for the extension of state rather than voluntary provision, which was a hallmark of liberal politics, came with the extension of the electorate in Britain to include the majority of male adults by the 1880s. This change not only converted what was known in continental Europe as the "social question" into a "parliamentary question," but it also initially conferred on the Liberal Party the votes and representatives of the newly enfranchised urban working class.[12] The subsequent creation of an independent Labour Party representative of working-class interests was made possible with the financial and organizational assistance of the trade-union movement, eventually robbing the Liberal Party of the critical mass of voters necessary to elect sufficient numbers of representatives to remain a national political force. The party of reform fell victim to the reforms it had promoted. The year after publication of *Road to Serfdom,* in 1945, the Labour Party was elected in another landslide, which brought about the implementation of the 1944 Education Act, the creation of the National Health Service, together with the provision of universal entitlements for pensions and unemployment.[13]

Although the supply side traces a similar chronology, its constraints are not quite so familiar. The British state was certainly "limited" for much of the nineteenth century, but this was of course only true for the inhabitants of Great Britain, and not for those of India or Australia. There was no especially complicated reason why, in the first half of the nineteenth century, the British state was domestically a "small" state. The wars of the eighteenth century, culminating in the Napoleonic Wars, all but ruined the state finances. Even if central government, such as it was, had sought widespread interference in the social and economic life of the country, it did not possess the financial means to do so. During the period 1822–1831, defense consumed 30 percent of central government resources, while debt servicing took up another 59 percent.[14]

Debt repayment made up almost a half of government spending until mid-century, falling eventually to around 10 percent at the end of the century.[15] Military spending moved in the opposite direction, and in Britain's case this meant primarily spending on the navy, which not only secured the seas for free trade but also enforced the abolition of the slave trade. By the end of the century, however, gunboat diplomacy had given way to a naval arms race with Germany, so that in the financial year 1913–1914 from a budget of £197.5m the navy took £48.8m. and the army £28.3m. Social services of all kinds—education, health insurance, pensions—took £32.1m. Revenue was overwhelmingly indirect, so that the costs of navy and army together (£79.1m) were almost matched by revenues from taxes on the sale of alcohol, tobacco, tea, and sugar alone (£71.5m).[16] A fiscal base so heavily skewed to taxation on such basic items of mass consumption proved unwieldy in wartime;[17] British war finance therefore had once more to borrow heavily in international markets, with repayment requiring a restructuring toward direct taxation together with a significant increase in the overall tax burden. The fiscal profile of government once again doubled from 1914 to 1920 because of the costs of war.[18] Defense had taken 44 percent of total expenditure in 1913–1914, debt services 14 percent, and social services (education, health, labor, insurance, and pensions) 19 percent. By 1925–1926 these figures had altered to defense 16 percent, debt servicing 46 percent, and social services 24 percent.[19]

All of this is to say that the chronology offered by Hayek for the decline of the liberal state is broadly correct, but not for the reasons he adduces. It was not "German ideas" that undermined classical liberalism, but the internal and external dynamics of industrialization and democracy—what in another language used to be called social progress. The state based on the rule of law along the lines that Mill articulated in 1859, and which underpins Hayek's critique of modernity, barely outlasted Mill's lifetime. Everywhere reform brought costs that required higher levels of taxation and consequent accountability in the expenditure of public money. The civil service reforms of the 1850s converted occasional emoluments to fixed salaries and pensions. The movement for the incarceration of convicted criminals, rather than their consignment to the gallows or transportation, brought increasing expenditures for both local authorities and central government. The regulation of private enterprise—factory inspection, hours of work for women and minors, railway safety, clean water, and waste disposal—extended the financial commitment of central government. Local government assumed responsibility for elementary education and from the 1890s developed a framework of vocational education in new technical colleges. The issue of how liberty and democracy might be secured in the world that such forces were to create became a critical one during the interwar period. Hayek was entirely silent on these developments.

The Road to Serfdom was, as noted earlier, a political, not an economic, tract. Hayek was a professor of economics, but in constructing his argument he made no use of economic reasoning even in its broadest sense. The classical liberalism that the book invoked promoted above all a conception of political freedom, underpinned by a parallel, but weaker, conception of economic liberty. Free markets, in this classical view, were a corollary of political liberty, and not the other way around.[20] The universality of political rights under a rule of law had only slowly been extended into the marketplace, usually in Britain a narrative related to freedom to participate in trade unionism. But since manual workers made up the overwhelming majority of the workforce, legislation on the freedom of association, labor contracts, working conditions, and hours of work was, in the nineteenth century, a very important part of "economic liberty," even though such rights are usually understood to be part of the history of the socialist movement. Even free trade, an international hallmark of the liberal state if ever there was one, was in the nineteenth century primarily a political, and not an economic, idea.[21] Although an economic argument for the gains from trade had been developed by Adam Smith and James Mill, cryptically articulated by David Ricardo in 1817, and fully elaborated by John Stuart Mill in 1829–1830,[22] none of these arguments informed the extension of free trade during the nineteenth century. Ricardo's argument from what was later known as comparative advantage addressed the rate of profit, not popular welfare; economic liberty was merely a condition for the realization of comparative advantages, and, unlike Smith's argument, played no special role in Ricardo's.[23] Moreover, Ricardo couched his argument in terms of the trade between England and Portugal in wine and wool (the Methuen Treaty of 1703), making it very easy for nonspecialists to confuse comparative with absolute advantage. This confusion has since been intrinsic to all public discussion of the gains from international trade.

What distinguishes neoliberalism from classical liberalism is the inversion of this relationship between politics and economics. Arguments for liberty become economic rather than political, identifying the impersonality of market forces as the chief means for securing popular welfare and personal liberty.[24] This was essentially Hayek's argument—that a society in which decision making was in large part centralized would undermine the welfare and freedom of its population. But just as Hayek failed to consider the developmental tendencies of political life, he also failed to take account of the changing nature of capitalist economies from the later nineteenth to the mid-twentieth century. Consequently, the centralization and bureaucratization that he attacks is an outcome of "foreign ideas," not the internal dynamic of business, welfare, and politics. For Hayek, the "market" is an abstract, not a substantive, entity; the "perfect market" is the counterpart of the liberal state. He appeals to classical liberalism but argues from economy to polity; his "road to freedom" now ran through the market to political liberty, and not the other way around. The fact that this argument was underpinned by a conception of the state borrowed from the nineteenth century was of secondary importance, since politics had now become the corollary of economics.[25] By the time Hayek was writing, democratic states everywhere had already assumed a significant responsibility for the welfare of their citizens, and governments were increasingly judged by the degree of success with which the prosperity of voters was secured. The postwar years were to reinforce this trend, not diminish it.

Political theory was never widely debated with any great enthusiasm or sophistication in twentieth-century Britain, and so this internal disconnection in Hayek's argument seems to have gone unnoticed. His work was taken up by individuals who argued almost exclusively in terms of economic, not political, liberties. When set against the history of liberalism in twentieth-century Britain, the placing of such liberal economic arguments within the political landscape is not a straightforward matter. "Liberalism" was a moveable feast. In later Victorian Britain, the Liberal Party was identified with issues such as Irish Home Rule, social and electoral reform, and promotion of the early development of what became the Labour Party, funded by the trade-union movement. Social welfare in Britain was a Liberal innovation, dating from the 1906 election following which Winston Churchill became Liberal president of the Board of Trade. Later on, when the Liberal Party had been eclipsed by the Labour Party, the figures whom Hayek most closely associated with the forces of collectivism, Keynes and Beveridge, were Liberals—not Labour, nor Conservative. The postwar Labour government did of course enact the legislation that created the welfare state, but the reflexes of British business at this time, as of also the Conservative Party, were strongly corporatist. It was a Labour government that in 1949 created the Monopolies (and Restrictive Practices) Commission to report on private-sector cartels and monopolistic firms, making it the first government in Europe to introduce legislation directed to the ending of restrictive practices and the promotion of competitive markets.[26] The Conservative Party remained the party of corporatism through the 1950s and 1960s, with the Liberal Party adopting increasingly social liberal policies. This changed first in 1970 with the election of Edward Heath's Conservative government on an uncompromising free market agenda. But Heath was also a supporter of European integration, later anathema to Margaret Thatcher, who in many respects revived the economic sentiments of postwar Liberals. In the meantime the Liberal Party, following a tortured chapter of accidents and incidents too arcane to be recounted here, became briefly the Liberal and Social Democratic Party, before settling upon its present title of Liberal Democratic Party. In 1997 the Labour Party was reelected under the New Labour banner, and in its second and third terms term began to complete implementation of reforms to health, education, and welfare that Margaret Thatcher had failed to carry through in the 1980s. But the final execution of centralized state planning for health, education, and welfare was achieved during the term of New Labour, building on a policy agenda that was supposedly the essence of Thatcherism. Characteristic of government policy in health and education in the early twenty-first century is a rolling program of reform and marketization in which the language of markets and choice is coupled with micromanagement on the part of central government departments.[27]

And so it is perhaps little wonder that liberalism has been left to economics, where at least matters seem to be a lot more straightforward.

Liberal Economics in Interwar Britain

The transition in the foundation of liberal argument from politics to economics outlined above found support in Britain from academic economists able to articulate clearly these new foundations. This was first made obvious in the dispute over tariff reform leading up to the 1906 election, when proponents of the "new economics" publicly supported free trade, while those economists who did not—William Cunningham, W. A. S. Hewins, William Ashley—are linked by the skepticism with which they viewed the development of contemporary economic thinking. During the 1920s a number of academic centers for teaching and research in economics developed, foremost among them being the London School of Economics, but also including Birmingham and

Manchester alongside Oxford and Cambridge. LSE economists stood out for
the clarity with which they linked the economics they taught to liberal ideas.
This tradition goes back to the founding professor of economics, Edwin Cannan.[28] Representative of his approach is his collection of essays and articles on
the conduct of the economy during World War I and after in which he asserts,
in his typically forthright style, that "Modern civilization, nearly all civilization, is based on the principle of making things pleasant for those who please
the market and unpleasant for those who fail to do so . . . ," adding ". . . whatever defects this principle may have, it is better than none."[29] The "protest" of
Cannan's title *(An Economist's Protest)* is against economic nationalism and the
delusions of economic management, combining relentless criticism of government regulation with support for international government.

Cannan had been an Oxford student in the 1880s, part of a generation that
with Ashley and Hewins had by the early 1900s turned away from the connection of reformist politics to economics.[30] But Cannan was a great admirer
of Jevons and sought to apply elementary economic principles to the work of
business and government. Although Cannan's understanding of economics
was by the 1920s generally regarded as rather old-fashioned, the style carried
over to many of his students, notable among them being Lionel Robbins and
Arnold Plant, two of the later MPS members from Britain. Cannan had upon
his retirement in 1927 been succeeded by Allyn Young, but with Young's premature death in 1929 Robbins, a 1923 graduate, was appointed to the chair of
economics. This was part of a clear transition in the school, in which new appointments were increasingly drawn from its own students. In 1930 Arnold
Plant returned from Cape Town as professor of commerce, and throughout
the following two decades Robbins and Plant were dominant figures at the
LSE. Coupled with a consolidation in the school itself, its students spread out
to other institutions. The *Calendar* records twelve graduates in commerce and
economics appointed in 1931 to posts in Britain, South Africa, India, New
Zealand, and Japan.[31] Robbins, who had visited Mises's *Privatseminar* in Vienna during the 1920s (see the Introduction to this volume) also brought
Hayek to London in the same year first as a visiting professor, then as a permanent appointment; while Robbins's presence is suggestive of the school's
established political character, there is no indication that Hayek had any independent impact on the work of the school or on its reputation.[32]

Robbins had been impressed by the published work of Hayek and von Mises,
and their influence is particularly clear in his notorious account of the depres-

sion. The American Crash of 1929 had not directly created an international depression, but it undeniably marked the end of a brief period of international economic recovery. Britain departed from the Gold Standard in September 1931 and responded to the growing crisis by electing a new national government the following month. This government proceeded to abandon free trade for protection, introducing commodity boards to promote and subsidize domestic production. These developments led Maynard Keynes to entirely recast his arguments on employment and trade, recognizing that the new policy regime could not simply be wished away. This was an important element in the drafting and composition of his 1936 *General Theory of Employment, Interest and Money.*

Set against this background, Robbins's *Great Depression* of 1934 is a doctrinaire tract lacking engagement with contemporary economic problems. This disconnect was noted at the time; the reviewer in the *Economic Journal* opened by noting that the study was made "from the standpoint of the analytical neo-individualism which has been developing in recent years at the London School of Economics" and further suggested that Robbins's objective was to vindicate "an elaborate and essentially abstract theory of the conditions of equilibrium."[33] Robbins's general argument was that prosperity would return only if the market were permitted to work without hindrance. He argued that central bankers seeking to promote reflation simply created greater fluctuations; and that the creation of a social insurance system had removed any incentive trade unions might have had to protect their members by agreeing to reductions in wages. Hence Robbins's policy argument was that central bankers should not seek to manage financial markets and that universal social insurance was a bad idea. The longest chapter in the book outlines a blueprint for recovery, which emphasizes the restoration of business confidence through the stabilization of international exchange, hence the restoration of the Gold Standard as the route to renewed growth and prosperity and the consequent reduction of unemployment.[34] Businessmen, Robbins argued, should be freed of regulation as well as the illusion that the state will prevent their ruin if they make mistakes.

> The property owner must learn that only by continually satisfying the demands of the consumer can he hope to maintain intact its value. Only in such conditions can we hope for the emergence of a structure of industry which is stable in the sense that it can change without recurrent catastrophe.[35]

He concluded by calling for limited government, a reflection of the fact that all over the world parliaments were assuming responsibility for more than they could effectively oversee. This was certainly true, but the utopian cast of this line of argument is plain.

The general character of this line of economic argument is not specifically "Austrian." Arnold Plant had constructed similar arguments during the 1920s, drawing on the economic principles he had learned from Edwin Cannan. Plant's first publication concerned the wage differentials secured by a segregated labor market, whether in South Africa or the American South, translating a denunciation by Lord Bryce of racial discrimination into the language of rent-seeking behavior. Poor whites, he argued, unable to compete on equal terms with blacks, employed political means to place blacks at a permanent disadvantage and hence extract a rent.[36] He maintained that such impediments to the working of the labor market impoverished black workers and reduced overall economic efficiency, and hence the welfare of all. Later, during the 1930s, he wrote two papers on patents and copyrights, which similarly identified these legal instruments as monopolistic in character, secured as a property right created by statute. This argument would later be translated and generalized into the language of rights to intellectual property, as Ronald Coase, Plant's student, was to point out in his biography of Plant.[37] In 1937 Plant took part in a (scripted) BBC radio discussion entitled "This Planning Business." John Strachey argued the case for planning by suggesting that modern capitalist enterprise was characterized by planful activity, which displaced market mechanisms, and that if modern government were to follow the lead of modern business this would naturally mean an extension of such techniques to public administration and social welfare. Plant, an expert on modern business who ran the LSE's graduate school of business, and whose knowledge of modern business practice was probably more extensive than that of any other contemporary academic, would have none of this.[38] He put forward simple free market principles so vigorously that the third participant, Harold Macmillan, the future Conservative prime minister, concluded that he had "never listened to a more hard-boiled conception of free Capitalism than that which he [Plant] advances."[39] According to Macmillan, these ideas belonged to the nineteenth, not the twentieth, century.

Macmillan was wrong on this matter. The principles that Plant advanced so ruthlessly were very much part of the twentieth century. They reflected the way in which modern economics was evolving into an apparently closed, self-referring system of thought suitable for teaching to young people and capable of ever-increasing technical elaboration—rather like Ramist logic in sixteenth-century France. Plant's arguments on labor discrimination and copyright employed very simple economic principles to great effect. But what distinguished the exposition of economic principles at the London School of Economics was a strong normative belief that such classroom principles could be translated unmediated into economic argument and policy agendas. What lent this, for the time, idiosyncratic belief resonance was the school's position in the expanding educational system. Alongside its regular daytime students there were also evening students for whom teaching was duplicated. In addition, as part of the University of London, the school offered its curriculum and courses to corresponding students throughout Britain and the Empire. Arnold Plant also ran a well-funded Commerce Degree Bureau that coordinated distance learning though the circulation of teaching materials and the marking of student essays by LSE staff. The school's pedagogic reach was therefore far greater than that of Oxford, Cambridge, or even Manchester and was aimed at a wider constituency. In the postwar expansion of economics teaching in school and college, the LSE could capitalize on this influence. The later MPS member Frederic Benham, a graduate who was also on the staff, had published a textbook of economic principles in 1938 to support its teaching in London and beyond, and this text remained in print until the 1960s.[40] The eighth edition of 1967 can be found heading the list of general economics textbooks in a survey of economics for schools dating from the early 1970s.[41] In the 1950s Benham's text was superseded at university level by that of Stonier and Hague, also directed to the London economics degree.[42] And when the first "modern" British economics textbook was published by Richard Lipsey, that too was written by a professor of the London School of Economics.[43] During the 1950s and 1960s the London School of Economics was far more representative of mainstream orthodoxy in Britain than either Oxford or Cambridge, and it was also able to project its version of modern economics to a far wider audience. By that time, however, arguments concerning the deficiencies of planning, together with its consequent inefficiencies and infringements of liberty, had moved on, since in the meantime the experience of the British economy in wartime had displaced that of World War I Germany, and the postwar welfare state and program of nationalization presented neoliberals with more immediate targets for their criticism.

Planning the War Economy

Economic advice had played very little direct role in the direction of the war economy in Britain during World War I; the World War II experience was to prove very different. Not only were economists recruited to assist in determining priorities, gathering information and generating usable statistics, but it was Robbins who ended up in charge of the main office, the Economic Section. Furthermore, in the later 1930s the government sought to direct productive capacity toward military ends. Aircraft production, for example, was a complex process, encompassing numerous functions and activities ranging from ministerial decisions on the types, qualities, and quantities of aircraft required by the RAF and the Fleet Air Arm, through the design and testing of prototypes by private companies, the evaluation of competing aircraft, the placing of orders, and finally the construction of airframes and engines. As early as March 1938, a formal decision was made to place orders regardless of financial constraint, seeking direct maximization of existing manufacturing capacity rather than working to the budgetary constraints that had earlier hindered the rapid production of modern types.[44] One month before the war began, the government created the Ministry of Supply to coordinate wartime production, and in May 1940 a Ministry of Aircraft Production was formed. At its peak in 1944 aircraft production employed some 40 percent of Britain's industrial workforce.[45]

Academic economists were quickly recruited to government service. In late 1939 a Central Economic Information Service was established, staffed by John Jewkes and Harry Campion from Manchester, and Austin Robinson from Cambridge. Churchill created a Statistical Section at the Admiralty where Roy Harrod, Tom Wilson, Bryan Hopkin, David Bensusan-Butt, and Douglas MacDougall worked for Lindemann, Churchill's scientific adviser. In June 1940 Lionel Robbins, R. F. Fowler, and James Meade were recruited, with further approaches being made to Richard Stone, Stanley Dennison, and Harold Wilson. In early 1941 the functions of the Service were divided between a new Central Statistical Office, headed by Harry Campion and Ely Devons, and an Economic Section, headed by Jewkes. When Jewkes left for the Ministry of Aircraft Production in September 1941, Robbins succeeded him as head of the Section.[46] Key British members of the MPS like Jewkes and Robbins—Robbins would draft the statement of aims, for example (see Introduction in this volume)—thus had extensive first-hand experience in government. Furthermore, any list of British economists working for the government during the war contains a significant proportion of those who, after the war, would be associated with the MPS, but very few of those younger economists assumed leading positions during the 1950s and 1960s.

There is now an extensive literature that details the involvement of British economists in wartime economic administration and the nature of their work. Two factors are of importance here. First, central direction of the UK's wartime economy did not seek to displace the private sector,[47] but as the major purchaser of goods and services the government assumed de facto direction of industrial output. This was especially clear in the work of the Ministry of Aircraft Production, which coordinated service demands with both the existing and new manufacturing capacity available to it. Second, those working in economic administration gained a unique insight into the varied problems of demand and supply that had for most of them previously been a purely abstract, theoretical matter. Their skills found new outlets. Bensusan-Butt studied the impact of air bombardment and concluded that in 1941 only one in five sorties got within five miles of the target. MacDougall devised a graphical representation of the phases of the moon coordinated with convoy routes to predict the nights when convoys would be most at risk from attack. Tom Wilson, aware of transport constraints, suggested that vehicles be shipped in a partially dismantled state to increase the flow of supplies to the Middle East and India without requiring more shipping space. The literature is full of similar examples of the government's very practical economic management activities in wartime in the early 1940s. Economists wrestled with mundane but intractable problems such as what to do with 300 Wellington bombers parked on Blackpool beach without propellers.[48] However doctrinaire academic economists might have been in peacetime, under wartime conditions they demonstrated a clear understanding of the complexity of economic administration and the delicacy of the interface between the work of government administration and the efficiency of the economy as a whole. Aircraft production in Britain was completely transformed as a result of their efforts, but not unfortunately its business structure.[49]

Before the war, aircraft construction had been essentially a craft industry. Part of the prewar program of expansion was aimed simply at the extension of production capacity, so that even obsolete types were turned out so that mass production techniques might be developed in a hitherto craft-based industry.[50] Car firms became component suppliers, and in this way over time familiarity with mass construction to higher engineering standards was transferred to postwar civilian consumer production. That this experience was not then translated into the postwar modernization of British consumer industries is a complex story involving the return of loaned American machine tools, depleting British plants of the only modern equipment they had,[51] the limited purchasing power of the British public, the diversion of the majority of scientists, engineers, and technicians to employment in the government sector, and, not least, the sheer inability of British management to innovate in the way that their German, French and Italian counterparts did—all of which countries still have domestically owned car firms.[52]

The British wartime economy was run with the assistance of many senior British economists, but the great majority returned to academic life in 1945 and 1946 to rebuild their departments and extend the discipline. Ely Devons returned to teach in Manchester but wrote up his four years' experience in the planning department of the Ministry of Aircraft Production as *Planning in Practice.*[53] This fascinating work details the increasingly complex business of building aircraft, which, throughout the war, "competed" in a very direct way with German, Japanese, and Italian products.

John Jewkes, Devons's Manchester colleague who had also spent over a year as director of statistics and programs in the Ministry of Aircraft Production, also produced his "memoirs," but his recollections were very different. Acknowledging Hayek's *Road to Serfdom,* he opened with the following *parti pris:*

> The fall in our standard of living to a level which excites the pity and evokes the charity of many other richer countries, the progressive restrictions on individual liberties, the ever-widening destruction of respect for law, the steady sapping of our instinct for tolerance and compromise, the sharpening of class distinctions, our growing incapacity to play a rightful part in world affairs—these sad changes are not due to something that happened in the remote past. They are due to something which has happened in the past two years. At the root of our troubles lies the fallacy that the best way of ordering economic affairs is to place the responsibility for all crucial decisions in the hands of the State.[54]

So what had happened in the preceding two years, 1946 and 1947, to bring about such a catastrophic state of affairs? The Bank of England was nationalized (March 1946), plans for a National Health Service were announced, the intention to nationalize the steel industry was made public (April 1946), plans for a united, independent India had begun (May 1946), bread rationing was introduced (May 1946), the King David Hotel in Jerusalem was blown up (July 1946), the Muslim League demanded a separate "Pakistan" (May 1946), nationalization of railways, ports, long-distance transport ,and canals was announced (November 1946), the coal industry was nationalized (January 1947), the meat ration was reduced (January 1947), and later that same year the Town and Country Planning Act was introduced to place the regulation of land use in the hands of local authorities. Though very selective, this list serves to draw attention to one important fact: owing partly to the experience of the war economy and partly to the international challenges presented by a declining empire, the British postwar government certainly did have an agenda for the extension of the public sector, but it was also faced with managing several other major and intractable problems. For one thing, the occupation of Germany brought with it a responsibility to feed the German population in the British Military Zone. Hence it became necessary to continue and even sharpen wartime rationing in Britain and reduce the daily caloric intake of the average German adult below 1,000 calories. The Palestine Mandate brought its own problems, and in India independence turned into a bloodbath, with 1,200 Muslims killed in the worst single incident in September 1947. And underlying all these problems was the fact that the clock was ticking on the American loan negotiated by Keynes, which had provided Britain with the dollars to continue its international trade following the abrupt cessation of Lend Lease one week after Japan surrendered. Parliament accepted the terms of the fifty-year loan in December 1946, obliging the British government to return sterling to convertibility within two years.[55] This was duly done on July 15, 1947, and then suspended once more on August 21, 1947 because most of the loan had by that time been expended defending sterling's parity.[56]

Reading through even a selection of such political and economic events and issues is sobering, even today. Jewkes spent several years during the war grappling with analogously intractable problems but appears to have learned little from the experience. The few substantial remarks in his broadside against "planning"—concerning, for example, the technical development of tanks and aircraft[57]—are highly tendentious, uninformative, and seemingly uninformed, especially when set against Devons's book. The writings of Peter Bauer, who would become a leading MPS development economist (see Plehwe, Chapter 7 in this volume), betray similar failings to those of Jewkes. During 1946 Bauer visited Malaya on behalf of the Colonial Office, and in 1948 he published a detailed study of the rubber industry.[58] In 1949 he moved on to study West African overseas trade, writing up his findings in a detailed monograph.[59] Common to both Bauer's and Jewkes's works is a detailed understanding of the impact of a regulated international trading system on domestic production structures and output, an understanding that is used to demonstrate the unanticipated problems created by regulation. But Bauer did not become well-known because of these works, nor did he refer to them later when arguing against state-directed development aid. Instead, he became famous as a critic of overseas aid in a series of essays and books published from the 1960s to the 1980s whose generality and sheer repetition belies the careful argument of his earlier work. Like Jewkes, the forcefulness of his critique of state and economy is inversely proportional to its substantive merits. This critique resonated outside the academy, but their colleagues did not take it with any particular seriousness. Nevertheless, Bauer was subsequently awarded a life peerage in 1982 by Margaret Thatcher, and in 2002, shortly before his death, he was the first recipient of the Milton Friedman Prize for Advancing Liberty, a biannual prize of $500,000 given by the Cato Institute.

Postwar Liberalism as Neoliberalism

Jewkes and Bauer might have expressed themselves with some stridency, but in the 1940s and early 1950s their basic argument was one shared by many academic economists, especially at the London School of Economics.[60] In his 1947 Marshall lectures, Robbins reflected on the lessons that might be drawn from wartime experience, or "what economic policy can do for the advancement of human welfare."[61] Noting that free prices had been abandoned early in the war, he nonetheless expressed his belief in the efficacy of free markets in terms that recall Cannan's remarks some twenty years earlier:

> I am inclined to think that the experience of war vindicates completely the doctrine of the textbooks, namely, that with *given* goods and a *given* distribution of income and capital—please note this second qualification—there is nothing like the market mechanism for getting the goods into, roughly speaking, the right hands.[62]

The conclusion that he drew from his wartime experience was not that the market was an ineffective mechanism for distributing goods, but that the problem lay in the "configuration of power to demand to which the market responds."[63] Inequities should be remedied not by interference with the market, but by acting directly upon them through taxes and subsidies. In this way freedom of choice in the market might be maintained, for "good government is no substitute for self-government and it is an essential function of the state to make as much self-government as possible available."[64] Robbins drew a clear line between the necessity of wartime regulation, where there was a pressing and an obvious objective, and the functioning of a peacetime economy, where no such objective existed and it was not government's place to choose one. He was, however, moderate in his assessment of the strains of a transition period, and also in passing disavowed more extreme views expressed in his *Great Depression,* in which he had overlooked "deep-seated possibilities of disharmony."[65]

But at about the same time that Robbins had delivered this recantation,[66] the first meeting of the Mont Pèlerin Society took place, and it was Robbins who drafted the final version of its statement of aims. The initial draft from which he worked (considered by those assembled to be too long) strongly asserted the centrality of competitive markets to the preservation of individual freedom, moving through ten points from this principle to general remarks on the need to strictly limit government activity.[67] It would not be unfair to say that this bald assertion of the centrality of free market mechanisms to political liberty is closer to the spirit of the Society than Robbins's subsequent more general statement where he instead emphasizes the "central values of civilization" and "the conditions of human dignity and freedom."[68] In that version, the market mechanism does not have pride of place in the defense of human freedom; instead, Robbins argues from traditional liberal values, but with one small exception: democratic political values do not have pride of place either.

Robbins, Plant, Stanley Dennison, and Jewkes were listed as members of the Society on its incorporation, although Plant attended neither the first nor any further meeting. If we examine the composition of British Mont Pèlerin Society membership, a background in academic economics dominates those British members with current university appointments, and the LSE and Manchester account for the majority of the economists.[69] Only a few of these British economists appear to have been especially active in subsequent MPS meetings. In 1950 Ronald Coase attended and addressed the membership on "Broadcasting in a Free Society"; in 1951 T. S. Ashton outlined his criticisms of the treatment of capitalism by historians, a meeting also attended by Benham and Bauer. Bauer attended many more meetings and delivered no less than six papers on development economics (crusading against foreign aid) at MPS conferences (see Plehwe, Chapter 7). British members who associated themselves most closely with the Society's activities were not younger academics, but chiefly employees or consultants linked to pressure groups or think tanks, such as Arthur Shenfield,[70] who in 1954 gave a paper on "Democracy, Socialism and the Rule of Law."[71]

Part of the reason that British economists played a relatively muted part in the early work of the MPS can be attributed to the time of its foundation. British academic economists were as a whole broad supporters of government policy in the 1950s, during the greater part of which the Conservative Party was in power. Given that political life was configured around business and labor, the only established position from which the Conservative government's policy could be publicly criticized was already occupied by the Labour Party. Each party of course had its shadings, from right to left. But militant criticism of state activity from any other direction would automatically place the critic on the fringes of the existing political spectrum. It was difficult to reconcile such a stance with an academic reputation in the postwar world. Ronald Coase (who by then was in the United States), for example, was known to be no socialist, but his general reputation has always been primarily that of an author of carefully argued and prescient articles on topical issues such as broadcasting rights, while the novelty of his arguments on social cost derived in great part from how he made use of actual legal disputes in studying the allocation of costs. Coase's writings lack the rhetorical flourishes typical in Bauer and Jewkes, and stand out for the precision with which argument is constructed and advanced.

Consequently, those who did adopt the role of "free market critics" did so from the margins, if not from outside the academy. Bauer's international reputation was as a propagandist for economic liberalism, not as an eminent economist; which was why he became Margaret Thatcher's favorite economist. Arthur Shenfield is presented by Hartwell as an "eminent economist," but in the postwar period the measure of eminence had become publication in the leading English-language academic journals, and there is no trace of this achievement for Shenfield. British economists generally adhered to the vision of peacetime market structure and function that Robbins had outlined in his 1947 lectures, but as economics became a more technical enterprise, so the linkage of economics to political liberty became a commonplace assumption that was considered unworthy of serious discussion.

British neoliberalism therefore became a current of thinking nurtured outside the academy and was not taken very seriously within it. Most significant for the subsequent development of neoliberal thinking was the creation of the Institute of Economic Affairs (IEA) in 1955. The moving spirit behind this organization was Antony Fisher, an entrepreneur and strong believer in free markets who had first attended a meeting of the Mont Pèlerin Society in 1951 and who in 1954 gave a paper on "The British Farmer and the Government."[72] The work of the Institute was chiefly in the field of economic journalism, publishing pamphlets and seeking influence on public opinion, opinion formers, and politicians. Critical to the success of the Institute, however, was the joint activity of Ralph Harris, sometime lecturer in economics at St. Andrews,[73] and Arthur Seldon, Plant's research assistant from 1937 to 1939.[74] For the first ten years of its existence, Harris and Seldon to all intents and purposes *were* the IEA. While developing a public profile through the later 1960s and 1970s, and gaining some influence over the returning Conservative government of 1970, their public reputation was unrelated to these academic roots. Instead, they foreshadowed the emergence of a new wave of journalists and commentators with connections to government, the prime example being Nigel Lawson, Thatcher's chancellor during the 1980s, whose career had begun during the 1950s in financial journalism.

The Conservative Party continued in power until 1964, so that the advocacy of markets and economic liberty cultivated by Harris and Seldon placed them on the fringes of British politics—perhaps not quite like the League of Empire Loyalists or Moral Rearmament, but not far off.[75] Fifteen years later this picture would dramatically change, of course. But in 1968 a young David Collard of Bristol University had already noted the rise of a new right:

> Hardly a week goes by without some conference of teachers, social workers or medical men being told that, for economic reasons, consumers must be charged directly for welfare services. . . . bits and pieces of the New Right's doctrine appear in various places, from the writings of Enoch Powell or the Bow Group to the propaganda of Aims of Industry, but it is most coherently expressed in the publications of the Institute of Economic Affairs (IEA). The IEA's output has been considerable.[76]

Collard was prescient indeed in his public warning that a "collective view can be discerned." He emphasized that the IEA's publications were directed against the welfare state, that they had been written by respected economists, and that they had begun to find a receptive audience among various professions closely linked to the welfare state—such as teachers, doctors, and social workers. He warned his academic colleagues against underestimating the new right and cautioned against a tendency to discount its significance, for "on the left . . . counter arguments have been based on instinct, sentiment and a vague distaste for the profit motive. In terms of economic theory there is a worthwhile piece of demolition work still to be done."[77] Collard clearly identified a central feature of neoliberal argument, the redefinition and reorganization of state functions:

> The market system is a spur to efficient production. Liberty itself depends on the free choice offered by market institutions and each advance of the public sector is a step along Hayek's "road to serfdom." The public sector is clumsy, inefficient and bureaucratic. Its pricing policies lead to shortages (and restrictions of choice) which can be remedied only by pushing taxation to unacceptably high levels. As far as possible, state-provided services should be taken into the private sector on normal market principles except for those hard cases really needing direct state intervention.[78]

Although the academic mainstream may not have been wrong to regard much of this argument as highly problematic, the left chose to ignore Collard's early recognition of the considerable influence of neoliberal doctrine forged jointly by British and foreign MPS members. The principal British economic events of the 1970s—the oil-price surge, inflation, entry into the European Community— coincided in the main with Labour governments, and in opposition the Conservative Party saw no need to set a new agenda for confronting government policy. Radical criticism of the Labour government came from the left, not the right. Such criticism ultimately served to unseat it, while also opening the Labour Party to an internal radicalization that was to render it unelectable for almost twenty years.

The defeat of Labour in 1979 by a Conservative Party led by Margaret Thatcher altered the terms of public debate. Perceiving the academic establishment to be arrayed on a spectrum from left-liberal to socialist, the Conservative government now turned for advice to individuals associated with the Institute of Economic Affairs and the Adam Smith Institute.[79] Think tanks and external advisers became a fixture in public administration, cutting out academic economists and diminishing their authority. In March 1981 when 364 economists signed a letter to *The Times* arguing that current government policy would further sharpen the rising rate of unemployment and factory closures, the outcome was a polarization of university and government to the lasting detriment of the university. At the same time, academic economics was transitioning into a formalized neoclassical orthodoxy whose purchase on public argument was increasingly at a discount.[80] Neoliberal "economism" increasingly dominated the public domain, a discourse of markets and liberty whose lack of intellectual credibility was no obstacle to its propagation and execution. When a New Labour government at last returned in 1997, it would extend and deepen this trend.

Notes

1. Friedrich Hayek, *The Road to Serfdom* (London: Routledge and Kegan Paul, 1944), 6.

2. John Stuart Mill, "On Liberty," in Mary Warnock (ed.), *Utilitarianism* and *On Liberty* (Oxford: Blackwell, 2003), 173.

3. The name "Liberal" was first adopted for the Whig Party by Gladstone in 1868, in which year the party won 61.5 percent of the vote. As the electorate extended to all male and female adults, a process completed only in 1928, so its share of the vote declined. In 1935, polling slightly above its numbers in 1868, it won 6.7 percent of the vote.

4. "The Nature and History of the Problem," in F. A. von Hayek (ed.), *Collectivist Economic Planning* (London: George Routledge, 1935), 1–40.

5. For a summary of the background to Mises's critique of economic planning, see my essay, "The Logical Structure of the Economic World—The Rationalist Economics of Otto Neurath," in *Strategies of Economic Order* (Cambridge: Cambridge University Press, 1995), chapter 6.

6. See my introduction to Otto Kirchheimer and Franz Neumann, *Social Democracy and the Rule of Law* (London: Allen and Unwin, 1987), 1–26, and more generally, Duncan Kelly, *The State of the Political. Conceptions of Politics and the State in the Thought of Max Weber, Carl Schmitt and Franz Neumann* (Oxford: Oxford University Press, 2003).

7. See the discussion of Schmitt in Phil Mirowski's Postface in this volume, "Defining Neoliberalism." Franz Neumann and Otto Kirchheimer both recognized the relevance and power of Schmitt's critique of democratic order; this point needs to be emphasized because it has been rather obscured by comparisons with Hayek.

8. Hayek, *Road to Serfdom,* 56. This formulation owes much to the principles underlying his essay "Economics and Knowledge," *Economica* N.S. 4 (1937), 33–54.

9. Mill, "On Liberty," 172.

10. These are the dates when it actually happened, not when it was meant to happen.

11. P. Gosden, *The Education System since 1944* (Oxford: Martin Robertson, 1983), 6, 36; and F. K. Ringer, *Education and Society in Modern Europe* (Bloomington: Indiana University Press, 1979).

12. By 1911, about 78 percent of the British population lived in towns of 3,000 inhabitants and over, as opposed to 35 percent for France, and around 50 percent for Germany. The British urban working class was by far the largest single section of the population, which was one factor that made the British working class unique.

13. It is itself a complicated story: see Nicholas Timmins, *The Five Giants: A Biography of the Welfare State* (London: HarperCollins, 1995). The "Five Giants" were identified by William Beveridge in 1942 as Want, Disease, Ignorance, Squalor, and Idleness.

14. P. Harling and P. Mandler, "From 'Fiscal-Military' to Laissez-faire State, 1760–1850," *Journal of British Studies,* 32 (1993), 49.

15. A. T. Peacock and J. Wiseman, *The Growth of Public Expenditure in the United Kingdom,* National Bureau of Economic Research Number 72, General Series (Princeton, NJ: Princeton University Press, 1961), 38–39. There is of course an important distinction to be made between transfers, current, and capital expenditure. The "rise of the welfare state" translates fiscally into the increase of central government transfers, benefits, and pensions becoming an increasingly significant part of public expenditure. These are strictly transfers between sections of the population, from taxpayers to beneficiaries, and are simply redistributional. But the point made here is that the government has to raise this money in the first place, even though transfers are not strictly "items of expenditure" like the salaries of civil servants or the development of new weapon systems; and that transfer payments related to "welfare" were historically preceded by transfer payments to pay off "warfare." Although much of government expenditure in the nineteenth century involved domestic redistribution (from the poorer to the richer classes, hence the reverse of what we would assume today), the fiscal structure was skewed heavily to indirect taxation, which thus both reinforced this redistributional character and severely limited the ability of governments to increase its revenues. This basic structure survived until World War I, which destroyed it for good.

16. E. V. Morgan, *Studies in British Financial Policy, 1914–25* (London: Macmillan, 1952), 89.

17. Direct taxes were of course collected annually. Since World War I began rather less than halfway through one tax year, even if the income tax had been a significant source of government revenue, the rates could in principle only have been altered in March 1915, taking effect from April 1915 and being collected during the latter half of 1916. By this time the war would have been over, or so it was thought until at least late 1915.

18. And the return to the Gold Standard in 1925 diminished the importance of the distinction between domestic and international public debt, imposing a general deflationary restriction on public finances.

19. Morgan, *Studies,* 98.

20. This contrasts with German "ordoliberals" who argued primarily for economic liberty, political liberty being a secondary consideration.

21. Agitation for free trade in the 1830s and 1840s crossed class boundaries and united both working and middle classes; the class-ridden historiography of nineteenth-century social movements, where the working class is part of the "history of socialism" and the middle class, of the "history of liberalism," has entirely obscured this linkage between the classes.

22. Mill, among other things, introduced the contrast of comparative and absolute advantage, terms that Ricardo does not use.

23. For an elaboration of this argument, see my essay, "Reading Trade in the *Wealth of Nations,*" *History of European Ideas,* 32 (2006), 57–89.

24. Public choice analysis completes this development by translating political theory into the terms of economics.

25. And so Hayek wrote in terms of a minimal state based on the rule of law, but he conceived social order as essentially market-based. His admirers tended to read him in terms of the latter rather than the former.

26. The Treaty of Rome contained articles on competition and restrictive practices, but on its signing in 1957 only Germany had actually established a Federal Office that might lend force to these principles, and it had done so just months before.

27. See, for example, John Mohan, "The Past and Future of the NHS: New Labour and Foundation Hospitals," www.historyandpolicy.org/archive/policy-paper-14.html (accessed March 2008).

28. Cannan taught short courses from the early years of the school, was made professor in 1907, and retired in 1926. His was never a full-time appointment, and he commuted daily to the school from his home in Oxford, where he also served on the City Council for several years.

29. Edwin Cannan, "Preface" to *An Economist's Protest* (London: P. S. King and Son, 1927), vi–vii.

30. For an account of this phase in the development of academic economics, see Alon Kadish, *The Oxford Economists in the Late Nineteenth Century* (Oxford: Oxford University Press, 1982).

31. "Student Appointments," London School of Economics and Political Science, *Calendar* 1931–1932, 427.

32. I have interviewed several students and teachers who were at LSE during the 1930s and 1940s, and none of them volunteered comments attesting to Hayek's impact in lecture room or seminar. Nor when directly asked did their remarks suggest that Hayek was a prominent person in the school. The dominating figures were Lionel Robbins and the (subsequently more obscure) Arnold Plant. This is also plain from the correspondence of representatives of the Rockefeller Foundation, whose financial support was so important to the school. Given Hayek's later eminence, his admirers have assumed that he must have been "always already famous" and their recollections adjusted themselves to suit this assumption. For an account of the LSE in the 1930s, see my forthcoming *Making Economics: The Formation of Economic Science and the British University 1805–1950* (Leiden: E. J. Brill, 2009).

33. H. D. Henderson, *Economic Journal*, 45 (1935), 117.

34. The exact nature of the contrast with Keynes on this point merits noting here, for neoliberals persist in confusing "Keynesianism" with the arguments of Maynard Keynes, whose work they do not seem to have read. For a particularly flagrant example of willful misrepresentation, see R. Cockett, *Thinking the Unthinkable: Think Tanks and the Economic Counter-Revolution 1931–83* (London: Fontana Press, 1995), especially 38, 46. Like Robbins, Keynes believed that recovery lay in a restoration of business confidence, but Keynes argued that this would only happen if central authorities

gave them "reasons to be cheerful." It was certainly not the function of government to supplant business decision making; rather, economic policy sets the framework in which decisions to invest and consume are made, and it is in the power of governments to stimulate business optimism as well as business pessimism. Arguing, as did Robbins, that the best policy is no policy simply wishes away the existence of markets and governments. John Maynard Keynes, *The General Theory of Employment, Interest and Money,* vol. 7 of *Collected Writings of John Maynard Keynes* (London: Macmillan, 1973), 46–50, 148–164.

35. Lionel Robbins, *The Great Depression* (London: Macmillan, 1934), 190.

36. Arnold Plant, "The Economics of the Native Question," published in *Voorslag,* Durban, May–July 1927; reprinted in A. Plant, *Selected Economic Essays and Addresses* (London: Routledge and Kegan Paul, 1974), 3–16.

37. Although in the process of translation Plant's negative view of property rights was transmuted into Coase's positive one; see Ronald Coase, "Arnold Plant" in his *Essays on Economics and Economists* (Chicago: University of Chicago Press, 1994), 182.

38. Plant's student Ronald Coase inaugurated the transaction cost approach to explain the existence of firms in his 1937 article "The Nature of the Firm." This filled a neoclassical black box and undermined a prevailing belief in the bureaucratic efficiency of deliberate planning ("organization") by drawing attention to problems of delegation (principal-agent relationships). The approach has given rise to the critical study of the limits of organizational efficiency and to a search for alternative ways of organizing (e.g., "simulating markets" within firms and public organizations. See Oliver E. Williamson and Sidney G. Winter (eds.), *The Nature of the Firm: Origins, Evolution, and Development* (New York: Oxford University Press, 1991).

39. Script in Plant Papers, file 180, British Library of Political and Economic Science Archive Department.

40. F. Benham, *Economics: A General Textbook for Students* (London: Sir Isaac Pitman & Sons, 1938).

41. Assistant Masters Association, *The Teaching of Economics in Secondary Schools* (London: Cambridge University Press, 1971), 166. Under "Advanced Level: Basic Texts" Benham, as revised by Frank Paish, is listed second after a more general work. Lipsey is listed tenth, Samuelson twelfth, and Stonier and Hague fourteenth.

42. A. W. Stonier and D. C. Hague, *A Textbook of Economic Theory* (London: Longmans, Green & Co., 1953).

43. R. G. Lipsey, *An Introduction to Positive Economics* (London: Weidenfeld and Nicolson, 1963).

44. M. M. Postan, *British War Production* (London: HMSO, 1952), 87.

45. Tom Wilson, *Churchill and the Prof* (London: Cassell, 1995), 56.

46. A detailed account of the entry of economists into wartime administration, and a survey of their activities, can be found in A. Cairncross and N. Watts, *The Economic Section 1939–1961: A Study in Economic Advising* (London: Routledge, 1989).

47. The only significant aircraft firm that was nationalized in the course of the war was Shorts of Belfast, and this was mainly for a purely practical reason: to stop it producing its obsolete heavy bomber.

48. Interview with Sir Alec Cairncross, in Keith Tribe (ed.), *Economic Careers: Economics and Economists in Britain, 1930–1970* (London: Routledge, 1997), 52.

49. The threat of aerial bombing led to a policy of plant dispersal in Britain, so that there was little incentive to create large firms, and none at all to emulate the large plants typical of the United States.

50. Hence the building of 3,100 obsolete Fairey Battle light bombers, whose performance in France during May 1940 was so lamentable—see M. Smith, "Planning and Building the British Bomber Force, 1934–1939," *Business History Review,* 54 (1980), 48–50.

51. The lamentable history of the British motorcycle industry is in part based on this problem, as contrasted with the Italian industry. When as a schoolboy in the mid-1960s I worked in two light engineering factories in South London, the mass of the older machinery was British, while the only modern equipment was German.

52. See David Edgerton, *Warfare State. Britain 1920–1970* (Cambridge: Cambridge University Press, 2006), chapter 2.

53. Ely Devons, *Planning in Practice: Essays in Aircraft Planning in War-time* (London: Cambridge University Press, 1950).

54. John Jewkes, *Ordeal by Planning* (London: Macmillan, 1948), vii.

55. As it turned out, the U.S. dollar would be the only convertible international currency until 1958.

56. As it was the duty of the government to do under prevailing international agreements.

57. Jewkes, *Ordeal,* 21. Problems with tank development were linked to the lack of suitable engine designs and a consequent reliance on available commercial models, and the constraint of the existing railway loading gauge—larger armored vehicles could not be carried on British tracks. It is for this same reason that the Eurostar carriage conforms to British dimensions and is considerably more cramped than Continental carriages.

58. Peter Bauer, *The Rubber Industry: A Study in Competition and Monopoly,* Publication of the London School of Economics and Political Science [no series no.] (London: Longmans, Green & Co., 1948).

59. Peter Bauer, *West African Trade: A Study of Competition, Oligopoly and Monopoly in a Changing Economy* (London: Cambridge University Press, 1954).

60. See Alan Peacock, "The LSE and Post-war Economic Policy," in his *The Political Economy of Freedom* (Cheltenham: Edward Elgar, 1997), 122–123.

61. Lionel Robbins, *The Economic Problem in Peace and War: Some Reflections on Objectives and Mechanisms* (London: Macmillan, 1947), 3.

62. Ibid., 5.

63. Ibid., 8.

64. Ibid., 18.

65. "I owe much to Cambridge economists, particularly to Lord Keynes and Professor Robertson, for having awakened me from dogmatic slumbers in this very important respect" (Robbins, *The Economic Problem,* 68).

66. The Marshall Lectures were delivered in "the Spring" of 1947, the preface to the printed version being dated May 1947.

67. The "Draft Statement of Aims" is printed in R. M. Hartwell, *A History of the Mont Pelerin Society* (Indianapolis, IN: Liberty Fund, 1995), 49–50, and the Introduction to this volume.

68. Hartwell, *History,* 41.

69. With an LSE connection: T. S. Ashton (also Manchester), Bauer, Benham, Coase, Frankel, Paish, Plant, Robbins, Schwartz, Yamey; with a Manchester connection: Ashton, Devons, Hagenbuch, Jewkes, Prest. Birmingham is the one other significant pole: Walters, Littlechild, Shenfield.

70. Shenfield (1909–1990) is a very shadowy figure whose wife had a *Who's Who* entry, but who, unusually, did not have one for himself. In 1948 he was appointed in Birmingham as assistant lecturer in economics (alongside Frank Hahn), but there is no record of how long he remained in this post. In the mid-1950s he was economic adviser to the Federation of British Industry. See some comments on his later career in Allister Heath, *Journal of the Institute of Economic Affairs,* 19, No. 2 (June 1999).

71. Mont Pèlerin Society, Inventory of the General Meeting Files (1947–1990), Liberaal Archief, Ghent, Belgium, various sessions.

72. Fisher had ended up in farming and introduced battery hen farming to Britain—an innovation that from today's perspective is suggestive of the priority neoliberals gave to economic efficiency over wider political liberties as articulated in modern debates on animal rights.

73. Where James Nisbet taught, having been appointed in 1935 and retiring as professor in 1970. Nisbet was a prominent Scottish advocate of laissez-faire, having published *A Case for Laissez-Faire* (London: P. S. King, 1929).

74. For the activities of the IEA, see Cockett, *Thinking the Unthinkable.* Cockett's account of the background to British neoliberalism up to this point is unreliable and tendentious. For example, when discussing the rise of government expenditure (p. 17), he selects 1870–1890 as his baseline, with which he compares 1926 and 1940. As argued above, two world wars played an important role in extending the reach of government in Britain, but this was in fact continuous with the eighteenth century, as David Edgerton has more recently documented. On p. 34 he divides the world into "liberals and Keynesians," apparently overlooking the fact that Keynes was a Liberal, as was, for instance, also James Meade. On p. 37, discussing "spiralling wage costs," he appears unaware that the price level fell in the 1930s and that developments in industrial structure led to a demand for more highly skilled labor, which would command higher

wages. There are numerous other such instances of distortion and misrepresentation in his account of the development of the British economy and of the debates that developed around this, both within academia and beyond.

75. This dimension is understandably absent from Cockett's heroic history of the IEA. A recent BBC documentary on British neoliberalism, *Tory! Tory! Tory!,* suggested that the general perception of Harris and Seldon during the 1950s and 1960s was that they were harmless eccentrics with little insight into the workings of government.

76. David Collard, *The New Right: A Critique,* Fabian Tract 387 (London: Fabian Society, 1968), 1.

77. Ibid.

78. Ibid.

79. Individual economists who found favor with the Thatcher government, such as Patrick Minford, Peter Bauer, and Alan Walters, remained unrepresentative of mainstream academic economists.

80. See the later sections of my entry, "Britain, Economics in (20th century)," in Stephen Durlauf and Lawrence Blume (eds.), *The New Palgrave Dictionary of Economics,* 2nd ed. (Basingstoke: Palgrave Macmillan, 2008).

3

Neoliberalism in Germany

Revisiting the Ordoliberal Foundations of the Social Market Economy

RALF PTAK

Germany's economic model has been frequently described as a *coordinated* market economy juxtaposed against the Anglo-Saxon *liberal* market economies of the UK and the United States. For many, Germany's post–World War II "social market economy" in particular constitutes an alternative model to harsher neoliberal systems (Nicholls 1994). A high degree of state interventionism is alleged to be strongly rooted in the history of Germany, which is also frequently held to be deficient in the cultural values of liberal individualism. Indeed, the origins of modern social security systems can be traced back to Bismarck's efforts in the late nineteenth century to protect workers from old age poverty and health-related risks not meliorated by market forces. But the promise of pensions and health insurance was at the same time meant to undermine the rapid rise of the Social Democratic Party in that era. Previous efforts to outlaw the first modern mass party had proved ineffective. Since the strong police state (and the military) were incapable of solving the problem, other means had to be found to limit the appeal of a working-class mass movement, which propagated revolutionary socialism at the time. Half a century later and after two devastating wars, the original model of a social market economy continued to display these ambiguities: ordoliberal economists, the German members of the larger neoliberal family of thought, conceived the social market economy in order to offset what they considered to be dangerous trends in the postwar economy. In light of the contemporary misunderstanding of the character of the original social market economy, it is difficult to explain why German trade unions, Social Democrats, and communists fought Ludwig Erhard's efforts to institutionalize the social market economy, why Margaret Thatcher propagated the German model on her way into Downing Street (Cockett 1994), and why Milton Friedman recommended the German model to Chile's dictator Pinochet after the coup (see Fischer, Chapter 9 in this volume).

A closer look at the history of German neoliberalism helps to clarify the puzzle. Ordoliberalism is substantially less different from other streams of neoliberal thought than many have thought, although the German tradition of a strong state certainly extends throughout the history of German ordoliberalism. But ordoliberalism had more to offer to the international evolution of neoliberalism than mere reiteration of a parochial German understanding of the state.

Many intellectual histories of neoliberalism tend to juxtapose German ordoliberalism and Austrian neoliberalism in order to emphasize the Germanic state tradition, which is difficult to reconcile with the market radical individualism that has been inspired by the marginalist revolution (most recently, Foucault 2004). A leading German ordoliberal, Hans Willgerodt, alerts his readers to the dangers, when considering the differences between related neoliberal concepts, as more important than what is common to all of them. According to Willgerodt, neoliberals acknowledge the need to complement traditional liberalism with important external alien elements, correct mistakes of the past, and transform doctrine in light of new insights and convictions. A better understanding of the role of the state is considered a key task on which true neoliberals would agree. While competition between liberal convictions may suggest a separation of ordoliberalism from related approaches, Willgerodt maintains that "in reality there exists only a difference in emphasis, and opportunities for an academic and political division of labor" (Willgerodt 2006, 55). Foucault (2004) correctly emphasized that German ordoliberals were indeed the *avant garde,* and they went further than other members of the neoliberal family in addressing the shortcomings of traditional liberalism. The ordoliberals collaborated in developing a new social theory of the economy, and strongly redoubled efforts to understand the relation between law and economics, for example. But Foucault underestimates the extent to which both German and Austrian neoliberal economists shared a particular (sociological) understanding of economics and fought a narrow econometric/technical understanding.

In order to substantiate this argument, we need to subject the historical origins and the evolution of ordoliberalism[1] to greater scrutiny. Even though some of the leading ordoliberals (Alexander Rüstow, Wilhelm Röpke, and Alfred Müller-Armack, for example) were more often than not located elsewhere than Freiburg, Walter Eucken's *Freiburger Schule* deserves special attention. English-language contributions to the history of German neoliberalism (and its impact on the social market economy) are rare. Most of the few contributions that exist have been written by German neoliberals in order to positively affirm their theoretical perspectives, and all fail to critically examine the hostility of key ordoliberals to parliamentarian democracy and their entanglements in the Nazi regime (Hutchison 1979; Watrin 1979; Giersch 1988; Vanberg 1988; Peacock and Willgerodt 1989a, 1989b; Leipold 1990; Nicholls 1994; for a notable exception, see Tribe 1995). Although German ordoliberals like to congratulate themselves on their defense of individual freedom and liberty, the history of German neoliberalism clearly reveals the limited, primarily economic understanding of freedom that is the common denominator of the different schools of neoliberal thought. Even so, conservative patriarchal ideas of society are more explicitly integrated into the German contribution.[2] A detailed account of the different stages in the evolution of German ordoliberalism (from the time of the Great Depression onward) will also clarify why and how German neoliberals, rather than the potentially more compatible socialists, conceived and promoted the social market economic model. Outside observers frequently fail to see the extent to which German exceptionalism has been a peculiar combination of both strong and yet limited state intervention. Privatization was high on the German agenda after World War II when many other countries were experimenting with nationalization, for example. Although comparative research on the post–World War II rise of Keynesianism has attempted to explain German exceptionalism in this regard (see Hall 1989), the rise of German neoliberals to key positions of power during the early years of the Federal Republic of Germany cannot be understood without taking a closer look at their previous intellectual, economic, and political activities.

This chapter is organized as follows. It starts with a discussion of some of the peculiarities of ordoliberalism in order to provide a better picture of

specifically German neoliberal developments. Next follows a detailed examination of the genesis of ordoliberal ideas during the Great Depression and
the subsequent developments leading up to a self-conscious ordoliberal doctrine (during the Nazi era and during the early years of the Federal Republic)
(the second through the fifth section). Owing to the importance of debates on
the relationship between ordoliberalism and the Nazis, an entire section (the
fourth) is devoted to this topic. Once the backdrop of the historical stages of
the development of ordoliberalism is in place, I will proceed to clarify how the
social market economy was conceived as a vehicle to implement ordoliberal
ideas (the sixth section).

Some Peculiarities of Ordoliberalism
(in Comparative Perspective)

Along the spectrum of neoliberalism, ordoliberalism is found at a range of
frequencies that owes some of its peculiarities to the specific German conditions encountered during the Weimar Republic and under Nazi rule. In contrast to the Austrian and Chicago emphasis on the rather abstract rule of the
law, the ordoliberals grant the visibly strong state a much more prominent
role in establishing and securing the capitalist market economy. This recognition of the role of the state is at the very center of ordoliberal efforts to theorize an ideal social order of capitalism and to design public policy to this end.
The specific term *policy of order (Ordnungspolitik)* was coined by the Freiburg
school, led by Walter Eucken and Franz Böhm, during the second half of the
1930s. Members of this school conceived of the need to theorize the frameworks that effectively structure the relationship between the state, the economy, and society in general. They thereby fostered an early understanding of
the important relationship between law and economics, relative to their neoliberal comrades. Their central goal in this task was to secure a socially embedded and well-functioning competitive order.

Other schools of neoliberalism do, of course, assign the state a highly significant role in ensuring a free market economy. Examples are the Central Bank
Authority, exercised in monetarist perspective; regulatory reform activities dedicated to promote privatization, such as the provision of school vouchers; and
deregulation and liberalization policies inspired by public choice theory. Yet in
the original conception of ordoliberalism, the theoretical understanding of the
state is far more explicit. As a result, important differences between factions

with regard to the neoliberal understanding of specific state functions persist to this day, say, with regard to antitrust conceptions featured in Freiburg as compared to the essentially pro-trust arguments from Chicago (compare Van Horn, Chapter 6 in this volume). Ordoliberalism ventured beyond a limited safeguarding and correcting role for the state in an effort to prevent abuse of monopoly power or to promote and stabilize competition. The state is instead employed to initiate and comprehensively ensure a competitive order. In the very first systematic ordoliberal book on competition theory (Miksch 1937), Leonhard Miksch, Eucken's most prominent student,[3] classified market competition as an "event" *(Veranstaltung)* to be organized by the state. The resulting mode of "liberal interventionism" (Rüstow 1932, 170) required the state to take active measures to establish a concrete system of competition and thereby translated theoretical models of a competitive market for practical purposes (Eucken [1952] 1990, 254). The static perception of perfect competition—informed by neoclassical equilibrium theory—manifestly differs from the dynamic understanding of competition that was later developed by Germanophone economists (including neoliberals), taking off from Hayek's concept of "competition as discovery process" (1968) in particular.[4]

The second peculiarity of Germany's ordoliberal contribution to neoliberalism was a dedicated effort to resolve what the German ordoliberals themselves conceived as "the social question." German neoliberals attempted to address issues of social cohesion in direct competition with widespread confidence in the efficacy of the welfare state, and they offered an alternative solution: the social market economy. They provided a theoretically grounded political program, and they elevated their concept into a significant point of reference in postwar Germany. A concerted campaign of neoliberal and business forces promoting Ludwig Erhard's social market economy started in 1945–1946, when the public debate addressed the question of how Germany's economy and society should be arranged. Initially, even the Ahlen program of the conservative Christian Democratic Party (CDU) featured socialization strategies (Ptak 2004). In this context, as early as 1953 Alexander Rüstow stressed that "the only consequent, properly thought-out, unified and independent program of economic policy from our side known to me is the one of so-called neoliberalism or 'Social Market Economy,' according to the fortunate coining of my colleague Müller-Armack who has just recently been appointed to the Federal Ministry of Economics. It is a program my friends and I, a group whose acknowledged mentor in Germany, Walter Eucken, died far

too soon, have been working at for years" (Rüstow 1953, 101). Certain concessions to competing visions of universal welfare were made in theory, and more
concessions had to be made owing to prevailing political power constellations.
But even if the pragmatic flexibility of neoliberalism Hayek had stressed[5] required a stronger dose of social liberalism in practice than most neoliberals
were willing to swallow for political reasons in postwar Germany, early on
ordoliberals were able to limit the welfare state, compared with other countries until the late 1950s. The ordoliberals were successful because of their own
special social scientific understanding of economics and their readiness to
cross disciplinary boundaries. To appreciate both the success and the limits of
their emphasis on social cohesion, we have to consider two prominent ordoliberals in particular.

It turned out to be of signal importance for neoliberalism that Wilhelm
Röpke and Walter Rüstow (both exiled from Germany by the Nazis) violated
disciplinary boundaries in an effort to provide the sociocultural foundations
necessary for a liberal economic order. They argued persuasively that a regulatory order comprised of legal and state institutions was not sufficient to properly embed the market economy in society. In order to give such an order further stability, a more comprehensive complement of sociopolitical concepts
was needed. German neoliberals, insistent on the need to pay strict attention
to questions of sociopolitical integration, deserve credit for acknowledging
the destructive potential of the market economy. At the same time, this debate
reflects a strange mix of steadfast belief in the market on the one hand and of
reactionary pessimism with regard to progress and the future on the other.
The pure ordoliberal design of a market society was ultimately doomed to fail
given these inherent contradictions, which resulted from the combination of
economic modernity and antimodern political, social, and cultural ideas.[6]

Wilhelm Röpke had launched broadsides against classical economic liberalism since the early 1940s. He claimed that classical writers had ignored the fact
"that the market economy constitutes a narrow sector of societal life only." Although the market economy was "simply [an] indispensable configuration" in
the economic sphere, where it would manifest itself in an "unadulterated and
genuine" way, on its own, it would be dangerous, if not indefensible, because
for all intents and purposes it would reduce humans to an unnatural existence:
"The market economy thus requires a firm framework, which we shall call in
short an anthropological-sociological frame" (Röpke 1946, 82f.).[7] It would
prove difficult to capture the full outlines of this frame, however. Both Rüstow

and Röpke addressed the perceived societal crisis from a perspective of fundamental cultural pessimism, along the lines Spengler had presented in his *Decline of the West* at the end of World War I.

One way to examine the ordoliberal effort to understand social reality in
that era is to recognize that it constituted a mix of social scientific observation and metaphysical speculation, which operated on three levels: First, the
spiritual-moral crisis was held to have caused the degeneration and structural
disintegration of society (Röpke [1942] 1979, 22ff.). Second was the crisis of
development of the mass society, which Röpke and Rüstow, but also Eucken,
as early as the beginning of the 1930s, had identified as the central reason for
the demise of the Weimar Republic. This phenomenon gained new prominence in the structural analysis of society under the label of so-called proletar-
ianization (Röpke [1942] 1979, 30). Third, the ordoliberals posited a crisis of
gigantism and bureaucracy (Röpke [1942] 1979, 103ff.; Rüstow 1950, 71) in addition to the critique of the central state, making reference to it in order to
harshly attack the impact of technical progress (Rüstow 1951), the development of large-scale enterprises (Röpke 1948a), the rapid urbanization of life
(Röpke 1946, 287), and the alleged overpopulation (Rüstow 1951, 389; Röpke
[1942] 1979, 28).

Both the thrust and the passion of this critique of what the ordoliberals perceived to be the disintegration of the modern capitalist society had a greater
affinity with conservative than with classic liberal positions. Röpke (1948b, 226)
himself acknowledged the relationship of his thought to "religious-conservative
streams." But even if it seems absurd that the prophets of market economic
forces of innovation would castigate the results of the economic dynamism, the
antimodernism evident in their social and cultural critique provided the basis
for one of the pillars of the ordoliberal program: stability and security for the
working class was prerequisite to securing the market economy. This program
fundamentally differed from left-wing calls for egalitarian redistribution.

Behind the ordoliberal analysis lurked the promise of a hierarchically structured society, a "natural order" that Eucken, Böhm, and Röpke had all evoked
and that had become a quasireligious Ordo talisman of the "new" liberalism
in Germany. The basic Ordo mind-set served not only as an ideological backdrop for a hierarchical social model,[8] but also as a way of providing legitimacy
for its supposedly irrevocable character. Ordo was regarded as the culmination
of Western high culture, defined in classically Eurocentrist fashion as the
zenith of human development. Eucken ([1952] 1990, 372) argued that Ordo

represented an "order, which accords with the essence of humans; this means an order in which proportion (measure) and balance exist."

But a number of problems arose as to how this general idea could be translated into concrete political concepts. A few cornerstones of Eucken's Ordo ideas, such as an estate model of social stratification,[9] elite rather than mass influence with regard to political decision making, protection and expansion of private property, and decentralization and subsidiarity as primary principles for the political and social structure, can be readily recognized in terms of basic doctrine. However, the rather metaphysical Ordo idea did not easily lend itself to use as a model for the implementation of a neoliberal political program in post–World War II Germany for reasons that are fairly obvious. According to Otto Veit (1953, 32), in a contribution to the *Ordo Yearbook,* it was nevertheless imperative to "achieve something that claws at metaphysics: to approximate the order of this world to the Ordo of the world of ideas." Ordoliberalism was challenged to bridge the gap between utopian ideals and the sordid facts on the ground, even when the facts were so unpleasant that many preferred to be dreamers.

Röpke and Rüstow made it their task to translate the metaphysic of Ordo into a concrete political program. They complemented the normative framework of the ordoliberal economy with an analysis of the transition from the present to the ideal future. Röpke (1946, 79 and 85; emphasis in original) called this dimension of the ordoliberal program *"structural policy"* designed to "no longer assume the social preconditions of the market economy . . . as given, but to modify them with a specific intent." Thereby a *"countermounted socio-political effort" (widergelagerte Gesellschaftspolitik)* was conjured to contribute to the stability of the market economic order. Rüstow conceptualized his sociopolitical aspirations as "Vitalpolitik"—emphasizing the ideological function of the "supra-economical" beyond concerns about the structural imprint of society. Rüstow (1950, 91) considered it of utmost importance to recognize "the superior importance of the vital and the anthropological, even within the economy, compared to technically economic aspects, which can be quantitatively measured."

While attending to the sound of a humanistic critique of narrow economistic thinking, it is important not to overlook the fact that the attacks were directed mainly against redistributive social and wage policies. Rüstow (1957b, 235) stressed "the origins of the term Vitalpolitik in opposition to a purely material social policy." It was not the demand for higher income, better working conditions, or shorter work time—classical labor movement demands, in short—that was considered to yield the determining indicator of the positive life situation of the "mass," but rather a policy "with an impact on the well being, a feeling of content of the individual human" (Rüstow 1957b, 235).[10] It was possible for Ordos to conceive of a sort of social subjectivism, according to which feelings of satisfaction (to be generated) would replace more mundane material solutions of the social question.

Taken together, Rüstow's social-psychological and ideological approach embodied in his concept of a Vitalpolitik, and Röpke's sociological "structural policy," were the linchpins of the ordoliberal political project. Central to both was an imperative to strengthen the capitalist social structure with the provision of determined and sustained support to small and medium-size enterprises and to family agriculture.[11] The members of the independent middle strata of society were considered the most important recruits for the ordoliberal policy project. They were to constitute the fertile soil ("Mutterboden," Röpke 1946, 224) of the desired order. Although they were extolled as the "healthy" core of an ailing society threatened by industrialization and mass culture, curiously, they were also considered an apolitical and uncompromised quantity still cognizant of "rendering to the king what is owed to the king, but also giving to god what belongs to god" (Röpke 1946, 223). In addition, the function of the middle strata as intermediate rungs in the climb up the social ladder was stressed time and again, not least by Müller-Armack (1947, 127), who referred in a more pragmatic manner to the reconciliation function of the "tremendously important intermediary and middle strata" of society. Thus, liberal ideas about social advance due to meritocracy were to some extent reconciled with considerations of natural hierarchy.

The reliance on a visibly strong state as evidenced by *Ordnungspolitik* (akin to Nazi ideology based on Carl Schmitt, as discussed later in this chapter) and an emphasis on the sociocultural foundations of individuals in the market economy (a key divergence from the anti-individualism of Nazi ideologies) became constitutive elements of Germany's "new" liberalism. The German ordoliberals sought their own response to the Social Question, in constant fear of what they regarded as the ultimate destructive powers of socialist organizing in mass production and society at large—exemplified by trade-union "monopolies" and the welfare state. They incessantly stressed the importance of sociopolitical integration, which was intended to mitigate the centrifugal forces of a market-oriented organization of society, by offering all and sundry alternatives to the proposals of social liberals and socialists. Whereas authoritarian elements of compulsory integration were emphasized in the first papers written by ordoliberals in the 1930s, this approach had to change after 1945—postwar circumstances no longer allowed embracing national-authoritarian approaches to sociopolitical integration. Conjuring an original neoliberal interpretation of the perennial Social Question thus became increasingly urgent: the critique of capitalist dynamics had moved to center stage in politics, while the trade unions and Social Democrats could no longer be prevented by force from competing in this field.

Without a doubt, early Anglo-Saxon neoliberal thought was inclined toward a more brazen individualism and tended to impose stricter standards as far as the government's concrete tasks of social policy were concerned, in comparison to German ordoliberal theory and practice. However, neither Hayek's sharp criticism of the frequently quoted weasel-word "social," nor his skepticism about the term *social market economy*,[12] should rashly be interpreted as mounting an implacable opposition toward the approach developed by German ordoliberals. Hayek certainly was afraid that using the term *social* would lead to a tendency to fortify the welfare state against the ordoliberal intention. On the other hand, Hayek and even his "Spiritus Rector," Mises, were keenly aware that the implementation of the market economy in Germany as a social market economy was a function of the specific political circumstances in West Germany after 1945. For without a flexible and pragmatic political approach, the reintroduction of a market economy would arguably have not even been feasible in the immediate aftermath of the war given widespread public awareness of and concern about the cooperation of capital, academia, and the Nazi rulers. Hayek biographer Alan Ebenstein (2001, 242), in contradiction to many attempts at cleanly separating Austrian and German versions of neoliberalism, notes:

> Hayek's discussion of the West German "social market economy" sheds light on his conception of optimal, or at least adequate, societal order. Relating a story about Erhard, Hayek recalled that "we were alone for a moment, and he turned to me and said, 'I hope you don't misunderstand me when I speak of a social market economy *(Soziale Marktwirtschaft)*. I mean by that that the market economy as such is social not that it needs to be made social." In *Law, Legislation and Liberty*, Hayek commented on the term "social market economy" that "I regret this usage though by means of it some of my friends in Germany (and more recently in England) have apparently

succeeded in making palatable to wider circles the sort of social order for which I am pleading.

As German economic historian Knut Borchardt (1981, 36) pointed out, especially with regard to the flexible conceptual approach of the social market economy, the basic agreement of the German ordoliberals with the ideas of Hayek (and vice versa) is mostly *underestimated.*

The Historical Origins of Ordoliberalism: The Great Depression

The emergence of ordoliberal theory and its relevance as the basis of the social market economy can be factored into different stages of development: The Great Depression, the period of Nazi rule, and postwar reconstruction— stretching from the late 1920s to the early 1950s. Not until the 1950s can one speak of a more or less coherent theory and practice of "new" liberalism in Germany, expressed by the special relationship between ordoliberalism and the social market economy. Even the term *ordoliberalism* occurred for the first time in 1950 and has been used as a widely accepted self-description since the late 1950s (see note 1), whereas the term *neoliberalism* originated in the 1930s and has been used only intermittently and ambiguously ever since (Walpen 2004, 73f.).

   Not unexpectedly, some vital roots of this new liberalism can be recognized in earlier lines of economic thought. Different versions of liberalism were present and influential during the nineteenth century in the German world (Raico 1999). During Wilhelminic Germany and the Weimar Republic, German social liberals like Friedrich Naumann and Walter Rathenau attempted to integrate Social Democrats into the ruling structure of the political system in order to broaden support for their global ambitions. The economic base of the Weimar liberals was grounded in competitive new industrial sectors in chemicals and electronics to which the center-right liberal parties were closely allied. A broader political alliance was considered necessary at that time to curtail the economic and political power of the old, primarily inward looking and monopolistically organized steel and coal industries, which generally backed reactionary right-wing parties. Leading steel and coal magnates maintained monarchist and militaristic perspectives, and consequently supported a variety of anti-Weimar movements of the radical right. The political battles between the liberal and reactionary forces were bound up with numerous economic issues. State regulation of prices for coal and steel was proposed by liberals to limit what was regarded as an economic and a political abuse of the existing market conditions, which allowed economic monopolies of Germany's old industrial core to control prices (Opitz 1973). Rathenau's arguments in favor of a public economic sector *(Gemeinwirtschaft)* were specifically aimed at integrating Social Democracy into the world market-oriented political coalition. His ideas had become targets for the early right-wing liberal attacks on social liberal "socialism," as in von Mises's major work *Die Gemeinwirtschaft.* In any case, the linear history of a continuous development from "old" to "new" liberalism as presented in many neoliberal histories of economic thought[13] misses a complicated process of conflicts and shifting alliances, in spite of all the efforts to trace the lineage of neoliberalism straight backward to one version of nineteenth-century liberalism.

The world economic crisis unfolding between 1929 and 1932 marked the explicit starting point for ordoliberalism in Germany, at a time when liberal economists in other countries did not have much reason to expect many liberal impulses from German academic economics. "The only influential and active circle of theorists that until 1933 struggled with great effort, yet to no avail, for a free economy" (Hayek 1983, 12) had been the group of the so-called Ricardians in support of "free trade" who were organized in and around the Verein Deutscher Maschinenbau-Anstalten *(VDMA),* the lobby of the export-oriented engineering industry. This group, which centered around Rüstow, who had led the VDMA's Department of Economic Policy since 1925, can be described as the nucleus of the new liberalism in Germany upholding free trade perspectives against the rising sentiment of regionalism and autarchy. Scholars like Hans Gestrich, Otto Veit, Hans Ilau, and Friedrich A. Lutz contributed to the reform of economic liberalism and held influential positions both in business associations and academia. They were to become leading representatives of German neoliberalism after 1945.

In the immediate aftermath of the Great Depression, essays written by Eucken, Rüstow, Röpke, and Müller-Armack in 1932 and 1933 had a remarkable impact on nascent ordoliberal thinking. Although these basic writings[14] covered different topics and emphasized alternative rationales, they marked the contemporary upheaval of liberal thinking. Eucken, Rüstow, Röpke, and Müller-Armack characteristically referred to the significance of the world economic crisis as the turning point of economic liberalism in Germany.

Without initially taking too much notice of each other, each of these authors tried to analyze the "crisis of capitalism" that had erupted since the late 1920s and announced a quest for a "new liberalism" (Rüstow 1932, 172). Their discussion focused on revision of liberal approaches to the state. The state was now newly identified as the momentous instrument needed to achieve the principles of a market economy. Despite significant differences in their analytical approach, all the authors were united in their effort to reject the common interpretation of the hitherto most severe crisis of the capitalist economy as proof of the failure of capitalism. However, they also regarded the world economic crisis as a wake-up call to search for a new theoretical and ideological justification for a free market economy, which all of them never doubted was the most effective economic system despite the Great Depression.

These early writings all made the explicit admission that classical theory had underestimated the necessity of a state taking active measures in ideal market economies, combined with scathing attacks on the actual political system of the Weimar Republic. It was largely the tendency toward the so-called *Wirtschaftsstaat* (Eucken's "economic state") that was harshly criticized and blamed for shifting political and economic power to various organized interests. Owing to the rise of powerful special interests, the state was considered the easy prey of political parties ("Staat als Beute": Rüstow 1932, 171). As a consequence, the state was rendered incapable of acting independently for the larger good, at least according to the early ordoliberals. They argued in favor of resurrecting the classical liberal dualism of state and society, but conceived of the need for a positive state authority superior to all the powers present in society. To posit "independent" state authority favorable to the functioning of the market thus required an active role in institutional design, one that resembles the subsequent efforts of public choice theory and rational choice-based neo-institutionalism.

Particularly during the early period, we have ample evidence that the emerging ordoliberal camp was not ready to accept public opinion formation under conditions of parliamentarian democracy, with people freely expressing and mediating diverging interests and economic positions (Ptak 2002). The ordoliberals' prescriptions were constructed according to the ideas of *Ordnungspolitik:* societal participation in decision making was to be reduced so as to affirm decisions taken on behalf of the public, all in the name of freeing the market economy from destructive group interests, turning it toward a competitive order, and letting it thereby realize its alleged inherent social potential.

The main pillar of ordoliberalism became the "strong state," which would supersede the weak *party and intervention state*. At the end of the Weimar Republic, those who would later became leading ordoliberals stood shoulder to shoulder with other reactionary and Nazi forces who sought a restriction of democracy as an absolute precondition to solve the economic and social crisis. In doing so, Rüstow and Müller-Armack in particular referred affirmatively to Carl Schmitt's theory of the state (Ptak 2004). The Schmitt notion that they found useful was that of the total state, which was considered weak rather than strong. Both the early ordoliberal writers and Schmitt[15] (to whom the ordoliberals unself-consciously referred during the Weimar years) maintained that such a weak state was the result of welfare state interventionism legitimated by parliamentarian democracy. This state was weak because it was at the mercy of the interest groups of the plural society. "The appearance referred to by Carl Schmitt with reference to Ernst Jünger as the 'total state,' " Rüstow explained at the Dresden meeting of the Vereins für Socialpolitik, "actually is the opposite: not state omnipotence, but state impotence. It is an indicator of pitiful weakness of the state, a weakness incapable of defending against the united onslaught of interest crowds. The state is pulled to pieces by avaricious interests" (Rüstow 1932, 171; compare Müller-Armack 1932, 196f.).

Neither Rüstow nor Eucken was keen to repress or disguise their critique of the democratization of the economy and society following the events of 1918–1919 and encapsulated within the Weimar Constitution.[16] Both blamed the introduction of parliamentarian democracy for destroying the dualism of state and society, which in the past had secured a balance between state authority and free individuals. They also contended that through its dependence on political parties and the popular vote the government lost authority and the ability to exert leadership in society. After 1919, government authority was based on the "principle of horse trading," according to Rüstow ([1929] 1959, 91). He regarded the search for political compromise in the context of the Weimar constitutional state as an effort to evade political responsibility, which deprived the state of its capacity to act. As a result, "things move for ages and ages . . . as if Germany is the country of unlimited political impossibilities" (Rüstow [1929] 1959, 94). In this paper delivered to the Deutsche Hochschule für Politik in Berlin, Rüstow also discussed the question of how to strengthen state leadership against parliamentarian democracy while respecting the Weimar Constitution. Once again referring to Carl Schmitt,[17] Rüstow suggested a version of chancellor dictatorship, which would open up the opportunity to "within certain

limits implement measures first, but later-on subject them to discussion in order to maintain democracy." At this point, Rüstow was apparently convinced
of the principle of plebiscitary leadership, although at the same time he did
emphasize a temporal character of dictatorship, "so to say a dictatorship on
probation" (Rüstow [1929] 1959, 99).

In addition to this display of an authoritarian bent, the early writings of Eucken, Rüstow, and Müller-Armack demonstrate that ordoliberal identity was
mainly fueled by an opposition to major contemporary economic and political
ideas, primarily against Marxist positions in general, but also against Keynesian
economic theory, which had emerged alongside neoliberalism. "This frontal
opposition explains its aggressive element" (Riese 1972, 27)—and has remained
inherent in ordoliberalism up until the present day. By masking this negation
as the starting point of building a theory, ordoliberalism eventually gained no-
toriety as a rather dogmatic theory designed to reassign legitimacy to the ideas
of competition and the market.[18]

The Nazi Era: Working on the Theoretical Foundations of Ordoliberalism

After its early formulations of culturally pessimistic perspectives during the
early 1930s, German ordoliberalism assumed the format of an economic school
of thought during the Nazi era. Its ambitions were to formulate universal economic policy principles with an eye to the whole of society. The circle around
Eucken in Freiburg came to be considered both the point of departure and
the theoretical backbone of later German ordoliberalism.

The work done by Eucken's group between 1933 and 1945 fostered the preconditions for the *Freiburger Schule,* which became the most highly regarded
academic institution of ordoliberalism after World War II—despite the rather
close entanglement of many of its members with the Nazi regime. The most
relevant basic texts and the preliminary work for subsequent manuscripts
came out of this period, yielding the broad theoretical foundation of ordoliberalism immediately after the end of World War II. Eucken succeeded Götz
Briefs as professor of economics at the Faculty of Law and State Sciences at
Freiburg University in 1927.[19] Once established there, Eucken began to lay the
groundwork for his own school of thought. His closest collaborator was an expert in business law, Franz Böhm, who taught in Freiburg between 1933 and
1936, at which point he was offered a visiting professorship in Jena. Böhm was

eventually deprived of his teaching privileges after he openly opposed the Nazi race policies. The core group of the early Freiburg school included another legal scholar, Hans Großmann-Doerth, who joined Eucken and Böhm in publishing the series *Ordnung der Wirtschaft* beginning in 1937.

During the Nazi period four volumes were published in this series, with a number of other manuscripts in various stages of preparation (Krause 1969, 191). The prime objectives of these works, as expressed by the title of the series, were, first, to establish a clear understanding of the fundamental regulatory principles conducive to order for the government's economic policies; and, second, to reveal the negative economic and social consequences of economic development based on previous liberal economic policy principles, which were subject to so much criticism following the onset of the Great Depression. Eucken's group was convinced that these negative effects could be controlled if the fundamental economic order principles the group advocated were honored. Böhm's volume, written to establish the political perspective on order *(Die Ordnung der Wirtschaft als geschichtliche Aufgabe und rechtsschöpfende Leistung),* was first published in 1937. This book assumed an important place in the later discussion on the social market economy (Haselbach 1991, 93), as did another volume on competition theory written by Miksch in the same year, but rewritten and published in 1947 under the title *Wettbewerb als Aufgabe—Die Grundsätze einer Wettbewerbsordnung.* Two books on monetary theory also published in the series were written by Lutz and Gestrich.

Arguably the most important book on the development and professional acceptance of ordoliberalism was Eucken's textbook *Grundlagen der Nationalökonomie* (1940/1943). His earlier (and less technical) book titled *National Economics—For What Purpose? (Nationalökonomie—wozu?),* published in 1938, already had contained a summary of the basic ideas of the *Grundlagen.* After concluding his long-standing studies on capital theory (taken up in the 1920s) with an article on temporal aspects of the production process that was published in 1937, Eucken started to expose historical school scholarship to a fundamental critique (Eucken 1938b). The Nazi regime had once again allowed the influence of the historical school to expand in German economics. Eucken's *Grundlagen* book focused on method and sought to produce a new synthesis of the "great antinomy" of historical and theoretical economics in Germany. Eucken developed pointed abstractions from which he derived ideal types that would help him develop a general theory of economic order, to "recognize the system of order and thus the structure of the economic order of *each* epoch and *every* people (Volk)." He believed his method would yield "useful tools" needed to describe the "concrete every day life . . . of every concrete economic order" (Eucken 1940/1943, 254f.; emphasis added). Eucken thus developed his theory of market forms by leaning heavily on Stackelberg, who juxtaposed two basic types of economic systems—a centrally directed economy and a market economy—with a large number of theoretically possible variations. However, Eucken only posited a market economy framed by a political order that he considered economically viable and amenable to human beings.

Eucken's core argument went as follows: Approaching a state of full competition was made possible by relying on an economic policy formulated by the state to destroy economic concentrations of power and the resulting dysplasias of the free economy. This liberal version of antitrust was a cornerstone of the ordoliberal program for the postwar period (Ptak 2004). For practical purposes, the concept of an order of workable competition had been further developed in Eucken's posthumously (1952) published *Grundsätze der Wirtschaftspolitik*. Eucken's wife, Edith Eucken-Erdsiek, and his assistant, K. Paul Hensel, completed that book in 1950. This work defined order as the realization of an economy characterized by the absence of power due to a consistent employment of constitutional and regulative principles in economic policy (Eucken [1952] 1990, 254ff.) This particular orientation would lead to serious conflicts among neoliberals with regard to the understanding of competition, the question of monopoly, and the relation between the state and the economy—a discussion that remains of vital importance today (see Lutz 1989 and Möschel 1989; compare Van Horn, Chapter 6 in this volume).

Apart from the positions held by Eucken and other members of the Freiburg group, we cannot neglect certain contributions of Ludwig Erhard, if only because he has been called the "father" of the social market economy. Erhard was both a key political broker with regard to implementation of the social market economy and helped pave the way for this theoretical model. Erhard, a Ph.D. recipient in microeconomics, worked in various fields of applied market and consumption research and consulting during the Nazi period. He also wrote a few theoretical pieces on fundamental questions relating to economic policy and order and was particularly interested in the impact of general political frameworks on price formation (1939a, b; 1942). These publications already display a close affinity to the emerging ordoliberal perspective, an affinity that becomes even more pronounced in Erhard's subsequent writing and is especially evident in his expertise on war financing and the consolidation of war debt ([1943–1944] 1977). Erhard's last personal academic assistant, Horst Friedrich Wünsche (1997, 155), claims that the ordoliberals had no direct impact on his political thought, but this disclaimer is hardly convincing given Erhard's rather close personal ties with many ordoliberals and the extent to which his theoretical position overlaps with their work. If the theoretical development of the "new" liberalism is fully documented, it is impossible to view Erhard's concept of a social market economy in isolation. Erhard was an avid participant in the ordoliberal mainstream, although his orientation and focus were geared toward the more practical side.[20]

Articles published by Böhm, Eucken, and Miksch in a 1942 book, *Der Wettbewerb als Mittel volkswirtschaftlicher Leistungssteigerung und Leistungsauslese (Competition as a means to increase and select national economic efficiency)*, edited by Klasse IV der Akademie für Deutsches Recht (AfDR),[21] took up a variety of topics closely connected to the Freiburg school's perspective on competition theory and policy. These contributions did not cover new ground in terms of theory, but they were nonetheless politically important. The involvement of ordoliberals in Nazi Germany's most important academic institution has been a subsequent topic of heated discussion in the historical literature. The ordoliberal contributions did indeed discuss the Nazi regime's economic policies in the most concrete ways, but they show no evidence for the frequent claims[22] that they were in fundamental opposition against the Nazis. Their contributions, rather, provide evidence that the ordoliberals constructively contributed to solutions of specific problems of the war economy, and they even seem to indicate their ability to grasp an opportunity "to gain influence on the programmatic efforts to plan for a post-war economic policy" (Haselbach 1991, 95). Arguments claiming that their activities in these circles should be regarded as secret resistance efforts and promotion of an "underground economy" (Schlecht 1981, 15) are unconvincing. Because of the importance of the issue, we will present a separate discussion of the relationships between ordoliberals and the Nazis in the next section.

During the same period, Röpke, Rüstow, and Müller-Armack further developed the groundwork for the "new" economic liberalism from a sociological point of view. The cultural turn of ordoliberalism (Haselbach 1991, 159ff.) was triggered by social, cultural, and philosophical currents that were held to cause the impasse seen in modern society. To meet this challenge, a phalanx of right-wing thinkers, including the ordoliberals, responded to the need to theorize culture from within their own reconstructive missions.[23]

As early as 1932, in his book *Entwicklungsgesetze des Kapitalismus,* Müller-Armack had contrasted capitalism with Marxist developmental theory, presenting capitalism as a process open to influence by "action" *(Tat)* and "will" *(Wille).* Decisive voluntarism could and would suffice to overcome the mounting crisis of capitalism. Not having published for some time thereafter, in 1941 Müller-Armack submitted his *Genealogie der Wirtschaftsstile,* a work on religious sociology dealing with the history of capitalist ideas. Following Max Weber, Müller-Armack analyzed interdependencies among religious-denominational developments and economic processes ranging from the sixteenth to the eighteenth century. In subsequent years he broadened his studies to the nineteenth and twentieth centuries, though these works were not published before 1945. His *Das Jahrhundert ohne Gott* (Century without god) eventually appeared in 1948, and his *Diagnose unserer Gegenwart* (Diagnosis of the present time) was published in 1949. The two books marked the timely completion of his transition from a fervent supporter of Italian fascism and Nazi Party membership in Germany during the 1930s to a proselytizer of (Protestant) Christianity as a key source for the postwar value orientation. Müller-Armack's studies as well as Röpke's and Rüstow's writings on cultural theory reflected their search for a philosophical foundation and for additional legitimacy in social theory for the economic orientation of ordoliberalism. Their joint efforts amounted "to nothing less than a plan to draft a social and cultural organization of society adequate for a capitalist market economy" (Haselbach 1991, 71). Röpke's trilogy—*Die Gesellschaftskrise der Gegenwart* (1942), *Civitas humana* (1944), and *Internationale Ordnung* (1945)—along with Rüstow's three-volume edition *Ortsbestimmung der Gegenwart* (1950, 1952, 1957), and last but not least the works by Müller-Armack, all located their research in the tradition of the Western world of Christianity. Supplemented by an austere conservative critique of culture, which was most evident in Röpke's work, the tradition of Christian culture was to become the lowest common denominator of an ordoliberal system that insisted on a foundation in strong moral standards. Christian values were thought to enable individuals to resist the temptations of planning. A new moral basis for economic action was deemed necessary for both ordoliberals and other people—not the least because of their entanglement in the Nazi regime.

Ordoliberalism and Nazism

The very fact that ordoliberalism developed a large part of its theoretical foundations within the temporal and geographical bounds of Nazi Germany raises
the important question, If and to what extent were ordoliberals influenced by
Nazi Germany in general and by Nazi economic policy considerations in particular? Repeated claims that the Freiburg school and Ludwig Erhard were a
staunch part of the opposition to the Nazis—claims that buttressed the legitimacy of the social market economy—deserve closer scrutiny.[24]

What certainly can be rejected as a mere cover-up is the claim that the ordoliberals who did not emigrate from Germany opposed, or even persistently resisted, the national socialist regime (e.g., Willgerodt 1998; Wegmann 2002,
55–72; Goldschmidt 2005). With the exception of the documented emigrants
(Wilhelm Röpke and Alexander Rüstow), such a revisionist history of the wartime ordoliberals is not supported by facts. Papers published in Freiburg between the mid-1930s and the beginning of the 1940s unquestionably reveal that
ordoliberal concepts were designed to be implemented under the auspices of a
Nazi government. In particular, Böhm's book on the order of the economy *(Die
Ordnung der Wirtschaft als geschichtliche Aufgabe und rechtschöpferische Leistung),*
published in 1937, leaves no room for speculation in this regard (Abelshauser
1991; Haselbach 1991, 84f.; Tribe 1995, 212; Ptak 2004, 90f.). The very lack of a
consistent economic policy under the Nazis—the Nazis' economic policy oscil-
lated wildly between planning and competition at least until the war—reinforced
the ordoliberals' hope of finding a sympathetic hearing for their authority-
supported model of competition (Herbst 1982; Abelshauser 1999).

At the same time, the economists who were on the road to ordoliberalism
were not (necessarily) National Socialist economists. In spite of the totalitarian character of Nazi-Germany, it is very important to recognize and understand that different lines of economic thinking coexisted in Nazi Germany.
Any analysis should therefore address the question of economics in Nazi-
Germany in order to adequately address distance from and complicitness with
the ruling powers and philosophies, as well as the changing perspectives and
fortunes of individual economists over time. One must consider the multi-
form ways of relating to the Nazi regime (1) before and after 1933, when parliamentarian democracy and labor movement opposition were eliminated;
(2) before and after 1938, when the pogroms against the Jewish population
started in earnest; and (3) before and after 1942, which marked both the year

when the Holocaust decision was taken and when the war fortunes turned against the Nazis in Stalingrad (Walpen 2004, 93f.).

After 1942, many people in Nazi Germany recognized that the war was lost and so attempted to distance themselves from the ruling Nazis (Roth 2004). Even if this was in a sense opportunistic, moving into opposition against the regime at that juncture did cost many lives, including the liberal economist Jens Jessen. Several members of the Freiburg school were questioned by the Gestapo, and some were imprisoned. However, any late participation in op-positional activities can hardly exonerate those right-wing liberal economists who had accommodated themselves to the regime before 1942 and deliber-ately lent their economic expertise to the Nazis for the bulk of the era. While early theoretical considerations of ordoliberalism were congenial to Nazi ef-forts to curtail certain special interests and trade unions in particular, the ordoliberal framework that promoted a strong and independent state could just as well be turned against the Nazi usurpation of power. This perspective was easier to articulate after the Nazis were toppled, but it should be noted that few expressed it before 1942.

With regard to more narrowly defined economic issues, the early ordoliber-als were continually at odds with other schools of economic reasoning that op-erated during the Nazi era. As a rather coherent theoretical circle within the ordoliberal spectrum, the *Freiburger Schule* particular tried to promote a com-petitive order before and even during wartime. By developing policy advisory roles, they saw a chance to fill the economic theory vacuum in Nazi Germany with an *authoritarian* competitive order. Even though one cannot assume a broad, overall congruence between ordoliberal positions and National Socialist ideology, the authoritarian element, which Böhm characterized as *kombinierte Wirtschaftsverfassung*[25] ("combined economic constitution") (1937), represents a much visited point of intersection with National Socialist ideology regarding regional self-sufficiency. Despite the ordoliberals' growing skepticism about Nazi Germany during the later phases of the wartime economy in particular, hope remained that the residual market economy could be preserved to create pro-market conditions that could be implemented after the war. Miksch as a journalist and Müller-Armack and Erhard as political advisers directly dealt with issues concerning the wartime economy and planning for the postwar pe-riod, and like many other economic professionals were at least indirectly en-tangled in National Socialist policies of expansion during much of the 1930s and 1940s (Ptak 2004). Tribe (1995) has mapped the respective attitudes of neoliberals ranging from Republican resistance (Röpke) to staunch conservatism (Eucken) and active Nazism (von Stackelberg). Other researchers try to excuse cooperating ordoliberals by speaking in rather obscure ways of exiles and "half exiles."[26] In any case, Wegmann (2002) and others who insist that a huge distance be maintained between ordoliberals and the Nazis fail to understand the considerable overlap of ordoliberal and Nazi critiques of parliamentarian democracy, trade unions, and the Communist Party in particular.[27]

Reading the early critiques of parliamentarian democracy in the oeuvre of German ordoliberals and Austrian school neoliberals reveals the obscure authoritarian tendencies that were operating just beneath the surface of many neoliberals. These tendencies have reemerged time and again in eras of perceived danger to the neoliberal cause. These weaknesses for repressive regimes recur in the history of neoliberalism, as evidenced by Hayek's and Friedman's support of "free market economic policies" under the leadership of Pinochet in Chile, for example (see Fischer, Chapter 9 in this volume).

The Early Triumph of Neoliberalism: Ordoliberalism in the Era of West German Reconstruction

The third stage of ordoliberal theory construction began in the immediate postwar period. Strictly speaking, it involved a debate about rebuilding a capacity for governance toward the end of the devastating war. Therefore, a priority for this stage was to put implementation back on the agenda, not least in concrete terms of pragmatic accommodation. Despite Allied reservations about a liberal economic and social policy and a widespread consensus supporting comprehensive economic planning, proponents of ordoliberalism succeeded in gaining lasting influence on the economic and social order of postwar Germany. Their decisive advantage over other intellectual trends in the immediate postwar period lay in the ordoliberal nucleus, namely, the *Freiburger Schule*, which had been able to continue their work during the National Socialist era. Left-wing oppositional economists either had emigrated or been eliminated.

Supporting the ordoliberals' efforts in Germany were neoliberal refugees who had obtained powerful academic positions in the UK (Hayek), the United States (Karl Brandt, Gottfried Haberler), and Switzerland (Röpke). The involvement of prominent ordoliberals (Eucken, etc.) in the post–1942 oppositional activities of national conservative forces provided legitimacy for the cadres, despite their considerable roles in economic policy making during the

Nazi era. It was the Cold War constellation, however, that cleared the way for the prevailing one-sided representation of ordoliberal opposition to Nazi rulers: nearly everyone was welcome in the alliance against the widely perceived communist threat.

Ordoliberals had occupied themselves with questions of postwar planning from 1942 to 1943 (Ptak 2004, 136ff.), Although few in number, they knew how to take advantage of the institutional vacuum of those chaotic days and rapidly gained influence over the elites in economics, politics, and academia. The extensive ordoliberal literature produced between 1945 and the founding of the Federal Republic in 1949 addresses five main themes: first, building an ideological front against collectivism in the form of the Soviet Union and its various Western varieties of economic democracy and planning; second, dissociating ordoliberalism from laissez-faire principles; third, justifying, modifying, and stating more precisely the principles of ordoliberalism *(Ordnungspolitik)*, and applying these economic policies ("arranged" market economy); fourth, developing a frame in search of a community of people directed by market economy principles; and fifth, producing a constructive draft designed to combine society and economy in terms of a third way between capitalism (as a historically outdated order) and socialism (as a current threat), which finally materialized in the social market economy.

Various reasons explain the success of the ordoliberals in influencing the public economic debate. First, the ordoliberals came up with a culturally coherent concept of economic theory at a time characterized by political, economic, and social turbulence. The normative character of the Ordo doctrine sketching a prospective harmony of economy and society was attractive to a largely insecure population; despite their sympathy for anticapitalist positions, people were reluctant to become part of any new experiments. The popularity of ordoliberal concepts was particularly based on an ingrained mistrust of laissez-faire capitalism and partly on a stance that was politically favorable to strict antimonopoly policy. But the popularity was also due to the absence of coherent and persuasively elaborated rival concepts of Keynesian provenance in support of democratic socialism in Germany. After distancing themselves to certain degrees from the ruling strata in the late Nazi regime, ordoliberals endeavored to cooperate with Western Allies at an early stage—before the end of the war (mainly through international contacts in Switzerland). The ordoliberal circle could also take advantage of the clean reputations of Röpke and Rüstow, both of whom had gained international respect as antifascist scientists. Capitalizing on Röpke as one of Erhard's and Adenauer's most influential advisers, but also on Rüstow, who as chairman of the *Aktionsgemeinschaft Soziale Marktwirtschaft* represented German neoliberalism in public, the Freiburg school benefited from earlier connections. Legitimacy provided by the exiled economists for this line of thought extended to the scholars who had stayed behind in Germany.

Probably more significant for the type of economics that came to dominate the German scene after the war was the actual balance of power that existed until the Federal Republic of Germany was founded. The most important economic and political decisions were taken between 1946 and 1948 during Allied occupation and before West Germany as an entity (including its new democratic institutions) was proclaimed and established (Abelshauser 2004). Even what it meant to qualify as a capitalist firm was redefined in this period (Djelic 1998). As a representative of the new liberalism and as head of the *Verwaltung für Wirtschaft* (*VfW,* meaning administration for the economy), it was up to Erhard to organize the transition from a wartime economy to a new civilian economic system. Ordoliberal positions on the *VfW* advisory board far outweighed representatives of other postwar models. Both the occupation law and the generous American sponsorship provided Erhard with tremendous power that enabled him and Miksch to achieve the "double market-economical reform" in 1948 (namely, currency reform and the end of price controls, the famous *Leitsätzegesetz*) almost singlehandedly. Parliament had hardly any control or oversight. The conservative political scientist Werner Kaltefleiter (1989, 68) describes Erhard's room to maneuver before 1949 as "dictator like power base" (compare Hayek 1983, 20, Schwarz 1992, 68; Hartwell 1995, 214), while Hirschman (1989) has stressed the role of U.S. occupation forces in Germany in keeping the advocates of Keynesianism repressed in Germany.

The disastrous postwar situation regarding food and health colored the entire situation in Germany, and an enormous shortage of supply would have been deciding factors in implementing domestic reforms after 1948. For Phillip Herder-Dorneich (1993, 13), the success of liberal reforms goes back to the German people, "who had experienced three years of social learning while almost starving to death." Economic planning experienced *then* reflected a kind of "children's fear" (Wallich 1955, 13). But the reforms were also facilitated by massive neoliberal propaganda, which denounced *all manner* of economic planning as another step toward poverty and deprivation. The Ordo postwar propaganda campaign succeeded in opening space for capitalism in the refined shape of the social market economy.

After the currency reform and the *Leitsätzegesetz* dating from 1948, ordoliberal implementation strategies with their veiled multilayer networks turned out to be quite effective. These strategies involved founding market-oriented think tanks at universities, intensifying international political networks via the Mont Pèlerin Society, and supporting economic journalism in the mass media. Ordoliberalism was avidly promoted in the pages of *Frankfurter Allgemeine Zeitung,* whose publisher, Erich Welter, had been Miksch's superior at the *Wirtschaftskurve* journal during the war. Many of the Ordos were swiftly integrated into the neoliberal thought collective. Practically all the leading ordoliberals, including Welter, Miksch, Röpke, Eucken, Müller-Armack, Böhm, Pfister, Dietze, K. F. Maier, F. W. Meyer, Ilau, Hensel, and of course Erhard, joined the Mont Pèlerin Society. Ultimately, ordoliberal positions on economic policy were significantly reinforced by the rapid increase in prosperity from the late 1940s onward.[28] The market-oriented reforms in postwar Germany were to a great extent stabilized and politically accepted because they were intellectually wedded to the concept of the social market economy. This concept was launched, not least as a result of the campaign launched by the dedicated employer organization Die Waage. Between 1952 and 1965, large West German enterprises channeled DM 16.11 million for a political publicity campaign, with the purpose of establishing the social market economy according to ordoliberal principles. The campaign proved quite successful, contributing to general election results that were highly favorable to the conservative-liberal parties, which were closely tied to the corporate sector (Schindelbeck and Ilgen 1999; Ptak 2004).

The Social Market Economy as the Launch Vehicle of Ordoliberal Concepts

The German neoliberal school managed to distance itself from classical liberalism by accepting authority for the shaping of economic policy, and by having the resources and capacity for design of a postwar new liberal policy for society at large. As far as economic theory was concerned, German ordoliberalism, unlike the Austrian school that emerged around Mises and Hayek, maintained a strong attachment to the neoclassical equilibrium model, as evidenced by

Eucken's formalistic market model. This situation may also have been overdetermined, since the American victors were busy inserting "good" neoclassical economics into the reconstructed German universities (Bernstein 2001). In addition, the newly established liberal interventionism was promoted because it was supposed to be aligned with timeless principles of market conformity.[29] When the doctrine was actually deployed, however, what this basically meant in practice was that political measures encountered their limits wherever they undermined the formation of what was perceived as an equilibrium price (Schiller 1958, 17).

The ordoliberal ideal of a competitive order deprived of political power and working in a steady state of perfect competition could never have served as a blueprint for postwar reconstruction. Ordoliberals perceived neoclassical economics to be in need of further amendment in order to be translated into practical experience. How could the imposition of a free market compel or encourage already existing monopolies and oligopolies to give up their dominant economic position? For that reason, one of the central questions of the social market economy languished unanswered: Which societal groups and social forces should be charged with the mandate to secure a competitive order committed to ordoliberal ideas, given the already existing pluralistic structures, particularly in parliamentary democracies? The ordoliberal model of a market embedded in various social and political institutions largely failed because of highly unrealistic expectations. Instead of tackling the current societal, social, and political conditions, it remained oriented toward an abstract ideal of society that displayed features of enlightened absolutism and preindustrial social structures.

At this point, the real functional significance of social market economy as a concept comes into play. Bridging the conceptual/practical divide was largely left to Müller-Armack, who turned this seeming deficiency into a thorough practical strategy of implementing a new liberalism in Western Germany. With hindsight, we have to acknowledge that Rüstow was correct when he referred to the "Social Market Economy as the realization of the neoliberal program" (Rüstow 1957c, 76). Müller-Armack's aim was to promote the social market economy as a strategy for transferring the principles of new liberalism into potentially hostile political and societal spheres without neglecting the ultimate neoliberal objective of creating a new kind of strong state. Müller-Armack was unabashed in paying tribute to the ordoliberal formation and giving advice to the political leadership. "Our theory," he explained at the 1953 annual meeting of the Mont Pèlerin Society, "is abstract; it can only gain broad public acceptance if it gets a concrete meaning and demonstrates the man in the street that it will redound to its advantage" (quoted from Roth 2001).

The fact that the social market economy was first and foremost a tool to attain a certain political objective, rather than a scientific theory per se, reveals why there is (still) no closed theory of the social market economy comparable to the older elaborate ordoliberal system. Aims and objectives were developed step by step in response to concrete political developments, rather than according to logical extrapolations and derivations from ordoliberal theory. Consequently, these aims and objectives display to a large extent flexibility and adaptability toward changing economic, political, and sociocultural conditions in society. Thus, it was because of the evolutionary character of Müller-Armack's approach that over the years tensions would arise relative to the dogmatic and normative character of ordoliberal theory in practice. "Whilst the ordoliberal concept provides a concrete program for the political caste, Müller-Armack's concept of Social Market Economy can, in a nutshell, be understood as a methodical principle" (Starbatty 1986, 16).

Indeed, two methodical principles determined the ultimate conceptual development of the social market economy: its evolutionary moment and the so-called irenic (meaning placatory or conciliatory) formula.[30] In this sense, the original version of the social market economy represents an economic concept based on the German variant of neoliberalism, but yielding to political exigencies all the way down its historical path. The irenic formula provided the ideological support deemed necessary to pacify looming class conflict. Yet, Müller-Armack was well aware that the irenic formula would not endure forever as a general conception without continuous adaptations to changing socioeconomic realities and shifting configurations of power. A certain dexterity was required in order to address, preempt, or even dissolve emerging structural conflicts: "Of course, the tense situation, likely to arouse social conflicts, is subject to historical change and requires us *to look for respective strategic formulas of this irenic balance again and again.* Therefore, the social market economy is," as Müller-Armack summed up the irenic idea in the early 1960s, "a *strategy in the societal sphere;* if it is successful and reaches its aim may never be decided exactly" (1962, 13; emphasis added).

Against this political economy background, we can now understand why it is so very hard to grasp the fundamental economic core of economic policy in the social market economy, though a few constants arguably determine Müller-Armack's evolutionary approach. Starbatty denotes three indispensable invariants: (1) preserving the market economy as a dynamic order; (2) preserving the social balance which maintains the suppression of conflicts; and (3) securing stability and economic growth through competition and financial policies (Starbatty 1982). These imperatives, in a way, characterize a neoliberal program, which is determined by a defensive and pragmatic character and by an extremely high political sensitivity toward uneasy societal circumstances.

Conclusion

Given the range of worldwide neoliberal concepts, ordoliberalism as a specific continental European current was largely formed in Germany—and also in Turkish and Swiss exile—from the 1930s to the 1950s. Its distinctive characteristic is an elaborately developed theory of the state, which is held to be indispensable for the constitution and stabilization of the continuously aspired competitive order. German ordoliberal concepts entail a strong authoritarian element, which is displayed in a fundamental skepticism toward democracy: In this sense, the ordoliberal market society is a morally grounded and socially formed competitive society that is supposed to curb the acknowledged destructive potential of markets and special interests.

This basic pattern is also visible in the conception of the social market economy, a curious offshoot of ordoliberalism. On the one hand, this concept can be assessed as a successful local implementation strategy for the transplantation of ordoliberal ideas into the West German postwar society of the 1950s. PR campaigns were successfully employed, in much the same way that one would sell soap or cars, to overcome the widespread skepticism of the West German people toward a market-oriented order of society. In any event, West Germany's noticeable economic success imbued the ideology with a kind of national identity. Later, however, the term *social market economy* turned out to be more of a problem than a boon because it was more and more perceived as a concept tied rather too closely to a specific format of economic success. Changing conditions for economic growth undermined not only the social market economy itself, but also the ideological efforts it entailed (a "third way") to legitimize market-oriented politics rather than some vision of comprehensive welfare. Since the trade unions and the Social Democratic Party learned to use the concept in the same opportunistic way as the ordoliberals, persuading governments to expand the welfare state under continuous reference to the social market economy, the model increasingly lost its original neoliberal content. Thus, the social market economy as a programmatic concept was gradually afflicted with dissolution, first and foremost because of the evolutionary structure and flexibility inherent in its own argument. Contemporary neoliberal strategies attempt to re-launch the original as a "new social market economy."[31]

With hindsight, we can call into question what remains with regard to ordoliberalism and the concept of social market economy. Overall, the approach based on the original ideal of ORDO, imagining a harmonic order of the market and a highly stratified society, has definitely failed, giving way to concrete forms of corporatism and antagonistic cooperation after Erhard's demise. Still, some elements have been adopted or have been revived—in both scientific and economic discussions that are of practical relevance right up to the present day. This is especially true for the approach based on *Ordnungstheorie* in general, and the thesis dealing with the interdependence of economic, political, and social arrangements in particular *(Interdependenz der Ordnungen)*. Ordoliberalism can in fact be considered an embryonic neo-institutionalist doctrine *avant la lettre,* though a close examination of the relationship of ordoliberalism and rational choice-based neo-institutionalism has yet to be carried out in any serious way. However, ordoliberalism as a specific German variety of neoliberalism has gradually converged with Austrian economics and Anglo-Saxon versions of neoliberalism, especially in the field of competition theory proper. The globalization of neoliberalism—powerfully advanced by neoliberal networks within and around MPS—has increasingly blurred the lines of original (German, Austrian, French, American) schools of thought. Hayek, for example, returned from the United States to Europe in 1962 to serve as economics professor in Freiburg: "Thus closes the circle," lectured Michel Foucault in 1978 at the Collège de France.

Notes

I am grateful to Dieter Plehwe both for numerous comments with regard to substantive issues and for his aid in translating this chapter. German quotes have been translated for easier reading.

1. According to Becker (1965, 41), the term *Ordoliberalismus* was first used by Moeller (1950, 224) to identify a specific neoliberal circle, the so-called Ordo-Kreis around Walter Eucken and his Freiburger Schule, which started to publish the *Ordo Yearbook* in 1948. The term was adopted for the first time in the twelfth volume of the journal *ORDO* by the editors Franz Böhm, Friedrich Lutz, and Fritz Meyer (pp. 32–47).

2. A better understanding of German ordoliberalism should prove useful for a re-examination of the relationship between neoliberalism and neoconservatism, and may thereby contribute to a better understanding of the roots of strategic alliances between neoliberals and the religious right in the United States, for example.

3. During World War II, Miksch, who had received his habilitation from Eucken in 1938, published highly relevant articles on issues concerning the wartime economy in a supplement of the business section of the *Frankfurter Zeitung*, called *Wirtschaftskurve*. This periodical is known to have echoed the wartime economy concepts of the planning office at the *Ministerium für Rüstung und Kriegsproduktion* (Ministry of Armament and Munitions). Immediately after 1945, Miksch became one of Ludwig Erhard's most influential advisers, initially as political consultant in the public relations department of the *Verwaltung für Wirtschaft*. In 1948, after having been appointed head of the *Grundsatzreferat der Preisabteilung* (meaning Miksch was responsible for drawing the main lines at the department for setting and controlling prices), he set up the *Leitsätzegesetz*, which marked the transition to a market economy in West Germany in the same way as the currency reform did. Furthermore, Miksch is considered to have invented the As-If-Theorem. According to this theorem, state authorities should fix a competition price, if market competition is insufficient or fails completely (Miksch 1948). Miksch had joined the Social Democratic Party and was one of the few Social Democrats who joined the Mont Pèlerin Society.

4. Dürr's first systematic analysis of ordoliberalism in fact suggests a complete distinction of ordoliberalism and neoliberalism primarily because of this difference: "The first and foremost difference between ordoliberalism and neoliberalism can be seen in the fact that the latter tries to further a 'competitive order' or 'workable competition' whereas the continental (German) ordoliberalism aspires to *veranstalten* a consistently 'ordered competition.' Secondly, the measures concerning the distribution of wealth and income display a more social liberal character" (Dürr 1954, 7). Similar efforts to amplify differences are soundly rejected by Wegmann (2002) and Nicholls (1984).

5. "There is nothing in the basic principles of liberalism to make it a stationary creed, there are no hard-and-fast rules fixed once and for all. The fundamental principle that in the ordering of our affairs we should make as much use as possible of the spontaneous forces of society, and resort as little as possible to coercion is capable of an infinite variety of applications" (Hayek [1944] 1991, 13).

6. Although we do not pursue it here, some authors have discussed this curious mixture of concepts in German thought under the rubric of "reactionary modernism"; see Herf 1984.

7. Rüstow (1950, 50) formulated his opinions in the same vein: "competition pure . . . means complete incoherence, complete shortage of social viscosity where it alone rules social relationships. A fortiori it depends in complementary ways and as a precondition on the counterweight of strong framing forces of a different kind, on ethical and sociological ties that are otherwise secured."

8. "The Ordo-thought took shape in the middle ages. It had a determining impact on the composition of the whole of medieval culture. It means the *meaningful* junction of the variety to a whole" (Eucken [1952] 1990, 372; emphasis in original).

9. The ordoliberal estate model was limited by its primary emphasis on the competitive order, which was not to be compromised. It was sympathetic to the idea of a hierarchical society without attaching any regulatory functions to it with regard to economic life. This was in stark contrast to the Catholic social doctrine.

10. Rüstow (1957a, 520) defined Vitalpolitik as "a policy, which consciously considers everything concerning the true well being of the human subject, her contentment and happiness, and aims at creating the preconditions for a life worth both living and defending."

11. The family was to be the principal social core of decentralized economic entities (Röpke ([1942] 1979, 31; Rüstow 1957b, 222).

12. "We owe a great enrichment of our language to the Americans, because they were the ones who coined the characteristic term 'weasel-word.' This little predator . . . can allegedly suck the content of an egg without doing any harm to the shell. This reflects the fact that weasel words deprive terms of their actual meaning as soon as they are added. . . . [T]he term 'sozial' is the weasel-word par excellence. Nobody knows what it actually means. But it is definitely true that a social market economy is no market economy . . . social justice is not justice—and I am afraid a social democracy is no democracy either" (Hayek 1979, 16).

13. See, for instance, Hayek, Sieber, Tuchtfeldt, and Willgerodt (1979), but cf. Willgerodt (2006).

14. Walter Eucken's *Staatliche Strukturwandlungen und die Krisis des Kapitalismus* (1932) and Alexander Rüstow's *Interessenpolitik oder Staatspolitik* (1932) are typically referred to as the real founding documents. In addition, Röpke's contribution on "Maximen rationeller Intervention" in his writing on state interventionism (1929) has been given pride of place from prominent neoliberals (see Hayek et al. 1979). To understand the critique of parliamentarian democracy, however, Rüstow's 1929 paper "Diktatur innerhalb der Grenzen der Demokratie" (dictatorship within democratic confines, published in 1959) is of considerable importance. Frequently mentioned are two works by Alfred Müller-Armack: his *Entwicklungsgesetze des Kapitalismus. Ökonomische, geschichtstheoretische und soziologische Studien zur modernen Wirtschaftsverfassung* (1932) and *Staatsidee und Wirtschaftsordnung im neuen Reich* (1933). Others refer to Franz Böhm's *Wettbewerb und Monopolkampf. Eine Untersuchung zur Frage des wirtschaftlichen Kampfrechts und zur Frage der rechtlichen Struktur der geltenden Wirtschaftsordnung* (1933), Hans Gestrich's *Liberalismus als Wirtschaftsmethode* (1930), and Wilhelm Röpke's "Epochenwende" (1933). On the early literature, compare Becker (1965, 41–43), Haselbach (1991, 19, 23f., 72f.), and Reuter (1999, 71ff.).

15. Schmitt (1933, 84; emphasis original) discussed different meanings of a "total state" in a presentation to industrialists. He identified first "a very strong state. It is *to-*

tal in the sense of quality and energy much like the fascist state claiming to be a 'stato totalitario,' which first of all indicates the exclusive control of the means of power by the state, and their employment to further increase its power. It refuses to transfer new means of power to its enemies and destroyers, and to undermine its power by whatever reference to liberalism, constitutionalism and the like. He can distinguish between friend and foe. . . . But there also exists another meaning of the word total state. . . . This type of total state is a state, which indiscriminately steps into all subject matters, all spheres of human existence, which does not know anymore a sphere free of the state, because it cannot distinguish between anything. It is *total in a purely quantitative sense, in the sense of pure volume, not of intensity and political* energy. . . . The contemporary German party state is *total due to weakness* . . . , due to the inability to resist the onslaught of parties and organized interests."

16. Later ordoliberal writers like Willgerodt (1998, 48) are eager to qualify the early ordoliberal critique of democracy: "It is thus not so much a matter of radically rejecting pluralism, but to oppose a wrong way of political participation of economic and social groups from a liberal point of view."

17. While Reuter (1999, 72) recognizes the agreement of the neoliberal founding papers with Schmitt's analysis of the state, "they did not draw his conclusions." According to Reuter, "the difference is clear: Rüstow demanded the return of the liberal state, which additionally was to be in charge of protecting competition by establishing rules and supervising compliance." Milene Wegmann (2002) completely missed the double meaning of the term *total state* in her effort to contradict researchers who have correctly emphasized a close relationship between Rüstow's and Schmitt's state theory.

18. Egon Edgar Nawroth emphasized "that neoliberal academics are not so much interested in a serious controversy about the problems raised but rather in a conversation within their own four walls. This essentially amounts to nothing more than relentlessly repeating one's own theses while ignoring fundamental objections with silence" (Nawroth 1961, 18).

19. The other two economic chairs were held by Karl Diehl, who was succeeded by Constantin von Dietze in 1937 and by Adolf Lampe.

20. This may also explain Erhard's reservations about pure theory as referenced by Wünsche. Not in the least due to Erhard's increasing political power in postwar Germany, Erhard occasionally rejected the advice of model theorists sharply. But he also declared himself an ordoliberal, occasionally at least (for example, when speaking to the Protestant working group of his Christian Democratic Party; see Erhard 1962, 592). On the occasion of Böhm's eightieth birthday Erhard wrote: "I would like to frankly acknowledge that my own contribution to this effort [the social market economy—R.P.] would not have been possible without Walter Eucken, Franz Böhm, Wilhelm Röpke, Alexander Rüstow, F. A. von Hayek, Alfred Müller-Armack and many others who joined me in thinking and debating" (Erhard 1975, 15).

21. The AfDR economics group, founded in 1940 and headed by Jens Jessen, encompassed a total of nine working groups on the themes of economic history, economic policy, social policy, agricultural policy, money and credit, financial economy, price policy, transport policy, international economics, and a coordinating central caucus on economics. The ordoliberals congregated mainly in the economics and price policy working groups. See Haselbach (1991, 94ff.) and Janssen (1998, 189ff.).

22. Blumenberg-Lampe (1973, 30); Janssen (1998, 193–195); Quaas (2000, 58).

23. See Rehberg (1999) for overlapping efforts against the negative implications of the "mass society" of Gehlen, Freyer, and Schelsky in the field of sociology.

24. Because "this neoliberal way of thinking," wrote Röpke in his Eucken obituary, provides an example of "how honest, clear thinking men devoted to freedom and the law answered to the rape of the human being by collectivism and totalitarianism. They earned their right to teach the world . . . about the impossibility to separate Freedom and the constitutional state from the freedom in the economic order" (Röpke 1950).

25. The ordoliberals bundled their normative concepts in the idea of a *Wirtschaftsverfassung*, that is, an organization of market economy under constitutional law. The idea of a *kombinierte Wirtschaftverfassung* was developed under the influence of Nazi Germany and referred to a combination of two *Lenkungsprinzipien* ("governing principles") within the scope of this economic system: on the one hand, indirect governing via competition, and on the other hand—where required—direct governing by the state. This proposal was devised by early ordoliberals and marks a compromise, taking into consideration the National Socialist primacy of politics without dispensing with an economic system dominated by competition.

26. "The introversion of the half-exile was often inimical to the conception of an indictment on a sufficiently grand scale, but in which the role of National Socialism would neither assume the megalomaniacal proportions of its own self-image, nor dwindle into pardonable insignificance. It was Röpke who indicated the culture and economy in which 'the German catastrophe' was but an incident. Rüstow . . . return[ed] with an indictment of the historical manifestations of much that West Germans were now eager to reappropriate, as well as much that they had reason to forget. The 'dark side of the economic miracle' was, in one sense, what the neo-liberals attacked; in another sense, it was they who provided the shadow, the third dimension. It was they who, while vigorously repudiating negative and destructive criticism of Ludwig Erhard's reforms, nevertheless sought to become the conscience, and on occasion the guilty conscience, of the social market economy" (Johnson 1989, 54). It should be noted that Johnson's chapter was part of an affirmative two-volume effort (Peacock and Willgerodt 1989; and Peacock and Willgerodt with Johnson 1989) to introduce German ordoliberalism to the English-language audience, edited and written mostly by MPS members.

27. Even Ludwig von Mises, whose Jewish background eventually necessitated his escape from the Nazis had—at least until 1927—sympathies for Italian fascism in one

area: according to Mises, it had accomplished an eternal achievement in the fight against socialism (Walpen 2004, 332f.).

28. Abelshauser (2004) challenged the ordoliberal interpretation of the "German Miracle" crediting pro-market reforms. High growth rates were rooted in the long-lasting phase of rebuilding the economy after the war, a modern system of production that was less damaged than many thought and in excellent international economic condition in the aftermath of the Korea crisis.

29. First thoughts on liberal criteria for economic interventions were presented by Ludwig von Mises in the 1920s, but they needed systematization according to Röpke (1929; [1942] 1979), however, without ever leading to clear-cut positions.

30. This irenic element is borrowed from the German sociology of religion and describes the claim to solve socioeconomic conflicts, inevitably emerging in market economies peacefully, that is, without neglecting social adjustments.

31. See Speth (2004); Kinderman (2005); and Plehwe (2006) for background and critical analysis of this "initiative for a new social market economy" (INSM).

References

Abelshauser, Werner. 1991. "Die ordnungspolitische Epochenbedeutung der Weltwirtschaftskrise in Deutschland: Ein Beitrag zur Entstehungsgeschichte der Sozialen Marktwirtschaft." In Dietmar Petzina (ed.), *Ordnungspolitische Weichenstellungen nach dem Zweiten Weltkrieg,* Schriften des Vereins für Socialpolitik, N.F., Bd. 203. Berlin: Duncker & Humblot, 11–29.

Abelshauser, Werner. 1999. "Kriegswirtschaft und Wirtschaftswunder. Deutschlands wirtschaftliche Mobilisierung für die Zweiten Weltkrieg und die Folgen für die Nachkriegszeit." *Vierteljahrshefte für Zeitgeschichte* 47(4): 503–538.

Abelshauser, Werner. 2004. *Deutsche Wirtschaftsgeschichte seit 1945.* Munich: Beck.

Akademie für Deutsches Recht (ed.). 1942. *Der Wettbewerb als Mittel volkswirtschaftlicher Leistungssteigerung und Leistungsauslese.* Schriften der Gruppe Wirtschaftswissenschaft, 6. Berlin: Duncker & Humblot.

Allen, Christopher. 1989. "The Underdevelopment of Keynesianism in Germany." In Peter Hall (ed.), *The Political Power of Economic Ideas: Keynesianism across Nations.* Princeton, NJ: Princeton University Press, 263–290.

Becker, Helmut Paul. 1965. *Die soziale Frage im Neoliberalismus. Analyse und Kritik,* Sammlung Politeia, 20. Heidelberg: Kerle u.a.

Bernstein, Michael. 2001. *A Perilous Progress.* Princeton, NJ: Princeton University Press.

Blumenberg-Lampe, Christine. 1973. *Das wirtschaftspolitische Programm der "Freiburger Kreise." Entwurf einer freiheitlich-sozialen Nachkriegswirtschaft. Nationalökonomen gegen den Nationalsozialismus.* Berlin: Duncker & Humblot.

Böhm, Franz. 1933. *Wettbewerb und Monopolkampf. Eine Untersuchung zur Frage des wirtschaftlichen Kampfrechts und zur Frage der rechtlichen Struktur der geltenden Wirtschaftsordnung*. Berlin: Heymann.

Böhm, Franz. 1937. *Die Ordnung der Wirtschaft als geschichtliche Aufgabe und rechtschöpferische Leistung*. Heft 1 der Schriftenreihe Ordnung der Wirtschaft, Franz Böhm, Walter Eucken, and Hans Großmann-Doerth (eds.). Stuttgart: Kohlhammer.

Borchardt, Knut. 1976. "Wachstum und Wechsellagen 1914–1970." In Hermann Aubin and Wolfgang Zorn (eds.), *Handbuch der deutschen Wirtschafts- und Sozialgeschichte*, Bd. 2. Stuttgart: Klett-Cotta, 685–740.

Borchardt, Knut. 1981. "Die Konzeption der Sozialen Marktwirtschaft in heutiger Sicht." In Otmar Issing (ed.), *Zukunftsprobleme der sozialen Marktwirtschaft*. Schriften des Vereins für Socialpolitik, NF 116. Berlin: Duncker & Humblot, 33–53.

Cockett, Richard. 1994. *Thinking the Unthinkable: Think-Tanks and the Economic Counter-Revolution 1931–1983*. London: HarperCollins.

Djelic, Marie-Laure. 1998. *Exporting the American Model*. New York: Oxford University Press.

Dürr, Ernst-Wolfram. 1954. *Wesen und Ziele des Ordoliberalismus*. Winterthur: Keller.

Ebenstein, Alan. 2001. *Friedrich Hayek: A Biography*. New York: Palgrave.

Erhard, Ludwig. 1939a. "Voraussetzungen und Prinzipen der Marktforschung." In Vereinigte Glanzstoff-Fabriken (ed.), *Marktforschung als Gemeinschaftsaufgabe für Wissenschaft und Wirtschaft. Festgabe für Conrad Herrmann*. Wuppertal: Weddigen, 29–44.

Erhard, Ludwig. 1939b. "Einfluß der Preisbildung und Preisbindung auf die Qualität und die Quantität des Angebots und der Nachfrage." In Georg Bergler (ed.), *Marktwirtschaft und Wirtschaftswissenschaft. Eine Festgabe aus dem Kreise der Nürnberger Schule zum 60. Geburtstage von Wilhelm Vershofen*. Berlin: Deutscher Betriebswirte-Verl., 47–100.

Erhard, Ludwig. 1942. "Die Marktordnung." In Karl Theisinger (ed.), *Die Führung des Betriebes. Festschrift zum 60. Geburtstag von Wilhelm Kalveram*. Berlin: Spaeth & Linde, 274–282.

Erhard, Ludwig. 1943–1944/1977. *Kriegsfinanzierung und Schuldenkonsolidierung*. Mit Vorbemerkungen von Ludwig Erhard, Theodor Eschenburg, Günter Schmolders. Faksimiledruck der Denkschrift von 1943/1944. Frankfurt am Main: Propylaen.

Erhard, Ludwig. 1962. *Deutsche Wirtschaftspolitik—der Weg der Sozialen Marktwirtschaft*. Düsseldorf: Econ.

Erhard, Ludwig. 1975. "Franz Böhms Einfluß auf die Politik." In Hans Sauermann and Ernst-Joachim Mestmäcker (eds.), *Wirtschaftsordnung und Staatsverfassung. Festschrift für Franz Böhm zum 80. Geburtstag*, Tübingen: Mohr, 15–21.

Eucken, Walter. 1932. "Staatliche Strukturwandlungen und die Krisis des Kapitalismus." *Weltwirtschaftliches Archiv* 36(2): 297–321.

Eucken, Walter. 1937. "Vom Hauptproblem der Kapitaltheorie." *Jahrbücher für Nationalökonomie und Statistik* 145: 533–564.

Eucken, Walter. 1938a. *Nationalökonomie-wozu?* Leipzig: Meiner.

Eucken, Walter. 1938b. "Die Überwindung des Historismus." *Schmollers Jahrbuch* 62(1): 63–86.

Eucken, Walter. 1940/1943. *Die Grundlagen der Nationalökonomie.* 3rd rev. ed. Jena: Fischer.

Eucken, Walter. 1952/1990. *Grundsätze der Wirtschaftspolitik.* Edith Eucken and K. Paul Hensel (eds.). 6th rev. ed. Tübingen: UTB.

Foucault, Michel. 2004. *Geschichte der Gouvernementalität II. Die Geburt der Biopolitik.* Frankfurt am Main: Suhrkamp Verlag.

Gestrich, Hans. 1930. *Liberalismus als Wirtschaftsmethode.* Berlin: Industrie- und Handels-Zeitung.

Gestrich, Hans. 1936. *Neue Kreditpolitik.* Heft 3 der Schriftenreihe Ordnung der Wirtschaft. Franz Böhm, Walter Eucken, and Hans Großmann-Doerth (eds.). Stuttgart: Kohlhammer.

Giersch, Herbert. 1988. "Liberal Reform in West Germany." *ORDO* 39: 3–16.

Goldschmidt, Nils (ed.). 2005. *Wirtschaft, Politik und Freiheit.* Freiburger Wirtschaftswissenschaftler und der Widerstand. Tübingen: Mohr Siebeck.

Hall, Peter (ed.). 1989. *The Political Power of Economic Ideas: Keynesianism across Nations.* Princeton, NJ: Princeton University Press.

Hartwell, Ronald Max. 1995. *A History of the Mont Pelerin Society.* Indianapolis, IN: Liberty Fund.

Haselbach, Dieter. 1991. *Autoritärer Liberalismus und Soziale Marktwirtschaft. Gesellschaft und Politik im Ordoliberalismus.* Baden-Baden: Nomos.

Hayek, Friedrich August von. 1944/1991. *The Road to Serfdom.* London: Routlege.

Hayek, Friedrich August von. 1968. *Der Wettbewerb als Entdeckungsverfahren.* Kiel: Institut für Weltwirtschaft.

Hayek, Friedrich August von. 1979. *Wissenschaft und Sozialismus.* Vorträge und Aufsätze des Walter-Eucken-Instituts, No. 71. Tübingen: Mohr.

Hayek, Friedrich August von. 1983. "Die Wiederentdeckung der Freiheit— Persönliche Erinnerungen." In VDMA (ed.), *Produktivität, Eigenverantwortung, Beschäftigung. Für eine wirtschaftspolitische Vorwärtsstrategie.* Cologne: Deutscher Instituts-Verl., 9–22.

Hayek, Friedrich August von, Hugo Sieber, Egon Tuchtfeldt, and Hans Willgerodt. 1979. "Wilhelm Röpke—Einleitende Bemerkungen zur Neuausgabe seiner Werke." In Wilhelm Röpke, *Ausgewählte Werke—Die Lehre von der Wirtschaft.* 12. Auflage. Bern: Haupt, v–xxxvi.

Herbst, Ludolf. 1982. *Der Totale Krieg und die Ordnung der Wirtschaft. Die Kriegswirtschaft im Spannungsfeld von Politik, Ideologie und Propaganda 1939–1945.* Stuttgart: DVA.

Herder-Dorneich, Phillip. 1993. *Soziale Marktwirtschaft als weltweites Modell. Versuch einer Neuformulierung.* Cologne: Walter-Raymond-Stiftung.

Herf, Jeffrey. 1984. *Reactionary Modernism: Culture and Politics in Weimar and the Third Reich.* Cambridge: Cambridge University Press.

Hirschman, Albert O. 1989. "How the Keynesian Revolution Was Exported from the United States, and Other Comments." In Peter Hall (ed.), *The Political Power of Economic Ideas: Keynesianism across Nations.* Princeton, NJ: Princeton University Press, 347–360.

Hutchison, Terence W. 1979. "Notes on the Effects of Economic Ideas on Policy: The Example of the German Social Market Economy." *Zeitschrift für die gesamte Staatswissenschaft* 135/4: 426–441.

Janssen, Hauke. 1998. *Nationalökonomie und Nationalsozialismus. Die deutsche Volkswirtschaftslehre in den dreißiger Jahren.* Marburg: Metropolis.

Johnson, Daniel. 1989. "Exiles and Half-Exiles: Wilhelm Röpke, Alexander Rüstow and Walter Eucken." In Alan Peacock and Hans Willgerodt, with Daniel Johnson (eds.), *German Neoliberals and the Social Market Economy.* New York: St. Martin's Press, 40–68.

Kaltefleiter, Werner. 1989. "Bedingungen für die Durchsetzung ordnungspolitischer Grundentscheidungen nach dem Zweiten Weltkrieg." In Wolfram Fischer (ed.), *Währungsreform und Soziale Marktwirtschaft.* Berlin: Duncker u. Humblot, 61–76.

Kinderman, Daniel. 2005. "Pressure from Without, Subversion from Within: The Two-Pronged German Employer Offensive." *Comparative European Politics* 3: 432–463.

Krause, Werner. 1969. *Wirtschaftstheorien unter dem Hakenkreuz. Die bürgerliche politische Ökonomie in Deutschland während der faschistischen Herrschaft.* Berlin: Akademie-Verlag.

Leipold, Helmut. 1990. "Neoliberal Ordnungstheorie and Constitutional Economics. A Comparison between Eucken and Buchanan." *Constitutional Political Economy* 1: 47–65.

Lutz, Friedrich. 1936. *Das Grundproblem der Geldverfassung.* Heft 2 der Schriftenreihe Ordnung der Wirtschaft. Franz Böhm, Walter Eucken, and Hans Großmann-Doerth (eds.). Stuttgart: Kohlhammer.

Lutz, Friedrich A. 1989. "Observations on the Problem of Monopolies." In Alan Peacock and Hans Willgerodt (eds.), *Germany's Social Market Economy: Origins and Evolution.* New York: St. Martin's Press, 152–170.

Miksch, Leonhard. 1937. *Wettbewerb als Aufgabe. Die Grundsätze einer Wettbewerbsordnung,* Heft 4 der Schriftenreihe Ordnung der Wirtschaft. Franz Böhm, Walter Eucken, and Hans Großmann-Doerth (eds.). Stuttgart: Kohlhammer.

Miksch, Leonhard. 1948. "Die Wirtschaftspolitik des Als-Ob." *Zeitschrift für die gesamte Staatswissenschaft* 105: 310–338.

Moeller, Hero. 1950. "Liberalismus." *Jahrbücher für Nationalökonomie und Statistik* 162: 214–240.

Möschel, Wernhard. 1989. "Competition Policy from an Ordo Point of View." In Alan Peacock and Hans Willgerodt, with Johnson, Daniel (eds.), *German Neoliberals and the Social Market Economy.* New York: St. Martin's Press, 142–169.

Müller-Armack, Alfred. 1932. *Entwicklungsgesetze des Kapitalismus. Ökonomische, geschichtstheoretische und soziologische Studien zur modernen Wirtschaftsverfassung.* Berlin: Junker und Dünnhaupt.

Müller-Armack, Alfred. 1933. *Staatsidee und Wirtschaftsordnung im neuen Reich.* Berlin: Junker und Dünnhaupt.

Müller-Armack, Alfred. 1941. *Genealogie der Wirtschaftsstile. Die geistesgeschichtlichen Ursprünge der Staats- und Wirtschaftsformen bis zum 18. Jahrhundert.* Stuttgart: Kohlhammer.

Müller-Armack, Alfred. 1947. *Wirtschaftslenkung und Marktwirtschaft.* Hamburg: Verl. für Wirtschaft und Sozialpolitik.

Müller-Armack, Alfred. 1948. *Das Jahrhundert ohne Gott. Zur Kultursoziologie unserer Zeit.* Münster: Regensberg.

Müller-Armack, Alfred. 1949. *Diagnose unserer Gegenwart. Zur Bestimmung unseres geistesgeschichtlichen Standorts.* Gütersloh: Bertelsmann.

Müller-Armack, Alfred. 1962. "Das gesellschaftspolitische Leitbild der Sozialen Marktwirtschaft." *Wirtschaftspolitische Chronik* 11(3): 7–28.

Nawroth, Egon Edgar. 1961. *Die Sozial- und Wirtschaftsphilosophie des Neoliberalismus.* Heidelberg: Kerle.

Nicholls, Anthony J. 1984. "Das andere Deutschland—Die Neoliberalen." *Zeitschrift für Wirtschaftspolitik* 33(2/3): 241–259.

Nicholls, Anthony J. 1994. *Freedom with Responsibility. The Social Market Economy in Germany, 1918–1963.* Oxford: Clarendon Press.

Opitz, Reinhard. 1973. *Ideologie und Praxis des deutschen Sozialliberalismus 1917–1933.* Dissertation, University of Marburg/Lahn.

Peacock, Alan, and Hans Willgerodt (eds.). 1989a. *Germany's Social Market Economy: Origins and Evolution.* New York: St. Martin's Press.

Peacock, Alan, and Hans Willgerodt, with Daniel Johnson (eds.). 1989b. *German Neoliberals and the Social Market Economy.* New York: St. Martin's Press.

Plehwe, Dieter. 2006. "Soziale Marktwirtschaft als Steinbruch?" In Ariane Berthoin Antal and Sigrid Quack (eds.), *Grenzüberschreitungen—Grenzziehungen. Implikationen für Innovation und Identität.* Berlin: Sigma Verlag, 353–386.

Ptak, Ralf. 2002. "Chefsache. Basta! Der Neoliberalismus als antiegalitäre, antidemokratische Leitideologie." In Norman Paech, Eckart Spoo, and Rainer Butenschön (eds.), *Demokratie—wo und wie?* Hamburg: VSA, 87–102.

Ptak, Ralf. 2004. *Vom Ordoliberalismus zur Sozialen Marktwirtschaft. Stationen des Neoliberalismus in Deutschland.* Opladen: Leske and Budrich.

Quaas, Friedrun. 2000. *Soziale Marktwirtschaft. Wirklichkeit und Verfremdung eines Konzeptes.* Bern: Haupt.

Raico, Ralph. 1999. *Die Partei der Freiheit. Studien zur Geschichte des deutschen Liberalismus.* Stuttgart: Lucius & Lucius.

Rehberg, Karl-Siegbert. 1999. "Hans Freyer—Arnold Gehlen—Helmut Schelsky." In Dirk Kaesle (ed.), *Klassiker der Soziologie.* Vol. 2: *Von Talcott Parsons bis Pierre Bourdieu.* Munich: Beck, 72–104.

Reuter, Hans-Georg. 1999. "Genese der Konzeption der Sozialen Marktwirtschaft." In Knut Wolfgang Nörr and Joachim Starbatty (eds.), *Soll und Haben—50 Jahre Soziale Marktwirtschaft.* Stuttgart: Lucius & Lucius, 67–95.

Riese, Hajo. 1972. "Ordnungsidee und Ordnungspolitik—Kritik einer wirtschaftspolitischen Konzeption." *Kyklos* 25: 24–48.

Röpke, Wilhelm. 1929. "Staatsinterventionismus." *Handwörterbuch der Staatswissenschaften,* 4. Auflage. Ergänzungsbd. Jena: Fischer, 861–882.

Röpke, Wilhelm. 1933/1962. "Epochenwende." In *Wirrnis und Wahrheit. Ausgewählte Aufsätze.* Erlenbach: Rentsch, 105–124.

Röpke, Wilhelm. 1942/1979. *Die Gesellschaftskrisis der Gegenwart,* 6. Auflage. Bern: Haupt.

Röpke, Wilhelm. 1944. *Civitas Humana.* Erlenbach-Zürich: Rentsch.

Röpke, Wilhelm. 1945. *Internationale Ordnung.* Erlenbach-Zürich: Rentsch.

Röpke, Wilhelm. 1946. *Civitas Humana,* 2nd rev. ed. Erlenbach-Zürich: Rentsch.

Röpke, Wilhelm. 1948a. "Klein- und Mittelbetrieb in der Volkswirtschaft." *ORDO* 1: 155–174.

Röpke, Wilhelm. 1948b. "Die natürliche Ordnung. Die neue Phase der wirtschaftspolitischen Diskussion." *Kyklos* 2: 211–232.

Röpke, Wilhelm. 1950. "Walter Eucken." *Neue Zürcher Zeitung,* March 25, 1950.

Roth, Karl-Heinz. 2001. "Klienten des Leviathan: Die Mont Pèlerin Society und das Bundeswirtschaftsministerium in den fünfziger Jahren 1999." *Zeitschrift für Sozialgeschichte des 20. und 21. Jahrhunderts* 16(2): 13–41.

Roth, Karl-Heinz. 2004. "Der 20. Juli 1944 und seine Vorgeschichte." In Karl-Heinz Roth and Angelika Ebbinghaus (eds.), *Rote Kapellen-Kreisauer Kreise-Schwarze Kapellen. Neue Sichtweisen auf den Widerstand gegen die NS-Diktatur 1938–1945.* Hamburg: VSA, 16–68.

Rüstow, Alexander. 1929/1959. "Diktatur innerhalb der Grenzen der Demokratie, Dokumentation des Vortrages und der Diskussion von 1929 an der 'Deutschen Hochschule für Politik.'" *Vierteljahrshefte für Zeitgeschichte* 7(1): 85–111.

Rüstow, Alexander. 1932. "Interessenpolitik oder Staatspolitik." *Der deutsche Volkswirt* 7(6): 169–172.

Rüstow, Alexander. 1945/1950. *Das Versagen des Wirtschaftsliberalismus,* 2nd ed. Bad Godesberg: Küpper vorm. Bondi.

Rüstow, Alexander. 1950. *Ortsbestimmung der Gegenwart. Eine universalgeschichtliche Kulturkritik, 1. Band: Ursprung der Herrschaft.* Erlenbach-Zürich: Rentsch.

Rüstow, Alexander. 1951. "Kritik des technischen Fortschritts." *ORDO* 4: 373–407.

Rüstow, Alexander. 1952. *Ortsbestimmung der Gegenwart. Eine universalgeschichtliche Kulturkritik, 2. Band: Weg der Freiheit.* Erlenbach-Zürich: Rentsch.

Rüstow, Alexander. 1953. "Soziale Marktwirtschaft als Gegenprogramm gegen Kommunismus und Bolschewismus." In Albert Hunold (ed.), *Wirtschaft ohne Wunder.* Erlenbach: Rentsch, 97–127.

Rüstow, Alexander. 1957a. *Ortsbestimmung der Gegenwart. Eine universalgeschichtliche Kulturkritik, 3. Band: Herrschaft oder Freiheit.* Erlenbach-Zürich: Rentsch.

Rüstow, Alexander. 1957b. "Vitalpolitik gegen Vermassung." In Albert Hunold (ed.), *Masse und Demokratie.* Erlenbach-Zürich: Rentsch, 215–238.

Rüstow, Alexander. 1957c. "Die geschichtliche Bedeutung der Sozialen Marktwirtschaft." In Erwin von Beckerath, Fritz W. Meyer, and Alfred Müller-Armack (eds.), *Festschrift für Ludwig Erhard, Wirtschaftsfragen der Freien Welt.* Frankfurt am Main: Knapp, 73–77.

Schiller, Karl. 1958. *Neuere Entwicklungen in der Theorie der Wirtschaftspolitik.* Vorträge und Aufsätze des Walter Eucken Instituts, Heft 1. Tübingen.

Schindelbeck, Dirk, and Ilgen Volker. 1999. *Haste was, biste was! Werbung für die Soziale Marktwirtschaft.* Darmstadt: Primus.

Schlecht, Otto. 1981. "Die Genesis des Konzepts der Sozialen Marktwirtschaft." In Otmar Issing (ed.), *Zukunftsprobleme der sozialen Marktwirtschaft.* Schriften des Vereins für Socialpolitik, NF 116. Berlin: Duncker & Humblot, 9–31.

Schmitt, Carl. 1933. "Starker Staat und gesunde Wirtschaft. Ein Vortrag vor Wirtschaftsführern." *Volk und Reich* 2: 81–94.

Schulz, Gerhard. 1985. "Über Johannis Popitz (1884–1945)." *Der Staat* 24(4): 485–511.

Schwarz, Gerhard. 1992. "Marktwirtschaftliche Reform und Demokratie—Eine Hassliebe? Überlegungen zur Interdependenz der Ordnungen beim Übergang von der Kommando- zur Wettbewerbswirtschaft." *ORDO* 43: 65–90.

Speth, Rudolf. 2004. *Die politischen Strategien der Initiative Neue Soziale Marktwirtschaft.* Düsseldorf: Hans-Böckler-Stiftung.

Starbatty, Joachim. 1982. "Alfred Müller-Armacks Beitrag zur Theorie und Politik der Sozialen Marktwirtschaft." In Ludwig-Erhard-Stiftung (ed.), *Symposion VIII.* Stuttgart: Fischer, 7–26.

Starbatty, Joachim. 1986. "Die Soziale Marktwirtschaft aus historisch-theoretischer Sicht." In Hans Pohl (ed.), *Entstehung und Entwicklung der Sozialen Marktwirtschaft.* Beiheft 45 der *Zeitschrift für Unternehmensgeschichte.* Stuttgart: Franz Steiner Verlag, 7–26.

Starbatty, Joachim. 2000. "Eine Neue Soziale Marktwirtschaft?" *Handelsblatt* 5.12.

Tribe, Keith. 1995. *Strategies of Economic Order. German Economic Discourse, 1750–1950.* Cambridge: Cambridge University Press.

Vanberg, Viktor. 1988. "Ordungstheorie" as Constitutional Economics—The German Conception of a "Social Market Economy." *ORDO* 39: 17–31.

Veit, Otto. 1953. "ORDO und Ordnung. Versuch einer Synthese." *ORDO* 5: 3–47.

Wallich, Henry C. 1955. *Triebkräfte des deutschen Wiederaufstiegs*. Frankfurt am Main: Knapp.

Walpen, Bernhard. 2004. *Die offenen Feinde und ihre Gesellschaft*. Hamburg: VSA.

Watrin, Christian. 1979. "The Principles of the Social Market Economy—Its Origins and Early History." *Zeitschrift für die gesamte Staatswissenschaft* 135(3): 405–425.

Wegmann, Milene. 2002. *Früher Neoliberalismus und Europäische Integration*. Baden Baden: Nomos.

Willgerodt, Hans. 1998. "Die Liberalen und ihr Staat—Gesellschaftspolitik zwischen Laissez-faire und Diktatur." *ORDO* 49: 43–78.

Willgerodt, Hans. 2006. "Der Neoliberalismus—Entstehung, Kampfbegriff und Meinungsstreit." *ORDO* 57: 47–89.

Wünsche, Horst Friedrich. 1997. "Erhards soziale Marktwirtschaft: von Eucken programmiert, von Müller-Armack inspiriert?" In Ludwig-Erhard-Stiftung (ed.), *Soziale Marktwirtschaft als historische Weichenstellung*. Bonn—Düsseldorf: ST Verlag, 131–169.

4

The Rise of the Chicago School
of Economics and the
Birth of Neoliberalism

ROB VAN HORN

PHILIP MIROWSKI

> Democracy, as viewed by libertarians . . . also implies, at best, a continuing process of relevant discussions and inquiry among professional truth-seekers or academic problem-solvers, who, though scrupulously detached from active politics and from factional affiliations, subtly and unobtrusively guide or arbitrate political debate by their own discussions.
>
> Simons 1948, 8

Our objective in the present chapter is to relate the sequence of events that led to the rise of the Chicago School of economics. This chapter in many respects is a revisionist story, grounded more directly in archival evidence than in the personal reminiscences that have tended to be the staple of this area in the past. It situates the rise of the school at a very critical juncture of events at a very specific date, namely, 1946. It subverts certain widely held notions about the history of economics, such as the mistaken conflation of the rise of the Chicago School with the larger rise to dominance of neoclassical economics in postwar America, or the supposed continuity of social doctrine that was thought to characterize the pre- and postwar Chicago School, as well as the belief that it was some "core scientific theory" that provided the backbone of the school, whereas the applications in such areas as law and business only came later. Although space limitations prevent us from giving a comprehensive account of the later shape of the Chicago School, this chapter nevertheless downgrades any idea that some abstract analytical characterization of the economy formed the nucleus around which the school crystallized (such as Reder's [1982] concept of tight prior equilibrium), and replaces it with explicit political orientation, something that weighed very heavily on the minds of all the main protagonists. Indeed, our central thesis is that the rise of the Chicago School must be understood as one component of a specific larger transnational project of innovating doctrines of neoliberalism for the postwar world.

This chapter diminishes the importance of certain figures who have often loomed large in the folklore, such as Frank Knight or Jacob Viner; it reevaluates the role of others, such as Milton Friedman; and it elevates to prime positions some neglected figures such as Friedrich Hayek, Henry Simons, and Aaron Director. The tale is studded with poignant ironies, such as the fact that the prime external contractor for the erection of the Chicago School would not then be accepted as a member in good standing of the Economics Department once it got off the ground; or that the prime architect so despaired of ever convincing the subcontractors to get the foundations laid that he committed suicide. Finally, the trademark Chicago doctrine of the supposed separation of positive from normative economics (Friedman 1953) assumes a strikingly ironic significance in the light of this account. Now that the Chicago School no longer exists in anything like its original form, we believe the time has finally arrived to tell the actual story in the fine detail that would satisfy the historian, rather than the ceremonial after-dinner speaker. But more importantly, this account begins to situate the Chicago School in the larger framework of the postwar creation of neoliberalism.

American Road Repairs: Hayek and Simons

As part of his larger campaign to warn the Western world about the imminent threat of left-wing totalitarianism, Friedrich Hayek (then still an economist at the London School of Economics) delivered a lecture at the Economic Club in Detroit, Michigan on April 23, 1945.[1] He was on a book tour promoting his surprise best-seller, *The Road to Serfdom* (1944). In Detroit he proselytized: "I think there is a great educational task to be fulfilled. We must make the masses of people learn and understand the problem that is before us, make them capable of discriminating between methods which will achieve the end and methods which are empty promises, and particularly tell them that there may be desperate palliatives like inflationary measures which in the short run may keep employment high, but in the long run make the situation much more difficult than it was before." Within two days of the event, Hayek met with the businessman Harold Luhnow—then president of the Volker Fund—in Chicago. Luhnow offered to provide financial support for Hayek in his educational quest, since he too had been searching for intellectual weapons to curb the power of government in the postwar era.

Luhnow had become president of the William Volker & Co., a national furniture distribution company and window-shade manufacturer located in Kansas City, Missouri in January 1938. Luhnow was a strident anti-New Deal conservative and was then in the process of converting a philanthropic fund originally intended to help the citizens of Kansas City into something completely different: a foundation to promote a rethinking of liberal politics in America. The Fund, which existed from 1932 to 1965, would play a major role in conservative intellectual politics in twentieth-century America. To pursue that end, Luhnow arranged the tête-à-tête with Hayek on April 24/25, 1945.[2]

At the meeting Luhnow sought to commission Hayek to write *The American Road to Serfdom*. The original text had been composed with a British audience in mind and perhaps had been pitched at too elevated a level of discourse for American audiences. Subsequently, Hayek in his later book *Hayek on Hayek* claims that he did not take Luhnow's offer seriously, but says that he spoke at length with his "great friend" Henry Simons about it in Chicago (Hayek 1994, 127). Hayek also claimed that he "had to report to Luhnow in the course of the journey that I couldn't do anything about it," and that he initially declined Luhnow's offer after returning to England. Nevertheless, Luhnow cabled back and gave Hayek the authority to determine the course of the project, including subcontracting the authorship of the revised *Road*, to which Hayek agreed (Hayek 1994, 127–128). However, an epistolary exchange between Hayek and Luhnow challenges Hayek's personal reminiscences: apparently, Hayek had been much more receptive to the opportunity, because he regarded it as potentially constituting something much more ambitious. Hayek actually wrote Luhnow from Chicago on May 3, 1945, before returning to England:

> My friend, Mr. Friedrich A. Lutz of Princeton, whom I had in the first instance in mind and who came to see me here in Chicago to discuss it, is quite willing to take part in it although he is for some time committed to other work, and feels that he will need two or three other people to work with him as a team. . . . It has since occurred to me that Princeton is not necessarily the best place and that there is a great deal to be said for conducting the investigation at the University of Chicago where there are a number of people whose collaboration would be extremely useful.[3]

As a sign of the seriousness with which the offer was regarded, other participants in "the first Chicago discussions of the project [included] Jacob Viner,
Robert Hutchins, Karl Brandt, and [Dean Robert Redfield]," in addition to
Simons and Lutz, and most probably Aaron Director and possibly Milton
Friedman.[4] Since he is often thought to have been unsympathetic to the politics of those involved, the early and close participation of Hutchins, the soon-
to-be chancellor of the University of Chicago, will prove important.[5] Hayek,
however, was not the only one who was ebullient about this prospect; so too
was Henry Simons of the Chicago Law School.[6]

Hayek and Simons's intellectual friendship dated back as early as 1934
when Hayek sent an appreciation of Simons's *Positive Program for Laissez Faire*
(SPRL, Hayek to Simons, December 1, 1934, box 3, file 40). By 1939, a close
comradeship had developed: Simons then commiserated with Hayek over the
British political landscape: "For England, however, it seems impossible to
hold out even a slender hope. England, to be sure, may still be saved, but not
by her own actions—only by the example of a wise and successful liberal program in the United States. So, I welcome your contribution to discussion here
and, hoping that you will again write for American readers, I suggest that this
may be the most useful contribution you can make toward the cause of liberalism in England and elsewhere."[7] Hayek had earlier praised *A Positive Program for Laissez Faire:* "I have the greatest sympathy for the general spirit
which it expresses and I feel that it does raise the problems which economists
ought to discuss to-day more than others."

During the 1930s, however, they did not fully concur on some issues, which
would later loom large: "I have grave doubts about the suggestion that all industries where perfect competition can not be restored should be socialized."[8]
Here Hayek referred to Simons's notorious policy recommendation in *Program*
that industries like the railroads, which had grown so concentrated as to be
nearly impossible to challenge or reform, be nationalized. Simons, however,
did not make such a seemingly anti-free market proposal on conventional socialist interventionist grounds, but rather on a purely classical liberal basis.[9]
Like Hayek, Simons believed that the liberal safeguard of freedom is the most
important objective for public policy, and denounced political control unless it
was unavoidably necessary to promote a freer market. Yet unlike most post-
1946 Chicago School economists, Simons deeply distrusted nearly all concentrations of power as inimical to both political and economic success: "*Thus, the
great enemy of democracy is monopoly, in all its forms:* gigantic corporations,

trade associations and other agencies for price control, trade-unions—or, in general, organization and concentration of power within functional classes" (Simons 1948, 43). Concentrations of power posed a threat to the "heart of the contract," and thus to relative prices, which should adjust freely to reach competitive equilibrium. Because the "heart of the contract" is the sine qua non of freedom, "A monopolist is . . . an implicit thief because his possession of market power leads to the exchange of commodities at prices that do not reflect underlying social scarcities" (De Long 1990, 606). Simons indeed believed that the proliferation of monopoly had led to the Great Depression. The role of government, therefore, should be to maintain a propitious market milieu—a legal and institutional framework, a correct level of currency, a definition of private property, an initial allocation of endowments—where competition, the agency of control, can function effectively.

Simons's "Positive Program" reads today more like a left-leaning attack on corporate prerogatives than anything we might associate with a neoconservative agenda, but in the 1930s it was situated well within the bounds of classical liberalism. After the abolition of corporate monopoly, Simons also proposed the abolition of private deposit banking predicated on fractional reserves; the revision of the tax system to achieve greater equality of wealth and income; and the "Limitation upon the squandering of our resources in advertising and selling activities" (1948, 57). One can easily appreciate why this program had attracted the attention of radical reformers, even though its chances of enactment were slim to negligible in that era. First and foremost on his reform agenda was "elimination of private monopoly in all of its forms" (1948, 57). Simons of course also recommended an array of other reforms to address the depression economy. For example, he was an early proponent of the "establishment of more definite and adequate 'rules of the game' with respect to money" (1948, 57).

From his marginal position at the Chicago Law School, with Volker's encouragement, Simons soon became the center of gravity for the group of Chicago economists Hayek had begun to imagine as a dedicated cadre to pursue his political goals.[10] This was more than a pipe dream because Simons enjoyed close personal relations with President Robert Hutchins, who would help in multiple ways to facilitate what Simons had come to call "the Hayek Project."[11] In expressing his admiration for Simons's financial savvy, Hutchins wrote: "It sounds to me as though you would get us a million dollars from Mr. Rockefeller and another million, by way of apology, from Harry Luce. When the money comes in, I will split it with you."[12] Most significantly, one should note that Simons felt altogether comfortable sharing his recommendations for staffing the Economics Department directly with Hutchins in 1946, even though he was not even a member of that department: "P.S. I hear that Milton Friedman, whom I was proposing for Lange's place, has been appointed to an associate professorship at Minnesota."[13] In the intellectual sphere, Simons and Hutchins shared a certain fondness for Adam Smith, perhaps regarding one another as embattled classical liberals.[14]

Though Hayek, Hutchins, and Director much respected and liked Henry Simons, the relationship Simons had with most members of the existing Economics Department, especially Frank Knight and Jacob Viner, was less than amiable during the war. In 1944, smoldering enmity between some members of the faculty senate, which included Viner and Knight, and the administration (mainly Hutchins) erupted when Hutchins delivered his January 1944 speech to the faculty, as recounted in his numerous biographies (Ashmore 1989; Dzuback 1991). In pursuit of a transvaluation of values that might render the University "a democratic and effective academic community," Hutchins, among other things, proposed the abolishment of "the farce of academic rank," in which "[the University] is still entangled," and he recommended a profound reorganization of University administrative power. This recommendation precipitated a pitched battle between the so-called six burghers of the Chicago campus, which included Knight and Viner, and the University administration.[15] It ranged over a raft of issues, ranging from bureaucratic structures to curriculum reform to the proper subjects of university research. Politics was never very far below the surface of these tumultuous events.

Faithful supporters of Hutchins, such as Simons and John Nef, an economic historian, soon embroiled themselves in conflict with the Economics Department.[16] Perhaps because of his warm relationship with Hutchins, Simons entered the fray, upbraiding the "six burghers" for what he thought obstreperous and counterproductive tactics. Apparently, Viner countered with a reprimand of his own, to which Simons rejoined: "You may be right in analyzing my case as a persecution complex. However, . . . you have recruited many dubious, timid, and diffident persons. This augments your power, for timid souls will not desert even though they regret having joined—you probably don't need them now anyway; and it increases your moral responsibilities."[17]

Given this heated exchange, the relationship between Viner and Simons most likely verged upon irreconcilable; simultaneously, the relationship between Simons and Knight was also turning sour. They were located on opposing sides of the bureaucratic battles, but there was something more in their growing antagonism. By the mid-1940s, Knight and Simons's research had undergone unprecedented divergence, and not just because they were now located in separate departments. Knight, according to Simons, was "increasingly preoccupied with philosophy and philosophies, not to mention historians, theologians, and anthropologists, et al., and is not deeply interested in concrete problems of economic policy."[18] Partly because of the divarication that now characterized their intellectual relationship, their personal relationship by early 1946 had grown distant and impersonal.

For all these reasons, when Hayek pointed in late 1945 to "a number of people whose collaboration would be extremely useful" at the University of Chicago, he may very well not have envisioned the close collaboration of Knight and Viner.[19] In fact, more likely, Hayek was leaning toward collaboration with Henry Simons (the central protagonist), Aaron Director, and possibly Milton Friedman. To facilitate and direct the collaboration, Simons wasted no time in drawing up an ambitious plan to recast the Chicago landscape.

Simons informed Hayek:

> I have contrived a project largely for what one might call ulterior purposes: (1) to get Aaron Director back here and into a kind of work for which he has, as you know, real enthusiasms and superlative talents. . . . Moreover, I have deliberately formulated the kind of project for which this University would be the natural location and for which Aaron would be the natural choice as head . . . I am sorry to have organized Lutz out of the picture— and hope he might be "organized in" again from time to time or permanently. He is probably the best choice for your kind of project; but Aaron seems a better choice for mine, if only by the nature off his own preferences and interests—although Lutz, in turn, would be a better choice for my project if it were located at Princeton.[20]

Shortly thereafter, in early June, Simons drafted two memoranda that laid out the proposals for a new research program. There Simons wrote: "A distinctive feature of 'Chicago economics,' as represented recently by Knight and Viner, is its traditional-liberal political philosophy—its emphasis on the virtues of dispersion of economic power (free markets) and of political decentralization."[21] Simons regretted that this philosophical orientation was "almost unrepresented among great universities, save for Chicago." Surveying the current landscape, Simons observed that the current Chicago liberal thinkers would encompass

Knight, Lloyd Mints, Viner, H. Gregg Lewis, and himself. But not all were suited to the task at hand. Lewis, Simons believed, was "long and frequently on leave." Knight was, Simon stated, increasingly preoccupied with matters not concerning economic policy, but concerning philosophy, history, theology, and anthropology. Outside economic interests and "special" writing and research tended to occupy Viner, according to Simons. So "that leaves Mints and Simons." Thus, Simons proposed the creation of an "institute" that would be comprised of various scholars dispersed across disciplinary boundaries at Chicago, an Institute: "without total reliance on departmental or university policy." Simons nominated Director, whom he deemed a steadfast liberal, as the permanent head of the project. Simons stipulated the following requirements: "[The leader] should be an essentially intellectual person, not a promoter, not politically ambitious or 'on the make,' not 'the administrative type,' not prominently identified with other organizations or public activity, and not adept at salesmanship or public relations." Simons suggested Milton Friedman be enrolled as part-time statistician, though he added that George Stigler or Allen Wallis would do as well.[22] For twenty years, Simons believed, the activities of the Institute should be restricted to publication of scholarly and semipopular literature to promote liberal ideas—"stimulated and facilitated rather than under contracts with participants." The Institute's other functions were conceived to include facilitating academic discussion, bringing in libertarian visiting professors, and neutralizing the pernicious influence of the Cowles Commission at Chicago. Ultimately, "The Institute should be mainly concerned with political philosophy and with major practical problems of economic policy"; he suggested monopoly, monetary policy and foreign trade. Given Simons's location, it was taken for granted that questions of law and economics would be treated on an equal footing. "It should not undertake major empirical research. . . . it should aim merely at influencing the best professional opinions and political action through such professional opinion, not directly." Simons added, "It should not, however, seek "to influence immediate political action." Simons then recommended Walter Lippmann, Arnold Plant, Lionel Robbins, Theodore Schultz, Garfield Cox, Wilber Katz, Karl Brandt, Frank Knight, Jacob Viner, Friedrich Lutz, Friedrich Hayek, George Stigler, and Allen Wallis as affiliates to sustain the Institute and to further its aims. Political orientation clearly provided the major litmus test.

Simons anointed Director as the prospective head of the Institute based on personal friendship and political perquisites. Simons revealed some of

his motives in an earlier missive to the department chair of economics in
1939:

> Finally, a purely personal note. Aaron has been more useful to me than all
> other [persons in] the University combined. He greatly influenced every-
> thing I have written and all my teaching here. Frankly, I find it hard to do
> writing which meets my own standards, or to make innovations in my
> courses, except in connection with a lot of discussion and exchange of ideas
> with persons of similar interests. . . . in spite of my efforts and good inten-
> tions of other people, I have been, *qua* economist, alone since Aaron left.
> Certainly I am worth more to the University with Aaron around than with-
> out him. . . . When he was back last Fall, I acquired again a delightful sense
> of belonging to a real (and rather numerous) community of economists
> hereabouts. . . . the intentions [among others in the department] become
> fruitful only with Aaron around to help us in the business of helping each
> other. (SPRL, Simons to Mr. Wright, February 20, 1939, box 8, file 10)

Aaron Director is therefore the third main protagonist in our account of
the origins of the Chicago School and represents the other major link to
Hayek.[23] After undergoing conversion from leftist politics in the early 1930s at
Chicago, Director had been working at the U.S. Treasury. In 1937, Director
sailed to England to write a dissertation under Viner on the quantitative history of the Bank of England. When the Bank unexpectedly thwarted his efforts, Director became more closely associated with Arnold Plant and Lionel
Robbins at the London School of Economics (LSE). In 1939, Director sailed
back to Washington, where he worked until 1946. In 1938, his sister Rose mar-
ried Milton Friedman.

Soon after arriving in London, Director met Hayek, and they came to regard each other as intellectual comrades in arms.[24] Director later became one
of Hayek's staunchest political allies in the United States, persuading the University of Chicago Press to publish *The Road to Serfdom* after numerous commercial publishers had turned it down. Not surprisingly, Director then
promptly wrote a laudatory book review for *The Road to Serfdom*: "There is
no economist writing in English more eminently qualified to do this job [ex-
ploring the ultimate political implications of abandoning the competitive sys-
tem]. In addition to . . . his repute as an economist, Professor Hayek is our
most accomplished historian of the development of economic ideas" (1945,
174). Director frequently commiserated with Hayek over politics from his own
perch in wartime Washington: "In a future war we must give some consideration

to economizing the use of authoritarian control, this not so much because it has alternative uses but because the supply of good controlled is very limited, and because its utilization may accustom us to accept it after the war is over" (1940, 360). Director's deep respect for Hayek would later prove pivotal in Director's decision to return to Chicago.

Shortly after Hayek met with the Chicago contingent, Simons stayed with Director in Washington, D.C., where they, along with Milton Friedman, Homer Jones, Herbert Stein, and Fritz Machlup, all discussed Simon's scheme in his memoranda and Hayek's suggestions.[25] Significantly, both Director and Simons wrote to Hayek in order to bring him up-to-date after the conclave. Simons reported that the men had bandied about ideas for compromises between his own ambitious scheme and various alternative short-term academic projects. Director's assessment was rather pessimistic, however. Most of the conclave attendants had concurred with Simons's memo in principle, but all had registered disagreement with Simons's more elaborate vision of a twenty-year project that aimed to advance the tradition of liberal economic doctrines and influence public policy. There was, for instance, some hesitation about Hayek's "Austrian" methodological proclivities. Instead, Director and the others "would assign more importance than he does to a certain amount of empirical investigation—directed of course to the central issue of maintaining competitive conditions. An investigation of the economies of scale and inevitability of monopoly suggest itself as an illustration. An incidental advantage of the inclusion of empirical work is greater 'saleability' so that it would not be necessary to insist on as on a period as twenty years. Assured existence for 8 to 10 years—perhaps even 5 or 6 years—might in fact imply some assurance of an extension to the maximum period of twenty years."[26]

In spite of Director's proffered suggestions, he bore disappointing news for Hayek and Simons: Director was inclined to remain in Washington for another three years. Hayek wrote Simons: "You will see from this that I am in full sympathy with your scheme. If I can keep Luhnow sweet till the right man is available we might well proceed on this combined scheme." Hayek then continued, "I have not yet had time carefully to study Director's scheme of a Free Market Study. . . . It seems to cover all points I had had in mind and much more and confirms me in my conviction that a great deal of work of this kind needs to be done, and needs to be done in America by persons thoroughly familiar with American conditions." Hayek advised Simons to informally tell "the various people who were drawn into the first Chicago discussions of the project, particularly Viner, Hutchins, Brandt and perhaps your Dean, that as none of the suitable people were available at the moment, the whole plan is for the time being postponed."[27]

In the meantime, Hayek had written Luhnow, dutifully informing him that, "for the time being [the] attempts to organise the investigation we discussed have failed."[28] Hayek, despite the setback, was "no less anxious to see the work done." To accomplish this, Hayek requested Volker funding for a trip to the United States to personally look into the situation. Possibly to persuade Luhnow to underwrite an alternative scheme, Hayek enclosed Simons's memorandum, which, Hayek stated, has "all the essentials of which I am in close agreement and which I therefore attach to this letter." Hayek concluded: "I enclose a memorandum which together with the second document explains in some detail the aims and organisation of the society which I have mentioned before. . . . I don't know whether I have succeeded in expressing in these memoranda why such an organization as I sketch there seems to me one of the best contributions in the fight against the evil which threatens all [mankind]." Here Hayek referred to his own nascent plans for a prospective International Academy, of which the Acton-Tocqueville Society was to have been a part. The outlines for the International Academy eventually metamorphosed into what later became the Mont Pèlerin Society (Hartwell, 1995, 27–28). It is important to realize that, for Hayek, these negotiations over Chicago and the parallel construction of what became Mont Pèlerin were all part of the same common endeavor.

In the Acton-Tocqueville Memorandum, Hayek wrote: "The tide of Totalitarianism which we have to counter is an international phenomenon and the liberal renaissance which is needed to meet it and of which first signs can be discerned here and there will have little chance of success unless its forces can join and succeed in making the people of all the countries of the Western World aware of what is at stake."[29] In August 1945 Hayek conceived of the *American Road* project at Chicago as a subordinate part of a larger and more comprehensive scheme—a political movement to counter the intellectual traditions that would, as Hayek thought, inexorably lead to the emergence of totalitarian regimes throughout the Western world.[30]

But here is where the objectives of the supposedly passive bankroller intruded. Despite Hayek's praise for Simons's memo, Luhnow expressed no interest in it and tellingly objected to Hayek's "International Academy" because "experience has already proven in too many cases that it is almost impossible to keep control of organizations of this sort and, frankly, our main interest is in the proposition we outlined to you."[31] A modicum of control of any such organization was of paramount concern for its patrons: they were not willing to underwrite just any arbitrary conclave of self-identified political liberals. Luhnow also reported that he had discussed Hayek's most recent letter directly with Hutchins, "asking whether it would be possible for the University of Chicago to bring you there for a seminar at your convenience." Hutchins had suggested Hayek contact him immediately to make arrangements. Luhnow agreed to underwrite Hayek's trip and emphasized once more that his primary objective was to find someone to compose a text that a layperson could comprehend, a plan for "a workable society of free enterprise." He suggested the book *How We Live* by Fred G. Clark (1944) as a stylistic model for the *American Road to Serfdom.* One doubts if Hayek had ever seen a copy, for if he had, he would have immediately soured on Luhnow. *How We Live* was a large-print book, with didactic pictures facing each page of "text," which itself consisted of single-sentence paragraphs written for people who still moved their lips as they read. The quality of argument resembled a fourth-grade civics textbook.

Hayek immediately responded to Luhnow; he proposed coming to Chicago in the spring of 1946. Hayek contacted Hutchins on November 5, 1945, and that same day gave Simons the go-ahead to facilitate arrangements.[32] Until the receipt of this letter, Simons had begun to despair; as he confided to Hutchins: "I am not remiss in telling you about the Hayek project, for there still is no further news. I have heard nothing. . . . The memos and their scheme, however, were obviously not well contrived to get funds from his particular 'angel.' "[33] Hutchins reassured Simons that Hayek had been in contact with Luhnow. Simons subsequently contacted Hutchins about his scheme outlined in his memorandum: "I hear that Milton Friedman, whom I was proposing for Lange's place, has been appointed to an associate professorship at Minnesota. My scheme thus requires raiding the Minnesota staff for two men, within a few years. Moreover, it might now be best under that scheme, to get Stigler first."[34]

Thus the Volker Fund financially supported and stage-managed Hayek's 1946 American tour; it reimbursed Hayek for all of his traveling expenses while in the United States and arranged for Hayek's sojourns or meetings at various universities.[35] After April negotiations in Chicago, in early May, Hayek wrote Luhnow that Chicago would be the preferable work site for the *American Road;* however, Hayek regretted that negotiations were dragging on: "I am getting nervous that I may not be able to put up a definite proposal before I go on the West Coast."[36] Hayek also informed Luhnow that he was inclined to set up something at Princeton if negotiations failed at Chicago.

Hayek thought that negotiations had flagged because Director had wanted to be granted permanent tenure and that negotiation had only regained steam after the Volker Fund offered to pay Director's law school salary for the first five years. Director later publicly admitted: "It was earlier decided that Chicago was the only place that was likely to accept such a project, and it was also decided that the law school was the only part of the University of Chicago that would accept such a project" (Kitch 1983, 181). Thus, while Hayek depicted the Law School as the intellectually ideal location in correspondence, it was in fact the only serious prospective location for the American Road Show; other universities tended to balk at the level of control that Volker sought to exert as a condition of funding. But this would later prove significant, since it illustrates the important fact that the subsequent "Chicago Schools" of both economics and the law were jointly incubated—one did not simply give rise to the other.[37]

Surely Hutchins's liberal bent went a long way toward facilitating the logistics for the Free Market Project, as it became known, and his attenuated scruples concerning taking money with strings attached did the rest. Perhaps this was because he was coming off the experience of the Metallurgy Lab in World War II, and as he admitted in an internal memo in June 1946, "It seems likely that within the next five years the Government will become, directly and indirectly, the principal donor of the University."[38] Hutchins was therefore looking for some private antistatist funding to offset the looming postwar influence of the federal government on Chicago intellectual life and the University at large. The existing Economics Department, given its wartime depopulation, was in no shape to boast a dominant ideological orientation or to attract external funds. The Cowles Commission, an externally endowed economics research institution, was mostly stocked with self-identified socialists. The department also sported a rump representation of older-style Institutionalist economists.[39] These factions would have surely scoffed at such an openly antistatist-oriented unit: but they were mostly kept out of the loop.

Director, Hayek stipulated, would be free to select his collaborators either from the University of Chicago or from outside the University.[40] The collaborators would expedite the composition of the *American Road to Serfdom* because the particular targeted research they would undertake could be integrated within the broader scope of the book: "These supporting studies fit in extremely well with plans of this kind which the Department of Economics and particularly Mr. Friedman has for some time considered, and the Department rather hopes that it will be able to continue these more specialized studies beyond the point and the date when their first results have been used for the book." In order to further assuage Luhnow's continuing worries, Hayek included a copy of a memorandum drafted by Friedman: "It shows how closely the plans of the Department of Economics fit in with the work on the book." Hayek also enclosed a copy of the *Outline of Organization for the Proposed "Free Market Study,"* dated May 23, 1946.[41]

The prospective Free Market Study sought to define the political promise of a new, more economically oriented liberalism: "The free market [is] the most efficient organizer of economic activity—[the Study will] emphasize and explain that the free market is systemic, rational, not chaotic or disorderly—, show how the free market performs some of the more difficult functions, such as allocating resources to their best use and distributing consumption through time." The project also intended to examine the relationship between the free market and political and personal freedom. For our purposes, however, it is more important to note that under the rubric of "the promise of the free market," the outline identified both private monopoly and public regulation as "The Menace to the Free Market," with the latter being deemed more "dangerous."[42]

The outline stipulated that Aaron Director would direct the study and be included as part of an executive committee, which was charged to organize "such further subsidiary or supplementary investigations as seem appropriate to secure a satisfactory conclusion of the main study, and for this purpose [engaged] qualified research workers from inside or outside of the University of Chicago."[43] The study would aim to produce, "within three years a work of a semi-popular character [*The American Road to Serfdom*] on the lines of the provisional outline attached to this memorandum, provided that the University of Chicago is willing to offer him [Director] a permanent position with the status of full professor." The proposal also outlined how the Volker Fund would stage-manage the American Road Construction Project:

[The] William Volker Charities Fund of Kansas City, Missouri, is prepared to provide for the finance of the study of a suitable legal and institutional framework of an effective competitive system and that it is willing to contribute for this purpose the expense of the members of an advisory committee consisting of persons sympathetic to the purposes of this investigation and whose advice is likely to assist in the work of the regular staff who might periodically meet in Chicago for the discussion of problems arising in connection with it.

Sometime after Hayek mailed the Free Market Study proposal to Luhnow, the Chicago Law Faculty formally approved it, with only the central administration of the University of Chicago needed to authorize final approval. However, the central administration balked at one stipulation of the Free Market Study during a preliminary vote on June 10: "that the faculty of the Law School of the University of Chicago is prepared to extend to Mr. Director an appointment as Research Associate with the rank of Professor and with permanent tenure, on condition that this salary be underwritten for a period of five years with funds from outside the University."[44] The administration objected to giving Director automatic permanent tenure after a Volker-funded five-year research stint.

Luhnow, who surely would have immediately been apprised of the outcome of the central administration's vote, scribbled a note to Hayek on June 18: "I'm not one to interfere when I ask someone to do a job for me. Just take your time. Be cautious, and be as sure of your men as possible. . . . It's in your hands."[45] Clearly, at this juncture Luhnow revealed his aggravation, if not his exasperation, because the proposal had failed so close to the finish line. However, in his reaction, he also demonstrated the persistence with which he was willing to pursue his vision of a special cadre of liberals devoted to developing a very specific agenda of doctrines to be planted and nurtured at Chicago.

Hayek responded to Luhnow with shocking tragic news: Henry Simons was dead; he had committed suicide on June 19. Hayek lamented: "I have just had the sad news that Henry Simons has suddenly died in Chicago. He was so much the intellectual centre of the group I had in mind and the attraction which made Director willing to go to Chicago that I cannot yet see what the consequences of it will be." Hayek continued, "I had become very fond of him. I wish I knew somebody to replace him. But if my scheme collapses as a result I really don't know where to turn."[46] Given the precise timing, it is difficult not to imagine some connection between Simons's suicide and the Director snafu. It thus seemed that the whole plot to pave the American Road had hit an insuperable obstacle.

Director, stunned by the dreadful news, wrote Hayek: "By now you will have learned of the great tragedy which has befallen us. My own loss is great in any event. It is magnified by the regret that I allowed myself to be persuaded to go on with your project. This may have taken Henry Simons' thoughts away from other problems. But rejection of the project by the administration added but another to the many disappointments he received from the University."[47] Immediately after this letter to Hayek, Director received even stranger news.

Wilber Katz, dean of the Law School, informed Director of an unfortunate misunderstanding between himself and Hutchins. Apparently, Katz and the rest of the Chicago Law Faculty had thought Director was to be appointed research associate with professorial rank for five years and then granted tenure; however, Hutchins, "from Hayek or otherwise," had understood that "a five-year appointment" without promise of tenure was under consideration.[48] Apprised of the apparent misunderstanding between the dean of the Law School and the president of the university, the central administration agreed to reconsider the proposal, only on condition that Director agreed to a five-year appointment with no guarantee of tenure.

Director was now feeling torn and nonplussed. He immediately penned another letter to Hayek: "I would like to know just what you think in the light of the changes which have taken place. Until I hear from you, I shall merely acknowledge receipt of the letter." Hayek responded: "[After] your letter, I do want to say that in a sense it would seem to me even more important than before that you should accept. It seems to me the only chance that the tradition which Henry Simons created will be kept alive and continued in Chicago— and to me this seems tremendously important. . . . And after closer acquaintance with Milton Friedman I believe that even without Henry Chicago is still much the best place where to do it."[49] Even at this stage, Hayek did not consider Friedman the linchpin of his Institute.

Hayek's reassurance must have lifted Director's spirits, for he replied promptly, informing Hayek that he would agree to accept the five-year post without promise of tenure. Director then pledged his allegiance to Hayek: "I need not assure you that I consider your project of the greatest importance, or of my permanent interest in the issues at stake. You know the source of my hesitation. Henry's death has of course accentuated this."[50] Thus, we observe that Hayek played the instrumental role in persuading Director to go to Chicago and in making the Volker project happen; furthermore, Friedman did not play any equivalent role. Director had written Hayek: "Milton Friedman may be in touch with you. I talked with him briefly; he is no longer as enthusiastic as he was, it may be because of his reaction to the practical implications for me."[51] This action, we argue, demonstrates Hayek's indispensable and pivotal role in the creation of the Chicago School.

Hayek then contacted Luhnow and informed him that arrangements had once again been reversed, insisting that Chicago was the best place and Director was the best man for their job, in spite of Simons's death. Moreover, Hayek alerted Luhnow that Allen Wallis intended to move from Stanford to Chicago: "Mr. Wallis, incidentally, would seem to me to be the obvious person to replace Henry Simons on the Managing Committee."[52] Subsequently, Katz wrote Luhnow, and Luhnow later responded:

> William Volker Charities Fund, Inc., accepts Dr. Hayek's proposal and we are prepared to contribute $25,000 per annum for three years in the course of which this study is to be completed. In addition, we agree to contribute a further amount of not more than $10,000 per annum for a period of two years to cover the salary of Mr. Director for the period of two years after the investigation is completed. Also we agree to defray the expenses of the members of the Advisory Committee as they are brought to Chicago for a discussion of this study, this also to include the expenses of Dr. Hayek for any trips he makes to Chicago in further supervision of this project.[53]

As soon as the show got on the road, Luhnow moved with alacrity to further assert his prerogatives over the Free Market Study by inserting some of his deputies into the process. After acceptance by Director and the official concurrence by the Chicago administration, Luhnow wrote Hayek: "We presume that the large Advisory Committee will be set up rather promptly and we believe that it should be well thought out and I would like to ask that Leonard B. Read and Loren B. Miller be included on this Advisory Committee." Luhnow also mandated that "the suggested Advisory Committee be submitted to Loren Miller for his examination before it is actually announced."[54] Luhnow thus ensured that men conforming to the Volker Fund's political philosophy would oversee the progress of the Free Market Study project, even from its outset. Hayek had no option but to agree.

Luhnow highly respected both Read and Miller; primarily because Luhnow, who sought to "keep control of organizations" he funded, shared the libertarian zeal and philosophical beliefs of both men. Luhnow regularly consulted Miller for advice about Hayek's endeavors. For instance, in early July of 1946,

Loren Miller had contacted Luhnow and expressed misgivings about the inclusion of Theodore Schultz on the Executive Committee. Luhnow concurred with Miller: "I have listened to comments of Schultz on the Chicago Round Table and I am inclined to agree . . . that he is not proper timber for the Executive Committee of a study of our sort."[55] Luhnow probably objected to what he considered lackluster libertarian enthusiasm in Schultz. Nevertheless, Hayek insisted that Schultz not be excluded: "If I am not mistaken somebody, contrary to Mr. Miller's view, had rather singled out Professor Schultz as the only reliable person of my group and I had then explained that he in fact was the one among them who I knew least, but that he was indispensable as head of the department of economics in Chicago. . . . But my impression is that he will be entirely neutral, although he may occasionally plead for compromises which I trust the other members of the committee will reject."[56] Luhnow later capitulated, and Schultz remained on the Executive Committee. Hayek, who clearly had felt that Friedman did not have a sufficiently influential connection with the Economics Department, insisted on including Schultz as an essential component of the committee. From 1946 onward, Hayek would often exert a commensurate strategic moderating influence wherever coalitions were being recruited to the neoliberal agenda, as in the Mont Pèlerin Society.[57]

In 1946, Leonard Read, a businessman and important figure in the postwar right, had obtained a loan from the Volker Fund to purchase property in Irvington, New York and create the Foundation for Economic Education (FEE), an organization the Volker Fund subsidized for many years.[58] Read tended to see the world in black and white, which was why he had earned Luhnow's trust: "There was no big tent in Read's world. There was only a core group of ideas. You could either take them or leave them . . . ." Not surprisingly, Read advocated an inflexible stratagem for defeating socialism: "to move beyond denunciation to 'upholding its opposite . . . expertly, proudly, attractively, persuasively' " (quoted in Hoover 2003, 188). Apparently, the late Simons was not judged sufficiently infused with political virtue for Read, because he would shortly criticize Simons's posthumously published *Economic Policy for a Free Society*:

> Some of us here have carefully gone over the galleys of "Economic Policy for a Free Society" by Henry Simons. We had hoped this was a piece we might assist in distributing, but it is so well loaded with the advocacy of collectivistic ideas, that it falls entirely out of our field. The book states many positions with which we are in agreement, but personally, I do not believe

that the cause of individual liberty and a free market economy will be aided by it. (Quoted in HPHI, Letter from Read to Director, November 24, 1947, box 58, folder William Volker Fund 1939–1948)

Once again, Hayek was called upon to smooth ruffled feathers and protect his fledgling project. He wrote Luhnow: "I am writing to draw your attention to Henry Simons' book, *Economic Policy for a Free Society* . . . it seems to me to represent the kind of attitude which must be taken if there is to be any prospect of preserving the competitive system and a free society generally . . . it is certainly in the spirit of that book that Director will conduct his investigation at Chicago."[59]

At this crucial juncture, we can observe the major protagonists engaged in intense negotiations as to what it would mean to launch a Chicago School of Liberal Economics. A number of things become apparent, which have been absent from previous historical accounts. First, it was the legacy of Henry Simons that was perceived to be at issue in the nascent formation. The mere fact of a seminar identifying itself as being "pro-free market" was not sufficient for concocting a credo to which all parties could subscribe. Second, Luhnow and the Volker officers were not mere pecuniary accessories to the rise of the Chicago School: they were hands-on players, determined and persistent in making every dollar count, supervising doctrine as well as organization. Third, all and sundry depended on Hayek to keep the project on an even keel: no one else on home ground seemed to possess as much intellectual gravitas or deft punctilio as Hayek. In particular, Frank Knight was nowhere to be seen in the archival records of these negotiations. But even with Hayek and Director pulling the strings, success was not a foregone conclusion.

After all, the stated objective was to produce an *American Road to Serfdom,* and this entailed something more than a minor adjustment of accent when transporting the text across the pond. The politics of postwar America presumed not only a powerful state, but also a configuration of powerful corporations whose international competitors had mostly been reduced to shadows of their former selves. In promoting "freedom," they were primarily intent on guaranteeing the freedom of corporations to conduct their affairs as they wished. Thus, the Volker Fund was not interested in bankrolling a classical liberal economic position resembling that of Henry Simons, for it did not adequately correspond to their objectives. American corporations did not fear concentrations of power and generally favored the existence of a powerful

Cold War state. It is our contention that the Volker Fund pushed for a reformulation of classic liberalism in the American context to conform to its Cold War antisocialist agenda.[60] The participants in the Free Market Study, and even eventually Hayek, would just have to learn to adjust to the emergent characteristic doctrines of neoliberalism.

Mont Pèlerin, Chicago, and the Postwar Construction of Neoliberalism

We cannot count the number of times one encounters a variation on the assertion that: "Frank Knight's main claim to fame is his undisputed position as the founder of the Chicago School of Economics."[61]

We indeed strenuously dispute this notion, on the basis of the information provided in the first section of this chapter. But beyond the factual error of mistaking Knight for the actual progenitors (Simons and Director and, most of all, Hayek), it is necessary to insist that identification of the founder of the Chicago School makes a profound difference to our understanding of the rise of neoliberal economics in the postwar period. We have our own personal doubts as to whether Knight could have successfully organized and orchestrated a weekend picnic,[62] much less a major transnational intellectual movement; but luckily that question need not be settled here. Rather, the misattribution of founder status to Knight has had two pernicious consequences: it has diverted attention away from the fact that the inauguration and establishment of the Chicago School constituted just one component of a much more elaborate transnational institutional project to reinvent a liberalism that had some prospect of challenging the socialist doctrines ascendant in the immediate postwar period. It also, unfortunately, muddies the conceptual outlines of the tenets of this resulting neoliberalism, such that a lucid comprehension of its economic and political infrastructure becomes effectively impossible.[63] In order to dispel the confusion, we need briefly to revisit the environs of Mont Pèlerin.

Once we acknowledge Friedrich Hayek's pivotal role in getting the Chicago School up and running by the fall of 1946, and then turn our attention to the first meeting of the Mont Pèlerin Society in Vevey, Switzerland, in April 1947, we can begin to appreciate the extent to which the dual start-ups of the two landmarks of the history of postwar neoliberal thought were intimately connected.[64] The MPS is generally regarded as the central locus of the development of neoliberal doctrine in the postwar world. Yet we observe that

Hayek provided both the intellectual impetus and the organizational spade-work for both the Chicago School and the MPS, while the initial funding for the Swiss meeting came from European funds raised from corporate sources by Albert Hunold and from American support provided mainly by the Volker Fund. Luhnow sent Miller and Read to monitor the proceedings and to re-port back on the fruits of his investment. Loren Miller must have liked what he saw because beginning with the second meeting in 1949, he became a ma-jor supporter of the movement in his capacity as trustee of the Relm and Earhart Foundations (Hartwell 1995, 45). In keeping with its long-horizon ap-proach, Luhnow continued to provide airfare for selected Americans to attend the Mont Pèlerin conclaves for a decade, only terminating its support in 1957.[65] Tellingly, on one occasion, the Volker Fund expressed interest in find-ing an entire U.S. platform for a MPS meeting, which Hayek estimated would cost $20,000 to $30,000.[66] Significantly, Director helped arrange for these foundations to bankroll such ventures.[67]

That MPS and the Chicago School were joined at the hip from birth is ver-ified by the fact that most of the major protagonists were present at the cre-ation of both organizations: Director, Friedman, Wallis, and Knight.[68] When the MPS was legally constituted, it was registered as a nonprofit corporation in Illinois, with offices formally listed as located in the University of Chicago Law School; Allen Wallis served as treasurer during the initial phase of 1948–1954 (Hartwell 1995, 45). But more importantly, just as in the Free Mar-ket Study at Chicago, the areas of expertise covered by the MPS were con-sciously expanded well outside any notional boundaries of disciplinary eco-nomics in the 1940s as a technical subject. Law, religion, history, and scientific philosophy would be as relevant as economics in the search for a rejuvenated liberal creed. This was exemplified in the six core principles enunciated at the founding of MPS:

1. The analysis and explanation of the present crisis so as to reflect its es-sential moral and economic origins.
2. The redefinition of the state's functions so as to distinguish more clearly between the totalitarian and the liberal order.
3. Methods of reestablishing the rule of law and of assuring its develop-ment so that individuals and groups are not in a position to encroach upon the freedom of others and private rights are not allowed to be-come a basis of predatory power.

4. The possibility of establishing minimum standards by means not inimical to initiative and the functioning of the market.

5. Methods of combating the misuse of history for the furtherance of creeds hostile to liberty.

6. The problem of creating an international order conducive to the safeguarding of peace and liberty and permitting the establishment of harmonious international economic relations. (Hartwell 1995, 41–42)

This broad range of topics and disciplinary backgrounds found representation within MPS because both Luhnow and Hayek suspected that economics was not going to be reoriented in a liberal direction from within. What was required was (harkening back to the Simons quote) a novel academy of professional problem-solvers, "scrupulously detached from active politics and from factional affiliations [who would] subtly and unobtrusively guide or arbitrate political debate by their own discussions." It is perhaps difficult for contemporaries to appreciate the extent to which something like this closed debating society constituted through top-down organization was felt to be anathema to the liberal right in midcentury. As Milton Friedman joked in a letter to Hayek, "our faith requires that we are skeptical of the efficacy, at least in the short run, of organized efforts to promulgate [the creed]" (in Hartwell 1995, xiv). But far from a mildly piquant irony, the phenomenon of capitulation to the oxymoron of an "anarchists' convention" was the key defining moment in the rise of the neoliberal movement. The ultimate purpose of institutions such as the MPS and the Chicago School was not so much to revive a dormant classical liberalism as it was to forge a neoliberalism better suited to modern conditions.[69]

The classical liberalism of the eighteenth-century philosophers was a theory of natural tendencies in human nature, which might have been stifled or misdirected by misguided understandings of the natural order. It took as its benchmark the "obvious and simple system of natural liberty [which] establishes itself of its own accord," as Adam Smith put it in Book IV of his *Wealth of Nations*. It was this conception of liberty that Friedman cited as the prior "creed": a political doctrine so transparent and robust that one did not need either to organize special cadres to argue out its core tenets or to forge cabals to encourage its practice. The previous theorists of classical liberalism had exhibited a tendency to be either such inveterate optimists that they would perceive no need for concerted political and social organization in the interests of liberty, or else curmudgeonly elitists who would feel soiled by participation in actual political activity. The building of political movements and the innovation of lasting institutions for the purpose of spreading liberal doctrines was not a natural part of the heritage of either wing of the tradition.

The term *neoliberalism* was apparently coined at the Colloque Walter Lippmann in Paris in 1938 (Denord 2001; also Chapter 1 in this volume; Lemke, 2001, 204) to herald the appearance of a new orientation toward the previous liberal tradition. The term was also briefly entertained by Milton Friedman (1951) to indicate the ambitions of Chicago and Mont Pèlerin. Interesting here are the repeated evocations of neoliberalisms before the fact, since it is our impression that much of the content and practice of the new position was in fact progressively worked out over the period 1946–1980, but not exclusively at Chicago and MPS. The topology and ecology of the New Right is a topic of much historiographic dispute that we cannot begin to confront here.[70] However, we believe this chapter makes a small contribution to the clarification of neoliberalism by recounting the origins of its most famous Anglophone intellectual citadel at the University of Chicago.

A doctrine as protean as neoliberalism resists simple definition, as noted by Dieter Plehwe in the Introduction; but a few salient features especially relevant to Chicago can be sketched here. The starting point of neoliberalism is the admission, contrary to classical liberalism, that its political program will triumph only if it acknowledges that the conditions for its success must be *constructed*, and will not come about "naturally" in the absence of concerted effort. This notion had direct implications for the neoliberal attitude toward the state, the outlines of what they deemed a correct economic theory, as well as the stance adopted toward political parties and other corporate entities that were the result of conscious organization, and not simply unexplained "organic" growths. In a phrase, "The Market" would not naturally conjure the conditions for its own continued flourishing, so neoliberalism is first and foremost a theory of how to reengineer the state in order to guarantee the success of the market and its most important participants, modern corporations. Neoliberals accept the (Leninist?) precept that they must organize politically to take over a strong government, and not simply predict it will "wither away."

It would take us too far afield to adequately characterize the neoliberal project in all its glory, particularly as it came to be erected at Chicago and Mont Pèlerin after the 1950s.[71] However, Chicago neoliberalism transcends the classical liberal tension between the self-interested agent and the patriotic duty of the citizen by reducing both state and market to the identical flat ontology of the neoclassical model of the economy. (The situation prevalent at MPS was much more complex.)[72] "Freedom" was recoded to mean only the capacity for self-realization attained through individual striving for a set of necessarily un-explained (and usually interpersonally ineffable) prior wants and desires. Once this new lexicon was firmly set in place, it became impossible within this dis-course to regard any economic transaction whatsoever as coercive (Smith 1998, 80), which was a massive departure from prior classical liberal discourse.

We should not venture to assert that Hayek or Director or Friedman had a clear vision that this would become their prime political creed from the outset in 1946; nor would they mutually concur in each and every respect as to how the project was to be pursued in the following decades. A detailed history of their individual conversion experiences still remains to be written. Thus in describing the broad tenets of neoliberalism, we do not wish to be seen as immediately positing a monolithic doctrine or fixed set of commandments to which any as-pirant had to subscribe under pain of banishment. The purpose of the MPS and the Free Market Study was to debate possible trajectories for the future of liber-alism, not prematurely chisel them in stone. Nevertheless, some striking depar-tures from classical liberalism grew out of the MPS and/or the Chicago School, and these have direct bearing on the widespread impression that there subsisted political continuity with prewar liberals like Simons, or indeed, Frank Knight.

Notoriously, it was the Chicago School that innovated the idea that much of politics could be understood as if it were a market process, and therefore amenable to formalization through neoclassical theory. Politicians, it was claimed, were just trying to maximize their own utility, as were voters. Unfor-tunately, this doctrine implied that the state was merely an inferior means of attaining outcomes that the market could provide better and more efficiently; and that in turn led to a rather jaundiced assessment of the virtues and bene-fits of democracy.[73] This doctrine was then associated with a rather unflatter-ing assessment of the intellectual qualities of the populace; for instance, edu-cation was no longer understood as the price to be paid to build a competent democratic citizenry, but rather as just another commodity that should go to the highest bidder (Mirowski, forthcoming). Because the vast masses of the poor were not in a position to buy very much of it, it was imperative that an elite cadre of experts should exert itself behind the scenes to shape and execute public policy, leading to a strong elitist strain within neoliberalism.

The reverse side of flattening the state/market distinction was a repression of overt considerations of power, both within economics and in neoliberal po-litical theory. Corporations, in particular, were inevitably characterized as pas-sive responders to outside forces. In economics, the only market actor accused of misusing power was the trade union, which was uniformly treated as illegitimate, whereas any other instance of market power, as in the case of monopoly or oligopoly, was either treated as harmless and temporary or attributed to some nefarious state policy (Van Horn, Chapter 6 in this volume). The unfocused character of power helped ratify their convenient popular notion that the neoliberals were bravely pitted against entrenched elites, little freshwater Davids to the bicoastal Goliath/Leviathan, appealing to their restive libertarian wing by making it seem they were not themselves mouthpieces for certain powerful interests. American economics had thus become well and truly politicized, while spokesmen like Friedman and Stigler would persist in claiming that it managed to exist poised outside of political discourse, partaking instead of the otherworldly virtues of science.

Knight, and possibly Hayek prior to the early 1950s, had decided that "science" was having a nefarious intellectual influence that threatened market liberties.[74] But Wallis and Friedman and their Chicago followers soon came to realize that it was a deadly error to set one's political commitments as pitted against science in the era of the Atomic Bomb. Their embrace of statistics and their evocations of the mystique of science thus became one of the major neoliberal calling cards of the Chicago School. This, in turn, led to one manifestation of the engineering mentality to be co-opted by the neoliberal right, in that ambitious schemes to reengineer the state from within (fixed money growth rules at the Federal Reserve; school vouchers to privatize public education; abolition of the draft; institutionalized corporate oversight of governmental medical and pharmaceutical regulation; flexible exchange rates between national currencies enforced by transnational regulators) tended to displace classical Burkean gradualism and conservatism. In a further imitation of natural science, freedom was redefined as a purely mechanical "choice" that could be exercised in each and every sphere of social life.

Road Kill in Chicago

Rather curiously, Hayek's relationship with the Chicago department he had done so much to help create also experienced some parlous twists and turns, just after he had succeeded in getting it up and running.

In May 1945, Hayek supposedly received and turned down "various offers of a permanent position in America."[75] Claude Robinson claimed he could secure a position at Princeton for Hayek (Hoover 2003). Hayek confided to

Röpke that he had turned these offers down because "I still feel my first duty is over here—though I do not know how long this feeling will survive in a position of which I am condemned to look at events without being able to do anything." Yet by the early months in 1947, Hayek strongly indicated that he wished to become a professor in the United States. His first choice was Princeton; his main reservation was the relatively meager salary. Hayek wrote Viner:

> [Most] teaching positions in the States are financially not attractive enough to compensate for the personal complications and extra financial burdens which a move to the States would in my case involve, while the various offers of a financially very advantageous character which I received while I was in the States were not of a kind I wished to consider. There might be some possibility that some of this money might be diverted to the Institute, although I do not particularly like the idea and also have some doubt whether it would still be available now my temporary notoriety is a matter of the past.[76]

After Hayek gained a feel for the nature of the prospect at Princeton, Luhnow and Robinson contacted Princeton on Hayek's behalf. However, Princeton refused to hire Hayek on such terms as they offered: "In the past, the Institute has not accepted, and in the future it probably cannot properly accept, funds as specifically allocated by the donors as would be implied by your offer." Hayek complained to Viner, who responded, "I think you are going to run into the same situation at any of the respectable institutions."[77]

Luhnow then approached Hutchins about hiring Hayek at Chicago. The possibility was raised of a position within the Economics Department. The deliberations occurred in the fall term of 1948, only two years after the launch of the Chicago School. The Economics Department, however, flatly refused to appoint Hayek. Friedman, by then an active member of the Economics Department, claimed to have had no say in the matter (Ebenstein 2001, 174), but we find this implausible. Others have noted Friedman's uncharacteristic defensiveness when queried about this incident (Caldwell 2004, 297n10). John Nef, who as chair of the Committee should have known the particulars, gave the following retrospective account:

> The Economics Department welcomed his connection with Social Thought, although the economists had opposed his appointment in Economics for years before largely because they regarded his *Road to Serfdom* as too popu-

lar a work for a respectable scholar to perpetrate. It was all right to have him at the University of Chicago so long as he wasn't identified with the economists. (Nef 1973, 237)

Ironically, after Hayek had worked so assiduously to bring about the collaboration of liberal-minded members of the Law School, Economics Department, and Business School, not one of these units could find it in their interest to extend Hayek an offer. Instead, Hayek was relegated to the Committee on Social Thought. Hayek's appointment to the Committee would require only the personal initiative of Hutchins, since it was widely regarded as his bailiwick. In fact, Hutchins met Luhnow in Kansas City to discuss the matter. Luhnow wrote:

> Among other things he asked us directly if we would have any interest in having you established at the University of Chicago. Our reply was that under certain conditions . . . meaning without too heavy a teaching load so that the major portion of your time could be devoted to research . . . we felt you could be interested and that the Volker Charities Fund would be interested in supporting your efforts at Chicago. You will probably hear direct from the University before long.[78]

Hayek eventually accepted the Volker-funded position in the Committee of Social Thought in 1950. Even though he had not received a position in the Economics Department, he nonetheless was paraded as a figurehead of the New Chicago to business magnates, invited to Hutchins's house to dine and deipnosophize with them. The neoliberal project was being advertised as philosophizing in full swing at Chicago, and, at least initially, Hayek was its public face.[79] Later, in August, Hayek remarked to his private secretary Charlotte Cubitt that he was forced from now on "to do everything for money" (quoted in Hoover 2003, 195). In retrospect, what else could he have expected?

Friedman Hits the Road

Aaron Director was hired, the Free Market Study was launched, and even Hayek ended up at Chicago, but what about the anticipated end product? The original *Road* was not just getting patched; some genuinely novel doctrines were being cooked up in the cement mixer, and therefore the completion date of the construction project kept getting delayed. We believe the more the makeover of Chicago economics succeeded, the less insistent became the belief that the whole project was about the popularization of a distinctly Hayekian doctrine. This perhaps explains why such an unlikely protagonist finally made good on the Volker contract.

For putative believers in the sanctity of contract, the Chicago cadre was amazingly cavalier about the terms of their agreement. This was no simple imperative to produce a text on time and within budget, or so it seemed; there were no penalties for default. Most notably, Aaron Director did not fulfill his original contractual obligation to finish the *American Road* by the spring of 1952, nor did he ever. Yet it is important to note that the Volker fund did not withdraw its funding out of dissatisfaction with Director; nor was Director expelled from Chicago for violating the original terms of his employment. Here we observe that, at least for the Chicago players, politics proved stronger than "the market." This is not to suggest that the Volker Fund was lax in applying pressure on Director. On several occasions, Hayek wrote letters to Luhnow to allay his worries that the project had gone astray. For example, near the close of the 1940s Hayek wrote Luhnow: "While I have not actually seen any of Mr. Director's manuscript I had many long and highly interesting discussions with him and have no doubt that he is doing very interesting work and has made good progress on his book. I don't think you or I need to regret the choice we made."[80] Moreover, on one occasion, Knight informed Hayek that he did not believe that the Volker Fund would purchase Director's airline ticket to attend the MPS meeting in Europe because of their dissatisfaction with Director's progress on the book. Nevertheless, the Volker Fund took the long view and helped Director and other Free Market Study members to revise the classical liberal doctrine and propagate the result through both technical and popularized outlets. Thus, in spite of their contractual failure in 1952, Director and the Free Market Study had pleased the Volker Fund in other ways, as evidenced by its continued largesse. And Volker's patience was eventually rewarded. Not Hayek, not Director, but Milton Friedman finally made good on the Free Market project, albeit a decade late.

Capitalism and Freedom, a corporate neoliberal version of *Road to Serfdom,* appears to have finally provided Luhnow with the book he had arguably paid for many times over. The Preface to the book reveals it is a Volker product through and through, although it neglects to mention the Free Market Study, or indeed, any of the rest of events we have related herein. The fact that the author was Friedman, and that publication took so long, reveals the patience, flexibility, and tenacity of the Volker Fund in pursuit of their political objectives. Not only did they get a document that recast conservative politics in a mold much different from that pioneered by Henry Simons, but also one that Luhnow would find more salubrious.

Interestingly, the subsequent history of *Capitalism and Freedom* shows that Friedman never suffered the supposedly deleterious consequences of stooping to popularization that were said to have dogged Hayek's career. This suggests that it was the *content* of the book rather than the mere fact of being low-balled toward the general public that was the prime determinant of its success. If anything, the 1962 book is far more simple-minded than its original inspiration. It claims that "economic freedom is an end in itself" (p. 8), only to absolve itself of ever having to define "freedom" (p. 26). In contrast to *Road,* it makes no effort to conduct a dialogue with socialists, nor indeed anyone else who might disagree with it. Politics is treated as either a market phenomenon or a pathetic joke, with nothing in between: for instance, it has the *chutzpah* to cite McCarthyism as "another example of the market in promoting freedom" (p. 20). "The wider are the range of activities covered by the market, the fewer are the issues on which explicitly political discussions are required" (p. 24). Friedman's corporate sponsors would certainly cheer that sentiment; but they would like his treatment of corporations even better. Market power was simply waved away with the Friedmanite recourse to the notorious doctrine of the *as if:* "I have become increasingly impressed with how wide is the range of problems and industries for which it is appropriate to treat the economy as if it were competitive" (p. 120). Monopoly, should it exist, is blamed on the government and is deemed to be relatively harmless. Patents are deemed not to be monopolies simply because they participate in the definition of property rights (p. 127). There is no such thing as a social or political responsibility of corporations (p. 133), and as a special bonus thrown to his patrons, Friedman proposed that the corporate income tax be abolished (p. 132). The education industry, he said, should be privatized, which includes spinning off ownership of those ridiculous state universities (p. 99). (It was a good thing the Free Market Project was sited at a private university!)

Crude argumentation of this ilk proved wildly popular in the American arena, as evidenced by the fact that the book has never gone out of print. Friedman accomplished what Hayek never did and what Director was apparently incapable of doing. The *Road to Serfdom* is an intricate and subtle tract compared to its confident bromides. But the major difference is that *Capitalism and Freedom* wore its own provenance on its sleeve: it was *proud* to be the work of an intellectual for hire, because all human discourse was essentially just a sequence of disguised market transactions:

> For advocacy of capitalism to mean anything, the proponents must be able to finance their cause. . . . Radical movements in capitalist societies . . . have typically been supported by a few wealthy individuals . . . a role of inequality in wealth in preserving political freedom that is seldom noted. (1962, 17)

A better testimonial to Luhnow could not be imagined.

Notes

This chapter received no outside funding or support, a fact bearing some relevance to its thesis. If anything, it has received unremitting discouragement at the hands of economists too numerous to mention. We would like to thank the following for their comments: Bruce Caldwell, Duncan Foley, Bernhard Walpen, Dan Hammond, Jamie Peck, and Roger Backhouse. Dieter Plehwe has helped us in ways too numerous to remember.

Archival Sources

GSPR   George Stigler Papers, Regenstein Library, University of Chicago
HPCU   Harold Hotelling Papers, Columbia University Archives,
HPHI   Friedrich Hayek Papers, Hoover Institution, Stanford University
HPRL   Robert Hutchins Papers, Regenstein Library, University of Chicago
KPRL   Frank Knight Papers, Regenstein Library, University of Chicago
MAHI   Fritz Machlup Papers, Hoover Institution, Stanford University
MPHI   Mont Pelerin Society Papers, Hoover Institution, Stanford University
SPRL   Henry Simons Papers, Regenstein Library, University of Chicago
TSPR   Theodore Schultz Papers, Regenstein Library, University of Chicago

1. For some of the details of Hayek sojourns in American between 1945 and 1950, see Hoover (2003, 184–197); for general biographical background, see Ebenstein (2001) and Caldwell (2004). The quote from his speech is taken from a copy in the Hayek Papers [henceforth HPHI] (box 106, folder 8, 15).

2. HPHI, Loren Miller to Allen B. Crow, April 24, 1945, box 58, file: William Volker Fund 1939–1948; Hayek (1994, 127). There is as yet no solid scholarly history of the Volker Fund; but see Piereson (2005).

3. In this letter we also learn that Luhnow offered to pay for a private secretary-research assistant for Hayek (HPHI, Hayek to Luhnow, May 3, 1945, box 58, file: William Volker Fund 1939–1948).

4. At this point, neither Director nor Friedman was a member of the Chicago faculty. Further discussion of the whereabouts of the individual participants, and reasons to believe Friedman and Director were involved at this early stage, can be found in Van Horn (2007).

5. See, for instance, Ashmore (1989, 269), where Hutchins is quoted as observing by July 1946 that "we have the most conservative economics department in the world." The curious motivations behind Robert Hutchins's participation in these events will require the further attention of historians, something that we cannot accord it here.

6. SPRL, Hayek to Simons, August 22, 1945, box 8, file 9. In 1939, Henry Simons had moved from the Economics Department to the Law School to teach "Economic Analysis and Public Policy." The typical explanation for Simons's appointment recounts a fierce dispute between the irascible Frank Knight and determined Paul Douglas (Kitch 1983; Stigler 1988). In this account, Douglas asserted that Simons was a lackadaisical scholar, and Knight objected and claimed Simons as his intellectual progeny. Eventually, Douglas relented, and Simons later received his Law School appointment, an appointment that may have materialized because, according to Kitch (1983), in 1939 the Law School had just initiated a special four-year legal program wherein high school graduates intending to practice law entered Chicago as undergraduates, and Simons helped ensure they received a broad-based social science education. It appears that the residual hostility in the Economics Department and the alteration in the curriculum of the Law School account for Simons's external appointment.

7. SPRL, Simons to Hayek, April 14, 1939, box 3, folder 40. The subsequent quote comes from SPRI, Hayek to Simons, December 1, 1934, box 3, file 40.

8. From SPRL, Hayek to Simons, December 1, 1934, box 3, file 40.

9. It will soon become important for our story to realize that Simons's uncompromising vision of classical liberalism as opposition to power in all its guises later proved an embarrassment to the subsequent neoliberal Chicago School. De Long (1990) provides an incisive critique of the later misrepresentation of Simons by later Chicago economists. Charles Hardy (1948) also provides a useful brief overview of Simons's work.

10. Hayek reported: "[Henry] was so much the intellectual centre of the group I had in mind" (HPHI, Hayek to Luhnow, June 25, 1946, box 58, William Volker Fund 1939–1948). We must stress that at this juncture the initiative did not come out of the Economics Department, a point central to the larger thesis of this chapter.

11. SPRL, Hutchins to Simons, July 14, 1942, box 8, file 11.

12. SPRL, Hutchins to Simons, November 5, 1943, box 3, file 58.

13. SPRL, October 6, 1945, box 8 file 9. Oskar Lange, the economist star of the Cowles Commission in the later 1930s and an avowed socialist, resigned his position at

Chicago in 1945 to return to his native Poland. Before leaving, Lange handpicked his successor to run Cowles to be Jacob Marschak. Incidentally, Friedman and Stigler were interviewed for posts in the Economics Department the following spring, but only Friedman was hired. The circumstances surrounding the hiring of Friedman in 1946 also require further attention that we cannot devote to it here.

14. Possibly Simons and Hutchins shared this propensity because Friedrich Lutz had been Hutchins's economics instructor: "I will have you know that Mr. Lutz and Miss Kyrk were my economics teachers" (HPRL, Hutchins to Simon Leland, May 12, 1942, box 83, folder 8).

15. KPRL, box 1 addenda, folder 3; Dzuback (1991, 197). The remaining burghers included Ronald S. Crane, Avery O. Craven, E. J. Kraus, and Sewall Wright. For more, see Dzuback (1991) and McNeill (1991). Director later reminisced: "Hutchins was not liked in the economics department" (in Kitch 1983, 176).

16. John Nef wrote to Knight: "Is it not a fact that your whole campaign is motivated by animus against the Committee on Social Thought, though you dare not mention it . . ." (TSPR, April 26, 1944, box 53, folder: "general university material").

17. SPRL, Simons to Viner, undated, box 8, file 7.

18. SPRL, undated, Memorandum I, box 8, file 9.

19. This is part of our case that the supposed continuity of the post–1946 Chicago School with the positions of Knight and Viner has been misleading. In the summer of 1947 Viner "refused an invitation to join the Mont Pèlerin Society, disdaining activity for 'political purposes' " (Hoover 2003, 190), and Viner later revealed he had little to do with the Chicago School that formed in 1946 (Patinkin 1981, 266). In light of this evidence, even though Viner was present at the initial meeting at Chicago and if Hayek hoped to implicate him in other schemes, Viner did not participate and most likely would not have taken part in subsequent events, had he not decamped to Princeton in 1946. This constitutes one of our major claims that the purported continuity of the Chicago School across the 1946 divide is mistaken.

20. SPRL, Simons to Hayek, May 18, 1945, box 8, file 9.

21. SPRL, undated, box 8, file 9. All of the following quotes come from Memorandum I, unless otherwise indicated. One should not interpret this as full agreement between the mentioned parties, but rather evidence of Simons promoting Chicago in ways he knew to be only partly faithful to events on the ground.

22. Wallis, after running the Applied Mathematics Panel at Columbia during the war, which included Friedman, Stigler, and Savage among its participants, was recruited to teach statistics at Stanford for the academic year 1945–1946, only to move to the Chicago Business School in the fall of 1946. See HPCU, box 6.

23. For biographical information, see Coase (1999) and Stigler (2005).

24. "I first met Professor Hayek while on a visit in England in 1938. However, as a student of economics, I have been familiar with Hayek's work for at least fifteen years . . . I consider Hayek's ideas worth projecting anywhere where there is free dis-

cussion and especially in the United States" (Director to Croswell Bowen, July 12, 1945, MAHI, file "Hayek").

25. Simons described Director's residence in a letter to Lutz: "You should spend a night or week-end [at Director's place]—as I know he'd want you to if his house was not momentarily full of parasitic Chicago friends like me" (SPRL, June 26, 1945, box 4, file 23). Incidentally, Simons closes: "P.S. Frank Graham and [Frank] Fetter may have some useful ideas for our conspiracy!"

26. SPRL, Simons to Hayek, July 2, 1945, box 8, file 9 and HPHI, Director to Hayek, July 2, 1945, box 73, folder 14 (emphasis added).

27. All quotes in this paragraph are from SPRL box 8 F 9, Hayek to Simons, August 22, 1945.

28. HPHI, Hayek to Luhnow, August 15, 1945, box 58, file: William Volker Fund 1939–1948.

29. August 1945, SPRL, box 8, F 9.

30. Although we cannot describe it here, the project encompassed both intellectual and political forms of mobilization. For examples, see Plehwe and Walpen (2005).

31. HPHI, Luhnow to Hayek, September 7, 1945, box 58, folder: William Volker Fund 1939–1948.

32. SPRL, Hayek to Hutchins, box 8, folder 9.

33. SPRL, September 4, 1945, box 8, file 9.

34. SPRL, Simons to Hutchins, October 6, 1945, box 8, folder 9. Simons had been urging the Economics Department to hire Stigler and Friedman since 1944: "Stigler and Hart we need now or very soon. Friedman should be 'kept on the shelf,' against the contingency of our having to replace Lange or Marschak, or against the possibility of Mr. Cowles offering funds for another major joint appointment" (SPRL, Simons to Leland, November 17, 1944, box 8, file 11). There is no evidence that Simons had the support of the Cowles Foundation in this plan. However, one letter suggests that Simons sought to diminish the influence of Cowles in the Economics Department. In August 1945, Simons writes: "If Lange is leaving, we should go after Milton Friedman immediately. It is a hard choice between Friedman and Stigler. We should tell the administration that we want them both." (SPRL, Simons to Leland, August 20, 1945, box 8, file 9). It appears that Simon forwarded a copy of the latter letter to Hutchins.

35. "I have contacted Dr. Hutchins today so that a definite commitment will come to you shortly from the University of Chicago and from Stanford University as well" (HPHI, Luhnow to Hayek, January 28, 1946, box 58, William Volker Fund 1939–1948) and HPHI, July 20, 1946, box 58, William Volker Fund 1939–1948.

36. HPHI, May 3, 1946, box 58, William Volker Fund 1939–1948.

37. The Volker Foundation later instituted the "Antitrust Project" at the Law School under the guidance of Director, upon the model of the Free Market Project described herein. This is further explored in great detail in Van Horn (2007) and in Chapter 6 of this volume.

38. Quoted in Gruber (1995, 265). Hutchins had a history of trying to start up externally funded politically oriented think tanks at Chicago. For instance, in consort with Paul Hoffmann, he had unsuccessfully attempted to nurture an "American Policy Commission" in 1941 (Raynor 2000, 181).

39. The complicated ecology of wartime Chicago is discussed in Rutherford (forthcoming) and Mirowski (2002).

40. The Volker Fund budget included funds to pay for visiting professors and like expenses. Director made good use of this capacity in the "Anti-trust Project" he ran at Chicago. On this, see Van Horn (forthcoming).

41. HPHI, Hayek to Luhnow, May 23, 1946, box 58, file: William Volker Fund 1939–1948. There are a number of documents bearing the names of different authors, which purport to outline the same Free Market Project. However, it is probable that the scheme of May 1946 was roughly identical to the one Director drew up in 1945.

42. See TSPR, May 23, 1946, box 39 (addenda), folder: Free Market Study. This more closely approximated Hayek's position on monopoly than it did Simons's position. This is discussed in greater detail in Van Horn (2007).

43. TSPR, May 23, 1946, box 39 (addenda), folder: Free Market Study.

44. Ibid.

45. HPHI, box 58, William Volker Fund 1939–1948.

46. HPHI, Hayek to Luhnow, June 25, 1946, box 58, William Volker Fund 1939–1948.

47. HPHI, June 31, 1946, box 58, William Volker Fund 1939–1948.

48. HPHI, June 28, 1946, box 58, William Volker Fund 1939–1948.

49. HPHI, July 1, 1946, box 58, William Volker Fund 1939–1948 and HPHI, July 10, 1946, box 58, William Volker Fund 1939–1948. This letter reveals that Hayek's acquaintance with Friedman came late in the process and that he had not been considered the primary partner in the project.

50. HPHI, July 15, 1946, box 58, William Volker Fund 1939–1948. Unfortunately, we do not know the exact source of Director's hesitation; one plausible explanation might be that Director feared this project might taint his career in the same way that the *Road to Serfdom* had tainted Hayek's, making future academic employment difficult in an American academic milieu. Indeed, this was the interpretation of John Nef (1973, 237). Another plausible explanation might be that Director felt some misgivings about returning to the University of Chicago because in 1934 an animus in the Economics Department toward his outspoken libertarian views may have played some role in prompting him to leave.

51. HPHI, July 1, 1946, box 58, William Volker Fund 1939–1948.

52. HPHI, July 20, 1946, box 58, William Volker Fund 1939–1948.

53. HPHI, July 29, 1946, box 58, William Volker Fund 1939–1948.

54. HPHI, Luhnow to Hayek, August 16, 1946, box 58, folder: William Volker Fund 1939–1948. Miller was a director of the Civic Research Institute in Detroit at the time.

55. HPHI, Luhnow to Hayek, August 16, 1946, box 58 folder: William Volker Fund 1939–1948. On Schultz's career, see Burnett (1980).

56. HPHI, August 26, 1946, box 58, folder: William Volker Funds 1939–1948.

57. This is discussed in detail in Walpen (2004); and Plehwe and Walpen (2005). We are claiming here that Hayek was especially sensitive to the interpersonal dynamics of building political coalitions in a way that many of the stalwarts of the Chicago School were not, and not that he was especially open to diversity of thought as a *sine qua non* of a liberal position, as was the case with, say, John Stuart Mill.

58. Gary North, a previous Volker staff member, refers to FEE as the granddaddy of all libertarian organizations (see "Leonard E. Read's Small Tent Strategy," www.lewrockwell.com/north/north117.html, last accessed October 13, 2008). In this article, North also portrays the powerful influence Read had on the liberal movement and his adamant, uncompromising philosophical stance. For more on Read, see Nash (1976) and Laurent (2006).

59. Hayek Papers, Hayek to Luhnow, December 8, 1947, box 58, folder: William Volker Fund 1939–1948.

60. Although the Volker Fund took measures to ensure that its agenda remained uncompromised in organizing the Free Market Study proposal and project, the oversight by no means ceased in other ways after the Free Market Study began. The interventions of the Volker staff at the University of Chicago after 1946 are too numerous to be covered in this chapter; see, however, Van Horn (2007).

61. Sally (1997, 123). For instance: "The central figure in the founding of the [Chicago] School was Frank H. Knight" (Hartwell 1995, xix). It is not a fallacy found only on the right: "It was Knight more than any other economist who was instrumental in creating an atmosphere at Chicago conducive to the production and dissemination of libertarian disciples" (Tilman 2001, 1).

62. "Knight was not the easiest chap to live with . . . everything was absurdly simple or simply absurd" (Samuelson 1991, 537).

63. Many previous attempts to inquire into the philosophy of Chicago School members have led into dead ends by neglecting the neoliberal imperative. See, for instance, Samuels (1976); Paqué (1985); Frazer (1988); Hirsch and de Marchi (1990); Teles (2008); and Tilman (2001). We cannot conduct a point-by-point comparison of Knight's doctrines with those of the later Chicago School in this chapter, although such an exercise would reveal the distance between their conceptions.

64. The sanctioned internalist history by Hartwell (1995) is distinctly uninformative about such intellectual and social matters. More serious historical work is beginning to appear, such as Walpen (2004); Plehwe and Walpen (2005); and Laurent (2006).

65. See Luhnow to Hayek, November 15, 1956, HPHI, box 58, folder: William Volker Fund.

66. To this proposed occasion, which would be hosted at the Westchester Country Club, New York, and which would "offer proximity to a number of places which would make an interesting 'tour,'" the Volker Fund would have promised at least

$5,000 (HPHI, Cornuelle to Hayek, May 7, 1951, box 58, folder: William Volker Fund 1949–1952).

67. HPHI, box 73, folder 14. Simons had initially helped Hayek become better acquainted with representatives of the American foundations, such as the Rockefeller Foundation, for helping with the promotion of his international society: "The main purpose of this letter is to pass along a suggestion of my friend William Harrell, Business Manager of the University. He points out that your scheme for intellectual cooperation with German scholars and historiographers—your Acton-Tocqueville Society—is a 'natural' for support by the Rockefeller Foundation" (SPRL, Simons to Hayek, July 2, 1945, box 8, folder 9). Rockefeller had been intermittently subsidizing Hayek since his Vienna days at Mises's business cycle institute.

68. George Stigler, who would only join the Chicago Department in 1956, was also present. Stigler (2005) gives an account of this meeting, but misrepresents the purpose of the meeting as a "celebration of classical liberalism."

69. The insistence on the divergence between classical liberalism and neoliberalism follows an extensive literature, which we can only point to here (Burchell et al. 1991; Barry et al. 1996; Gray 1989; DeLong 1990; Smith 1998; Lemke 2001; Walpen 2004; Plehwe and Walpen 2006; Harvey 2005; Laurent 2006).

70. Some relevant citations are Nash (1976); Paqué (1985); De Long (1990); Lemke (2001); and Laurent (2006).

71. See, however, Walpen (2004); Laurent (2006); Van Horn (2007); and Mirowski, Postface in this volume).

72. Hayek's own trajectory diverged fairly far from this generalization. See Paqué (1985); and Walpen (2004). Among neoliberals at MPS, the acceptance of neoclassical economic theory as core doctrine took a very long time to become relatively accepted.

73. This hostility to democratic processes is discussed at much greater length in Amadae (2003); and Mirowski (2005). Nominally left-wing versions of neoclassical theory, such as that represented by Cowles, also tended to share this attribute. See Mirowski (2002, chapter 6).

74. Hayek's late conversion from denouncing scientism to flirting with naturalistic doctrines of mind and evolution are discussed in Mirowski (2002) and (2007)

75. HPHI, box 79, F 1, Letter from Hayek to Röpke May 27, 1945.

76. HPHI, box 56 F 2, July 13, 1947, Hayek to Viner.

77. HPHI, Robert Oppenheimer to Luhnow, May 25, 1948, box 58, William Volker Fund 1939–1940 and HPHI, July 30, 1948, box 58, William Volker Fund 1939–1940.

78. HPHI, Luhnow to Hayek, September, 1948, box 58, William Volker Fund 1939–1948.

79. The British ambassador to the United States reported in March of 1945: "Wall Street looks on Hayek as the richest goldmine yet discovered and are peddling his views everywhere" (quoted in Hoover 2003, 184). For example, Hayek and Hutchins entertained "Laird Bell, Chairman of the Board of Trustees of the University [of

Chicago]; John Ivy, an oil operator from Huston, Texas; Meyer Kestenbaum, President of Hart, Schaffner and Marx; William J. Kelly, President of Machinery and Allied Products Institute; Oscar Mayer, President of Oscar Mayer & Company, meat packers; John L. McCaffrey, President of International Harvester Company; and Hermon D. Smith, Vice-President of Marsh & McLennan, Insurance" (HPHI, Hutchins to Hayek, January 12, 1950, box 55, folder 1).

80. HPHI, March 10, 1950, box 58, folder 17.

References

Amadae, S. M. 2003. *Rationalizing Capitalist Democracy.* Chicago: University of Chicago Press.

Ashmore, Harry. 1989. *Unseasonable Truths.* Boston: Little, Brown.

Barry, Andrew, Osborne, T., and Rose, Nikolas (eds.). 1996. *Foucault and Political Reason—Liberalism, Neoliberalism and the Rationalities of Government.* London: UCL Press.

Bowler, Clara Ann. 1974. "The Papers of Henry C. Simons." *Journal of Law and Economics* 17(1): 7–11.

Bronfenbrenner, Martin. 1962. "On the 'Chicago School of Economics.'" *Journal of Political Economy* 70: 72–75.

Buchanan, James. 1991. "Frank H. Knight." In Edward Shils (ed.), *Remembering the University of Chicago.* Chicago: University of Chicago Press.

Burchell, Graham, Gordon, Colin, and Miller, Peter (eds.). 1991. *The Foucault Effect.* Chicago: University of Chicago Press.

Burnett, Paul. 1980. *The Visible Land: Theodore Schultz and the Liberal Turn in Agricultural Economics.* University of Pennsylvania, Ph.D. thesis.

Caldwell, Bruce. 2004. *Hayek's Challenge: An Intellectual Biography of F. A. Hayek.* Chicago: University of Chicago Press.

Clark, Fred. G. 1944. *How We Live.* Princeton, NJ: Van Nostrand.

Coase, Ronald. 1998. "Aaron Director." *New Palgrave Dictionary of Law and Economics.* London: Macmillan.

Coats, A. W. 1963. "The Origins of the 'Chicago School(s).'" *Journal of Political Economy* 71: 487–493.

Davenport, John. 1946. "The Testament of Henry Simons." *University of Chicago Law Review* 14: 5–14.

De Long, J. Bradford. 1990. "In Defense of Henry Simons' Standing as a Classical Liberal." *Cato Journal* 9: 601–618.

Denord, Francois. 2001. "Aux Origines du neo-liberalism en France." *Le Mouvement Social* 195: 9–34.

Director, Aaron. 1940. "Does Inflation Change the Economic Effects of War?" American Economic Review 30(1) Supplement: 351–361.

Director, Aaron. 1945. "Review of 'The Road to Serfdom' by Friedrich A. Hayek." *American Economic Review* 35: 173–175.

Director, Aaron. 1946. "Simons on Taxation." *University of Chicago Law Review* 14: 15–19.

Dzuback, Mary Ann. 1991. *Robert M. Hutchins*. Chicago: University of Chicago Press.

Ebenstein, Alan. 2001. *Friedrich Hayek*. New York: St. Martin's Press.

Emmett, Ross. 1998. "Entrenching Disciplinary Competence." In Malcolm Rutherford and Mary Morgan (eds.), *From Interwar Pluralism to Postwar Neoclassicism*. Durham, NC: Duke University Press, 1998.

Frazer, William. 1988. *Power and Ideas: Milton Friedman and the Big U-turn*. Gainesville, FL: Gulf/Atlantic.

Friedman, Milton. 1951. "Neoliberalism and Its Prospects." *Farmand* 17(February): 89–93.

Friedman, Milton. 1953. *Essays in Positive Economics*. Chicago: University of Chicago Press.

Friedman, Milton. 1962. *Capitalism and Freedom*. Chicago: University of Chicago Press.

Friedman, Milton. 1974. "Schools at Chicago." *University of Chicago Magazine* (Autumn): 11–16.

Gray, John. 1989. *Hayek on Liberty*. London: Routledge.

Gruber, Carol. 1995. "The Overhead System in Government-sponsored Academic Science." *Historical Studies in the Physical and Biological Sciences* 25(2): 241–268.

Hammond, J. Daniel. 1992. "Interview with Milton Friedman." *Research in the History of Economic Thought and Methodology* 10: 91–118.

Hardy, Charles Oscar. 1948. "Liberalism in the Modern State: The Philosophy of Henry Simons." *Journal of Political Economy* 56(4): 305–314.

Hartwell, R. Max. 1995. *A History of the Mont Pelerin Society*. Indianapolis, IN: Liberty Fund.

Harvey, David. 2005. *A Short History of Neoliberalism*. New York: Oxford University Press.

Hayek, Friedrich. 1994. *Hayek on Hayek*. Chicago: University of Chicago Press.

Hayek, Friedrich. 1994 (1944). *The Road to Serfdom*. Chicago: University of Chicago Press.

Hennecke, Hans Jorg. 2000. *Friedrich August von Hayek: Die tradition der Freiheit*. Dusseldorf: Verlagsgruppe Handelsblatt GmbH.

Hirsch, Abraham, and de Marchi, Neil. 1990. *Milton Friedman*. Ann Arbor: University of Michigan Press.

Hoover, Kenneth. 2003. *Economics and Ideology*. Lanham, MD: Rowman & Littlefield.

Hutchins, Robert M. 1934. "The Autobiography of an Ex-Law Student." *University of Chicago Law Review* 1: 511–518.

Kitch, Edmund W. (ed.). 1983. "The Fire of Truth: A Remembrance of Law and Economics at Chicago, 1932–1970." *Journal of Law and Economics* 26: 163–234.

Knight, Frank. 1999. *Selected Essays*. 2 vols., ed. by Ross Emmett. Chicago: University of Chicago Press.

Laurent, Alain. 2006. *Le Libéralisme Américain: Histoire d'un détournement*. Paris: Les Belles Lettres.

Leeson, Robert. 1998. "The Early Patinkin-Friedman Correspondence." *Journal of the History of Economic Thought* 20(4): 433–448.

Lemke, Thomas. 2001. "The Birth of Bio-politics: Michel Foucault's Lecture at the College de France on Neo-liberal Governmentality." *Economy and Society* 30: 190–207.

Levi, Edward H. 1966. "Aaron Director and the Study of Law and Economics." *Journal of Law and Economics* 9: 3–4.

McNeil, William. 1991. *Hutchins' University*. Chicago: University of Chicago Press.

Meltzer, Bernard D. 1966. "Aaron Director: A Personal Appreciation." *Journal of Law and Economics* 9: 5–6.

Miller, H. Laurence. 1962. "On the 'Chicago School of Economics.'" *Journal of Political Economy* 70: 64–69.

Mirowski, Philip. 2002. *Machine Dreams: Economics Becomes a Cyborg Science*. New York: Cambridge University Press.

Mirowski, Philip. 2005. "Sleights of the Invisible Hand: Economists' Postwar Interventions in Political Theory." *Journal of the History of Economic Thought* 27(March): 87–99.

Mirowski, Philip. 2007. "Naturalizing the Market on the Road to Revisionism: Caldwell on Hayek's Challenge." *Journal of Institutional Economics* 3: 351–372.

Mirowski, Philip. Forthcoming. *ScienceMart™*. Cambridge, MA: Harvard University Press.

Nash, George. 1976. *The Conservative Intellectual Movement in America since 1945*. New York: Alfred A. Knopf.

Nef, John. 1973. *Search for Meaning: Autobiography of a Nonconformist*. Washington, DC: Public Affairs Press.

Paqué, Karl. 1985. "How Far Is Vienna from Chicago?" *Kyklos* 38: 412–434.

Patinkin, Donald. 1981. *Essays on and in the Chicago Tradition*. Durham, NC: Duke University Press.

Piereson, James. 2005. "Funding a Movement." *The Insider*, Summer: InsiderOnline .org.

Plehwe, Dieter, and Walpen, Bernhard. 2006. "Between Network and Complex Organization: The Making of Neoliberal Knowledge and Hegemony." In Bernhard Walpen, Dieter Plehwe, and Gisela Nuenhoffer (eds.), *Neoliberal Hegemony: A Global Critique*. London: Routledge.

Raynor, Gregory. 2000. *Engineering Social Reform: The Rise of the Ford Foundation and Cold War Liberalism, 1908–59*. New York University, Ph.D. thesis.

Reder, Melvin. 1982. "Chicago Economics: Permanence and Change." *Journal of Economic Literature* 20: 1–38.

Rutherford, Malcolm. Forthcoming. "Chicago Economics and Institutionalism." In Ross B. Emmett, ed., *The Elgar Companion to the Chicago School*. Cheltenham: Edward Elgar.

Rutherford, Malcolm, and Morgan, Mary (eds.). 1998. *From Interwar Pluralism to Postwar Neoclassicism*. Durham, NC: Duke University Press.

Sally, Razeen. 1997. "The Political Economy of Frank Knight: Classical Liberalism from Chicago." *Constitutional Political Economy* 8: 123–138.

Samuels, Warren (ed.). 1976. *The Chicago School of Political Economy*. East Lansing, MI: MSU Press.

Samuelson, Paul A. 1991. "Jacob Viner." In Edward Shils (ed.), *Remembering the University of Chicago*, 533–547. Chicago: University of Chicago Press.

Samuelson, Paul A. 1998. "How Foundations Came to Be." *Journal of Economic Literature* 36(3): 1375–1386.

Simons, Henry C. 1948. *Economic Policy for a Free Society*. Chicago: University of Chicago Press.

Smith, Vardaman. 1998. "Friedman, Liberalism, and the Meaning of Negative Freedom." *Economics and Philosophy* 14: 75–94.

Stigler, George. 1974. "Henry Calvert Simons." *Journal of Law and Economics* 17(1): 1–5.

Stigler, George. 1988. *Memoirs of an Unregulated Economist*. New York: Basic Books.

Stigler, Stephen. 2005. "Aaron Director Remembered." *Journal of Law and Economics* 48: 307–311.

Teles, Steven. 2008. *The Rise of the Conservative Legal Movement*. Princeton, N.J.: Princeton University Press.

Tilman, Rick. 2001. *Ideology and Utopia in the Social Philosophy of the Libertarian Economists*. Westport, CT: Greenwood Publishing.

Van Horn, Robert. 2007. *The Origins of the Chicago School of Law and Economics*. Notre Dame University, Ph.D. thesis.

Walpen, Bernhard. 2004. *Die Offenen Feinde und Ihre Gesellschaft*. Hamburg: VSA Verlag.

PART TWO

Arguing Out Strategies
on Targeted Topics

5

The Neoliberals Confront
the Trade Unions

YVES STEINER

From the mid-1930s through the 1960s, trade-union participation in economic and industrial regulation policies, along with their political importance and membership, increased constantly in the Western world. Whether in the United States, Britain, or Switzerland, unions became a key actor in the pursuit of a concerted national income policy. In West Germany, unions became associated with the economic and political reconstruction of the country; to a lesser extent, the same thing occurred in France, in Belgium or in Italy. Everywhere in Western countries, the wage-bargaining process was recast as a fundamental element in a compromise between employees and employers, even in several cases under the supervision of the state.

The postwar generation of neoliberals gazed on this phenomenon with some alarm. In their opinion, arrangements between organized labor and capital paved the way to the institutionalization of a quasi-corporatist regime, which implied a terrible threat to the market economy and, in their view, a free society. That is precisely what one of the most prominent of neoliberal thinkers, Friedrich A. Hayek, argued in his famous pamphlet published in 1944, *The Road to Serfdom* (Hayek: 1993 [1944], 145–148). In fact, Hayek identified this issue as the thorniest question that neoliberals would have to tackle in the postwar world. Co-founder with Wilhelm Röpke and Albert Hunold of the Mont Pèlerin Society (MPS),[1] Hayek stressed the degree to which that question was important for the neoliberal movement at the founding meeting of the Society in April 1947. Indeed, after having deplored the "uncertainty and vagueness" of classical liberal ideas on union policy, Hayek delegated to the MPS the task of formulating "an appropriate program of labor or trade-union policy." As he insisted, "if there is to be any hope of a return to a free economy, the question of how the powers of trade-unions can be appropriately delimited by law as well as in fact is one of the most important of all the questions which we must give our attention" (Hayek 1949, 117).

Indeed, the MPS would undertake to address the trade-union issue on numerous occasions during the 1950s. According to Hartwell, this issue was the third most important theme covered by the MPS between 1947 and 1959.[2] More than twenty MPS members can be identified as actively discussing it during that period. It is also important to note that numerous neoliberal authors, many of them MPS members, published extensively on this topic in the 1950s.[3] Hence, this period appears to be crucial to understanding how neoliberals came to forge their discourse on unions. As the permanent debating society in charge of the restoration of liberal ideas in the 1950s (Plehwe and Walpen 1999; Denord 2002), the MPS seems to be a good place to begin an examination of the internal debates within neoliberal circles, particularly on the union issue. The MPS thus will serve as the focus of this chapter.

The Society was an intellectual arena in which theoreticians of particular schools of thought—mainly ordoliberalism, the Austrian School, and the Chicago School—exchanged and confronted each other's ideas. But the MPS was also a place to hobnob with some luminaries of the intellectual faction of the capitalist elites, persons in close contact with several highly influential businessmen (both in Switzerland and the United States) who supported the Society financially from its foundation.[4] Thus, MPS discussions often began with theoretical issues but rapidly moved on to practical issues in direct connection with the types of problems that the capitalists had to confront, such as the union question.

Using archival sources,[5] this chapter surveys these debates. It seeks to evaluate the extent to which MPS members succeeded in formulating, as Hayek pleads in 1947, "an appropriate program of labor or trade-union policy" during the 1950s. Contrary to what has often been asserted about early neoliberalism, we find in this period no agreement; no dominant consolidated position emerges on that question inside the MPS. In fact, MPS members who took the floor on this issue during the 1950s meetings turned out to be strongly divided between those who considered some form of arrangement between employers and trade unions beneficial, and those who, like Hayek, rejected it as a danger-ous departure from liberalism. To a large extent, the former constituted the majority until the mid-1950s: during this first period, these two rival neoliberal approaches on trade unions seem to have been regarded within MPS as merit-ing equal consideration, and hence being of equal importance. At the end of the decade, however, those who urged limitation of cooperation between orga-nized labor and capital became dominant in neoliberal circles.

The Sanguine Neoliberal Attitude toward Unions

At the end of the 1940s, one can roughly describe the dominant position on unions within the MPS as entertaining a not unfriendly stance toward them. At the outset, many MPS members were willing to argue that valuable coop-erative arrangements between trade unions and employers existed elsewhere, particularly in Europe. From their experience, it seemed that labor leaders could come to understand the ways that their own interests converged with those of their employers. Besides, it could be argued that a nationally central-ized wage-bargaining process resulted in certain political benefits for the capi-talist class. This faction argued that the unions' open-minded attitude might permit some form of inclusion in the conduct of the enterprise, at least in sev-eral specific areas such as social policy.

The influential Swiss economist and diplomat William E. Rappard was one of the more important MPS members who supported such views on la-bor. At that time, Rappard was the director of the prestigious *Geneva Institute of International Studies,* which invited Hayek, Mises, Röpke, and Rüstow, among others, to lecture on liberal policies during the 1930s.[6] Rappard was the author of important scholarly works on labor questions since the 1910s, in particular on labor legislation, and was a distinguished specialist of the Swiss industrialization in the nineteenth century (Rappard 1914). The diplomatic activities that occupied his time after World War I brought him in contact with Swiss elite circles. From that time onward, Rappard maintained close re-lations with several governmental officials and economic elites, especially with a most influential Swiss industrialist and diplomat, Hans Sulzer. When Swiss employers associations and unions negotiated the famous 1937 agreement (known as *La Paix du Travail*) that prohibited the use of strikes and public protests by unions, Rappard was a close observer who appreciated the usefulness of this pact. At the maiden 1947 MPS Conference, during the session on unions, Rappard openly supported the idea that such a pact could have been regarded as highly beneficial with reference to the Swiss case: "the [Swiss] labour leaders are closely tied up with the whole economic process. They were shown and convinced that wage rises, for instance, would be bad for the country as a whole and in the long run for the worker themselves." To Rappard, the MPS task should be "to educate the trade unions leaders, and members, to a conception of solidarity of employers' and employees' interests" (Graham 1947, 204). He concluded that "we should certainly not . . . disregard the things which *are* in the common interests of the employers and employees. Without a minimum of solidarity, no human society is possible" (Graham 1947, 210; emphasis by Rappard).

During this meeting, Rappard did not find himself isolated on this particular issue. Most European MPS participants were inclined to favor a collaborative attitude between employers and employees.[7] Furthermore, this perspective came in the short term to be dominant in the MPS. In 1949, for example, the Society opted to revisit the union issue again in a dedicated meeting (Steiner 2005). Interestingly, the main theme of debate turned out to be the participation of labor in the conduct of enterprise, something that presupposes the existence of an active partnership between the employer and the unions. Like Rappard in 1947, many MPS members were convinced that a program of labor leaders' education in the benefits and necessity of adhering to principles of a free society should be a cornerstone of a neoliberal agenda. German ordoliberals, such as Franz Böhm[8] and Leonhard Miksch,[9] promoted a paternalistic version of the agenda, one in which a modicum of indoctrination was necessary in order to "change the ideology of the workers" and to convince them to accept their vocation as the group on which the free society would have to be based (Böhm 1949, 2; Miksch 1949, 1).[10] However, Böhm foresaw the complication that an education in the foundational principles of the free society would equally tend to encourage their willingness to participate directly in the governance of such a society, and thus, in the guidance of business conduct (Böhm 1949, 3). The ideological integration of unions into the operation of the free society threatened to transgress the limits of their involvement in economic activities, and in particular, in the firm, the very heart of capitalist enterprise.

Not unexpectedly, other MPS members found this prospect unappealing. At the same meeting, other members sought to clarify to what extent they would allow unions to be involved in the conduct of the enterprise. For example, Karl Paul Hensel, another ordoliberal, proposed to codify the rights and duties of unions and employers in a sort of "industrial labor constitution." At that time as assistant to Walter Eucken, one of the founding fathers of ordoliberalism,[11] Hensel was very anxious to regulate the conflict between labor and capital at the point where it originated, that is, inside the enterprise, and therefore to improve the legal position of the trade unions, which he described as being as weak as possible in the German context. Thus, Hensel prognosticated that neoliberals might make use of this industrial labor constitution to abolish existing ". . . one-sided prerogatives" and to equalize ". . . the rights derived from property in material goods with those derived from the working power within an industrial enterprise" (Hensel 1949, 13); but also to institutionalize the claims of the laboring partners to the net income (Hensel 1949, 16) and the selection of managers (Hensel 1949, 17). Hensel also sought to channel the influence and participation of unions through the system of works councils. Interestingly, his proposals resembled in many respects the subsequent German co-determination system (*Mitbestimmung*). Hensel's enterprise-level representation of workers endorsed a very limited version of co-determination, however, compared to the much further reaching demands of Germany's trade unions of a democratic reconstitution of the capitalist economy. Union proposals for co-determination centered on trade-union influence on economic decision making beyond the enterprise at sector and macroeconomic levels (e.g., directing investment flows), for example (compare Deppe, Von Freyberg, and Kievenheim. 1969). Hensel's endorsement of a co-management of social affairs by worker elected councils at the enterprise level was close to the legal stipulations of the Mitbestimmungsgesetz of 1952, though Germany's trade unions eventually succeeded in undermining the efforts to limit trade-union influence to some extent by securing strong ties of individual works council members and the trade unions. Hensel instead aimed at constraining trade-union influence. He never referred to the concept of "co-determination" as such, and he counseled caution regarding the organization of joint labor-management committees that advise management on concrete business issues.[12]

Albert Hunold was not as reluctant as Hensel to appeal to a kind of solidarity (even he would never use such terminology) between employers and employees. During 1949, Hunold served as the MPS secretary and its main fundraiser, but he had also enjoyed close connections with Swiss elites since the 1930s.[13] With regard to European social policy, Hunold was tireless in denouncing increasing state intervention, particularly in Germany, Belgium, Holland, and Switzerland. Yet when it came to the issue of trade unions, he described as legitimate two different types of formal combination between employers and unions in social policy: the first one at the industrial level *(community of trade)*, the second at the firm level *(community of enterprise)*. In both cases, he believed that these combinations would tend to encourage and reinforce labor participation in the conduct of business. Union representatives, for example, would conduct surveillance on corporate management, especially on financial issues that would be closely connected with the enterprise social policy. Such arrangements would also provide a "fifth column in the enterprise itself . . . to the most extreme elements of the workers" (Hunold 1949, 3). Nevertheless, Hunold was convinced that the community of trade and the community of enterprise would have to be supported. As he said,

> both organisations, the internal managerial community of enterprise, as well as the corporate community of trade, could and should be used in order to create better understanding between labour and management, to create social peace. . . . Both organisations, if managed properly, could be a considerable counter-weight against state's social policy, against welfare-state which must be considered as one of the great danger of our time. (Hunold 1949, 5)

Sharing Hunold's concern was Stanley Dennison, an English economist who along with Hayek shouldered responsibility for preparing the whole 1949 meeting on labor participation.[14] As Dennison argued in his own paper, English joint labor-management control could be considered to be quite successful on one point. It had indeed proved an acceptable way to prevent the arbitrary intervention of the British Ministry of Labor in the conduct of business, which "contains a worst threat to our social order than does a good deal of monopoly in a labour market which is still essentially organised as a balance of opposing forces. . . . Here I find my sympathies in Britain with the trade unions however much their monopolistic tendencies, together with many of their policies, are to be deplored, in the main they are still, in Britain at least, one of our bulwarks against worse evils; and, paradoxically enough they are one of the few remaining props of a market economy in labour" (Dennison

1949, 10). As for Hunold, as long as it was sufficiently hedged round with limits, labor participation could be countenanced as a temporary expedient in order to prevent disruptive public interventions in the conduct of business, especially those considered as anathema from the neoliberal standpoint.

To a great extent, this neoliberal approach on unions was characteristic of the positions of ordoliberal thinkers like Franz Boehm, Goetz Briefs, or Carlo Mötteli in the 1950s (Böhm 1952; Briefs 1952).[15] To them, the "classical" form of unions had changed irreversibly after World War I in Europe, and perhaps since the mid-1930s, even in the United States. From then on, unions were considered to be fully recognized by the law, by employers, and by public opinion. They had attained the status of politically legitimate quasi-public institutions, with indispensable functions for the stability of the social order. The German language of "social partnership" between capital and labor attributed to unions a quasi-official place of honor in the economic process and, consequently, in its regulation. Briefs coined the term *befestigte Gewerkschaften* (fastened/stabilized unions rather than "well-entrenched"). Such a powerful position rendered it impossible to simply resist union demands for co-determination in postwar Germany, for example. Briefs warned that the co-determination system could be a first step on the road to a political and economic system ultimately ruled by the trade unions. His warnings against the "trade-union state" were prominently featured in *Frankfurter Allgemeine Zeitung*, for example, and served as a rallying point for the opposition against the trade-union agenda on co-determination. Briefs's extremely corporatist concept of the present social order foreclosed coercive state regulation (except for emergency circumstances), but insisted on a voluntary commitment of trade unions to their role as stabilized, and thus stabilizing, institutions. They should not try (in any way) to change the existing order as well as the existing relationship of social forces because this would automatically threaten their attained status as "fastened" (which means: respected) unions. Briefs believed that trade-union demands for co-determination as a concept of joint leadership of production constituted an attempt to fundamentally change the existing order. "Industrial democracy" would change the relationship of forces to the advantage of trade unions and would open the road to the "trade-union state." In this context, the defense of the free society had to be developed on two levels.

On the fundamental level, a more "friendly" attitude to the unions appeared to be a timely and judicious means to reinforce moderate labor leaders as against their comrades who wanted to radicalize workers' organizations. Educating those open to persuasion concerning the tenets of a free market society would be the preliminary perquisite of the neoliberal program. Once they were sufficiently indoctrinated, the next level would be to usher them into the antechambers of the conduct of enterprise. Nonetheless, their participation in the structures of management was understood as harboring all manner of dangers. Economically speaking, their interventions could disturb business investment—and thus, earnings—by substituting political criteria (maintaining employment, employee purchase power, etc.) for economic rationality. It would be easy to portray union participation as the Sorcerer's Apprentice, with the tendency to misallocation of resources inside the enterprise becoming a threat to the entire price system. Thus, it was taken as a necessary corollary that labor's participation in management had to be limited to social and personnel matters. Above all, safeguards would have to be in place to restrain their presence where their voices could disturb investment choice. All of these ideas, far from being purely theoretical abstractions, formed the ideological basis of the German employer associations' discourses on co-determination in postwar Germany and during the 1950s.

The Neoliberal Big Chill

The neoliberal version of a calculated companionship of mutual interest and integration between unions and employers had been dominant inside MPS circles since the end of 1940s. However, a few key MPS members refused to consider any such alliance as the correct attitude of a refurbished liberalism. Since 1944 Hayek, for example, strongly criticized a "deliberate collaboration between organized capital and organized labor" because it would be conducive to the growth of monopolies and detrimental for the larger community (Hayek 1993 [1944], 148). During the 1947 founding meeting at Mont Pèlerin, Hayek refrained from tackling the issue; but he persuaded his old Austrian compadre Fritz Machlup to stand as the main speaker of the session on unions (with Rappard intervening as well).[16] Hayek chose Machlup for his long experience with business organizations and his interest in industrial organization. During the social and political agitation of the Red Vienna, Machlup had served time as a businessman for his father, a minor cardboard-manufacturing industrialist. Until 1933, Machlup managed the family business (Ybbstaler Pappenfabriken) and extended its activities in Hungary (Elso Magyar Cartonlemezgyar). In 1927, Machlup became a prominent member of the Board of the Austrian Cardboard Manufacturers Cartel.

In the 1940s, Machlup had devoted sustained attention to the labor question, notably for the American Chamber of Commerce (ACC). In that capacity, he had sporadically lectured ACC members on industrial issues. In November 1946, he received an offer from William K. Jackson, ACC president and United Fruit Corporation chairman, to deliver a paper on wage determination to an ACC Economic Institute gathering. Jackson signaled: "we strongly believe that nothing today threatens our competitive economy more, at this particular time, than the superficiality with which we generally see the issues in our collective-bargaining controversies" (Jackson to Machlup, November 25, 1946, HIA FMP, 30.14). But Jackson also enlisted Machlup's help in changing current attitudes toward wage determination prevalent among ACC members. Indeed, the ACC was then divided between firms that had already accepted New Deal policies and labor practices with their consequences for the collective bargaining machinery and nonunion firms that had resisted such a trend. Thus, according to Jackson, this particular ACC meeting was intended to serve as a rallying point for nonunion enterprises, fortifying those who wanted to hear some protolibertarian voices on union policy.[17]

Prompted by Jackson, Machlup agreed to read a paper on "Monopolistic Wage Determination as a Part of the General Problem of Monopoly"[18] at the Economic Institute in January 1947 (Machlup 1947). In this paper, Machlup argued that American unions did not learn the hard lessons from the past: there was no evidence they were ready to moderate their wage demands. To the contrary, he raised the specter of the economic and political danger of spreading syndicalism and of a labor monopoly, in particular on control over real wages. He also looked askance at government regulation of wage rates resulting from collective bargaining. His proposals for reform were to break down large unions to smaller size (by prohibiting industrywide wage bargaining) and to prohibit state intervention during the wage-bargaining process. At the 1947 Mont Pèlerin Conference, Machlup essentially developed the same argument as that in his ACC pamphlet (Graham 1947, 202–203).[19] The only change in the presentation was a proposed extension of his analysis to the whole Western world. As in the United States, a free labor market was said to be nonexistent in England and in France because of state interventions. In both countries, legislation fosters a monopoly situation in favor of labor, and hence unions can manipulate wage determination. To restore full employment, Machlup suggests curbing labor monopoly power in four ways: educating union leaders, prohibiting state aid to unions, eliminating closed shop rules, and, in particular, downsizing the average union. The downsizing proposal, which Machlup considered politically feasible, sought to limit the union size to that of the plant level and to prohibit any combination between different unions.

Rappard's interventions were in fact a reaction against Machlup's speech. The Swiss economist reprimanded his MPS comrade for omitting the efficiency of existing relationships between employers and employees in European countries, especially in Germany and Switzerland. Rappard summarized Machlup's position as "strongly affected by US policy" (Graham 1947, 204). Machlup retorted by describing as "romantic" Rappard's vision of responsible union leaders restraining their wage increases simply because somebody had taken the time to educate them (Graham 1947, 215). Machlup was also troubled by those who placed their faith in industrial peace: "Industrial peace is something we should be afraid of, as it can only be bought at the cost of further distortion of the wage structure. I am most afraid of Professor Iversen's proposal for wage determination by State, and consider it to be the end of democratic government" (Graham 1947, 215). Other MPS members, though in the minority, also made efforts to challenge Rappard, Iversen, and their comrades.[20] For our present purposes, it will suffice to recount the case of Vernon Watts, who made the longest intervention during this session.

In 1947, Vernon O. Watts[21] was an economic adviser at the Foundation for Economic Education (FEE) in New York. Originally, he had not been invited by Hayek to the Mont Pèlerin Conference. However, an American businessman who helped to finance the conference, Harold L. Luhnow, imposed Watts and three other FEE staff members on Hayek and the meeting, as escorts for FEE boss Leonard Read. Since 1946, Luhnow had financed the FEE through his foundation, the Volker Fund. Other FEE financial supporters in that era constituted the hard core of nonunion firms, such as B. F. Goodrich, DuPont, General Electric, General Motors, or Sun Oil Company. From the 1940s onward, the FEE was one of the most active organizations devoted to promulgating free enterprise ideology in the United States. In the 1950s, the FEE devoted its efforts to discredit New Deal liberalism and to undermine the power and legitimacy of organized labor (Fones-Wolf 1994, 8; Jacoby 1997, 232, 242; 326–327n.17). During this period, Vernon Watts participated in this campaign by publishing articles and pamphlets, most notably a bitter critique of unions (Watts 1954).[22] In 1947, Watts ardently testified that "concentrations of economic power [are] necessary for incentive purposes" in case of capitalist firms, but interestingly, not for unions. The reason for the differential, wrote Watts, was that the unions have imposed their power by using legalized violence. As for Machlup, dismantling large unions was a matter of neoliberal necessity. And finally, Watts exhorted people like Rappard to forget "their liberal philosophy" and "absolute moral codes" in face of the terrible threat that unions constitute (Graham 1947, 211). Here we observe the kind of splits over practical policies that motivated the initial rejection of classical liberalism and underpinned the quest for a neoliberalism.

In 1947, Machlup and Watts's nascent position reflected the first halting steps of a neoliberal literature on unions toward the position that analyzed them in terms of monopoly power and delegitimated this labor monopoly power because it was established by legalized coercion. This important literature emerged in the 1950s, almost all of which was connected with the MPS or its Volker-funded affiliate, the FEE.[23] This literature appeared as the counterpart in economics of the concurrent political assault on American unions and those in business or in government that supported them. For example, these works promoted an extremely critical stance on the national wage-bargaining process, arguing that this machinery was just an attempt from unions combined with compromised employers to manipulate prices to the detriment of consumer sovereignty. What tended to get highlighted was the existence of an alliance between unions and employers that was viewed as an important departure from true liberalism. However, these attacks against union-employer alliances emerged in a context in which, contrary to the situation in Europe, American business was profoundly unorganized and divided on New Deal policies (Gordon 1998). Part of the neoliberal agenda was to draw stark lines between those who would count as being "compromised" and those who escaped unscathed. It was also a time when nonunion employers began a large assault against those in the business sector who had been seen to have collaborated too closely with unions.

Because of the way the lines were being drawn, it is not surprising that those who financially supported the antiunion economic discourses and those who operated through anticommunist organizations or free market institutions, like the FEE, turned out to be one and the same. It was the case for J. Howard Pew (Sun Oil Company) and Jasper E. Crane (DuPont), two major funders behind MPS activities. In the 1930s, both men initiated the earliest campaigns against the New Deal via the National Association of Manufacturers. Fiercely anticommunist, Pew and Crane invested in FEE and its campaigns in favor of free enterprise ideology (see Chapter 8 by Phillips-Fein in this volume). In 1947, Crane became a MPS member; Pew did as well in 1954. Both had been major donors to the MPS since 1958.

Inside the MPS, the position represented by Machlup or Watts on unions remained dormant until the end of the 1950s. Other MPS members such as William Hutt did take the floor during the decade in order to support a point of view similar to that of Machlup or Watts.[24] However, the situation changed dramatically at the Princeton meeting (1958), the first gathering of the Society at a university and the first held in the United States. This particular meeting was entirely financed by Jasper Crane and his business associates. Because of his pre-eminent role in financing the meeting, Crane sought to intervene massively in the meeting's program to the detriment of Hayek, who served more as a secretary than as an intellectual organizer of this meeting (Steiner 2007, chapter 4).

At Crane's bidding, Hayek organized a full session on the problems of unions, essentially based on the works of Sylvester Petro.[25] Indeed, far from a general session on unions, the talks were devoted mainly to Petro's recent book, *The Labor Policy of the Free Society* (1957), in which he denounced the fact that, as he saw it, American unions possessed too much legal power and threatened the existence of the free enterprise society. His denunciation was based on an historical analysis demonstrating that "coercive" union practices such as the union shop had been progressively integrated in the U.S. legal framework. Unions are legally protected when they act to oppress employees and employers, a situation that Petro describes as a union's "legal coercion." As in his 1957 book, Petro urged in his MPS paper drastic changes in then-contemporary U.S. labor law, in particular the dismantling of the Norris-LaGuardia Act of 1932[26] and the abolition of the National Labor Relations Board. Finally, Petro insisted that all of these suggestions "in their present form . . . are tailored to the here and the now—the United States in the mid-twentieth century. [But] I believe that they would *in general* fit fairly well the conditions in any developed market economy" (Petro 1958; emphasis by the author). As in the case of Machlup in 1947, the American experience was thought to be easily extrapolated elsewhere, when it came to neoliberal theory.

Also invited by Hayek and Crane to give his point of view on the question was Harold Gregg Lewis,[27] who pursued the same theoretical line as Petro (Lewis 1958, 5). According to Lewis, the monopolizing activities of American unions resulted in a wage increase of 5 percent or more each year. In his view, the inflation rate inevitably followed this trend. This "significant labour monopoly problem" illustrates the growing economic influence of unions that tended to be correlated with the growth of union membership after the mid-1930s. "The main cause [of both trends was] a change in public policy toward trade unions" (Lewis 1958, 1) where the turning point appeared to be the Norris-LaGuardia Act. In addition, this change in public policy encouraged "awful" union practices (discriminatory limitation on admission to union membership, closed shop, boycott, and even racketeering). Lewis deplored the fact that in economics no serious discussions had occurred on "labor monopoly, its causes and consequences, and the relation, if any, of labor monopoly to the unpretty features of unionism" (Lewis 1958, 3). Proposals to counteract these deleterious consequences were deemed necessary, and Lewis proceeded to explore some of them.[28] He suggested a vast legal reform program to reduce labor monopoly in order "to purge the law of its pro-monopoly features" (Lewis 1958, 6). He called for the elimination of the Norris-LaGuardia Act, the National Labor Relations Act (which provided the legal framework of the National Labor Relations Board), and the legislation, including minimum wage laws, designed to protect or promote labor monopoly. But even that draconian proposal did not seem sufficient to Lewis, who then proposed what he called a "*limitist approach*" in unionism matters: to prohibit all large-scale concerted action among employers and employees (Lewis 1958, 7). His proposals also encompassed intervention in the organization of unions and prohibition of membership in the union as a condition of employment at the plant level. All of these proposals should be considered as the reorientation of existing structures toward competitive unionism and, eventually, a freely competitive labor market.

Only one MPS member invited by Hayek (and Crane) disagreed with Petro and Lewis: the German ordoliberal Hans Ilau.[29] He contributed little more than a severe critique of Petro's book, and the key problem he isolated was that concerning inflation: Petro, as well as Lewis, could not comprehend why and how trade-union policy caused inflation (Ilau 1958, 1). In particular, Petro appeared to argue that coercion and intimidation were the main causes of inflation, to the exclusion of monetary aspects. By comparison with the United States, in West Germany coercion and intimidation were putatively less present—the closed shop was unknown, for instance—but inflationary effects seemed to occur nonetheless. Indeed, and particularly since the mid-1950s, West German unions had been very successful in their wage negotiations, without recourse to what others were calling coercion. But this success was not the primary source of inflation: "the rise of wages in Germany . . . has not been due to coercion by unions, but to the *favourable business conditions*. . . . Therefore it is more accurate to say that an inflationary situation caused this marked rise of wages than to say that the rise of wages caused an inflationary situation" (Ilau 1958, 3; emphasis mine). Ilau prognosticated that the first cause of an inflationary situation lay in a phenomenon of "imported inflation," which was a consequence of a too-low German exchange rate. "Therefore I think that monetary policy is a far more important factor for the value of money than labor-relations legislation" (Ilau 1958, 3). In such a context, Ilau disagreed with proposals for the elimination of the right to strike or the right of self-organization, such as those by Lewis. According to Ilau, "politically it is not conceivable to abolish these institutions in a free society. Therefore the only problem is to endeavor to prevent inflation risk due to the abuse of these rights by labor unions. This seems to me the central point. I do not believe that labor legislation can do much here" (Ilau 1958, 4). Ilau instead saw that the way forward was to domesticate trade-union leaders and thereby accustom labor unions to accept wage moderation, as well as to prevent recourse to strikes, as in the Swiss case since 1937. "The difficulty as well as the great task is to create a similar attitude in the minds of labor leaders throughout the free world" (Ilau 1958, 4). This was the task that he sought to place on the MPS agenda, before any changes in labor legislation, which he regarded as potentially coercive and antidemocratic.

In Princeton, Ilau must have felt quite isolated in defending such views during this session on unions. Only two other men took the floor to express their support for Ilau: Goetz Brief and the Swiss publicist, Bieri.[30] Ilau thus became the lonely standard-bearer for his German ordoliberal fellows, as for Rappard and Hunold at the beginning of the 1950s. Ilau continued to preach that stable and beneficial arrangements can occur between industrialists and workers. In his view, the legal disarmament of trade unions was not the essence of a free society, but rather its repudiation. Inside the MPS, this perspective tended to disappear in the 1960s, as political "freedom" became increasingly conflated with economic freedom for the capitalist.

Reprise

Traditionally, Hayek's position on unions has been enshrined as the foundation of the neoliberal standpoint on this question (Schulten 2004, 71–76).[31]

According to Hayek, unions are a perversion of the "spontaneous order," and as such, an exception to the rule of law. Indeed, governments have failed to prevent the unions' use of coercion and violence, since their behavior has been protected by law. This unlimited power allowed unions to occupy powerful positions in the wage-bargaining process, or in some instances, in the conduct of enterprise. In both cases, employers are portrayed as helpless, unable to resist union power and thus forced to accept wage increases. Unions are thus put in the artificial position of being able to manipulate wages in relative terms. However, if wages are distorted in this way, costs and prices will be misallocated. In such a situation, the market, as a device for signaling changes in supply and demand, is disrupted and unemployment results on the labor market. In this manner of framing the situation, unions represent the foremost threat to the economic order and free society. Consequently, Hayek urged a legal disenfranchisement of unions and the restoration of a well-functioning rule of law.

The bulk of these arguments came from Hayek's key writings on unions at the end of the 1950s, following a decade of intense disputation inside the MPS on the same topic (Hayek 1959, 1960, 1984). However, Hayek's standpoint reflects only one side of the discussions that occurred in neoliberal circles during the 1950s. In the plurality of neoliberal viewpoints expressed on unions, Hayek opted for the most radical version, the one least tolerant of the very existence of unions. This was the version that scholars like Machlup and Petro, both former students of Mises, supported from 1947 to 1958. As this chapter has demonstrated, this view was fostered primarily in the American context and reflects the political and social interests of an ultraconservative fraction of employers, who regarded existing European practices with disdain. In opting for contempt, Hayek explicitly rejected another potential neoliberal position, which considered that a solidarity of interests between capital and labor could sometimes be appropriate and beneficial. The hostility to this alternative position went far beyond mere disputation over appropriate economic and social theory. Hayek felt it necessary to condemn those comrades who defended it and to describe such an alliance between employers and employees as "the crudest type of socialism, commonly known as syndicalism" (Hayek 1959, 292). In his *Constitution of Liberty* (chapter 19 on Labor Unions and Employment), Hayek simply omits neoliberal authors who were advocates of the alternative, only referring to "serious" neoliberal authors such as Machlup, Hutt, Petro, and Mises. From that time forward, the Hayekian position became the dominant neoliberal perspective on unions, notably because those who defended a more cooperative view with unions lost their influence in neoliberal circles.[32] This shift is all the more important to consider in the present context, given that in many other theoretical disputes within the MPS, Hayek was not able to prevail.

It is nonetheless important to emphasize that, behind these divergences of opinion,[33] an essential point of convergence exists. All the papers distributed on the unions' problems in the MPS explicitly or implicitly took as a fundamental trope of argumentation that government interference in the functioning of the market economy must have harmful consequences. But that did not, by itself, nail down the neoliberal position on unions. For several authors, the nexus of harm was that governments failed to prevent the use of coercion and violence by unions. For them, it was a travesty that this coercive power was now legally protected. For those who were less revulsed by the mere existence of trade unions, an arrangement between the unions and employers could be viewed favorably if it would neutralize the prospect of conflict between them and prevent further state interventions in business relations. In this sense, the variety of positions on trade unions takes place on a continuum characterized by differences in assessment of the right platform from which to position oneself with regard to the welfare state. Thus, this plurality of opinions can be also interpreted as an essential strength[34] of the neoliberal discourse on unionism.

Notes

1. Extant histories of the MPS are Hartwell (1995); Walpen (2004, chapters 1–3).

2. See Hartwell (1995, 225). Seven sessions on this topic were organized during the meetings of this period on the dates (1947, 1949, 1954, 1958). After 1960, however, the MPS gave less attention to that question. Again according to Hartwell, MPS members revisited the trade-union problem during two complete sessions between 1960 and 1969, three between 1970 and 1979 and two between 1980 and 1989. To my knowledge, it appears that in 1984 the MPS tackled the labor issue for the last time, during a full session on the rise and fall of trade unions at its twenty-fifth meeting.

3. See, for instance, McCord Wright (1951); Machlup (1952); Petro (1957); Chamberlin, Bradley et al. (1958); Bradley (1959). For the British political situation, see Cockett (1995).

4. In the Swiss case, the Society received help from two influential businessmen in postwar Switzerland—the banker Rudolf Speich and the industrialist Hans Sulzer, who eventually became members of the Society. In the U.S. case, the Society was supported by the Volker Fund and the Foundation for Economic Education. Created in 1946, the

FEE was financed by the Volker Fund and firms such as General Motors and DuPont. Key American businessmen who supported the MPS were Harold L. Lunhow, Jasper E. Crane, and J. Howard Pew, all MPS members (Steiner forthcoming, chapter 2).

5. This material comprises the papers distributed before the MPS meetings in 1949 and 1958. Unfortunately, the papers in circulation at the 1954 meeting are not available. However, for several sessions, transcripts of discussion can be accessed (1947, 1958). Correspondence and elements of secondary literature complete the material.

6. A biography in French on Rappard exists (Monnier 1995). On his role at the MPS founding meeting and his precious help in supporting this meeting, see Busino (1990).

7. Among others: the Belgian industrialist Henri de Lovinfosse and economists such as Carl Iversen, Karl Brandt, Maurice Allais, and to a certain extent, John Jewkes.

8. With Walter Eucken and Hans Grossmann-Doerth, Frans Böhm co-founded the so-called German ordoliberal school of economics during the 1930s. At the end of the war, he became professor in Freiburg and eventually in Frankfort. Böhm was a member of the *Christlich Demokratische Union Deutschlands* (CDU) and a member of the Parliament between 1953 and 1965. He also participated in Germany's economic reconstruction, notably regarding the legal aspects of cartels and competition.

9. Between 1923 and 1925, Miksch was a member of the Nazi Party. He earned a degree (1926) and a doctorate, supervised by Walter Eucken, in 1929, both in economics at the University of Freiburg. Until 1944, Miksch was engaged in journalism at the *Frankfurter Zeitung*. After the war, he became the economic adviser of Ludwig Erhard, then director of the office for the administration of the economy, and future Bundesminister of Economic Affairs. In 1949, Miksch was appointed professor of economics at Mannheim, before becoming professor of fiscal economics at Freiburg in 1949.

10. Inversely, both Böhm and Miksch are suspicious of employers' ability to defend the free economy: they are interested in, but they are not ready to accept, "the duties and commitments which are the consequences of freedom" (Miksch 1949, 1).

11. Hensel wrote his dissertation under Eucken's supervision in 1951. After Eucken's death in 1950, he published Eucken's famous book, *Grundsätze der Wirtschaftspolitik* (1952).

12. By the mid-1960s, Hensel withdrew from his early position in support of limited co-determination. He started to strongly criticize the co-determination system as well as other forms of *"economic democracy"* (Hensel 1989 [1966], 137–139).

13. Hunold served as secretary of the Zurich Stock Exchange (1930–1945) and of the Zurich Bank Association (1940–1945). Between 1945 and 1946, he was also director of the Credit Suisse Zurich and after 1947, managing director of the Swiss Watch Industry, an association of Swiss watch manufacturers.

14. Beginning in October 1948, Hayek worked closely with Dennison to draft a program for the 1949 Seelisberg meeting and to recruit some speakers (Hayek to Dennison, October 9, 1948, Friedrich Hayek Papers (hereafter FAH), Hoover Institution

Archives, 73.10; Dennison to Hayek, October 18, 1949, FAH, 73.10). Interestingly, Hayek proposed inviting Hutt as a replacement for Machlup, who was unable to attend the meeting in 1949 (Hayek to Dennison, February 10, 1949, FAH, 73.10). This proposal came from Machlup, who persuaded Hayek to include Hutt in the Seelisberg meeting (Hayek to Machlup, January 26, 1949, Fritz Machlup Papers (hereafter FMP), Hoover Institution Archives, 36.17; Machlup to Hayek, February 3, 1949, FMP, 36.17). This detail will be of importance, as we will show below.

15. Economist Carlo Mötelli was a Swiss journalist at the prestigious *Neue Zürcher Zeitung*. His friend Albert Hunold, and, to a certain extent, William Rappard, were both largely inspired by ordoliberal theories, particularly the works of Wilhelm Röpke and Alexander Rüstow.

16. With Gottfried Haberler, Fritz Machlup was Hayek's assistant at the *Osterreichisches Institut für Konjunkturforschung,* an institute founded in 1927 by Hayek's mentor Ludwig von Mises and financed by the Rockefeller Foundation. Machlup did his dissertation under Mises's supervision. Both Hayek and Machlup were active participants in Mises's *Privatseminar* in the 1920s.

17. Apart from Machlup, two other future MPS members read a paper during the conference: Leo Wolman (National Bureau of Economic Research) on "Collective Bargaining and Economic Liberalism" and Felix Morley (*Human Events,* Editor) on "The Meaning of Economic Liberalism."

18. Machlup received $150 for his contribution. Moreover, the final text was published in the form of a pamphlet (Jackson to Machlup, November 25, 1946; Machlup to Jackson, November 27, 1946, FMP, 30.14).

19. Moreover, Hayek prevailed upon him to bring copies of his pamphlet for distribution during the session. However, these copies sent by the Chamber of Commerce did not reach the Mont Pèlerin in time (Machlup to Keller, March 21, 1947, FMP, 30.14; Keller to Machlup, May 2, 1947, FMP, 30.14).

20. They were mostly American and English: Frank Graham (chairman), Frank Knight, John Davenport, Stanley Dennison, Michael Polanyi, and Vernon Watts.

21. Watts was hired by the Los Angeles Chamber of Commerce, of which Leonard Read was executive director in 1939. In 1946, Watts followed Read in New York in order to set up the FEE.

22. This pamphlet was distributed at the 1954 MPS meeting in Venice (Watts to Hayek, June 10, 1954, HIA FHP, 80.6).

23. See, for instance, McCord Wright (1951); Machlup (1952); Petro (1957); Chamberlin, Bradley et al. (1958); Bradley (1959); Friedman (1962).

24. See William H. Hutt's paper during the 1949 meeting in Seelisbserg; or those of L. A. Hahn, at the Bloemendaal meeting in 1950, and Ludwig von Mises, in Beauvallon in 1951 (Hutt 1949; Hahn 1950; Mises 1951). Also, in 1956, Hayek and Wilhelm Röpke, both MPS founding members, strongly diverged on the role of unions at the Berlin meeting. As reported by a Swiss journalist and MPS member, Ernst Bieri (*Neue Zürcher*

Zeitung), Röpke was unconvinced by Hayek's severe condemnation of unions. To Röpke, they proved their usefulness in the defense of free economy as the Swiss case demonstrated. Condemnation of unions per se was then an absurdity (Bieri 1956).

25. A law professor at the New York University (NYU), Sylvester Petro was a former student of Mises's seminar at NYU, where Petro met people such as Henry Hazlitt, Israel Kirzner, and Murray Rothbard. Petro's *Labor Policy in a Free Society* is a strong indictment of American labor law and of labor unions as they function in the United States. This book, dedicated to Mises, had considerable influence on Hayek and served as one of the main sources of inspiration for Hayek's own works on unions, in particular *The Constitution of Liberty* (1960).

26. The Norris-LaGuardia Act was the first U.S. federal law that prohibited "yellow dog contracts" or other contracts in which a worker agreed as a condition of employment not to join a union.

27. Harold Gregg Lewis served as professor at the Department of Economics at the University of Chicago from 1939 to 1975. He was deeply involved in labor economics during the 1950s, and he is considered one of the founding fathers of modern labor economics. He was the author of *Unionism and Relative Wages in the United States,* published in 1963, which was the distillation of a six-year project research funded by the American Enterprise Association on "The Relative Wage Effects of Unionism." In the mid-1950s, Lewis also served as a coordinator in a program financed by the United States Agency for International Development (USAID) in order to upgrade the teaching of economics in Latin America, in particular in Chile, where he ran the program from 1956 to 1967. For further biographical information, see Biddle (1996).

28. To a large extent, the analysis as well as the proposals sketched by Lewis resembled those of Roscoe Pound (Pound 1957, 21) and obviously those of Petro's 1957 book. See in particular Petro's analysis of the legal coercion (Petro 1957, 44–48) of the legal destruction of equity in labor relations in the United States (Petro 1957, 125–132, 272–289). Proposals such as the abrogation of the Norris-LaGuardia Act or the abolition of the National Labor Relations Board are presented in his chapter 19.

29. Hans Ilau was a former student of Walter Eucken. After receiving his Ph.D., Ilau did not pursue a professor's career. After the war, he became administrator of the Board of the Rhine Main Bank. In 1958, he was director of the Chamber of Industry and Commerce in Frankfurt.

30. "The trade unions on the one hand and the employers on the other hand, are still adversaries but they are no longer feel [*sic*] as enemies. I believe one should take such a favourable situation as a starting point for renewing and expanding the doctrine of a free society and a free economy. . . . It is our task to convince to workers that what is good for the economy as a whole is good for themselves and that in the market lies their very interests. The danger therefore, is not in the institutions—per se— but in the manner in which institutions may be used and applied." See the Princeton meeting transcripts (E. Bieri*),* HIA MPS, 13.1.

31. See also the critical analysis of F. A. Hayek's position on unionism by R. Richardson and the comment on Richardson's paper by B. C. Roberts (Richardson 1997; Roberts 1997).

32. In particular, after the so-called Hunold affair when, in 1961, Hunold, Röpke, Brandt, Rustöw, and twelve other MPS members left the Society (Hartwell 1995, 100–133; Denord 2002). On the role of Bruno Leoni during this conflict, see Walpen (2004, 145–151).

33. On unions, another well-known divergence can be seen between Milton Friedman and the other contributors to McCord Wright's book. Friedman argued that the impact of trade unions on wage structure was not generally as important as expected in then-orthodox economics (McCord Wright 1951, 202–259).

34. "With a more detailed and historical analysis, it becomes evident that the neoliberalism is not singular, but plural. From basis-common elements he knows indeed very various developments. That plurality of neoliberalism is not a weakness, but constitutes a strength in the context of a Hegemony Theory standpoint" (Plehwe and Walpen 1999, 206).

References

Biddle, J. 1996. "H. Gregg Lewis." In Warren Samuels (ed.), *American Economists of the Late Twentieth Century,* 174–193. Cheltenham: Edward Elgar.

Bieri, E. 1956, September 7. "Das Programm der Freien Gesellschaft. Tagung der Mont Pèlerin Society in Berlin." *Neue Zürcher Zeitung,* (Zurich).

Böhm, F. 1949. "Labour and Management." Mont Pèlerin Society, 2nd General Reunion, Seelisberg, Switzerland.

Bradley, P. D. (ed.). 1959. *The Public Stake in Union Power.* Charlottesville: University of Virginia Press.

Briefs, G. 1952. *Zwischen Kapitalismus und Syndikalismus: die Gewerk schaften am Scheideweg.* Berne: Francke.

Busino G. 1990. "William Rappard, le libéralisme 'nouveau' et les origines de la Mont-Pèlerin Society." *Revue Européenne des Sciences Sociales,* 88, 205–216.

Chamberlin, E., Bradley, P. D., et al. 1958. *Labor Union and Public Policy.* Washington, DC: American Enterprise Association.

Cockett, R. 1995. *Thinking the Unthinkable: Think-Tanks and the Economic Counter-Revolution 1931–1983.* London: Fontana Press.

Dennison, S. R. 1949. *Labour and Management.* Mont Pèlerin Society, 2nd General Reunion, Seelisberg, Switzerland.

Denord, F. 2002. "Le prophète, le pèlerin et le missionnaire—La circulation internationale du néo-libéralisme et ses acteurs." *Actes de la Recherche en Sciences Sociales,* 145, 9–20.

Deppe, F., Von Freyberg, J., and Kievenheim, C. 1969. *Kritik der Mitbestimmung. Partnerschaft oder Klassenkampf.* Frankfurt: Suhrkamp.

Durr, W. 1954. "Dirigismus im Feuer der Kritik." *Schweizer Monatshefte,* 34 (8), 539–542.

Eucken, W. 1952. *Grundsätze der Wirtschaftspolitik.* Berne and Tübingen: Francke & Mohr Verlag.

Fones-Wolf, E. 1994. *Selling Free Enterprise: The Business Assault on Labor and Liberalism, 1945–60.* Chicago: University of Illinois Press.

Gordon, C. 1998. "Why No Corporatism in the United States? Business Disorganization and Its Consequences." *Business and Economic History,* 27, 1, 29–46.

Graham, F. (ed.). 1947. *Wages and Wage-Policy.* Conference Proceedings of the 1st Meeting of the Mont Pèlerin Society at Mont Pèlerin, Switzerland. Stanford, CA, Hoover Institution Archives, 202–215.

Hahn, L. A. 1950. "Keynesian Monetary and Fiscal Policy." Mont Pèlerin Society, 3rd General Reunion, Bloemendaal.

Harris, R., and Seldon, A. 1959. "The Tactics and Strategy of the Advance to a Free Economy." Mont Pèlerin Society, 10th General Reunion, Oxford.

Hartwell, R. M. 1995. *A History of the Mont Pelerin Society.* Indianapolis, IN: Liberty Fund.

Hayek, F. A. 1949. " 'Free' Enterprise and Competitive Order." In F. A. Hayek, *Individualism and Economic Order,* 107–118. London: Routledge & Kegan Paul.

Hayek, F. A. 1950, September 20. *President's Circular.* Archives fédérales. Berne (Switzerland), Fonds Rappard (J.I.149 1977/135), vol. 75.

Hayek, F. A. (ed.). 1954. *Capitalism and the Historians.* Chicago: University of Chicago Press.

Hayek, F. A. 1959. "Unions, Inflation and Profits." In P. D. Bradley (ed.), *The Public Stake in Union Power.* New York: University of Virginia Press.

Hayek, F. A. 1960. *The Constitution of Liberty.* London: Routledge & Kegan Paul.

Hayek, F. A. 1984. *1980s Unemployment and the Unions.* London: Institute of Economic Affairs.

Hayek, F. A. 1993 [1944]. *The Road to Serfdom.* London: Routledge.

Hensel, P. K. 1949. *Industrial Labour Constitution in the Competitive Economy.* Mont Pèlerin Society, 2nd General Reunion, Seelisberg, Switzerland.

Hensel, P. K. 1989 [1966]. "Problems of Workers' Democracies." In Peacock A. and H. Willgerodt (eds.), *German Neo-Liberals and the Social Market Economy.* New York: St. Martin's Press.

Hunold, A. 1948, September 19. *Procès-verbal de la séance du Comité des Directeurs— Bâle,* Archives fédérales, Berne (Switzerland), Fonds Rappard (J.I.149 1977/135), vol. 75.

Hunold, A. 1949. *Managerial and Corporate Social Policy in Opposition to State Social Policy.* Mont Pèlerin Society, 2nd General Reunion, Seelisberg, Switzerland.

Hutt, W. H. 1949. *Trade Unions and the Price System.* Mont Pèlerin Society, 2nd General Reunion, Seelisberg, Switzerland.

Ilau, H. 1958. *Labor Unions, Freedom and Inflation.* Mont Pèlerin Society, 9th General Reunion, Princeton, NJ.

Jacoby, S. 1997. *Modern Manors: Welfare Capitalism since the New Deal.* Princeton, N.J.: Princeton University Press.

Lewis, H. G. 1958. "Labor Unions and Labor Monopoly in the United States." Mont Pèlerin Society, 9th General Reunion, Princeton, NJ.

Lewis, J. 1984. *Industrialisation and Trade Union Organization in South Africa, 1924–1955: The Rise and Fall of the South African Trades and Labour Council.* Cambridge: Cambridge University Press.

Machlup, F. 1947. "Monopolistic Wage Determination as a Part of the General Problem of Monopoly." In *Wage Determination and the Economics of Liberalism.* Washington, DC: Chamber of Commerce of the United States.

Machlup, F. 1952. *The Political Economy of Monopoly: Business, Labor, and Government Policies.* Baltimore, MD: Johns Hopkins University Press.

McCord Wright, D. (ed.). 1951. *The Impact of the Union: Eight Economic Theorists Evaluate the Labor Union Movement.* New York: Augustus M. Kelley.

Miksch, L. 1949. *Attempt of Liberal Program.* Mont Pèlerin Society, 2nd General Reunion, Seelisberg, Switzerland.

Mises, L. 1951. "Profit and Loss." Mont Pèlerin Society, 4th General Reunion, Beauvallon.

Mises, L. 1980. "Profit and Loss." In L. Mises. *Planning for Freedom,* 108–150. South Holland, IL: Libertarian Press.

Monnier, V. 1995. William E. Rappard, défenseur des libertés, serviteur de son pays et de la communauté internationale. Geneva: Slatkine.

Petro, S. 1957. *The Labor Policy of the Free Society.* New York: Ronald Press.

Petro, S. 1958. "Free Employee Choice as a Basis of Labor Policy." Mont Pèlerin Society, 9th General Reunion, Princeton, NJ.

Plehwe, D., and B. Walpen. 1999. "Wissenschaftliche und wissenschaftspolitische Produktionweisen im Neoliberalismus—Beiträge des Mont Pèlerin Society und marktradikaler Think Tanks zur Hegemoniegewinnung und—eraltung." *Prokla* 115 (2): 203–235.

Pound, R. 1957. *Legal Immunities of Labor Unions.* Washington, DC: American Enterprise Association.

Rappard, W. E. 1914. *La Révolution industrielle et les origines de la protection légale du travail en Suisse.* Berne: Staempfli & Cie.

Richardson, R. 1997. "Hayek on Trade Unions: Social Philosopher or Propagandist?" In S. Frowen (ed.), *Hayek: Economist and Social Philosopher,* 259–273. New York: St. Martin's Press.

Roberts, B. C. 1962 [1959]. *Trade Unions in a Free Society—Studies in the Organisation of Labour in Britain and the USA.* London: Institute of Economic Affairs.

Roberts, B. C. 1997. "Comments on 'Hayek on Trade Unions: Social Philosopher or Propagandist?' by Ray Richardson." In S. Frowen (ed.), *Hayek: Economist and Social Philosopher*, 275–280. New York: St. Martin's Press.

Roper, I. 2005. "Can the Third Way Recast the Link?" In M. Harcourt and G. Wood (eds.), *Trade Unions and Democracy—Strategies and Perspectives*, 62–81. Manchester: Manchester University Press.

Schulten, T. 2004. *Solidarische Lohnpolitik in Europa—Zür Politischen Ökonomie der Gewerkschaften*, 362. Hamburg: VSA-Verlag.

Steiner, Y. 2005. "Ce marché qui rassemble et qui divise les Firsthand Dealers in Ideas de la *Mont Pèlerin Society*." In G. Bensimon and J.-P. Potier (eds.), *Histoire des représentations du marché*, 476–494. Paris: Michel Houdiard Editeur.

Steiner, Y. Forthcoming. *Réunir, puis réduire le néolibéralisme: La Société du Mont-Pèlerin et ses sociabilités savante et patronale*. Lausanne, Université de Lausanne, Thèse de doctorat.

Watts, V. O. 1954. *Union Monopoly, Its Cause and Cure*. Los Angeles: Studies of the Foundation for Social Research.

Walpen, B. 2004. *Die Offenen Feinde und ihre Gesellschaft. Eine hegemonietheoretische Studie zur Mont Pèlerin Society*. Hamburg: VSA Verlag.

Wilson, T. 1958. *Trade Unions in Britain*. Mont Pèlerin Society, 9th General Reunion, Princeton, NJ.

6

Reinventing Monopoly and the Role of Corporations

The Roots of Chicago Law and Economics

ROB VAN HORN

Introduction

Once upon a time, classical liberals were wary of monopoly as inherently inimical to democracy because in their view it undermined a necessary condition for democratic politics to flourish, namely, a competitive market. In the 1930s, Henry Simons, a respected University of Chicago professor and self-proclaimed classical liberal, described monopoly in all its forms—including large corporations—as "the great enemy of democracy."[1] As World War II drew to a close, however, the heirs to liberalism—both in Europe and the United States—worried that they needed to create a more robust liberal doctrine to prevent its demise and to stave off the looming threat of totalitarianism. To accomplish this feat, they organized a few like-minded souls to investigate and discuss the multifarious areas of the classical liberal doctrine dealing with business organization, including monopoly and corporations.

In April 1947, those embattled few founded the Mont Pèlerin Society (henceforth MPS). Attended by both Europeans and Americans, the MPS served as a forum for general intellectual debate. In its early years, the discourse ranged widely from unions to economic development to liberalism and Christianity to agriculture policy to free enterprise to political crisis.

Significantly, the very first meeting of the MPS in 1947 touched on the issues of competition and monopoly, signaling the importance of these concepts in the program of reinvigoration of liberalism.

For MPS members, the issue of monopoly loomed so large primarily because of the way their opponents on the left had framed it. The left had been arguing that since the start of the twentieth century monopoly had been expanding apace throughout the United States and Western Europe, such that the bulk of the economy—owing to this inexorable growth—would inevitably soon be controlled by monopolies.[2] The left predicted that the forces of competition would continue to prove ineffectual in the face of such growth. Consequently, they insisted that the only rational solution was socialist control of the economy. This tenet of the program of the left threatened the very cogency of liberal optimism and was one of the major motivations for the MPS liberals to rethink liberal doctrine. However, efforts to reformulate liberalism did not only happen at MPS meetings; they also occurred at select institutions with related research objectives.

This resulting division of effort conformed to the vision of Friedrich Hayek, who played a principal role in setting up two such research initiatives at the University of Chicago. In one such initiative, known as the Free Market Study (FMS) project, Hayek—through repeated efforts—secured the requisite funds and recruited the necessary individuals.[3] He persuaded Aaron Director to head up the project.[4] In addition to the aptly named Director, the FMS comprised six other steadfast liberals at Chicago: Edward Levi (a law professor), Frank Knight (an economics professor), Garfield Cox (dean of the Business School), Wilber Katz (dean of the Law School), Theodore W. Schultz (chair of the Economics Department), and Milton Friedman (an economics professor)—several of whom were also present at the premier MPS meeting.[5] The FMS commenced meeting at the Chicago Law School in 1946 and was concluded around 1952. Though avowed to study and describe "a suitable legal and institutional framework of an effective competitive system" (Coase 1998, 603), the FMS predominantly researched the issues of monopoly and corporations, transforming the fundamental economic approach to these issues and giving birth to a significant tenet of neoliberalism. In 1953, Director further deployed these nascent premises in structuring another focused research endeavor.

As the FMS wound down in 1951, Hayek helped secure the funds for another law-school-based project, the Antitrust Project (1953–1957), with Director again at the helm and with Edward Levi—by then dean of the Law School—as second in command. Though it initially aimed to concentrate on the issue of monopoly, continuing where the FMS had left off, the Antitrust Project subsequently enlarged its focus to numerous areas of antitrust law. Nevertheless, it preserved the investigation of monopoly as a collateral but an important aim. This chapter documents the years of painstaking efforts of the Chicago neoliberals—as they would later be called—to reformulate the classical doctrine with respect to monopoly and corporations, and their deployment of these changes to help reinvigorate the liberal position toward antitrust issues.

Given, however, that the MPS project of reconstruction was a transnational effort, the Chicago contingent was not the only group investigating these issues. In 1951, as Friedman observed, "The doctrine sometimes called neoliberalism . . . [had] been developing more or less simultaneously in many parts of the world" (1951a, 91). A German cadre, later known as ordoliberals, or German neoliberals, was also occupied in reconsidering the classical liberal conceptions of monopoly and corporations, and in developing what became known as ordoliberal competition policy. However, unlike the Chicagoans, the Germans had begun their efforts in the mid-1930s (Gerber 1998, 234–235); by the late 1930s, the theoretical foundations of ordoliberalism were more or less in place.[6] Despite the fact that both groups actively participated in the MPS, these two research initiatives turned out to be largely disengaged in practice, each influenced by different institutional and legal components within their respective country.[7] Nonetheless, for our purposes, both constituted subsets of a larger neoliberal initiative.

Given the limitations of space, it is not feasible here to cover both the German ordoliberals and Chicago neoliberals in their quest to redefine monopoly in the immediate postwar period. The primary focus here will be on the efforts of the Chicago group. But before charting the development of the Chicago neoliberals, this chapter compares Chicago's position circa 1947 regarding monopoly and corporations with that of the German ordoliberals. At that juncture, these two groups had relatively similar attitudes toward monopoly and corporations. In order to demonstrate this similarity, I will turn to the first MPS meeting. Its participants included steadfast Chicago defenders of freedom, such as Director and Friedman, and staunch German ordoliberals, such as Walter Eucken and Wilhem Röpke. This turns out to have been the only meeting in the first two decades at which a representative of the Chicago School addressed the issues of monopoly and corporations. Specifically,

Director delivered a lecture on the topic, "Free Enterprise or Competitive Order." The aspect that is quite telling about this disquisition is that Eucken and other ordoliberals present voiced no substantial objections to Director's claims. Because scholars typically portray the Chicago position on monopolies and corporations as inherently contrary to the ordoliberal position, this seems to be a surprising occurrence.[8] I will explain the surprising reticence of the ordoliberals by arguing that in 1947 ordoliberalism and the incipient Chicago School shared an important common premise. Both schools of thought lauded and respected the work of the renowned classical liberal Henry Simons.

This chapter explains how and why Chicago came to renounce its classical liberal heritage with regard to monopoly and competition. The chapter is divided into four sections. In the first, I will summarize the ordoliberal position, paying particular attention to monopoly, corporations, and competition policy.[9] Next, I will examine Director's MPS address and then show what common ground the two approaches shared through the classical liberal, Henry Simons. Although the later development of ordoliberalism is not charted here, a brief characterization will prove useful to demonstrate how radical the subsequent developments of Chicago neoliberalism in the 1950s really were.

The second section begins with a general description of the FMS and then moves on to examine the claims of three key members of this project: Aaron Director, Milton Friedman, and Edward Levi. By detailing early developments within the project, I will scrutinize the professed views of Director and Friedman, the two principals of the project, on monopoly and corporations. I will also point to sources from 1947 to suggest Levi's views on these same subjects. A description of these three individuals' views of monopoly and corporations will show that even during the early years of the FMS (1946–1949) all three still sounded very much like classical liberals, despite their explicit commitments to reformulate and recast liberalism in new, more robust directions.

The third section looks at each individual in turn, showing how his opinion during the later years of the FMS (1950–1952) or during the period immediately following the FMS sharply diverged from his earlier opinions, thus providing evidence of the timing and emergence of neoliberal doctrine at Chicago (at least with regard to these particular topics). Notably, the birth of neoliberal competition theory occurred roughly four years after the FMS commenced; this was a notably short period of time.[10] By contrast with Henry Simons, the triumvirate of Director, Friedman, and Levi began to advocate the idea that monopoly, in all its forms, was almost always undone by the forces of competition; and consequently that a relatively sanguine attitude should be adopted toward both monopoly and large corporations. The corporations were said to have approximated the impersonal ideal of the market, even in what would appear, by conventional measures, to be fairly concentrated markets.

After demonstrating Director, Friedman, and Levi's right turns, I will, in the fourth section, provide an overview of the Antitrust Project. This discussion will consist primarily of an analysis of the Antitrust Project's manifesto (Director and Levi 1956), demonstrating how reformulation of the classical liberal doctrine during the FMS provided the backbone for the hybrid antitrust neoliberalism that emerged during the course of the Antitrust Project. Essentially, Director and Levi (1956) demonstrated an unprecedented skepticism about the extension of monopoly power via exclusionary practices, such as tying arrangements or price discrimination, and a concomitant disdain for adjudication or legislation that regarded these practices as per se deleterious or per se illegal.

The Antitrust Project gave rise to a prodigious number of publications, many of which depended on the fundamental presuppositions advanced during the latter years of the FMS. From the outside, it may have seemed that Chicago law and economics was incubated during the period of the Antitrust Project, but in fact it took root earlier, during the operation of the FMS.[11] Thus, the origins of Chicago law and economics (not to mention postwar Chicago economics) are unmistakably traced to the effort of Director and others at Chicago to revamp the classical liberal doctrine—especially as it had been espoused by Henry Simons—during the course of the FMS. For this reason, Chicago law and economics should be regarded as one of the pathbreaking neoliberal movements in modern intellectual history.

Before turning to a detailed description of the FMS and its undertakings, it is important to keep in mind that reconceptualization of liberal doctrine at the University of Chicago occurred under external solicitation from a politically motivated benefactor, the Volker Fund. The Volker Fund bankrolled both the FMS and the Antitrust Project, as well as a myriad of future research projects at Chicago, and directly exerted its influence throughout the duration of those projects. During the middle years of the FMS (around 1950), the Volker Fund went so far as to threaten to eject Director from his leadership role in the FMS because the Volker Fund refused to accept certain tenets of classical liberalism, namely those espoused by the deceased Chicago economist Henry Simons.[12] As the FMS wound down, in 1951, Jacob Viner—a classical liberal and renowned economist who left Chicago for Princeton in 1946—recollected his experience at a Volker-funded conference headed by Director and Levi at the Chicago Law School:[13] "[Everything] about the conference except the unscheduled statements and protests from individual participants were so patently rigidly structured, so loaded, that I got more amusement from the conference than from any other I ever attended . . . even the source of the financing of the Conference, as I found out later, was ideologically loaded."[14]

Chicago and the Ordoliberals Set Out in Sweet Harmony

Scholars almost invariably portray the Chicago School and ordoliberalism as propounding contrary major premises regarding monopoly. For example, Chicago neoliberals are said to maintain that competition has a self-correcting power, which ensures that monopoly power is short-lived. Ordoliberals, on the other hand, are not champions of self-healing competition: "Ordoliberal policy does not rely exclusively on the long-term process of self-healing of the overall society [through competition], but protects the individual's economic freedom of action as a value in itself against any impairment of excessive economic power" (Möschel 2001, 5). Although such characterizations are in broad outline correct, they tend to lead to the blinkered generalization that Chicago liberals and German liberals have always been at loggerheads over the issue of monopoly (and the issue of corporations). In fact, in the immediate postwar period, these two schools held relatively similar positions on these issues. One reason was their intellectual inspirations had a common ground: Henry Simons.

As one student of ordoliberalism has observed, "With regard to competition policy Simons' programme, especially (1934), inspired Eucken" (Meijer 1994, 30). In fact, around 1950, at Groningen University economics students had been assigned Simons (1948) as required reading (Meijer 1994, 28). In the immediate postwar period, Aaron Director, like Eucken, nurtured a deep respect for Simons's work. After Simons's suicide, Director played a principal role in compiling Simons's oeuvre for publication. In the Prefatory Note of *Economic Policy for a Free Society,* Director stated: "[Simons] was a first-rate economic theorist. . . . He had no illusions about the great obstacles to the re-creation of a free-market society. . . . We have to believe that the additional work which

Henry Simons would have accomplished will ultimately be done by others" (p. vii). Therefore, since Director—as will be argue below—sounded very much like Simons in his MPS address, it is no surprise that Eucken had no major objections to Director's talk.[15] Before turning to it and a comparison of his claims to those of the ordoliberals, it is useful to provide a brief sketch of ordoliberalism, especially its position concerning monopoly, corporations, and antitrust policy in the 1940s.

Ordoliberalism, like classical liberalism, maintained that a free enterprise system was necessary for a free, prosperous, and equitable society.[16] Unlike classical liberals, ordoliberals advocated that a competitive economic system should be grounded in a specific "constitutional" framework; this, according to Gerber (1998), was the signature contribution of ordoliberalism and its significant departure from classical liberalism. For ordoliberalism's vision of society to become a reality, society needed both a political constitution and an "economic constitution." The political and legal decisions that would give rise to society's economic system would determine the nature of its economic constitution. Ultimately, the economic constitution must be grounded in ordoliberal economic theory; ordoliberals therefore appointed themselves de facto lawmakers. Specifically, the economic constitution should construct an economy with "complete competition" wherein no firm would possess the power to coerce another firm. Like Simons and classical liberals, ordoliberals feared governmental and nongovernmental concentrations of power. They were convinced that Nazi Germany emerged as a result of the misuse and abuse of political and economic power, which crushed liberalism.[17] Hence, under ordoliberalism, the legislature "made" the law; the executive had virtually no political and economic power; and the judiciary ensured that policy implemented by the legislature was consistent with the economic constitution.

Even though the economy is grounded in a "constitutional" framework, an *Ordnungspolitik* (order-based policy) must be designed to implement society's economic constitution. Markets must be maintained and created through prudent nondiscretionary government policy. According to the ordoliberals' understanding of *Ordnungspolitik,* government policy decisions needed to flow from and be constrained by the economic constitution. Thus, "Government did not 'direct the process' of the economy. It merely established the 'forms' or structural conditions within which those processes could function effectively" (Gerber 1998, 248). Ordoliberals called this "indirect regulation," which comprised "constitutive" and "regulative" principles. Constitutive

principles—the fundamental principles of economic policy—served to establish the form of the economic system. They included monetary stability, open
markets, private property, contractual freedom, liability, and policy consistency. Regulative principles flowed from constitutive principles, functioning
to maintain the efficaciousness of constitutive principles. Competition law,
for example, was a regulative principle. Like other types of regulative principles, competition law not only had to be embedded in constitutive principles,
but also had to be symbiotically related to other regulative principles, such as
monetary policy and trade policy.

Ordoliberals considered competition law the keystone of their program:
"Monetary and other policies designed to foster competition would have little
effect, ordoliberals argued, if firms could act in concert in setting prices or determining output, or if firms with economic power could use that power to
foreclose opportunities for competition" (Gerber 1998, 250). Competition law
served both to create and protect the conditions of complete competition; "it
had to block the anti-competitive mechanisms which society can spawn"
(Lemke 2001, 195). It sought to prevent monopoly power, to extirpate existing
monopoly power, and—if dissolution was not feasible—to control conduct
stemming from monopoly power. Ultimately, it served to eradicate private monopoly power, such as cartels and, importantly, exclusionary practices. In general, in keeping with the classical liberalism exemplified by Director in 1947 and
by Simons, ordoliberals sought to eliminate monopolies, minimize "big business," and support an economy comprised of small and medium-sized firms.

In 1947, Director believed that authority had either supplanted individualism or ominously threatened to supplant it in short order. In brief, state intervention had become regrettably ubiquitous. Director maintained that state
intervention had destroyed or nearly destroyed the competitive order because
liberals lacked solutions to conflicts between social interests and the results of
free enterprise. Director supported the idea of a reconstituted liberal: "The
theory of liberalism must be extended to include a prescription of the role of
the state in making private enterprise the equivalent of competitive enterprise" (p. 77).[18] However, in promoting these changes, Director was adhering
to the classical liberalism of Simons.

In keeping with Simons, Director steadfastly believed that the liberal doctrine needed, above all else, to champion freedom by "promoting the dispersion of power necessary for competitive order" (pp. 77–78). Notably, Director
observed that a substantial amount of monopoly power existed in the free

enterprise system. To create a working competitive order, Director, like Simons, advocated state action on three fronts: (1) preventing private monopoly; (2) controlling combinations among workers and businesses; and (3) providing monetary stability. Because of the scope of issues examined in this chapter, we shall restrict ourselves to addressing only (1) and (2).

Regarding industrial monopoly, although Director maintained that international trade normally provided a check on industrial monopoly, he admonished that this was not a sufficient check. Antitrust law was also needed to play a critical role. Concerning the United States, Director indicated that antitrust law had lessened but not eliminated private monopoly. He suggested that heightened antitrust enforcement and additional policy measures were necessary to deal with the substantial extent of industrial monopoly. For Director, additional policy measures were needed to target patent law and to address the inequality of income and inequality of wealth that stemmed from exercised monopoly power. Regarding patent law, he stated: "A study of the American antitrust cases discloses the crucial importance which patents on inventions have played in creating and maintaining industrial monopoly."[19] Regarding the inequality of income and wealth, he asserted, "Some of the existing income inequality of income and inequality of wealth reflects the monopoly power of industry."[20]

Interestingly, Director asserted that antitrust laws were "mere stopgap measures."[21] Radical corporate reform also needed to be undertaken. He maintained that classical liberalism failed to adequately address the scope of power of corporations and trade unions. Concerning corporations, he asserted:

> The unlimited power of corporations must be removed. Excessive size can be challenged through the prohibition of corporate ownership of other corporations, through the elimination of interlocking directorates, through a limitation of the scope of activity of corporations, through increased control of enterprise by property owners and perhaps too through a direct limitation of the size of corporate enterprise.[22]

Significantly, the first MPS member in the transcript to respond to Director's disquisition was Eucken. Eucken pointed out that Director erroneously presumed that the government should directly address the monopoly problem. "[The monopolist] is more afraid of competition than of government control. What is required is an independent supervisory authority guided by law and not by Parliament."[23] Eucken based his comment on a key premise of ordolib-eralism: The autonomous monopoly office, the enforcer of competition law, should be immune from political influence and should be guided in assessment by established legal strictures. These legal strictures needed to be grounded in an economic constitution.

At this juncture, despite the fact that Director did not support an eco-nomic constitution and an independent monopoly office, he shared Eucken's disdain for concentrated power because it undermined freedom. Thus, both were utterly convinced that monopoly needed to be prevented. Moreover, both harbored strong reservations against large corporations; each disapproved of the ramifications of that power for the market and for society.

This common ground proved transient, however. Director and the FMS members would soon take the development of liberal doctrine in a radically different direction than that favored by the German ordos. As the following section illustrates, it took a few years for a sharp break from the classical liberal position of Simons to transpire. After the neoliberal position concerning mo-nopoly, corporations, and antitrust law emerged, there was an ironic turn of events; it now seemed that Simons had more closely evoked the ordoliberals, not the Chicago neoliberals. As one historian of economic thought observed, "In general, the West Germans' program resembles Henry Simons" (Oliver 1960, 118). With this in mind, we turn to the FMS and chart the emergence of trademark Chicago doctrine concerning monopoly.

Haunted by Classical Liberalism: The Early Years of the FMS

Although Hayek and the Volker Fund had cooperated to bring about the com-position of an *American Road to Serfdom,* Aaron Director—the individual anointed with this primary responsibility—never finished the book by the con-clusion of the FMS around 1952.[24] The first half of the FMS essentially was de-voted to debate over several possible trajectories of a reconceptualized liberal doctrine, whereas the last half basically served to consolidate a chosen trajec-tory. It is evident, however, that from 1946 to 1947 Director and Friedman were more than a little unclear as to how to accomplish this convergence; and that at that point in time Levi still clung to his classical liberal convictions.

The FMS met bimonthly, especially in 1946 and 1947. In the early FMS meetings, as in his 1947 MPS disquisition, Director conveyed an unwavering conviction that the liberal doctrine needed to be reformed. Director sought research grounded in empirical analysis and devoted to investigation of the facts underlying economic policy.[25] A palpable corollary of such an analysis would be the facilitation of the development of a more robust liberal policy. Although the FMS could have pursued numerous research avenues, after the first couple of meetings, it quickly narrowed its focus to issues concerning monopoly and corporations. This suggested the FMS members' desire to respond to the left's understanding of monopoly.

At a meeting in mid-November, Director and the members tackled the issue of industrial concentration. Director proffered two alternative explanations for industrial concentration: "Of course we could start from the position that existing concentration has already reached a point which makes it objectional from a political point of view, or again we may start from the position that the existing concentration results in the most efficient use of resources and does not eventuate in significant departures from competitive behavior."[26] In suggesting that the existing concentration was politically objectionable, Director showed he still nurtured a soft spot for classical liberalism. Considering this quote in the light of Director's 1947 MPS lecture, we see that Director leaned more toward the notion that monopoly was more a part of the problem than of the solution.

By the end of November, FMS members turned their attention to barriers to entry. Conventionally, the barriers considered included the availability of raw resources—like iron ore and vanadium; the control of methods or means of distribution—like exclusive dealerships or advertising trademarks; unfair competition—like boycotts, predatory activities, bribery, or sabotage; and the control over credit resources and the reluctance of financial institutions to extend this credit. The fact that the FMS members thought it prudent to entertain the issue of barriers to entry is telling; as Herbert Hovenkamp pointed out, the Chicago School would eventually become known for maintaining that barriers to entry were essentially a myth.[27] Nonetheless, the FMS once again discussed the issue of barriers to entry in February 1947.

Addressing the FMS members, Director pointed out that numerous government barriers to entry had been erected, supposedly to protect consumers. He acknowledged that the government restrictions most likely served to encourage adequate standards of performance, and stated, "As the standards are frequently, if not always, promoted by those who have a private interest in restricting entry it would not be surprising if the social interest were subordinated to the private interest."[28] Thus, Director partly indicted corporations and other private firms for responsibility in installing barriers to entry. In effect, he maintained that corporations used their political power to direct government authority. By doing so, Director again revealed a classical liberal bent: conventional liberals tended to fear a concentration of corporate power because it threatened the sovereignty of democratic government. When Director's statement is considered alongside his MPS disquisition—where he strongly objected to the power of corporations and claimed that the government must regulate and restrict their power—it is clear that the source of the problem of such barriers to entry is laid at the doorstep of the corporations, not the government. This position stands in stark contrast with the later Chicago position, which states that corporations capture the regulatory process, and hence government cannot be trusted to devise economic policy.

At one meeting in early January 1947, Friedman proposed that the FMS should devote time and resources to investigating the issue of the separation of corporate ownership and corporate control, mainly because of the social problems that stemmed from this divergence of interest. He stated: "[The] separation of ownership from control has important social disadvantages. It encourages utilization of resources for purposes other than maximization of their return; greatly facilitates the securing of monopoly positions; and gives rise to private economies of scale that are not matched by social economies."[29] Friedman's proposed remedy was to increase the ownership interest of the corporate directors. "By identifying ownership with control," he believed, "the proposal would eliminate many of the present abuses of the corporate form. It would immediately eliminate holding companies . . . it would make mergers more difficult; . . . These effects would themselves retard the tendency (if it exists) toward increasingly large and monopolistic organizations and stimulate the breakdown of existing giant corporations."[30] Thus, in 1947 Friedman advanced a standard premise of classical liberalism: large corporations and monopolies posed a serious social problem that had to be addressed by public policy.

During this same period of time, Edward Levi[31] also revealed his classical liberal bent by advocating a frontal attack on monopoly and concentrated industries. In April 1947, Edward Levi sat down with Wendell Berge[32] and James Martin[33] (whom he called "valiant fighters against monopoly") at the Chicago Round Table to discuss the issue of monopoly in the light of antitrust law enforcement and antitrust law legislation in Germany and the United States (Levi, Berge, and Martin 1947, 2). The three men commiserated about the virtual ubiquity of entrenched monopoly power in both countries. As Levi pointed out, "the fact of the matter is that there is enormous concentration in the American economy today and an enormous amount of monopoly" (p. 3). "It will take men who are willing to go against size as such and to see to it that the American way of life—the competitive way—is preserved" (Levi, Berge, and Martin 1947, 19). In a 1947 article, Levi lamented this concentration, attributing its cause partly to ineffectual antitrust law enforcement.

To curtail concentration and monopolization, Levi put forward some policy recommendations, one of which included cracking down on vertical integration. "Usually in an integration case, however, the effort is made to use ownership of one part of an industry to dominate another part—at least that is what separates the integration case from the straight monopolization case" (Levi 1947, 180). Levi recommended: "Here an intent to monopolize may have to be found, and may well be only in a plan recognized as such because of restrictive arrangements, price cutting, or fraud—earmarks of the abuse category" (p. 180). In short, Levi maintained that vertical integration coupled with "abuses," such as price-cutting, provided sufficient evidence of intent to monopolize, and hence constituted grounds for illegality. After the birth of neoliberalism, however, Levi would come to maintain the contrary proposition.

The Birth of Neoliberalism: Monopoly Is Not the Great Enemy of Democracy

By 1951 the principal protagonists at Chicago came to see themselves as advocates of a new and distinct version of liberalism. In one instance, they even used the term *neoliberalism*. This suggests that the principals were conscious that a reformulation had at least begun to materialize (even as the *American Road to Serfdom* languished).

Although Director never himself employed the term *neoliberalism* in his scant few publications, his brother-in-law, Milton Friedman, did employ it self-referentially in his 1951 article entitled "Neoliberalism and Its Prospects."[34] Friedman's 1951 manifesto did not seek to fully lay out a cogent doctrine of neoliberalism; instead, it pointed toward some salient features of neoliberalism and compared them to the superseded classical liberalism. According to Friedman, nineteenth-century liberals maintained that the state should restrict its activities to the preservation of order and enforcement of contracts. Friedman pejoratively labeled it a negative philosophy in which "Laissez-faire must be the rule" (1951a, 91). One glaring flaw of nineteenth-century liberalism, according to Friedman, was that "it failed to see that there were some functions the price system could not perform and that unless these other functions were somehow provided for, the price system could not discharge effectively the tasks for which it is admirably fitted" (p. 91). Hence, Friedman specified that the state must indeed play a positive role: "Neoliberalism would accept the nineteenth century liberal emphasis on the fundamental importance of the individual, but it would substitute for the nineteenth century goal of laissez-faire as a means to this end, the goal of the competitive order. . . . The state would police the system, establish conditions favorable to competition and prevent monopoly, provide a stable monetary framework, and relieve acute misery and distress" (pp. 91, 93). This reconceptualization of the state became one of the hallmarks of MPS neoliberalism, as argued throughout this volume.

Friedman later dropped the terms *neoliberal* and *neoliberalism* (for reasons not explored here), but assertions that the principals at Chicago espoused a novel version of liberalism continued apace. For instance, Director suggested something very like this in a nationwide radio broadcast (Director, Brown, and Weaver 1955).[35] Nonetheless, the strongest evidence that Director and others came to regard classical liberalism as a hoary superseded doctrine is to be found in their arguments during the latter half of the FMS.

Aaron Director

The neoliberal reorientation toward monopoly first made its debut in Director's book review of Charles Lindblom's *Unions and Capitalism* (Director 1950). Director maintained that because of competitive forces emanating from the supply side of the market, competitors would supplant any monopoly that attempted to permanently restrict its own supply. According to Director, the market system through the "corroding influence of competition" (p. 165), has the "effective tendency" to "destroy *all* types of monopoly" (p. 166; emphasis added). Thus, competition became Director's philosopher's stone, and the only way the stone would lose its prodigious powers was whenever government intervened. Director maintained that history had demonstrated that without the intervention of government, "competitive tendencies have triumphed over the exclusive or restrictive tendencies" (p. 166). Among most economists and jurists of the 1950s, however, it would have been an outrageous oxymoron to maintain that competition existed even in the face of monopoly.[36] Therefore, by 1950, Director had become an acolyte of an unprecedented faith in the forces of competition.

In keeping with his change in attitude toward monopoly during the fifth year of the FMS, Director in 1951 expounded on his revised views of corporations from an arena circumscribed by economic issues since, according to Director, political issues were irrelevant for policy analysis.[37] This blithe conjuring away of "politics" as an irrelevant residual consideration for economists would become another hallmark of the Chicago School. To explore this matter further, we will now turn to the problem of monopoly.

Building on the premise that competitive forces undermine monopoly, Director claimed that if the corporate form had contributed to the emergence of a monopoly, it also would have simultaneously contributed to the demise of that monopoly—even if it seemingly facilitated a large-scale organization with monopoly powers. Implicitly conjuring Hayek's "road to serfdom," "The road to monopoly even with neutral rules is not a one-way road" (1951, 20). Furthermore, Director maintained that monopoly power did not get projected from one market to another; thus, a monopoly in the product market could not perniciously or selfishly manipulate the labor market or the capital market.

Similarly, Director asserted that a corporation, in spite of its size or the level of concentration of its market, could not hinder free choice in the labor market or any other market. In fact, according to Director, the corporate form was ideal not only because it neither hindered nor promoted monopoly, but also because it approximated the impersonal ideal of the market. Director sanguinely opined that, as with monopoly, the competitive forces would control corporations and ensure they approximated the ideal of competition. According to Director, this even applied to large corporations that gained their size via vertical or horizontal merger.

Furthermore, Director maintained that, although the separation of corporate ownership and corporate control did seem to be an issue in certain precincts, the capital market tended to narrow the divergence. Director stated that "the reduction in the price of shares occasioned by the divergence of interest will make it profitable for alternative sources of supply of control to purchase such shares for the very purpose of removing the divergence of interest" (p. 24). Again, the correction occurred through the palliative forces of competition, in keeping with Director's unprecedented faith in the pervasive efficacy of competition.

Less than five years after the FMS began, Director's 1946 speculation about the power of competition—that is, "monopoly tends to disappear and competition to revive even where once dormant"—became for the Chicago School an assertion of fact—that is, competition undermines all forms of monopoly. This marked a crucial watershed in the emergence of neoliberalism at Chicago and a crucial departure from ordoliberalism. Furthermore, in 1951, Director maintained—despite his 1947 claims at the MPS meeting that corporate power needed to be curtailed to foster a competitive order—that concentrated industries, with a full complement of large corporations, tended to be competitive. Unlike Simons and ordoliberals, he claimed that corporations—even big, behemoth corporations—approximated the impersonal ideal of the market. This change in attitude toward large corporations and concentrated industries marked another salient departure from classical liberalism. Like Director, his brother-in-law, Milton Friedman, adopted a similar position when it came to monopoly.

Milton Friedman

In 1947, in keeping with classical liberalism, Friedman had expressed concern about problems with monopoly. He had also expressed concerns about the corporate form that stemmed from the divergence of corporate ownership and control. However, after the lapse of four years, Friedman revealed his newfound neoliberal bent toward monopoly in an article published in France. One aim of his 1951 article was to describe the American free enterprise system to his European audience, who, he felt, mistrusted and misconstrued the American free enterprise system. In the course of doing so, Friedman departed from the classical liberal doctrine in several ways.

Friedman, contravening Edward Levi's 1947 contention that monopoly was ubiquitous in the United States, contended that such a depiction of monopoly was fallacious. Friedman suggested that prescriptions to ameliorate the purported monopoly problem were iatrogenic. By contrast to his 1947 worries, Friedman then maintained that monopoly persists only when it receives open support from government—suggesting that the divergence between corporate ownership and control had a nugatory influence on the persistence of monopoly (1951b, 17). Participation in the FMS seemed to have changed Friedman's mind.

Friedman now argued that actions of monopoly were conspicuous and actions of competition were inconspicuous: "monopoly is highly 'visible,' and draws attention to itself whereas the workings of competition are devious and hidden" (1951, 15). Moreover, like Director, Friedman asserted that competitive forces inherently limited the power of monopoly. As a result, Friedman portrayed the market power of monopoly as relatively benign, stating that "the effective power of [industrial and labor monopoly] over prices and wages tends to be considerably exaggerated" (p. 16). Friedman later stated, "I have become increasingly impressed with how wide is the range of problems and industries for which it is appropriate to treat the economy as if it were competitive" (1962, 120). Moreover, unlike Simons and the ordoliberals, Friedman concluded that private monopoly should be preferred to public monopoly and public regulation of monopoly (p. 28).[38]

Unlike classical liberals who feared the political and economic effects of monopoly power, henceforth Friedman adopted a relatively sanguine attitude. Classical liberals expressed misgivings about the concentrations of power that monopoly represented. With his scope narrowed to economic considerations, Friedman countered that inimical competition curbed monopoly power. The compelling empirical data that had supposedly swayed his opinion was nowhere to be seen. Classical liberals had suggested instead that monopoly eventually suppressed competition. Director and Friedman turned this distinction on its head, asserting that competition eventually suppressed monopoly.

Edward Levi

In 1947, Levi lamented the ubiquity of monopoly as the curse of concentration in numerous industries in the United States. Like Simons, at that time Levi saw forms of monopoly as the root of society's problems.

By the mid-1950s, Levi came to propound the opposite viewpoint. In 1956, he and Director wrote, "Since economic theory demonstrates that the presence of monopoly is much more often alleged than confirmed . . . less rather than more regulation ought to be prescribed" (p. 344). Moreover, contrary to Levi's 1947 claim, jointly he and Director also maintained that abuses of the firm, such as price-cutting, cannot create or enhance monopoly power (p. 290). They went so far as to claim, "In point of fact even a firm with complete monopoly power over prices and output cannot both get the advantage of such power and impose additional coercive restrictions on suppliers and customers" (p. 290).

By this time, Levi had adopted a relatively sanguine attitude toward monopoly and toward its persistence. Moreover, just as with Director and Friedman, Levi regarded the effects of monopoly as relatively benign, lamenting the benighted antimonopoly policy of the status quo U.S. antitrust laws, which ig-

nored modern economic theory (i.e., Chicago neoliberal economic theory). In 1953, shortly after the birth of neoliberalism at Chicago and shortly before Levi's volte-face, the Chicago-based Antitrust Project commenced. This project deserves to be remembered as the first self-consciously applied neoliberal project at Chicago. In 1957, after Levi's transformation, Levi joined the MPS. Since he had begun to participate in the revision of an important aspect of legal and social theory, it became a foregone conclusion that he would be ushered into the transformative intellectual experience at the heart of the "thought collective."

Pro-Trust Antitrust: The Antitrust Project

As with other distinctively neoliberal projects, the Antitrust Project had its fair share of MPS members (Aaron Director and John Jewkes) and future members (Edward Levi, John McGee, and William Letwin). Headed by Director and assisted by Levi, the Antitrust Project comprised both postdoctorate and post-juris doctorate students and visiting professors: a Chicago Law School graduate, Robert Bork,[39] a Committee on Social Thought Ph.D. graduate, William Letwin,[40] a former Department of Justice employee, Ward S. Bowman,[41] a Ph.D. graduate from Vanderbilt University, John S. McGee,[42] and a visiting scholar from Britain, John Jewkes[43] (Kitch 1983, 201–202). From 1953 to 1957,[44] these individuals collaborated to produce a prodigious number of articles and one book:

1. Letwin's articles, which included: Letwin (1954, 1956, 1959a, 1959b) and covered the law of restraint of trade and the history of the Sherman Act
2. Director and Levi's (1956) article on exclusionary practices
3. McGee's (1958) article on predatory pricing
4. Bowman's (1955) work on resale price maintenance
5. Bowman's (1957) article on tying arrangements
6. Jewkes et al.'s (1958) book on sources of innovation
7. Bork (1954) and Bowman's (1955 and 1957) articles on vertical integration
8. McGee's (1956) piece on price discrimination
9. Jewkes's (1953a and 1958) articles on government regulation of business[45]

Reminiscing on his experience with the Antitrust Project, John McGee reported that when he arrived at Chicago he "thought that the whole issue was monopolization" (Kitch 1983, 205). However, the scope had expanded with

alacrity to encompass manifold antitrust law issues, and yet the investigation of
the issue of monopoly remained ancillary for the purpose of many of the articles. Despite the broad range of antitrust issues that the Antitrust Project addressed, the leitmotif of most of the articles was that monopoly power could
not be extended through a laundry list of "abuses," such as tying arrangements
and resale price maintenance. In fact, this was essentially the explicit purpose
of Director and Levi (1956)—an umbrella article that incorporated the major
premises of other individual specialized Antitrust Project articles. Herbert
Packard, a legal scholar, perceptively regarded this article as the culmination of
the Antitrust Project: "If there is a 'Chicago school' of antitrust thought, its
manifesto is presumably the [1956] article by Levi and Director on Trade Regulation" (1963, 55–56). Thus, this article will be used to demonstrate the shape
of the emerging Chicago neoliberalism in the field of antitrust.

To comprehend the neoliberal claims advanced by Director and Levi (1956),
the sharp departures from the classical liberal doctrine during the course of the
FMS must be considered, for the premises of the FMS regarding monopoly and
corporations formed the underlying assumptions for the neoliberal premises of
the Antitrust Project. With this in mind, the following analysis will proceed as
follows: (a) some historical and terminological observations of antitrust law generally and exclusionary practices specifically and a brief note on the classical liberal perception of exclusionary practices; (b) a summary and critique of Director and Levi's argument; and (c) a description of how their analysis depended
on the FMS and an examination of some crucial neoliberal developments.

Director and Levi's manifesto was not intended to be a comprehensive
statement of the Chicago neoliberal position on antitrust law. Like the canon
of the Antitrust Project, it only covered a portion of United States' antitrust
law. Moreover, in the 1960s and 1970s, Ward Bowman, Robert Bork, John
McGee (all Antitrust Project members), George Stigler, and Richard Posner
made important contributions to refine and explicate the Chicago neoliberal
position on antitrust law, broadening their analysis far beyond the scope of
the initial Antitrust Project.

Exclusionary Practices: What Exclusion?

Antitrust casebooks (e.g., Posner 1974) list nearly all the topics covered by the
Antitrust Project under the rubric of exclusionary practices, that is, any practices that preclude or prevent competitors from entering the market. These

practices include price discrimination, vertical integration, tying arrangements, and resale price maintenance. In the 1940s and 1950s, the Supreme Court often treated such practices as deleterious for competition and considered them tantamount to abuses, deeming illegal per se some of these practices, such as resale price maintenance and tying arrangements. However, per se rules were not always part of U.S. antitrust law.

As Director and Levi (1956) observed, in the first twenty years of the Sherman Act, antitrust lawsuits frequently targeted businesses that were of enormous relative size gained through mergers and acquisitions and that overtly engaged in practices regarded as abusive. The quintessential example of this trend is the classic *Standard Oil* case. Standard Oil—a gigantic corporation—formed as a result of a number of mergers and acquisitions, and in this 1911 case, the United States government charged Standard Oil not only for being an unlawful monopoly that needed to be broken up into thirty-four independent companies but also for engaging in abusive practices, such as predatory pricing.

After *Standard Oil,* businesses were more often targeted that were not of great relative size, suggesting that enormous size coupled with abusive practices was not necessary for finding illegality. Instead, as Director and Levi pointed out, various types of practices such as tying arrangements, vertical integration, and exclusive dealing were increasingly declared either per se illegal or highly questionable without the consideration of monopoly power. Although Director and Levi questioned nearly all of these declarations of the Supreme Court, Henry Simons—a classical liberal at the University of Chicago—would have generally concurred with the Court: "The problem is that of selecting for proscription certain practices and arrangements, highly useful or essential for restraint of competition, which are not essential or highly useful for the conduct of competitive enterprise. . . . More narrowly, it is a problem of depriving corporations of powers and privileges which were unwisely granted, have been patently abused, and are quite unnecessary for effective organization or efficient operation and management" (1948, 101). Moreover, by maintaining that unambiguous and unequivocal rules of the game should guide antitrust enforcement, Simons repudiated the use of the rule of reason by the courts. Under the rule of reason, the courts had to determine whether an unreasonable restraint of trade occurred.[46] Not surprisingly, Henry Simons lambasted the rule of reason: "There must be explicit and unqualified repudiation of the so-called 'rule of reason'" (1948, 58).[47] Simons claimed that the rule of reason granted absurd powers to corporations (pp. 42–43).

Before turning to Director and Levi's implicit endorsement of a rule of reason analysis and their argument concerning the treatment of abuses, we consider their general argument and their reassessment of the United States industrial pattern, which crucially depended on the FMS. In a nutshell, Director and Levi argued that *their* understanding of economics did not justify the applications of the antitrust laws in the 1940s and 1950s. They disagreed with what they labeled "the drive for certainty and automaticity" on the part of the courts—particularly in the form of the incipiency doctrine that aimed to catch questionable anticompetitive conduct in its early stages. For Director and Levi, a dangerous implication of the drive for certainty and the reliance on numerous per se rules to help achieve greater certainty would result in the enfeeblement of the common law foundations of antitrust law, thereby precluding the antitrust laws from weathering future possible NRA attempts.[48] To Director and Levi's dismay, the drive for certainty unjustifiably rested on certain economic doctrines, doctrines that were no longer applicable because of the shift in the industrial pattern.

The FMS project sponsored Warren Nutter's investigation of the extent of monopoly in the United States[49] and Fred Weston's UCLA-based project that investigated the extent of mergers in the United States.[50] The Nutter investigation concluded that the extent of monopoly had not quantitatively increased in the last fifty years, and the Weston project concluded that the absolute size of large firms in the 1920s through the 1940s had been due to internal growth and that mergers had a nugatory effect on the level of industrial concentration in this period. In keeping with these conclusions, Director and Levi maintained that the industrial pattern of the United States was much less concentrated than what was commonly believed to be the case. Furthermore, because large firms had resulted from internal growth rather than by merger and acquisition, Director and Levi maintained that cutting down these firms would perniciously punish firms for utilizing economies of large scale—a fear of the U.S. federal courts.

Thus, Director and Levi suggested that the United States had entered a new era because of the dramatic shift in the industrial pattern, and, as a result, the application of the theory monopoly—an economic doctrine regularly relied on by the courts—was no longer apt: "The application of the monopoly concept to industries with three or four large units leads to curious anomalies" (1956, 287). According to Director and Levi, in connection with this shift in industrial pattern, the courts had applied the concepts of abuses and collusion to firms of less than clear monopoly size out of a misguided apprehension that such firms would gain monopoly power via abuse or collusion. Director and Levi maintained that the courts had egregiously and widely applied the concept of abuses and collusion in such a way that contravened economic theory.

The courts, Director and Levi maintained, understood abuses to be exclusionary devices to expand or obtain monopoly power. For example, they stated, "Thus when vertical integration is concerned, the inquiry is often as to the 'leverage' of the device" (p. 289). However, according to Director and Levi, the courts' treatment of abuses presupposed that a firm could obtain monopoly power via the use of the so-called abuse, and this underlying premise opposed Director and Levi's economic theory.

After briefly emphasizing that the foundation for the doctrine of abuses or coercive restrictions rested on questionable legislative grounds, Director and Levi stated: "The economic teaching gives little support to the idea that the abuses create or extend monopoly" (p. 290). According to Director and Levi, some monopoly power was necessary to impose a coercive restriction; otherwise a firm's total cost would be higher than total revenue. Because of the reduction in price, the firm would invariably lose some of its original power, and a consequence of the reduction in price was a decrease in revenue—suggesting that a firm's original power did not depend, as classical liberals contended, on political power. Thus, the coercive restriction would be sensible only if it took the form of price discrimination, and as a means of price discrimination, the restrictions would be merely an enjoyment of the original monopoly power, not an extension of it (p. 290). To emphasize the ubiquity of this economic principle, Director and Levi cited the instance of pure monopoly: "In point of fact even a firm with complete monopoly power over prices and output cannot get the advantage of such [original] power and impose additional coercive restrictions on suppliers and customers" (p. 290), thereby suggesting that exclusionary practices do not enhance or support monopoly power and thus implying that such practices are relatively benign. Granted Director and Levi suggested that there are exceptions to this general economic rule, but they implied such exceptions were relatively rare and opined that the responsibility for finding these exceptions rested with the courts.[51]

Having laid out this economic analysis, Director and Levi turned to the legal issue of abuses: "We have suggested that in most instances the supposed abuses neither support nor enlarge monopoly power" (p. 291). In patent tying cases, for instance, when the courts spoke of this device as an attempt to expand patent monopoly, the courts—according to Director and Levi—misconstrued economic reasoning: "[We] believe that the [tying] practices . . . can be explained best as methods of charging different prices to different customers and not as extensions of monopoly to other areas" (p. 292). In short, a central assumption of Director and Levi's analysis was that the imposition of certain types of coercive restrictions by a firm is tantamount to the imposition of price discrimination by that firm because of the aforementioned precondition for coercive restrictions. Director and Levi also utilized this assumption in their brief analysis of another restrictive practice, vertical integration. Contrary to Levi's 1947 claim, they maintained that "Vertical integration . . . often appears explainable as a method price discrimination" (p. 293).[52] Director and Levi also critiqued the restrictive practices, such as exclusive dealing; however, because their analysis did not provide a further understanding of the development of the neoliberal doctrine, we will forego further summary.

Although Director and Levi conceded that their economic analysis did not necessitate a change in the status quo law because the courts may reason that the law has more to do with rules of fair conduct—an alternative to the position of Director and Levi that carried some weight in 1956—than with adherence to economic analysis, they pointed out: "The important point, however, is that the restrictions or abuses will not in most cases carry with them the normal incidents of monopoly" (p. 294). In other words, price discrimination, whatever its permutation, did not adversely influence competition or surreptitiously tend to create monopoly. Although Director and Levi did not explicitly reject rules of fair conduct at this juncture in their argument, they emphasized: "Clarification of the economic basis thus presents the opportunity of choice for the law" (p. 294).

Next, Director and Levi briefly turned to the application of the idea of collusion. With regard to collusion, Director and Levi focused primarily on the issue of price-fixing agreements. They acknowledged that when price fixing occurs among members of an industry that control a large market share in terms of sales, the adverse consequences for the market can be predicted with some certainty. However, when price fixing occurs among firms with an insignificant combined market share, "there is less foundation for [illegality]" (p. 295). Although Director and Levi acknowledged there were meritorious arguments for declaring price fixing illegal in all instances—even when it is unclear if the agreement will actually affect price—they stated: "The extension of the Sherman Act into the remoter nooks and crannies of commerce, because of the broadened view of commerce among the states, however, may be thought to raise some questions as to the worthwhileness of a prohibition of all forms of price fixing regardless of the market effect" (p. 295).

Director and Levi concluded:

> The problems are difficult, and the law is not likely to meet them directly. [We do not] mean to suggest that the law must alone move within the confines of changing fashions in such theory. The law indeed can have a life of its own. But in this field of law more than any other, the general presumptions are of such a character that they cannot be readily isolated from the corresponding presumptions which dominate economic theory. We do suggest that in the future there may well be a recognition of the instability of the assumed foundation for some major antitrust doctrines. And this may lead to a re-evaluation of the scope and function of the antitrust laws. (p. 296)

In this prescient final paragraph, Director and Levi laid a foundational neoliberal premise, which would develop into a more extreme form in the coming years: Antitrust law should utilize economic theory, and Director and Levi had in mind the special brand of economic theory they espoused—not the versions of imperfect competition theory espoused by the Cowles Commission or MIT (Mirowski 2002). That is, when courts decide cases, reformulated Chicago economic theory should be employed as background theory. This implies that notions of rules of fair conduct should not be the sole basis of antitrust law decisions, which included principles such as small businesses should have the right to compete.[53] This neoliberal premise underlay many of the articles of the Antitrust Project.

However, some other important neoliberal developments composed the argument of Director and Levi, and most of these developments were grounded in the major premises of the FMS. This suggests that Director and Levi's 1956 article is the culmination of not just the Antitrust Project but also the FMS for the version of Chicago law and economics in the 1950s. Director and Levi's interpretation of the industrial pattern on which they based their analysis dovetails with the FMS contributions of Warren Nutter and Fred Weston. Of course, this interpretation drove Director and Levi's analysis, which led them to conclude that the economic principles of monopoly no longer applied to most firms of large size in the 1950s—creating a new problem of size for the courts—and implied that large corporations may approximate the impersonal ideal of the market and not threaten relative prices.

Moreover, the fact that Director and Levi justified collusion in the form of price fixing in some instances is a violation of classical liberalism, which argued that prices must adjust freely to reach a competitive equilibrium and reflect underlying social scarcities. A threat to freely adjusting prices was thenceforth treated as tantamount to a threat to freedom.

In keeping with Director's 1951 analysis, Director and Levi suggested that an analysis of political power was irrelevant to economic analysis. They argued that the utilization of a coercive restriction required "the price which would be charged without the restriction [to be] reduced" (p. 290). For such a condition to hold, it must be assumed that only economic factors bear on the circumstance in which the coercive restriction will be utilized. If political power facilitated the implementation of a coercive restriction, this necessary condition would fail to hold. Moreover, like Friedman in 1951, Director and Levi displayed a sanguine attitude toward monopoly.

Perhaps most importantly, Director and Levi affirmed and clarified that, aside from a special instance, monopoly would be undermined by competition (Director 1950). They suggested that this occurred when the monopoly exercised its monopoly power. In doing so with coercive restrictions, a loss of revenue would occur. Thus, in a sense, the profit motive of the firm would discourage the use of monopoly power. This faith in competition to undermine monopoly is a crucial neoliberal development, and its implication for antitrust law, for Director and Levi, was that coercive restrictions ought not be per se illegal, but rather that a case-by-case inquiry is necessary to determine if the exercised monopoly power qualifies as the "special case" (p. 290). Given the fact that Director and Levi classified this instance as a "special case" and given the extraordinary legal costs such a case-by-case inquiry would involve, the apparent logical implication would be the futility of an analysis to determine if the "special case" applied because a cost-benefit analysis probably does not merit it.

By maintaining that abuses did not in most instances substantially lessen competition or tend to create monopoly and by suggesting that the courts needed to conduct an industrial inquiry to determine whether industry is and is not dominated by a monopoly, Director and Levi, in effect, espoused a rule of reason analysis by the courts under such circumstances, which Simons—as indicated above—claimed granted absurd powers to corporations.

Conclusion

In a period of just ten years (1946–1956), the contents of liberalism at Chicago underwent a radical transformation. Director and other neoliberal advocates and converts no longer regarded monopoly as the great enemy of democracy, much less a force to be broken up by the hammer of U.S. antitrust law. Rather, they argued that not only was monopoly not deleterious to the operation of the market, but also that it was a negligible symptom attributable to ill-functioning ham-fisted activities of government. Moreover, they no longer re-garded large corporations as corpulent political bodies that would not be toppled—even under the pressure of market forces.[54] Rather, they character-ized corporations—even behemoth corporations—as relatively benign entities that naturally gave rise to the market conditions that would eventually under-mine them. In other words, the string of victories that allowed a large corpora-tion to dominate the market would invariably be pyrrhic victories. In the light of these neoliberal tenets, exclusionary practices—practices typically regarded as pernicious to the operation of the market—were portrayed as basically short-lived price discrimination, ephemeral to the operation of the market.

The ordoliberals, however, held steadfast to their belief that monopoly, large corporations, exclusionary practices, and other concentrations of eco-nomic power or utilizations of economic power were harmful to the operation of the market. Like Simons, the ordoliberals feared that economic power per-niciously threatened society's freedom by eliminating competition: "For Eu-cken and his colleagues, history . . . had demonstrated that competition tended to collapse, because enterprises . . . were frequently able to acquire such high levels of economics power that they could eliminate competition" (Gerber 1998, 250). The Chicago neoliberals had no such reservations. In the 1960s and 1970s, when they turned their attention to other areas of law, they gave no weight to considerations of economic power in their analyses.

The area of antitrust law would not be the only area of law that would be graced with attention by those at or associated with Chicago. Tort law and prop-erty law—as well as numerous other areas—would also receive the attention of neoliberals. In *Economic Analysis of Law*, first edition, Posner emphasized that one "can . . . find economic analyses of crime control, accident law, contract damages, race relations, judicial administration, corporations and securities reg-ulation, environmental problems, and other areas of central concern in the con-temporary legal system" (1972, ix). Furthermore, other projects at Chicago would later transform the economic approach to various areas of law based on some of the very same fundamental premises nurtured at the FMS and the An-titrust Project. The Volker Fund also bankrolled a Law and Economics Program later set up in the Chicago Law School. Initially overseen by Director and derived from the Antitrust Project, the Law and Economics Program provided research fellowships for law and economics, which benefited several notable law professors: Ronald Coase, Kenneth Dam, Edmund Kitch, and Richard Posner (Coase 1993, 247–248).[55] The Law and Economics Program thus guaranteed the next generations of neoliberals an opportunity to debate, develop, and disseminate their ideas. Nonetheless, history reveals that the roots of Chicago law and economics still remain firmly anchored in the FMS and the Antitrust Project. Chicago law and economics still presumes that monopoly is relatively benign and that corporations are not a political and an economic problem. It doesn't fear either monopoly or corporations as the great enemy of democracy. In the end, Chicago law and economics rejected Simons' and the ordoliberals' necessary condition for freedom: "It seems clear, at all events, that there is an intimate connection between freedom of enterprise and freedom of discussion and that political liberty can survive only within an effectively competitive system," a system without gigantic corporations and monopoly (Simons 1948, 43).

Notes

All archival material is quoted with permission. The author would like to thank T. Paul Schultz, Princeton University, and the Ghent Archive in Belgium. The author would also like to thank Phil Mirowski, Dieter Plehwe, Bruce Caldwell, Dave De-Long, Steve Medema, Warren Samuels, Dan Hammond, the referees for Harvard Press, and Monica Van Horn for helpful and thoughtful feedback.

Archival Sources

MPS1947LA Records of the 1947 meeting, Mont Pèlerin Society, Liberaal Archief, Ghent, Belgium
TSPR Theodore Schultz Papers, Regenstein Library, University of Chicago
VPML Jacob Viner Papers, Mudd Library, Princeton University

1. For evidence of Simons's classical liberal bent, see De Long (1990).
2. See, for example, Burns (1936); Tarshis (1946).
3. For a detailed account of how this transpired, see Chapter 4 in this volume.
4. For a detailed account of Director, see Van Horn (forthcoming). It is ironic that Director came to Chicago to head this project, because in the mid-1930s the Economics Department had refused to renew Director's contract, thereby forcing Director to leave and seek work in Washington, D.C. The reader may also refer to Chapter 4 in this volume for some background on Director.
5. Director, Friedman, and Knight attended the MPS meetings in the late 1940s.

6. See Ptak, Chapter 3 in this volume.

7. "In Germany, after 1945 the problem was the opposite: how to create a state that did not yet exist on the basis of non-state domain of economic liberty" (Lemke 2001, 196).

8. Typically, scholars who portray the Chicago position on monopolies and corporations as contrary to the ordoliberal position include, for example, Moschel (2001).

9. Note that "competition policy" was treated as basically synonymous with "antitrust law."

10. At Chicago, shortly thereafter, Director influenced George Stigler and John McGee, causing each to repudiate classical liberal tenets (Stigler 1988, 99–100; Kitch 1983, 206).

11. For insights into how some historical accounts overlook the importance of the FMS for Chicago law and economics, see Chapter 4 in this volume.

12. Simons committed suicide in 1946, as described in Chapter 4.

13. Viner demonstrated his classical liberal credentials on issues concerning monopoly in a 1959 address on the intellectual history of laissez-faire at the University of Chicago Law School. There he admonished, "In any case, monopoly is so prevalent in the markets of the western world today that discussion of the merits of the free competitive market as if that were what we were living with or were at all likely to have the good fortune to live with in the future seem to me academic in the only pejorative sense of that adjective" (1960, 66). Invoking Henry Simons, Viner called for a challenge to monopoly practices: "given the prevalence or danger of substantial intrusion of monopoly into the market, the logic of the laissez faire defense of the market against state-intervention collapses and there is called for instead, by its very logic, state-suppression or state-regulation of monopoly practices, which one may wish to call, as Henry Simons called it, an instance of 'positive laissez faire' " (p. 67).

14. See VPML, November 24, 1969, Viner to Don Patinkin, box 53, folder: Patinkin, Don).

15. Notably, Friedman acknowledged that he learned from both Simons and Eucken (Friedman 1962, 28). Friedman later stated, "I've gone back and reread the Positive Program [see Simons (1948)] and been astounded at what I read. To think that I thought at the time that it was strongly pro free market in its orientation" (Kitch 1983, 178). However, in the third section of this chapter we will see that he came to disagree with both Simons and Eucken about monopoly.

16. The description of ordoliberalism in this section draws primarily from Gerber (1998). For other sources on ordoliberalism, especially their competition policy, see Gerber (1994); Hildebrand (1998, chapter 3); and Moschel (2001). In this volume, see Ptak, Chapter 3. Although some may object that ordoliberalism was not fully formed, Ptak states that by the late 1930s the theoretical foundations of ordoliberalism were in place. In fact, in 1948, the *Ordo Yearbook,* which gave rise to the name "ordoliberalism," was launched (Tribe 1995, 1295). Of course, after World War II, ordoliberal policy needed to be further developed and then implemented through the key concept of the

"social market economy," "a carrier of ordoliberal programming and social engineering" (Ptak 2004 and see Ptak, Chapter 3 in this volume).

17. "In this perspective, the collapse of democracy in Germany is not caused by a functioning market economy, but rather the consequence of the fact that such an economy did not exist. From the viewpoint of the Ordoliberals, the Third Reich was the inevitable result of a series of anti-liberal policies" (Lemke 2001, 193).

18. Records of the 1947 Mont Pèlerin meeting, Liberaal Archives, Ghent, Belgium. Henceforth cited as MPS1947LA.

19. MPS1947LA, 79

20. Ibid., 84

21. Ibid., 79

22. Ibid., 80

23. Ibid., 85

24. The information on the FMS in this section comes from TSPR, box 39 (addenda), folder: Free Market Study.

25. Two empirical investigations funded in part by the FMS were Nutter (1951) and Weston (1953). Interestingly, the empirical research was published after the neoliberal claims started to emerge. Moreover, the extent to which the empirical research supports the neoliberals' claims is questionable; see Van Horn (2007).

26. See TSPR, November 15, 1946, box 39 (addenda), folder: Free Market Study.

27. Hovenkamp (1985).

28. See TSPR, February 26, 1947, box 39 (addenda), folder: Free Market Study.

29. See TSPR, undated, box 39 (addenda), folder: Free Market Study.

30. See ibid.

31. Levi received his law degree from the University of Chicago in 1935 and his J.S.D. degree from Yale in 1938. From 1940 to 1945, he served as special assistant to the attorney general, and worked under Thurmond Arnold in the Antitrust Division of the Department of Justice. Coming to the University of Chicago Law School in 1946, Levi worked as a professor. From 1950 to 1962, he served as dean of the University of Chicago Law School, becoming president of the University of Chicago in 1968.

32. Berge resigned as the assistant attorney general in charge of the Antitrust Division of the United States Department of Justice a week prior to the colloquy.

33. James Martin, at the time of the discussion, was the chief of the Decartelization Branch of the United States Office of Military Government for Germany.

34. Friedman's article appeared in *Farmand,* a publication edited by the MPS member Trygve Hoff (1895–1982), who attended the premier meeting in 1947. Incidentally, Hoff published an anniversary edition of *Farmand* in 1966, which contained articles by numerous MPS members—including Friedman, Stigler, Machlup, Hayek, Leonard Read, and John Jewkes.

35. Director stated: "I am speaking of the 'older kind of liberals.' These people recognize that, while the democratic method is preferable to other alternative methods,

nevertheless the majority decision involves a substantial amount of coercion; and it seems to me, as a consequence of that, if we are interested in maximizing individual freedom, we must keep those activities which are taken on the majority principle to a bare minimum and leave as much as possible—and to me that includes a great deal— to be decided by the voluntary decisions of individuals, singly or in relations with other individuals and groups" (p. 5).

36. In 1950, the status quo would have maintained that monopoly precluded competition and thus necessitated government intervention.

37. The fact that Director confined his analysis to the domain of economics is a neoliberal move. See Director (1951, 18).

38. Friedman stated, "Walter Eucken, a noted German liberal, observing public monopoly in German railroads, found the results so distasteful that he concluded public regulation would be a lesser evil. Having learned from both, I reluctantly conclude that, if tolerable, private monopoly may be the least of the evils" (p. 28).

39. Robert Bork obtained his J.D. in 1953, and he remained with the Antitrust Project for two years. In 1955, he worked at Kirkland, Ellis, Hodson, Chaffetz & Master, a corporate law firm, located in Chicago and New York City. In 1962, with the help of Ward Bowman, Bork obtained a position at Yale (Bork 1977, 235). Eventually, in 1982, Bork would be appointed to the U.S. Court of Appeals for the District of Columbia Circuit. In 1987, President Ronald Regan nominated Bork for the United States Supreme Court, and the Senate refused to confirm his nomination. Bork's 1978 book, *The Antitrust Paradox,* has supported the reasoning of numerous Supreme Court cases (Bork 1978; Kovacic 1990; *Contemporary Authors* 2004).

40. After his Antitrust Project stint, in 1956, Letwin obtained a position at MIT in the Industrial School of Management.

41. Bowman, who had been working in the Chicago Law School before the Antitrust Project commenced, spent his final year with Director in 1956 at the University of Chicago Law School. In 1957, he obtained a position as associate professor of law and economics at the Yale Law School (Bowman 1957, 19).

42. By 1957, McGee obtained an associate professorship in the University of Chicago Business School; in the 1960s, he moved to the University of Washington (Bowman 1957, 19).

43. Present at the premier MPS meeting, Jewkes was in the Economics Section of the War Cabinet and then later at the Ministry of Aircraft Production during the war (Cockett 1995, 57). In 1947, he joined Merton College, Oxford University, where he served as professor of economic organization. At the time the Antitrust Project began, he was a visiting professor from Merton College (Jewkes 1953b). By 1958, Jewkes had returned to England (Jewkes 1958).

44. Although it is unclear when the Antitrust Project formally ended, it is indisputable that the original group dispersed by 1957, with most of the members remaining through 1955.

45. See Priest (2005, 353–354).

46. According to the rule of reason, "The courts were to determine reasonableness by considering the conditions leading to the adoption of the restraint, the effects of the restraint, actual and probable, and the intentions of the participants, as indicated by their actions" (Dietz 1951, 8).

47. Simons called for the courts to spurn the rule of reason because "[when] lawyers try to draw a line between lawful and unlawful restraint of trade, they invariably end up with something that looks like the silhouette of a roller-coaster. . . . The purpose may be laudable; but the result is that few people get caught, rather fortuitously, and the growth of monopoly, with perhaps some formal modification, proceeds apace" (101).

48. The National Recovery Administration (NRA) was an early New Deal piece of legislation that started in 1933 (later abolished by the Supreme Court in 1935). It essentially suspended antitrust law for two years, and it supervised the development of codes of fair competition. Consequently, the common law foundation of antitrust trust law became less important.

49. See Nutter (1951).

50. See Weston (1953).

51. They stated: "But except of this special case, there is no clearly apparent advantage to a firm with monopoly power as against one without such power" (p. 290).

52. Director and Levi rejected the traditional objection to vertical integration, tying arrangements, and exclusive arrangements on the grounds of scant evidence: "It will be said that vertical integration like exclusive arrangements and tying clauses increases a competitor's capital requirements, and so places him at a disadvantage. We have already indicated that our belief in the need for further exploration and clarification of that line of argument" (p. 293).

53. For elucidation of this principle, see Hovenkamp (1985, 225).

54. In 1943, Henry Simons stated, "The efficiency of gigantic corporations is usually a vestigial reputation earned during early, rapid growth—a memory of youth rather than an attribute of maturity. Grown large, they become essentially political bodies, run by lawyers, bankers, and specialized politicians, and persisting mainly to preserve the power of control groups and to reward unnaturally an admittedly rare talent for holding together enterprise aggregations which ought to collapse from excessive size" (1948, 246).

55. Coase came to the Chicago Law School in 1964, Posner in 1969, and Dam in 1960. Kitch obtained his law degree at Chicago in 1964, and he served as a professor from 1965 to 1982. Coase is now professor emeritus at the Chicago Law School, and Posner still teaches there. Coase and Posner are both MPS members.

References

Bork, Robert. 1954. "Vertical Integration and the Sherman Act: The Legal History of an Economic Misconception." *University of Chicago Law Review*, 22: 157–201.

Bork, Robert. 1977. "Ward S. Bowman Jr." *Yale Law Journal*, 87: 235–236.

Bork, Robert H. [1978] 1993. *The Antitrust Paradox: A Policy at War with Itself.* New York: The Free Press.

Bowman, Ward S. 1953. "Toward Less Monopoly." *University of Pennsylvania Law Review,* 101(5): 577–641.

Bowman, Ward S. 1955. "Prerequisites and Effects of Resale Price Maintenance." *University of Chicago Law Review,* 22: 825–873.

Bowman, Ward S. 1957. "Tying Arrangements and the Leverage Problems." *Yale Law Review,* 67: 19.

Burns, Arthur R. 1936. *The Decline of Competition.* New York: McGraw-Hill Book Co.

Coase, Ronald. 1993. "Law and Economics at Chicago." *Journal of Law and Economics,* 36: 239–254.

Coase, Ronald. 1998. "Aaron Director." In Paul Newman (ed.), *The New Palgrave Dictionary of Economics and the Law.* New York: Macmillan.

Cockett, Richard. 1995. *Thinking the Unthinkable.* New York: HarperCollins Publishers.

Contemporary Authors. 2004. "Robert H. Bork." E-document: Thomson Gale.

De Long, J. Bradford. 1990. "In Defense of Henry Simons' Standing as a Classical Liberal." *Cato Journal,* 9: 601–618.

Dietz, Arthur T. 1951. *An Introduction to the Antitrust Laws.* New York: Bookman Associates.

Director, Aaron. 1950. Review of Charles E. Lindblom, *Unions and Capitalism.* *University of Chicago Law Review,* 18: 164–167.

Director, Aaron. 1951 "Conference on Corporation Law and Finance." *University of Chicago Law School,* 8: 17–24.

Director, Aaron, Stuart Gerry Brown, and Richard M. Weaver. 1955. "Who Are Today's Conservatives?" *University of Chicago Round Table.* #881.

Director, Aaron, and Edward Levi. 1956. "Trade Regulation." *Northwestern University Law Review,* 51: 281–296.

Friedman, Milton. 1951a. "Neoliberalism and Its Prospects." *Farmand,* February 17: 89–93.

Friedman, Milton. [1951b] 1952. "Free Enterprise." *University of Chicago Roundtable.* #744.

Friedman, Milton. 1953. "What Is American Capitalism?" *University of Chicago Roundtable.* #794.

Friedman, Milton. 1962. *Capitalism and Freedom.* Chicago: University of Chicago Press.

Gerber, David. 1994. "Constitutionalizing the Economy: German Neo-liberalism, Competition Law." *American Journal of Comparative Law,* 42: 25–85.

Gerber, David. 1998. *Law and Competition in Twentieth Century Europe.* Oxford: Clarendon Press.

Hildebrand, Doris. 1998. *The Role of Economic Analysis in the EC Competition Rules.* Boston: Kluwer Law International.

Hovenkamp, Herbert. 1985. "Antitrust Policy after Chicago." *Michigan Law Review,* 84: 213–284.

Jewkes, John. 1953a. "The Nationalization of Industry." *University of Chicago Law Review,* 20(4): 615–645.

Jewkes, John. 1953b. "Monopoly and Economic Progress." *Economica,* 20(New Series)(79): 197–214.

Jewkes, John. 1958. "British Monopoly Policy 1944–56." *Journal of Law and Economics,* 1: 1.

Jewkes, John, David Sawyers, and Richard Stillerman. 1958. *The Sources of Invention.* New York: St. Martin's Press.

Kitch, Edmund W. (ed.). 1983. "The Fire of Truth: A Remembrance of Law and Economics at Chicago, 1932–1970." *Journal of Law and Economics,* 26: 163–234.

Kovacic, William E. 1990. "*The Antitrust Paradox* Revisited." *Wayne Law Review,* 36: 1413–1471.

Lemke, Thomas. 2001. "The Birth of Bio-politics: Michel Foucault's Lecture at the College de France on Neo-liberal governmentality." *Economy and Society,* 30: 190–207.

Letwin, William. 1954. "The English Common Law Concerning Monopolies." *University of Chicago Law Review,* 21: 355–385.

Letwin, William. 1956. "Congress and the Sherman Antitrust Law." *University of Chicago Law Review,* 23: 221–258.

Letwin, William. 1959a. "The First Decade of the Sherman Act: Early Administration." *Yale Law Journal,* 68: 464–495.

Letwin, William. 1959b. "The First Decade of the Sherman Act: Judicial Interpretation." *Yale Law Journal,* 68: 900–929.

Levi, Edward H. 1947. "The Antitrust Laws and Monopoly." *University of Chicago Law Review,* 14(2): 153–183.

Levi, Edward H., Wendell Berge, and James Martin. 1947. "Are We against Monopoly?" *University of Chicago Round Table Pamphlets,* #477.

Liggio, Leonard P., and Tom G. Palmer. 1988. "Comment: *Freedom and the Law:* A Comment on Professor Aranson's Article." *Harvard Journal of Law and Policy,* 11(3).

McGee, John S. 1956. "Price Discrimination and Competitive Effects: The Standard Oil of Indiana Case." *University of Chicago Law Review,* 23: 398–473.

McGee, John S. 1958. "Predatory Price Cutting: The Standard Oil (N.J.) Case." *Journal of Law and Economics,* 9: 135.

Meijer, Gerrit. 1994. "Walter Eucken's Contribution to Economics in an International Perspective." *Journal of Economic Studies,* 21(4): 25–37.

Mirowski, Philip. 2002. *Machine Dreams.* New York: Cambridge University Press.

Moschel, Wernhard. 2001. "The Proper Scope of Government Viewed from an Ordoliberal Perspective." *Journal of Institutional and Theoretical Economics,* 157: 3–13.

Nutter, G. Warren. 1951. *The Extent of Enterprise Monopoly in the United States, 1899–1939.* Chicago: University of Chicago Press.

Oliver, Henry M. 1960. "German Neoliberalism." *Quarterly Journal of Economics,* 74(1): 117–149.

Packard, Herbert L. 1963. *The State of Research in Antitrust Law.* New Haven, CT: Walter E. Meyer Research Institute of Law.

Posner, Richard. 1972. *Economic Analysis of Law.* Boston: Little, Brown.

Posner, Richard A. 1974. *Antitrust: Cases, Economic Notes, and Other Material.* St. Paul, MN: West Publishing Co.

Priest, George L. 2005. "The Rise of Law and Economics: A Memoir of the Early Years." In F. Parisi and C. K. Rowley (eds.), *The Origins of Law and Economics.* Northampton, MA: Locke Institute.

Ptak, Ralf. 2004. "Vom Ordoliberalismus zur Sozialen Marktwirtschaft." Sationen des Neoliberalismus in Deutschland. Opladen: Leske und Budrich.

Simons, Henry C. 1948. *Economic Policy for a Free Society.* Chicago: University of Chicago Press.

Stigler, George. 1988. *Memoirs of an Unregulated Economist.* New York: Basic Books.

Tarshis, Lorie. 1946. *The Elements of Economics.* Boston: Houghton Mifflin.

Tribe, Keith. 1995. Review of A. J. Nicholls, *Freedom with Responsibility. Economic Journal,* 105(432): 1294–1295.

Van Horn, R. 2007. *The Origins of the Chicago School of Law and Economics.* Ph.D. thesis, Department of Economics, Notre Dame University, South Bend, IN.

Van Horn, R. Forthcoming. "Aaron Director." In Ross Emmett (ed.), *The Elgar Companion to the Chicago School.* Northampton, MA: Edward Elgar.

Viner, Jacob. 1960. "The Intellectual History of Laissez Faire." *Journal of Law and Economics,* 3: 45–69.

Weston, J. Fred. 1953. *The Role of Mergers in the Growth of Large Firms.* Berkeley: University of California Press.

7

The Origins of the Neoliberal Economic Development Discourse

DIETER PLEHWE

Neoliberalism and Development (Economics) Reconsidered

When a key group of concerned neoliberal intellectuals associated with Friedrich August von Hayek met in 1947 to start up the Mont Pèlerin Society, the "Third World" was not present on the agenda of the founding conference. A wide range of political economy issues aired at this opening meeting have subsequently been repeated: "politicization of economic life, the nature and working of the market economy, the problems of public finance, monetary instability and the problems of inflation, agricultural policy and agricultural fundamentalism, trade unions and wage policies, capitalist and socialist productivity, and the welfare state and social security." "The only major new subject introduced after 1947," stated MPS member and historian Max Hartwell (1995, 39), "was underdevelopment, about which, especially in the papers of P. Bauer and S. H. Frankel, there was omniscient understanding."

Pace Hartwell, the purpose of this chapter is to shed light on the ambiguous character of the neoliberal development discourse of the Mont Pèlerin Society. Starting in 1951 at the Beauvallon (France) conference, the group placed the topic of development on the agenda at four of the eight general meetings that took place during the 1950s. The area created a remarkable set of problems for the group in search of a sufficiently defined neoliberal identity. A closer examination allows us a glimpse into the wide spectrum of opinions and the extent of disagreement within this transnational group of intellectuals dedicated to renew liberalism. We can also observe some of the ways in which certain opinions were subject to a strategic selection process, though methods and approaches featured in some discarded works continued to inform a neoliberal core message on development.

Disagreement between neoliberal scholars on development in the 1950s should not be surprising, since development economics constituted an entirely new academic (sub)discipline informing national and international development policies in the aftermath of World War II and thus provided ample opportunities for a wide variety of approaches in the beginning. Traditional neoclassical economics—at the time still centered on equilibrium theory and full competition—seemed of little use in this field. While its shortcomings with regard to explaining labor market problems provided room for economists inspired by Keynes to inform employment strategies, urgently needed theoretical, conceptual, and empirical information needed to tackle pervasive problems of underdevelopment also emerged from a wide variety of heterodox development economists and seemed to provoke another "Keynesian revolution" of sorts (Hirschman 1981). Although the academic hierarchies and selection mechanisms typically found in established disciplines had yet to be developed, there were not many (neo)liberal economists who figured prominently at the time as potential gatekeepers and guardians of authoritative knowledge in the formative period of the new discipline of development economics. Traditional economists in fact objected to the formation of a specialized subdiscipline in principle and looked with dismay at the central roles allotted to "the state" and "planning" by many scholars in development economics.

Exacerbating matters for the scholars and practical men in search of neoliberal identities was the emergence of many new nation-states that, in the process of decolonization, were eager to experiment with extensive state planning. Frequently, these states chose to model their industrial system on the Soviet pattern, though without subscribing to bolshevism. Many Western industrialized countries eager to secure allies against the Soviets regarded such (noncommunist) planning efforts with some sympathy. According to many Western experts, the emerging international development financing and aid regime was to provide crucial funding for state-led development planning in the postcolonial world. In the eyes of (MPS) neoliberals, a dangerous liaison between planning-minded leaders in developing and developed countries threatened to undermine the free market system. Theoretical and practical challenges abounded, and "underdevelopment" arguably constituted even *the* new question for a renewed liberalism in a rapidly changing world (Steiner 2005).[1]

Although dedicated efforts to address development issues from a neoliberal perspective were developed in the early 1950s, their impact was not widely noticed until the late 1970s, and not before the 1980s did neoliberal expertise attain the status of authoritative development knowledge. At this point, worried members of the development community in the field first observed, and critically examined, a contemporary "neoliberal counter-revolution" (Toye 1993).

Possibly because of the considerable time lag between the genesis and conspicuous impact of neoliberal development economics, historiographers following Toye (1993) have dated the rise of the alleged neoliberal "counter-revolution" to the late 1970s and early 1980s. By those years, Thatcher and Reagan had been elected, and hence powerful right-wing arguments in favor of free market capitalism were being made in the analysis of the global debt crisis (Colclough 1991; Toye 1993; Leys 1996). Until the late 1970s, even critical scholars like Robert Cox (1979) did not identify a neoliberal camp as such when trying to describe major discourse coalitions in development. More recent intellectual histories (Ariffin 2001; Jolly 2004) once again speak rather vaguely about "free market approaches." The constitution of a powerful neoliberal cadre in development economics and politics several decades earlier remains overlooked.

Contrary to widely held convictions about the neoliberal "counter-revolution," I will argue that neoliberal development discourse emerged together with modernization and radical paradigms, and thus also preceded more comprehensive left-wing theories (dependency theory, world systems theory), which appeared in the 1960s (Leys 1996, 8–11). While Ascher (1996) correctly suggests that "in terms of historiography . . . the conventional interpretation of . . . a clash between so-called structuralists and neoclassical approaches, with the eventual victory of the neoclassicists, is profoundly misleading" (Ascher 1996, 315), his "evolutionary" perspective resembles the counter-revolution story rather too closely. Ascher observes the "rise and dominance of a *diluted* neoclassicism in methodology and epistemology, and an antistatist doctrine that nonetheless is still pursued by and through state institutions" (Ascher 1996, 313; emphasis added). Ascher failed to examine the institutional, sociological, and anthropological perspectives "diluting neoclassical economics," in a new body of neoliberal development literature that emerged in the course of the 1950s. Partly because of the common failure to better identify and recognize the neoliberal critique of neoclassical economics, his account does not explain the noted paradox of an alleged "antistatist" doctrine underpinning policies "nonetheless" pursued by and through state institutions.

The early contributions of leading neoliberal development theorists such as Peter Bauer and Herbert Frankel emphasized by MPS historian Hartwell were indeed crucial in setting the stage for the later dominant neoliberal streams of thought on the subject area. Yet their "omniscient" knowledge and expertise constituted but one element in a larger family of more or less stringent (neo)liberal and conservative streams of development thinking that at times uneasily coexisted within and around the Mont Pèlerin Society.[2] Upon closer inspection, it appears that earlier neoliberal scholars had been severely hampered in aligning their perspectives on development issues owing, first, to a sometimes hysterical *anticommunism* prevailing during the 1950s. As a consequence, many members of the emerging neoliberal camp relegated questions of development economics to second place behind international security concerns. Second, a strong commitment to *colonial economics* explains the dominance of conservative intellectual baggage over future-oriented neoliberal perspectives, which can be easily detected in the works of many early members of the neoliberal network.

Starting from what in the course of the 1950s appeared to be a rather heterogeneous group of right-wing liberal and conservative speakers, one can nevertheless identify the common straits of an early neoliberal development discourse and a new and positive neoliberal program that has escaped notice so far. I will argue that Bauer's contributions to MPS conferences in the late 1950s have been crucial primarily for clarifying the intellectual battle lines with regard to development economics and politics—both in the neoliberal camp and in the field in general.

The remainder of this chapter will closely scrutinize the formative period of development debates in and around the Mont Pèlerin Society to clarify the immense political value of Bauer's insight and to suggest that the alleged neoliberal "counter-revolution" actually developed *parallel* to the alleged original "revolution" within development economics in the 1950s. Deepak Lal— himself a member of the Mont Pèlerin Society—has been one of the few who have noted that "there has, however, *always* been some opposition to these [heterodox mainstream] views" (Lal 2000 [1983], 5; emphasis and brackets added). The focus on the Mont Pèlerin Society not only helps shed more light on the early neoliberal "opposition" in the academic field, but also can serve to reveal the social, political and economic dimensions of neoliberal discourse production beyond academia, which have not been subject to sufficient scrutiny in the research on the ascendance of neoliberal development theory.[3]

The analysis will proceed in chronological order. I will first establish how and why development theory arrived on the agenda of organized neoliberalism. An examination of presentations at the early (1950s) conferences will follow, in combination with an analysis of other publications of some authors, and there will be an analysis of the links between some of these scholars and activists who held positions in corporations, business associations, foundations, think tanks, politics, or the media. Strong dissent within the MPS notwithstanding, neoliberalism will become visible as a well-established, albeit quite diverse, scientific and political force operating in a truly pluralistic development landscape during the 1950s.

When and How Did Development Arrive on the Neoliberal Agenda?

Beyond local strongholds in different countries (like Germany, the UK, the United States, and France), MPS had an early presence in the developing world (e.g., South Africa, Mexico, Brazil) and a number of intellectual allies in others (e.g., India) as we shall see shortly, which was partly due to the colonial history of these countries. Reliable transnational links dating back to Mises's *Privatseminar* conducted in Vienna during the 1920s and the results of émigré networking of Hayek in the UK and Haberler in the United States during the 1930s and 1940s (see Feichtinger 2001) were an invaluable asset when MPS members started to examine the field of development economics and politics during the 1950s. They reinforced previously existing links and forged new transnational alliances in order to strengthen collaborative scientific and political efforts: "When [MPS member] Friedman joined C. W. Guillebaud as coeditor of the Cambridge Economic Handbook series in 1956," for example, "they decided to commission [MPS member] Bauer and B. S. Yamay to write the development text" (Strassmann 1976, 278). In his own account, MPS member Harberger (1996) notes that "good economics" was brought to Chile beginning in 1955.

MPS members (at the London School of Economics, in Freiburg and Chicago, for example) were already engaged in the ensuing development de-

bates when the issue was first addressed at the fourth MPS conference in Beauvallon, France in 1951. Similar to the way that the MPS conferences addressed
many issue areas ("Liberalism and Christianity," "Liberalism and European Integration," "Liberalism and Socialism," "Liberalism and Agriculture," "Liberal-
ism and Democracy," Liberalism and Racialism," "Liberalism and Colonialism";
see Liberaal Archief 2004), a panel on "Liberalism and the Underdeveloped
Countries" was organized to apply "neoliberal norms and principled beliefs" to
the field of development. The novel topic was originally proposed by Ludwig
von Mises, according to the September 7, 1950 circular on the preceding MPS
council meeting (MPS Circular 1950, quoted in Steiner 2005). Liberalism and
the underdeveloped countries, along with three other topics proposed by Mises
(the nature and functions of profits; the treatment of capitalism by the historians; an analysis of the pro-Soviet bias outside of Russia) eventually constituted
the full program of the 1951 Beauvallon meeting (cf. Liberaal Archief 2004).
Why did von Mises propose the new topic?

Although von Mises did not concentrate on development economics as
such, his whole oeuvre displays a keen interest in capitalist development in
general. In addition, there are specific reasons for his sensitivity to the issue of
developing countries. Most importantly, von Mises was fully aware of the political controversies surrounding the course of development planning in many
so-called Third World countries preceding the post–World War II discourse
because he had been invited in 1941 by (later MPS member) Luis Montes de
Oca, the former director of Mexico's central bank, to fortify antiplanning
forces in Mexico in their uphill battle against the reform efforts of the Cárde-
nas presidency. Von Mises stayed in Mexico in 1942 as visiting professor at the
National University of Mexico (Harper et al. 1971, ix). His sojourn yielded a
book on the economic problems of Mexico, including a proposal to privatize
Mexico's railroad system (Mises 1998 [1943]; see Plehwe 2002 for further details). Furthermore, von Mises worked at the Foundation for Economic Education (FEE) in Irvington on Hudson together with the prominent journalist
and MPS member Henry Hazlitt. The FEE was an early partisan think tank
leaning strongly to market radical libertarianism (compare Phillips-Fein in
Chapter 8 of this volume). FEE published both Hazlitt's general critique of
U.S. foreign policy based on financial aid (Dollar Diplomacy), and its application to the emerging field of development politics after President Truman's
Point Four speech. Hazlitt's political journalism likely reinforced Mises's sensitivity to the political importance of the subject matter with regard to forging

a new liberal identity (cf. Steiner 2005). Both Mises and Hazlitt, of course, belonged to the core group of intellectuals who, next to Friedrich August von Hayek and MPS secretary Albert Hunold, were most important in organizing the Mont Pèlerin Society (Walpen 2004). Finally, the new addition to the agenda of the neoliberal thought collective is hardly surprising given the presence of MPS members in developing countries. The important role Mises played in particular for a large group of neoliberal intellectuals in developing countries is reflected in a two-volume collection of essays titled "Towards Liberty" in his honor published by another MPS related partisan think tank, the Institute for Humane Studies, in 1971. The sponsoring committee included the Mexican MPS member Gustavo R. Velasco. The first volume is organized by country and features MPS member contributions from Argentina, Guatemala, Mexico, and Peru apart from European Countries, the United States, and Japan (Harper et al. 1971). Other political factors to be considered when answering the question of why development was placed on the MPS agenda will be discussed below. It is clear, however, that the ensuing post–World War II development debates were situated at the confluence of a whole range of critical issues (such as the character of the state, the role of international trade, and the influence of socialism), which at the time caused concerned neoliberals sleepless nights.

A critical study of the varieties of neoliberalism present within and around the Mont Pèlerin Society, as evidenced by the speakers and contributions to the Beauvallon and subsequent general meetings, is crucial, however, to understand that earlier MPS scholarship in development did not conform to the particular Mises wing of neoliberalism. Nor was later "neoclassical economic thinking" just "diluted" by absorbing parts of the wisdom generated by structuralist and heterodox thinkers of the left who figured prominently in the field of development economics during much of the post–World War II history of development economics. The development discourse within the Mont Pèlerin Society provides ample evidence of a wide range of opinions within the neoliberal group and sheds light on the historical, institutional, sociological, and anthropological economic traditions of the right that are extremely important to an understanding of certain transformations of neoclassical economics (e.g., with regard to the understanding of competition, labor, knowledge, the law and the state, and dynamics of development and change in general). There exists ample evidence (presented later in this chapter) for the great struggle involved in framing a new perspective based on a fairly clear and sufficiently defined neoliberal worldview. Ludwig von Mises probably did not anticipate that he would open a Pandora's Box when prompting the topic on the agenda.

The Cold War and the Invention of Underdevelopment

The year 1947 marked the serious beginning of the Cold War, with the Truman Doctrine proclaiming a fight against communism wherever. In March 1949, Truman announced what would become known as the *point four* program to aid developing countries, a program based on a *modernization* vision of science and technology designed to meet universal development needs around the globe, especially in underdeveloped areas and countries. Esteva (1992, 6) argues that Truman "invented" the term *underdevelopment* in the contemporary sense in his presidential address by using the word *underdeveloped* for the first time in this context, though Cooper (1997) explains the substantive affinities of earlier *colonial development* discourses in Europe (which had emerged in reaction to anticolonial movements). Unconvinced by the president, conservative Republicans in the United States continued to question the rationale of *economic* development aid during both the Truman and Eisenhower administrations, and argued in favor of foreign *military* aid instead to meet the communist challenge. As a result, unilateral spending of the United States fell far short of the amount envisioned by modernization theorists during the 1950s (Latham 2000; Pearce 2001; Gilman 2003).

Despite the inevitable deflation of grand development schemes, Bretton Woods, the United Nations, and various U.S. government institutions were established toward the end of and shortly after World War II, and started to develop exploratory investigations and programs. Important works directly addressing developing countries and development issues include Prebisch and Singer's structuralist arguments pointing toward a secular trend of deteriorating terms of trade for primary producers. At the same time, international organizations and regimes like the General Agreement on Tariffs and Trade (GATT) were successfully helping to resurrect fledgling world trade.

Domestically, social liberalism was on the rise in many Western countries: the Labour Party won the 1945 elections in England, and Germany's Christian Democrats worked on the Ahlen program, accepting the possible need of socialization of certain means of production. The U.S. Marshall Plan backed the economic recovery of Western Europe, Japan, and the colonial territories, though important U.S. institutions were ambiguous with regard to economic planning abroad (Hirschman 1989). In any case, economic recovery solidified the split between (capitalist) Western and (socialist) Eastern Europe. In the United States, McCarthyism started to target (alleged) communists in 1951: The prevailing wisdom for much of the 1950s and 1960s expressed a "Cold War mentality" (Walpen 2004, 118–120), which was well reflected in the discussions at MPS conferences on development topics.

The 1951 Beauvallon Conference: Export-Oriented Traditional Production

The first MPS general conference to cover issues related to the emerging neoliberal development discourse was the fourth time the steadily growing group gathered—for five days in September in Beauvallon, France.[4] The final topic discussed at the 1951 general meeting over the course of two days addressed "Liberalism and the Under-Developed Countries."

Carlo Mötteli's discussion of the meeting for the Swiss daily *Neue Zürcher Zeitung* omitted the contributions by S. Herbert Frankel, Peter T. Bauer, and Frederic C. Benham to the conference (Liberaal Archief 2004, 23). In stark contrast to Hartwell's (1995) emphasis on Bauer and Frankel, his summary stated that Louis Baudin, Wilhelm Röpke, and John Jewkes "had the most penetrating analysis to offer of development plans on the collectivist pattern, while Henry Hazlitt . . . criticized President Truman's Point Four program rather severely. The net result . . . may be . . . that there can be no general therapy for the development of under-developed countries. . . . Hasty and ill/considered schemes will merely make things easier for Communism." If it is sometimes difficult to find authors openly professing to neoliberalism, Mötteli was unafraid of displaying neoliberal self-confidence: "But while *the old system of laisser faire, laisser aller is as much out of the question in underdeveloped areas as elsewhere,* hope exists that the *principles and policies of neoliberalism* will find a promising field of activity and development there" (Mötteli 1951, 23; emphasis added).

Unfortunately, only Benham's[5] paper is available in the MPS Archive in Ghent. Additional information on the early MPS debates can be inferred, however, by drawing on subsequent publications, which allow documentation of the close interaction of MPS scholars present at Beauvallon. A wide range of rather traditional staples of knowledge grounded in colonial economics is hard to overlook in the collective effort *in search* for neoliberal perspectives at the time. While Benham conformed with Mötteli's caveat about specific local circumstances in the developing world requiring exceptions from any generalized approach, he nevertheless went on to make "some sweeping generalizations in order to bring out . . . some fundamental conclusions, namely that the main road to economic progress for underdeveloped countries is to increase their output per worker in agriculture and to specialize on producing for export those goods and services in which they have a comparative advantage" (Benham 1951, 1). Benham argued that *industrialization* strategies failed to understand that, historically, industrializing Britain was dependent on the preceding improvement of agriculture. In contrast to the British experience, contemporary developing countries were held to immediately benefit from international trade if they specialized in *traditional production for export.* Benham rejected diversification strategies (from agriculture to industry), especially if they increased protectionism. He even cast doubt on widely propagated education efforts (alphabetization campaigns, etc.) because they "would be very expensive" and because it is not "clear how a general non-technical education would have any immediate effect on output" (Benham 1951, 5).

Benham stressed overpopulation and a preference for leisure rather than work as intrinsic obstacles to development. Apart from invoking stereotypes typical of Victorian anthropology prevalent in the comparative developmental discourse of nineteenth-century evolutionism (Pieterse 2001, 19), it is not difficult to see Benham developing a systematic counterargument against the emerging industrialization and modernization strategies based on import substitution and selective protectionism. Benham's paper displays an important contradiction in this regard: Given his emphasis on "free trade" (Benham helped translate Haberler's book on international trade),[6] it is interesting that Benham regards a local lack of certain inputs in industrial manufacturing and insufficient local markets as important obstacles to industrialization in developing countries (Benham 1951, 8–9), while emphasizing the benefits accruing to developing countries from international exports of traditional (i.e., agricultural and raw materials) production. Why should developing countries not import missing inputs and export manufactured goods to the larger consumer markets? Hong Kong and Singapore obviously were not yet the neoliberal poster children of export-oriented industrialization.

Benham's thinking basically remained confined within the framework of nineteenth-century colonial economics.[7] The recommended concentration on the primary sector (and export specialization in competitive areas thereof) were strategies that would not challenge the prevailing global division of labor and were thus in line with (conservative) interests in the industrialized countries still in control of colonial territories (securing continued and improved access to primary inputs and avoiding potentially new competition for their own industrial exports to the regions). Although the focus of Benham (and other MPS development experts, as we shall see) was in line with traditional liberal colonial economics on export-oriented agriculture (and other raw materials), it is nevertheless easy to see how his reasoning in opposition to *import substitution industrialization* (ISI) was an early and rudimentary form of what can be presently regarded as generalized free trade strategies (despite the emphasis on exports displayed in the *export-oriented industrialization,* or EOI, paradigm that came to displace it). Since lowering barriers to imports is considered quintessential to EOI, *international* trade, and not *national* development, was the predominant guiding principle.

Unlike a collection of papers given at the Beauvallon conference on the related topic of "Capitalism and the Historians,"[8] which was subsequently published, the plan to publish the papers on "Liberalism and Underdeveloped Countries" failed. While Mötteli's (1951) report on the development discussion does not provide much detail with regard to the content of the first neoliberal deliberations in the development field, we can learn a bit more about the content of the MPS meeting's papers and discussions by reading Wilhelm Röpke's subsequently (1953) published article. It appeared in the fifth issue of *ORDO,* the premier neoliberal academic journal in Germany (founded by MPS members Walter Eucken and Franz Böhm), and benefited tremendously from the neoliberal network of intellectuals and their encounter at MPS meetings.

Röpke's Early State of the Neoliberal Art in Development

Wilhelm Röpke's[9] (1953) broad overview warned against the dangers related to the new favorite term *development,* especially since most powerful countries (the United States) and international organizations (e.g., the United Nations) lent gravitas to the mushrooming development knowledge and expertise. Röpke honestly acknowledged that he relied heavily on the work of the French economist Gaston Leduc,[10] a fellow MPS member, in writing his paper. Röpke suggested that many issues of the present development debate had previously been discussed under the topic "industrialization of new countries," and he considered it advantageous that the term *development* is neutral with regard to the type of economic activity to be achieved. This would allow consideration of original (agricultural) production instead of industrialization.[11] He also attacked the close link between "collectivists" and "state planners" in Western developed countries and like-minded leaders in developing nations. While recognizing that "developmentalism" was conceived to shield underdeveloped countries from Soviet influence and that it reversed some of the previous protectionist practices in Western countries, he nevertheless regarded state planning and collectivism as the main features of developmentalism as ill-conceived strategies that would ultimately destroy freedom, market exchange, and democracy in both developing and developed countries. According to Röpke, the new ideology was related to the equally detrimental ideologies of full employment, the welfare state, and international integration (Röpke 1953, 69).

Röpke linked the origins of collectivist developmentalism to the prehistory of the International Bank for Reconstruction and Development (World Bank Group) and to the genesis of Truman's Point Four Program. He cited Henry Hazlitt's (1950) book, *Illusions of Point Four,*[12] to let his readers know that the leader of the U.S. Communist Party, Earl Browder, had anticipated President Truman's core idea in 1944 (Röpke 1953, 68n.4). Röpke then attacked the "narrow economism/technicism" of development economics, which he defined as a lack of consideration of a wide range of spiritual and moral as well as sociological questions (Röpke 1953, 71). Contrary to liberation theories, he considered *decolonization*—not colonization—as a historically unique expansion of Western culture around the world at the expense of traditional cultures. Although Western responsibility for the cruelties of colonialism and the prevailing misery in developing countries called for active sympathy, Röpke nevertheless counseled to meet the erroneous beliefs of leaders in developing countries with strong resistance and straightforward criticism (Röpke 1953, 74).

Industrialization strategies were doomed to fail, according to Röpke, owing to the lack of a "liberal tradition" required to succeed in manufacturing. Throughout the Third World, with the exception of some Latin American countries, Röpke thought he observed a lack of punctuality, reliability, the inclination to save and to create—entrepreneurship for short. A successful approach, he believed, would require recognizing the "subtle and complicated process" of development, "flexible adaptation," "smart connections to the existing," and "slowly growing"—just the opposite of the goals of planners (all quotes from Röpke 1953, 77). Röpke relied on Herbert Frankel's Beauvallon

contribution[13] to attack the ignorance of development planners, and he referred to other work by Frankel to authorize the distinction between (acceptable) infrastructure planning and (misguided) investment and planning for
market-oriented production. And he relied on Frederic Benham's contribution
for an example of the successful export-oriented development of traditional
agriculture (supporting small-scale industrialization in Malaya) in contrast to
"overindustrialization" in Turkey, Australia, and South Africa (Röpke 1953, 85).

Röpke pointed out that the overwhelming share of industrial production
remained highly concentrated in just a few countries, in spite off the dedicated efforts to industrialize new countries. To back this assertion, he quoted
a recent study of his Beauvallon co-speaker and fellow MPS member John
Jewkes.[14] Jewkes argued that the inherent advantages of industrialization, science, and technology lead to benefits accruing to industrialized nations, and
these had described precisely the reasons for import-substituting industrialization strategies: dedicated efforts were needed in order to break the "vicious cycle of poverty" and to overcome the dependencies resulting from the prevailing global division of labor, according to Myrdal and others. Röpke assured
his readers, however, that traditional production was *not* inferior, and he fore-
casted improving terms of trade for primary commodities in the long run for
those developing countries that dedicated their efforts to this sector. The crisis of raw materials production and trade in the aftermath of the Great Depression was regarded as the key culprit in erroneous thinking (of Prebisch and
Singer, without mentioning them) (Röpke 1953, 88–89).

In line with Benham and colonial economists, Röpke thus called for export-
oriented traditional production. Instead of industrialization, he recommended
diversifying the organizational structure of agricultural producers. Family
farms should specialize in export crops without becoming fully dependent on
market income. Röpke referred to Peter Bauer's work on rubber regulation in
support of his argument. But he also called on the West to remove protective
tariffs and on leaders in developing countries to promote land reform (Röpke
1953, 93). Röpke thus rejected contemporary critiques of traditional production (claiming a generally low productivity of agriculture). He suggested that
this sector was more likely to absorb large parts of the growing population
than any industrial alternatives. Ultimately, Röpke concluded, not much
could be done to overcome the fundamental problem: the lack of capital
(availability) due to the low propensity to save, the absence of capital markets,
and the inadequate banking systems. Consequently, capital would necessarily
have to come from the outside. He considered private investment (though

beneficial) completely insufficient in terms of what would be needed. The crucial issue was the very condition under which development planning was supposed to occur: according to Röpke, private investment would be undermined by creating political conditions inimical to private investors. He did not trust the international rule of law due to the composition of prospective UN membership: Europe's vote was observed to be outnumbered soon by new developing countries, assisted by the "anti-imperialist screaming" of the Russian representatives of world communism (Röpke 1953, 104).

An examination of Benham and Röpke's contributions reveals the links between a number of scholars and writers in Europe and the United States found within the orbit of the Mont Pèlerin Society, including some of the much later well-known "counter-revolutionaries" (e.g., Haberler and Bauer) as early as 1951. Röpke refers almost exclusively to the work of neoliberals organized in the MPS: Frederic Benham, Peter Bauer, Herbert Frankel, and Henry Hazlitt, as well as John Jewkes and Gaston Leduc. While dismissing with disdain the antiagrarian "mentality" of Manoilesco and a few individuals advancing "socialist propaganda" (Röpke 1953, 85 and 70, respectively), advocates of industrialization and planning strategies mostly remained unnamed. These anonymous writers of international agency and task force reports were reprimanded with evidence presented from the neoliberal pool of individual scholars and practical "experts."[15]

At this point the MPS group displayed an understanding of development economics that still uncomfortably resembled traditional colonial economics underpinned by Victorian anthropology: According to Benham, people lacked the propensity to save, and according to Röpke, there was a lack not only of entrepreneurs, but also of a class and the spiritual-moral preconditions that could eventually generate entrepreneurs. Advancing industrialization strategies thus were considered ill-conceived strategies for various reasons, pursued by a dangerous—Jekyll and Hyde like—alliance of Western socialists and government elites in the developing world. Although industrialization was at the same time considered likely to fail and therefore to be counterproductive as well with regard to the declared goal of keeping the Soviets out, it was suggested that societies move further toward the "totalitarianism" of planning.

Although such a group was unlikely to play a strong role in the emerging development debate (except for the advocacy of free trade and private investment promoting the GATT, for example), key elements of the later success of the neoliberal discourse are readily visible: Neoliberals insisted on the "diversity" of developing countries, objected to industrialization as a universal solution, and displayed an appreciation for frequently neglected issues of agriculture and traditional production (see Ascher 1996). The emphasis on diversity could be considered rhetorical rather than substantial, but given the readiness for generalized solutions related to export-oriented traditional production, scholars in and around MPS nurtured skepticism against the very way structuralists applied neoclassical modeling tools and emphasized detailed local knowledge with regard to history, people, and institutions. It was not the interest in sociology and institutions that separated Röpke and, say, Myrdal, but rather different varieties of sociology and institutional perspectives alongside a different normative and epistemological understanding of economics.

Whereas Röpke's thinking in particular was nostalgic in some ways, both Benham's and Röpke's reasoning already contained programmatic neoliberal elements of change: conservative reform was prescribed, requiring concessions both from developed countries and from feudal landowners in developing countries. Neoliberal scholarship thus displayed its own moments of critique of the status quo. But we cannot yet observe great confidence in a neoliberal *economic* perspective. The developmentalist argument was primarily countered with general sociological, moral, and historical arguments. A strongly felt need to engage in revisionist historiography can be observed on industrialization, which played an even greater role in later MPS conferences addressing the history of colonialism, for example. Another quite obviously dominant concern over Soviet expansion also became more prominent at later MPS conferences, before Peter Bauer managed to comprehensively challenge foreign aid strategies, and to develop a more coherently neoliberal development perspective. Before revisiting the MPS conferences of the second half of the decade, it is helpful again to briefly consider the general historical background for the 1957 (St. Moritz) and 1958 (Princeton) conferences.

The Bandung Era: Consolidation of the Third World

The 1957 MPS conference took place in St. Moritz two years after the Bandung (Indonesia) conference organized by the governments of newly independent Indonesia, Ceylon (Sri Lanka), India, and Pakistan. The Bandung conference "was a result of their frustration with the political logjam surrounding new membership in the United Nations. By 1953/54 no new members had been inducted into the organization since the acceptance of Indonesia in January 1950. The 1955 meeting in Bandung was attended by delegations from 29, primarily new, nation-states or nationalist movements in Asia and Africa" (Berger 2004, 11–12). The political logjam at the UN had resulted mainly from the Cold War rivalry of the superpowers. Thus, Mark Berger aptly captures various organizing efforts of newly independent countries still fighting anticolonial movements as "the overall consolidation of Third Worldism . . . grounded in the post-1945 conjuncture of decolonization, national liberation and the Cold War" (ibid., 11). The Bandung conference specifically addressed the issue of French colonialism in North Africa: The war that was then being waged in Algeria to prevent decolonization was into its second year. In 1957, Ghana, under the leadership of Kwame Nkrumah, was the first (former British) colony in Southern Africa to gain independence. Only five years later the United Nations would admit no less than fifty new members (sixteen in Africa), which basically doubled UN membership.

Rapid economic development in the defeated nations of Germany, Japan, and Italy was largely credited to the Marshall Plan, the U.S. international credit and aid program that also helped consolidate the Western (North Atlantic Treaty Organization—NATO) military alliance. Beyond Europe and Japan, this apparent economic and political success seemed to validate President Truman's 1949 "point four" vision to win the ensuing Cold War: improving living standards by helping governments in underdeveloped countries acquire industrial *and* agricultural equipment and skills. Because the USSR was perceived to be the dominant threat to world stability, the development programs run by various agencies at the time eventually supported many state-led and even socialist development programs in countries such as Nehru's India that kept a political distance from the Soviet Union.

Decolonization, and concomitantly rising "Third Worldism," continued to present enormous challenges to neoliberal perspectives. The revolutionary aspirations of the popular masses in the Third World, utopian egalitarianism, an emphasis on a strong and centralized state to accomplish development, and international alliances all combined with rhetorical commitments to transnational unions (pan-Arabism, pan-Africanism, etc.) in favor of regional integration and redistribution (Berger 2004, 34). At home, most neoliberals were worried about a disturbing willingness of leading politicians from both the right and the left to embrace expanded state management of the economy and foreign aid.

Apropos Decolonization: Feeble Liberalism Abroad
and at Home: St. Moritz

Seven years after Beauvallon, the topic of development moved up on the MPS's agenda,[16] owing to the rising challenge of Third Worldism in general and to a specific "German" discussion within the neoliberal camp in particular. In St. Moritz, eighty-five members (including Peter Bauer, Herbert Frankel, and Karl Brandt as important academics in the development field) and fifty-nine guests (including publisher Eugen Rentsch, who published a whole series of neoliberal contributions to the field of development in the early 1960s)[17] assembled for a week in September 1957 to discuss the topics "Colonialism and Liberalism" followed by panels on "Liberal Philosophy," and "European Integration." Recognizing the context is important to understand the early quarrel of neoliberals with the consolidation of "embedded liberalism" (Ruggie 1982). The effort of MPS circles to rewrite colonial history (emphasizing civilizing effects rather than exploitation), however, was sparked by the writing of one of their own, namely, the reflections of German MPS member Alexander Rüstow[18] on colonial imperialism. Rüstow's book had prompted Hayek to place the topic at the top of the agenda. Lined up in the discussion were Karl Brandt (Stanford), Arthur Shenfield (London), Edmond Giscard d'Estaing (Paris), and P. T. Bauer (London), all of them pitted against Rüstow, who presented the part on colonial imperialism, the third of his three-volume *Ortsbestimmung der Gegenwart,* to his fellow neoliberals. Rüstow spoke last, but we will reverse the order to ascertain what it was in Rüstow's writing that aroused the intellectual leadership of the MPS at the time to arrange for this discussion in the first place. In fact, there were two Rüstows speaking: Rüstow the decidedly *Christian* neoliberal and Rüstow the uncompromising *neoliberal* Christian. While the decidedly Christian neoliberal persona was fully in line with the dominant opinions reflected in the other papers, Rüstow's uncompromising neoliberal Christian guise caused great irritation.

The first Rüstow started his analysis by combining the terms of colonialism and imperialism to blame the *absolutist state's* thirst for power for the earliest and most brutal application of colonial imperialism in an apparent effort to separate the term *imperialism* from *capitalism.* The liberal Hobson (1965 [1902]), of course, had originally established this link by way of his critical examination of British imperialism during the time of the Boer War; Marxists like Lenin, Luxemburg, and Hilferding relied heavily on Hobson's work. Instead of characterizing a specific epoch of capitalist development, Rüstow turned imperialism into a universal category of state power indicated by foreign policy "behavior." Such a phenomenological approach allowed Rüstow to treat the Spanish and Portuguese conquistador in the same manner as nineteenth-century Western imperialism and twentieth-century Soviet efforts to expand communism. Needless to say, little effort was wasted on searching for different reasons and causes for only superficially similar policies: then and now, here and there, Rüstow found the same causes for imperialism—centralized state power.

At the same time, Rüstow chastised the West for the epoch of discoveries, blaming avarice, addiction to power, and sadism as the strongest motivations of the early expansionism. His critical discussion of the early ideologies developed to legitimize the conquista—including the denial of human status to the native peoples in the conquered territories—does not lack clarity. And while he praised church efforts to humanize colonial practices, as well as general efforts to improve the medical, educational, and technical standards of living in the colonies, he emphasized the continued abuse of power as well as what he regarded as the unintended consequences of some of the progress made (e.g., famines linked to rapid population increase). In Rüstow's analysis, anything positive weighs "feather light" compared to the crimes committed under the auspices of colonial imperialism, a "seamless chain of heaviest crime against humanity" committed over half a thousand years and continuing to his days of writing (Rüstow 1957, 506).

As background to his fears regarding these crimes, Rüstow points to the feelings of hatred and revenge that have accumulated and built up in four continents. Though not ready to explode everywhere right away, these feelings, he says, are only waiting to be exploded by bolshevism against "us." Rüstow urged his contemporaries to find a solution to the most pressing problem causing the present crisis of humankind, and he warned countries that still had colonies to leave in good grace instead of waiting to be thrown out. White settlers were singled out as the gravest problem for anticolonialism, notably in South Africa. Rüstow's "common-sense" approach led him to ask rhetorically what one could expect from the victims of colonial imperialism other than copying Western behavior: "Is Nasser not exactly the type of a dashing General Governor?" (Rüstow 1957, 515). To sum up, he argued, in a strongly felt Christian spirit, that "we" still lack any consciousness of guilt toward our victims of centuries-old colonial superimposition and lack any sense of penitence.

Subsequently, however, the focus of Rüstow's contribution shifted considerably. The second Rüstow went on to reject "typical" accusations against colonial powers as allegedly preventing colonial people from attaining a cultural development similar to "ours." He interprets all progress in this direction as a result of colonization; thus, colonized people might be happier without the external enforcement of civilization, but they would also be left more "backward" (ibid., 516). He goes on to ask what kind of model the West has to offer to liberated colonies that could compete with bolshevism. Rüstow dismissed Anglo-Saxon parliamentarian democracy as an option and asked political scientists to assist the intelligentsia of former colonies to develop a model that would help to combine the indispensable elements of dictatorship with a minimum of democratic freedom. Such a model would eventually also "help us" (Rüstow, 1957, 517). Thus, a core feature of his thought in the 1920s—the perceived need of a *strong* state to overcome alleged problems of "parliamentarianism" reminiscent of Carl Schmitt's argument (see Ptak, Chapter 3 in this volume; Walpen 2004, 332–333)—remained essentially unchanged despite his clear and unequivocal rejection of the Nazis. In any case, Rüstow's approach led him *to support* Truman's Point Four Program in order to help Third World countries to avoid searching for needed capital in Russia, although he cautioned against naïve optimism due to the local circumstances. "At the same time the time is pressing in the highest degree" (Rüstow, 1957, 517).

Rüstow's effort to reconcile his neoliberal ideas and his Christian ethos moved him closer to the increasingly social liberal mainstream, but too close for his neoliberal confreres, despite strong commonalities in defending certain aspects of the record of colonialism and in supporting limitations on democracy. Much like Truman, however, Rüstow rejected the "old imperialism."[19] Such a position was likely to concern MPS members who had listened to Hazlitt's critique of the Point Four Program and Röpke's rejection of an ill-timed Christian emphasis on *Western guilt.* Three papers explicitly or implicitly responded to Rüstow's argument: Arthur Shenfield's "Liberalism and Colonialism," Edmond Giscard d'Estaing's "Liberalisme et Colonialisme," and Karl Brandt's "Liberal Alternatives in Western Policies toward Colonial Areas." None of the three authors shared Rüstow's concern for Western colonial crimes.

    Shenfield,[20] much like Rüstow, did not want to reserve the term *imperialism* for "relatively liberal, rapidly abdicating empires of the West." Instead of

pointing to the centralized state in general, he singled out the "two great im-
perialisms of our age," namely, Hitler's Germany and Stalin's Russia. Shenfield considered anticolonialism rather than colonialism the "aggressive"
party. Identified with nationalism,[21] Shenfield believed that anticolonialists
weakened the West from within, laying "it open to attacks of its enemies."
The British colonies, for example, were said to have constituted a major obstacle against Japanese aggression in World War II. And security concerns did
not diminish after the war: "In a world in which the West is at bay, no liberal
can support the replacement of Western dominion by power vacua. Even if
self-determination may be accepted as a liberal doctrine—and it cannot without qualification [*sic!*]—the security needs of the West must override it where
necessary" (Shenfield 1957, 1).

While privileging security, Shenfield conceded that the defense of the West
could not at all times and in all places be equated with fighting anticolonialism. He feared that France would ruin itself by holding on to Algeria, even if
the motivation were just. "There are times and places where a sphere of influence is still possible but dominion is not" (Shenfield 1957, 4). He proceeded to
turn the argument on the "deterioration of the quality of government" after
decolonization *primarily* against the colonizing countries: "It may not become
even Britain to talk about high standards of public conduct when the British
electoral game has fallen in large measure to the level of mass bribery of the
"under-privileged" (Shenfield 1957, 5), Ultimately, liberalism was considered
most sophisticated if it was taught to independent people—who, if they would
understand sophisticated liberalism, could even see the dangers of self-
determination, according to Shenfield. In any case, assistance to the former
colonies should be tied to conditions as a weak alternative to imposing "good
government (and in particular the rule of law)." The declared goal to prevent
communism might fail, Shenfield stated, because raising standards of living
might awaken the desire for more rapid progress, "which is in fact impossible
under any system but which communism may plausibly offer to deliver"(Shenfield 1957, 6). Although Shenfield emphasized how Western security redirected
attention to the dilution of liberalism in the West, the other speakers felt an
even stronger need to revise the history of colonialism.

Edmond Giscard d'Estaing (1892–1982)—the father of French president
Valéry Giscard d'Estaing—headed the Société Financière Française et Coloniale
(Denord 2003, 401). He served as president of the International Chamber of
Commerce when he addressed the MPS conference to alert his audience to the

"simplification grossière" of presenting colonialism as the domination of one country by another. According to Giscard d'Estaing, colonialism was a civilization process embedded in a long history of co-penetration. Certain dynamic people just naturally exercised influence over others. Giscard d'Estaing also emphasized historical and regional differences that prompted developing countries to recognize just how far they had advanced with regard to political and economic sovereignty. Apparently unaware of what seems to be but a small irony, he wrote this belief in the middle of the French war to prevent Algeria from becoming independent. Only a few professional agitators believed that political independence was sufficient to create wealth, according to this wealthy Frenchman. Since nomadic people in the desert could not produce, let alone consume, the oil that was available there, he argued, oil could be turned into wealth only if it was exported to the industrialized world: "Il est impossible de voir là la moindre trace de colonialisme" (Giscard d'Estaing 1957, 3). It was crucial with regard to the postcolonial future that political sovereignty should not harm the rest of the world. The former colonies were called upon to reconcile their political independence with economic solidarity.

Karl Brandt[22] objected against measuring human action by idealistic standards: "It is essential for our discussion that we consider it taboo to select certain historical incidents of misconduct of colonial powers as arguments . . . because every one of them can be counterbalanced by even more deplorable evidence on the other side. . . . This latter remark should be redundant, but the latest discussion of the colonial problem in Germany calls for it" (Brandt 1957, 2). While acknowledging the need to create conditions to advance freedom and welfare in the West and in the underdeveloped countries, Brandt emphasized that the "colonial question involves the *priority issue of security* of the Western world and defense against infiltration and expansion of the Soviet orbit into the retarded areas via militant nationalism and emotionally fired racism" (2; emphasis added). The Germans and Japanese allegedly criticized the colonial powers France and Great Britain because they had lost their own colonies. This caused "bad feelings," Brandt alleged, "and led to "ideological defection" from the defense against the Soviet attack "with its underlying commercial opportunism" (1957, 2). He demanded that the critique of colonialism be aimed at "those who practice it now with the plain intent to enslave peoples" (p. 2). The French effort to hold on to Algeria was clearly not to be regarded as such a case. They "need our friendly understanding and practical assistance rather than harsh condemnation based on lack of factual information and a lack of any will to understand of what is at stake" (p. 6). In a detailed comparison of the different colonial areas, Brandt emphasized the accomplishments of the colonizing countries with regard to both development and decolonization: "To put it bluntly, the West has no reason to be ashamed of its history of colonial expansion despite many errors in detail and the sad shortcomings of all human action" (p. 8).

Although Brandt had no time to consider the darker sides of colonialism, he did proceed to construct a positive program, and in doing so, he hinted at some persisting problems of colonial history. His perspective on the "political and social goals of the West" included a demand for *equal access* to education and training, *equal pay* for equal quality of work, gradual *abolition of a privileged status* for white people, *private property* as central precondition for human dignity, and the responsibility of individuals and as the basic incentive (p. 11). In this address, Brandt bequeathed us with a concise statement of core aspects of MPS neoliberalism: "the philosophy of freedom and human dignity, and a market economy *governed by* social conscience and responsibility of *an elite* of citizens" (p. 7; emphasis added).

The 1957 conference report in *Neue Zürcher Zeitung* was written by Helmut Schoeck, the MPS's chief theorist of *envy*. The Atlanta-based sociologist (Emory University) went beyond the other speakers at the conference in positively defining imperialism as the geographic expansion of a system of order (rule of law, etc.) (Schoeck 1957, 7). He praised colonialism for having brought "about everything" to those areas with regard to political organization and the rule of law. Schoeck subjected Rüstow to harsh criticism, pointing out that Rüstow did not concentrate on the colonial crimes committed by Russian settlers and military. He considered Rüstow's emphasis on *Western* colonial crimes as possibly more damaging than known declarations against the testing of atomic weapons (Schoeck 1957, 7). According to Schoeck, foreign aid amounted to nothing but misallocation of resources. He thus completely missed the elements of a positive neoliberal program presented by Brandt, although he can hardly be blamed for doing so, given the rather small amount of space allocated to this message compared to the presentation of overriding concerns for "security."

Unfortunately, we do not know what Peter Bauer and Herbert Frankel as the most prominent development economists present at the conference had to say with regard to the deliberations in St. Moritz, but Bauer's later writing on colonialism shows the lasting impact of the MPS exercise in revisionism with regard to colonial history. Bauer is certain "that it is untrue that the west has caused the poverty of the underdeveloped world, whether through colonialism or otherwise." Instead he suggested that it was important "to identify groups and sections in both rich and poor Countries who stand to gain from acceptance of the idea of western responsibility for the poverty of underdeveloped countries, and to examine the reasons for their success in propagating this idea, especially in the west" (Bauer 1971, 148).

Princeton, 1958: The "New Orthodoxy" and the Impertinence of Foreign Aid

One year after St. Moritz, and for the first time in a highly prestigious U.S. environment (at Princeton University)[23], development was again high on the MPS agenda. A total of seventy-eight members and sixty guests assembled in New Jersey. US$42,875 had been raised from thirty-five donors, which allowed reimbursement of travel expenses for participants from Europe, Latin America, and South Africa. The fund-raising success was credited to Fritz Machlup's efforts to plan the Princeton meeting in general and to "Jasper Crane of the DuPont Company, an early member of the Society, [who] had persuaded enough donors to meet the costs" (Hartwell 1995, 100) in particular.

The first paper on development was delivered by Eugênio Gudin[24] in a panel on agriculture that otherwise featured papers opposing agricultural protectionism in Europe and the United States (see Liberaal Archief 2004). Gudin described unfavorable geographic and climatic conditions for agriculture in Latin America (with few exceptions, in Argentina). But countering the prevailing perception of price and income instability in the agricultural sector, he made a double distinction between annual and perennial agricultural products, and between durable and perishable products. Such differences and a "higher or a lower price elasticity of demand makes it difficult to speak of 'agricultural produce' in general. Generalization here often leads to confusion, as is also the case when 'Latin American' economic problems are discussed as a whole" (Gudin 1958, 2). According to Gudin, no "disguised unemployment" (*pace* Arthur Lewis) was possible in countries where "land is still quite abundant in relation to population" (Gudin 1958, 3), though he refrained from discussing the issue of access to land. According to Gudin, disguised unemployment was often confused with low productivity.

Gudin argued against the myth of industrialization. At the time, high levels of unemployment in Europe and the United States demonstrated that the depression had affected the industrialized countries as well. Another argument in favor of industrialization—the Economic Commission for Latin America (Prebisch) perspective of an "inevitable trend" of worsening terms of trade for agricultural producers—was subjected to a detailed critique drawing on the work of Jacob Viner, Charles Kindleberger, and his fellow MPS members Bauer and Haberler. With all the cards stacked against industrialization strategies—the "recurrence of the long repeated, resilient and unscientific argument of Manoilesco" (Gudin 1958, 5)—Gudin eventually argued in favor of investment in agriculture (and education and health) as promising areas for rapid development. He emphasized the need for special *domestic* agricultural investment because different conditions did not allow the import of expertise from developed countries. Gudin called for agrarian reforms, though he rejected left-wing demands (for radical redistribution of land): Economists would point out the need to increase productivity and the availability of credit to "increase the cake." He rejected the complaints of small farmers about the difficulties of obtaining credit and about the prevailing high interest rates. But he conceded that (low) credit worthiness of small farmers and (high) risk involved in agricultural lending might require the involvement of government institutions (Gudin, 1958, 6).

Without mentioning Theodore W. Schultz's work—*Food for the World*, which appeared in 1945, and *The Economic Organization of Agriculture*, released in 1953—Gudin outlined a positive program that contained elements that were strikingly similar to proposals made by Schultz.[25] Schultz of course won a Nobel Prize for his "pioneering research in economic development . . . with particular consideration of the problems of developing countries" (Meier 1987, 15). When Schultz redirected his earlier emphasis on human capital to agriculture, he consulted the work of development economists during the 1950s. He was "appalled by their treatment of the role of agriculture" (Schultz 1987, 20). Instead of concentrating on preexisting structural constraints and demands for industrialization as the main way out of poverty, Schultz's analysis focused on growth opportunities and investment in agriculture (not least in research and human capital). He helped to establish the doctrine that even poor farmers are "economic men" sensitive to incentives and prices. Herbert Frankel explained in a speech at the Princeton meeting of the MPS how traditional communal practices in South Africa effectively constrained individual farmers (printed in *MPS Quarterly* I, 1959, 16–19): Again, we find a peculiar mix of neoclassical and sociological/institutional approaches within the neoliberal group of intellectuals, now focusing on constrained agricultural entrepreneurship in developing countries. A voice from Brazil arguing in favor of home-grown agricultural competencies arguably provided more support for a neoliberal development perspective than European voices in defense of colonialism. The other major obstacle preventing a more genuinely neoliberal development perspective was removed by Peter Bauer, at least theoretically.

Two papers by Peter Bauer[26] in a panel dedicated to underdeveloped countries (chaired by Arthur Shenfield) can easily be considered the most important contributions on the topic at Mont Pèlerin conferences up to that point. Bauer's work reflects the completion of the original constitution of the neoliberal discourse: economic arguments no longer appeared to be secondary to security concerns. Bauer's work also more clearly defined the "enemy" (state-led development discourse). Although he did not personally present his work in Princeton—he had to travel to Pakistan—his papers and the subsequent discussion were considered important enough to be fully documented in the first volume of the *Mont Pèlerin Quarterly* published in April 1959.[27]

John Davenport *(Fortune)* presented Bauer's article, "Economic Growth and the New Orthodoxy," which had been published in the May 1958 edition of *Fortune,* and Bauer's paper "Regulated Wages in Under-Developed Countries" (an amended version of a University of Virginia Lecture delivered in May 1958). In his *Fortune* article, Bauer claimed that the new development orthodoxy in the transatlantic world was based on a fallacy. The very division of the world into a developed and an underdeveloped area, he claimed, and the underlying analysis of a "vicious cycle of poverty" requiring special economic development measures were fallacious. He specifically attacked Gunnar Myrdal[28] because of the political acceptability his arguments had gained through their sponsorship by the UN and national organizations. Bauer also focused on the foreign aid proposals of Walt Rostow and Max Millikan, the leading proponents of modernization development theory.

In awareness of prevailing security concerns, Bauer suggested that he neither condemned all government economic assistance nor wanted to minimize the Russian threat. But planning would yield the opposite results of what was aimed for on the one hand, and development should not be reduced to growth, a simple increase of the volume of goods and services on the other: "It is an increase in goods and services that people want and have freely chosen," Bauer argued, "it is a widening of human options. This kind of freedom is obviously jeopardized by systems of statist compulsion" (Bauer 1958a, 142).

Bauer thus introduced a normative dimension in support of capitalist development requiring qualitative analysis. He conceived of a need to distance himself from *positivistic* measurement because of wealth per capita statistics (which Gunnar Myrdal and other "planners" relied on), which he considered arbitrary in regard to the division of rich and poor, and slighting real income "not subject to easy measurement, especially when human satisfactions are taken into account" (Bauer 1958a, 142).[29] Bauer opposed the notion that developing countries were locked into poverty (as statistics seemed to indicate): "nations, like individuals, are constantly moving up and down in the scale, and it is the final trend that counts" (2). He also argued that statistics were misleading because they misrepresented development progress (better health, etc.) that could lead to worsening per capita income figures. Instead of the "colossal aggregate," he proposed considering the "enormous diversity of the areas in question" (Bauer 1958a, 142–143).

If the "vicious cycle" argument was correct, formerly poor nations could not have advanced, Bauer argued, nor would the "massive accumulation of capital" by poor immigrants in many underdeveloped areas have been possible. He cited the cash crops of the rubber industry in Malaya and West Africa as examples of rapid—though admittedly uneven—growth spurred by *private* investment. Bauer warned against identifying low-level development with stagnation because of a lack of industry. Though admitting that industrial investment is measured more easily, Bauer argued that agricultural investment is "highly important in the early stages of economic advance" and essential (food) to the fundamental needs in most countries (Bauer 1958a, 143).

Bauer also suggested that agriculture had remained important in many cases, as it had in the United States, Canada, and New Zealand, and that the amount of industry a country needed was specific to each individual case. He held the absence of government intervention rather than the type of economic activity to be important. Despite the lack of raw materials and a small domestic market, Bauer stated, Hong Kong rapidly industrialized through "private initiative and enterprise."[30] "Unfortunately, it is just these forces that advocates of the new orthodoxy seem to distrust" (Bauer 1958a, 194).

Bauer attacked foreign aid, even when it was dedicated to improvement of the infrastructure. Developing countries, he wrote, did not need elaborate infrastructures to enjoy rapid development, though he mostly feared "the propensity of many governments not only to try to finance roads and harbor developments, but at the same time to finance, and indeed own, all kinds of manufacturing enterprises from steel mills to chemical plants" (Bauer 1958a, 195).He presented resulting budgetary and foreign exchange difficulties as the real causes for the request of foreign aid. Although aid could initially be useful to set a process in motion, Bauer objected to supplying aid to countries that subsequently failed to severely limit the sphere of government activity. Bauer also attacked "forced savings" through taxation, because taxation would only lead to the growth of government bureaucracy. He singled out Myrdal in his effort to identify alleged common-sense government planning and socialism presented as the only solution—and backed by Western agencies—due to a perceived lack of private savings and investment in the developing world. According to Bauer, the resulting government expansion would instead lead to a misallocation of capital. Even worse, forced saving would discourage private saving and investment—an idea presaging later crowding out theories. At the same time, Bauer was eager to extend the critique of government ownership to government programming because even if a state did not own an industry, government intrusion would likely hamper rather than facilitate development. Bauer suggested that advanced nations had not relied on such measures in their early development and that they had found it difficult to manage in wartime. Bauer eventually used Paul Rosenstein-Rodan's work (if disingenuously) as witness to government ineffectiveness because this representative of the new orthodoxy had written about the lack of qualified personnel in developing countries needed to actually carry out programming tasks (Bauer 1958a, 198).[31]

Bauer clearly stressed fundamental choices beyond practical considerations. Enhanced government planning, he asserted, "enhances the intensity of political struggle" whereas the "higher liberties and freedoms we cherish—freedom of the press, freedom of assembly, freedom of the ballot—have all been built up and buttressed by certain economic institutions, including respect for private property and a system . . . that responds to individual choices made in the marketplace" (Bauer 1958a, 198). In his eyes, the West was about to give away a successful system in support of a system championed by the Soviet Union.

There obviously was little room for balanced reflections of possible merits in the tradition of List (infant industry protectionism, etc.), evidenced in the catching-up process of the United States, Germany, or Japan (vis-à-vis England), or even of the UK vis-à-vis the Netherlands (e.g., with the Navigation

Acts supported by Adam Smith). Bauer's policy for progress suggested funding policies that were diametrically opposed to the recommendations of the alleged new orthodoxy: minimize state ownership and planning, and promote private (foreign) investment instead of suppressing it. He called for professions of faith in the world economy. Strong signs of rebounding world trade and the West's significant investment in the former colonies augured well for progress. Even more important than trade and investment was what "the people do for them- selves": freed from restrictions, Bauer trusted that "middle-class or 'bourgeois' virtues" would prevail. He was not shy (if disingenuous again) to cite Karl Marx as key witness: In the *Communist Manifesto,* Marx *and* Engels of course had observed that the bourgeoisie draws in all nations, "even the most barbar- ian, into civilization" by way of rapidly improving all instruments of produc- tion and communication. According to Bauer, history definitely had to end here. Owing to prevailing political conditions, much remained to be done—in the field of development and labor economics, for example.

Whereas Bauer argued in his *Fortune* article that the true development restric- tions were recently developed political constraints, his second paper, "Regu- lated Wages in Under-Developed Countries" (Bauer 1958b), applied this rea- soning to the labor market in developing countries. Labor market problems of course featured prominently both with regard to the rise of the Keynesian "rev- olution" and the emergence of "development economics." Arthur Lewis's work on "disguised underemployment" in agricultural societies was akin to Keynes's work with regard to unemployment in industrialized countries: neoclassical equilibrium theory was considered to apply to a special (optimal) case only, and the recognition of limits of traditional economics paved the way for neces- sary variations in economic analysis and policy prescriptions for a real world featuring too many examples of disequilibrium (or low-level equilibrium; see Hirschman 1981).

Bauer's discussion directed attention to *regulation* of wages and work hours. A motto quoted from a report of the South African Industrial Legisla- tion Commission in 1935 contained the core message of Bauer's paper: "In an unregulated market, the available supplies or numbers determine the wage, but, under regulated conditions, wages determine the numbers" (Bauer 1958b, 1). Although Bauer admitted difficulties in determining the extent to which wage regulation existed and mattered, he referred to an International Labor

Organization (ILO) publication on minimum wages supporting his claim "that regulated wages affect economic activity over a wide area of the underdeveloped world" (Bauer 1958b, 2). The rise of wage regulation was blamed on organized labor conspiring with established employers, interests in planning, vested interests in the new bureaucracies involved in wage regulation, and an "international emulation effect": international organizations (particularly the ILO) and foreign governments encouraged local politicians to develop labor legislation akin to that in the developed world to avoid being considered backward (Bauer 1958b, 3).

The impact of wage regulation, Bauer said, had destroyed the major competitive advantage of developing countries: abundance of cheap labor. Bauer contrasted the rapidly growing East Asian economies and India to argue that "contrived scarcity" injured "prospects for economic growth" (Bauer 1958b, 4).

Bauer denied the existence of disparities in bargaining power between capital and labor and the exploitation of workers. Only the absence of "independent competing alternatives" allowed exploitation in his framework: "Even illiterate poor workers will be paid what they are worth, if employers can obtain their services only by competing for them" (Bauer 1958b, 8). Since wage regulation stifled growth and limited employment, employers were denied opportunities to compete and were more likely to be forced to become exploitative (Bauer 1958b, 9). "Contrived scarcity," he suggested, had led to a misallocation of resources, whereas diminished current production and future growth potential had led to a reduction in national income (equated to the volume of possible investment) and to a "lesser flexibility and adaptability of the economy" (Bauer 1958b, 9).[32]

In 1958 it was Ernst Bieri[33] who summarized the Princeton conference for *Neue Zürcher Zeitung (NZZ)*. He covered neither the presentation of Bauer's papers nor the subsequent discussion. Bieri warned against romantic illusions about foreign aid for farmers in the Third World. He called for investment in infrastructure to promote the transition away from farming in the *industrialized* world, and he repeated calls to continue focusing on agriculture rather than industry in the developing world. *NZZ* authors continued to paint a rather conservative picture of the MPS to the outside world by *not* reflecting the formation of the distinctly neoliberal development discourse. Contrary to the impression that was promulgated, we can gather further evidence in support of a new direction and program from the first volume of the *MPS Quarterly* (edited by Hunold).[34]

John Davenport *stressed* the "positive program" contained in Bauer's work in response to frequent accusations levied against the neoliberal right of "just being negative" (*MPS Quarterly* 1 1959, 7): Foreign *private* investment combined with the adequate efforts of developing countries, "which can develop normally and naturally by sticking to well-tested economic principles—the principle of sound money, for instance, and the principle of limited versus unlimited government" (Davenport 1959, 7).[35] However, David McCord Wright felt that in order to not be perceived in a purely negative fashion, "we will have to give some direct aid in addition to the military aid, as a *diplomatic move* more than anything else" (*MPS Quarterly* 1, 1959, 8; emphasis added).

Some of the participants were at odds with Davenport's presentation of Bauer's principled position against foreign aid. Gudin did not agree with some statements of Davenport (who apparently had suggested "that blank cheques" were a common foreign aid practice), and he referred to his fellow MPS member Erik Lundberg's position on private foreign investment: "sometimes it is very costly to the country which receives it" (*MPS Quarterly* 1, 1959, 23), because second-rate machinery had been imported at high interest rates, for example. Gudin also would "not include Professor Nurkse's book and theories among those which have been mentioned by Bauer as the 'planifactor sort of people' " (*MPS Quarterly* 1, 1959, 21).

Obviously using blunt instruments to define the adverse discourse, Bauer helped to (over)define what in retrospect appears to be a dominant and coherent structuralist paradigm of *development economics* in the immediate postwar period. Considering the "confusions" that prevailed among MPS members with regard to the development discourse—lack of confidence in the market and support for state aid—the more nuanced positions within the opposing camps arguably had to be ignored to achieve sufficient contrast between the camps, and to positively define and align neoliberal *perspectives* over the coming years: Peter Bauer's foundational academic contribution, the Cambridge handbook *The Economics of Underdeveloped Countries* (commissioned by C. W. Guillebaud and Milton Friedman), had in any case already appeared in 1957, as had his *Economic Analysis and Policy in Underdeveloped Countries* (Cambridge/Duke). It would still take some time, of course, until the *Economist* could report on May 4, 2002 that Bauer was to the idea of the Third World as Hayek was to socialism. Lord Bauer's obituary would be titled "A Voice *for* the Poor" (p. 93; emphasis added).

Although a lot of work remained to be done on the road to intellectual hegemony, the group of neoliberal development theorists was already well established by 1958. The Mexican MPS member Gustavo R. Velasco mentioned visits by Louis Baudin, a recent lecture by Frankel in Mexico City, as well as talks and general statements at MPS meetings by the founding members Allan Fisher and Friedrich August von Hayek in his contribution to the Princeton discussion. Gudin relied on Lundberg, Frankel referred to Ferrero, and so forth. Although the positions of MPS members like Röpke, Benham, or Bauer diverged in important ways, they heavily relied on each other as seen in their overlapping arguments against state interventionism and planning. Further research is needed to more precisely establish if and to what extent academic publications drew on a pool of talent organized in the invisible and transnational college of the MPS.

Fortune's Davenport eventually went far beyond Bauer by adding some details to the foreign aid discussion. His remarks illuminate some of the early victories scored by the neoliberal/neoconservative camp in the United States. He pointed out that Rostow and Millikan's proposals (to which Bauer had referred) only required the recipient country to establish a system of forced savings and to present a development plan. Davenport shared the information with his audience that the Kennedy/Cooper resolution to back India's five-year plan with substantial U.S. aid had been *defeated,* though he cited a certain Mr. Morley to stress that this resolution was "a fairly frightening phenomena" (*MPS Quarterly* 1959, 7). The quoted Mr. Morley, like Milton Friedman, was on the advisory board of the American Enterprise Association (AEA), which subsequently became the American Enterprise Institute (AEI). Peter Bauer's *United States Aid and Indian Economic Development* was published by the Association in 1959 (with an introduction discussing the flaws of the Kennedy/Cooper resolution). Already in 1954, AEA had published Karl Brandt's work on agricultural price controls, a topic that was also of interest to Milton Friedman at the time (see Strassmann 1976, 282).

Davenport added another detail (reminiscent of Röpke's 1953 association of development, full employment, the welfare state, and planning) and sum-

marized Bauer's papers to describe "this whole theory of economic development . . . [as] part and parcel of the theory of the Welfare State" (p. 6). The
planned economy and the welfare state defined what could not be considered
among principled neoliberal perspectives of development, which in turn had
to be developed to figure out what the state and other forces should do in an
effort to eventually come up with a positive, potentially competitive program.

Davenport clarified the way in which an important link between neoliberal
and security concerns remained after all. Unlike Bauer's works, Davenport's
left no doubt about which international policy the United States should develop. If there had been no communist menace requiring costly military efforts, he wrote, "it might well have been possible to be a little more indulgent
toward the Welfare State and some of its experiments. . . . I think, however,
that in the grim situation in which we stand we can go much further. We can
say, 'The Welfare State is not only wrong in principle. It is, in this setting of the
need to maintain a firm military position, a complete impertinence'" (MPS
Quarterly 1, 1958, 8).

Conclusion: 1950s Pluralism in Development Theory

Looking back at the early MPS conferences, we note a growing self-confidence
within the neoliberal camp with regard to the development theme. Although
many intellectual and real components and circumstances needed for the subsequent rise to hegemony were still missing, many internal obstacles had been
identified and addressed: Peter Bauer in particular clarified the neoliberal vision with regard to foreign aid. Bauer overcame the previous lack of confidence
in entrepreneurship and market relations in the developing world within the
neoliberal group of scholars and intellectuals steeped in colonial economics.
Bauer's work manifestly documents a neoliberal reasoning in which economic
considerations are no longer subordinate to security concerns. Other contributions recognized and addressed specific needs with regard to capitalist agriculture in developing countries, and the manifold battle lines with competing discourses were more readily identified: the neoliberal *war of position* (Gramsci)
could be fought more easily toward the end of the 1950s. At this point in time,
organized neoliberals in science and politics had already developed an important network of intellectuals (as well as a few think tanks and corporate and political foundations) across borders, which operated in a more pluralist environment. A wide variety of perspectives articulated the emerging and evolving

constellation of social forces between and within the First, Second, and emerging Third Worlds.

Ascher (1996, 314) recognizes the early pluralism when he refers to Hirschman, who argued in 1981 that in the early (and formative) period of the field "neoclassical economics was competing with Marxism, neo-Marxism, and a distinctive development economics," although neither Ascher nor Hirschman recognized the distinctiveness of the neoliberal participants in the debate. Meier and Seers (1984, 22) came somewhat closer in their effort to describe Western *mainstream* pluralism of the early days: "Some may choose to summarize the mainstream development economics of the 1950s as being structural, shaped by trade pessimism. . . . But there were crosscurrents, and the period was characterized by vigorous debate over some leading issues. Especially notable were controversies over balanced growth versus unbalanced growth, industrialization versus agriculture, import substitution versus export promotion, planning versus reliance on the market price system. The debates of some of these issues are still unresolved."

The early formation of the distinctly *neoliberal* discourse and the transnational social forces nurturing it in any case have escaped due attention. A future analysis of the neoliberal development discourse and thought collective as evidenced by MPS conferences and networks from the 1960s to the present time is likely to yield a better understanding of why many debates of longstanding issues are still unresolved indeed.

Notes

1. Parallel to my own research at ICAS/NYU (2004/5), Yves Steiner at the Centre Walras Pareto—Université de Lausanne has been conducting his Ph.D. research ("L'affrontement des néolibéralismes au coeur du renouveau libéral: les débats de la Société du Mont-Pèlerin (1947–1960)" on this topic. (Compare his chapter on trade unions, Chapter 5 in this volume). This chapter has benefited strongly from his critical comments.

2. Development issues were discussed at sixteen of the thirty-two general meetings between 1947 and 1998 by a total of 110 MPS members and guests (including Anne Krueger and Jagdish Baghwati; see Liberaal Archief, 2004). In addition, a total of thirty speakers discussed development issues at nine of seventeen regional MPS meetings held between 1966 and 1990, according to the conference programs available at the Hoover Institution's MPS archive. While Peter Bauer and Herbert Frankel contributed most frequently to the conferences (six and four times, respectively), Hartwell (1995) fails to help understanding the long-term collective effort.

3. Toye (1993) and Colclough and Manor (1991) do not venture far beyond an ideological critique of individual authors and the field's intellectual history. Toye briefly alerts his readers to the significant role played by the Institute of Economic Affairs and news media (Toye 1993, 93–94), and Colclough (1991, 7 and 22–23n5) alerts us to the fact that "some neo-liberal economists secured strategic advisory or executive posts in government and international agencies." For an introduction to more than one hundred neoliberal think tanks around the globe founded or run by MPS members, see Plehwe and Walpen (2006).

4. The conference was attended by fifty-three participants and six guests, eighteen from the United States, and all the others from Europe (Hartwell 1995, 92). MPS membership had grown to 167. Funding was raised by F. M. Morisot "on behalf of a group of French members and Friends," according to Hartwell (1995, 92). In fact. the meeting was financed by the Centre National du Patronat Français (CNPF), a key employer organization that also founded the French Association de la libre entreprise (ALE) at the price of nearly 2 million francs (equivalent to contemporary €39.000) in 1947. ALE was directed by Georges Villiers, the president of the CNPF, and led by Georges Morisot, an engineer at Michelin (see Denord, Chapter 1 in this volume).

5. Frederic C. Benham was part of the British LSE group of liberals that gathered around Robbins. He carried LSE influence to Singapore and Australia, where he was a lecturer at the University of Sidney from 1923 to 1930 (Apel 1961, 17; Hartwell 1995, 18). Benham helped translate Gottfried Haberler's (1968) *The Theory of International Trade, with Its Applications to Commercial Policy.* At the time of the Beauvallon conference, Benham served as economic adviser to the government of Malaya (Hartwell 1995, 89). Two years later Röpke (1953, 84) referred to him as a financial adviser to the British governor of Singapore. His textbook, entitled *Economics,* appeared in 1949 in its fourth edition (compare Tribe, Chapter 2 in this volume).

6. "Haberler is one of the great figures of international economics of the twentieth century. He played a crucial role in the construction of the modern pure theory of international trade by introducing the opportunity cost approach (which replaced the confusing real-cost approach espoused particularly by Viner) This new approach clarified the nature of the gains from trade and the law of comparative advantage and went beyond Ricardo's special constant cost case. . . . In addition, Haberler's classic textbook . . . has laid the foundation for much later work. It sorted out (and usually demolished) many arguments for protection" (Corden 1987, 84; compare Bair, Chapter 10 in this volume).

7. "Industrialization was not part of colonial economics because the comparative advantage of the colonies was held to be the export of raw materials for the industries in the metropolitan countries" (Pieterse 2001, 5).

8. This 1954 collection (edited by Hayek) was published "by a commercial publisher, with Society support but without its imprimatur" according to Hartwell (1995, 93). He thus freely admits the hiding away of organizational ties between the contributing

scholarly individuals. The book was in fact published by both University of Chicago Press and Routledge. The historical revisionism in this area, with particular regard to Marxist accounts of the history of industrialization (aiming to contradict claims about a decline in living standards of workers; see Hartwell 1995, 94), played a prominent role in the development discourse as evidenced in Benham's paper. The interdisciplinary composition of the MPS deliberately sought by Hayek evidently eased the promotion of interdiscourses.

9. Wilhelm Röpke was an economics professor at Philipps University, Marburg, during the Weimar Republic. An early conservative opponent of the Nazis, he fled Germany for Switzerland (via Amsterdam and Istanbul). After the war, he became a key activist of the neoliberal and neoconservative right. His idea to found a neoliberal journal was eventually merged with Hayek and Hunold's initiative to found the MPS. Röpke frequently contributed to MPS meetings and served as president from 1961 to 1962 when he resigned over the Hunold/Hayek affair (Walpen 2004). Zmirnak (2001) links his heart attack in 1962 leading up to his eventual death in 1964 to the tumultuous ending of his leadership in the MPS.

10. Leduc's (1952) report "Le sous-devéloppement et ses problèmes" was originally written as a report to the Congrès des Economistes de langue française (Röpke 1953, 64). Leduc was a co-founder of the French neoliberal think tank Association pour les Libertés Economiques et le Progrès Social (ALEPS; see Denord, Chapter 1 in this volume). Between 1961 and 1978, Leduc contributed five papers to MPS conferences. He served as MPS president from 1974 to 1976.

11. Apart from the affinities to colonial economics, Röpke's nostalgic reasoning considers industrialization truly a mixed blessing in the West because of its tendency to help destroy the original culture through economic and political centralization. Röpke wanted every man to be a farmer (cf. Zmirnak 2001, 179–180).

12. Henry Hazlitt (1894–1993) was a highly influential New York-based journalist writing for *Newsweek,* the *Wall Street Journal, the New York Times, the Nation, the American Mercury, the Freeman,* and the like. He won fame for his popular scientific *Economics in One Lesson* (1946). A founding member of MPS and the U.S. Philadelphia Society, Hazlitt contributed five papers to MPS meetings. Murray Rothbard described Hazlitt's paper (subsequently published by the Foundation for Economic Education in 1951) as a "brief pamphlet" in which his 1947 analysis "Will Dollars Save the World?" was applied to foreign aid (www.mises.org/hazlitt/hazlittbib.asp).

13. S. Herbert Frankel (1903–1996) taught in Johannesburg, London, and Oxford, and published widely in development economics and monetary theory. Frankel contributed three papers to MPS meetings, chaired one session, and was an active participant in various discussions of development and labor issues.

14. John Jewkes (1902–1988), an Oxford economist, was a founding member and president of the MPS (1962–1964).

15. Interestingly, Röpke refers several times to Ragnar Nurkse and discusses his work with great care. Nurkse's critique of disguised unemployment, of Keynesian employment strategies, of endogenous capital formation, and of forced savings are all

positively noted, though Röpke blamed him for mistakenly assuming a general constraint on profitable expansion of original production (Röpke 1953, 98–100). Despite his association with the structuralist paradigm, Ragnar Nurkse was closely tied to the emerging neoliberal group of scholars. He had participated in Mises's *Privatseminar,* and the Austrian Institute for Trade Cycle Research financed his 1935 study *Internationale Kapitalbewegungen* (Feichtinger 2001, 187 and 193, respectively).

16. The 1956 Berlin conference also featured a paper on underdeveloped countries. Unfortunately, Louis Baudin's "Soviet Expansionism in the Under-developed Countries" is not available at the Ghent Archive (see Liberaal Archief 1994). However, the primary concern of the 1956 conference was "The challenge of Communism and the response of liberalism" (the conference title).

17. Albert Hunold (ed.), 1961: *Entwicklungsländer. Wahn und Wirklichkeit.* Erlenbach-Zürich (including the discussion of the 1960 Kassel meeting of MPS), *Lateinamerika—Land der Sorge und der Zukunft.* Erlenbach-Zürich 1962, *Afrika und seine Probleme,* Erlenbach-Zürich, 1965.

18. Alexander Rüstow (1899–1966), professor of economics, opposed the Nazis in Germany and eventually fled to Istanbul. After World War II, he held a chair in economics and social sciences at the University of Heidelberg, and headed the Alfred Weber Institute. His *Ortsbestimmung der Gegenwart* (three volumes) is sometimes placed next to Popper's *Open Society,* Hannah Arendt's "Elemente und Ursprünge totaler Herrschaft," and Adorno and Horkheimer's "Dialektik der Aufklärung." Together with Wilhelm Röpke, Rüstow determined the crisis of liberalism in its economism. The threat of totalitarianism required a complete new beginning in the social sciences, they argued at the founding conference of the MPS (Walpen 2004, 58). Rüstow helped to set up and run the early German quasi-partisan think tank Arbeitsgemeinschaft Soziale Marktwirtschaft (in support of Erhard's social market economy; see Schindelbeck and Ilgen 1999). Within MPS, Rüstow participated in seven panels between 1950 and 1961, and he intervened three times in the development deliberations.

19. "The old imperialism—exploitation for foreign profit—has no place in our plans. What we envisage is a program of development based on the concepts of democratic fair dealing" (Truman cited in Esteva 1992, 6).

20. Arthur Shenfield was an LSE-trained economist with focus on labor and the law who worked at the Institute of Economic Affairs. He was a member of the Longbow group, launched in 1965 after the Tory defeat in 1964 to form a coherent conservative philosophy (Cockett 1995, 165). Hartwell emphasizes that Shenfield was a distinguished economist, though he did not hold a university position. Shenfield delivered no less than thirteen papers to MPS general meetings between 1954 and 1986, served three times as a chairman of panels, and, as acting president of the Society, delivered the president's lecture in 1974. At MPS meetings, Shenfield mostly spoke on trade-union issues. Only once did he again venture out into the development-related sphere, calling for the abolition of the International Labor Organization in his 1984 paper.

21. Shenfield's co-speaker Giscard d'Estaing went even further in this direction. He understood anticolonialism as an "explosion de xénophobie, du coté negative, c'est-à-dire de racisme, due coté positif" (Giscard d'Estaing 1957, 2).

22. Karl Brandt (1899–1975) was the founder and director (1929–1933) of the Institute of Agricultural Market Research at the Berlin University of Agriculture (later absorbed by Humboldt-Universität). Brandt was one of the 167 academics rescued in 1933 by the New School for Social Research (in collaboration with the Rockefeller Foundation). He eventually joined the faculty of the Food Research Institute at Stanford University (founded in 1921 with financial support from the Carnegie Corporation) and served on President Eisenhower's Council of Economic Advisers (1958–1961). A founding member of MPS, Brandt presented papers or chaired panels ten times between 1947 and 1962. He quit the Society in 1962 and called for its liquidation because its atmosphere of friendship and cooperation had been destroyed and because of the Hunold/Hayek affair (Hartwell 1995, 136–137; Walpen 2004, chapter 3). But he later presented a paper at the 1970 conference in Munich (Liberaal Archief 2004).

23. Ironically, the Princeton and subsequent Oxford meetings almost witnessed the collapse of the transnational neoliberal community instead of an increasing reputation. Hartwell (1995, 100–103) blamed Albert Hunold's authoritarianism in managing the MPS, but Hunold and others were at odds with Hayek and others on the fundamental tasks of the MPS, pitting political against long-term intellectual goals (see Walpen 2004, 131–138). Unfortunately, Hartwell provides no detailed background on Machlup's concerns over the American organizing committee's discussion of the Princeton conference *program*. Other research demonstrates conflicts of interests between *donors* (including members) and *academic intellectuals* as a possible further element of the substantive conflict between the Hunold and Hayek camps (see Phillips-Fein, Chapter 8 in this volume). In a rare departure from the usual restraint on political declarations, the Princeton meeting issued a proclamation signed by about twenty MPS members. The proclamation expressed gratitude for the United States' "historical role . . . in the present struggle for the survival of liberty and human dignity against the forces of Communist tyranny, aggression and subversion" (*MPS Quarterly* 1959, 8). This would suggest a link between Hunold and U.S. donor interests, contradicting somewhat Hartwell's narrative of Hunold "endangering" all the arrangements.

24. E. Gudin (1886–1986), an engineer by training, taught economics and served in the Ministry of Agriculture. He was a Brazilian delegate to the IMF Directorate from 1951 to 1956, and he was vice president of the International Economic Association in 1959. Gudin joined MPS in 1954. Beyond one paper and two further interventions in Princeton, no further record of interventions exists at general meetings. Together with Roberto Campos and José Merquior he was one of the most important neoliberal intellectuals in Brazil (Gros 2003, 123).

25. During the MPS discussion on Bauer's papers (see below), Romulo Ferrero refers to "the great agricultural authority . . . Prof. Schultz" whose point against disguised unemployment was more or less repeated "only a few days ago" by Professor

Gudin (*MPS Quarterly* 1959, 24). On Schultz's role at Chicago, see Van Horn and Mirowski, Chapter 4 in this volume).

26. Peter T. Bauer (1915–2002) arguably was the most prominent development economist in the ranks of the MPS. Born in Hungary, Bauer came to Cambridge in the UK to study economics in the 1930s. On the basis of his fieldwork in Africa and Southeast Asia, he rejected the "dual economics" (Hirschman) perspective, and he vigorously opposed national planning and foreign aid. Bauer mainly taught at LSE until his death in 2002. Margaret Thatcher awarded Bauer the lordship in 1983 (on a recommendation by Bauer's fellow MPS member Sir Alan Walters (http://politics.guardian.co.uk/politicso bituaries/story/0,1441,710597,00.html). Between 1951 and 1990, Bauer contributed to nine MPS meetings (contributing eight papers and chairing a panel). Bauer eventually received the first Milton Friedman Prize of the CATO Institute, worth half a million U.S. dollars (www.cato.org/special/friedman/bauer/index.html, accessed April 10, 2005).

27. In addition to John Davenport's (*Fortune*) presentation, seven interventions reflecting the cosmopolitan character of the MPS (by Canadian economist David McCord Wright, Mexican legal scholar Gustavo R. Velasco, Japanese economist Nobutane Kiuchi, development economist S. Herbert Frankel, Ludwig von Mises, Eugenio Gudin, and the Peruvian legal scholar Romulo A. Ferrero) were documented.

28. The *MPS Quarterly* editor (Hunold) also alerted readers to "another article (by Bauer) . . . published in 'Economic Journal' . . . 1959 . . . , a splendidly written critical analysis of the ideas expressed in three books recently published by Gunnar Myrdal" (*MPS Quarterly* 1, 1959, 26).

29. Quality-of-life (anticonsumerist) arguments later became popular on the left, and development statistics became an important area of contestation. The Economic Freedom of the World Indexes (by Frazer Institute and the Heritage Foundation) were originally conceived at MPS meetings. While Cuba does well in the UN human development index, it is at the bottom of the Economic Freedom index (see Plehwe and Walpen 2006).

30. Bauer does not discuss U.S. protectionist measures against Japan (the "voluntary export restraints" established in 1957), which led Japanese investors to start production in Hong Kong (Bonacich et al. 1994). Jennifer Bair brought this to my attention.

31. Rosenstein-Rodan would probably have suggested developing missing qualifications. In general, neoliberal scholars apply a two-level argument: planning and redistribution does not work in principle, but even if the ideal plan could be designed, implementation would be impossible.

32. Bauer used South Africa's skilled white labor force to illustrate his argument. These privileged workers succeeded in fending off new entrants (poor white and black workers) by wage regulation and an "industrial color bar enforced by custom and trade unions" (Bauer 1958b, 12). Apartheid in this perspective was caused in no small measure by the institution of wage regulation, though it would be interesting to understand what Bauer referred to as "custom." The South African case particularly bolstered his claim of the (negative) effects of wage regulation beyond the economic sphere.

33. Ernst Bieri (1920–), theologian, worked (like Carlo Mötteli) for *Neue Zürcher Zeitung* (from 1946 to 1966) and for the Swiss Bank Julius Bär. He joined the MPS in 1956–1957.

34. This publication was controversial from the beginning, and later, disagreement would erupt, also owing to the journal, "more or less . . . a personal initiative by Hunold" (Hartwell 1995, 103).

35. Ludwig von Mises seconded the idea of emphasizing the enormous importance of foreign private investment that was not accounted for in Ricardo's trade theory, and Kiuchi reported that planners in Japan had to scrap the first five-year plan because the economy grew much faster than planned (*MPS Quarterly* 1, 1959, 20 and 15, respectively).

References

Apel, Hans-Eberhard. 1961. "Edwin Cannan und seine Schüler." Die *Neuliberalen an der London School of Economics.* Tübingen: J. C. B. Mohr (Paul Siebeck).

Ariffin, Yohan. 2001. *Généalogies du discours du développement—Idées, doctrines et technologies politiques.* Université de Lausanne, Ph.D. thesis.

Ascher, William. 1996. "The Evolution of Postwar Doctrines in Development Economics." In A. W. Coats (ed.), *The Post-1945 Internationalization of Economics,* 312–336. Durham, NC: Duke University Press.

Bauer, Peter. 1958a. "Economic Growth and the New Orthodoxy." *Fortune,* May 1958, 142, 143, 194, 196, and 198.

Bauer, Peter. 1971. *Dissent on Development: Studies and Debates in Development Economics.* London: Weidenfeld & Nicolson.

Berger, Markus T. 2004. "After the Third World? History, Destiny, and the Fate of Third Worldism." *Third World Quarterly* 25, 1, 9–40.

Bieri, E., 1958. "Der Stand des Liberalen Denkens." (Offprint from *Neuen Zürcher Zeitung,* September 14–16, 1958, 8 p.)

Bonacich, E., L. Cheng, N. Chinchilla, N. Hamilton, and P. Ong. 1994. *Global Production: The Apparel Industry in the Pacific Rim.* Philadelphia: Temple University Press.

Caldwell, Bruce. 2005. The Road to Serfdom. Editor's Introduction. Unpublished manuscript.

Cockett, Richard. 1995. *Thinking the Unthinkable: Think Tanks and the Economic Counter-revolution, 1931–83.* London: Fontana.

Colclough, Christopher. 1991. "Structuralism versus Neo-liberalism: An Introduction." In Christopher Colclough and James Manor (eds.), *States or Markets? Neo-liberalism and the Development Policy Debate,* 1–25. Oxford: Clarendon Press.

Colclough, Christopher, and James Manor (eds.) 1991. *States or Markets? Neo-liberalism and the Development Policy Debate.* Oxford: Clarendon Press.

Cooper, Frederick. 1997. "Modernizing Bureaucrats, Backward Africans, and the Development Concept." In Frederick Cooper and Randall Packard (eds.), *International Development and the Social Sciences: Essays on the History and Politics of Knowledge,* 64–92. Berkeley and Los Angeles: University of California Press.

Corden, Max. 1987. "Comments." In Gerald Meier (ed.), *Pioneers in Development.* Second Series, 84–91. Oxford: Oxford University Press.

Cox, Robert. 1979. "Ideologies and the New International Economic Order: Reflections on Some Recent Literature." *International Organization* 33 (2): 257–302.

De Vries, Margaret Garritsen. 1996. "Comments." In A. W. Coats (ed.), *The Post-1945 Internationalization of Economics,* 357–363. Durham, NC: Duke University Press.

Denord, François. 2003. "Genèse et institutionnalisation du néo-libéralisme en France (années 1930–années 1950)." Unpublished Ph.D. thesis, Ecole des Hautes Études en Sciences Sociales, Paris.

Esteva, Gustavo. 1992. "Development." In Wolfgang Sachs (ed.), *The Development Dictionary,* 6–25. London: Zed Books.

Feichtinger, Johannes. 2001. *Wissenschaft zwischen den Kulturen. Österreichische Hochschullehrer in der Emigration 1933–1945.* Frankfurt am Main–New York: Campus Verlag.

Gilman, Nils. 2003. *Mandarins of the Future: Modernization Theory in Cold War America.* Baltimore, MD: Johns Hopkins University Press.

Gros, Denise Barbosa. 2003. *Institutos Liberais e Neoliberalismo no Brasil da Nova República.* Porto Alegre: Fundação de Economia e Estatística Siegfried Emanuel Heuser.

Haberler, Gottfried. 1968. *The Theory of International Trade: With Its Applications to Commercial Policy.* Trans. Alfred Stonier and Frederick Benham. New York: Augustus M. Kelley Publishers.

Hall, Peter (ed.). 1989. *The Political Power of Economic Ideas. Keynesianism across Nations.* Princeton, NJ: Princeton University Press.

Harberger, Arnold C. 1996. "Good Economics Comes to Latin America, 1955–1995." In A. W. Coats (ed.), *The Post-1945 Internationalization of Economics,* 301–311. Durham, NC: Duke University Press.

Harper, F. A., F. A. von Hayek, Henry Hazlitt, Leonard E. Read, and Gustavo R. Velasco (eds.). 1971. *Towards Liberty.* Menlo Park, CA: Institute for Humane Studies.

Hartwell, R. Max. 1995. *A History of the Mont Pèlerin Society.* Indianapolis, IN: Liberty Fund.

Hazlitt, Henry. 1950. *Illusions of Point Four.* Irvington-on-Hudson, NY: Foundation for Economic Education.

Hirschman, Albert O. 1981. "The Rise and Decline of Development Economics." In Albert O. Hirschman (ed.), *Essays in Trespassing: Economics to Politics and Beyond,* 1–24. Cambridge: Cambridge University Press.

Hirschman, Albert. O. 1989. "How the Keynesian Revolution Was Exported from the United States, and Other Comments." In Peter Hall (ed.), *The Political Power of Economic Ideas: Keynesianism across Nations*, 347–360. Princeton, NJ: Princeton University Press.

Hobson, John. 1965 [1902]. *Imperialism: A Study.* Ann Arbor: University of Michigan Press.

Hunold, Albert (ed). 1961. *Entwicklungsländer. Wahn und Wirklichkeit.* Erlenbach-Zürich: Eugen Rentsch Verlag.

Hunold, Albert (ed.). 1962. *Lateinamerika—Land der Sorge und der Zukunft.* Erlenbach-Zürich: Eugen Rentsch Verlag.

Hunold, Albert (ed.). 1965. *Afrika und seine Probleme.* Erlenbach-Zürich: Eugen Rentsch Verlag.

Jolly, R. 2004. *UN Contributions to Development Thinking and Practice.* Bloomington: Indiana University Press.

Lal, Deepak. 2000 [1983]. *The Poverty of "Development Economics."* Cambridge, MA: MIT Press.

Latham, Michael E. 2000. *Modernization as Ideology.* Chapel Hill: University of North Carolina Press.

Leduc, Gaston. 1952. "Le sous-développement et ses problèmes." *Revue d'Economie Politique,* May, 133–189

Leys, Colin. 1996. *The Rise and Fall of Development Theory.* Bloomington: Indiana University Press.

Liberaal Archief. 2004. The General Meeting Files of the Mont Pèlerin Society (1947–1998). Ghent: Liberaal Archief (www.liberaalarchief.be/MPS.pdf).

Meier, Gerald M. (ed.). 1987. *Pioneers in Development.* Second Series. Oxford: Oxford University Press.

Meier, Gerald M., and Dudley Seers (eds.). 1984. *Pioneers in Development.* Oxford: Oxford University Press.

Mises, Ludwig von. 1998 [1942]. *Problemas Económicos de Mexico: Ayer y hoy.* Mexico City: Instituto Cultural Ludwig von Mises.

Mitchell, Timothy. 2002. *Rule of Experts: Egypt, Techno-politics, Modernity.* Berkeley: University of California Press.

Mötteli, Carlo. 1951. "The Regeneration of Liberalism." *Swiss Review of World Affairs* November, 21–23.

MPS Quarterly = The Mont Pèlerin Society Quarterly, Vol. 1, No. 1, April 1959.

Pasche, Cécile, and Suzanne Peters. 1997. "Les premiers pas de la Société du Mont-Pèlerin ou les dessous chics du néolibéralisme." *Les Annuelles* 8(8): 191–230.

Pearce, Kimber Charles. 2001. *Rostow, Kennedy, and the Rhetoric of Foreign Aid.* East Lansing: Michigan State University Press.

Pieterse, Jan Nederveen. 2001. *Development Theory: Deconstructions/Reconstructions.* London: Sage.

Plehwe, Dieter. 2002. "Neoliberale Ideen aus der nationalen Peripherie ins Zentrum gerueckt: Der Fall Mexiko." *Journal fuer Enwicklungspolitik (Austrian Journal for Development Studies)* 18(3): 249–264.

Plehwe, Dieter, and Bernhard Walpen. 2006. "Between Network and Complex Organization: The Making of Neoliberal Knowledge and Hegemony." In Dieter Plehwe, Bernhard Walpen, and Gisela Neunhöffer (eds.), *Neoliberal Hegemony: A Global Critique,* 27–50. London: Routledge.

Röpke, Wilhelm. 1953. "Unterentwickelte Länder." *Ordo* 5: 63–113.

Ruggie, John Gerard. 1982. "International Regimes, Transactions, and Change: Embedded Liberalism in the Postwar Economic Order." *International Organization* 36(2): 379–415.

Schindelbeck, D., and V. Ilgen. 1999. *"Haste was, biste was!" Werbung für die Soziale Marktwirtschaft.* Darmstadt: Primus Verlag.

Schoeck, Helmut. 1957. "Der Stand des Liberalen Denkens. Jubiläumskongress der Mont Pèlerin Society in St. Moritz, September 1957." *Neue Zürcher Zeitung* vom 14/16. September (Separatabdruck).

Schultz, Theodore W. 1987. "Tensions between Economics and Politics in Dealing with Agriculture." In Gerald M. Meier (ed.), *Pioneers in Development,* Second Series, 17–38. Oxford: Oxford University Press.

Steiner, Yves. 2005. *L'affrontement des néolibéralismes au coeur du renouveau libéral: les débats de la Société du Mont-Pèlerin (1947–1960).* Université de Lausanne, Ph.D. thesis.

Strassmann, W. Paul. 1976. "Development Economics from a Chicago Perspective." In Warren J. Samuals (ed.), *The Chicago School of Political Economy,* 277–294. East Lansing: Michigan State University.

Toye, John. 1993. *Dilemmas of Development.* Oxford: Cambridge University Press.

Walpen, Bernhard. 2004. *Die offenen Feinde und ihre Gesellschaft.* Hamburg: VSA.

Zmirak, John. 2001. *Wilhelm Röpke: Swiss Localist, Global Economist.* Wilmington, DE: ISI Books.

MPS Papers Quoted (Liberaal Archief)

Bauer. P. T. 1958b. (Presented by J. Davenport.) *Regulated Wages in Under-Developed Countries.* 17 p.

Benham, Frederic C. 1951. *Liberalism and Underdeveloped Countries.* 9 p.

Brandt, Karl. 1957. *Liberal Alternatives in Western Policies toward Colonial Areas.* 13 p.

Giscard d'Estaing, E. 1957. *Libéralisme et Colonialisme.* 4 p.

Gudin, Eugênio. 1958. *Agriculture. South America.* 6 p.

Rüstow, Alexander. 1957. *Kolonialimperialismus.* (Offprint from A. Rüstow, Ortsbestimmung der Gegenwart. Band 3, Herrschaft oder Freiheit?, 506–518).

Shenfield, A. A. 1957. *Liberalism and Colonialism.* 6 p.

8

Business Conservatives and the Mont Pèlerin Society

KIM PHILLIPS-FEIN

Historians of the conservative intellectual movement in the United States have generally depicted the thinkers who rejected liberalism in the 1940s and 1950s as idiosyncratic and iconoclastic figures on the margins of American life. "What seems, in retrospect, most remarkable about the leaders of this movement in these early years was their tenacity in the face of an often hostile environment," writes historian George H. Nash, in his magisterial 1976 analysis of the rise of conservatism as an intellectual force.[1] This historical judgment largely echoes the beliefs of the participants themselves. Many conservative intellectuals of the early postwar period—a group that includes traditionalist philosophers like Richard Weaver and Russell Kirk as well as the Austrian economists and early libertarians—felt themselves to be sharply at odds with the rest of the modern world, out of step with the commonly accepted faiths of their day. They saw themselves as especially distant from the business world, which they believed had accepted the basic tenets of New Deal liberalism.[2]

But the early history of the Mont Pèlerin Society suggests that intellectual critics of New Deal liberalism—especially those who were most active in developing the network of neoliberal thinkers—did not entirely lack support among businessmen. For within the American business community, opposi-

tion to the New Deal and to Keynesian political economy did not cease with
the end of World War II. On the contrary, a small community of business leaders who had been ardent opponents of the New Deal during the 1930s continued their political work in the 1940s, the 1950s, and beyond. This group,
which included retired executives, businessmen from small companies, and
management at larger corporations, tried to fight the power of New Deal liberalism in a variety of ways—by struggling to change labor law to make it less
sympathetic to unions; by disseminating strategies companies could use to
fight unionization of their employees; and ultimately by supporting candidates who could take their message into electoral politics. This small community of businessmen was delighted to learn of the work of Friedrich Hayek
and Ludwig von Mises, and they helped to form a supportive network for the
Austrian thinkers in America. A few even became deeply involved with the
Mont Pèlerin Society (MPS), providing financial support that was critical for
the MPS's growth and development. Although these businessmen were not
exactly neoliberal in their orientation—they lacked a high level of theoretical
sophistication, and, in general, they did not develop a perspective geared toward using the state to further the power of the market—they found much to
identify with in the MPS project and the work of Hayek and Mises.[3]

These business critics of New Deal liberalism supported a wide range of organizations during the 1940s and 1950s. Some of the groups they worked with,
like the National Association of Manufacturers, focused on mobilizing businessmen themselves, disseminating antiunion strategies and orchestrating public relations campaigns. Others, like Fred Schwarz's Christian Anti-Communist
Crusade, were populist organizations seeking to educate ordinary citizens about
the threat of the far left.[4] But one of the most significant areas of activity for
business conservatives in the postwar years was in creating and funding conservative think tanks such as the Foundation for Economic Education (FEE) and
the American Enterprise Association (AEA—the organization eventually
changed its name to the American Enterprise Institute). These think tanks were
devoted to articulating an economic philosophy centered on the idea of the free
market and disseminating this vision to intellectual elites—journalists, politicians, businessmen, and academics. Such intellectual organizations were, in a
sense, the ideal social technology for business conservatives. Through funding
think tanks, the business opponents of the New Deal could bring ideas reflec-
tive of their broad political views—not simply their immediate interests—into
the intellectual life of the nation, and they could do so regardless of whether or

not such ideas could command support in elections or compel a mass-based organization. The partisan think tanks functioned almost like a political party, in terms of developing and refining ideology and relating it to matters of immediate concern. Yet their great strength from the standpoint of the businessmen who funded them was that they were able to operate without any real need for a popular organization.

The Mont Pèlerin Society differed in important ways from the FEE and AEA, which sought to popularize free market economic ideas and to intervene in policy debates. By contrast, Friedrich Hayek, the founder of the MPS, wanted to create an organization that would serve as a space of free intellectual inquiry, where social scientists and expert thinkers devoted to the idea of the free market could meet to discuss and refine their thought. The remove of the MPS from the rough-and-tumble world of policy debate, as well as the central roles played by European, non-American intellectuals in the organization, might have seemed to make it an unlikely candidate for support from American businessmen. But the Society, along with the domestically oriented, partisan political think tanks, benefited from the active participation of the network of American business conservatives. This was most evident in the fund-raising drive for the first American meeting of the MPS in Princeton in 1958, which the Society pursued almost entirely at the behest of Jasper Crane, a former executive of the DuPont Chemical Company who did the brunt of the fund raising from other businessmen to raise money for the meeting. Crane's enthusiastic commitment to building the American meeting, as well as the participation of the other businessmen whom he sought to involve in the group, suggests a different view of the Society's history, and in turn, of the intellectual history of the postwar right—one in which the lines between business conservatism and the world of intellectual life cannot be so neatly drawn.

This is not to suggest that the ideas developed by the intellectuals of the MPS were directly influenced by the funding role played by men like Crane, but rather that American business conservatives viewed the development of free market philosophy with great interest, recognizing it as an elegant, sophisticated statement of their world-view. Nor is it to argue that the relationship between the intellectuals and their patrons in the business world was always smooth or easy. On the contrary, the businessmen feared that intellectual organizations would prove insufficiently loyal in the political arena and that their unrestrained agenda would mean that they advanced arguments that did not necessarily help the political cause. Hayek's relationship with Crane and with his other business supporters was at times rocky and strained, as the Austrian thinker had no intention of allowing his Society to become either a propagandistic organization or a plaything for rich men. By and large, however, both the businessmen and the intellectuals understood their usefulness to each other. The relationship between Hayek and Crane was an early example of a businessman providing financial and political support for free market ideas—as many more would in subsequent years, helping the ideology of the marketplace become ever more prestigious and powerful as the twentieth century went on.

Moreover, the relationship between the MPS and business conservatives suggests the important and often unrecognized role that international thinkers played in the rise of the American right. The conservative movement in the United States is often thought to reflect a distinctly American set of individualistic values and a uniquely American antipathy to powerful central governments. But the history of the MPS and its interactions with the business right indicates that the ascendance of free market ideology cannot be understood solely as an American phenomenon, for it grew in tandem with the development of an international community of economists, political scientists, and other academics committed to the vision of dismantling the welfare state and reconfiguring society to allow the market greater freedom.

Seeking a Bible of Free Enterprise

Jasper Elliot Crane, the MPS's most active business supporter in its early years, was born in 1881 in Newark, New Jersey. The child of local elites, Crane attended Princeton, and shortly thereafter began his lifelong association with the DuPont Company. He became a vice president of the company, and worked there until his retirement in 1946. The DuPont Company had been one of the centers of opposition to the New Deal during the 1930s. Pierre du Pont, the company's president, and his brothers Lammot and Irénée, were prominent conservative activists throughout the New Deal decade. While Pierre du Pont had initially been a supporter of the Democratic Party in the election of 1932, largely because of the Democrats' opposition to Prohibition, he and his brothers quickly grew disillusioned with Roosevelt and frightened by what they perceived as strident attacks on business in the midst of the Great Depression. In 1934, the du Ponts founded the American Liberty League, an organization that claimed to be devoted to teaching the American people about "the right to work, earn, save, and acquire property and to preserve the ownership and lawful use of property when acquired," and in the process, mobilizing a vast popular movement against the initiatives Roosevelt was undertaking.[5] In reality, the group mostly issued shrill broadsides against the New Deal, warning of the new era of class conflict and government tyranny that was arising in the United States. As one pamphlet put it, the New Deal represented "the attempt in America to set up a totalitarian government, one which recognizes no sphere of individual or business life as immune from governmental authority and which submerges the welfare of the individual to that of the government."[6]

The American Liberty League failed to attract substantial popular or intellectual support. Journalists portrayed it as an organization dominated by a few very rich people, striking out to protect their class interests. Few intellectuals were involved with the League; its speakers were mostly businessmen, lawyers, and Democrats associated with Al Smith (Roosevelt's opponent in the primary election). The organization quietly disappeared following Roosevelt's reelection in 1936. The failure of the League suggests the weakness of conservatism in Depression America, especially as an intellectual force. As one historian has put it, during the era of the New Deal in the United States, "a coherent body of conservative thought scarcely existed, except to the extent business philosophers had shaped absolutist ideas of laissez-faire to advance the interests of private enterprise."[7] Those intellectuals and writers who did criticize the New Deal—thinkers like Frank Knight, Albert Jay Nock, Henry Simons, and Walter Lippmann—frequently had little use for businessmen either. Some viewed business as complicit in the New Deal, while others saw it as inherently lacking in ethics and political principles. Either way, the old world of laissez-faire championed by the Liberty League seemed dead.[8]

Although Crane attended some League functions and surely knew of its activities, he was not a major participant. During the 1930s, he gave the occasional public speech critical of the general direction of American politics. But his real political involvement began only after he retired from DuPont in 1946. Following this dramatic year, which saw not only the advent of the Cold War but the largest strike wave in American history, Crane quickly became active in a variety of organizations, all of which were dedicated to the general proposition that liberalism, even more than Soviet communism, was the gravest danger facing the United States in the postwar period. In the late 1940s and early 1950s, Crane served as a trustee for the Foundation for Economic Education. He played a central role in the National Association of Manufacturers, where he chaired a Committee on Cooperation with Churches, which sought to dissuade churches from allying themselves with "movements to win greater social protection and advantage for labor."[9] Along with his friend J. Howard Pew, the president of Sun Oil, Crane took on a leadership position in the National Council of Churches, a lay organization devoted to winning control over the mainline Protestant church back from the liberals and socialists whom they believed had won control over the Federal Council of Churches.[10]

But even as he grew more deeply engaged in the world of political activism, Crane sought a firmer theoretical and intellectual grounding for his work. This was not simply a personal mission for him; rather, he felt that it was of the deepest political significance. Ideological incoherence, he thought, was one of the greatest obstacles faced by opponents of liberalism. As Crane wrote to a friend in 1945, he had been deeply impressed by another friend's idea that "Christianity made little progress until in the Second Century it had the writings of the New Testament; Communism got nowhere until Marx wrote Das Kapital (read by very few people at first but gradually gaining enormous influence); National Socialism needed Mein Kampf to be effective." Crane was looking, as he put it, for the "New Testament of capitalism," the " 'bible' of free enterprise."[11]

Finding the Prophet

Crane met Hayek during one of Hayek's trips to the United States following the publication of The Road to Serfdom. The two were introduced in May 1946 by Loren Miller, of the Detroit Bureau of Governmental Research, shortly after William H. Luhnow (who worked for the Kansas City-based Volker Fund, a foundation funded by a furniture manufacturer) proposed to Hayek that he write a "Road to Serfdom" about trends in the United States.[12] Miller, who had helped arrange a public talk for Hayek in Detroit, thought that Crane would be interested in the project. The two men had dinner together in New York a few weeks later, along with Leonard Read of the Foundation for Economic Education and Ludwig von Mises (Read had become one of the strongest supporters of Hayek's old teacher, going so far as to help Mises publish his magnum opus Human Action, and Mises would soon start to work for the FEE). At that New York meeting, Crane and Hayek discussed Hayek's plans for what would become the Mont Pèlerin Society.[13] The two men were a bit skeptical about each other. "They seem to be doing very good work, though rather different in character from that which we are contemplating here," Hayek wrote to Luhnow shortly after the meeting.[14] Meanwhile, Crane wrote to Miller, asking him whether Hayek was Jewish and expressing his fears that "a group, half of whom were Jews, would not be apt to be tinged with the collectivist thought that is characteristic of reformed Jewry."[15] A few days later, he followed up with an anxious telegram, telling Miller that he feared that the men who might work with Hayek were "dubious or semisocialist" and that even in *The Road to Serfdom,* Hayek had introduced "a note of compromise" that, "if carried further by unsound men, [would] result in positive harm." Crane told Miller that he hoped Hayek would consult with Ludwig von Mises before starting any new intellectual organization or project.[16]

Hayek's next contact with Crane came in the preparations for the first meeting of the MPS. In return for paying the travel expenses of American members going to Switzerland, Luhnow and the Volker Fund requested permission to invite some of their own picks: Walter Lippmann, F. A. Harper of FEE, Yale economist Fred Fairchild, and most of all Crane (who, Luhnow wrote to Hayek, could be expected to pay his own way).[17] Hayek was immediately doubtful about Crane's participation, although he suggested that perhaps he could attend as an observer, if not as a full member. "After some discussion with my Swiss friends," he wrote to Luhnow, "it had been agreed that for this first conference we should ask as members only people who are in the first place scholars or writers, in order to avoid any impression that the conference has been instigated by any business interests."[18] Two days later, Hayek wrote to Crane to tell him that from a strategic standpoint, it was not a good idea for businessmen to participate in the initial meeting: "I think you will agree that experience has shown that any effort in the sphere of ideas, if it is to be effective, must avoid even the appearance of being dependent on any material interests, and that for that reason we have been careful not to include in the list of persons originally invited, anyone, however sympathetic with our aims, who might be thought by the public to represent specific interests."[19]

Crane's response to Hayek indicated his deepening interest in the Society and his willingness to be involved—he even showed a distinct enthusiasm for taking a backseat role to the scholars. He agreed with Hayek that businessmen and dilettantes should not be publicly associated with the Society: "The conclusions reached, the philosophy developed, the suggestions made, and the points raised for further inquiry will have, coming from men of the highest scholarship, profound influence in the realm of ideas." Perhaps most surprisingly, the specifically nonpragmatic program of the MPS appealed to Crane.

The new organization should not, he thought, attempt to get involved in politics, or even to participate in the types of broad ideological campaigns being organized by the National Association of Manufacturers. "To attempt wide propaganda would in my opinion be quite unwise and would indeed weaken the potential usefulness of the society. That, as the need for it becomes manifest, can be carried on by other instruments created for that very purpose."[20]

Still, Crane declined an invitation from Hayek to attend the first meeting even as an observer. And despite his enthusiastic expressions of support, his fears about the ideological heterogeneity of the MPS only intensified after the first meeting. In June 1947, Crane wrote to Hayek that he was disappointed by reports (likely coming from Leonard Read of FEE) that there were "accepters of collectivism" at Mont Pèlerin: "Are you quite sure that all of the American members, as I know some of them to be, are quite dependable?"[21] Hayek responded with a warning against the "tendency to create an unreasoning orthodoxy which treats traditional liberal principles as a faith rather than a problem on which reasonable people may differ." But Crane was not impressed by the call to intellectual diversity.[22] He argued that "the membership should be as far as possible composed of people who are sincerely devoted to the principle of human liberty," and urged Hayek to "scrutinize" future recruits with "great care." Such fears notwithstanding, he did agree to join the MPS as a full member.[23]

Even after joining the group, Crane continued to have doubts about the ideological direction of the organization. In 1948, he sent one of his friends a list of the new MPS members, in the hopes that the friend would review it to make sure everyone was ideologically sound.[24] In 1949, Crane wrote an angry letter to Hayek about a paper by Frank Knight, "The Determination of Just Wages," which Knight had written for the Society's annual meeting. (Knight failed to attend the meeting, so it never was presented publicly.) The paper argued, among other things, that wealth was becoming progressively more concentrated in the United States, a point that Crane denounced as an idea "which stems from Karl Marx." To make matters worse, Knight had written that "nineteenth century liberalism naively over-emphasizes freedom," a point Crane found "really shocking:" as he concluded, "Unless we uphold the sanctity of the individual and cherish moral ideals, we are lost."[25]

Yet despite his lingering uncertainty, Crane was not willing to give up on the Society. At the end of 1948, he sent a copy of Hayek's article, "The Intellectuals and Socialism," to his close friend and fellow activist, the Sun Oil executive

J. Howard Pew. "I am a member of this Mont Pelerin Society," Crane wrote to Pew. "We will get some things of value from the foreigners, even though they cannot understand our American idea of liberty."[26]

Despite Crane's long-standing ambivalence toward the Society, Hayek sought to cultivate him as a potential donor to the group, at some points gently implying that his financial contributions would be helpful, asking him for help directly at others. In the early years of the MPS, funds were a perennial source of anxiety. Efforts to raise money to fund travel to conferences frequently failed, leaving the Society dependent on the contributions of small think tanks like the Volker Fund. The conservative businessmen who bankrolled many of the initial think tanks—Lewis Brown of Johns-Mansville, a major roofing and insulation corporation, who founded the American Enterprise Association, and B. E. Hutchinson, a Chrysler executive and NAM regular who gave generously to organizations like FEE—were not interested in the Mont Pèlerin Society. Many conservatives in the business community shared Crane's chariness about giving money to European intellectuals to do nothing in particular except meet and talk to one another. The Rockefeller Foundation declined to make money available to the Society, on the grounds that it would create a precedent for funding requests from "Communist and dirigiste" organizations.[27] In addition to the broader questions of strategy and politics, American businessmen may have been anxious about donating to the Society in part because of a 1950 congressional investigation of the American Enterprise Association. The investigation pointed out that the group seemed to violate federal lobbying laws because it was funded almost entirely by corporations, and newspaper reports lambasted the organization as a "big business" group.[28]

Because of the MPS's trouble in raising money, Crane's openness to the organization, however qualified, must have made Hayek hope that someday he would be willing to donate funds. Late in 1948, Hayek wrote to Crane in pointed tones of the difficulties he had faced raising money: "While I see daily how for the international contacts of the leftish groups, and particularly the Communists, almost unlimited means seem to be available and in consequence the closest co-ordination of their systematic efforts possible, I have so far failed to obtain any funds to speak of for similar endeavors on the liberal side."[29] Early in 1952, Hayek decided to more explicitly ask Crane for donations to fund an American meeting of the Society. He anticipated that this meeting would cost about $30,000 to $40,000, and hoped that Crane and six or seven other people would contribute $5,000 each.[30] Crane responded that while he would be happy to give money, and thought the conference a "very desirable affair," the requested $5,000 would be "too big a share for me to take." He suggested a few additional people for Hayek to contact: the salt magnate Sterling Morton ("he is very wealthy"), the Alfred P. Sloan Foundation, even the Rockefeller and Carnegie Foundations (Crane did not know of the earlier frustrations with the foundations).[31] Crane's reluctance to become a fundraiser ultimately helped to doom the plans for an American meeting in the early 1950s. As Hayek wrote in a November 1952 circular to the Society's membership, "The fact is that I simply have not found an American Dr. Hunold."[32]

Building the Church: The First American Meeting

In 1956, Crane's attitude toward the Society shifted. In November 1956, directly following the reelection of President Dwight D. Eisenhower, Crane wrote to Hayek to press him on organizing an American meeting of the MPS, saying he thought it a "very important move." Through such a meeting, "the American public, and particularly the thinking people, would learn . . . of the widespread advocacy of the liberal philosophy and its strong intellectual foundations."[33] Hayek responded in language that seemed designed to urge Crane to step up as an organizer, saying that while he, too, thought an American meeting was of the greatest importance—"any further development of the Society, indeed its fruitful further existence, depends largely on the possibility of holding an American meeting"—he himself was unable personally to devote the time to raising money for such a meeting. "Unless some friends will take over the effort of fund-raising for an American meeting, I see no prospect of success."[34]

In a sharp departure from his 1952 position, Crane agreed to take a leading role in fund-raising for the meeting, assuring Hayek, "I will be ready to make an active effort to secure the necessary financial aid for such a meeting." He urged Hayek to invite J. Howard Pew ("a sound libertarian and a most generous supporter of worthwhile activities") to join the Society, especially since Pew would be able to raise and donate money to make the meeting possible, and he again mentioned Sterling Morton, who Crane thought "might be a large financial supporter of the Mont Pelerin Society." Crane's suggestions of business supporters reflected a larger desire to change the composition of the Society's membership and to encourage exchange between businessmen and scholars. It also likely reflected his earliest concerns about the ideological consistency of the group. He concluded his note with a prominent postscript that

seemed targeted at Hayek's early reluctance to include executives in the organization: "While the membership of the Mont Pelerin Society is and should
be predominantly academic, I believe a small admixture of dedicated businessmen is desirable. As the European members get to know them, or I sup-
pose I should say us, they may lose some of their distrust of capitalists."[35]

What accounted for Crane's changed attitude toward the Society and his
new interest in raising money for an American meeting? It may have reflected
a shift in the nature of business activism following Eisenhower's reelection.
Prior to the Eisenhower years, the business opponents of New Deal liberalism
hoped that the Republican Party, once back in power, would undo the New
Deal. But instead Eisenhower's "moderate Republicanism," which accepted a
Keynesian framework sympathetic to limited government involvement in the
economy, and which treated liberal social programs and labor unions as necessary bulwarks against economic strife and social disorder, solidified the
political transformations of the New Deal era. In the 1940s and early 1950s,
business activism had largely consisted of broad public education campaigns
regarding the virtues of free enterprise, featuring newspaper advertisements,
mass-printed brochures, and other similar efforts informed by the desire to
impact political culture as quickly as possible by reaching as many people as
possible. They sought to carry out an essentially populist strategy, believing
that getting their point of view across was all that was needed to regain the
confidence of the masses. In the mid-1950s, however, following the disappointments of the Eisenhower era, conservative activists began to feel that
they would be more successful if they tried to shape the opinions of smaller
numbers of more influential people. They began to target their projects at academics, clergy, journalists and politicians—people whom they felt would
have a disproportionate impact on the larger culture. A letter from William
Grede—president of Grede Foundries, a past president of NAM and a member of the Board of the Federal Reserve Bank of Chicago (and, subsequently, a
member of the John Birch Society)—responding to a solicitation for donations from a NAM "education" campaign summarizes the shift in opinion:

> I would say that I have recently become convinced that broad public edu-
> cation programs are very expensive, not only in total but in terms of dollars
> per unit of result. I recognize that there is a terrific amount of left-wing
> propaganda, but most of it is free because about fifty years back they suc-
> cessfully carried on a revolution in the so-called "intelligentsia"—the opin-
> ion molding groups. I have come to the conclusion that more good will be

accomplished with the same money by investing it in a counter-revolution in this field. Convincing, for instance, the leaders in the education field, and especially the economics education field, at our universities of the soundness of our position, the education of university professors in the fields of sociology and economics in the sounder principles and then in the installation of these kinds of people on our faculties.[36]

Grede became a contributor to the Mont Pèlerin Society, and it seems likely that Crane's own ideas regarding strategy moved along these same lines at about the same time. (Grede went even further and began to fund-raise himself for the Society—as he wrote in one of his letters, "A few of the contacts I have made in Europe convince me that there is a small group that is fighting back and at the very same sources that started the socialist revolution of probably fifty years ago. They are beginning to make some headway.")[37]

Once Crane committed to the plan of an American meeting of the MPS, he at last lived up to Hayek's hopes as a fundraiser. Crane diligently raised money for a year and a half, sending letters to dozens of prominent conservative businessmen and to small right-wing foundations. His initial pitch sought to persuade businessmen that the esoteric group mattered:

> While freedom in economic affairs still seems to be losing ground politically throughout most of the world, there is at least one encouraging sign. Among educators there is more awareness of the concept of freedom, and increased interest in it. Some of them even evidence a retreat from collectivist philosophy, which has so long dominated academic thinking, and a groping toward a better understanding of liberty. This is important, because what the highbrows upstairs talk about today has such a decisive influence on the public opinion of tomorrow.[38]

Crane urged the prospective donors to contribute to funding an American meeting: "It is ironic that an organization to advance the ideas which have found their fullest expression in America has never had a meeting here."[39]

Many potential donors turned Crane down. But he was able to persuade thirty-three wealthy individuals to contribute to fund the American meeting (he himself contributed $5,000, the very amount that he had deemed too much only a few years earlier). The du Pont family and DuPont executives donated to the meeting. A small conservative foundation named the Relm Foundation gave $5,000, as did J. Howard Pew. New York financier Jeremiah Milbank (who would later play an important role in the small group of businessmen and conservative activists who drafted Senator Barry Goldwater to run for the presidency in 1964), the United Fruit Company, U.S. Steel, the Ford Motor Fund, and the Milliken Foundation (run by Roger Milliken, a textile manufacturer and major backer of Barry Goldwater, who shut down his factories entirely after a union drive won) each contributed $1,000. The Winchester Foundation contributed $3,000 at the behest of wealthy lawyer Pierre Goodrich, and the Frederick Nymeyer Foundation, run by a business consultant, gave $1,000. Smaller contributions came from Henning Prentis (of Armstrong Cork Company), Sterling Morton of Morton Salt, retired Chrysler chair of finance B. E. Hutchinson, the Beech Aircraft Corporation, and Grede Foundries, as well as foundations like the Kennametal Foundation.[40] The total amount collected for the meeting was about $40,000.

Yet Crane's new level of participation, which Hayek had so long sought, was not without its complications. As Crane grew more active as a fundraiser, he also began to try to intervene more directly in the internal life of the Society—leading to a set of conflicts that are entirely absent from the official history of the MPS.[41] Because Crane was raising money, he sought at many points leading up to the meeting to influence the program and even the membership of the group. Commenting on a draft of the program, Crane wrote, "I only hope there is no slip-up by which any compromisers with basic principles would get on the program. That sort of thing seemed to me to be very regrettable at St. Moritz, but using the program that you have laid out it is not to be anticipated at Princeton." He was especially concerned with the chairmen that Hayek would select, writing that he hoped they would be "men of extraordinary competence and soundness."[42] After reading an essay by Wilhelm Roepke, Crane wrote Hayek an anxious letter, expressing fears that Roepke would "attack laissez faire in the American meeting," and urging Hayek to think about how to have the "maximum degree of prevention of attacks on free enterprise in the American meeting."[43]

Other members of the Society felt uncomfortable about the degree to which Crane was attempting to shape the American meeting. Fritz Machlup, a Johns Hopkins professor and treasurer of the society, wrote to Hayek after a meeting of the financial committee, "Crane began with a discussion of your program. I did not like the idea that this Committee should at all get into a matter which is entirely in your prerogative, but I did not say anything as Crane began with a nice statement that he would not like to interfere but he had a great interest in the program because of his assurances to the various donors."[44] Hayek responded, "Crane is sometimes a little bit of a nuisance but on the whole I have been fairly successful at disregarding suggestions from him I did not like."[45]

Meanwhile, Crane regularly consulted with his friends at the Foundation for Economic Education and other activists and businessmen about the best ways to quietly influence the program. This was an uneasy process, in part because of long-standing tensions between the FEE and the MPS. The FEE, founded in 1946 by Leonard Read, the charismatic former president of the Los Angeles Chamber of Commerce, sought to revive "freedom philosophy," sending polemical newsletters to its mailing list of over 28,000 subscribers and reissuing classic works of market philosophy like Frédéric Bastiat's *The Law* and the writings of William Graham Sumner. Although Read admired Hayek tremendously and adopted his vision wholeheartedly, Hayek and others in the MPS had long been wary about the FEE and about its strength in the American free-market intellectual scene, viewing the FEE as an overly strident, simplistic organization that alienated as many people as it persuaded. Karl Brandt, for example, wrote that the FEE was "radical" and issued "cheap propaganda."[46] Crane, on the other hand, considered the FEE "Number One in the institutions for the maintenance of freedom."[47]

The members of the FEE were well aware of the Society's condescension. F. A. Harper, one of FEE's staff libertarians, wrote to Crane, "Anyone who is acutely sensitive to such things knows how much the officials of the Mont Pelerin Society are on guard against invasion and capture by FEE, or any group strongly centered around FEE." The source of this discomfort, in Harper's view, was the Society's insistence on appearing to be a space of neutral intellectual inquiry, an attitude that the politicized FEE roundly rejected: "We have acquired the label of intolerance to views differing from our own . . . and the price we must pay for it is a degree of 'cold shoulder,' a strong feeling of suspicion whenever we appear to aggress."[48] At first, Leonard Read, the head of FEE, was lukewarm about the idea of an American meeting. "Considerable expense is involved and I merely wonder if it's worth the candle," he wrote to Crane.[49] Nonetheless, Crane consistently solicited Read's opinions (and those of Harper) on the program, although he was aware that he had to keep his efforts to do so secret from Hayek. For example, in September 1957 he barred Read from attending a meeting with Hayek: "While FEE men must be on guard to make certain of the program for the proposed meeting in the United States next year, this should be done with a maximum degree of tact, as the officers of the Society might resent any suggestion of domination by the FEE."[50] At the same time, Crane himself felt that the FEE was certainly on a par with the Society. In a fund-raising letter to Irenee du Pont, he wrote, "The Mont Pelerin Society is an international group which has been largely influenced by FEE, though that connection is played down as we don't want the foreigners to think we are trying to run the show."[51]

Crane's deepening involvement in the conference ultimately came to threaten the Society's prized intellectual independence. Because he raised the money for the conference, Crane believed that he had the right to ultimately determine its program. As he wrote to his friend Rose Wilder Lane—the daughter of Laura Ingalls Wilder and a conservative writer and activist in her own right with whom Crane conducted a voluminous correspondence—he "had no reluctance at all . . . to insist on sound statements from the speakers at the Mont Pelerin conference." He explained that while he did not want to be "tactless so as to defeat my very purpose," he had told Hayek that "I must thoroughly approve of the program if I am to raise the money for the meeting."[52] He was especially interested in one point: he (and the other businessmen donors) wanted Ludwig von Mises to play a more central role in the conference than Hayek had originally envisioned. Philip Goodrich, a conservative lawyer and an activist who contributed to the meeting, wrote to Crane to tell him that he believed Mises should be invited to play a prominent role in the conference. "This is Hayek's society, of course, in the sense that he has been President of it for a long time but there is also in this First American Meeting a top place for Von Mises."[53] Crane relayed the message to Hayek. Hayek responded by telling Crane that he would permit Mises to give a keynote address—and even suggesting that Goodrich could speak after Mises if he so desired.[54]

Crane tried to bring businessmen into the Mont Pèlerin Society. In early June, he sent Hayek a long list of people to invite to the conference, including B.E. Hutchinson (a retired chairman of the finance committee at Chrysler and a financial supporter), Charles Hook (the chairman of Armstrong Cork Company), Lammot du Pont Copeland (a DuPont vice president), James Rogers of the Ingersoll Milling Company, Robert E. Woods of Sears, Roebuck, Bradford B. Smith of U.S. Steel, Roger Milliken, Olive Ann Beech (president of Beech Aircraft Corporation), and Bernard Kilgore, president of the *Wall Street Journal*.[55] Hayek complied in some cases, but in others he drew the line. Crane suggested inviting Ray Murphy, chairman of Equitable Life Insurance Company, whom Hayek not only asked to the meeting but also requested to deliver a paper. The company responded that Murphy had retired—but that his successor, James F. Oates, would be delighted to prepare and read the paper for the Society. Hayek turned this offer down.[56]

Crane also wanted to bring the European visitors from Princeton—where the meeting was to be held—out to view the wonders of American industry in the West. "I am exceedingly anxious that they see something of America beside the Atlantic Seaboard, for one of the great values of the meeting of the Mont Pelerin Society is that these foreign economists, political scientists, historians, and other educators, who know nothing of America, should receive on this visit to the United States some idea of the American way of life, cultural values, and philosophy," he wrote to John Holmes, an executive of the Chicago meatpacking firm Swift & Company.[57] He hoped to be able to guide the foreign visitors on a trip to visit the "the stock yards, one of the big banks"—and in particular, to tour corporations with conservative leadership, like Thompson Products and Sears Roebuck, both of which were led by men who were conservative activists (Fred Thompson and General Robert E. Wood).[58] In the end, Crane's vision of taking the scholars to Chicago, Cleveland, Detroit, and beyond proved to exceed the limits of the budget and administrative capacity of the conference. But instead, on breaks from their meeting, the thinkers gathered in Princeton visited Levittown, Tidewater Oil Company, U.S. Steel's Fairless Works, and DuPont.[59]

The American meeting of the MPS took place on September 8–13, 1958, at Princeton. It was the largest conference in the history of the Society, with the most extensive program.[60] The keynote addresses were by Ludwig von Mises (on "Liberty and Property,") by conservative journalist Felix Morley (on "The Meaning of Freedom,") and by donor P. F. Goodrich ("Why Liberty?"). The program included panels on inflation (including papers by Milton Friedman and journalist Henry Hazlitt) and the welfare state (businessman and John Birch Society member William Grede gave a paper on the "Moral Effects of the Welfare State"). But the conference did not go as smoothly as Crane had wished. It was at this meeting that Hayek and others began to become acutely aware of the strange behavior of their original patron, Dr. Albert Hunold. At the meeting, Hunold's behavior was erratic and belligerent. He demanded changes in the menus that Crane had carefully ordered, refused to speak to the host representing Princeton University and the Graduate College, and got into screaming arguments with various people at the Princeton Inn (including Alfred de Grazia, a Princeton professor who had volunteered to oversee details at Princeton during the meeting). He failed to make appropriate arrangements

with the public relations agency, Hill and Knowlton, which had been contracted for the Society, and he also abandoned responsibilities for arranging
the Western trip. Worst of all, "from the platform he made slurring references
to the foolish policies of the United States, hardly becoming one who was a
guest in this country," and "his economics seemed at variance with that professed in the aims of the Mont Pelerin Society."[61] Hayek and others blamed
many of the failures of the meeting—the lack of publicity, the fact that the
Western trip did not come off—on Hunold.

From Crane's point of view, Hunold's breakdown must have indicated the
ultimate limitations of the MPS as a political vehicle. Despite all his careful
work, the meeting still had been disrupted by unpredictable Europeans. At the
same time, the mounting tensions with Hunold, which would nearly break the
MPS apart in future years, may have had another lesson for Hayek and others:
the danger of allowing donors and businessmen to play too great a role in determining the direction of the MPS. For whatever reason, Crane's participation
in the MPS seems to have declined following the high point of the American
meeting, although he still remained a general supporter of its aims.

While the American meeting gave the intellectuals new reasons to fear the
strings that seemed to come with the involvement of donors, the conference at
Princeton did not mark the end of the broader relationship between businessmen and the high theorists of the Mont Pèlerin Society. On the contrary, the
connections between the business world and that of think tanks and intellectual organizations would only deepen over the years to come. Conservative
foundations such as the Lilly Endowment and the Relm Foundation continued in the 1960s to donate money to subsidize the travel costs associated with
Mont Pèlerin Society meetings to places as far-flung as Japan and even
Venezuela.[62] At the 1964 meeting, Milton Friedman and Hayek circulated a
prospectus for a book series on "Principles of Freedom," in which prominent
free market intellectuals would write short popular volumes for an audience of
undergraduates and lay readers; they had already attracted numerous corporate
sponsors for the series, including GE, DuPont, Shell Oil, and U.S. Steel.[63] Free
market economists—including Society members—spoke at meetings of the
National Association of Manufacturers, the Los Angeles Chamber of Commerce, and the Crotonville School of General Electric. Their books were
owned by leading conservatives in the business world, like Lemuel Boulware,
who pioneered antiunion strategies at GE during the 1950s.[64] In short, the men
of the Mont Pèlerin Society not only drew financial support from businessmen

and invited them to their conferences; they were well-known within conservative circles in the corporate world. And while Hayek was not setting labor policy at American corporations, his ideas helped to legitimate the rising tide of antiunion sentiment throughout business in the late 1950s. The ideas and arguments of the neoliberal thinkers helped to transform the opposition to unions and the welfare state from reactionary politics to good judgment in the public mind. What is more, Crane's support for the Society anticipated the increase in political activity and funding for conservative think tanks that would come about during the tumultuous 1970s—for example, the role played by businessmen like Joseph Coors in funding the Heritage Institute during the 1970s.

The connections between wealthy donors like Crane—whose participation and imaginative commitment to the MPS went far beyond simply giving money to taking an active role in fundraising and organization for the conference—and intellectuals like Hayek are key to understanding the rise of the postwar right. Recognizing these relationships helps us to see the material basis for the postwar right. Seeing the networks between businessmen and intellectuals demands that we take account of the influence of free market thought on the core group of businessmen who remained critical of New Deal liberalism, and the extent to which they came to understand their antipathy to labor unions and the welfare state in terms of a struggle for freedom against the forces of collectivist tyranny. The motives of businessmen like Crane reflected a broad vision of society and their place within it, and cannot be reduced to short-term economic interest. They were motivated by a broad sense of political values, by a sweeping philosophical program, even more than a sense of immediate financial need. In his 1960 work, *The Constitution of Liberty,* Hayek himself paid an implicit homage to Crane and the other businessman-activists who clustered around the MPS. The leadership role played by individuals who could offer financial support to organizations representing their beliefs, he wrote, was of special importance when it came to supporting unorthodox ideas in "politics, morals and religion." If "minority views are to have a chance to become majority views," they would need to rely upon the financial support of wealthy iconoclasts.[65] It was language that must have been dear to Jasper Crane's heart.

Notes

1. George H. Nash, *The Conservative Intellectual Movement in America since 1945* (Wilmington, DE: Intercollegiate Studies Institute, 1998), 28.

2. For one example of the conservative self-image, see the memoir of *National Review* publisher William Rusher, *The Rise of the Right* (New York: William Morrow, 1984).

3. For a discussion of the role of money and wealth in building the postwar right, see David Chappell, "The Triumph of Conservatives in a Liberal Age," in Jean-Christophe Agnew and Roy Rosensweig (eds.), *Companion to Post-1945 America* (Malden, MA: Blackwell, 2002), 312. The question of whether the business conservatives were "neoliberal" is complicated. They were generally most interested in reversing the New Deal, especially with regard to labor unions, so in the sense of wanting to move society back to an earlier point, they were certainly conservatives. In addition, their sense that they understood a set of underlying social laws and principles about the way that society should operate, and that activists in social movements were ignorant of these, gave them a certain skepticism about labor unions and policies encouraging economic redistribution, and in this respect as well they were akin to conservatives of old. At the same time, they were enthusiastic about capitalism and the market, in contrast to thinkers such as Russell Kirk and Richard Weaver. In addition, they were rarely completely consistent—they were not opposed to various uses of the state to further the interests of business. And Jasper Crane—of special significance for this chapter—wrote that he wished that he could still call himself a "liberal." For the purposes of this chapter, however, I will refer to them as conservatives, both because of the intellectual logic of doing so and because historically they affiliated themselves with a political movement that had little ambivalence about adopting the word.

4. See Lisa McGirr, *Suburban Warriors: The Origins of the New American Right* (Princeton, NJ: Princeton University Press, 2001), especially 98–102.

5. Robert F. Burk, *The Corporate State and the Broker State* (Cambridge, MA: Harvard University Press, 1990), 144. Burk's book is an excellent history of the political evolution of the du Ponts.

6. Jouett Shouse, "The New Deal vs. Democracy," speech given on June 20, 1936, pamphlet in Edith Phillips Collection, Hoover Institution. Also see Frederick Randolph, "The American Liberty League, 1934–1940," *American Historical Review,* 56, No. 1 (October 1950), 19–33.

7. James MacGregor Burns, *Roosevelt: The Lion and the Fox* (New York: Harcourt, Brace, 1956), 156.

8. For some examples of the work of these other critics of the New Deal, and their ambivalence toward business, see Henry Simons, *Economic Policy for a Free Society* (Chicago: University of Chicago Press, 1948); Frank Knight, *Freedom and Reform: Essays in Economic and Social Philosophy* (New York: Harper & Brothers, 1947); Walter Lippmann, *An Inquiry into the Principles of the Good Society* (Boston: Little, Brown and Company, 1937); Michael Wreszin, *The Superfluous Anarchist: Albert Jay Nock* (Providence, RI: Brown University Press, 1971); Rick Tilman, *Ideology and Utopia in the Social Philosophy of the Libertarian Economists* (Westport, CT: Greenwood Press, 2001).

9. Elizabeth Fones-Wolf, *Selling Free Enterprise: The Business Assault on Labor and Liberalism* (Urbana and Champaign: University of Illinois Press, 1994), 220.

10. Ibid., 237–238.

11. Jasper Crane to Loren Miller, September 14, 1945; November 13, 1945; Jasper Crane Papers, box 51, Hagley Museum and Archive, Wilmington, Delaware.

12. Loren Miller to Jasper Crane, May 3, 1946. Friedrich Hayek Papers (FH), box 58, folder 16. Hoover Institution, Stanford University. The chapter by Rob Van Horn and Phil Mirowski in this volume (Chapter 4) is the best discussion of the way that Hayek came to America, exploring his connections with the Volker Fund in great depth.

13. Jasper Crane to Loren Miller, May 21, 1946. JCP, box 51.

14. Hayek to Luhnow, May 23, 1946. FH, box 58, folder 16.

15. Crane to Miller, June 3, 1946. JCP, box 51.

16. Crane to Miller, June 12, 1946. JCP, box 51.

17. Luhnow to Hayek, January 27, 1947. FH, box 58, folder 16.

18. Hayek to Luhnow, February 5, 1947. FH, box 58, folder 16.

19. Hayek to Crane, February 7, 1947. FH, box 73, folder 1.

20. Crane to Hayek, March 7, 1947. FH, box 73, folder 1.

21. Crane to Hayek, June 3, 1947. FH, box 73, folder 1.

22. Hayek to Crane, June 19, 1947. FH, box 73, folder 1.

23. Crane to Hayek, September 5, 1947. JCP, box 52.

24. E. E. Lincoln to Crane, July 14, 1948. JCP, box 52. Lincoln expressed a variety of doubts and said that he was uncertain what purpose the new organization would serve.

25. Crane to Hayek, October 17, 1949. JCP, box 52. One wonders whether Crane's religiosity may have fed into his skepticism about the Mont Pèlerin Society.

26. Crane to Pew, December 28, 1948. JCP, box 52.

27. Brandt to Hayek, April 12, 1949. FH, box 72, folder 36.

28. "Lobby Inquiry Finds 'Big Business' Group," *New York Times,* December 30, 1950; "Lobby Probers Turn Spotlight on Business-Backed Group," *Washington Post,* December 30, 1950.

29. Hayek to Crane, January 31, 1949. JCP, box 52.

30. Hayek to Crane, January 17, 1952. JCP, box 52.

31. Crane to Hayek, February 29, 1952. JCP, box 52.

32. Mont Pelèrin Society, President's Circular, November 1952. JCP, box 52.

33. Jasper Crane to Friedrich Hayek, November 21, 1956. JCP, box 52.

34. Hayek to Crane, November 30, 1956. JCP, box 52.

35. Crane to Hayek, December 13, 1956. JCP, box 52.

36. William Grede to C. S. Rogers, July 20, 1954. FH, box 74, bolder 15.

37. William Grede Fundraising Letter, undated but circa July 12, 1955. FH, box 74, folder 15.

38. Crane Fundraising Letter, April 25, 1957. JCP, box 52.

39. Ibid.

40. Fritz Machlup, "Final Financial Statement on Princeton Meeting," May 20, 1959. Sent to Jasper Crane, William Curtiss, John Davenport, Lawrence Fertig, and Friedrich Hayek, FH, box 78, folder 1.

41. This is R. M. Hartwell's *A History of the Mont Pelerin Society* (Indianapolis, IN: Liberty Fund, 1995). Hartwell mentions Crane's role in raising money for the meeting, but says nothing about the debates that ensued about the program.

42. Jasper Crane to Friedrich Hayek, January 9, 1958. FH, box 73, folder 1.

43. Crane to Hayek, November 19, 1957. FH, box 73, folder 1.

44. Fritz Machlup to Friedrich Hayek, January 31, 1958. FH, box 78, folder 1.

45. Friedrich Hayek to Fritz Machlup, February 10, 1958. FH, box 78, folder 1.

46. Brandt to Hayek, June 28, 1949. FH, box 72, folder 36.

47. Crane to du Pont, November 19, 1957. JCP, box 52.

48. Harper to Crane, October 1, 1957. JCP, box 52.

49. Read to Crane, June 13, 1957. JCP, box 52.

50. Crane to Read, September 25, 1957. JCP, box 52.

51. Crane to du Pont, November 19, 1957. JCP, box 52.

52. Crane to Rose Wilder Lane, November 21, 1957. JCP, box 52. This note was in response to a long missive from Lane, with whom Crane kept up a voluminous correspondence, in which she berated him for having any sense that "it is improper for the man who pays the fiddler to dictate the tune." It was, she said, "a fallacy promulgated by the eggheads—who get the money, but because they cannot earn it in a free market, must affect to despise money, and money-earners, in an effort to protect their own self-respect." Lane to Crane, November 15, 1957.

53. Excerpts from letter written by Pierre F. Goodrich to Jasper Crane. FH, box 73, folder 1.

54. Friedrich Hayek to Jasper Crane, March 3, 1958. JCP, box 52.

55. Jasper Crane to Friedrich Hayek, June 6, 1958. FH, box 73, folder 1. Fritz Machlup, the treasurer of the Society, never appreciated the influence Crane had over invitations. A year later, when the Society was planning a meeting at Oxford, Machlup wrote to Hayek, "Crane wants to bring people to Oxford. Personally, I do not believe that the people whom he proposes have in the past contributed a great deal to our meetings, or are likely to do so in the future. It would be my preference to save our funds for more important purposes in the future." Machlup to Hayek, June 18, 1959. Box 78, folder 1, Friedrich Hayek Papers.

56. Friedrich Hayek to Ray Murphy, April 21, 1958, FH, box 78, folder 11. R.I Nowell to Friedrich Hayek, May 5, 1958, FH, box 78, folder 20.

57. Crane to John Holmes, May 7, 1958. JCP, box 52.

58. Crane to Frederick Nymeyer, October 25, 1957. JCP, box 52.

59. Jasper Crane to Friedrich Hayek, list of individuals and companies to thank, September 19, 1958. JCP, box 53.

60. R. M. Hartwell, *A History of the Mont Pelerin Society* (Indianapolis, IN: Liberty Fund, 1995), 100.

61. Confidential Memorandum of Delinquencies of A. Hunold, Secretary of the Mont Pelèrin Society, in Connection with Its American Meeting in Princeton, September 8–13. September 17, 1958. JCP, box 52. It is unclear who wrote this document.

62. Hartwell, *A History of the Mont Pelerin Society,* 145–148, 155.

63. Dieter Plehwe, draft of essay, "Reconstructing Neoliberal (MPS) Development Economics and Politics," 20. The results of this initiative are not altogether clear, and the subject merits attention from future researchers. Another area for future research might be the funding sources of the Philadelphia Society, an intellectual organization that resembled an American branch of the MPS.

64. See Kimberly Phillips-Fein, "Top-Down Revolution: Businessmen, Intellectuals and Politicians Against the New Deal, 1945–1964." Columbia University, Ph.D. dissertation, 2005.

65. Friedrich Hayek, *The Constitution of Liberty* (Chicago: University of Chicago Press, 1960), 125.

PART THREE

Mobilization for Action

9

The Influence of Neoliberals in Chile before, during, and after Pinochet

KARIN FISCHER

Introduction

The dictatorship of Augusto Pinochet in Chile (1973–1989) has attracted special attention among those seeking to better understand the role of neoliberal ideas in economic and social engineering. But already before Pinochet's coup d'état, Chile was considered a "laboratory" by Chicago economist Theodore Schultz (Valdés 1995, 126). And Chile served later as a showcase for the alleged merits of neoliberal reform agendas promoted elsewhere.[1] Despite the brutal repression of the opposition under the Pinochet dictatorship, neoliberal economists in fact have been widely praised both inside and outside of Chile for their policy advice against protectionist, socialist, and populist tendencies, which were thought to undermine a private property market economy, as well as growth and development prospects. Whether the result of or despite the authoritarian regime, Chile's post-coup economic development record is widely regarded as relatively better than that of other Latin American countries. But because of the global awareness of the Pinochet regime's abysmal human rights record, Chile has never enjoyed a "model" status similar to the East Asian "tiger" economies.[2]

Although a lot of time has passed and Chile has become a stable democracy, considerable disagreement and debate persists regarding Chile's road to neoliberalism. In spite of the extensive research that has been done on the "Chicago boys" (see Valdés 1995), the role of neoliberal intellectuals and the significance of the mobilization of a particular set of ideas need to be more fully considered when explaining the development of neoliberalism in Chile. To improve our understanding of the role of intellectuals and ideas, it is necessary to reexamine the changing roles and social positions of neoliberal intellectuals *before, during, and after* the Pinochet dictatorship.

Two years after the coup in 1973, an economic team referred to as the "Chicago boys" occupied positions within Chile that permitted them to successfully introduce a new development model into the country. In an effort to redirect the domestic economy toward global competition, the previous import substitution model was replaced by an export orientation. Many tariff and nontariff barriers were abolished in due course, and anti-inflationary strategies were pursued by means of highly restrictive monetary and fiscal policies. The thoroughgoing reorganization of the economy was yoked to equally wide-ranging social changes aimed at no less than a reconfiguration of the relations between capital, the state, and labor—eventually codified in a new constitution. As yet there is no agreement, even among scholars skeptical of the success of the coup, on the key question: how much weight should be given to neoliberal intellectuals and ideas in transforming Chilean society?

The Pinochet regime fostered highly personalized channels of communication with the "economic change team" and allowed it a high degree of autonomy in the pursuit of neoliberal planning activities and structural reforms. This has been confirmed by insiders such as the "godfather" of the Chicago boys, Arnold Harberger: "Given that there was a military government, the idea that they were willing to cede economic authority to a group of technocrats made that transition easier than it would have been in a democratic context of the same time and place" (Harberger 1999). Yet Harberger did not subscribe to the perspective of scholars who argued that a radical break with long-established institutional arrangements and the exaction of high social costs involved in the neoliberal adjustment process necessarily required an authoritarian political system (Foxley 1986; Martínez and Díaz 1996). To counter the position of these scholars, Harberger cited the experience of other countries that had carried out neoliberal reforms: "Then what happened is that one democratic government after another in Latin America adopted virtually identical reforms. . . . So you can't say that these reforms are inevitably shackled to a military government" (Harberger 1999).

As an early proponent of the Chilean economic policy transformation, Harberger can be said to have made an affirmative assessment of the technocratic power of "independent" professional economists. This has been seconded by some of the key Chilean players: In 1971, before the events of the Pinochet coup, one critic of the Chicago boys claimed that "the Chileans who returned from Chicago after 1960 are even more Friedmanite than Friedman himself" (Mario Zañartu, quoted in Valdés 1995, 206). Institutional sociologists have critically examined the highly professional involvement and ideological cohesion apparent in the Chilean project, likewise to emphasize the influence of bureaucratic technocrats empowered to design a new legal and economic framework. By emphasizing professional academic, technocratic, and bureaucratic dimensions, however, scholars who focus on the role of ideas neglect the content of scientific and technocratic knowledge when explaining the rise of neoliberalism in Chile and elsewhere.[3] Scholars who emphasize interest group networking insist that the individuals who succeeded at Chicago sought to introduce their neoliberal vision of social order, rather than simply to apply "science" in some value-free and professional manner.[4] Even before these Chilean scholars served in powerful government and private-sector positions, they—together with high-ranking military officers, representatives of big business, and other right-wing factions—played an important role in obstructing the Allende government (Imbusch 1995; Silva 1996; Fischer 2002). Nevertheless, thus far those scholars have paid scant attention to other important academic and intellectual developments of Chilean (and foreign) neoliberalism.

We can, therefore, still subject to further scrutiny the multifaceted mobilization and transformation of knowledge and ideas involved in Chile's economic and social transformation,. Although each of the approaches cited above has greatly enhanced our knowledge of Chile's road to neoliberalism, we cannot adequately explain the power and relative influence of neoliberal intellectual entrepreneurship in Chile through theories that elevate "technocracy" (economic professionalism), "domestic institutions" (the military dictatorship), or "interest groups" (power elite networking) to center stage without considering the transnational evolution of Chilean neoliberalism.

This chapter focuses on the historical trajectories of neoliberal knowledge and ideas in Chile. Starting in the 1950s, I examine more closely the organizational efforts made to introduce neoliberal thinking in Chile, in conjunction with the early careers of economists trained abroad in neoliberalism. I will argue that we need to consider Chile as a crucial site for transnational neoliberal resistance against the dominant postwar development paradigms of state-driven modernization, import substitution, and social reform. In the next section, I will reexamine the networking and coalition-building activities of the different "counter-revolutionary" political and ideological factions in the 1970s. As we shall see, neoliberal intellectuals were embroiled on multiple fronts in the effort to overthrow the socialist government of Salvador Allende. Only later was a Chilean understanding of a "new liberalism" imposed to crystallize this process. In this regard, it is essential to recognize the role of Chilean legal scholars in addition to the local economists. In the last section of the chapter, I will explain how and why the content of neoliberalism has changed several times in Chile in reaction to important events, above all in reaction to the severe economic crisis in 1982. Here it will be imperative to recognize and explore the role of other foreign sources of neoliberal economics and social philosophy (such as public choice and Austrian economics) in addition to the Chicago School. I will thus argue that neoliberalism in Chile cannot be readily understood on the basis of some clearly defined, prepackaged, one-size-fits-all set of ideas, and then be simply identified with generic antidemocratic authoritarianism. Rather, we need to examine diverse neoliberal intellectuals in terms of their motives, their individual reasoning quirks; and their actions in context; only then can we fully understand how neoliberals and their ideas have been mobilized and adapted so successfully. Both the domestic and international stories can be integrated by always keeping one eye on the international Mont Pèlerin Society, where Chilean and foreign neoliberals worked closely together.

Setting the Stage

Arranging the Transfer of Neoliberal Ideas: The Catholic University–Chicago Connection

In the 1950s, various programs were initiated to introduce and strengthen Western economics in Latin America's academics. Of particular importance in this regard were U.S. efforts to "modernize" the curriculum in economics and to provide training grants to Latin American students to come to the United States. American resources were deployed with the goal of training new economic personnel, thereby providing a bulwark against Marxist positions, which were accorded considerable importance in the new development discourse established after World War II. Although many academics involved in the U.S. Point Four Program supported what later culminated in Walt Rostow's "modernization paradigm," the effort also recruited neoliberal strongholds like the University of Chicago, which was hostile to the strong emphasis on state planning that dominated the developmental mainstream in the West at the time.[5]

The Point Four efforts to organize a transfer of economic ideas and methods were aimed at Latin American countries. Chile arguably figured more prominently in the "battlefield of ideas" than other countries, if only because the United Nations Economic Commission for Latin America (ECLA) had been established in Santiago in 1948 and had become a bastion of the structuralist approach to the causes of uneven development. Raúl Prebisch, ECLA's general secretary, promoted the import substitution development strategy. Within this framework, a selective retreat from the world market was prescribed to enhance regional economic cooperation and alter the international division of labor to the advantage of the newly industrializing countries (Prebisch 1950, 1961). ECLA therefore contributed to an intellectual climate that attracted critical development theorists from all over the Americas, including the Chicago School heretic Andre Gunder Frank.

Efforts to nurture neoliberal ideas in Chile culminated in 1956 with the agreement that the economics faculty of the Catholic University of Santiago (Universidad Católica, CU) signed with its counterpart at the University of Chicago. The so-called Project Chile was conceived as part of the U.S. Point Four Program of technical assistance and economic aid to underdeveloped countries. It was conducted by the International Cooperation Administration, or ICA (today the Agency for International Development, or AID) (Fontaine 1988, 23). The origins of the agreement can be traced to the conversations of the chair of the Economics Department at Chicago, Theodore Schultz,[6] with Albion Patterson, director of the ICA and technical cooperation at the Institute of Inter-American Affairs in Chile. Schultz was particularly concerned with education and human capital as they related to economic growth. He accordingly proposed a project entitled "Technical Assistance to Latin America," and "wanted to use Chile as a laboratory to test his theories."[7]

An earlier signal event in the formation of a neoliberal thought collective in Chile was a congress of Latin American universities that took place in Santiago in 1953. The Catholic University representatives, President Alfredo Silva and law professor Julio Chaná, successfully thwarted a plan to establish a research institute on regional economic development under the auspices of their progressive counterpart, the University of Chile. After his successful intervention, Chaná was rewarded with the post of dean of the economic faculty at the Catholic University, and he immediately began to reorganize the faculty. Together with Patricio Ugarte, a commercial engineer trained in the United States and responsible for the Point Four Program in Santiago, Chaná spearheaded the establishment of an institute dedicated to investigating and promoting foreign investment. Their first attempt to institutionalize neoliberal research perspectives was frustrated by strong opposition from nationalist professors and progressive members of the faculty, who argued that a liberal approach imported from the United States was inappropriate for CU (Valdés 1995, 122f.).

A second attempt, launched in 1955, succeeded in overcoming these obstacles and led to Project Chile. Patterson, Chaná, and Ugarte eventually signed a treaty of cooperation, and members of the Chicago department (T. W. Schultz, Earl J. Hamilton, Simon Rottenberg, and Arnold Harberger) traveled to Santiago to work out the concrete terms of a future training program. Despite continuing opposition from some university council members, an agreement with the Economics Department of the University of Chicago was finally signed in March 1956. As a result, approximately thirty Chilean economists were trained in Chicago between 1956 and 1964. The exchange program also attracted graduates from the University of Chile and succeeded in substantially altering the way economics was taught in the whole Chilean University system.[8]

After the official end of Project Chile in 1964, the recruitment and training of students continued with funds from the Economics Department of the University of Chicago, AID, the Ford and Rockefeller Foundations, the Organization of American States, the Chilean Central Bank, and Chile's planning office, ODEPLAN (Oficina de Planificación Nacional). In addition, the Ford Foundation donated $750,000 for a ten-year period to the Center for Latin American Economic Research at the University of Chicago. In the course of three decades, more than 150 Chilean students received their training in Chicago (Biglaiser 2002, 275f.). During the 1960s, Latin American graduate students made up one-third of the total stock of students in Chicago's Economics Department (Harberger 1999). This long-term investment in the transfer of neoliberal ideas to Chile was especially important because the intellectual climate was steadily trending in the opposite direction, as a result of the widely perceived failure of the policies carried out within the modernization paradigm. Alternative approaches based on the radicalized structuralist paradigms of the world system and dependency theories had increasingly gained currency in ECLA. Latin American development theorists stressed the lopsided integration into the capitalist world market and the exploitative role of foreign capital and multinationals. Influenced by numerous anticapitalist movements in the Third World, the "dependency approach" became the most important underdevelopment paradigm during the 1960s and 1970s. Policy proposals advocated "(collective) self-reliance" and the severing of ties to the capitalist world economy ("delinking").[9]

Such countercurrents notwithstanding, the Chile-Chicago exchange program was very successful in realizing its promoters' expectations. After their return to Chile, the young economists brought their freshly acquired knowledge into the conglomerates or filled academic posts at Catholic University. Economists affiliated with the ruling Christian Democratic Party entered state agencies in the 1960s under President Eduardo Frei. Chicago-trained and other neoliberal economists secured important positions in the Central Bank (e.g., Alvaro Bardón, Carlos Massad, Jorge Cauas),[10] the budget agency, and the supraministerial planning office ODEPLAN. Immediately after the coup, ODEPLAN would become the "operational basis" of the economic change team that designed the economic transformation.[11]

New Projects of the Right: A New Party and the Gremialista Movement

Throughout the 1960s, the traditional right lost ground in Chile. To prevent the victory of the socialist candidate Salvador Allende, the parties of the right felt compelled to back the moderate Christian Democrat Eduardo Frei in the 1964 presidential elections. In response to electoral defeat—the Liberals fell from twenty-eight seats to six, and the Conservatives from seventeen to three—Liberals, Conservatives, and nationalist groups founded the National Party in 1966. The new party, exhibiting a style reminiscent of that of conservative governments at the beginning of the nineteenth century, advocated a strong authoritarian nationalism. "Interest group-led" party politics was to be replaced by a government relying on "neutral" experts, with an emphasis on private property and entrepreneurship. The new right thereby tried to distance itself from the traditional right, which was now disparaged as opportunistic and oligarchic, always seeming to be at the service of vested interests (Vergara 1985, 61f.).

At the same time, another radical right-wing movement emerged at the Catholic University. The so-called *gremialista* movement ("guildism") became a gathering point for teachers and students, who claimed to rescue the university and society as a whole from the "Christian-Marxist clutch" (Arriagada 1998, 76ff.). The universities in general and CU in particular served as an important political arena mirroring the social and ideological climate in society: when the Christian Democratic government proposed a far-reaching educational reform that would give poorer segments of the population increased access to Chile's elitist universities, violent clashes erupted between right-wing and reformist factions (Huneeus 1998).

The *gremialista* movement would ultimately provide an essential recruitment base for the pro-coup coalition. Established by Sergio Guzmán, a law professor at the CU and later one of the intellectual leaders of the military regime, his ideological project was based on corporatist ideas grounded in ultraconservative Catholicism. The gremialists sought to replace party politics with an authoritarian corporatist regime. Business interest groups and professional organizations *(gremios)* were assigned key roles in a system of functional representation that was to control and moderate the discretionary political power of the state (Teichman 2001, 25; Valdivia and de Zárate 2003, chapter 5). In Guzmán's words, *gremialismo* is based on the autonomy of intermediate organizations of society, which all have their very own objectives, without being instrumentalized by "collectivist" ideologies, governments, or political parties. Combined with a strong emphasis on an authoritarian Catholic value code, the *gremialismo* discourse had a strong impact on those who felt threatened in the face of an "overpoliticized" and increasingly polarized historic situation: primarily middle-class sectors and small entrepreneurs (cf. Cristi 1999, 2000; Montecinos and Markoff 2001).

The battleground at the university brought together the returning Chicago economists, who began to occupy leading positions in student and university bodies at CU, and the *gremialistas.* Many of the economists who designed the socioeconomic reforms of the post-coup period actively participated in the *gremialista* movement—the only *radical* political entity in the fight against what was perceived as a Chilean "road to socialism" inside and outside the campus (Lavín 1986; Huneeus 1998).

Building Up Networks: Big Business, Neoliberal Economists, and the Military

In the face of the political shift to the left, with the Frei administration initiating an agrarian reform alongside educational reforms and other redistribution measures, the right-wing forces in Chile began to forge direct contacts and networks within and outside the public sphere. Crucial protagonists in this regard were the representatives of the conglomerates (O'Brian and Roddick 1983; Silva 1996). Many of the top leaders of the conglomerates either were trained in Chicago (Manuel Cruzat, head of the Cruzat-Larraín group, for example) or collaborated closely with the neoliberal economists from the late 1950s onward. On behalf of these powerful groups, the economists conducted courses at SOFOFA (Sociedad de Fomento Fabril / Federation for the Promotion of Industry), the industrialists' association, to win private-sector converts for their ideas. Important public channels were opened by media mogul Álvaro Saieh, who also had a Ph.D. from Chicago, and by the publisher of the influential daily newspaper *El Mercurio,* Agustín Edwards. The Edwards group was one of the conglomerates involved in the printing, paper, and packing industries, as well as in finance, mining, and consumer goods production (Silva 1996; also see Dahse 1979).

Agustín Edwards eventually became a key actor in an informally organized cabal that would play an important role in shaping the prospect of a military coup against the duly elected government of Salvador Allende. Together with Hernán Cubillos, head of the *El Mercurio* newspaper, and ex-Navy officer Roberto Kelly, he founded the *Naval Brotherhood of the South Pacific* (Cofradía Náutica del Pacífico Austral) in 1968. The Brotherhood was initially conceived as a leisure club for boating aficionados. It was quickly turned into a political circle comprised of actors who saw their economic and social interests endangered by the political developments and increasingly felt that they could not maintain their position within the given institutional order. The first plans for a military coup originated in the ranks of this "Brotherhood" (Corvalán Marquéz 2001, 223f.).

Agustín Edwards founded Chile's first neoliberal think tank CESEC (Center for Social and Economic Studies)[12] whose main task was to attack the mixed-economy perspectives still popular in leading business circles. Members of the think tank drew up the economic program of the right-wing candidate Jorge Alessandri in the 1970 presidential elections, the emblematic figurehead of *gremialism.*[13] Of course, he could count on the active support of Jaime Guzmán, who also contributed to his election manifesto and led his youth organization. Interestingly, at that time the free market ideas of the CESEC economists were to some extent opposed by Alessandri's political team, which favored the traditional right-wing perspectives of a corporativist closed economy. However, *gremialista* leader Jaime Guzmán was successfully mediating between the market radical and the corporatist factions backing Alessandri and thereby helped to avoid public disagreements with regard to these issues. Although neoliberal economic ideas were not high on Alessandri's agenda, the campaign was successful in winning important adherents to the Chicago ideas among key businessmen. Moreover, it brought neoliberal economists together with *gremialistas* in joint concrete action—and forced them to compromise over the common goal (O'Brian and Roddick 1983; Silva 1991, 392).

After Allende's election victory in 1970 and in the face of the nationalization and collectivization of enterprises, SOFOFA, headed by representatives of the conglomerates, stepped up its counteractivities. Moving well beyond mere propaganda work, the supply of daily consumer goods was interrupted in an attempt to provoke backlash. Along these lines, SOFOFA organized entrepreneurial boycotts and a collapse of private transportation. In 1971, the association explicitly dedicated itself to an overthrow of the government; the Chicago-trained economist Sergio Undurruga was charged with coordinating the SOFOFA task groups security, propaganda, and economic policy (Delano and Traslaviña 1989, 23f.; Corvalán Marquéz 2001, 225).

The informal "Monday Club" (see Table 9.1) activities of the CESEC staff and members of the *Naval Brotherhood* were pivotal in mobilizing the economic group and in drawing up an economic counterprogram. Starting in 1971, they began to meet regularly in the *El Mercurio* office of Hernán Cubillos. Contacts were developed with "disappointed *Freístas*," Christian Democrat-affiliated economists who were willing to join the insurgency. Naval officer Roberto Kelly was especially important in the effort to broaden the coalition.

Table 9.1   Key actors in Chile's radical market reform I
(Names of MPS members in italics)

	The economic subnetwork with military, technocratic, conglomerate links: Naval and Monday Club Network
José Toribio Merino	Naval Brotherhood, military junta, responsible for economic matters; with formal position in the government
Hernán Cubillos	Naval Brotherhood, Monday Club, head of *El Mercurio*, Edwards group, CESEC, economic research group; minister of foreign affairs (1978–1980)
Agustín Edwards	Naval Brotherhood Club, head of Edwards group, CESEC, research group
Javier Vial	Monday Club, head of BHC group, Chicago economist

Manuel Cruzat	Monday Club, head of Cruzat-Larraín group, Chicago economist, Ph.D. in business administration Harvard; "El Ladrillo" team
Orlando Sáenz	Monday Club, Edwards group, president of SOFOFA, Chicago economist, "El Ladrillo" team; with formal position in the government. He was widely believed to be involved with the right-wing terrorist group Patria y Libertad.
Roberto Kelly	Former navy officer, Monday Club; with formal position in the military government (minister-director of ODEPLAN), Chile's representative to BID (1979–1980)
Emilio Sanfuentes	National Party, Edwards group, CESEC, Chicago economist, "El Ladrillo" team, economic editor of *El Mercurio*; with formal position in the military government (economic adviser in central bank)
Pablo Baraona	Monday Club, Chicago economist, Cruzat-Larraín group, BHC (bank of Vial group), Edwards group, SOFOFA, CESEC; with formal position in the military government
Sergio de Castro	Chicago economist, director of the Faculty of Economics (CU), Edwards group, "El Ladrillo" team, co-founder of think tank CEP (1980), with formal position in the military government
Juan Carlos Méndez	Monday Club, Chicago economist, ODEPLAN; with formal position in the military government (budget director at the Finance Ministry)
Sergio Undurraga	National Party, Chicago economist, "El Ladrillo" team
Ernesto Silva	Monday Club, Chicago economist, "El Ladrillo" team
Juan Villarzú	Originally Christian Democrat–affiliated economist, Monday Club, Chicago economist, budget director after the coup
Jorge Cauas	Originally Christian Democrat–affiliated economist, MBA Columbia University, director of the Faculty of Economics (CU), "El Ladrillo" team, co-founder of CEP; with formal position in the military government
Carlos Massad	Originally Christian Democrat–affiliated economist, Chicago economist, president of the Central Bank
Alvaro Bardón	Originally Christian Democrat–affiliated economist, Monday Club, Chicago economist
Andrés Sanfuentes	Originally Christian Democrat–affiliated economist, Chicago economist, "El Ladrillo" team, with formal position in the military government

Sources: Silva (1991); Mönckeberg (2001); de Castro (2002); Teichman (2001); additional research by the author.

He acted as liaison to Pinochet and Admiral Merino, who was responsible for
economic affairs under the military regime. Kelly became minister of planning
at ODEPLAN immediately after the coup. It has been reported that it was
Kelly who recommended the neoliberal shock program to Pinochet in 1975
(Fontaine 1988; Arriagada 1998). The Monday Club developed an economic reform program, which eventually gained fame as "El ladrillo," or "the brick"
(CEP 1992). It was implemented after 1975 when the radical market fraction
within the Pinochet junta achieved control over economic policy making.

The network activities encompassed neoliberal economists, representatives
of big business, the navy (which was in charge of constitutional matters, economics, finance, and mining after the coup), and the *gremialista* movement.
With regard to intellectual resources, they could rely on academics poised and
able to conceptualize a radical counterprogram of political economy. The academics in question did not restrict themselves to the academic sphere. Quite a
number of key neoliberal economists were ready and willing to help create political circumstances favorable to testing their ideas in the "real world," rather
than to simply wait for an occasion to do so. Intellectual projects, in their turn,
were dependent on crucial external partners in order to succeed. Big business,
always an important political actor in Chilean history, provided critical funding and media channels indispensable to influence public opinion and to
destabilize the existing system. Last but not least, the military provided the
necessary force to overthrow the duly elected Allende government when the
right-wing opposition forces lost all hopes of achieving their ends through
electoral change. Examining the question of intellectual leadership within this
coalition, it is important to further discuss the role of neoliberals vis-à-vis the
gremialistas in particular.

It is often said that the neoliberal economists and the *gremialistas* came
from totally different intellectual backgrounds, the neoliberal economists being "scientific" free market apologists and the *gremialistas* being corporatists
with Hispanic authoritarian values (see, for example, Silva 1991, 393). Distinguishing the intellectual perspectives of neoliberals and *gremialistas* is not easily done, however. Many of the economists who reentered the Catholic University upon their return from Chicago in fact actively participated in the
gremialista movement. Among the economists who represented the *gremialistas* in university bodies or participated actively in the movement were Juan
Carlos Méndez, Miguel Kast, Pablo Baraona, and the MPS-members Arturo
Fontaine Talavera and Cristián Larroulet. The dean of the economic faculty,
Sergio de Castro, was on the list of *gremialista* candidates; the director of the

economic faculty and later finance minister, Jorge Cauas, was also close to the movement (Lavín 1986; Fontaine 1988, 31; Huneeus 1998).

Apart from overlapping membership, the ideology of leading *gremialistas* can neither be simply juxtaposed to neoliberal worldviews nor be understood in a categorical manner. The leading figure of the movement, Jaime Guzmán, defended the capitalist economy in his writings, which was rather atypical for adherents to corporatism. His explicit defense of capitalism was coupled with a strong antistatism rooted in a traditional Catholicism: in the social doctrine formulated by Pope John XXIII, Guzmán perceived private property rights and private enterprise as timeless and permanent values. He strongly invoked the principle of subsidiarity that is held to protect society against the state. Guzmán's corporativist capitalism perspective thus shared the antistatism and references to self-organization with neoliberal perspectives. Furthermore, Guzmán's intellectual development from the 1960s to the 1980s reveals a diminished reference to encyclical and corporatist principles (Vergara 1985; Cristi 2000). This shift may be due to Guzmán's intensified cooperation with the economic change team. He first encountered neoliberal thinking during the Alessandri election campaign in 1970 when he mediated between the neoliberal economists and Alessandri's corporatist-minded supporters. In 1971 he joined the Monday Club and the CESEC think tank (Fontaine 1991, 252).

Radical Market Reform under Military Rule

After the military coup in September 1973, it took about two years before the neoliberal faction ascended to positions of authority, which enabled technocrats to advance their far-reaching reorganization program. Some analysts have proposed that the insurrection against Allende was motivated by a prior decision to establish a new type of institutional order in the country. That is far from true. The military coup was based on a coalition of forces, aligned against the Popular Unity government (Martínez and Díaz 1996). Initially, the insurrection only determined that the future of the country would be decided by some combination of different forces represented in the junta.

With regard to a new neoliberal design of the institutional order, signals were mixed during the first two years of the new regime. The economic policy agenda was still dominated by a gradualist strategy advocating a modern "mixed" economy. Internal conflicts within the junta concerning the appropriate response to the economic situation were particularly visible between the navy and the air force, with the air force taking charge of labor and social affairs. The navy had the closest contact with neoliberal cadres, whereas air force commander Gustavo Leigh, Pinochet's principal rival for control of the junta, was the most prominent supporter of corporatist policies and sometimes was even called a Keynesian (Valenzuela 1993; Kurtz 1999, 409). Leigh was eventually expelled from the junta in 1978. Because of the internal differences, in the early years the regime apparently feared that a radical neoliberal shock program would harm important pro-coup social actors and hence threaten the long-term viability of political restructuring (Valdivia and de Zárate 2003, chapter 3).

Though falling short of fundamental institutional reforms, the initiatives launched immediately after the coup already advanced the neoliberal agenda by reversing major economic reforms of previous governments. The junta returned nationalized enterprises to their former owners (approximately 260 domestic firms) and compensated U.S. multinationals affected by expropriation measures. Price controls were eliminated and interest rates were freed. Beyond these privatization and deregulation efforts, the regime sought to stabilize macroeconomic variables in a more traditional fashion. Certain pre-coup contracts were to come into their own with regard to medium- and long-term planning: The junta commissioned the *gremialista* leader Jaime Guzmán to prepare a new political constitution in its first meeting in the morning of September 13. Guzmán was also responsible for the most important political document of the first phase, the *Declaration of Principles* launched in March 1974. This document went far in proclaiming the need for a sharp break with the past and in announcing a "new institutional order," although the precise character of the new order still sparked internal debate. However, inroads within the junta allowed key neoliberals to advance within the state agencies.

Navy and army officers rather than air force leaders were assigned leading economic policy positions, and both neoliberal and gremialist academics were called into key advisory positions (see Cañas Kirby 1997, 61f.). The more technical aspects of the ministry's tasks were designed and carried out by civilian undersecretaries. Pinochet himself made such staffing decisions, and thus the leading civilian positions involved a dual allegiance: to the minister in charge (typically a military man) and directly to Pinochet. This configuration is important in understanding the long-term trajectory of the reform policies instituted under the military regime: Although there were frequent changes at the minister level, the reform team worked continuously in loyalty to Pinochet.[14]

Undersecretaries were often recruited from ODEPLAN, the most pro-market reform institution within the government until the early 1980s. From early on, the planning ministry was accorded a high degree of autonomy within the administration. It thereby assumed the functions of a government laboratory or think tank in charge of researching and coordinating various reform projects in separate policy areas. The guiding force behind ODEPLAN was the *gremialista* and Chicago economist Miguel Kast. As subdirector (1975) and director (1978), he recruited like-minded economists and other professionals (agrarian engineers, for example) and thereby turned ODEPLAN into an ideologically cohesive think tank with a reliable network of experts who were closely linked to all the important institutions and agencies of the government.[15]

The Neoliberals' Ascent (1975–1978)

The post-coup stabilization strategy to control principal macroeconomic variables failed. Although prices were liberalized, inflation remained on a relatively high level, decreasing somewhat only from 508 percent in 1973 to 376 percent the year after. The continuously high level of inflation undermined aspirations to significantly increase the influx of foreign investment. Prices fell mainly because of declining internal demand, which resulted from the reduction of public expenditures and wages. The country's trade deficit increased because the price for Chile's copper, the principal export commodity, fell considerably in 1974. The rapid rise of oil prices after the formation of OPEC further depressed the country's fledgling manufacturing activities (Olave Castillo 1997; Ffrench-Davis 2003).

When it became evident that the economy was in a recession in 1975, a window of opportunity for a radical neoliberal transformation opened. First, decision-making powers were further concentrated in Pinochet's hands. He had disempowered the air force and continued purging civil and military officials who were opposed to a radical "shock treatment" approach. The analytical and educational work of the neoliberal economists around Pinochet had apparently borne fruit: Pinochet became convinced that only a radical shock treatment could effectively counter the ongoing crisis. Several sources point to a significant role of MPS members, and Milton Friedman in particular, in providing legitimacy for a radical program of neoliberal shock therapy. Friedman met Pinochet during his first visit to Chile at the end of 1974, and the personal meeting was followed up by an exchange of letters. Friedman recommended a radical program centered on severe budget cuts, monetary reform, and free trade.[16] Pinochet pointed out that much of what Friedman had recommended was part of the national recovery plan proposed by his treasury secretary, Jorge Cauas, who was to become "super minister" in charge of the stability program (Friedman and Friedman 1998, 594). Friedman's trip was funded by Javier Vial, the head of the BHC (Banco Hipotecario de Chile) group, which was close to the Chicago economists (Delano and Traslaviña 1989, 39; González-Rossetti, Chuaqui, and Espinosa 2000, 37).

Just as important for this watershed appears to be the curious fact that Pinochet and his closest advisers distrusted the politicians of the right, whom they considered a serious potential threat to their own position of power. Therefore, they disapproved of demands for a restoration of "oligarchic" order and land tenure (Martínez and Díaz 1996). Neoliberal free market ideas thus meshed nicely with junta calculations of preservation of a monopoly of political power. The Chicago-gremialist coalition of economists also had a competitive advantage owing to its previous work on a coherent economic recovery plan ("El ladrillo"). Apart from these internal factors, a number of external conditions argued for shock therapy. As a result of the ongoing economic crisis, Chile had to rely heavily on the external inflow of capital. Multinational lenders like the Paris Club were reluctant to lend to Chile, however, mainly because of the regime's human rights abuses. The appointment of the economic reform team mitigated this consideration: through their university background, they had personal and professional ties to officials from international organizations, which increased the credibility of Chile's government with lenders. Pinochet's leading academics thus served as "intellectual brokers" between the government on the one side and the International Monetary Fund (IMF) staff and international capital on the other (Teichman 2001). Chile had entered into a standby arrangement with the IMF as early as 1974, but few of the Fund's conditions had been met. Disappointed with Chile's performance, the Fund dictated a much harsher set of measures to defeat inflation and restore price stability and external balance in 1975. Pinochet's decision in favor of shock treatment and monetarism helped to facilitate better relations with the IMF (Fourcade-Gourinchas and Babb 2002, 548) and diminished the need for external funding from other sources, which would have required significant improvement in his regime's human rights record.

With Pinochet's decision to adopt a radical shock treatment, the neoliberal economists led by Kelly and Kast at ODEPLAN and by de Castro at the Fac-

ulty of Economics occupied the most significant positions of economic responsibility in 1975 (see Table 9.2). The new finance minister, Jorge Cauas, was
given additional power over every agency related to the Ministry of Finance as
well as over ten other ministries, giving him effective control over economic
decision making. The "Pinochet of the economy," Sergio de Castro, was placed
at the helm of the Ministry of Economics. Miguel Kast was named deputy director of ODEPLAN, and his staff supervised implementation of ministerial
tasks (Fontaine 1988).

The monetarist shock treatment, along with the establishment of a free
trade regime, deregulation of finance sector activities, and a second wave of
privatizations of traditional (and profitable) state-owned companies,[17] were
the primary components of the first neoliberal package (Tironi 1982; Olave
Castillo 1997, 53–105). Profound restructuring was further enabled by access
to foreign credit, which helped to control the adverse effects of the shock
treatment—namely, soaring imports due to overvaluation of the peso, dein-
dustrialization due to import competition, and rapidly rising unemployment.

Beginning in 1976, the economy slowly recovered. At the time, neoliberals
claimed credit for the economic recovery, although they would later blame the
crisis of the 1980s on the military government's reluctance to heed their advice. Implicitly recognizing that monetarist policies alone could not halt inflation, revaluations of the exchange rate were introduced that successfully
forced down inflation under 100 percent. Rising world market prices for copper and a stronger growth of exports improved the country's balance-of-
payments position. The new development strategy still included some incentives for nontraditional exports, but the focus was on export sectors with solid
comparative advantages. Earlier strategies of import substitution designed to
broaden the country's industrial base were rescinded. Chile affirmed its commitment to free trade and financial liberalization by its resignation from the
Andean Pact in January 1977 and the removal of obstacles to foreign financial
investment (Ffrench-Davis 2003). The traditional import substitution regime
was effectively abolished.

Public Choice Theory in Practice: Seven
Modernizations (1979–1981)

In 1978 Pinochet declared that the process of basic *economic* reconstruction
was complete. At the same time, he introduced a new reform agenda, which

Table 9.2 Key actors in Chile's radical market reform II
(Names of MPS members in italics)

Name	The political subnetwork of Chicago and Catholic University–trained academics with technocratic, conglomerate, and *gremialista* links	
	Education and civil society activities	Official government functions
Sergio de Castro	Chicago economist, *gremialista* movement, dean of the Faculty of Economics (CU), Edwards group, "El Ladrillo" team	Adviser to Ministry of Economic Affairs, minister for economic affairs (1975–1976), Chile's representative to BID (1975–1976), minister of finance (1976–1982), founder of CEP (1980)
Andrés Sanfuentes	Chicago economist, "El Ladrillo" team	Adviser to Central Bank, adviser to Budget Bureau
Sergio Undurruga	Chicago economist, "El Ladrillo" team, courses at SOFOFA	
Jorge Cauas*	Director of the Faculty of Economics (CU), close to the *gremialistas*, "El Ladrillo" technical team, founder of CEP; MBA Columbia University	Vice governor of Central Bank (1974), minister of finance (1974–1976)
Sergio de la Cuadra	Chicago economist, Vial & Edwards group, SOFOFA, CESEC	Chair of the advice committee on tariff policy at the Finance Ministry (1975), vice governor Central Bank (1977–1981), governor of Central Bank (1981–1982), minister of finance (1982–1984)
Pablo Baraona	Chicago economist, *gremialista* movement, Cruzat-Larraín group/BHC, Edwards group, SOFOFA, CESEC	Adviser to Ministry of Agriculture, vice governor Central Bank (1974–1975), governor of Central Bank (1975–1976), minister of economic affairs (1976–1978; 1988–1989), Chile's representative to BID (1976–1979), minister of mining (1989)
Sergio Fernández	Close relationship with Pinochet, Kast, Guzmán; founder of the pro-Pinochet party UDI	Minister of labor (1976), minister of the interior (1978–1982, 1987–1988)

Jaime Guzmán	Gremialista leader, founder of the pro-Pinochet party UDI (1991)	Legislative Commission (1974–1981)
Miguel Kast	Gremialista, Chicago economist (1983)	Subdirector (1975) and minister director of ODEPLAN (1978–1980), minister of labor (1980–1982), governor of Central Bank (1982)
Rolf Lüders	Chicago economist, BHC (bank of Vial group), dean of the economic faculty CU (1968–1971)	Director of the financial market development program OAS (1971–1974), member of the Legislative Commission (1974–1981), bi-minister of finance and the economy (1982–1983), Chile's representative to BID (1982–1983)
José Piñera*	Cruzat-Larraín group, CU economist, Harvard (postgraduate)	Minister of labor (1979–1980), minister of mining (1981–1982)
Hernán Büchi*	MA Columbia University, close to Chicago team since 1975	Subsecretary of economic affairs (1979–1981), deputy minister of health (1981–1983), minister director ODEPLAN (1983–1984), banking supervisor (1984–1985), finance minister (1985–1989), candidate for the presidency in 1989
Carlos Cáceres*	MBA Cornell University, ITP Harvard University	Governor of Central Bank (1982–1983), Chile's representative to BID (1983–1984), minister of finance (1983–1984), minister of the interior (1988–1990)
Cristián Larroulet	Chicago economist, gremialista movement, think tank CEP	Key figure in the Legislative Commission, head of planning ministry ODEPLAN (1981–1982), head of the cabinet at Ministry of Finance under Büchi (1985–1989)

* Did not study in Chicago but actively participated in the economic team. Büchi's MPS membership is uncertain.
Sources: Silva (1991); Mönckeberg (2001) Teichman (2001); additional research by the author.

aimed at extending a market approach to many spheres of society. The new program became known as the seven modernizations and included a new constitution with institutional reforms in labor, education, health, regional decentralization, agriculture, and justice policies. The "whole social structure of the country [was] opened up as a potential field for experimentation, based upon the pure truth of rational choice and the calculus of marginal utility" (Martínez and Díaz 1996, 92). Pinochet's announcement of the seven modernizations clearly bore Guzmán's trademark and provides further evidence of the cooperation of neoliberal economists and gremialists.[18]

Whereas the Chicago School's monetary, regulation, and competition theories served as talismans with regard to Chile's monetary and fiscal policies, the Virginia School's public choice theory pioneered by MPS members Buchanan and Tullock (Amadae 2003; Pitt, Salehi, and Eckel 2004) is important in better comprehending Chile's reform agenda for labor relations and the privatization of the country's social security and education systems (Stepan 1985). Partly as a result of the "Chicago" focus characterizing Chile's road to neoliberalism, the Virginia School's influence has been underemphasized and conflated with that of the Chicago School.[19] Public choice theory focuses on an economic theory of government and thus directly addresses the domain of political science. The Virginia School's Gordon Tullock (1972) was the first to proudly describe the new theoretical and methodological efforts as "economic imperialism."

Buchanan and Tullock (1962) identified the state as a central problem of neoclassical economic theory. Whereas traditional neoclassical analysis had little to say about the state, neoclassical welfare economics assumed the existence of a benevolent and efficient state capable of correcting market failures. Buchanan and Tullock then expanded on the Chicago School interest group and state agency models confined to regulatory politics (e.g., regulatory capture theories developed by MPS members Stigler and Posner) by developing a universal economic theory of politics. All policies, including those carried out in the name of the public, are explained by economic interests represented by conspiring coalitions of voters and by the capacity of politicians to shape such coalitions based on their interest in maintaining their positions of power. Inefficient consequences in the political marketplace were solely blamed on the fallacies of political decision making: "We can summarize public choice as a theory of governmental failure" (Buchanan 1979, 178).

Buchanan (1982) delivered a highly abstract paper titled "Limited or Unlimited Democracy" to the Mont Pèlerin Society meeting in Viña del Mar in Chile in 1981, which some construed as a critique of the host country's recent history. Buchanan stated that if limited democracy was a polity predisposed to disable a political market that would otherwise promote the most efficient allocation of scarce resources, the only meaningful task of the government would be to deprive the polity of its ability to do so. Public choice theory thus sought to limit democracy and to depoliticize the state in order to enable unconstrained market forces to guide human interaction. Since the Pinochet regime was committed to using its governmental powers in precisely this manner, Buchanan's paper provided theoretical support for the regime, even if it did not openly endorse authoritarian rule. Other MPS members, such as the Chilean government official Carlos Cáceres (1982), made a more straightforward case for authoritarian rule at the Viña del Mar meeting.

Both Buchanan and Tullock were frequent guests in Chile (Stepan 1985, 341). In the course of the seven modernizations transformation process, the Center for Public Studies (Centro de Estudios Públicos / CEP) and the Foundation of the BHC conglomerate sponsored Buchanan and Tullock (as well as Hayek and Friedman) to hold seminars. Arguably the most important Chilean intellectual inspired by the Virginia School was José Piñera,[20] the minister in charge of labor reform and privatization of the social security system. He claimed that the reforms created "the basis of a new political, economic, and social reality" (*Qué Pasa,* December 27, 1980). Piñera stressed the importance of propaganda work for the military, the staff of advisory bodies, and public servants in general, who needed to be cajoled to implement the reforms. He envisioned the transformation of the entire government into a huge university, featuring continuous conferences, educational meetings, and lectures for the military academies, all generating a high volume of papers (Piñera 1990, 1992; see also González-Rossetti et al. 2000). The neoliberal utopia of a society self-regulated by the market seemed to be just within reach, fostered of course by a military regime with absolute political power.

The labor reform agenda as laid out in the 1979 Plan Laboral exemplified the ways in which public choice theory was applied in Chile. Existing trade unions were made illegal, and workers were denied the right of collectively bargaining over wages and working conditions. The new law allowed only weak trade unions and forced them to compete with each other rather than to unite in order to improve the competitive position of labor vis-à-vis owners and management. Collective bargaining rights were hampered in several ways. Basic wage increases offsetting inflation were mandated by law, and individuals were granted the right to bargain for wages and conditions regardless of "collective" agreements, although employees in both the public and service sectors were exempted from this rule. The declared goal of the Plan Laboral was to "create rewards and structures that depoliticize automatically by the systematic insistence on market and individual-choice principles" (Stepan 1985, 323 quoting Chilean representatives). As Foxley (1986, 105) concludes, "free markets, decentralization, and political immobilization and control were all achieved at once."

Much has been written about Chile's social security reforms, which were also designed to replace collective and state-controlled instruments by "individualized" market contracting. The whole pension system was turned over to private enterprises, although members of the armed forces continued to receive comprehensive state guarantees. Legally mandated security for the investment of individuals provided for a minimal pension only. The government thereby opened up a vast new market. Capital collected on the basis of individual insurance contracts with workers and employees eventually amounted to approximately 20 percent of Chile's gross domestic product (GDP) after ten years. While the private schemes were presented to the public as a liberating device for the individual, two of the Chilean conglomerates (BHC and Cruzat-Larrain) quickly gobbled up no less than two-thirds of the market (O'Brian and Roddick 1983; Mönckeberg 2001, 209–230).

Space limitations prohibit detailed attention here to the wide range of reform efforts linked to the seven modernizations program. Intellectual doctrines formulated in Chicago were not marginalized during this second phase of neoliberal mobilization of knowledge. With reference to Harberger's ground rent theory, land use and housing in Santiago were relieved of all regulation and subjected to the market mechanism, for example (Oppenheim 1999, 152ff.; Sabatini 2000). As a consequence, the Chilean welfare state was weakened, but the authoritarian state was not. The new social security market was controlled by the conglomerates with the closest connections to Pinochet. The regime was thus able to fortify its power base. However, the poor performance of the conglomerates during the 1980s gave even the newly empowered customers the feeling that neither neoliberalism nor the junta could keep the original promises that had been made.

"Authoritarian Freedom": A Hayekian Constitution for Chile

The discussions at the 1981 MPS meeting in Pinochet's Chile kept returning to the concept of freedom. Nevertheless, a critique of the lack of political freedom and democracy in Chile was notably absent from the contributions of MPS members Friedman, Tullock, Watrin, Frickhöffer, Hartwell, Irvine, and Shenfield, all of whom complimented Buchanan and Cáceres on the list of speakers (see CEP 1982). Frickhöffer (1982) affirmatively likened Pinochet's efforts to the post–World War II German efforts to secure a social market economy under Ludwig Erhard. Milton Friedman recommended that other developing countries follow the Chilean example of economic reorganization without mentioning the touchy subject of authoritarian rule.

Hayek did not participate in the meeting, but *Estudios Públicos* published a paper he had originally given at the MPS regional conference held in Tokyo in 1966 on the topic of "Principles of a Liberal Social Order" (Hayek 1982). This paper is important to consider in relation to the arguably most consequential effort of the military regime: to institutionalize neoliberalism by designing and implementing a new constitution. In none of his public statements did Hayek intimate that he was overly troubled by the lack of democracy in Chile. In a letter to the editors of *Frankfurter Allgemeine Zeitung,* he suggested that each Pole would be happy if he/she were fortunate enough to escape to Chile (Hennecke 2000, 349). On another occasion, in 1981, when a journalist from Venezuela's *Daily Journal* asked him about totalitarian governments in Latin America, Hayek answered: "Don't confuse totalitarianism with authoritarianism. I don't know of any totalitarian governments in Latin America. The only one was Chile under (former Marxist president Salvador) Allende. Chile is now a great success. The world shall come to regard the recovery of Chile as one of the great economic miracles of our time" (quoted in Ebenstein 2001, 300). Buchanan joined Friedman in avoiding specification of the concrete "limitations" of democracy, while Càceres openly justified the Chilean military rule as a defensive measure.

One year before MPS leaders decided to choose Chile (of all places) for their regional gathering, the military regime enacted a new constitution in September 1980, which was slated to become effective in March 1981. The constitution was drafted by *gremialista* leader Jaime Guzmán, who from the beginning served as the architect of the legal and constitutional framework of the military government. The constitution was not only named after Hayek's book *The Constitution of Liberty,* but also incorporated significant elements of Hayek's thinking. Above all else, the constitution placed a strong emphasis on a neoliberal understanding of freedom. Guzmán's version of freedom is intrinsically connected to private property, free enterprise, and individual rights.

Individual freedom in his interpretation can only evolve in a radical market order. The constitution was dedicated to guarantee such an order without constraining any economic activities. In order to protect free market conditions and individual freedom against "totalitarian attacks" or "democratic intervention," the constitution stipulated the necessity of a strong central state authority to guarantee the established rule of law, and thus above all is hampered in the application of discretionary governmental power. Exempted were measures to uphold the status quo inasmuch as Guzmán aggressively supported the continuing state of emergency, which legalized the use of whatever discretionary powers were deemed necessary to quell oppositional forces. Human rights typically guaranteed by constitutions were not considered absolute in the Chilean version and were to be severely restricted "when a society undergoes turmoil or heavy challenges."[21]

Guzmán clearly drew on Hayek in distinguishing between authoritarianism and totalitarianism in order to justify a state's use of repressive measures when they are required, and deployed tools to shield a free market order against perceived totalitarian (= socialist) tendencies. During his second visit in Chile, Hayek had clarified his understanding of (neo)liberalism in this regard in an interview for *El Mercurio:* "A dictatorship can restrict itself and a dictatorship which deliberatively is restricting itself can be more liberal in its policies than a democratic assembly which has no limits"[22] (Hayek 1981). Not surprisingly, Hayek went to some lengths to bestow legitimacy on the new Chilean constitution, since he had been personally consulted by the Chilean government in the process leading up to the final draft. During his first visit to Chile in 1978, Pinochet had invited him to a personal meeting. Hayek's influence extended beyond the merely personal, however. One member of the commission in charge of drafting the constitution, Carlos Cáceres, was a close follower of Hayek and eventually joined the MPS in 1980 (Walpen and Plehwe 2001).

Vergara (1985, 106–133) has carefully reconstructed the internal discussions and negotiations that led to the final document. Interestingly, nationalists, neoliberals, and the *gremialistas* agreed on certain key elements—notably, the "necessity" to redefine and limit democracy to a "restricted" or "protected" sphere. While many elements of Hayekian neoliberalism provided the backdrop for an understanding of the Chilean constitution, they were recombined with traditional patriarchal and authoritarian concepts of the state.[23] The adoption of neoliberal principles in flexible and pragmatic ways within the constitution process can be further illustrated by turning to the next stage of developments. When the economy experienced a severe crisis in 1982, Pinochet was forced to recalibrate the economic policy orientation and to modify his regime's internal power structure.

Crisis and Restructuring of the Neoliberal Project (1982–1989)

Chile's economic crisis in 1982 was caused by a combination of external and internal factors. Among the external factors, the steep fall of the price for copper due to the global crisis was devastating, given the preponderance of copper in Chile's total exports. The uncontrolled financial liberalization, in combination with heavy borrowing of the Chilean conglomerates, were large factors in the country's economic recession. Credit had been incurred overwhelmingly for consumption purposes and for the takeover of enterprises, instead of investment in productive capacity. Rapidly declining growth, a growing balance-of-payments deficit, rocketing interest rates, and the insolvency of hundreds of firms in the manufacturing sector ensued. Sixteen private financial institutions (out of fifty) went bankrupt. Some of the most highly indebted conglomerates that were at the center of the neoliberal coalition disappeared from the Chilean economic map (Rozas and Marín 1988, 1989).

The sharp rise in the price of the dollar forced the government to intervene in the private administration of pension funds and the banking system. The two largest banks, BHC of Vial and Banco de Santiago of Cruzat-Larraín, came under state control. At the beginning of 1983, three financial institutions were liquidated, another five were taken over by the state, and two banks were subjected to a special regime of state oversight. The Central Bank then assumed responsibility for their external debt. Huge amounts of private debt were thus transferred to the state. The state—otherwise considered the biggest threat to humankind in neoliberal and conservative critiques of the welfare state—bailed out the private capitalist class at home and abroad.[24] In the face of looming economic collapse, the regime was forced to redirect economic policy. Nonetheless, the basic features of the neoliberal development model either remained in place or were resurrected after the crisis. What explains the resilience of the neoliberal economic framework and the maintenance of the neoliberal economic cadre?

The discussion concerning the appropriate reaction to the country's economic crisis exposed a rift within Pinochet's economic team. Minister of Finance Sergio de Castro stubbornly supported the regime of fixed exchange rates and "automatic adjustment," which had been introduced in 1979 during his tenure, and opposed the devaluation of the peso. Confronted with the growing fears of business leaders suffering from high interest rates and alarmed by the growing number of bankruptcies, he nevertheless stood by his understanding of neoliberalism, declaring that only the strongest and most competitive should survive. De Castro was left high and dry by the majority of his "El ladrillo" comrades who opted for devaluation—a decision that Pinochet himself soon seconded (Fontaine 1988, 154ff.).

De Castro was forced to resign from office at the beginning of 1982, as were also the minister of the interior, Sergio Fernández, and the mining minister, José Piñera. They were all replaced by military officers, corporate officers, and neoliberals who had proven more willing and flexible with regard to neoliberal principles in the short run. The regime devalued the currency and introduced various measures to protect domestic business. The new superminister of finance and economics was another MPS member, the Chicago-trained economist Rolf Lüders, who had been vice president of the BHC group before being called to office. Lüders decided to direct government support to indebted enterprises and to save the private banking system by way of state intervention, or, in his own words, "to rescue the financial system but not their owners" (Lüders 1993, 163). He subsequently appointed MPS member Cáceres president of the Central Bank and initiated negotiations with the IMF.

In order to destroy the opposition movement and to quell the mounting social protest, the regime proclaimed another state of siege, invoking traumatic memories of 1973. Fear of a return to the "chaos" of the Popular Unity era, with the military standing at the ready, stymied the protesters and the middle classes (Silva 1996, 2001). Another crucial task for the regime was to secure the confidence of the private sector through recruitment of wider entrepreneurial interests. Apart from the conglomerates, small and medium-sized enterprises (gremios) were co-opted. While the export-oriented development model was not in principle open to negotiation, it was modified to more strongly align international and domestic industrial and financial interests on the one hand and export-oriented agricultural interests on the other in support of the government. Minimum prices for key crops like wheat were established, and the government subsidized farm credits and renegotiated debt on highly favorable terms to promote the production of export crops. A temporary increase in import tariffs on agricultural produce and redirected export subsidies, combined with a drastic reduction in the cost of labor, was instituted to provide a favorable climate for a competitive agrobusiness industry. By way of developing a strategy of separate negotiations and "segmented responses" to "specific demands," the regime managed to split the business *gremios* (Campero 1993).

Arguably the most crucial factor in quickly resuming the neoliberal course was the materialization of foreign private capital and multilateral loans. Chile started negotiations with the International Monetary Fund in 1982 and international creditors in 1983. The country's recent expansionist policies threatened to be undermined by financial restrictions imposed by the IMF, which exercised strong pressure on the regime to return to a stricter fiscal policy. In addition, the World Bank and the Bank for International Development demanded immediate "normalization" of ownership of affected banks and firms, and the privatization of public enterprises (Silva 1991, 397). Accordingly, no agreement was achieved in the first round of negotiations, but informal discussions continued. These negotiations reinforced the position of the radical policy network of neoliberal economists inside and outside the state, and promoted the formation of a cohesive and effective international policy network involving World Bank and IMF officials (Teichman 2001, 78f.).

The key figure in the negotiations that would return the country from "crisis management" to a pronounced neoliberal policy was Hernán Büchi, who served as superintendent of the banking sector. He had been close to the Chicago team since 1975 and held important posts in the government (see Table 9.2). In 1985 he was appointed finance minister by Pinochet, and thus the second generation of economists was promoted. Apart from Büchi, some members of the old policy network were integrated into negotiations, especially the former finance minister de Castro. IMF officials briefed de Castro, who in turn kept Pinochet informed at regular meetings. Apparently, not all members of the old economic cadre believed in the new orientation. An interviewee told me that some continued to strictly oppose the state management of private debt, in the sense that the Central Bank bought the overdue debt of private banks and conglomerates, and was consequently forced to resolve the burgeoning public-sector deficit. This recollection supports the findings of Montecinos (1998, 84, 89). She quotes the "Chicago boys," who denied that they had acted in favor of the private-sector conglomerates, and insisted on the "patriotic" character of their mission.

According to the interviewee, it was Chile that helped pave the way for the technocratic management of the debt crisis in favor of the interests of international lenders, which subsequently put pressure on the other highly indebted countries in Latin America and Eastern Europe to pursue a similar path. The "plan chileno" followed the principle of "negotiations instead of confrontation" and introduced new programs such as the structural adjustment loans and debt swaps that were later employed in Mexico, Venezuela, Argentina, and Brazil. In affirmation, Hernán Somerville, chief foreign debt negotiator from 1983 to 1988 and a high banking official after the Pinochet regime, confirms that the "plan chileno" had been the blueprint for the Brady Plan (Somerville 1992, 114).

Finance Minister Hernán Büchi (1985–1989) continued to implement neoliberal reforms in a relatively short horizon and thereby succeeded in restoring the confidence of the international financial agencies (Silva 1991, 398). On the basis of Büchi's economic program, Chile negotiated three structural adjustment loans in 1985, 1986, and 1987. Uncontested measures of the adjustment program consisted of tariff reductions and privatizations. The reluctance of some members of the World Bank's executive board to lend to Chile because of continuing human rights abuses strengthened the bank's and the IMF's ability to ensure orthodoxy: senior officials were willing to risk the disgrace and trouble of being involved in Chilean affairs only if the agreement was "flawless" on economic policy grounds (Teichman 2001, 53, 80). In sum, the role of the multinationals was crucial: they were intimately involved in the development of a new economic program that returned Chile to the path of market reform, and helped to reinstall its strongest supporters in the state such as Pablo Baraona (minister of the economy 1987, mining minister 1988) and Fernández, who returned as interior minister.

Büchi not only handled the renegotiation and payment of the external debt, but also designed a coherent response to the crisis in the national financial system and restored the credibility and legitimacy of the overall economic model (Martínez and Díaz 1996, 97). The regime established interest rate controls and adopted a new banking law in 1986, which imposed depositary requirements and strict bank supervision. The principal export model was consolidated after the crisis, though nontraditional exports (mainly agricultural and related products such as wine and fruit, forest products such as pulp, and food products such as fish meal) were now promoted with substantial state incentives, such as special credit lines, and export promotion agencies. The new growth strategy consisted of a deflationary adjustment and restriction on internal demand in order to create favorable terms for export.

When economic indicators finally showed signs of recovery in 1985, a new round of privatizations were imposed. The privatization process included firms that were nationalized during the crisis and some of the strategic sectors that had been still excluded in the 1970s. State enterprises in the steel, sugar, and chemical industries, in aviation, energy, and telecommunications, as well as some copper mines, were turned over to the private sector. Everything was sold except for the remaining state copper firm and the state petroleum company. Most of the enterprises had been highly efficient and had so far generated surpluses for the state. Although small investors and employees were invited to purchase shares of the newly privatized enterprises—the regime promoted a propaganda discourse of "popular capitalism"—the process of concentration and centralization of capital resumed. The participation of foreign capital was mostly organized through joint ventures. Debt-for-equity swaps were so popular that, by 1988, nearly $2 billion of hard currency had entered the economy, leading to an intricate intertwining of foreign investors and domestic capitalists through the joint purchase of privatized firms. Members of the economic team participated in the newly formed directorates, thus reflecting the revival of many old coalitions.[25]

Altogether the measures taken to overcome the crisis were conceived as state interventionism designed to rescue the neoliberal model. Pinochet himself (quoted in Martínez and Díaz 1996, 98) considered the period "a case of sidestepping to recover strength." The measures taken consolidated and deepened the social relations in support of the previously established and promoted export-oriented mode of production.

Continuity of the Neoliberal Project after the Transition to Democracy

In October 1988 Pinochet lost the plebiscite, which had been required by the constitution.[26] A union of the center-left parties—the *Concertación*—won the first elections that took place a year later. The regime's candidate, Hernán Büchi, was defeated by Patricio Aylwin, a Christian Democrat. The members of the neoliberal team were now barred from high positions in government. Despite the new coalition government and the postdictatorship opportunities, practically all observers concur that the neoliberal model of economic policy by and large remained in place. Why was this the case?

A crucial factor ensuring continuity had been the "pacted transition" between the party leaders of the Concertación and the representatives of the regime. Not only was the legal framework kept in place—the transition took

Table 9.3 Fields of activity of neoliberals after transition to democracy (Names of MPS members in italics)

Name	Entrepreneurial activities	Civil society activities
Pablo Baraona	Director of subsidiaries of SQM (chemical industry)	Rector of the private university, Universidad Finis Terrae; council member of CEP
Alvaro Bardón		Director of the Institute of Public Policies (Instituto de Políticas Públicas) of Finis Terrae University, dean of the Universidad Finis Terrae
*Hernán Büchi**	President and vice president of various companies (insurance, chemical and metal-processing industry, food production; publishing house Copesa); member of the directorate of one of Chile's largest business conglomerates (Quiñenco, Luksic group)	Columnist, co-founder of Instituto Libertad y Desarrollo, current president of its International Economy Center; president of the Universidad del Desarrollo; founder and director of the Fundación Internacional para la Libertad (FIL); university professor; candidate for the presidency in 1989
Carlos Cáceres	Entrepreneur, director and president of various companies and joint-stock companies (tobacco, wholesale, food production, electricity); director of Fundación Chile (created in 1976 by the government and U.S. ITT Corporation to develop innovations and human capital)	Co-founder of the Instituto Libertad y Desarrollo in 1990, current president of the board and president of its entrepreneurial council; rector and vice president of the Universidad Adolfo Ibáñez (1990–2001); leading figure in Agustín Edwards Foundation, Paz Ciudadana (Citizens' Peace); vice president of Mont Pèlerin Society; member of Legionarios de Cristo; consultative board of Fundación Friedrich A. Hayek (Buenos Aires); university professor
Jorge Cauas	Director of BCI (bank) and Cruz Blanco Seguros (insurance company of Manuel Cruzat group)	Director of the Institute of Engineering (University of Chile); council member of CEP and its Commission on State Reform

Sergio de Castro	Director of SQM (chemical industry) in 1988, real estate activities, stockholder of various joint-stock companies; partner of Saieh's media empire Copesa	Founder and council member of CEP; council member of Universidad Finis Terrae
Cristián Larroulet		Columnist; co-founder and executive director of the Instituto Libertad y Desarrollo; professor and dean of the economic faculty of the Universidad del Desarrollo, director of the Universidad del Desarrollo, head of the economic team of UDI's frontman Lavín
Rolf Lüders		Professor of economics (Catholic University) and editor of the journal *Cuadernos de Economía*; consultant to the World Bank, United Nations, and Agency for International Development of the United States, among other institutions
José Piñera	Entrepreneur; international adviser for pension reform	Founder and president of the International Center for Pension Reform (Santiago); founder and president of the think tank Proyecto Chile 2010; chairman of the Cato Institute and co-chairman of its Project on Social Security
Andrés Sanfuentes	President of the national bank	Co-founder of the Instituto Libertad y Desarrollo

Sources: Mönckeberg (2001); additional research by the author. Büchi's MPS membership is uncertain.

place within the confines of the 1980 constitution—but also the structure of the state in terms of socioeconomic organization remained intact: "What *continuismo* provided for the democratic administrations was stability. It led to business support for democracy, it brought renovated socialists and Christian Democrats together around an economic strategy, and it provided a set of macroeconomic indicators that were perceived as desirable for further liberalisation" (Barton 2002, 363). Moreover Chile's social structure had been substantially transformed in ways that seem to confirm the argument of neoliberals that only a profound change in the culture and value system (rather than more ephemeral institutions) would be able to protect the neoliberal trajectory. The final triumph of the neoliberal thought collective was that former opponents eventually came to embrace it, thereby endowing it with new legitimacy. Although the foundations of the neoliberal model survived the return to parliamentarian democracy, Chile's neoliberals did not leave the future to chance.

The members of the neoliberal team had to vacate most of their posts at the center of power,[27] but they carried on their economic careers, filling important positions in corporations and civil society (see Table 9.3). They developed major activities in the academic world, the media, and international advisory services. Especially important was the establishment of private universities and think tanks. Three weeks after the installation of the first democratic government and his electoral defeat, Hernán Büchi, together with his MPS colleagues Cristián Larroulet and Carlos Cáceres, founded the Instituto Libertad y Desarrollo (ILD). The new partisan think tank soon became the "flagship in the battle of ideas." It covered a wide spectrum of activities ranging from opinion polls, academic publications, and commentaries in the media to conferences and seminars, all designed to influence public opinion in lasting ways. Although the directorate was split between the two right-wing parties (the National Party and the Independent Democratic Union [UDI]), the ILD was responsible for the government program of the serial UDI presidential candidate Joaquín Lavín. Chile's most internationally oriented right-wing think tank today participates in the International Foundation for Liberty (headed by Mario Vargas Llosa) and cultivates relations all over the world, though special attention is paid to Latin America, Eastern Europe, and the Far East. In 2000, the ILD hosted the biannual reunion of the Mont Pélerin Society (Libertad y Desarrollo 2005).

Apart from the ILD, the already mentioned Centro de Estudios Públicos (CEP) plays an important role in maintaining the neoliberal spirit. Its leading figures are Jorge Cauas, Pablo Baraona, and MPS members Sergio de Castro and Arturo Fontaine. The CEP enjoys strong backing from the Chilean conglomerates; it functions both as a neoliberal bridgehead in politics and as a meeting place for entrepreneurs and government officials. Among its fields of activities are sponsorship of debates on long-term neoliberal ideas. CEP publishes the *Revista de Estudios Públicos* and provides training for foreign (primarily Latin American and Eastern European) economists. Through its well-organized and well-financed activities, the central figures of the original neoliberal team continue to maintain a high profile in Chile.

Conclusion: The More Things Change, the More They Stay the Same

Chilean history provides us with a rich case study of the multifaceted mobilization and transformation of knowledge, and the effective political strategies of organized neoliberals. What conclusions might be drawn from our account? First, contrary to much of the secondary literature, neoliberalism in action has been more than a rote application of Chicago economic orthodoxy. The Chilean economic transformation was also guided—at different moments—by Virginia School and Austrian approaches. Furthermore, neoliberal scholars have shown considerable flexibility with regard to the "local" adaptation of theoretical approaches as well as political strategy.

The Chilean path to neoliberalism reveals different stages of development consisting of different tasks, theoretical positions, and modes of political rationality. To simplify, the first stage, *proto-neoliberalism,* covers the period from the mid-1950s to the end of the 1960s. The organized neoliberals focused primarily on projects outside the state. Think tanks, university institutes, and the media served as key institutions to build up cadres and a coherent counter to the dominant *Zeitgeist* in order to gain influence in the public sphere. The primary task was conceived as an ideological critique of the socialist/import substitution tendencies. The second stage, *rollback,* was put into effect between 1973 and 1975. The military regime destroyed the fundamentals of the import substitution model and its social relations through repression, the return of the expropriated enterprises, and the abolition of price supports. The next phase, *rollout,* started in 1975. The vanguard theorists widely entered in state positions, becoming organized state cadres, and implemented the monetary, regulation, and competition theories of the Chicago School. The ultraorthodox measures realized in the period 1975–1978 were aimed at the core of the economy and included the introduction of a free trade regime and the deregulation of the domestic and financial markets accompanied by further privatizations. After the economic reconstruction, the *extension* and, thus, *deepening* of neoliberalism as a program were effected between 1978 and 1981. The key reference was to the Virginia School public choice theory, wherein the market approach was extended to other spheres of society (viz., seven modernizations). The crisis of 1982–1983 provided the occasion for a *substantiation* phase of the neoliberal project under new conditions, requiring a greater amount of concerted state intervention to safeguard neoliberalism. The adjustment to external power relations and the socialization of debt demanded a reshuffling of the economic team, but ensured the continuity of the neoliberal model. The period 1983–1989 can be characterized as the *revival* phase of neoliberalism. Under Büchi, a state-led structural adjustment of the export-oriented economy was engineered. The path from an administration of the crisis to pronounced neoliberal policies mirrored the explicit demands of the international finance organizations.

Although the regime's proxy candidate for the presidency, Hernán Büchi, lost in the reinstated democratic elections, the institutional framework secured cultural hegemony and the *persistence* of the neoliberal model. Neoliberalism in Chile (and elsewhere) cannot be equated with authoritarianism and military dictatorship, ignoring continuities during and after the transition to democracy. It is precisely the mutability of neoliberal knowledge and its flexible relationship with power that sustained essential components of the neoliberal model and the neoliberal path in Chile.

Whereas from a purely Chilean point of view, the modification of the internal power structure and the abandonment of some orthodox elements of the neoliberal program in the course of the 1982–1983 crisis might be interpreted as ending a "radical neoliberalism" and opening up a "pragmatic phase" (Silva 1991, 2001), from a global standpoint it was exactly the fine-tuned adjustment to external and internal requirements that ensured the continuity of the neoliberal project. The partly reconstituted economic team made a pact with the global centers of power, the financial institutions, thus securing the neoliberal path. Chile not only figured as a role model in the "solution" of the international debt crisis, but also embarked on a coherent export-oriented development strategy. Under Büchi's aegis, a new regime of state-led export-oriented industrialization was set in motion, without altering the social relations around the development strategy (the seven modernizations) that had been previously implemented. Büchi and his alliance appeared as managers of a new industrial policy that included a commitment to increase exports and to preserve the domestic base at the same time. The state provided the old and new incentives in order to achieve competitiveness in the new nontraditional export sectors and to increase internal savings and investment. Simultaneously, it created favorable conditions on a macroeconomic level through devaluation, temporary tariff protection, regulation of the financial system, and a strict policy of wage controls.

Sergio de Castro was made the scapegoat and his public reputation suffered, but that was not allowed to interfere with the commitment to the overall economic model and to the dominance of the community of neoliberal economists. He took part in the selection of his successors and shortly thereafter again played an important role in debt negotiations and policy formulation. His staying power is further revealed by the fact that Sergio de Castro, the intellectual leader of the 1970s, and Rolf Lüders, the manager of the crisis, shared a common ideological home: they both joined the Mont Pélerin Society in 1982.[28] When ousted from their state positions, the neoliberal protagonists continued their work from within civil society: provided with channels of communication, think tanks, and public reputation, they continue to influence the transformation of contemporary Chile.

Notes

1. This notion was promoted in the PBS television series *The Commanding Heights,* broadcast January 10, 2000. There Milton Friedman is quoted as saying, "the really important thing about the Chilean business is that free markets did work their way in bringing about a free society."

2. The editors of *Frankfurter Allgemeine Zeitung,* Germany's neoliberal flagship among the nationwide print media, refused to print an article by Friedrich August von Hayek titled "True Reports on Chile" (Wahrheitsgetreue Berichte über Chile), for example. The daily paper did not even offer space to Hayek in its letters to the editors' section. Hayek eventually published his efforts in defense of economic and social policies under Pinochet in a small booklet published by Hanns-Seidel-Stiftung affiliated with Bavaria's Christian Social Union Party (see Walpen and Plehwe 2001, 67–69 for details).

3. See Silva (1991); Centeno and Silva (1996); Montecinos (1998); Fourcade-Gourinchas and Babb (2002) for a general discussion of the political dimensions of "technocratic power"; in the U.S. context see Fischer (1996).

4. Hence, one cannot take at face value some of the writings of Milton Friedman, for instance, on the boundaries between "positive" and "normative" economics. For more on this issue, see Van Horn and Mirowski, Chapter 4 in this volume.

5. Consult Biglaiser (2002) with regard to Packenham (1973); see Plehwe, Chapter 7 in this volume.

6. For the relationship of Schultz to the neoliberal ascendancy at Chicago, see Van Horn and Mirowski, Chapter 4 in this volume.

7. See Biglaiser (2002, 274); Harberger (1999); Silva (1991, 390); Valdés (1995, Chapter 5).

8. Among the first grant holders who went to Chicago were later economics minister (1975–1976) and finance minister (1976–1982) Sergio de Castro, who joined the MPS in 1982, and Ernesto Fontaine and Carlos Massad from the University of Chile. Among the first to achieve the Ph.D. were Rolf Lüders (member of the Legislative Commission 1974–1981, bi-minister of finance and the economy 1982–1983 and MPS member since 1982), Sergio de Castro, Ernesto Fontaine, and media mogul Alvaro Saieh (Delano and Traslaviña 1989, 13–16). They were trained by MPS members Becker, Friedman, Stigler, and Harberger (though Harberger joined MPS later in 1994).

9. See, for example, Frank (1967); Caputo and Pizzaro (1970); Amin (1973).

10. Bardón was a Chicago economist who particpated in the conspiratorial pro-coup coalition. Cauas received his MBA at Columbia University, but he was a personal friend of Harberger. At the time of his appointment, Cauas was working for the World Bank; he later gave up his political affiliation with the Christian Democrats and was eventually appointed finance minister after the military coup in 1974. Arnold Harberger served as an adviser for both Massad and Cauas (see Harberger 1999).

11. ODEPLAN was created in 1967 during the presidency of the Christian Democrat Eduardo Frei. The office was in charge of coordinating projects across ministries. Among the young economists working at ODEPLAN were Álvaro Donoso, Ernesto Silva, Ernesto Fontaine, Sergio de la Cuadra, and Juan Carlos Méndez (Fontaine 1988, 46; see Tables 1 and 2). See Vergara (1984); Fontaine (1988); Silva (1991, 1996); Huneeus (1998).

12. Following Valdés (1995, 227), CESEC was established in 1963; other sources date it as 1968 (see Silva 1991; Soto 2003).

13. The prominent entrepreneur Jorge Alesssandri had been president from 1958 to 1964. His politics of "technocratic liberalism" (inflationary measures, liberalization of trade, devaluation) was frustrated by the traditional right and the "rentier protectionism" of the entrepreneurial class. Under the military government, he became a member of the state council (Moulian 2006).

14. See Delano and Traslaviña (1989, 27ff.); González-Rossetti, Chuaqui, and Espinosa (2000).

15. ODEPLAN created numerous cooperation treaties with the Catholic University (thus shifting considerable funds to the Economics Department) and granted scholarships to study abroad. These activities played a decisive part in the building and maintenance of a skilled reform team throughout the military government, and in assuring the allegiance of its members to the regime.

16. For the long run, Friedman recommended a social market economy along the lines his fellow MPS members had developed for Germany immediately after the war (see Ptak, Chapter 3 in this volume).

17. The privatization process (of 507 public firms in 1973, 70 remained in 1976) certainly strengthened the private sector and led to a rapid increase in concentration of private property in the Chilean economy: a handful of conglomerates acquired the offered enterprises at relatively low prices, including financial institutions. However, the transfer of state property to the private sector remained incomplete. At the beginning of the 1980s, the state still owned six of the country's top ten enterprises, all of them in strategic sectors (copper, electricity, oil, and transport; see Rozas and Marín 1988, 1989).

18. See Guzmán's articles in his journal *Revista Realidad;* Valenzuela (1993); Cañas Kirby (1997, 82f.).

19. See Vergara (1985); Valenzuela (1993); Valdés (1995, 52–81), cf. Stepan (1985) and Walpen and Plehwe (2001).

20. Piñera was a UC economist who did his postgraduate work at Harvard University before serving under Pinochet. After his political career ended, he took an active role in the Chilean business sector and developed numerous think tank activities. He works as an adviser for pension reforms (e.g., in Eastern Europe). He attended the MPS regional meeting in Cancún (1996) where he gave a lecture on the Chilean pension system (see Piñera undated).

21. Guzmán, cited in Huneeus (1998, 24); see also Moulian (1997, 240–252); Cristi (2000, Chapters 1 and 5). The first amendments to the constitution of 1980 were made in November 2005; the 2006 elected government of Michelle Bachelet promised to change a key restrictive element for civil authority, the electoral law ("sistema binominal").

22. Spanish original: "Una dictadura se puede autolimitar y una dictadura que deliberadamente se autlimita puede ser más liberal en sus políticas que una asamblea democrática que no tiene límites" (Interview with F. A. Hayek, *El Mercurio*, April 19, 1981).

23. Vergara leaves no doubt which group adapted more during the process of constitutional debate, observing the "neoliberalization of the *gremialistas*" (Vergara 1985, 168).

24. When the nationalized banks were rapidly privatized after economic recovery, the government did not require a repayment of taxpayers' expenditures (Martínez and Díaz 1996, 59).

25. See Martínez and Díaz (1996, 55f.); Fazio (1997); and Kurtz (1999, 422). A telling example is the directorate of SQM, the flagship of the chemical industry that was fully privatized in 1988. Members of the directorate included the former ministers Carlos Cáceres, Sergio de Castro, and Enrique Valenzuela; Sergio de la Cuadra, Pablo Baraona, and Hernán Büchi were appointed in the 1990s (Mönckeberg 2001, own investigations). Compare Rozas and Marín (1989, 56) on the recomposition of the directorate of Banco de Chile.

26. Although 54.7 percent eventually succeeded in ousting Pinochet from office by choosing the *No* option, one should not forget that 43 percent of the population still supported Pinochet at this juncture. As stipulated in the 1980 constitution, Pinochet also remained commander-in-chief until 1998. Subsequently, his position as "Lifelong Senator" protected him from trial until the judicial process was initiated in 2001.

27. The exclusion from higher ranks was not complete. A consensual formula between the Pinochet and the incoming governments designated the composition of the board of the Central Bank, for example. Both administrations nominated two members; an economist who gave guarantees to both parties was made president. According to the new finance minister, Alejandro Foxley, this solution "was a way of showing the country, the private sector, and the international financial community that the Concertación is committed to the economic stability of the country" (*El Mercurio*, December 7–13, 1989, quoted in Montecinos 1993, 35).

28. The key figure, Hernán Büchi, is also rumored to be a MPS member, but we were unable to verify his membership.

References

Amadae, Sonja. 2003. *Rationalizing Capitalist Democracy: The Cold War Origins of Rational Choice Liberalism*. Chicago: University of Chicago Press.

Amin, Samir. 1973. *Le développement inégal. Essai sur les formations sociales du capitalisme périphérique*. Paris: Editions de Minuit.

Arriagada, Genaro. 1998. *Por la razon o la fuerza: Chile bajo Pinochet*. Santiago: Editorial Sudamericana.

Barton, Jonathan R. 2002. "State Continuismo and Pinochtismo: The Keys to the Chilean Transition." *Bulletin of Latin American Research* 21 (3), 358–374.

Biglaiser, Glen. 2002. "The Internationalization of Economics in Latin America." *Economic Development and Cultural Change* 50 (2), 269–286.

Buchanan, James. 1979. *What Should Economists Do?* Indianapolis, IN: Liberty Press.

Buchanan, James. 1982. "Democracia Limitada o Ilimitada." *Estudios Públicos* 6, 37–51.

Buchanan, James, and Gordon Tullock. 1962. *The Calculus of Consent*. Ann Arbor: University of Michigan Press.

Cáceres, Carlos Francisco. 1982. "La via chilena a la Economia de Mercado." *Estudios Públicos* 6, 71–87.

Campero, Guillermo. 1993. "Los empresarios chileno en el régimen militar y el post-plebiscito." In Paul W. Drake and Ivan Jaksic (eds.), *El difícil camino hacia la democracia en Chile 1982–1990*. Santiago: FLACSO, 243–303.

Cañas Kirby, Enrique. 1997. *Proceso politico en Chile, 1973–1990*. Santiago: Editorial Andres Bello.

Caputo, Orlando, and Roberto Pizarro. 1970. *Imperialismo, dependencia y relaciones económicas internacionales*. Santiago: CESO.

Centeno, Miguel Angel, and Patricio Silva (eds.). 1996. *The Politics of Expertise: Technocratic Ascendancy in Latin America*. London: Macmillan.

CEP. 1982. Conferencia Mont Pelerin. *Estudios Públicos* 6, segundo trimestre 1982. Santiago: CEP.

CEP. 1992. "El ladrillo. Bases de la política económica del gobierno militar chileno." Santiago: Centro de Estudios Públicos (online at www.cepchile.cl/dms/lang_1/cat _794_inicio.html, accessed June 7, 2007).

Corvalán Marquéz, Luis. 2001. *Del anticapitalismo al neoliberalismo en Chile.* Santiago: Editorial Sudamericana.

Cristi, Renato. 1999. "Jaime Guzmán, capitalismo y moralidad." *Revista de Derecho* 10, 87–102.

Cristi, Renato. 2000. *Pensamiento Político de Jaime Guzmán: Autoridad y Libertad.* Santiago: LOM.

Dahse, Fernando. 1979. *El mapa de la extrema riqueza. Los Grupos Económicos y el Proceso de Concentración de Capitales.* Santiago: Editorial Aconcágua.

Delano, Manuel, and Hugo Traslaviña. 1989. *La herencia de los Chicago boys.* Santiago: Las Ediciones del Ornitorrinco.

Downs, Anthony. 1957. *An Economic Theory of Democracy.* New York: Harper & Row.

Ebenstein, Alan. 2001. *Friedrich Hayek: A Biography.* New York: Palgrave.

Fazio, Hugo. 1997. *Mapa actual de la extrema riqueza en Chile.* Santiago: LOM.

Fazio, Hugo. 2000. *La transnacionalización de la economía chilena: Mapa de la Extrema Riqueza al año 2000.* Santiago: LOM.

Ffrench-Davis, Ricardo. 2003. *Entre el neoliberalismo y el crecimiento con equidad. Tres décadas de política económica en Chile.* 3rd ed. Santiago: J. C. Sáenz.

Fischer, Frank. 1996. "Die Agenda der Elite. Amerikanische Think Tanks und die Strategien der Politikberatung." *PROKLA. Zeitschrift für kritische Sozialwissenschaft,* 104, 26 (3), 463–481.

Fischer, Karin. 2002. "Neoliberale Transformation in Chile: Zur Rolle der ökonomischen und intellektuellen Eliten." *Journal für Entwicklungspolitik (Journal of Development Studies)* 18 (3), 225–248.

Fontaine Aldunante, Arturo. 1988. *Los economistas y el Presidente Pinochet.* Santiago: Zig-Zag.

Fontaine Talavera, Arturo (ed.). 1991. "El miedo y otros escritos: El pensamiento de Jaime Guzmán E." *Estudios Públicos* 42. Santiago: CEP.

Fourcade-Gourinchas Marion, and Sarah L. Babb. 2002. "The Rebirth of the Liberal Creed: Paths to Neoliberalism in Four Countries." *American Journal for Sociology* 108 (3), 533–579.

Foxley, Alejandro. 1986. *Latin American Experiments in Neo-Conservative Economics.* Berkeley: University of California Press.

Frank, Andre Gunder. 1967. *Capitalism and Underdevelopment in Latin America: Historical Studies of Chile and Brazil.* New York: Monthly Review Press.

Frickhöffer, Wolfgang. 1982. "La implantación de una economía de mercado: el modelo alemán y el modelo chileno." *Estudios Públicos* 6, 89–98.

Friedman, Milton, and Rose D. Friedman. 1998. *Two Lucky People.* Chicago: University of Chicago Press.

González-Rossetti, Alejandra, Tomas Chuaqui, and Consuelo Espinosa. 2000. "Enhancing the Political Feasibility of Health Reform: The Chile Case. LAC-HSR Health Sector Reform Initiative/Data for Decision Making (DDM) Project." Online at www.hsph.harvard.edu/ihsg/publications/pdf/lac/PolicyChile1 .pdf, accessed June 7, 2007.

Green, Donald P., and Ian Shapiro. 1994. *Pathologies of Rational Choice: A Critique of Applications in Political Science.* New Haven, CT: Yale University Press.

Harberger, Arnold. 1996. "Good Economics Comes to Latin America, 1955–1995." In A. W. Coats (ed.), *The Post-1945 Internationalization of Economics.* Durham, NC: Duke University Press, 301–311.

Harberger, Arnold. 1999. "Interview with Arnold Harberger by David Levy." *Revista Acta Académica,* No. 25, 79–99 (November). San José: Universidad Autónoma de Centro America.

Hayek, Friedrich. 1981. "De la Servidumbre a la Libertad (Interview with Lucia Santa Cruz)." *El Mercurio,* April 19, 1981, D1–D2. Online at http://www.liberalismus.at/Texte/mercurio.php.

Hayek, Friedrich. 1982. "Los principios de un orden social liberal." *Estudios Públicos* 6, 179–202.

Hennecke, Hans Jörg. 2000. *Friedrich August von Hayek: Die Tradition der Freiheit.* Düsseldorf: Verlag Wirtschaft und Finanzen.

Huneeus, Carlos. 1998. "Tecnócratas y políticos en el autoritarismo. Los 'ODEPLAN boys' y los 'gremialistas' en el Chile de Pinochet." *Revista de Ciencia Política* 19 (2), 125–158.

Imbusch, Peter. 1995. *Unternehmer und Politik in Chile. Eine Studie zum politischen Verhalten der Unternehmer und ihrer Verbände.* Frankfurt am Main: Vervuert Verlag.

Kurtz, Marcus J. 1999. "Chile's Neo-Liberal Revolution: Incremental Decisions and Structural Transformation, 1973–1979." *Journal of Latin American Studies* 31, 399–427.

Lavín, Joaquín. 1986. *Miguel Kast: Pasión de vivir.* Santiago: Zig-Zag.

Libertad y Desarrollo. 2005. *15 Años Trabajando por la Libertad y Desarrollo, 1990–2005.* Santiago: LyD.

Lüders, Rolf J. 1993. "El estado empresario en Chile. Las bases de su desarrollo hasta 1973, y la privatización durante el Régimen Militar." In Daniel L. Wisecarver (ed.), *El modelo económico chileno.* 2nd ed. Santiago: CINDE, 133–169.

Martínez, Javier, and Alvaro Díaz. 1996. *Chile: The Great Transformation.* UNRISD: Geneva.

Mönckeberg, María Olivia. 2001. *El Saqueo de los Grupos Económicos al Estado chileno.* Santiago: Ediciones B.

Montero, Cecilia. 1997. *La revolución empresarial chilena.* Santiago: Cieplan/Dolmen Ediciones.

Montecinos, Veronica. 1993. "Economic Policy Elites and Democratization." *Studies in International Comparative Development* (28):25–53.

Montecinos, Veronica. 1998. *Economists, Politics and the State: Chile 1958–1994.* Amsterdam: CEDLA Publications.

Montecinos, Verónica, and John Markoff. 2001. "From the Power of Economic Ideas to the Power of Economics." In Miguel Angel Centeno and Fernando López-Alves (eds.), *The Other Mirror: Grand Theory through the Lens of Latin America.* Princeton, NJ: Princeton University Press, 105–150.

Moulian, Tomás. 1997. *Chile actual: Anatomía de un mito.* Santiago: LOM.

Moulian, Tomás. 2006. *Fracturas: De Pedro Aguirre Cerda a Salvador Allende (1938–1973).* Santiago: LOM.

O'Brian, Phil, and Jackie Roddick. 1983. *Chile: The Pinochet Decade: The Rise and Fall of the Chicago Boys* (additional material from Jon Barnes and James Painter). London: Latin America Bureau.

Olave Castillo, Patricia. 1997. *El proyecto neoliberal en Chile y la construcción de una nueva economía.* México, D.F.: Instituto de Investigaciones Económicas, UNAM & Ediciones El Caballito.

Oppenheim, Lois Hecht. 1999. *Politics in Chile: Democracy, Authoritarianism, and the Search for Development.* 2nd ed. Boulder, CO: Westview.

Packenham, Robert A. 1973. *Liberal America and the Third World: Political Development Ideas in Foreign Aid and Social Science.* Princeton, NJ: Princeton University Press.

Piñera, José. 1990. *La revolución laboral en Chile.* Santiago: Zig-Zag.

Piñera, José. 1992. "Chile: el poder de una idea." In Barry B. Levine (ed.), *El Desafío Neoliberal. El fin del tercermundismo en América Latina.* Santafé de Bogotá: Editorial Norma S.A.

Pitt, Joseph, Djavad Salehi, and Douglas Eckel (eds.). 2004. *The Production and Diffusion of Public Choice Political Economy.* Malden, MA: Blackwell.

Plehwe, Dieter, and Bernhard Walpen. 1999. "Wissenschaftliche und wissenschaftstheoretische Produktionsweisen im Neoliberalismus." *PROKLA* No. 2, 203–235.

Prebisch, Raúl. 1950. *The Economic Development of Latin America and Its Principal Problems.* New York: United Nations/Economic Commission for Latin America.

Prebisch, Raúl. 1961. *Economic Development, Planning and International Cooperation.* Santiago: ECLA.

Rozas, Patricio, and Gustavo Marín. 1988. *Estado autoritario, deuda externa y grupos económicos.* Santiago: CESOC.

Rozas, Patricio, and Gustavo Marín. 1989. *1988: El "mapa de la extrema riqueza" 10 años despues.* Santiago: Ediciones Chile América CESOC.

Sabatini, Francisco. 2000. "Reforma de los mercados de suelo en Santiago, Chile. Efectos sobre los precios de la tierra y la segregacion social." *EURE* 26 (77), 49–80.

Silva, Eduardo. 1992. "The Political Economy of Chile's Regime Transition: From Radical to 'Pragmatic' Neo-Liberal Policies." In Paul Drake and Iván Jaksic (eds.), *The Struggle for Democracy in Chile.* Lincoln: University of Nebraska Press, 98–127.

Silva, Eduardo. 1996. *The State and Capital in Chile: Business Elites, Technocrats, and Market Economics.* Boulder, CO: Westview Press.

Silva, Patricio. 1991. "Technocrats and Politics in Chile: From the Chicago Boys to the CIEPLAN Monks." *Journal for Latin American Studies* 23, part 2, 385–410.

Silva, Patricio. 1998. "Neoliberalism, Democratization, and the Rise of Technocrats." In Menno Vellinga (ed.), *The Changing Role of the State in Latin America.* Boulder, CO: Westview Press, 75–92.

Silva, Patricio. 2001. "Democratisation and State-Civil Society Relations in Chile, 1983–2000: From Effervescency to Deactivation." Paper presented at the International Conference, "The Role of Civil Society in Conflict Resolution," National University of Ireland, February 14–16, 2001.

Silva, Patricio. 2006. "The Politics of Neoliberalism in Latin America." In Richard Robison (ed.), *The Neo-Liberal Revolution.* London: Palgrave, 39–57.

Somerville Senn, Hérnan. 1992. "La renegociación de la deuda externa chilena." *La transformación economica de Chile.* Cuadernos Universitarios, Serie Debates No. 1, 107–118. Santiago: Universidad Nacional Andrés Bello.

Soto, Ángel. 2003. *El Mercurio y la difusión del pensamiento político económico liberal. 1955–1970.* Santiago: Centro de Estudios Bicentenario.

Stepan, Alfred. 1985. "State Power and the Strength of Civil Society in the Southern Cone of Latin America." In Peter B. Evans, Dietrich Rueschemeyer, and Theda Skocpol (eds.), *Bringing the State Back In.* Cambridge: Cambridge University Press, 317–343.

Teichman, Judith A. 2001. *The Politics of Freeing Markets in Latin America: Chile, Argentina, and Mexico.* Chapel Hill: University of North Carolina Press.

Tironi, Ernesto B. (1982). *El modelo neoliberal chileno y su implemantación.* Santiago: CED.

Tullock, Gordon. 1972. "Economic Imperialism." In J. M. Buchanan and R. D. Tollison (eds.), *Theory of Political Choice.* Ann Arbor: University of Michigan Press, 317–329.

Valdés, Juan Gabriel. 1995. *Pinochet's Economists: The Chicago School in Chile.* Cambridge: Cambridge University Press.

Valdivia, Verónica, and Ortiz de Zárate. 2003. *El golpe después del golpe. Leigh vs. Pinochet: Chile 1960–1980.* Santiago: LOM.

Valenzuela, Arturo. 1993. "Los militares en el poder: la consolidación del poder unipersonal." In Paul W. Drake and Iván Jaksic (eds.), *El difícil camino hacia la democracia en Chile 1982–1990.* Santiago: Flacso. English edition: *The Struggle for Democracy in Chile, 1982–1990.* Lincoln: University of Nebraska Press (1991).

Vergara, Pilar. 1985. *Auge y caida del neoliberalismo en Chile.* Santiago: FLACSO.

Walpen, Bernhard, and Dieter Plehwe. 2001. " 'Wahrheitsgetreue Berichte über Chile'—Die Mont Pèlerin Society und die Diktatur Pinochet." 1999. Zeitschrift für Sozialgeschichte des 20. und 21. *Jahrhunderts* 2, 42–70.

Wisecarver, Daniel L. 1992. *El Modelo Económico Chileno.* Santiago: CINDE.

IO

Taking Aim at the New International Economic Order

JENNIFER BAIR

In the context of the recently proclaimed New International Economic Order, the United Nations Center on Transnational Corporations (UNCTC) was established by the UN Economic and Social Council in 1975.[1] This New York–based organ of the UN Secretariat was created to assist the work of another new body, the Commission on Transnational Corporations, which was charged with negotiating a code of conduct for multinational corporations. In less than two decades, the UNCTC was defunct, and the Commission's effort to adopt and implement a code of conduct had been abandoned. Yet in 1999, just a few years after the Center was officially disbanded by the General Assembly, multinational corporations reemerged on the UN scene when Secretary General Kofi Annan announced the launch of a new partnership between UN agencies and international business. This new venture, known as the Global Compact, underscored a dramatic shift in the United Nations' attitude toward multinational corporations (MNCs); the old debates of the 1970s and 1980s about how efficacious a code of conduct might prove in regulating MNC conduct have been replaced by efforts to leverage what Annan described as "the enlightened self-interest of companies" to developmental and social ends.

The transformation in development theory and policy that the trajectory from code to compact represents extends beyond the institutional arena of the United Nations and its embattled experiment with MNC regulation. Prevailing views on a range of issues relating to economic growth and industrialization were challenged as part of "the counterrevolution in development economics" that occurred during the last quarter of the twentieth century (Toye 1993). As a global debt crisis unfolded over the course of the 1980s, widening the gulf separating First and Third Worlds and casting ever greater doubt on the feasibility of import-substituting regimes, a new orthodoxy was being consolidated. Famously summarized by John Williamson as "the Washington Consensus" (Williamson 2004), this neoliberal model prioritized macroeconomic stabilization, liberalization, and privatization as the prescription for the developmental cure. Rejecting "the dirigiste dogma" (Lal 1985) that had haunted and halted the development efforts of poorer countries, the Consensus promoted a market-led paradigm that proscribed the kinds of interventionist strategies embraced by much of the developing world during its short-lived struggle for the New International Economic Order (NIEO).

Although the relationship between the defeat of the NIEO and the triumph of neoliberalism has received little scholarly attention, John Toye, in an exception to this general neglect, argues that "the threat of an NIEO, particularly one imposed by the South and supported on moral grounds by influential public opinion in the North, acted as a strong spur to the counterrevolution in development policy" (Toye 1993, 180). In this chapter, I revisit the rise and fall of the NIEO in order to excavate some of the intellectual and institutional foundations of that counter-revolution. Specifically, and in keeping with the project of this edited volume to analyze the foundations of contemporary neoliberalism, and especially the activities of individuals and organizations associated with the Mont Pèlerin Society (MPS), I focus on how four economists (university professors who are also MPS members) and one MPS-related think tank sought to shape the development debate before, during, and after the specific period of the NIEO.

The chapter proceeds in four sections: First, I review the foundations of the NIEO project, highlighting the key events that precipitated the developing world's efforts to transform the international economy via the institutional vehicle of the United Nations. Having outlined the main elements of the NIEO platform and its fate at the UN through the early 1980s, I consider how the work of Gottfried Haberler, Karl Brunner, Peter Bauer, and Deepak

Lal informed and contributed to the promotion of a counter-revolution in development economics that took aim at the NIEO's agenda for reform. Third, I focus on a particular front in the battle for the NIEO—the protracted and ultimately unsuccessful effort to draft a UN Code of Conduct on Multinational Corporations. In the fourth and final section, I discuss the Heritage Foundation's United Nations Assessment Project, which was an effort by Heritage to discredit and defuse the UNCTC, the Code of Conduct project, and indeed the broader NIEO agenda at the United Nations.

Collectively, this analysis underscores the extent to which the NIEO and its proponents were interpreted as a threat to an embattled "liberal international economic order" (Lal 1985). The Third World's perceived radicalism generated a sense of alarm in certain quarters that helped mobilize support for positions and policies that were being advocated in some academic and political circles. Thus, the developing world's struggle for reform of the international economy created an opening in the existing regime and in this sense provided an opportunity structure that did indeed facilitate a shift in the prevailing order, though not the one envisioned by the NIEO's supporters. Indeed, the defeat of the NIEO agenda both signaled and consolidated the ascendancy of the Washington Consensus as the dominant development paradigm.

Revolution from Within? The New International Economic Order at the UN

Although the New International Economic Order was officially proclaimed in 1974, its declaration at the United Nations was the culmination of a movement that began two decades earlier, with the Bandung conference of non-aligned countries in April 1955. The Non-Aligned Movement was initiated by African and Asian countries to address issues arising from decolonization, but by the second half of the 1950s Latin American states were seeking to join forces at the UN with these new nations for two reasons. First, the sheer increase in the number of UN members diluted the ability of Latin American countries to exercise power in the General Assembly through bloc voting. Second, governments in the region were seeking to enlist broad support among developing countries for the policies being promoted by the Economic Commission for Latin America (ECLA) and its director, Argentine economist Raúl Prebisch. The creation of the European Economic Community (EEC) in 1958, which many Third World governments feared would negatively impact their export performance, seemed to reinforce the view that developing countries had similar interests at stake with regard to the international economy.[2]

Thus, a mutual interest in putting economic development issues more squarely on the UN agenda served to secure an alliance between the African and Asian nations of the Non-Aligned Movement and the Latin American countries. When representatives from the three regions met in Geneva for the first United Nations Conference on Trade and Development (UNCTAD) during the spring and summer of 1964, they formed the Third World caucus known as the G-77, which proceeded to play an important role in lobbying for UNCTAD's institutionalization. The creation of UNCTAD as a permanent organ of the General Assembly was established by UN resolution no. 1995 in December 1964, and in early 1965, the General Assembly approved the appointment of Raúl Prebisch as that body's first secretary-general.

During its first decade of existence, UNCTAD scored some modest victories (most notably, agreement on the principle of a Generalized System of Preferences for developing-country exports), but it also sustained bruising losses on critical fronts, such as commodity agreements and international monetary reform (Toye and Toye 2004). Although UNCTAD II in 1968 and UNCTAD III in 1972 produced little in the way of progress on the G-77 agenda, the developing countries nevertheless appeared to ratchet up their rhetoric in the early 1970s. During the 1972 UNCTAD meeting in Chile, Mexican President Luis Echeverría proposed that the UN undertake the drafting of a "Charter on the Economic Rights and Duties of States," which would include, among other tenets, the right of states to the full exercise of national sovereignty over natural resources.

If the G-77's efforts for reform of the international economy were principally pursued through UNCTAD, the Non-Aligned Movement (NAM) served as a parallel source of support. The early 1970s witnessed a shift in what had been the NAM's primarily political focus, as the movement began devoting greater attention to economic concerns (Gwin 1977; McCulloch 1977). During the fourth summit of the NAM in September 1973, President Houari Boumedienne of Algeria, host of the Algiers meeting, called for a special session of the United Nations "with a view to establishing a new system of relations based on equality and common interests of all states" (Marshall 1994). This meeting, which would take place in spring 1974, was the Sixth Special Session of the General Assembly, at which the G-77 countries officially launched the NIEO project.

In terms of content, the NIEO platform represented more continuity than change, as it contained vague proposals for reform that the G-77 had advocated for some time. However, what was different, and dramatically so, was the international context in which the Third World was making its demands. The vertiginous increase in the price of oil engineered by OPEC in late 1973 created a perception on the part of several key G-77 members that the balance of international power had tilted in their favor. The fact that Northern countries, which even before the acute crisis precipitated by the embargo were concerned about the price and supply of oil, had agreed to a special meeting of the UN General Assembly devoted to development issues also emboldened the G-77, and the bloc's increasing radicalism culminated in the contentious Sixth Special Session of the General Assembly in March-April 1974.[3]

Appropriately enough, the Special Session opened with a two-hour address from President Boumedienne, who as an active player in OPEC, aptly embodied the North's oil crisis-induced anxiety.[4] As its pièce de résistance, the Sixth Special Session featured the adoption of UN resolution no. 3201, which declared "the establishment of a new international economic order." The NIEO platform consisted of twenty wide-ranging principles, including the inalienable right to "permanent sovereignty of every State over its natural resources and all economic properties . . . including the right to nationalization or transfer of ownership to its nationals."[5] This new order was to be based on "equity, sovereign equality, interdependence, common interest and cooperation among all states irrespective of their economic and social systems, which shall correct inequalities and redress existing injustices, making it possible to eliminate the widening gap between all the developed and the developing countries and ensure steadily accelerating economic and social development in peace and justice for future generations."

The NIEO's proponents contended that the gap separating the Third World from the developed countries could only be narrowed if the international trading system were reformed in such a way as to correct the "biases" against developing countries that were alleged to be inherent in it. This rationale for the NIEO's program of structural reform rested largely on the influential work done by Raúl Prebisch while head of the United Nations Economic Commission on Latin America. Much of the research conducted by the economists at ECLA purported to show a historical decline in the terms of trade for primary commodities, which Prebisch argued allowed the rich countries to reap most of the technological advances engendered through industrialization.

Prebisch and his colleagues at ECLA thus agreed with the prevailing view of the modernization theorists—that is, that industrialization was the requisite linchpin of any development effort. But they took issue with modernization theory's claims that the primary constraints on successful industrialization in the Third World were institutional and/or cultural. Instead, they argued that they were structural, and rooted in the nature of international trade patterns—that is, the exchange of primary commodities from the periphery for manufactured goods made in the core. On the basis of this analysis, Prebisch concluded that developing countries should pursue autonomous industrialization, and prescribed a regime of import substitution toward that end.

Prebisch's work undoubtedly provided an important justification for the NIEO platform, but his seminal thesis alleging deteriorating terms of trade for primary commodity exporters was published in 1950, more than two decades earlier. Thus in explaining why the NIEO emerged when it did, one must look to contemporary events, and specifically to the Arab oil embargo of 1973. The sense of economic and political dislocation generated by the oil shock, and the portentous predictions of the Third World's coming "resource power" that the energy crisis was thought to augur, were of decisive importance in explaining why the G-77 countries, despite having failed to secure most of the objectives laid out at the first UNCTAD conference ten years prior, nevertheless viewed the Sixth Special Session as an auspicious opportunity to advance their agenda (Doyle 1983).

From the perspective of the developing country coalition, there were seven primary areas on which progress had to be made in order for the New International Economic Order to be realized. First was implementing a system of "commodity price stabilization through the negotiation of price floors below which commodity prices would not be allowed to fall. The second was a scheme of preferential tariffs, or allowing exports of Third World manufacturers to enter First World markets at lower tariff rates than those applied to exports from other industrialized countries" (Bello 1998, 209). Third, the G-77 countries sought an increase in foreign aid and, fourth, alleviation of the debt burden. Reform of multilateral institutions in order to increase the voice of the Third World was the fifth action item on the NIEO agenda. Sixth, various forms of developing country protectionism deemed necessary to promote autonomous industrialization through import substitution were to be legitimated, including increased control of MNCs operating in the Third World. The seventh and related point was an enhancement of technology transfer

from the North to the South, which eventually resulted in work by UNC-
TAD on a code of conduct for technology transfer (Doyle 1983).

Most of these principles were contained in the founding document of the
NIEO, UN resolution no. 3201, adopted during the Sixth Special Session. It was
followed by three other resolutions pertaining to the NIEO: "Programme of Action on the Establishment of a New International Economic Order," which was
also adopted during the Sixth Special Session; "Charter of Economic Rights and
Duties of States," dating from the twenty-ninth session of the General Assembly
and adopted in December 1974; and, "Development and International Cooperation," which was passed in September 1975 during the Seventh Special Session
of the General Assembly. Karl Sauvant, a close observer of the NIEO's evolution
at the UN, who later became head of UNCTAD's investment division, concluded that, with the adoption of these four documents, "the developing countries had succeeded in making development—the establishment of the New International Economic Order—the priority item on the international agenda"
(1977b, 4). In fact, the long denouement of the NIEO was already underway by
the time Sauvant's laudatory assessment appeared in print.

The period between late 1973 and 1975 was not the germinating stage of the
new international economic order advocated by the G-77, but rather the
high-water mark of what proved to be a brief and ultimately ineffectual period
of reform. While in retrospect it may appear obvious (and to some, inevitable)
that this challenge to the existing order would prove unsuccessful, the NIEO's
fate seemed far less certain at the time. In fact, when the Seventh Special Session of the General Assembly was held in September 1975, some delegates and
analysts judged the NIEO's prospects for success as moderately bright. The
tone of the G-77 at the Session was less confrontational than it had been a
year prior, as suggested by the Group's decision to omit from the position paper it prepared for the meeting a few of the more controversial items on the
NIEO agenda, including permanent sovereignty over natural resources, producers' associations, and control over multinational corporations.

A number of observers of the Seventh Special Session concluded that, for
their part, the rich countries were more receptive to the G-77's proposal for a
new dialogue on development than they had been earlier, though it was clear
that considerable distance continued to separate the two camps and that the
United States, Japan, and the European Community were unwilling to accept
the proposition that structural transformation of the international economy
was a prerequisite for the outcomes sought by the G-77. Still, some analysts

offered positive assessments of the meeting: "although there is still no agreement between the rich and poor countries on the substance of fundamental
issues, there now exists an explicit commitment to negotiate. This commitment led to the optimism of participants at the Session; it indicated that, after
a standstill of more than a decade, development diplomacy may be newly en-
ergized" (Gosovic and Ruggie 1976, 327). Yet others pointed out that the
changes that had occurred between the Sixth Special Session in spring 1974
and the Seventh Special Session in fall 1975 improved the bargaining position
of the developed countries at the expense of the G-77. While the former meeting had taken place "in the final moments of a historic commodity boom and
in the height of the resource scarcity 'scare,' the Seventh Special Session occurred after many commodity prices had dropped precipitously and after the
effects of world inflation, recession, and higher oil prices in the less-developed
states had become well-documented" (Gwin 1977, 107).

Indeed, most discussions chronicling the trajectory of the NIEO focus on
how the G-77's challenge to the existing order rose and ebbed with the flow of
political and economic events during the 1970s. The uncertainty created by
growing instability in the global economy at the beginning of the decade was
followed by OPEC's audacious move to regulate petroleum output, and thus
control the world market price for oil—an apparent coup in international
economic relations that reverberated throughout the developing world and
precipitated the G-77's increasingly assertive posture at the UN. It was in this
context that the NIEO was launched, and while in objective terms the obstacles confronting the G-77 were still formidable, the international environment, characterized for the moment by Southern solidarity and Northern apprehension, was perceived by the developing countries as being exceptionally
propitious for advancing their agenda of structural reform (Rothstein 1984).
However, the window of opportunity that the Third World perceived to have
been opened by the events of that winter was brief. Following the initial shock
of the oil crisis, the industrial economies adjusted rather briskly to the
prospect of paying more for energy, and as Northern confidence returned,
Southern solidarity waned, thanks in part to the economic difficulties higher
fuel prices caused for the so-called NO-PEC members of the G-77 that found
themselves on the wrong side of the "oil divide."

Though it was not the transformation sought by proponents of the New International Economic Order, the 1980s did bring dramatic changes to the developing world. For many countries, the new order arrived in the form of a

Third World debt crisis, which, in turn, ushered in the era of structural adjustment, as the international financial institutions attempted to chart a course through that crisis. Although World Bank president Robert McNamara had hoped that the appointment of an Independent Commission on International Development could provide renewed focus and direction to the North-South debate, the recommendations made by that Commission, headed by former West German president Willy Brandt, were greeted with skepticism by U.S. and Western European governments when they were released in early 1980. Offering support for several of the proposals advanced by the G-77 under the aegis of the NIEO, the Brandt Commission report was more warmly received by the developing countries. However, it failed to reinvigorate the North-South dialogue, which was publicly acknowledged to be at a stalemate later that year during the 11th Special Session of the United Nations, when a number of G-77 members refused to promulgate the International Development Strategy for the Third Decade, despite having previously agreed to the document (Doyle 1983).

As something of a last-ditch effort to renew negotiations and overcome the impasse between North and South, Mexican President José López Portillo agreed to host a summit of leaders from twenty-two developing and developed countries in Cancún, Mexico. Although the organizers hoped that the meeting's intimate and unstructured format would encourage a new round of dialogue, the October 1981 summit proved instead to be the NIEO's death knell (Toye and Toye 2004). It is perhaps best remembered for the speech in which Ronald Reagan, foreshadowing the decisive turn in development discourse already under way, exhorted Third World leaders to embrace the "magic of the market."

Between 1979 and 1982, Margaret Thatcher, Ronald Reagan and Helmut Kohl came to power in the UK, the United States, and West Germany, respectively. Their electoral victories are generally regarded as the key political events marking neoliberalism's ascendance. The policies advocated by all three governments on key issues such as international trade and foreign aid were consistent with the market-led, export-oriented development model celebrated in President Reagan's 1981 speech at Cancún. Within a decade, Reagan's vision would be the new orthodoxy, widely diffused across the (after 1989, rather anachronistically named) Third World. Yet as various contributions to this book document, the ideas on which the new international development agenda was based predate neoliberalism's political triumph. Even as import-substituting industrialization strategies were disavowed and discredited over the course of the 1980s, throughout that decade and well into the next, proponents of the view that economic freedom and market competition are the best guarantors of development persisted in their fight against any regulatory or redistributive policies at the international level, which they regarded as inimical to the effective functioning of the free enterprise system. Although one can dispute the extent to which the G-77's agenda ever posed a clear and present danger to the existing order, it is evident that dedicated efforts to secure a liberal international economic regime continued well past the point at which the NIEO could be considered a viable threat.

In the remainder of the chapter, I examine more closely some of the efforts contributing to the emergence and consolidation of the neoliberal development paradigm, focusing first on four academic economists whose work addressed the debate regarding the causes of growth and development (or the lack thereof) in the Third World. Following this discussion, I describe how this debate played out with regard to one particular plank in the NIEO platform—the effort to draft a UN code regulating multinational corporations. Finally, I discuss one of the best known American think tanks associated with MPS, the Heritage Foundation, whose opposition to the NIEO and the United Nations more generally culminated in an initiative called the United Nations Assessment Project.[6]

My focus on MPS-connected actors does not imply a causal argument that organized neoliberals are responsible for the defeat of the G-77's agenda at the United Nations, nor do I want to suggest that their efforts explain why policymakers in the global South turned toward the Washington Consensus when they did. An adequate explanation for the wave of economic liberalization that broke over the developing world from Mexico to Morocco during the 1980s must acknowledge the extent to which these reforms were enabled by events in the international political economy, and especially a profoundly destabilizing Third World debt crisis, as Dani Rodrik (1994) has persuasively argued. However, by looking at the arguments and activities of individuals and institutions engaged in the debates of the period, we can add to this conventional, macro-level analysis another layer of understanding, one that is enabled by examining how and where the ideas and positions that orient much of today's development discourse were formulated and fostered, both before and after the relatively brief period of the G-77's campaign for reform. Thus, by revisiting the largely forgotten episode of the NIEO, I aim to provide a different perspective on the making of a neoliberal development model—namely, one that highlights the interaction of both political and economic opportunity structures, as well as the mobilization of intellectual and organizational resources in the articulation and dissemination of a new orthodoxy.

Dissent on Development: Haberler, Brunner, Bauer, and Lal on Trade and Aid

Economists Gottfried Haberler, Karl Brunner, Peter Bauer, and Deepak Lal helped shape the contours of the development debate during the second half of the twentieth century, and they contributed in various ways to what Toye refers to as the "counter-revolution in development economics." While Toye dates the counter-revolution from the late 1970s, the material presented in this section, which extends from Gottfried Haberler's 1957 report on the General Agreement on Tariffs and Trade (GATT) to a 2005 article by Deepak Lal, encourages a different periodization. It suggests that the seeds of this transformation were sown well before the specific period of the NIEO, and that the ideas that underlie it continue to be developed by scholars today, who draw on these earlier arguments while also updating them to reflect what are represented as ongoing challenges to the liberal international economic order.

While I draw out some of the common threads that run through their work, the four economists discussed in this chapter are by no means a coherent group: Haberler was an expert on international trade theory and policy; Brunner was a pioneering monetarist; and both the late Peter Bauer and Deepak Lal were development economists. I chose to discuss these figures because their work engages some of the key issues that were at stake in the NIEO, and because each has been a member of that network of neoliberal intellectuals and organizations discussed throughout this volume, the Mont Pèlerin Society. Although their work ranges widely over many themes in development economics, I focus on trade and aid, beginning with Haberler's intervention in the terms of trade controversy, which was a prime point of contention in the North-South debate.

As noted earlier, reform of the international trading regime was a principal objective of the NIEO's proponents. The rationale for such reform rested largely on a contention famously advanced by the first secretary-general of UNCTAD, Raúl Prebisch—namely, that the terms of trade were deteriorating over time for exporters of primary products. The so-called Prebisch-Singer thesis was accepted by many of the economists working at the United Nations, including those serving under Prebisch at the Economic Commission for Latin America and later UNCTAD, but it was regarded as controversial in the discipline at large. Following the key publications that disseminated the secular decline argument (Prebisch 1950; Singer 1950) , the Prebisch-Singer thesis was roundly attacked by academic economists, particularly in North America, with criticisms ranging from vehement denunciations (e.g., Jacob Viner) to somewhat more measured, if still unfavorable, assessments (e.g., Gerald Meier) (Dosman 2001).

Gottfried Haberler was among the trade economists of the day who weighed in on the controversy. Born in Austria in 1900, Haberler studied in Vienna with two of the principal figures in the history of the Austrian School of economics, Friedrich von Wieser and Ludwig von Mises. He later left the country and took a position in Geneva with the League of Nations' Economics Intelligence Service (EIS) before immigrating to the United States. In 1936 he joined the economics faculty at Harvard, where he taught until 1971. He later became the American Enterprise Institute's (AEI) first resident scholar, and like fellow Austrian economist and MPS member Fritz Machlup, he was associated with AEI until his death in 1995.

In 1975 Haberler was appointed to head a panel of experts commissioned by GATT to assess the terms of trade for primary commodities. The report produced by this commission, published in 1958 under the title *Trends in International Trade* but universally referred to as the Haberler Report, has been called a "turning point in GATT history" because it called for a range of measures aimed at expanding international trade and the role of developing countries within it (Evans 1968). Among its findings, the Commission confirmed that the prices of primary products had declined 5 percent since 1955, while the prices of industrial goods rose 6 percent over the same period. The Haberler Report also expressed concern about the implications of commodity price fluctuations for developing countries and voiced support for a buffer-stock scheme to help stabilize the earnings of raw material exporters.[7]

In their discussion of the Haberler Report, Toye and Toye suggest that the GATT Commission's findings supported the Prebisch-Singer side in the terms of trade controversy, which was well underway by the time of its publication. The authors also note that the Report prefigured several of the policy recommendations that would be associated with UNCTAD during Prebisch's tenure there—a resonance the authors find surprising, "given Haberler's criticism of the Prebisch-Singer hypothesis the following year" (2004, 215). Yet this apparent contradiction between Haberler's criticism of the Prebisch-Singer hypothesis and the findings outlined in the report, which bears his name, may be resolved by a closer consideration of both.

Haberler delivered his verdict on the Prebisch-Singer thesis in 1959 during lectures he gave in Cairo to commemorate the fiftieth anniversary of the National Bank of Egypt, and his assessment relied heavily on numerous critiques that had already been made by others. Although he did not dismiss the Prebisch-Singer thesis as impossible, Haberler faulted the analysis as very weak in empirical support. Furthermore, he argued that even if there had been a decline in the terms of trade in the recent past, there was no reason to assume that it would continue in the future, and no justification for basing policy recommendations on that assumption (Toye and Toye 2004, 133–134). In fact, none of the criticisms that Haberler offered of the Prebisch-Singer thesis are inconsistent with the conclusions reached by the GATT-appointed commission one year earlier: The Haberler Report did document a decline in commodity prices relative to those of industrial goods over a several year period in the mid-1950s, but it did not endorse the thesis of a secular decline in the terms of trade for raw material exporters. Its major complaint was not with the qualitative nature of trade between the rich and poor countries, but rather with the quantity of trade, and specifically with the consequences of market barriers constructed by developed-country governments. In "quiet and guarded language," the report's authors conceded that there was some merit to the developing-country grievances against the existing trade regime (Michalopoulos 2000), but they maintained that these complaints could be resolved through improved market access, and therefore more trade. The Haberler Report thus offered little in the way of ammunition for the G-77 countries when they appealed to the Prebisch-Singer thesis in making the case for the NIEO fifteen years later.

As noted earlier, the Prebisch-Singer thesis provided an intellectual rationale (and some might argue, a scholastic pretext) for the NIEO agenda in two ways. First, the secular decline argument was felt by the G-77 countries to buttress the case for reform of the international trade regime. Second, it helped justify another plank in the NIEO platform—an increase in foreign aid, which the NIEO's proponents argued "was transformed from being charity to being compensation, a rebate to the Third World for the years of declining commodity purchasing power" (Bello 1998, 209). However, the G-77's efforts to shift the aid discourse in this way were not entirely successful; the inefficacy of aid and the illegitimacy of Third World claims, moral or otherwise, on First World resources were themes that appeared frequently in the writings of the NIEO's critics, including the three economists discussed in the remainder of this section.

Karl Brunner was among the most important contributors to the development of monetary economics in the second half of the twentieth century. Several of Brunner's influential publications were co-authored with his former student and fellow MPS member Allan Meltzer (cf. Weller and Singleton 2006), with whom Brunner created the Shadow Open Market Committee in 1973 to appraise (often critically) the policies of the Federal Reserve's Open Market Committee. Yet while he is best known for his contributions to monetary analysis and policy, having coined the term *monetarism* to describe the approach most closely associated with Milton Friedman and the Chicago School (Brunner 1968), Brunner was also keenly interested in questions of epistemology and philosophy of science. These issues came to receive more explicit attention in Brunner's work over time as he developed "a gradual understanding that economic analysis offers a systematic approach to the whole range of sociopolitical reality" (Brunner cited in Laidler 1991, 634).

Brunner received his Ph.D. in economics from the University of Zurich in 1943 and taught at the universities of Konstanz and Bern, as well as at UCLA and Ohio State University before joining the economics faculty at the University of Rochester in 1971. At the time of his death in 1989 at the age of 73, Brunner was Fred H. Gowen Professor of Economics and director of the Center for Research in Government Policy and Business at Rochester. In addition to teaching and research, Brunner invested substantial energy in organizing conferences and meetings, including two events that survived Brunner himself and attest to his lasting influence. The first of these, the Konstanz Seminar on Monetary Theory and Monetary Policy, dates from 1970, at which time Brunner held a chair in economics at the University of Konstanz. Brunner organized the event with two goals: (1) to promote monetarism in Europe, particularly among European policymakers, who remained more strongly influenced in the early 1970s by the Keynesian paradigm than their North American counterparts; and (2) to narrow what Brunner saw as a lamentable gap in the quality of research and teaching in Europe compared to the United States, and accordingly to improve economics departments in European universities, especially in Germany and his native Switzerland.

Another influential initiative that Brunner spearheaded in the 1970s was the annual interdisciplinary series called the Interlaken Seminar on Analysis and Ideology (later renamed the Karl Brunner Symposium). The Interlaken Seminar, which continued throughout the 1980s and early 1990s, provided a forum for participants to explore wide-ranging methodological and epistemological questions across different disciplinary and policy domains. Brunner himself held strong views on such issues. He advocated that all endeavors of social science broadly conceived, not just economics, should accept the postulate of a "resourceful, evaluating, maximizing man"—a slightly modified version of *Homo economicus* to be contrasted with a sociological view of the subject. Once man's nature is understand as essential and invariant, the challenge for social scientists becomes clear: to design whatever institutional framework "offers the best chance, never an absolute guarantee, that this self-interested behavior will be channeled into socially productive directions beneficial to members of society" (Brunner cited in Laidler 1991, 637).

Brunner considered the NIEO to be an example of the misguided proposals that result when policymakers fail to recognize the importance of designing institutions that encourage the accommodation of individual self-interest with societal good. In a series of stinging essays on economic development in the Third World, Brunner characterized the NIEO as the "New Marxian-Leninist Manifesto" and a key "instrument in the worldwide battle to transform the free societies according to the prevailing totalitarian pattern" (Brunner 1996a, 161).[8] Brunner expressed particular concern that First World governments did not appreciate the magnitude of the threat because they dismissed the organizational vehicle of this "ideological assault on the West," the United Nations, as a highly ineffective, and thus generally benign, institution. But even if the numerous UN resolutions expressing support for the NIEO could be dismissed as empty rhetoric, and even if there was little in the way of empirical evidence that the G-77 was advancing its agenda, Brunner urged caution:

> Any particular event or occurrence . . . may have modest or even negligible significance, but their cumulative effects over many years still emerge with a serious weight. Moreover, even minor concessions supplemented with an array of new committees, commissions, or agencies open new avenues for the exploitation of the 'institutional weapon.' " (Brunner 1996a, 156)

Brunner refuted the claim that foreign aid to the Third World could be viewed as a form of restitution for the West's historical sins, since colonization had brought significant material progress to the Third World: "Justification of the NIEO in terms of an established 'right' based on 'past exploitation' should eventually be recognized as a theme without support in reality. It remains, however, a powerful ideological weapon to lure the support of a gullible western intelligentsia for the persistent raids on the wealth of western nations" (Brunner 1996a, 152). Despite all the NIEO's rhetorical emphasis on the right of developing countries to economic sovereignty and self-determination, the leaders of the G-77 were primarily intent on securing their own wealth and privilege. While the ruling oligarchs of the developing world advocate "the establishment of a socialist economy with eroded property rights and a political-administrative machinery replacing markets over a wide range of activities," the policies they endorse would actually worsen instead of improve life for the masses (Brunner 1996b, 183). Many of Brunner's criticisms of the NIEO were developed more fully in the work of Peter Bauer, whom Brunner references at length in his explication of colonialism's salutary effect on the Third World's economic development.

Born Pieter Tamas (later Peter Thomas) in Budapest, Lord P. T. Bauer studied at Cambridge and spent most of his academic career at the London School of Economics, from which he retired in 1983. Although Africa was his primary area of interest, Bauer wrote on a wide range of topics during a long career, including population policy, commodity stabilization, exchange rates, and property rights, as well as foreign aid and entrepreneurialism, the two issues for which his work is perhaps best known. Much of Bauer's later work took square aim at the "intellectual barbarism" of orthodox development economics, which he faulted for being methodologically flawed, politically motivated, and lacking in intellectual rigor (Bauer 1979). Chief among his complaints was that most development economists, failing to understand the central role of markets and the free enterprise system in generating growth, had, at least historically, wrongly endorsed dirigiste models, which were inimical to genuine development.

Advocacy of international aid, or what Bauer preferred to call "government to government transfer," is one of the grave errors for which development economists stand accused. Bauer argues that such aid does not and cannot promote economic growth in the Third World; where development has occurred, foreign assistance played no meaningful role in the process. Given the inefficacy of such transfers, why do arguments for foreign aid persist? Bauer suggested that "Western guilt" was the principal impetus behind such flows

(Bauer 1977). In fact, if the Third World transformed itself into a lobbying group for ever greater amounts of assistance, the rich countries are primarily to blame since, in Bauer's view, the demand for foreign aid was created by the very act of giving it, with the original sin dating back to U.S. president Harry Truman's misguided Point Four Program of 1949 (Bauer 1984).

Intent on debunking the idea that development assistance is a moral imperative to redress extant inequalities, Bauer argues that neither Western guilt nor humanitarian concern can justify resource transfers from rich-country governments to poor-country governments. He acknowledges that foreign aid is viewed by some as restitution for past wrongs instead of as charity, but Bauer rejects this assertion, concluding that "contact with the West has been the prime agent of material progress in the Third World" (Bauer 1984, 57). The prima facie evidence for this causal argument is the observation that those Third World countries with close historical ties to the First World are better off than other developing countries whose exposure to the West has been less extensive.

As for the specific argument of the NIEO—that aid be regarded as compensation to commodity exporters adversely impacted by changes in the terms of trade—Bauer is skeptical that a secular decline has occurred. However, he avers that if the Prebisch-Singer thesis were correct, exchange between developing and industrial countries would still be welfare-enhancing for both parties: "even if the terms of trade of the South were unfavourable on some criterion or other, this would mean only that the South had not benefited as much from its contacts with the West as it would have done had prices been more favourable. The peoples of the South are certainly better off than if they had no trade to have terms about" (Bauer 1984, 58).

Peter Bauer's career as a development economist spans the entire period examined in this chapter. His earliest publications on the rubber industry in Africa appeared prior to the publication of the Prebisch-Singer thesis in 1950 (Bauer 1946), and his final book, *From Subsistence to Exchange,* appeared in 2000. Throughout, he viewed himself as a maverick development economist, neglected by a mainstream opposed to his substantive views and his mode of argumentation, as he eschewed the trend in economics toward ever more sophisticated mathematical modeling. Deepak Lal, whose writings on development echo many of the themes championed by Bauer, addressed the question of Bauer's standing among development economists in his contribution to a 1987 issue of the *Cato Journal* devoted to Bauer's work.[9] Attributing Bauer's marginalization to a conflict between the "Weltanschaung" of Austrian economics, with which Bauer's work is identified, and that of mainstream economics, Lal laments the methodological narrowness of the latter, which proceeds from "an epistemologically unsound positivist view of economics as a science" and leads many to dismiss the work of figures, like Bauer, who fail to express their findings within the field's dominant rhetoric of mathematics.

Yet in the same article Lal also acknowledges that Bauer is not only no longer dismissed as a dissenting voice within his field, but that his contributions are being increasingly recognized and celebrated. Indeed, by the time of Bauer's death in 2002, his views were closer to mainstream development economics than those of Gunnar Myrdal, a frequent target of Bauer's criticism who received one of two Nobel Prizes awarded in economics in 1974, the same year that the NIEO was declared by the G-77.[10] Although the Nobel eluded Bauer, he was awarded the Cato Institute's first Milton Friedman Prize for Advancing Liberty in 2002.[11] As one article lauding the choice noted, many of Bauer's "formerly heretical insights" have become "part of a new conventional wisdom" (*Economist* 2002). In fact, Bauer anticipated many of the most celebrated themes in what Lal (1987) calls the "new political economy"; chief among these is a profound skepticism toward the state, frequently regarded as a self-interested bureaucracy inclined toward predatory behavior, and the argument that government intervention in market processes encourages rent-seeking dynamics that are inimical to productive economic activity and genuine development (Krueger 1974; Bhagwati 1982).

The fourth and final economist discussed in this chapter is Deepak Lal, whose essay "Markets, Mandarins, and Mathematicians" (1987) is cited several times in the preceding discussion of Bauer. Lal, an Indian-born economist who was educated at Oxford, served as a research administrator at the World Bank in the 1980s before becoming the James S. Coleman Professor of International Development Studies at the University of California at Los Angeles. In a body of work that extends from the 1970s through the present, Lal has sought to affirm what he calls the "liberal international economic order" or LIEO (a phrase presumably coined to contrast with the NIEO neologism), most notably in a well-received book, *The Poverty of Development Economics*. Originally released by the Institute of Economic Affairs, the noted British think tank, later editions of the book were subsequently published by Harvard University Press and MIT Press.

Among the topics that Lal addresses in his critique of postwar development economics is foreign aid. While demurring that he finds the debate over foreign aid exaggerated in relation to its importance, Lal nevertheless opposes such aid (or official development assistance, as it is generally known) on two grounds. Like Bauer, Lal first rejects the argument that the South has a right to aid from the North, since such a moral claim rests on the false assertion that there is an international community bound by a single shared ethical standard. Second, insofar as citizens of the North are concerned about the poverty of their counterparts in the South, there is no guarantee that transfers from rich-country taxpayers to the governments of poor countries will, in fact, benefit the poor.[12] Yet Lal notes approvingly of aid programs that come in the form of technical assistance, of the sort occasionally provided by the World Bank, for example, and his overall assessment of the dangers of foreign aid are far more measured than Bauer's vehement denunciations: "My conclusion, therefore, is that both the Left and the Right have trained their big guns on a target which at worst does little harm and at best can do, and has done, some good in the Third World" (1985, 57).

Echoes of another theme prevalent in Bauer's writings on foreign aid, Western guilt, can also be found in Lal's treatment of the subject. In a recent article warning of the "threat to economic liberty from international organizations," Lal offers a critical assessment of the World Bank, writing that the institution's "foreign aid arm—IDA—largely serves as an instrument for assuaging Western guilt. A useful analogy is with the money people give to street people, knowing full well that this will be used to fuel their drug habits or alcoholism, as it makes them feel virtuous" (2005, 517). Yet despite these apparently similar perspectives on foreign aid, John Toye emphasizes that Bauer and Lal differ in one important respect. Whereas Bauer rejects the value of aid entirely, Lal does not dismiss the possibility that it can be used to successfully leverage policy reforms. Indeed, when it is made conditional on the adoption and implementation of desirable policy, Lal views aid as the "catalyst which makes sound academic advice politically effective" (1993, 94).

Although Lal wrote little on the NIEO, a pamphlet that he authored for the Fabian Society in 1978 "seeks to provide some understanding of the historical and psychological roots of these [the G-77's] demands." Lal interpreted the South's aggressive posture in its confrontation with the North as an attempt by developing country elites to mobilize Western ideas (specifically national self-determination and equality) in pursuit of their own ends: "the elites of the Third World remain conscious of their country's vulnerability to any determined exercise of Western military power, and also of the potential threat to their positions vis-à-vis their subjects through subversion by the West. The fear that Western economic power, expressed through transnational corporations, could be used to exert pressure through economic destabilization to sow discontent between the rulers and the ruled, continues to be a serious worry for Third World leaders. Hence their strident calls for respect for national sovereignty and codes of conduct for multinationals" (Lal 1978, 7).

Lal's negative appraisal of the NIEO can be contrasted with a near contemporary assessment offered by Jagdish Bhagwati—a fellow Indian-born economist and Columbia University professor since 1980. In 1977, Bhagwati edited a volume featuring papers that had been presented at a May 1976 conference on the North-South conflict funded by the Ford Foundation. In his editor's introduction, Bhagwati noted the emergence of increasingly prominent critics of the NIEO who sought to discredit the G-77 agenda by denouncing developing country governments: "the argument that 'we cannot allow ourselves to be pushed around into giving aid to an undeserving, corrupt Third World' has several adherents in fashionable intellectual circles in the United States. This attitude of hostility to developing countries has been reinforced by the subtle but propagandistic caricaturing of the positions of developing countries in regard to the NIEO by conservatives and neoconservatives alike in the United States. *Ignoratio elenchi* is a favorite fallacy of intellectuals who are prominent, rather than eminent; it works very well in its intended purpose, but it must be exposed" (1977, 10). In the event it is not clear which "prominent rather than eminent" intellectuals Bhagwati is targeting in this passage, the reader is referred to a clarifying footnote: "Variations on this basic theme have appeared in articles by Daniel Patrick Moynihan, Peter Bauer, and others, in American magazines such as *Commentary*" (Bhagwati 1977, 23).

In the same chapter, Bhagwati offered a measured assessment of the South's position and the North's response to the G-77's agenda. Among the planks of the NIEO platform that Bhagwati considered most reasonable, and indeed necessary, was the regulation of multinational corporations. Concluding that "there is now clearly scope for a code of conduct on multinationals (MNCs) and their activities in developing countries," he notes that "until now the developing countries that worried about the MNCs were considered to be somewhat bizarre, if not depraved and corrupted by socialist doctrines." Referring to a series of events, including the dramatic overthrow of President Allende in Chile, Bhagwati goes on to note that "nothing works to cure one of illusions faster than to be proved naïve by unpleasant revelations. Thus the awareness seems to have grown in influential circles in both the developing and the developed countries that MNCs are a good thing but need to have their international conduct regulated by explicit codes and legal sanctions, including the extension of trust-busting legislation to internal operations in the social interest" (1977, 19–20).

It might appear surprising that an economist who has been one of the most eloquent and consistent defenders of the position that globalization and trade benefit the poor (Bhagwati 2005) could have endorsed what seems today to be a decidedly illiberal idea: the regulation of MNC activities in developing countries. Yet Bhagwati's views were widely shared in the late 1970s; Many observers agreed that the increasing size and influence of multinationals warranted some kind of international guidelines to regulate their activity, and several argued that a carefully crafted instrument could benefit multinational corporations as much as the governments that hosted them (McCulloch 1977; Davidow and Chiles 1978). In fact, as early as 1970, two defenders of MNCs had called for the creation of an "agreement based on a limited set of universally accepted principles" (Goldberg and Kindleberger 1970, 323). Although these were mainstream views, they were certainly not universal, and as the remainder of this chapter chronicles, the regulation of MNC activities via a United Nations code of conduct became one of the most contested planks in the NIEO platform.

The UNCTC and the Battle for a Code of Conduct

When the United Nations Center on Transnational Corporations was created in 1974 by the Economic and Social Council (ECOSOC), it was hailed as "a landmark in the development of the institutions needed for a New International Economic Order" (De Seynes 1976).[13] By that time, multinationals were figuring prominently in academic as well as political debates. The publication of Raymond Vernon's *Sovereignty at Bay* had focused attention on the implications of foreign direct investment in the Third World (Vernon 1971), and contemporary events, particularly in Latin America, generated anxiety about the extent to which powerful MNCs were meddling in the domestic affairs of host countries. But it was specific concern about the activities of ITT in Chile that led, in July 1972, to the creation of a Group of Eminent Persons appointed by the secretary general to study and report on the issue of multinationals. The twenty-member Group held three plenary sessions in the fall of 1973 and the spring of 1974, conducting hearings in New York and Geneva that included expert testimony from corporate and labor leaders, as well as from academics and advocates.[14]

In the spring of 1974, members of the Group drafted their final report, which relied both on the expert testimony given during the hearings and on a background document prepared by the UN Secretariat (UN pub. sales no. §.74.II.A.5). Among its key recommendations, the Group of Eminent Persons proposed the creation of a commission on multinational corporations, an independent research center to support the work of the commission, and preparation of a code of conduct that would regulate MNC activities in developing countries. These recommendations were reflected in the NIEO Programme of Action, which was adopted later that same spring, on May 1, 1974. This Programme "urged that all efforts should be made to formulate, adopt, and implement an international code of conduct for transnational corporations:

a) To prevent interference in the internal affairs of the countries where they operate and their collaboration with racist regimes and colonial administrations;

b) To regulate their activities in host countries, to eliminate restrictive business practices and to conform to the national development plans and objectives of developing countries, and in this context to facilitate, as necessary, the review and revision of previously concluded agreements;

c) To bring about assistance, transfer of technology and management skills to developing countries on equitable and favorable terms;

d) To regulate the repatriation of the profits accruing from their operations, taking into account the legitimate interests of all parties concerned;

e) To promote reinvestment of their profits in developing countries."

Within the UN Secretariat, primary responsibility for this task was assigned to the newly created Center on Transnational Corporations, which began its work in November 1975 with a staff of twelve. The UNCTC consisted of three branches: an Advisory Services division, which would assist developing country governments in their negotiations with MNCs; an Information Analysis division, which would gather data on multinational companies; and a Policy Analysis division charged with supporting the Commission's work on the Code of Conduct. The actual drafting of the Code was carried out by a working group composed of experts from the country-members of the Commission.[15]

Initially, expectations were high that work on the Code would be concluded quickly; one staffer wrote in a 1977 article that the Commission expected to finalize the Code in 1978 during its fourth session (Sauvant 1977a; cf. Ries 1977). As noted earlier, the idea of such a code had broad support at the time, inside as well as outside the Commission, even if there remained considerable vagueness or disagreement regarding what specific provisions it should contain. Although the U.S. representative to the United Nations reiterated his country's opposition to the New International Economic Order at the end of the 7th Special Session of the General Assembly in 1975,[16] Secretary of State Henry Kissinger nevertheless voiced support for a code of conduct regulating MNCs when he addressed the Assembly, suggesting it was among the least objectionable (if perhaps still not welcome) proposals on the table.

Although the effort to develop a code of conduct regulating multinationals was part of the broader NIEO agenda, the UNCTC (and the Commission which it served) nevertheless enjoyed something of an independent existence. Its status in this regard was underscored by the fact that the Center reported to ECOSOC, not UNCTAD, the body most closely identified with the G-77's position in the North-South debate. The Center's first director, Klaus Sahlgren, who came to the position from a post at GATT and led the Center until 1982, actively sought to avoid the CTC's identification with the NIEO project. Sahlgren viewed the Center's approach to the Code as less confrontational and more businesslike than work on the NIEO that was being conducted elsewhere at the UN. Reflecting years later on the Code project, Sahlgren remarked that the members of the Group of Eminent Persons, the staff at the Center, and the representatives and experts from different countries who served on the Commission agreed that it was important for the CTC to preserve "a neutral, impartial image in the eyes of its clients, which were both West and South, and also business. . . . The Code gave some concrete content to the NIEO. . . . Now personally I felt, and I still feel vindicated that the NIEO was a naïve mistake. It produced nothing and consumed a lot. Our [UNCTC] exercise could have been a signal to members—to the world, to put it a little bit pompously—that the NIEO could also mean something realistic and useful, like the code, instead of trying to introduce socialist concepts on the global scale" (Salhgren 2002).

During much of this early period, various corporate leaders (particularly from Europe) had a positive relationship with the CTC staff, as did the International Chamber of Commerce, which, like the major trade union federations, regularly sent delegates to meetings of the Commission. By the late

1970s, however, relations had cooled somewhat, and although meetings between corporate officials and members of the Center's staff conducting research on their enterprises had occurred with some frequency during the CTC's early years, a number of companies displeased with the results of these studies quit cooperating. A few went so far as to visit director Klaus Sahlgren, who listened to their complaints while defending the Center's independence (Mousouris 2003).

By 1978, the Commission had produced an annotated code of conduct, with brackets indicating passages on which consensus had not been reached (Feld 1980). According to Sotiris Mousouris, a longtime staff member at the Center, by the early 1980s Commission members had agreed to about 80 percent of the text: "We made fantastic progress in most of the provisions on labor, environment, human rights, on consumer protection, on obligations of home and host countries, on transfer pricing, on clarity of laws, on disclosure of information, and so on. One of the stumbling blocks that we never overcame . . . was the question of which law would apply in the case of nationalization and compensation. The host countries said national law. The western countries said international law. Other related problems were issues of jurisdiction, transfer of profits, settlement of disputes, and political intervention" (Mousouris 2003).

Several key disagreements about the status and scope of the Code were resolved during the eleven separate negotiating sessions that occurred during the first five years of the Commission's existence. There was, first, the fundamental question of to whom the Code would be addressed. Several developed countries proposed that the Code should outline responsibilities for host country governments as well as MNCs. The G-77 countries initially balked at this suggestion, which they felt would elevate multinationals to the status of sovereign states (Dell 1990). By 1980, the developed country-position prevailed, and the Commission proceeded to draft a two-part Code that outlined obligations for MNCs, as well as for the foreign governments that hosted them. The Southern countries also compromised with regard to the question of the Code's binding versus voluntary nature: While representatives to the Commission from the G-77 countries initially wanted observance of the Code to be obligatory, most quickly realized that only a voluntary Code would have any chance of success.

A more vexing issue arose when representatives to the Commission from the Soviet bloc insisted that their multinationals should be exempt from the Code. In their view, enterprises under the direction of socialist states operated according to different principles than their profit-oriented counterparts in capitalist economies. The OECD countries adamantly rejected this line of reasoning, and for years the status of the Second World's MNCs remained a contentious issue. Finally, the Commission confirmed in 1987 that the draft Code, upon becoming operational, would apply "to all enterprises that operate across national boundaries and in any field of activity, irrespective of whether they are privately owned, state owned, or of mixed ownership" (Dell 1990, 87–88). Thus, while the socialist countries agreed that their multinationals would be subject to the Code, they refused to call these firms corporations, leaving transnational enterprises as the compromise, if rather expansive, term.

Nationalization and expropriation proved more intractable issues, however. The OECD countries wanted a reference to what they asserted was "customary international law," including specific language about the right of foreign investors to "prompt, adequate, and effective" compensation. This position was rejected by several of the G-77 countries, whose representatives insisted that there was no consensus on what constituted "customary international law" in the first place. Furthermore, they argued that no international regulation regarding nationalization could supersede domestic law and be made binding on host country governments in the event of a dispute with foreign investors. This conflict fueled further disagreements. For example, the G-77 countries maintained that subsidiaries of MNCs should "insure that nationals of the host country can manage and operate the enterprise at all levels," but this position generated alarm within the OECD camp since it was "an obvious prerequisite for successful nationalization and/or expropriation by the host country government" (Feld 1980, 54).

By 1980, members of the Economic and Social Council were expressing dissatisfaction with the pace of the Code-drafting effort, noting in an ECOSOC resolution (1980/60) that "the progress made in the formulation of a code of conduct has not met the expectations of all." The same resolution went on to urge an expeditious conclusion to the process, concluding that "a universally accepted, comprehensive and effective code of conduct . . . will make an essential contribution to the new international economic order." Work on the Code continued, at least nominally, throughout the 1980s, but prospects for success were rapidly diminishing (Fatouros 1980; Hamilton 1984). Although agreement on two-thirds of the draft Code had been reached, the distance separating the Northern and Southern positions on the remainder was substantial.

When a full draft of the Code was finally completed in May 1990, a vote on it was scheduled for November of that year. However, the prospects for its adoption did not appear bright. In congressional hearings, U.S. Deputy Assistant Secretary of State Jane Becker testified that the United States would oppose the Code when it was brought to a vote at the United Nations. Characterizing the instrument as "obsolete," she noted that it would provide "only marginal benefit to the United States and American investors," and that it did not provide any protections that could not be secured through the more desirable options of bilateral investment treaties and GATT (BNA 1990, 1584–1585). The vote planned for November 1990 was postponed and rescheduled for 1991, but this deadline came and went as well. By this point, the Code was increasingly regarded as an anachronistic relic of the NIEO, "so divorced from reality in recent times that the attention of most Government representatives and international business leaders has shifted elsewhere" (Kline 1990, 2).

Negotiation of the Code was formally suspended in 1992. With the Commission that it was designed to support no longer working on the Code, the Center on Transnational Corporations became increasingly embattled, and later that year the UNCTC was dispersed.[17] Some of its staff were relocated from New York to Geneva and folded into UNCTAD's Division on Investment and Technology, where they helped launch the annual *World Investment Report,* a new flagship publication that reflected well the change in attitudes at the United Nations toward multinationals (Bair 2007).

One concrete outcome of the work done by the UN on multinationals is the impetus it provided for similar exercises. At the same time that the Code of Conduct on Transnational Corporations was being negotiated, UNCTAD was pursuing two other, more specific projects: the International Code of Conduct on the Transfer of Technology (begun in 1978 and abandoned in the early 1990s) and the Set of Multilaterally Agreed Equitable Principles and Rules for the Control of Restrictive Business Practices (adopted in 1980). Perhaps even more notable was the decision taken by the Organization for Economic Cooperation and Development (OECD) to pursue its own code project, resulting in the OECD Guidelines for Multinational Enterprises, which were adopted by member governments in 1976. This set of recommendations, which encourage multinationals to observe the policies of host country governments, was formulated not long after the UNCTC began its work on a Code of Conduct. Although the OECD guidelines differ in important respects from the UN draft code, there were several meetings between staff members at the UNCTC and the OECD in which ideas and information were exchanged. Even if the OECD project can, and to some extent should, be seen as an attempt to co-opt the UNCTC's work in this area, it is doubtful that the Guidelines for Multinational Enterprises would have been developed and adopted as rapidly without the pressure created by the United Nations' parallel efforts.

Yet if one can point to the OECD Guidelines as a positive legacy of the UNCTC, by the time of the Center's demise in the early 1990s, the entire Code-drafting effort was viewed by some as an unfortunate patrimony of the Cold War. For example, in Sandrine Tesner's recounting of the UNCTC's demise, the Code did not so much fail as fade away from lack of relevance. She describes the "quiet burial of negotiations on the Code of Conduct on Transnational Corporations" in 1992:

> Trying not to call undue attention to the failure of these discussions, the president of the 46th General Assembly reported that "delegations felt that the changed international economic environment and the importance attached to increasing foreign investment required a fresh approach." In fact, in the 1980s as negotiations had moved from the charged atmosphere of the NIEO, differences on the content of the code had progressively been narrowed to the point where a text acceptable to all parties was within reach. The legacy of these discussions, however, and the suspicion they inspired because of their historic linkage to the NIEO, made it preferable to give up the entire enterprise. In the 1990s, the CTC gave up its hostile tune to multinationals and began to praise their positive impact on job creation, technology transfers, and the facilitation of access to global markets by developing countries. (Tesner 2000, 23)

What is missing from Tesner's account of the CTC's demise is some sense of the context in which the need for a "fresh approach" became so apparent. While Tesner suggests that the abandonment of the Code project reflects "the changed international economic environment," she fails to note the attacks that had, for some time, been waged against the UNCTC and other elements within the UN associated with the G-77's agenda. Perhaps most notable among these attacks were the efforts of the Heritage Foundation discussed next.

The Heritage Foundation's United Nations Assessment Project

In 1973, Ed Feulner and Paul Weyrich, two young staffers working for a Republican congressman in Washington, D.C., decided to establish a new and different kind of think tank in the nation's capital. Feulner and Weyrich envisioned an activist organization with an independent research operation that would be dedicated to influencing policy debates in a way that the venerable and well-established American Enterprise Institute did not. Within a few years, thanks largely to seed money provided by the Coors Foundation, the Heritage Foundation emerged as the first and arguably most effective of a new breed of "advocacy think tanks." The organization's Board of Trustees, drawn mostly from the private sector, appointed Ed Feulner as president of Heritage in 1977.

By the time Feulner assumed the mantle at Heritage, he could boast of an impressive resume as a conservative activist. Together with William Buckley, Milton Friedman, and Donald Lipsett, he helped establish the Philadelphia Society in 1964—an effort that grew out of deep disappointment among conservatives over Republican candidate Barry Goldwater's defeat in the U.S. presidential election. The founders of the Philadelphia Society envisioned it as "an American version of the Mont Pèlerin Society, begun by F. A. Hayek in Europe twenty years before" (Edwards 1997, 186). A decade later, at the age of 32, Feulner himself would be made a member of MPS, and two decades after that, in 1996, he would be elected president of that organization.

The Philadelphia Society was founded while Feulner was completing an MBA degree at the University of Pennsylvania's Wharton School. Upon graduating from Wharton, Feulner decided to continue his studies as a nondegree student at the London School of Economics. Among the professors that Feulner would later name as influences on him during this period were Peter Bauer, whose seminars introduced him to new ideas regarding foreign aid for developing countries, "about which I had previously gotten the conventional wisdom from 'experts' like Walt Rostow" (Feulner quoted in Edwards 1997, 188). While studying at the LSE, Feulner also worked part-time at the Institute of Economic Affairs (IEA), the London-based think tank that was closely associated with the policies pursued by Margaret Thatcher as prime minister. The experience of working at the IEA reportedly taught Feulner about the power of ideas, supported by research, to shape political debates and influence public policy.

Although Feulner reported that MPS was the inspiration for the Philadelphia Society, it was the IEA's tactical and organizational model that Feulner embraced for the Heritage Foundation. In Hayek's vision, MPS was a long-term project: a loose but focused network of individuals dedicated to the development and debate of neoliberal ideas and their advancement in different spheres of society, including academe, the media and the private sector, as well as government. Despite internal disagreements about the extent to which MPS should intervene in a more public way in policy debates, the Society has remained a relatively low-profile organization, albeit with a considerable number of high-profile members. Instead of promoting its agenda via direct participation in the political process, MPS opts for a patient strategy of continually reexamining and renewing neoliberalism in thought and practice (Plehwe, Walpen, and Neunhoffer 2006). The Heritage Foundation, on the other hand, seeks a more immediate form of influence, paying paramount attention to the marketing of its ideas, chiefly to members of the media in a position to disseminate them, and to public officials, for whom Heritage prepares concise and unsophisticated summaries of key issues that can be digested en route to congressional votes—what Feulner refers to as the organization's "pioneering use of shorter policy papers for busy policy makers" (Feulner 2002, 73).

This self-conscious marketing of ideas to political figures culminated in Heritage's well-known manifesto, *Mandate for Leadership,* "a comprehensive blueprint for the incoming Reagan team" (Diamond 1995, 210). With an eye to what Heritage's leaders wagered would be a Democratic defeat in the 1980 presidential election, a team began work on the *Mandate* project in late 1979, around the same time that Ronald Reagan announced his candidacy for the Republican nomination. Consisting of twenty volumes and several thousand pages, the report outlined an inclusive conservative agenda for the new administration. Two days after Reagan's victory in the November 1980 presidential election, Ed Feulner and two of his colleagues from Heritage met with several members of Reagan's staff, each of whom was presented with a copy of *Mandate for Leadership.* Among them was Edwin Meese, one of Reagan's closest advisers and future U.S. attorney general, who had followed the preparation of *Mandate for Leadership* over the course of the preceding year while serving as Reagan's deputy campaign director. In fact, Meese's relationship with the Heritage Foundation continued for years after that 1980 meeting: Upon leaving the Reagan administration, he became the Ronald Reagan Distinguished Fellow in Public Policy and Chairman of the Center for Legal and Judicial Studies at the Heritage Foundation.

Several contributors to Heritage's *Mandate for Leadership* went on to positions in the new administration, including William J. Bennett, who would eventually serve as secretary of education (a cabinet post that *Mandate* had recommended be eliminated), future Interior Secretary James Watt, and James Malone, who would serve as the head of the U.S. delegation to the United Nations conference on the Law of the Sea.[18] While the close relationship between

Heritage and the Reagan White House was widely noted, the American Enterprise Institute could boast of sending an even larger number of alumni to the new administration. Among the twenty-seven members of AEI that went to work for Reagan was Jeane Kirkpatrick, who was named U.S. ambassador to the United Nations in December 1980.[19]

By the time Kirkpatrick became U.S. ambassador to the United Nations, Heritage had grown into an organization with forty employees and an annual operating budget of US$5.3 million in 1980 (Feulner 2002). The Foundation's staff more than doubled over the next five years to 100 employees, and its budget doubled over the same period as well, to $11.5 million in 1985. This amount slightly exceeded the entire operating budget for the United Nations Center on Transnational Corporations in the same year, as Heritage itself revealed: One of the many short position papers prepared by Heritage analysts (known as "Backgrounders") noted that the UNCTC received $11.4 million in funds for the UN's 1984–1985 budget cycle (Brooks and Pilon 1986).[20]

From the Foundation's earliest days, Heritage had called for a decrease in U.S. financial support for the UN. In addition to being an early proponent of reduced dues to the United Nations, Heritage analysts singled out specific organizations within the UN apparatus it considered prime candidates for budget cuts, including UNCTAD and the United Nations Educational, Scientific, and Cultural Organization (UNESCO). In 1982, Heritage launched an initiative called the United Nations Assessment Project, which, according to one policy analyst for the project, was developed in "response to the general perception in the United States that the UN was not very conducive to promoting U.S. interests" (*Multinational Monitor* 1989). Concerned about the use of the United Nations as an "institutional weapon" by the Eastern bloc and the Third World countries that were presumed to be under Soviet influence, Heritage urged the U.S. government to be steadfast in its opposition to the G-77 agenda.[21]

In a series of more than 100 Backgrounders, Heritage assailed the UN system, reserving its strongest criticism for UNCTAD and the UNCTC, which were seen as the leading promoters of an anti-American and anticapitalist agenda at the United Nations: "The United Nations has a long history of attacking the free enterprise system. A key element in this is the campaign against multinational corporations. . . . A leader in this attack is the New York-based Center on Transnational Corporations" (Heritage Foundation 1987). A 1983 Backgrounder pointed to the UNCTC as a prime example of Communist influence at the United Nations (Pilon 1983). Heritage argued that the NIEO was a vehicle for Soviet manipulation of the Third World and a grave threat to American interests. Furthermore, the misguided and ineffective policies its supporters promoted would simultaneously deprive the world's poorer countries of a brighter future: "Despite the collectivism, the Orwellian language, the sloppy scholarship, the increasing preoccupation with extraneous political issues, and the unconstitutional trend toward closed meetings, the most serious criticism of the UNCTAD is that, if adopted, the program sought by the radical leaders of the G-77 and the secretariat would actually make it more difficult for Third World nations to grow and develop" (Michalak 1984).

Among the several books that Heritage published as part of the United Nations Assessment Project is the provocatively titled volume *A World without a U.N,* featuring a foreword by former U.S. deputy ambassador to the United Nations Charles Lichtenstein. In a chapter discussing the UN and economic development, the authors warn that while "there is little new about NIEO emphases on grant aid, reduction of trade barriers, preferential market access for exports of developing countries, planning, and alleged deterioration of the terms of trade for raw materials exports . . . there is a new, disquieting strain in the NIEO proposals. Article 2 of the Charter of Economic Rights and Duties of States, for instance, is directed toward the regulation of transnational corporations and foreign investment and the authorization of nationalization and expropriation, with compensation to be determined by the courts of the nationalizing country" (Erickson and Sumner 1984, 3–4).

Heritage's own evaluation of its United Nations Assessment Project is highly favorable. Several specific actions that Heritage had championed, including U.S. withdrawal from UNESCO and the closing of the United Nations Center on Transnational Corporations were achieved. In a 1998 article urging the United States to pay some of its $1.3 billion in outstanding dues to the organization, the *Wall Street Journal* noted that the UN "has adopted more than half of the specific reforms demanded by the Heritage Foundation's United Nations Assessment Project in a series of 1983 and 1986 recommendations. Some of the unadopted reforms either are no longer relevant (e.g., an agency that was to be altered was eliminated) or have been partially implemented" (Kasten 1998). In fact, in his laudatory history of Heritage written to commemorate the Foundation's twenty-fifth anniversary, Lee Edwards recounts a visit to the Heritage Foundation's offices by then UNCTAD-president Gamani Corea, occasioned by the publication of a highly critical Heritage study. According to Edwards, "stories about Corea's 'dressing down' at the foundation raced through the

United Nations. Several months later, Corea resigned, his departure credited by observers to the confrontation at Heritage as well as the foundation's half-dozen pungent analyses" (Edwards 1997, 78).

Although it is not surprising that Heritage's leadership sees evidence of its influence on developments at the United Nations, some skepticism about this account of events is warranted. Corea's resignation from UNCTAD likely had as much to do with the embattled status of his Integrated Programme for Commodities as it did with any "dressing down" he received from Heritage staff. More generally, the Reagan administration was already warmly disposed toward many of the proposals that would be advanced by the Heritage Foundation's United Nations Assessment Project, including the closing of the United Nations Center on Transnational Corporations. In fact, U.S. opposition to the UNCTC was most likely a decisive factor in Boutros Boutros-Ghali's decision to fold the Center into UNCTAD as part of the reforms he made upon becoming secretary general in 1992.

Yet one of the lessons to be learned from the Mont Pèlerin Society's long-term vision of building the neoliberal movement is that rather than cultivate complacency, success should inspire the setting of new goals and the identification of new targets. Twenty years after the demise of the NIEO, the promoters of the LIEO are still waging numerous battles involving the United Nations. The director of foreign affairs for the Cato Institute recently published an edited volume, *Delusions of Grandeur: The United Nations and Global Intervention,* calling for a reexamination of the UN's role in numerous areas, including economic development. Deepak Lal has warned of the growing influence of NGOs at the United Nations, and concludes that the "web of multilateral organizations created at the end of the Second World War to promote a new LIEO ... are increasingly becoming the purveyors of a 'new dirigisme' " (2005, 517). In April 2004, the late American Enterprise Institute senior fellow and former U.S. ambassador to the United Nations Jeane Kirkpatrick testified before the U.S. Congress regarding the Law of the Sea Treaty. Urging against the Treaty's ratification, Kirkpatrick noted that during the 1970s, "the Treaty came to be viewed as the cornerstone of the New International Economic Order and of the associated efforts to use U.N. regulatory power as an instrument for restructuring international economic relations and redistributing wealth and power. The General Assembly is the institution through which the NIEO operates. It operates on the principle of one country, one vote" (Kirkpatrick 2004).

The transition from past ("the Treaty came to be viewed") to present tense ("the NIEO operates") in Kirkpatrick's remarks is instructive. To suggest that the NIEO functions today through the institution of the General Assembly is to reinscribe the danger that the G-77 agenda poses thirty years after it was declared at the Sixth Special Session, and in so doing to efface the dramatic transformation that has occurred within the international political economy in the intervening three decades. If this transformation seems obvious, the role played by networks of neoliberal intellectuals and organizations in securing it remains an ongoing debate to which this volume aims to contribute, if not resolve. While the success of the neoliberal revolution in the development sphere was fully secured only in the 1980s, and in the context of a Third World debt crisis that dramatically reconfigured the contours of the North-South debate, this chapter has emphasized the agency of individuals and organizations in articulating and promoting the policies and positions that were mobilized against the NIEO. These policies and positions continue to be marshaled by those invested in securing the liberal international economic order against whatever new threats appear on the horizon.

Notes

1. I am grateful to Will Milberg, David Levy, John Toye, and the editors for their comments on earlier drafts. I would like to thank the staff at the Modern Reading Room of the Bodleian library at Oxford University for assistance in accessing the papers of Sidney Dell, the directors of the United Nations Intellectual History Project for allowing me to consult oral histories of UN staff associated with the NIEO and the UNCTC, and those current and former UN staff in Geneva and New York whom I interviewed for this project.

2. These fears were shared by U.S. President John Kennedy. In part, they motivated the launch of what would become the Kennedy Round of tariff reductions through GATT, as well as the Alliance for Progress in Latin America (Toye and Toye 2004).

3. President Boumedienne's request for a special session of the General Assembly dedicated to raw materials and development was intended partly to defuse an earlier French proposal for a UN conference devoted exclusively to energy. Although the United States was not enthusiastic about the Algerian proposal, the Europeans embraced it, hoping that the meeting would provide opportunities to address developed country concerns (Gosovic and Ruggie 1976, 321).

4. As another symbolic demonstration of this perceived power shift, President Boumedienne's speech was given in Arabic at a time when it was not an official UN language.

5. Quotations taken from the text of General Assembly resolution no. 3201 (S-VI), "Declaration on the Establishment of a New International Economic Order." This resolution was adopted without a vote.

6. The policies and positions that Heritage advocates may be more widely recognized as conservative or neoconservative than neoliberal in the domestic political context. The relationship between neoconservatism and neoliberalism in the United States is contested by adherents and opponents of each school of thought. See Harvey 2005 for one discussion.

7. However, the Haberler Report did not endorse measures to raise or stabilize raw material *prices* (as opposed to export *earnings*). This issue, along with indexation, would prove a critical fault line in the negotiations over international commodity agreements in the decade to follow.

8. Similarly, Lal (1978, 10) argued that the rhetoric of equality mobilized by Third World states as a justification for the NIEO in part "represents the transfer of the Marxist notion of class and class warfare to the international scene."

9. This special issue of *Cato Journal* (volume 7, number 1), titled "Development Economics after Forty Years," amounts to a festschrift for Bauer and includes papers by three of the four economists discussed in this chapter (Bauer, Brunner, and Lal), as well as two other MPS members (Alvin Rabushka and Alan Walters).

10. The other Nobel Prize in economics in 1974 was awarded to Friedrich von Hayek.

11. Margaret Thatcher, who granted Peter Bauer his peerage while she was prime minister of Britain, was a member of the international selection committee for the Friedman Prize. The second recipient of the biennial Friedman Prize in 2004 was Hernando de Soto (see Chapter 11 by Mitchell in this volume).

12. Compare Lal's formulation to Bauer's oft-cited claim that aid is an excellent method of transferring money from poor people in rich countries to rich people in poor countries.

13. ECOSOC resolution 1913 created both a Commission on Transnational Corporations and a subsidiary body called the Information and Research Center on Transnational Corporations. The Center on Transnational Corporations was expected to "develop a comprehensive information system on the activities of transnational corporations by gathering information made available by Governments and other sources, and by analyzing and disseminating such information to all Governments." It was also charged "to conduct research on various political, legal, economic and social aspects relating to transnational corporations, including work which might be useful for the elaboration of a code of conduct and specific arrangements as directed by the Economic and Social Council."

14. During the course of these hearings, ousted Chilean president Salvador Allende was killed. Amid concerns about the role of ITT in the activities leading up to the military coup preceding Allende's death, the events in Chile had a sobering effect on the Group and its staff (Mousouris 2003).

15. The Commission on Transnational Corporations included representatives from Africa, Asia, and Latin America (who collectively comprised two-thirds of the Commission), while the developed world was represented by ten OECD members and five countries from the socialist bloc.

16. Although it rejected *the* new international economic order advocated by the G-77, the United States insisted it was willing to entertain discussions about *a* new international economic order, thus setting in motion a terminological dispute that continued at the UN for several years.

17. The UNCTC was officially disbanded in 1995 with passage of General Assembly resolution 49/130.

18. The Law of the Sea Treaty (LOST) was an NIEO initiative that the Reagan administration strongly opposed as a particularly misguided and dangerous element of the G-77 platform. President Clinton signed the treaty in 1994, but it has not been ratified by the Senate. See Eckert (1979) for an early assessment of the treaty and Bandow (2005) for a more recent statement of opposition.

19. Kirkpatrick returned to the AEI after leaving her post at the UN, becoming a senior fellow and director of the Institute's Foreign and Defense Policy Studies.

20. By 2000, Heritage's budget of $38 million represented well more than half the amount of that year's budget for the United Nations Conference on Trade and Development ($65.4 million). UNCTAD's budget had peaked in 1995 at $79.4 million.

21. In fact, the NIEO was the subject of one of Feulner's earliest publications for Heritage (Feulner 1976).

References

Bair, Jennifer. 2007. "From the Politics of Development to the Challenges of Globalization." *Globalizations* 4 (4): 486–499

Bandow, Doug. 1985. "Totalitarian Global Management: The UN's War on the Liberal International Economic Order." *Policy Analysis* No. 61, October 24.

Bandow, Doug, 2005. "Don't Resurrect the Law of the Sea." *Policy Analysis* No. 552, October 13; available online at www.cato.org/pubs/pas/pa/552.pdf; accessed February 2006.

Bauer, P. T. 1946. "The Working of Rubber Regulation." *Economic Journal* 56: 391–414.

Bauer, P. T. 1977. *Western Guilt and Third World Poverty.* Washington, DC: Georgetown University, Ethics and Public Policy Center.

Bauer, P. T. 1979. "Development Economics: Intellectual Barbarism." Pp. 41–58 in *Economics and Social Institutions: Insights from the Conferences on Analysis and Ideology,* Karl Brunner (ed.). Boston: Martinus Nijhoff Publishing.

Bauer, P. T. 1984. *Reality and Rhetoric.* London: Weidenfeld and Nicolson.

Bauer, P. T. 2000. *From Subsistence to Exchange and Other Essays.* Princeton, NJ: Princeton University Press.

Bello, Walden. 1998. "Bretton Woods Institutions and the Demise of the UN Development System." Pp. 207–227 in *Between Sovereignty and Global Governance: The United Nations, the State, and Civil Society,* Albert Paolini and Anthony Parvis (eds.). New York: St. Martin's Press.

Bhagwati, Jagdish. 1977. "Introduction." Pp. 1–24 in *The New International Economic Order: The North-South Debate,* Jagdish N. Bhagwati (ed.). Cambridge, MA: MIT Press.

Bhagwati, Jagdish. 1982. "Directly Unproductive Profit-Seeking (DUP) Activities." *Journal of Political Economy* 90 (October): 988–1002.

Bhagwati, Jagdish. 2005. *In Defense of Globalization.* New York: Oxford University Press.

BNA (Bureau of National Affairs). 1990. *International Trade Reporter* (October 17): 1584–1585.

Brooks, Roger, and Juliana Geran Pilon. 1986. "The United Nations Is Not Exempt from Budget Belt Tightening." Heritage Backgrounder #492, February 28.

Brunner, Karl. 1968. "The Role of Money and Monetary Policy." Federal Reserve Bank of St. Louis *Review* 50 (July): 9–24.

Brunner, Karl. 1996a [1978]. "First World, Third World and the Survival of Free Societies." Reprinted as pp. 143–171 in *Economic Analysis and Political Ideology: The Selected Essays of Karl Brunner, volume 1,* Thomas Lys (ed.). Cheltenham, UK: Edward Elgar.

Brunner, Karl. 1996b [1976]. "The New International Economic Order: A Chapter in a Protracted Confrontation." Reprinted as pp. 172–187 in *Economic Analysis and Political Ideology: The Selected Essays of Karl Brunner, volume 1,* Thomas Lys (ed.). Cheltenham, UK: Edward Elgar.

Davidow, Joel, and Lisa Chiles. 1978. "The United States and the Issue of the Binding or Voluntary Nature of International Codes of Conduct Regarding Restrictive Business Practices." *American Journal of International Law* 72: 247–271.

Dell, Sidney. 1990. *The United Nations and International Business.* Durham, NC: Duke University Press.

De Seynes, Philippe. 1976. "Transnational Corporations in the framework of a New International Economic Order." *CTC Reporter* 1 (December): 15.

Diamond, Sara. 1995. *Roads to Dominion: Right-Wing Movements and Political Power in the United States.* New York: Guilford Press.

Dosman, Edgar. 2001. "Markets and the State in the Evolution of the 'Prebisch Manifesto.' " *CEPAL Review* 75: 87–102.

Doyle, Michael. 1983. "Stalemate in the North-South Debate: Strategies and the New International Economic Order." *World Politics* 35 (3): 426–464.

Eckert, Ross. 1979. *The Enclosure of Ocean Resources: Economics and the Law of the Sea.* Stanford, CA: Hoover Institution Press.

Economist. 2002. "A Voice for the Poor." May 2.

Edwards, Lee. 1997. *The Power of Ideas: The Heritage Foundation at 25 Years*. Ottawa, IL: Jameson Books.

Erickson, Edward W., and Daniel A. Sumner. 1984. "The U.N. and Economic Development." Pp. 1–21 in *A World without a U.N.*, Burton Yale Pines (ed.). Washington, DC: Heritage Foundation.

Evans, John W. 1968. "The General Agreement on Tariffs and Trade." *International Organization* 22 (1): 72–98.

Fatouros, Arghyrios. 1980 "The UN Code of Conduct on Transnational Corporations: A Critical Discussion of the First Drafting Phase." Pp. 103–126 in *Legal Problems of Codes of Conduct for Multinational Enterprises*. Boston: Kluwer.

Feld, Werner J. 1980. *Multinational Corporations and U.N. Politics*. New York: Pergamon Press.

Feulner, Edwin. 1976. *Congress and the New International Economic Order*. Washington, DC: Heritage Foundation.

Feulner, Edwin. 2002. "The Heritage Foundation." Pp. 67–85 in *Think Tanks and Civil Society*, James McGann and R. Weaver (eds.). Piscataway, NJ: Transaction Publishers.

Goldberg, Paul, and Charles Kindleberger. 1970. "Toward a GATT for Investment: A Proposal for Supervision of the International Corporation." *Law and Policy in International Business* 2: 295–323.

Gosovic, Bratislav, and John Gerard Ruggie. 1976. "On the Creation of a New International Economic Order: Issue Linkage and the Seventh Special Session of the UN General Assembly." *International Organization* 30 (2): 309–345.

Gwin, Catherine B. 1977. "The Seventh Special Session: Toward a New Phase of Relations between the Developed and Developing States?" Pp. 97–117 in *The New International Economic Order: Confrontation or Cooperation between North and South?* Karl P. Sauvant and Hajo Hasenpflug (eds.). Boulder, CO: Westview Press.

Hamilton, Geoffrey. 1984. "The Control of Multinationals: What Future for International Codes of Conduct in the 1980s?" Geneva: Institute for Research and Information on Multinationals.

Harvey, David. 2005. *A Brief History of Neoliberalism*. New York: Oxford University Press.

Heritage Foundation. 1987. "The Center on Transnational Corporations: How the U.N. Injures Poor Nations." Heritage Foundation Backgrounder #608.

Kasten, Robert, Jr. 1998. "The U.N. Has Earned Its Back Dues." *Wall Street Journal*, September 23.

Kirkpatrick, Jeane. 2004. Testimony before the Armed Services Committee, April 8; available at http://armed-services.senate.gov/statemnt/2004/April/Kirkpatrick.pdf Kirkpatrick, Jeane.

Kline, John. 1990. "A New Environment for the Code." *CTC Reporter* 29 (Spring): 2–6.

Krueger, Anne. 1974. "The Political Economy of the Rent-Seeking Society." *American Economic Review* 64 (June): 291–303.

Laidler, David E. W. 1991. "Karl Brunner's Monetary Economics—An
    Appreciation." *Journal of Money, Credit and Banking* 23 (4): 633–658.
Lal, Deepak. 1978. *Poverty, Power and Prejudice: The North-South Confrontation.*
    Fabian Research Series 340. London: Fabian Society.
Lal, Deepak. 1985. *The Poverty of Development Economics.* 2nd ed. Cambridge, MA:
    Harvard University Press.
Lal, Deepak. 1987. "Markets, Mandarins, and Mathematicians." *Cato Journal* 7(1):
    43–70.
Lal, Deepak. 2005. "The Threat to Economic Liberty from International
    Organizations." *Cato Journal* 25 (3): 503–520.
Marshall, Peter. 1994. "Whatever Happened to the NIEO?" *Round Table* 83 (July):
    331–340.
McCulloch, Rachel. 1977. "Economic Policy in the United Nations: A New
    International Economic Order?" Pp. 17–52 in *International Organizations,
    National Policies and Economic Development,* Karl Brunner and Allan H. Meltzer
    (eds.). Amsterdam: North-Holland Publishing Company.
Michalak, Stanley. 1984. "U.N. Conference on Trade and Development Part 1:
    Cheating the Poor." Heritage Backgrounder #348, May 3.
Michalopoulos, Constantine. 2000. "The Role of Special and Differential
    Treatment for Developing Countries in GATT and the World Trade Organiza-
    tion." World Bank Policy Research Working Paper 2388. Washington, DC:
    World Bank.
Mousouris, Sotiris. 2003. Interviewed by Richard Jolly for the United Nations
    Intellectual History Project (UNIHP), Athens, Greece, February 11. Interview
    transcript accessed in the offices of the UNIHP, City University of New York
    Graduate Center, May 2005.
Multinational Monitor. 1989. "The U.S. and the U.N.: The Heritage Foundation
    Point of View." July–August.
Pilon, Juliana Geran, with Stanislav Levchenko. 1983. "Moscow's U.N. Outpost."
    Heritage Backgrounder #307, November 22.
Plehwe, Dieter, Bernhard Walpen, and Gisela Neunhoffer (eds.). 2006. *Neoliberal
    Hegemony: A Global Critique.* New York: Routledge.
Prebisch, Raúl. 1950. *The Economic Development of Latin America and Its Principal
    Problems.* New York: United Nations Economic Commission on Latin America.
Ries, Charles. 1977. "The 'New International Economic Order': The Skeptics' View."
    Pp. 63–84 in *The New International Economic Order: Confrontation or Cooperation
    between North and South?* Karl P. Sauvant and Hajo Hasenpflug (eds.). Boulder,
    CO: Westview Press.
Rodrik, Dani. 1994. "The Rush to Free Trade in the Developing World: Why So
    Late? Why Now? Will It Last?" Pp. 61–88 in *Voting for Reform,* Stephan Haggard
    and Steven B. Webb (eds.). New York: Oxford University Press.

Rothstein, Richard. 1984. "Regime-Creation by a Coalition of the Weak: Lessons from the NIEO and the Integrated Programme for Commodities." *International Studies Quarterly* 28 (3): 307–328.

Sahlgren, Klaus. 2002. Interviewed by Yves Berthelot for the United Nations Intellectual History Project (UNIHP), Kaorppoo, Finland, July 19–20. Interview transcript accessed in the offices of the UNIHP, City University of New York Graduate Center, May 2005.

Sauvant, Karl. 1977a. "Controlling Transnational Enterprises: A Review and Some Further Thoughts." Pp. 356–403 in *The New International Economic Order: Confrontation or Cooperation between North and South?* Karl P. Sauvant and Hajo Hasenpflug (eds.). Boulder, CO: Westview Press.

Sauvant, Karl P. 1977b. "Toward the New International Economic Order." Pp. 3–19 in *The New International Economic Order: Confrontation or Cooperation between North and South?* Karl P. Sauvant and Hajo Hasenpflug (eds.). Boulder, CO: Westview Press.

Singer, Hans W. 1950. "The Distribution of Gains between Investing and Borrowing Countries." *American Economic Review, Papers and Proceedings* 40 (May): 473–485.

Tesner, Sandrine, with Georg Kell. 2000. *The United Nations and Business: A Partnership Recovered.* London: Macmillan.

Toye, John. 1993. *Dissent of Development: Reflections on the Counter-revolution in Development Economics.* 2nd ed. London: Blackwell.

Toye, John, and Richard Toye. 2004. *The U.N. and Global Political Economy: Trade, Finance, and Development.* Bloomington: Indiana University Press.

Vernon, Raymond. 1971. *Sovereignty at Bay.* New York: Basic Books.

Weller, Christian E., and Laura Singleton (2006) "Peddling Reform: The Role of Think Tanks in Shaping the Neoliberal Policy Agenda for the World Bank and International Monetary Fund." Pp. 70–88 in *Neoliberal Hegemony: A Global Critique,* Dieter Plehwe, Bernhard Walpen, and Gisela Neunhoffer (eds.). New York: Routledge.

Williamson, John. 2004. "A Short History of the Washington Consensus." (CP/OL; available at www.iie.com/publications/papers/williamson0904-2.pdf; accessed April 2005.)

II

How Neoliberalism Makes Its World

The Urban Property Rights Project in Peru

TIMOTHY MITCHELL

To Friedrich Hayek and his fellow neoliberals, the individualist and none-galitarian society that neoliberalism envisaged was not a natural condition. They did not expect it to emerge spontaneously once the powers of the state were reduced, as nineteenth-century liberals had believed. The neoliberal order was an economic and social project to be built by capturing and reorganizing political power. In postwar Europe and North America, however, they could not hope to accomplish this project by entering politics directly. Politics, they argued, is governed by the prevailing climate of opinion. The postwar world of ideas was inhospitable to radical individualism. To capture political power, they would first have to alter the intellectual climate.

Hayek proposed that political technologies could be developed to engineer changes in the general climate of opinion. These technologies had to operate on those second-tier thinkers he called "intellectuals." In contrast to the "scholar or expert in a particular field," he wrote in an essay published in 1949 in the *University of Chicago Law Review,* those who perform intellectual functions—principally journalists and school teachers, but also media commentators, film makers, writers of fiction, and many others—are "second-hand dealers in ideas" (Hayek 1949). These people control the distribution of expert knowledge to ordinary members of the population. The task of the neoliberal movement was to design its own network of dealerships. By altering the distribution of ideas among the second-hand dealers, neoliberalism would try to change the world.

Half a century later, the worldwide spread of neoliberal projects appeared to demonstrate the success of these new intellectual technologies. But what exactly were their methods? What kinds of sociotechnical arrangements did they develop?

As several contributions to this volume explain, an important innovation was the think tank. The prototype for this new instrument of intellectual engineering was the Foundation for Economic Education (FEE), established in 1946. The previous year, on a visit to the United States, Hayek had met Harold Luhnow, head of Volker & Co., the country's largest wholesale interior furnishings business.[1] Luhnow helped finance the creation of the FEE, set up in Irvington-on-Hudson, an affluent suburb of New York City, in March 1946. He also funded the Free Market Project at the Law School of the University of Chicago, established in the autumn of 1946, from which the Chicago School of Economics developed, financed Hayek's appointment to the Committee on Social Thought at Chicago, and supported the founding of the Mont Pèlerin Society in April 1947 (see Plehwe, Introduction, and Van Horn and Mirowski, Chapter 4, in this volume).

Backed with funds from corporations and their owners, usually channeled through private foundations, think tanks repackaged neoliberal doctrines in forms that "second-hand dealers" could retail among the general public. Doctrine was supported with evidence presented as "research," and was translated into policy documents, teaching materials, news stories, and legislative agendas. Ideally, the think tank was to be led by an "intellectual entrepreneur," who would energize the sales team and be its spokesperson.

In London in 1955, another businessmen, Antony Fisher, founded the Institute of Economic Affairs with Hayek's encouragement, following a visit to the Foundation for Economic Education in 1952. The IEA further developed these methods and then helped establish a number of think tanks in other countries including the United States. Many of these partisan think tanks were founded and run by members of the Mont Pèlerin Society (see Plehwe and Walpen 2006 for an overview). The think tanks transformed neoliberalism from an intellectual philosophy into a set of practical political tools.

We should not assume that Hayek's own understanding of the role of intellectuals adequately accounts for the success in spreading the project of

neoliberalism. Hayek himself was indebted to the marketing and public relations methods developed by men like Fisher, who had a background in business and marketing.[2]

As the movement spread, it was also indebted to something more: an ability to transform its economic ideas and slogans into demonstration projects.

Like all sciences, economics faces the task of persuading people that what it
says is true. To strengthen its arguments, it must sometimes try and put them
to the test. But compared to laboratory sciences, it faces a particular difficulty
in establishing empirical evidence. The sociotechnical world that economics
describes cannot easily be rendered testable. For this reason, compared to
many other sciences, economics attaches less importance to having clear tests
and often seems to pride itself on not needing them. The manipulation of statistical data provides the most common way around this difficulty, while experimental economics offers a more specialized approach. Occasionally, however, academic economics employs another method for advancing and testing
its arguments. It is sometimes able to use the world as a laboratory.

When academic economics conducts experiments in the world-as-laboratory,
it encounters an interesting situation. The world is already full of economic experiments. These occur on a variety of scales, from the trial of a new commercial
product to the design of an entire market mechanism (Guala 2001; Callon 2007;
Muniesa and Callon 2007).

Among the most ambitious forms of economic experiment in recent decades have been the attempts in numerous countries to reformat the economy
as a whole, in programs of neoliberal economic restructuring (see Fischer,
Chapter 9 in this volume). The scale of these experiments offers unusual opportunities for putting economic arguments to the test. Such tests are interesting, not so much for the facts they confirm—the evidence never seems
complete enough to establish conclusive arguments—as for what they tell us
about how neoliberal facts about the economy are produced. They illuminate
the relationship between neoliberal economics and the object it studies—
including the role of think tanks and other intermediaries in this relationship.

Elsewhere I have argued that the idea of "the economy" is a surprisingly recent product of sociotechnical practice, emerging only in the mid-twentieth
century (Mitchell 1998, 2002, 2005a, 2008). Before then, economists did not
use the word "economy" in its modern sense. From around the 1930s, new
forms of consumption, marketing, business management, government planning, financial flows, colonial administration, and statistical work brought

into being a world that for the first time could be measured and calculated as though it were a free-standing object, the economy. Economics claimed only to describe this object, but in fact it participated in producing it. Its contribution was to help devise the forms of calculation in terms of which sociotechnical practice was increasingly organized. Economics, it follows, is important not just for what it says but for what it does.

The neoliberal movement has a peculiar relationship to wartime and postwar national projects for making "the economy." On the one hand, neoliberalism came into being as a movement of opposition toward "the economy." If the economy was in part a product of Keynesian and other forms of planning, calculation, and management, neoliberalism opposed this with the rival concept of the market, whose principles of operation were portrayed as an alternative to the administrative management of "the economy." On the other hand, as neoliberal think tanks proliferated and began to circulate and promote the ideas of neoliberal academic economists, they became increasingly involved in economic experiments in the world at large. These experiments took place in a world already formatted with the help of economic expertise, whether in the form of earlier Keynesian economic planning or of more recent neoliberal projects.

What is the relationship between these varieties of economic knowledge? How does the production of neoliberal economic knowledge assist in the wider circulation of neoliberal projects? Conversely, how does the unfolding of neoliberal experiments in the world help produce the experimental knowledge of the academy? And what is the role of neoliberal think tanks as intermediaries in this process?

In December 2004 the World Bank reported the completion of an ambitious and widely discussed economic experiment, the Urban Property Rights Project in Peru (World Bank 2004). The project addressed an issue found in almost every country of the global South. Large populations migrating from the countryside to the city have housed themselves by building neighborhoods that are not planned or regulated by the state. In many countries, these informal neighborhoods contain a majority of the urban population, most living without adequate municipal services or sufficient access to employment and income. The World Bank supported a crash program in Peru to transform the country's informal urban neighborhoods into legal, state-regulated housing.

The plan was to set up a simple procedure for registering the ownership of property and thereby turn millions of people into the formal owners of the homes they had built.

The plan promised much more than the regularization of property rights. The government and the World Bank believed that creating property owners offered a simple and inexpensive means to end widespread poverty. Holding formal title would enable ordinary people to use their homes as collateral for loans. The loans would provide capital for starting small enterprises, enabling every household to produce potential entrepreneurs. Formalization would also increase the value of the property, in the case of Peru perhaps doubling the price of the average 100-square-meter lot. By spending only $66 million ($38 million borrowed from the World Bank and the balance from its own revenues), the government would create $1.75 billion in economic benefits (World Bank 1998, 9).

The plan was developed from the work of the internationally known Peruvian entrepreneur and development economist Hernando de Soto. Founder of the Instituto Libertad y Democracia (Institute for Liberty and Democracy) in Lima, de Soto became the country's leading advocate of neoliberal reorganization in the 1980s and 1990s. He argued that informal housing and other forms of unregulated and illegal economic activity were a symptom not of economic backwardness but of overregulation by the state. Simplifying the process of registering property ownership would turn dead assets into live capital and transform every home owner into a capitalist entrepreneur (de Soto 1989, 2000).

The Institute for Liberty and Democracy carried out a pilot property-registration program in Lima in 1992–1994, building on an earlier U.S.-funded scheme it had introduced in the 1980s. The 1992–1994 program gave formal title to about 200,000 households. Two years later, the government launched a comprehensive urban titling program, targeting the capital and seven other cities, which together accounted for about 90 percent of the country's informal housing (World Bank 1998, 5). It later extended the program to another six urban areas. When completed in 2004, the program had registered a further 1.2 million households and issued 920,000 property titles (World Bank 2004, 8).

The program appeared to have a remarkable effect, though not the one anticipated. A number of studies of the Peruvian experiment found that property titles had no significant effect on access among the poor to business credit (Cockburn 2000; Field and Torero 2002; and other studies cited there).[3] Mortgage lending did eventually increase, but only after a new government abandoned de

Soto's neoliberal prescriptions and began to subsidize low-income mortgages.[4] However, another study found an unexpected change in the economic lives of those who became formal property owners: they began to work harder.

Obtaining title to their property seemed to increase the average number of hours that members of a household worked by 17 percent. The data suggested that over time, as the effect of titling intensified, the total number of hours worked might increase by 40 percent. There was also a redistribution of labor from work within the home to employment outside and from children to adults. Property titling was associated with a 47 percent decrease in the number of hours worked inside the house and a 28 percent reduction in the use of child labor (Field 2003, 3, 37).

To explain these findings, the author of the study, Erica Field, hypothesized that acquiring formal title freed members of the household to spend more time outside the home, based on the intuition that in the absence of a formal title people had to stay home to protect their property from being seized by others. A further intuition suggested that adults had a comparative advantage over children in defending the home, so in the absence of secure property rights children were more likely to be sent out to work. Once the property was secured with a formal title, children could stay home and adults could take over children's jobs outside the household (Field 2003, 7–8, 12).

The reports of this unexpected but remarkable consequence of property ownership were widely circulated. Alan Krueger, a senior economist at Princeton University, devoted a column in the business section of the *New York Times* to the paper's findings (Krueger 2003). Another well-known economist, Bradford DeLong at the University of California, Berkeley, singled out the same paper on his widely read weblog for making him "extremely hopeful about the future of economics" (DeLong 2003).[5]

For reasons I will explain, the paper's findings concerning the impact of property titling seem to me implausible. I will suggest a number of features of Peruvian politics and urban settlement that offer alternative explanations for the apparent increase in hours worked—explanations more closely linked to the implementation of the titling program and to its location within the wider networks of neoliberalism.

There were particular reasons why the research on the Peruvian experiment was able to reach such extraordinary conclusions. The research experiment was made possible by the political experiment that it studied. The political actors and the practical arrangements that shaped the property rights experiment shaped the conclusions reached in the experiment on the experiment. Uncovering how this happened will enable us to understand the relationship between the experimental process of making economies and the making of economics.

There were also particular reasons for the popularity of the paper, despite the implausibility of its findings. First, it suggested that the Peruvian property rights experiment confirmed in an unexpected fashion a leading tenet of neoliberal doctrine: that the right of private property is the fundamental requirement for economic development and that securing this right and reaping its benefits can be accomplished by establishing the proper rules and institutions (North 1981, 1990). Since the 1960s, the neoliberal movement had nurtured what became known as "the property right paradigm" (Alchian and Demsetz 1973). At the 1965 Mont Pèlerin conference, held in Stresa in northern Italy, Armen Alchian presented one of the earliest papers on this theme, "Some Economics of Property Rights," derived from research on corporate decision making carried out at the RAND Corporation (Alchian 1961, 1965). Harold Demsetz presented his paper on "The Exchange and Enforcement of Property Rights" (1964) at the same meeting (Mont Pèlerin Society 2003). The property rights literature provided a way for economists to acknowledge the role of corporations, governments, and other complex arrangements of agency and power, by simplifying them into individual actors governed by rules of property. It identified the absence of private property rights or the existence of communal rights as a source of uncertainty and potential instability. This work of simplification prepared the ground for the development of New Institutional Economics, which became a major branch of neoliberal thought. The discovery that securing their property ownership appeared to enable the poor of Peru to escape insecurity and get on with making money was an exciting confirmation of these fundamental doctrines of neoliberalism.

A second reason for the popularity of the paper was that its claims about Peruvian property rights echoed the arguments of neoliberal opponents of development planning. Peter Bauer (1984), the leading neoliberal critic of state-led development, had been arguing since the 1950s that the citizen of the Third World is a natural entrepreneur, whose capitalist spirit is stifled by the policies of the colonial and developmental state. The main reason why people in the South are poor, Bauer and his followers argued, is that the state's bureaucratic regulations and its failure to protect property rights discourage people's natural propensity to work hard and make a profit (see Plehwe, Chapter 7, and Bair, Chapter 10, in this volume). (In 2002, the Cato Institute celebrated Bauer's influence by awarding him the second biannual Milton Fried-man Prize for Advancing Liberty. Hernando de Soto, who served on the selec-tion committee for the award in 2002, was the next recipient of the prize, in 2004.) As we will see, organizations within the neoliberal movement subse-quently made use of the paper on Peru as an important source of evidence for the claims of Bauer and his followers.

A third reason for the popularity of the paper was that it enabled the spon-sors of the project in Peru, the World Bank and the Institute for Liberty and Democracy, to ignore its failures and describe its outcome as a success. The World Bank had to face the failure of the project to produce its intended re-sult, an increase in lending to the poor. It seized on the fact that the project's beneficiaries appeared to be working longer hours as an unexpected but wel-come outcome (World Bank 2004, 11). Meanwhile, the Peruvian organization responsible for the original scheme, de Soto's Institute for Liberty and Democracy, had fallen out of favor in Lima and was pursuing opportunities to design and implement similar experiments in other countries, including Mex-ico, the Philippines, and Egypt. Unable to point to evidence that the original project achieved its promised outcome, the ILD cited the apparent increase in working hours in its efforts to win funding for further projects abroad (Insti-tute for Liberty and Democracy n.d.).

Among academic economists, including those not associated with the neo-liberal movement, there was one more reason for the popularity of the re-search paper. It seemed to offer a solution not only to the problems of the world's poor but to the problems of economists.

Like all scientists, economists face the problem of how to persuade people that what they say is true. The abstract quality of many economic models can sometimes make them useful as political blueprints but difficult in practice to put to the test. Setting up experiments using human subjects is expensive, com-plex, and unreliable. The alternative is to use what actually happens in eco-nomic life as information against which to test an explanatory model. But this too presents difficulties. Economists readily admit that not everything is observ-able or measurable. The changes in a variable whose effect one is studying may be due to a factor outside the model. And the agents whose actions one is study-ing come with different preferences and abilities, which can affect the outcome. For example, in the Peruvian case, those planning to work outside the home might be more inclined to seek property rights, resulting in a process of self-selection (Rosenzweig and Wolpin 2000; Angrist and Krueger 2001).

One answer to these problems is to set up a natural experiment, that is, a situation in which the sociotechnical arrangements whose effect one wants to study are altered as a result of some event or circumstance "beyond the immediate control of the investigator" (McGinnis 1964). The typical case is one in which a change in government policy or legislation affects some members of a population but not others, creating a variation in the data that is random; or, if not random, at least unconnected or "orthogonal" to any unobservable factors that might be affecting the outcome one is trying to explain (Rosenzweig and Wolpin 2000, 828).

Economists who praised and publicized the study of the effects of the property titling program in Peru found it valuable not only for what it discovered about property rights but for the way in which it made the discovery: by using the titling program to carry out a sophisticated natural experiment (Krueger 2003). A study that merely compared the hours worked by people who had formal ownership of their houses with those who had not received title could not produce convincing evidence of the effect of formal ownership on employment. The extra hours that formal owners worked might be due to any number of unobserved factors.

To avoid this problem, the study exploited the variation created by the fact that the titling program was carried out in different stages. It began in certain neighborhoods in Lima and in subsequent years spread in a staggered pattern to other neighborhoods of the capital and to other cities. Rather than compare those households that obtained property titles with those that did not, the study compared the number of hours worked in the year 2000 by households eligible to obtain title (whether or not they actually obtained it) in neighborhoods already reached by the program, with hours worked by those eligible in neighborhoods the program had not yet reached. As a precaution, the author also compared the difference in working hours between those *ineligible* to obtain title (because they possessed formal title before the program began) in neighborhoods reached by the program and those ineligible in neighborhoods not yet reached, and subtracted this difference from the first.

This was an elegant construction of a natural experiment. It made clever use not just of the household survey data collected by the Peruvian agency responsible for the titling program, but of the staggered timing and other features of the program itself.[6] Among those who singled out the research for praise were scholars such as Krueger and DeLong, who were interested in promoting not a neoliberal political agenda but more empirically supported arguments in the discipline, and in the case of Krueger, strong advocates of the use of natural experiments.

A natural experiment in economics is not an experiment carried out in nature. It is an establishing of facts carried out in a world that has been organized to make it possible for economic knowledge to be made. Latour refers to this organizing work as "metrology," meaning "the gigantic enterprise to make of the outside a world inside which facts . . . can survive" (Latour 1987, 251; see also Mitchell 2002, chapter 3). Experiments to establish the facts of economics depend on projects carried out in the wider world to create sites where economic knowledge can gain a purchase. These sites, though larger than an ordinary laboratory, are nevertheless quite closely defined spaces—specific neighborhoods in particular cities of Peru, the local offices of a development organization and a neoliberal think tank, the text of a survey questionnaire and its administrators, the offices of a parent organization in Washington that provides the funds. As Latour points out, to provide a secure site for establishing facts, these locations must be well connected to one another. The interconnections establish the routes along which facts can travel and be confirmed. They also shape what kinds of facts can survive. To understand the outcome of the academic experiment in Peru, we must understand these routes created by the larger neoliberal political experiment. This requires us to trace the wider story of the Peruvian reforms and the political and intellectual arrangements of which they form a part.

The Peruvian property titling experiment was the outcome not only of political forces at work in Peru, but also of the expansion of the neoliberal movement in the late 1970s and 1980s. In 1977, Antony Fisher helped William J. Casey, a Wall Street tax lawyer well connected in New York financial circles, establish the International Center for Economic Policy Studies, later renamed the Manhattan Institute (O'Connor 2008, 344). In the same year, Edwin Feulner, a later president and trustee of the Mont Pèlerin Society, took charge of the struggling Heritage Foundation, which he had helped set up four years earlier, and turned it into a productive neoliberal think tank. A third neoliberal organization, the Cato Institute, was established at the same time in San Francisco. The year 1979 marked an important turning point for the movement. The election of the Thatcher government in Britain brought to power several figures associated with Fisher's Institute of Economic Affairs. The appointment of the monetarist economist Paul Volcker as chairman of the Federal Reserve marked a similar turning point for the neoliberal movement in the United States (Harvey 2005). In 1980, an election campaign organized by William Casey placed Ronald Reagan in the White House and brought large numbers of neoliberals into administrative and policy-making positions.

At the same time, plans were being drawn up to extend the neoliberal movement to other parts of the world. On New Year's day 1980, Hayek wrote a letter to Fisher, to be used for the purpose of raising funds for this expansion. "I entirely agree with you," Hayek wrote, "that the time has come when it has become desirable to extend the network of institutes of the kind of the London Institute of Economic Affairs." With the hyperbole required for fund raising, he added that "[t]he future of civilization may really depend on whether we can catch the ear of a large enough part of the upcoming generation of intellectuals all over the world fast enough. And I am more and more convinced that the *method* practiced by the IEA is the only one which promises any real results." He continued: "In building up that institute and trying the technique elsewhere, you have developed a technique by which more has been achieved in the right direction than in any other manner. This ought to be used to create similar institutes all over the world and you have now acquired the special skill of doing it. It would be money well spent if large sums could be made available for such a concerted effort."[7]

By 1981, the fund raising was successful enough for Fisher to establish the Atlas Foundation for Economic Research. He took its name from *Atlas Shrugged*, Ayn Rand's novel of 1957 depicting the vital role played by experts and men of ideas and the virtues of the right of private property and of a self-interested individualism threatened by the powers of government (see Mühlbauer 2006). The foundation's goal was to coordinate activities and corporate funding among the network of European and American think tanks and to extend it by developing and financing a group of neoliberal organizations outside Western Europe and the United States. De Soto was to be the first and most successful outcome of this initiative.

In November 1979 Hayek had traveled to South America and addressed a conference in Lima on "Democracy and the Market Economy" organized by Hernando de Soto. At that time Peru was in the process of moving from military rule to civilian government. The conference was intended to show the strength of the democratic right in Peru and to introduce right-wing intellectuals and politicians to the ideas of Hayek and his leading Latin American dis-

ciple, Manuel Ayau (Bromley 1990). A Guatemalan businessman educated in
the United States, Ayau had discovered neoliberalism at the Foundation for
Economic Education, and in 1959 he established the first neoliberal think tank
in Latin America, the Centro de Estudios Economico-Sociales, in Guatemala
City (Weston 2001). He became a member of the Mont Pèlerin Society in
1964 and in 1978–1980 served as president.[8] As MPS president, he helped de
Soto organize the Lima meeting, and the meeting led to the founding of the
Institute for Liberty and Democracy the following May.

Hayek put de Soto in touch with Fisher. The Atlas Foundation helped set
up and fund the ILD, one of the first of a new generation of neoliberal think
tanks in the South. "Antony gave us enormous amounts of information and
advice on how to get organized," de Soto later recalled. "It was on the basis of
his vision that we designed the structure of the ILD. He then came to Lima
and told us how to structure the statutes, how to plan our goals, how to build
the foundation, what to expect in the short and long term" (Frost 2002, cited
in Chafuen 2004). Supported by the Atlas Foundation and by the wider neoliberal movement, de Soto emerged over the following two decades as one of
the movement's most effective entrepreneurs.[9]

Although described as a Third World intellectual discovered by Hayek in
Lima, de Soto already had links with the neoliberal movement and a long professional experience in organizations involved in international trade and development. His father had served as secretary to Bustamente y Rivero, president
of Peru from 1945 to 1948, then worked abroad with the International Labour
Organization in Geneva and Washington, and later served as Peruvian ambassador to Switzerland. De Soto grew up partly in Switzerland and the United
States and returned to Geneva in the mid-1960s to study at the Graduate Institute of International Studies (Clift 2003; Vargas Llosa 1987). The institute was
a stronghold of the neoliberal movement in Europe: William Rappard, who
co-founded the Institute in 1928 and directed it until 1954, recruited as faculty
both Ludwig von Mises and Wilhelm Röpke, two of the founding members of
the Mont Pèlerin Society. Rappard himself gave the opening address at the society's first meeting in Switzerland in 1947 (Ebeling 2000). De Soto then
worked in Geneva for the General Agreement on Tariffs and Trade, an organization with close ties to the Graduate Institute of International Studies and
whose policymakers early on included prominent neoliberals like Gottfried
Haberler (compare Bair, Chapter 10 in this volume), and then as executive
head of the International Council of Copper Exporting Countries (CIPEC),

the cartel organization formed in 1967 by the governments of Peru, Chile, Zaire, and Zambia. His supporters later included Stephan Schmidheiny, the billionaire heir of the Swiss cement and construction materials conglomerate Holderbank AG, who was active in neoliberal organizations.[10]

De Soto organized the meeting with Hayek and Ayau in 1979, the year he moved back to Lima. He tells the story of how he initially tried to set himself up in business as the representative of a group of investors who had purchased the rights to gold placer deposits. The mining enterprise failed after the investors went to review their concessions in the rain forest and found hundreds of local people already panning for gold without concessions (Berlau 2003). De Soto had discovered the problem of informal property claims. His contacts in the European and North American neoliberal movement offered an answer to the problem.

De Soto's European background and connections were seldom mentioned by his neoliberal supporters. His credibility and growing authority as a popular development economist came to depend on his identity as a neoliberal from the Third World, willing to describe the poverty of the global South as a self-inflicted injury unconnected to its relationship to the North.[11] "Instead of seeing the developing world as victims of capitalism, Hernando argues, 'We're inflicting our own wounds,'" reported Andrew Natsios, the administrator of the U.S. Agency for International Development. "Since he is Peruvian, he can make this argument credibly" (quoted in Kleiner 2004). The credibility turned De Soto into a very useful asset for the neoliberal movement: "During the years I spent with Antony [Fisher] at Atlas," wrote Alex Chafuen (2004), who succeeded Fisher as the organization's president, "I couldn't recall any conversation, any speech about think tanks, or any fundraising letter where he did *not* mention Hernando."

Atlas schooled de Soto in the advocacy and research tactics of the think tank. Further support and training came from related official sources in Washington. In 1983 neoliberals in the Reagan administration set up the Center for International Private Enterprise, housed within the new National Endowment for Democracy, to support organizations in the developing world advocating neoliberal political programs.[12] CIPE developed a "toolkit" that spelled out the tactics to be used: create an advocacy team, identify key issues relevant to the target audience, research the issues, establish a goal, create a message and an advertising campaign, form grassroots advocates, work with the media, and become part of the governmental process (Center for International Private Enterprise,

2003). The following year CIPE awarded its first grant—to support de Soto's Institute for Liberty and Democracy. To build popular support for neoliberalism, the ILD identified its political issue not as property rights in general, or as the property rights of mining companies or other corporations, but as the problem of informal housing. It began studying informal communities in Lima and contracted with the Lima municipal government to run a scheme to register informal housing. This was the start of the twenty-year program that culminated in the $66 million program financed by the World Bank. In 2003, reviewing two decades of efforts to support neoliberal organizations in developing countries, CIPE in Washington described this first project in Peru as still its most successful initiative (Center for International Private Enterprise, 2003).

Supported from abroad, De Soto's institute grew in size, developed its advocacy campaign, and inserted itself into the processes of government. During the administration of Alan Garcia, in the second half of the 1980s, it became directly involved in policy making. ILD lawyers drew up proposals for property-rights legislation and administrative reforms. To promote the legislation, the ILD produced television commercials that, borrowing from American state lottery commercials, invited people to dream: "What would you do if you had capital?" By 1991, the Institute had a staff of 100. Victor Endo, an ILD lawyer who later worked at the World Bank, claimed that the think tank became "a kind of school for the country. Most of the important ministers, lawyers, journalists, and economists in Peru are ILD alumni" (Kleiner 2004).

In 1987 the ILD published a book based on its research and reform programs, under the title *El Otro Sendero* ("The Other Path"), subtitled "The Economic Answer to Terrorism." Its authors were de Soto and two of his collaborators, Enrique Ghersi Silva, a lawyer-economist influenced by the Chicago law and economics movement (see Van Horn, Chapter 6 in this volume) and subsequently a member and director of the Mont Pèlerin Society, and Mario Ghibellini, a writer. De Soto's organization of the team that produced the book exemplified the role of the neoliberal intellectual entrepreneur. "My contribution was that of the businessman," he explained. "I set my goals, identified my limitations, and obtained the resources to achieve the first and offset the second" (De Soto 1989, xxix).

The neoliberal movement transformed the book and de Soto into an international phenomenon. In 1989 the book was published in English in the United States, with its marketing ambitions reflected in a new subtitle: "The Invisible Revolution in the Third World."[13] Ghersi and Ghibellini's names were removed from the title page, leaving de Soto as the only named author. The Peruvian novelist Mario Vargas Llosa, an ex-leftist converted to neoliberalism by de Soto, it is said, and about to become the U.S.-backed candidate in the 1990 Peruvian presidential election (Rothbard 1995, 323–33), contributed a preface. The book carried endorsements from President George H. W. Bush, Richard Nixon, and several others. The Atlas Foundation selected the book for its first Sir Antony Fisher Memorial Award, a prize named after de Soto's recently deceased patron. Promoted with prizes, reviews, and endorsements from the network of European and American neoliberal think tanks and foundations, it became a worldwide bestseller.

In 1990 Alberto Fujimori was elected president of Peru. De Soto, who had abandoned Vargas Llosa's faltering candidacy in favor of the populist rival, became his principal political adviser. The new government instituted one of the most drastic neoliberal financial stabilization plans yet seen, and the country fell into recession.[14] In 1992 de Soto resigned from the government, after a dispute over Fujimori's refusal to challenge the armed forces. De Soto pursued his pilot titling program in Lima, with Japanese funds; but by 1994 the breakdown of the relationship between the government and the ILD stalled the project. He looked abroad and embarked on work advocating programs to end world poverty through property titling in Egypt and several other countries (Mitchell 2007). He used this work as the material for his second book, *The Mystery of Capital* (De Soto 2000). With endorsements from Margaret Thatcher, Milton Friedman, and other prominent neoliberals and prizes from neoliberal organizations, the book became another international bestseller.

In March 1996 the Peruvian government passed a law on property formalization and established an agency, COFOPRI (Comisión de Formalización de la Propiedad Informal), to take over the ILD program and turn it into a national scheme, recruiting members of the ILD team. In 1998 the World Bank stepped in with a loan for the completion of the program. Research funded by the bank showed that the program had failed to achieve its goal: property titling had produced no increase in credit to the poor. Concerned by the failure, in 2000 the World Bank carried out a survey of informal neighborhoods. The survey's primary purpose was to encourage commercial banks to lend money to the neighborhoods by providing them with data that would reduce the cost of assessing the creditworthiness of low-income households. It was this survey that became the basis for the "natural experiment" whose extraordinary results attracted such attention.

This outline of the history of neoliberal experiments in Peru indicates the extensive work involved in reorganizing the country in ways that made the subsequent research experiment possible. Contacts were made, advocacy training was organized, funding was arranged, fieldwork was undertaken, goals were established, political alliances were formed, elections were won, technologies were put in place to survey properties and record their ownership, and questionnaires were distributed and returned. All this experimentation and programming belongs to the work of economics. It organizes the world in ways that provided neoliberal economics with the opportunity to produce its facts.

We can now return to the natural experiment and consider an alternative interpretation of its results, one that is more closely related to the implementation of neoliberal economic experiments whose wider history has just been outlined. This alternative account will follow the work of economics, examining the processes that make some facts possible and not others.

The reliability of the experiment's findings can be questioned for a number of reasons. First, no plausible evidence is offered to support the author's intuition that households without a formal ownership document have to keep people at home to defend the property from being seized by others, or that gaining this document suddenly removes the alleged need for self-defense. The intuition is backed only by an anecdote from a World Bank report and the writings of Hernando de Soto. Evidence available in the same World Bank documents suggest a contrary view: Peru's informal urban communities are described as having very strong collective organizations and a great variety of neighborhood mutual-help arrangements. Typically, a squatter neighborhood was formed by a single village, whose members would plan their relocation collectively in advance, allocate each family a building plot, and reproduce the communal associations of the village in the new location. None of this indicates a situation in which people feel so threatened they must stay home to guard their individual properties. (The World Bank also reports that titling programs tend to weaken these neighborhood associations.) Evidence from other studies suggests that the security of informal households depends on a wide range of factors and is not necessarily dependent on possession of formal title (Gilbert 2002).

What makes the intuition plausible is that it resonates with the work of neoliberal institutional economists like Douglas North and neoliberal theorists of development like Peter Bauer. It *assumes* that a world without formal property rights is anarchic and that once the proper rules are in place a natural spirit of self-interested endeavor will be set free. It derives its plausibility more from the reader's familiarity with certain texts of neoliberal economics than from any knowledge of informal communities.

Second, even if it were the case that giving people a title document frees them from the need to defend their houses and enables them to go elsewhere to work, there must be some source of all the new jobs. Yet the paper offers no explanation of the source of the demand for the dramatic increase in employment and no aggregate data to suggest it occurred. It would be difficult to find such data, as the 17 to 40 percent increase in hours worked outside the home was alleged to take place during the second half of the 1990s, a period of sharp economic decline.[15]

Third, the paper's argument depends on the assumption that the informal neighborhoods of different Peruvian cities are similar to one another and that the sequence in which the titling program entered different cities and neighborhoods was random. The staggered implementation that made a natural experiment possible must be unrelated to any local differences that might influence the extent to which people in different neighborhoods work outside the home. The paper claims to resolve the possibility of nonrandom city timing by including city-level fixed effects in the regression estimates. However, more than half the survey neighborhoods already reached by the titling program were in one city, Lima. Different neighborhoods of the capital were reached by the program at different times. If there were significant reasons for introducing the program in some neighborhoods of Lima before others and for later extending it to certain neighborhoods of certain provincial cities before others, and if there were significant differences among these neighborhoods, this might offer a more reasonable explanation for the outcome of the experiment. Simply allowing for city-level fixed effects would not capture the possible interaction among this range of differences.

The experiment was unable to test whether differences among neighborhoods were affecting the rate of employment outside the home. The author claims such differences can be ignored, on the grounds that eight district-level poverty indicators (rates of chronic malnutrition, illiteracy, fraction of school-aged children not in school, residential crowding, adequacy of roofing, and the proportion of the population without access to water, sewerage, and electricity) were similar for program and nonprogram neighborhoods (Field 2003, 16 and table 1). The author also claims that detailed information on the sequencing of the program in Lima supports this interpretation (Field 2003, 53, figure 1).

There are two problems with these claims. First, indirect indicators of poverty levels, such as residential crowding or access to electricity, may be unable to capture major differences between different kinds of neighborhoods with different patterns of employment. Later in this chapter I illustrate significant differences in the case of one city that played an important role in the survey results. Second, the detailed evidence on the sequencing of the program shows the opposite of what is claimed. There was nothing random about the order in which the political experiment was carried out.

Information in the paper itself shows that the first wave of titling (1992–1995) occurred only in the center of Lima (where squatters would be more established and employment outside the home more accessible), while most of the later titling was in outlying districts. The first wave also focused on the wealthiest informal neighborhoods (seventeen out of nineteen program sites were in districts of poverty level four, the level of least poverty, and the other two in poverty level three) (Field 2003, 53, figure 1).[16] The World Bank also says that the order was not random, but rather was based on "ease of entry" to the neighborhood. The bank's Peruvian program office reported that the order depended on "geographical situation, feasibility to become regularized, dwellers' requests, existing legal and technical documents, and linkages with other institutions involved in the existing obstacles" (Field 2003, 16n31, citing Yi Yang 1999). The paper places this information in a footnote.

This evidence suggests a number of alternative explanations for the fact that households in neighborhoods titled early worked more hours, and were more likely to be employed outside the home, than those that the titling program had not yet reached. The first wave of titling took place in the center of the country's largest city and in its least impoverished informal district. The location of the district and the relative lack of impoverishment provide several possible reasons why its inhabitants would find more opportunities for work, especially for work outside the home. The fact that the accessibility of neighborhoods and other aspects of feasibility of titling influenced the choice of subsequent areas to be titled offers a further reason for the employment pattern.

It is also significant that the first wave was a pilot project, run by de Soto's Institute for Liberty and Democracy rather than the government. It was intended to demonstrate the feasibility of a rapid formalization program, the centerpiece of the neoliberal reforms adopted by the new government of Alberto Fujimori, whom de Soto initially served as a principal adviser. Anxious to raise both domestic political support and international development funds for the program, there would have been clear incentives to choose the right kinds of neighborhoods for the demonstration. (De Soto's resignation from his position in the Fujimori government, in protest at the president's acquiescence in the alleged involvement of the Peruvian armed forces in the narcotics trade, occurred as the program began. So the pilot titling project had to push forward de Soto's political agenda against a particularly strong current.) As we will see, this was only one possible way in which the project's need to demonstrate the truth of neoliberal economic theory entered into the kinds of economic knowledge it later helped produce.

There is a further way in which the political implementation of the titling program affected the sequence in which cities and neighborhoods entered into it. De Soto described the regularization of property rights as *El otro sendero,* "The Other Path"—or as his book's subtitle explained, "the economic answer to terrorism." The reference was to the Sendero Luminoso, the Shining Path, the Maoist revolutionary movement that in the 1980s controlled large areas of the central Andean highlands of Peru. The populism of de Soto's neoliberal program, emphasizing the virtues of property rights for the poor, was intended as an answer to the more radical property redistribution programs of the revolutionaries—as well as to the problems of large-scale urban migration caused by years of warfare in the countryside between the rebels and the Peruvian armed forces.[17] The war against the Sendero Luminoso and its effect on one particular city shaped both the property rights experiment and the research experiment to which it gave rise.

Table 11.1 lists the cities in the order in which they entered into the program, and indicates for each city the number of survey households located in neighborhoods that the program had reached ("program") and the number in districts not yet reached ("no program").

The table shows that, following a pilot project in Lima (1992–1994), the titling program was launched in Lima and in Peru's second largest city, Arequipa, in 1995–1996 and 1996–1997, and then expanded to the other coastal cities (Trujillo, Chiclayo, Piura, and Chimbote). Only toward the end of the project was it extended to two locations in the interior of the country—Huancayo in the central mountains and Iquitos in the tropical lowlands of the Amazon. As a result, two-thirds of the households not yet reached by the program when the survey was carried out (1,200 out of 1,808) were located in Chimbote and the two inland towns, and half of these (600) in just one place, Huancayo.[18]

Table 11.1   Distribution of households in survey sample

City	No program	Program	Total
Lima	209	501	710
Arequipa	11	150	160
Trujillo	108	52	160
Chiclayo	131	49	180
Piura	149	51	200
Chimbote	480	120	600
Huancayo	600	0	600
Iquitos	120	20	140
Total	1,808	942	2,750

Note: Cities listed in order of timing of program entry.
Source: Field 2003, Appendix C.

Huancayo is a city with a different recent history from the other cities of Peru. Located in the central highlands, it is the regional capital of an area of rich farmland and impoverished, mostly Quechua-speaking farmers, which in the 1960s gave birth to both the Sendero Luminoso and Túpac Amaru revolutionary movements. By the 1980s, the region had become a continuous battle zone in the war between government forces and the rebels. Tens of thousands were killed or disappeared, and hundreds of thousands fled the countryside and settled in new informal neighborhoods in Huancayo and other towns.[19]

Lima and the other coastal cities, traditionally centers of the country's creole elite, had attracted rural migrants over a longer period, since the 1940s and especially the late 1960s. In many cases, the migrants were drawn by opportunities for employment offered by industrialization and the service economy. Huancayo had previously enjoyed a somewhat mobile population dependent on seasonal agricultural labor, but by the 1990s was flooded with impoverished refugees, cut off from the countryside, and living in neighborhoods subject to frequent military raids but beyond the day-to-day control of government forces (Stepputat and Sørensen 2001). While refugees also fled to the outlying neighborhoods of Lima and other coastal cities, in the informal neighborhoods of Huancayo they constituted a large majority of the population.

After the war ended in 1992, two kinds of projects were launched to address the problems in Huancayo.[20] First, international humanitarian organizations set up well-funded aid programs in the city, offering neighborhood soup kitchens, medical services, and other basic relief, and then job-creation schemes based on street-vending, artisanal labor, and other household-based income generation. Second, the government, anxious to draw the refugees back into the countryside, offered an alternative assistance program to support the regeneration of agriculture. The refugees took advantage of these rural incentives, but typically without moving back to the countryside. As the economic shock caused by Fujimori's neoliberal reforms made waged employment in the city increasingly difficult to find, a majority of migrants began looking to the countryside as a source of urban incomes. Households developed distinctive "mobile livelihoods," traveling to the villages to sow and harvest and for other occasional tasks, sometimes leaving behind one or two members of the household to mind the fields and animals, but the rest returning to the city (Stepputat and Sørensen 2001, 783–786).

The informal urban neighborhoods of Peru are not, it turns out, similar to one another. The migrant communities of Huancayo, the city that provided one-third of the survey sample of households in neighborhoods waiting to be titled (and zero percent of those already reached by the titling program), had a quite distinctive political economy. Impoverished by war and isolation, they had relatively few opportunities for daily employment outside the household. But in the 1990s a plethora of international NGOs supplied food rations and healthcare along with opportunities for home-based income generation, while farming provided urban households with an occasional but significant income. These arrangements suggest a more plausible explanation for how households of similar basic levels of nutrition, literacy, access to municipal services, and other indicators of relative well-being might have very different levels of regular employment outside the home. Taken together with the evidence regarding Lima—that the choice of neighborhoods and the sequence in which the program reached them was not random—and similar evidence for other neighborhoods in other cities, this evidence indicates the variety of explanations that arise from following carefully the implementation of the larger experiment. They are explanations that have nothing to do with the impact of formal ownership on an imagined need to stay home and defend one's property.

The Peruvian urban property titling program indicates some of the difficulties in constructing natural experiments. I have explored these difficulties in detail, not to fault a particular piece of research but because there is more we can learn from them.

First, the possibility of the natural experiment depended on a prior and larger economic experiment. The attempt to test the impact of property ownership on the propensity to work was possible because Peru had become the site of a large-scale neoliberal experiment in the formalization of property rights and the formation of entrepreneurial subjects. Millions of citizens and hundreds of thousands of households had been drawn into an experiment designed to demonstrate that a simple procedure for acquiring property rights would lead to a transformation in economic action and a dramatic improvement in well-being.

The idea of a "natural" experiment is misleading.[21] The so-called natural experiment typically depends on some prior political intervention—in other words, a project or an experiment of some sort, which arranges the sociotechnical world in a way that offers further opportunities for experimentation. This intervention must be beyond the direct control of the investigator. But that does not insulate the second experiment from the effects of the first.

Second, there is seldom only one big experiment going on. The details of the Peruvian case suggest that problems may have arisen from the intersection of a number of related experiments. On the one hand, there was the difference between de Soto's original pilot project, intended to achieve certain local and international effects by demonstrating not so much the long-term benefits of property rights as the immediate viability of a high-speed, low-cost, titling program. Such concerns may have shaped the selection of neighborhoods for the pilot program in ways that affected the later study. On the other hand, there was the intersection of different government and NGO programs to deal with the threat and after-effects of a revolutionary attempt to introduce a very different kind of property experiment. The government and the World Bank justified the titling program in part because the regulation of informal housing offered the state a way to assert its political authority over neighborhoods that had often been beyond its control during the years of attempted revolution. But in Huancayo, the city at the center of the region of insurrection, this project intersected in unpredictable ways with other more urgent interventions. The research experiment, in ways I have indicated, was unable to keep these intersecting experiments from shaping its results.

The property titling program in Peru, moreover, was not just a local experiment in neoliberalism. It was the outcome of a much longer project for the expansion of neoliberal economic arrangements, a project in which Peru and Hernando de Soto, as we have seen, became important relay points.

The outcome of the experiment does not end with the publication and circulation of its findings. These were now available to be folded back into further projects and experiments of neoliberalism, helping to secure the facts of economics.

The Foundation for Teaching Economics offers summer courses and other programs to promote the teaching of neoliberal versions of economics in colleges and high schools. It belongs to the same network of political organizations as the groups that first funded and helped to organize de Soto and the ILD. Its chairman, William Hume, is a member of the Heritage Foundation, and it is funded by groups such as the John Templeton Foundation and the Scaife Foundation, which have close ties to Heritage, the Mont Pèlerin Society, and many other organizations within the neoliberal movement.

In 2004 the foundation published on its website a complete teaching unit with ready-made lectures for use in high school classrooms, entitled "Is Capitalism Good for the Poor?" (Foundation for Teaching Economics 2004). The lectures were written by academic economists and reviewed for publication by two of the foundation's advisers, Douglas North and Milton Friedman. After an introductory lecture on concepts and terms, the first substantive lecture is entitled "Property Rights and the Rule of Law." The lecture begins by proposing that in developing countries the most significant obstacle to improving the lives of the poor is the absence of clear property rights. The rest of the lecture supports this claim by making three arguments: that property rights create incentives to invest, that they create the means of investing by providing collateral for loans, and that they further promote development by freeing people from protective activities so that they can engage in productive activities. As evidence for the first two points, it cites the work of Hernando de Soto, and for the third point the paper on urban property titling in Peru by Field.

The results of the natural experiment made possible by the programs of neoliberalism were written into further neoliberal projects. The organization of experiments, both caged and in the wild, would continue.

Michel Callon (1998) suggests that economics should be approached not as a form of knowledge that pictures the world but as a performative activity. Economics participates in what Callon calls the per-formation of the worlds to which it belongs, meaning both their formation and their performance, by helping to set up sociotechnical agencies/arrangements *(agencements)*. These agents and arrangements can be thought of as instances of a wider process of experimentation (Callon 2007). The sociotechnical worlds we inhabit are shaped by a continuous series of experiments. The experiments sometimes bring together the caged economics of the academy and the broader projects of economics in the wild—the economics of think tanks, foundations, corporations, development programs, government agencies, NGOs, and others outside the confines of academic economics. The economy itself, I have argued (Mitchell 2005a, 2008), came into being in the mid-twentieth century as the outcome of such projects of experimentation and calculation.

What happens when caged economics meets economics in the wild? One discovers that the world outside is not really a wilderness; it is more like a reservation. This discovery should not be surprising. As we have stated, a "natural experiment" in economics is not an experiment that takes place in nature. It is an experiment that typically takes advantage of certain programs, policies, or political-economic processes that have arranged the sociotechnical world in a way that makes experimentation possible. The investigator does not control these wider experiments, but he or she relies on them. Although the forms of this reliance will be different in different cases, the possibility of economic experimentation depends on the larger programs, which constitute what we call the economy. The experiment works on prior experiments.

This dependence has important consequences. The outcome of the experiment will be shaped by the earlier experiments that made it possible. Not every research project will produce facts as improbable as those examined here. But the prior experiments will make some kinds of data available and not others; will provoke certain intuitions that appear to make sense of them and not others; will suggest one set of arguments derived from these intuitions and not others; will give them the plausibility they need to circulate when other arguments would fail to impress; will provide academic economics with material to promote a more empirical approach to the discipline; and will offer routes to feed the conclusions back into further political projects and programs.

Academic economics often appears extraordinarily abstract and almost indifferent to the practical world of everyday economic calculation. My argument that the work of economics contributes to the making of the economy might appear to attribute excessive influence to such a discipline. The question of what economics does, however, can only be addressed by following it at work. Taking a particular experiment and tracing the narrow but well-signposted paths that connect it to other projects offers the way to a more expansive understanding of the work of economics in general and of the work of neoliberal economics in particular.

Notes

A preliminary version of this chapter was presented at a workshop at New York University on April 30, 2005, and was published as Mitchell (2005b). I am grateful to Andrew Barry, Michel Callon, Julia Elyachar, Vincent Lepinay, Tomaz Mastnak, Dieter Plehwe, Sarah Radcliffe, and Sanjay Reddy for their comments.

1. The business, William Volker & Co., was founded by Luhnow's uncle, William Volker, who died in 1947. The funding was disbursed through the family's foundation, the William Volker Fund (Blundell 2001, 34; Boutros 2004).

2. Fisher made his wealth by introducing the factory farming of chickens in Britain. He established Buxted Chickens, the country's first and largest manufacturer of prepackaged, factory-produced poultry, after his visit to the Foundation for Economic Education in New York in 1952. F. A. Harper, who had taught economics at Cornell University, advised Fisher to visit the university's industrial project for the production of chickens. The profits from Buxted Chickens financed the creation of the IEA (Frost 2002).

3. For a further discussion of the assumptions at work in de Soto's schemes, see Mitchell (2007). A former Peruvian banker (who was subsequently an official in an international development agency) offered the following explanation for the unwillingness of the banks to lend to the poor: "If you lend money to someone who has spent years getting $10,000 together to build a home, and then they mortgage it to start a business and it fails, are you going to foreclose and send three kids out in the street? You stick with the middle class instead, where the worst that happens is you take away their TV" (Kleiner 2004).

4. The government of Alejandro Toledo, elected in 2001, introduced an emergency economic program, whose centerpiece was the creation of the Fondo MiVivienda, a state subsidy for low-income mortgages from commercial banks and finance companies, designed to create jobs in construction and simultaneously support the country's ailing commercial banks and construction industry. (See International Finance Corporation 2005, and Fondo MiViviendo n.d.) The World Bank (2004, 10) was then able to report, without explanation, a sudden increase in mortgage lending to the poor as though it were a consequence of its property titling program.

5. The paper was the main part of a doctoral thesis at Princeton. In a further sign of the positive reception of the research, its author subsequently accepted a faculty appointment in the Department of Economics at Harvard.

6. The data consisted of 2,750 households distributed across all eight cities where the titling program was introduced. The survey randomly sampled cluster units of ten households at the neighborhood level within each city. The number of clusters from

each city was based on the city's share of residents eligible to receive title. The survey did not record whether households had actually obtained title under the program (Field 2003, 15–16). This may be because the survey was carried out in response to the failure of property titling to increase the supply of credit to the poor. Its primary purpose was to promote lending by commercial banks and finance companies by collecting information that would reduce the cost of assessing the creditworthiness of potential borrowers (World Bank 2004, 12–13).

7. F. A. Hayek Letter to Antony Fisher, January 1, 1980. Available at www.atlasusa .org/pdf/2004yearinreview.pdf.

8. In 1972 Ayau founded the Universidad Francisco Marroquin in Guatemala City, a private university dedicated to the teaching of neoliberal political and economic ideas (Weston 2001).

9. For a discussion of de Soto's entrepreneurship beyond Peru, see Mitchell 2007.

10. Schmidheiny later funded the publication of a German translation of *The Other Path* (de Soto 1992) through the FUNDES Foundation, of which he was president.

11. The point here is not that de Soto's cosmopolitan background disqualifies his views. It is that his return to Lima and presentation as a person from the Third World gave his opinions a credibility and a usefulness to the neoliberal movement that they could not have had coming from Geneva.

12. The National Endowment for Democracy is ostensibly a nongovernmental organization, created and funded by the U.S. Congress. The Center for International Private Enterprise is one of its four constituent organizations and is described as a nonprofit organization affiliated with the United States Chamber of Commerce and funded by NED and the United States Agency for International Development (Lowe, n.d.).

13. A new U.S. edition, published in 2002 in the aftermath of the terrorist attacks of September 11, 2001, reverted to the original subtitle.

14. Following the 1990 "Fujishock," the proportion of Peruvians living in poverty increased to 54 percent; the percentage of the workforce underemployed or unemployed rose from 81.4 in 1990 to 87.3 in 1993; and real wages fell by 40 percent between 1990 and 1992 (Roberts 1996, 97).

15. Peru's per capita gross domestic product actually decreased in 1998 and 1999, by −2.2 percent and −0.8 percent (United Nations Economic Commission for Latin America and the Caribbean 2001, 69, table 55).

16. The paper wrongly states that the first wave "covers districts spanning poverty levels 2–4" (none are shown in level two districts) (Field 2003, 17).

17. After the Peruvian government began to adopt de Soto's plans, a series of attacks carried out against the ILD were attributed to Sendero Luminoso, including a car bombing of its offices on July 20, 1992 (de Soto 2002, xi).

18. When the program ended in 2004, Huancayo accounted for only 2 percent of the property titles it had awarded; Lima and Arequipa accounted for 67 percent (World Bank 2004, 5, map 1).

19. Peru's Truth and Reconciliation Commission, which published its final report in 2003, estimated that in the fighting from 1980 to 2000 between 600,000 and 1 million people were displaced and more than 69,000 were killed or disappeared. The Fujimori government was accused of using death squads and of other crimes against humanity. The Sendero Luminosa, which originally struggled for land reform and other social rights, became increasingly totalitarian, driving populations from their villages and creating prison camps that used forced labor (Norwegian Refugee Council 2004).

20. The U.S. Agency for International Development helped plan and fund both initiatives, as part of a $58 million program (1995–2002) for "Increased Incomes of the Poor" (United States Agency for International Development 1999).

21. Rosenzweig and Wolpin (2000) acknowledge the problem with the label by introducing the phrase "natural 'natural experiments'" to distinguish supposedly more natural arrangements, such as the differences among twins separated at birth—never merely a natural event.

References

Alchian, Armen A. 1961. "Some Economics of Property." RAND Corporation, P-2316. Santa Monica, CA: RAND Corp., May 16.

Alchian, Armen. 1965. "Some Economics of Property Rights." *Il Politico* 30: 816–829.

Alchian, Armen A., and Harold Demsetz. 1973. "The Property Right Paradigm." *Journal of Economic History* 33, no. 1: 16–27.

Angrist, Joshua D., and Alan B. Krueger. 2001. "Instrumental Variables and the Search for Identification: From Supply and Demand to Natural Experiments." *Journal of Economic Perspectives* 15, no. 4: 69–85.

Bauer, Peter T. 1984. *Reality and Rhetoric: Studies in the Economics of Development.* Cambridge, MA: Harvard University Press.

Berlau, John. 2003. "Picture Profile: Providing Structure to Unstable Places." *Insight on the News,* July 8. Available at http://www.insightmag.com/media/paper441/news/2003/07/08/Features/Picture.Profileproviding.Structure.To.Unstable.Places-440788.shtml; posted July 3, 2003, accessed May 11, 2005.

Blundell, John. 2001. *Waging the War of Ideas.* London: Institute of Economic Affairs.

Boutros, David. 2004. "The William Volker and Company." Western Historical Manuscript Collection in Kansas City. Available at http://www.umkc.edu/whmckc/Scrapbook/Articles/Volker.pdf; accessed March 4, 2008.

Bromley, Ray, 1990. "A New Path to Development? The Significance and Impact of Hernando De Soto's Ideas on Underdevelopment, Production, and Reproduction." *Economic Geography* 66, no. 4 (October).

Callon, Michel. 1998. *The Laws of the Markets.* Oxford: Blackwell.

Callon, Michel. 2007. "What Does It Mean to Say that Economics Is Performative?" In *Do Economists Make Markets? On the Performativity of Economics,* edited by

Donald MacKenzie, Fabian Muniesa, and Lucia Siu. Princeton, NJ: Princeton University Press, 311–357.

Callon, Michel, Cécile Méadel, and Vololona Rabeharisoa. 2002. "The Economy of Qualities." *Economy and Society* 31, no. 2: 194–217.

Center for International Private Enterprise. 2003. "How to Advocate Effectively." In *Annual Report 2003: The Business Case for Democracy: A Retrospective of CIPE's Accomplishments 1983–2003*, p. 30. Available at http://www.cipe.org/about/report/2003; accessed May 2005.

Chafuen, Alejandro A. 2004. "In Tribute to Hernando de Soto." Available at http://www.atlasusa.org/reports/chafuen_desoto.php; accessed April 3, 2005.

Clift, Jeremy. 2003. "Hearing the Dogs Bark." *Finance and Development,* December, 8–11. Available at http://www.imf.org/external/pubs/ft/fandd/2003/12/pdf/people.pdf; accessed April 1, 2004.

Cockburn, Calderon J. 2000. *Regularization of Land in Peru: Landlines.* Cambridge, MA: Lincoln Institute of Land Policy.

DeLong, J. Bradford. 2003. "The Future of Economics." Available at http://www.j<->bradford-delong.net/movable_type/archives/001385.html; accessed April 7, 2004.

Demsetz, Harold. 1964. "The Exchange and Enforcement of Property Rights." *Journal of Law and Economics* 7 (October): 11–26.

De Soto, Hernando. 1989. *The Other Path: The Invisible Revolution in the Third World.* English translation of De Soto et al. (1987). New York: HarperCollins.

De Soto, Hernando. 1992. *Marktwirtschaft von unten: Die unsichtbare Revolution in Entwicklungsländer.* German translation of de Soto et al. (1987). Zurich and Cologne: Orell Füssli Verlag.

De Soto, Hernando. 2000. *The Mystery of Capital: Why Capitalism Triumphs in the West and Fails Everywhere Else.* New York: Basic Books.

De Soto, Hernando. 2002. *The Other Path: The Economic Answer to Terrorism.* Reprinted edition of De Soto (1989), with a new preface. New York: Basic Books.

De Soto, Hernando, Enrique Ghersi Silva, and Mario Ghibellini. 1987. *El otro sendero: la revolución informal.* Lima: Instituto Libertad y Democracia.

Ebeling, Richard M. 2000 "William E. Rappard: An International Man in an Age of Nationalism." *The Freeman* 50, no. 1. Available at http://www.fee.org/publications/the-freeman/; accessed January 31, 2008.

Field, Erica. 2003. "Entitled to Work: Urban Property Rights and Labor Supply in Peru." Available at http://rwj.harvard.edu/scholarsbio/field/field.htm.

Field, Erica, and Maximo Torero. 2002. "Do Property Titles Increase Credit among the Urban Poor? Evidence from Peru." Mimeo. Princeton University, Princeton, NJ.

Fondo MiViviendo. n.d. "Misión y Visión." Available at http://www.mivivienda.com.pe/Informacion_Institucional/fmv_Mision.asp; accessed April 29, 2005.

Foundation for Teaching Economics. 2004. "Is Capitalism Good for the Poor?" Available at http://fte.org/capitalism/; accessed April 15, 2005.

Frost, Gerald. 2002. *Antony Fisher: Champion of Liberty.* London: Profile Books.

Gilbert, Alan. 2002. "On the Mystery of Capital and the Myths of Hernando de
     Soto." *International Development Planning Review* 24, no. 1: 1–19.
Guala, Francesco. 2001. "Building Economic Machines: The FCC Auctions." *Studies
     in History and Philosophy of Science* 32, no. 3: 453–477.
Harvey, David. 2005. *A Brief History of Neoliberalism.* Oxford: Oxford University Press.
Hayek, Friedrich von. 1949. "Intellectuals and Socialism." *University of Chicago Law
     Review* 16, no. 3: 417–433.
Institute for Liberty and Democracy. n.d. "Some of the ILD's Practical
     Achievements." Available at http://www.ild.org.pe/pdf/annex/Annex_01.pdf;
     accessed April 4, 2005.
International Finance Corporation. 2005. "IFC Increases Technical Assistance for
     Mortgage Markets in Central America and Peru." March 16. Available at http://
     www.ifc.org/ifcext/lac.nsf/Content/PressReleases; accessed April 29, 2005.
Kleiner, Art. 2004. "The Philosopher of Progress and Prosperity." *Strategy + Business*
     (Summer). Available at http://www.strategy-business.com/press/article/04203.
Krueger, Alan B., 2003. "Economic Scene: A Study Looks at Squatters and Land
     Titles in Peru." *New York Times,* C:2.
Latour, Bruno. 1987. *Science in Action: How to Follow Scientists and Engineers through
     Society.* Cambridge, MA: Harvard University Press.
Lowe, David. n.d. "Idea to Reality: A Brief History of the National Endowment for
     Democracy." Available at http://www.ned.org/about/nedhistory.html.
McGinnis, R. 1964. "Experiments." In *A Dictionary of the Social Sciences,* edited by
     Julius Gould and William L. Kolb. New York: The Free Press.
Mitchell, Timothy P. 1998. "Fixing the Economy." *Cultural Studies* 12, no. 1: 82–101.
Mitchell, Timothy P. 2002. *Rule of Experts: Egypt, Technopolitics, Modernity.* Berkeley:
     University of California Press.
Mitchell, Timothy P. 2005a. "Economists and the Economy in the Twentieth Century."
     In *The Politics of Method in the Human Sciences: Positivism and Its Epistemological
     Others,* edited by George Steinmetz. Durham, NC: Duke University Press, 126–141.
Mitchell, Timothy P. 2005b. "The Work of Economics: How a Discipline Makes Its
     World." *European Journal of Sociology* 47, no. 2: 297–320.
Mitchell, Timothy P. 2007. "The Properties of Markets." In *Do Economists Make
     Markets? On the Performativity of Economics,* edited by Donald MacKenzie, Fabian
     Muniesa, and Lucia Siu. Princeton, NJ: Princeton University Press, 244–275.
Mitchell, Timothy P. 2008. "Culture and Economy." In *The Sage Handbook of
     Cultural Analysis,* edited by Tony Bennett and John Frow. Thousand Oaks, CA:
     Sage Publications, 447–466.
Mont Pèlerin Society. 2003. Inventaris van de Algemene Congresdocumenten
     (1947–1998) / Inventory of the General Meeting Files (1947–1998). Ghent:
     Liberaal Archief. Available at http://www.liberaalarchief.be/MPS2005.pdf;
     accessed February 13, 2008.

Mühlbauer, Peter Josef. 2006. "Frontiers and Dystopias: Libertarian Ideology in Science Fiction." In *Neoliberal Hegemony: A Global Critique,* edited by Dieter Plehwe, Bernhard Walpen, and Gisela Neunhöffer. London: Routledge, 156–170.

Muniesa, Fabian, and Michel Callon. 2007. "Economic Experiments and the Construction of Markets." In *Do Economists Make Markets? On the Performativity of Economics,* edited by Donald MacKenzie, Fabian Muniesa, and Lucia Siu. Princeton, NJ: Princeton University Press, 163–189.

North, Douglas C. 1981. *Structure and Change in Economic History.* New York: W. W. Norton.

North, Douglas C. 1990. *Institutions, Institutional Change and Economic Performance.* Cambridge: Cambridge University Press.

Norwegian Refugee Council. 2004. *Peru: New IDP Law and Proposed Compensation Programmes Raise Hopes for the Displaced.* Geneva, Global IDP Project, Norwegian Refugee Council. Available at http://www.db.idpproject.org/Sites/idpSurvey.nsf/wCountries/Peru.

O'Connor, Alice. 2008. "The Privatized City: The Manhattan Institute, the Urban Crisis, and the Conservative Counterrevolution in New York." *Journal of Urban History* 34, no. 2: 333–353.

Plehwe, Dieter, and Bernhard Walpen. 2006. "Between Network and Complex Organization: The Making of Neoliberal Knowledge and Hegemony." In *Neoliberal Hegemony: A Global Critique,* edited by Dieter Plehwe, Bernhard Walpen, and Gisela Neunhöffer. London: Routledge, 27–50.

Roberts, Kenneth M. 1996. "Neoliberalism and the Transformation of Populism in Latin America: The Peruvian Case." *World Politics* 48, no. 1: 82–116.

Rosenzweig, Mark R., and Kenneth I. Wolpin. 2000. "Natural 'Natural Experiments' in Economics." *Journal of Economic Literature* 38, no. 4: 827–874.

Rothbard, Murray N. 1995. *Making Economic Sense.* Auburn, AL: Mises Institute.

Stepputat, Finn, and Ninna Nyberg Sørensen. 2001. "The Rise and Fall of 'Internally Displaced People' in the Central Peruvian Andes." *Development and Change* 32: 769–791.

United Nations Economic Commission for Latin America and the Caribbean, 2001. *Statistical Yearbook for Latin America and the Caribbean 2001.*

United States Agency for International Development. 1999. Congressional Presentation FY 2000: Peru. Available at http://www.usaid.gov/pubs/cp2000/lac/peru.html; accessed May 3, 2005.

Vargas Llosa, Mario. 1987. Preface to Hernando de Soto, Enrique Ghersi Silva, and Mario Ghibellini, *El otro sendero: la revolución informal.* Lima: Instituto Libertad y Democracia. Preface republished in English as "In Defense of the Black Market," translated by Alfred J. Macadam. *New York Times Magazine,* February 22.

Weston, William. 2001. "The Intellectual Portrait Series: A Conversation with Manuel Ayau." The Online Library of Liberty, a project of Liberty Fund, Inc.

MP3 audio file. Available at http://oll.libertyfund.org/title/972; accessed January 8, 2008.

World Bank. 1998. "Project Appraisal Document on a Proposed Loan in the Amount of US $38 Million Equivalent to the Republic of Peru for an Urban Property Rights Project." Report no. 18245 PE. Washington, DC: The World Bank.

World Bank. 2004. Implementation Completion Report (SCL-43840). On a Loan in the Amount of US $36.12 Million to the Republic Of Peru for an Urban Property Rights Project. Washington, DC: World Bank.

Yi Yang, Zoila Z. 1999. "COFOPRI, an Experience of Land Tenure Regularization in Informal Settlements in Perú: Regularisation Process Case Study at the Saul Cantoral Settlement." Paper prepared for the Advanced International Training Programme, Housing and Development, Lund Institute of Technology School of Architecture.

Postface

Defining Neoliberalism

PHILIP MIROWSKI

There are plenty of reasons to be wary of Wikipedia in the modern world, not the least of which is that some of the referees for this volume sternly warned me that it would be unseemly and undignified to make extended reference to it in a serious scholarly setting. I would like to begin here by suggesting that a quick bout of websurfing on Wikipedia can teach us numerous deep lessons about the ways in which neoliberalism has come to insinuate itself into much of Western culture since the events recounted in this volume, defining its modern incarnation. Our major theme will be: what holds neoliberals together first and foremost is a set of *epistemic* commitments, however much it might be ultimately rooted in economics, or politics, or even science. It didn't start out like that; but a half-century of hard work by the neoliberal thought collective has wrought a program that rallies round a specific vision of the role of knowledge in human affairs. Furthermore, Wikipedia itself owes its very conception to explicit neoliberal doctrine, something that I hope will eventually give all those apologists for its virtues pause. What may initially seem a cyber-detour is intended to illustrate how the efforts of the neoliberal thought collective have culminated in the last sixty years in a reasonably coherent and effective set of doctrines, even though when it started out, and for

sometime thereafter, it was very hard for Mont Pèlerin participants and their
fellow travelers to come to agreement over ideas and politics, much less settle
upon a stable common denominator that justified their existence and their
hopes for the future.

Just because my colleagues and I in this volume have hewn faithfully to the
canons of historical research in repeatedly pointing out crucial differences and
disagreements among our protagonists at various junctures, the reader should
not therefore conclude that there is no such phenomenon as "neoliberalism."
As Friedrich Hayek insisted in his opening address to the very first meeting of
the Mont Pèlerin Society on April 1, 1947, "Common work on the more detailed outline of a liberal order is practicable only among a group of people
who are in agreement on fundamentals, and among whom certain basic principles are not questioned at every step."[1] There were struggles and even purges
along the way (e.g., Hartwell 1995, chapter 5), but that should not disguise the
fact that Mont Pèlerin did eventually forge agreement on some fundamentals.
Indeed, we can and should come to appreciate the fact that the neoliberal
project managed to converge over time on a shared political philosophy and
worldview, despite the debates and struggles described in this volume. Prior to
this wrap-up, everything in this volume has sought to portray the neoliberals
in their process of Becoming; now it is time to come to terms with their
modalities of Being in the modern world. Much of this discussion revolves
around issues of content and meaning of the nature of knowledge; but we also
briefly consider how a "science studies" orientation can help to inform our
understanding of neoliberalism.

Wayward Wikipedia

In the following, I reproduce some excerpts from a rather heated and prolonged critique of the quest to compose an entry for the term *neoliberalism*
that took place within Wikipedia, the "free encyclopedia that everyone can
edit" in 2005.[2] The main home page is prefaced by the quote: "I do believe
this is the future of civil society."

> EDITOR: This term neoliberalism is used FAR too much in all the articles.
> I have never personally heard it used outside of Wikipedia. I do like the
> term insofar as it seems to highlight a good concept most people never use
> a specific word for, and in that sense is a good word. However, because of its
> seemingly non usage in real life, it can be really confusing. . . .

—Err . . . the term is widely used outside of Wikipedia, although I suspect mostly by its enemies rather than neutral parties. However, a quick web search will demonstrate to you that it is indeed a commonly used term to describe the attendant concept, and thus should remain as is.

—Is the term "neoliberalism" ever used by the neoliberals themselves?

—Yes. Many economists describe themselves as "neo-liberal economists."

—Really? Do you have any references? I have never found from the net any site in English which would describe itself "Neoliberal," and given my interests I would, if there would be many of them. There are a lot of sites criticizing neoliberalism, but none defending it or even representing it. . . .

—I think the problem here is that the term liberal has different meanings depending on the context. In the United States, the word liberal is generally used as a synonym for progressive, and is generally meant in a social context. In Europe (with the notable exception of the Liberal Democrats in Great Britain), the word tends to refer to a movement toward liberalization of markets. This is not a social, but instead an economic concept. . . .

—This is not entirely true. The term "neo-liberal" is not used by economists to mean the same thing as "liberal" in the classical sense. In fact, many economists will say something along the lines of "economically liberal" or "classically liberal" in order to specifically differentiate this worldview, which is what you describe, from a "neo-liberal" worldview, which does include both economic and social elements. A neo-liberal is someone who believes that the typical concerns of the liberal left—economic equality, etc.—can be furthered best within a free-market system. Please view the American Heritage definition for support of this statement. It is very difficult to argue successfully that the term "neo-liberal" is misused by Americans, since the term describes an American phenomenon. Western Europe generally uses the term derisively, to refer to American policy in general. In truth, it is a very vague term . . .

—Neoliberals call themselves "libertarians" in the USA, but the use has now spread a bit also in Europe . . .

—"Libertarian" is not the same thing as a neoliberal. Neoliberalism is an economic philosophy, whereas libertarianism is a socio-political philosophy that happens to include support for free-market economics. More importantly, most libertarians are hard-core *anti-interventionists!* What is called neoliberalism is the same as what most libertarians derisively call "liberventionism." . . .

Why on earth is Hayek on this page? Yes, Thatcher read his fine books and misunderstood them, but her policies didn't follow too closely to Hayek's bigger picture! If he is mentioned, at least it could be made clear that Hayek was a whig, a classical liberal.

—As the discussion of Locke in the article states, that paradigmatic classical liberal was a mercantilist: so state intervention in the economy was fine for classical liberals. Hayek liked to present himself as a classical liberal, but he was only able to do so by misrepresenting what classical liberals actually thought about the proper role of the state in the economy. That discussion has then went [*sic*] wrong. . . .

—If you look at the entry on liberalism in the Stanford Encyclopedia of Philosophy (which is written by experts) on the other hand, you will find that the case can not be made that "every notable thinker in the classical liberal canon after [Locke] aggressively fought for free markets." The Stanford entry says that "the seeds of this newer [welfare state] liberalism can be found in Mill's On Liberty." So there is ambiguity in classical liberalism about whether free markets are good or not.

—Hayek needs to be there since he was part of the meeting that first coined the term "neoliberalism" in 1938, and was to later form the basis for the Mont Pèlerin society. . . .

—Does anyone know whether Milton Friedman's *Capitalism and Freedom,* often cited as the font of neoliberalism, actually uses the term "neoliberalism"? Also, if it does, does anyone know whether this is the first use of the term?

—Actually, the term is considerably older. The first recorded usage (according to the Oxford English Dictionary) dates from 1898, when it was used by the co-operative economist Charles Gide to describe, in a somewhat pejorative manner, the neoclassical economics of Maffeo Pantaleoni. . . .

Wiki's entry associates "neoliberalism" with Robert Solow, Robert Mundell, Bradford DeLong, and Gregory Mankiw. . . . Milton Friedman is also mentioned as a "Neoliberal," however he has many times suggested abolishing IMF . . . I took off Stiglitz and Sen by this page, because, although they could be considered defenders of globalization, they are both strong opponents of neoliberalism . . . Prof Stiglitz is critical of "laissez-faire" policies, so to someone where neo-liberal = laissez-faire colonialism, he isn't a neo-liberal . . .

—Thus, isn't it fair to conclude that this is a political label rather then an existing entity? Something used for propaganda purposes but without contents?

—No. The difficulty in labeling individuals "neoliberal" is precisely an effect of neoliberalism being a diffuse and contested political ideology/project not tied to a single organization. That there are varieties of neoliberalism does not mean that the concept is entirely without merit. It is a political label and an academic label rather than an entity. This does not mean its use implies propaganda rather than simply a pejorative.

—How can it be a political label if no one labels himself as neoliberal? What you mean by neoliberal is just liberal? Do you know any neoliberal academic or politician which is a neoliberal icon or pundit? Which are his theses or the books where he exposes his program and what are the differences from the liberal one? Do you mean that Friedman is a neoliberal but he just doesn't know it?

Wikipedia's "discussion" function permits us to eavesdrop on America thinking out loud here; and it seems that many of these laborers in the cyber-vineyards treat politics much the same way they treat pornography: they can't define it, they haven't a clue where you can buy it, but they know it when they see it. It is not so much that they are sometimes wrong, as it is more distressing that they seem to have no way of knowing when and if they have ever gotten it right. And it's not just the linguistically challenged Americans who seem flummoxed, nor is it confined to the ranks of callow amateurs. Neoliberalism turns out to be anything but an easily and clearly defined contemporary political philosophy once we venture beyond popular representations, such as market radicalism, neoclassical economics, monetarism, or the journalistic mania for attributing coherent thought systems to politicians: Thatcherism, Reaganism, and Howardism, to name but a few. When the Zapatista movement called for global resistance against the NAFTA project in 1994 and sparked resistance to corporate globalization in general, neoliberalism was widely identified with U.S. superpower, unilateralism, and sometimes a forbidding borderless "global empire" (Hardt and Negri 2000). The puckish Slavoj Žižek has glossed neoliberalism as the doctrine, "You are free to do anything as long as it involves shopping." Leading intellectuals of the left thus have frequently, if unwittingly, contributed to the great confusion surrounding neoliberalism.[3] More recently, David Harvey (2005) has simply conflated neoliberalism with neoclassical economics. Earlier, Pierre Bourdieu (1998) and his followers popularized the notion of "pensée unique" or "strong discourse," where neoliberalism amounts to nothing more than a bland version of economism. Such misrepresentations would seem to suggest that neither the Austrian tradition in economics nor rational choice neo-institutionalism and its efforts to engage in the design and reform of a wide range of institutions would count as neoliberal. Various lawyers and political activists, who really should know better, treat it as an ideological movement that disempowers the state (McCluskey 2003).

And then there is the paranoia problem: just how pervasive is neoliberalism? One thing that is evident from their website is how much Wiki-worriers harbor dark suspicions about the extent to which economists, social theorists, and politicians purportedly "on the left" should legitimately be characterized as neoliberal. It almost smacks of a bad 1950s science fiction picture: Is Joseph Stiglitz *one of them?* How about Tony Blair? Or Bruno Latour? If the task at hand is to begin to clarify neoliberal scholarship and ideology, then simplistic notions of a placement on a left/right continuum clearly has not proven sufficient.

But before we turn to the task of defining modern neoliberalism, let us tackle the paranoia problem head on. To understand how Wikipedia can so egregiously misrepresent neoliberalism as a topic, we first need a better understanding of Wikipedia itself. And here, the first thing we discover is that many on the contemporary left seem to be flummoxed when it comes to grasping some basic facts of the modern neoliberal regime. Here is one representative example, chosen entirely at random:

> Mass media have acted as a pseudo-public sphere. . . . Wikipedia is surprisingly good proof that collaborative work by amateurs can provide balanced and reliable information. . . . A Wikipedia entry is a living and constantly changing organism, reflecting the current state of negotiations between people of vastly differing opinions on a subject. (Aufderheide 2007)

Our experience with the "neoliberalism" entry in Wikipedia should alert us that there is an element of wishful thinking in this portrait of the Net Information Commons as a political wonderland. Although one would expect the Internet to be chock-full of techno-utopian advertisements for itself, it would be more prudent to consult the critical perspectives of those who have had substantial experience as Wiki-workers, and can separate the hypostasis from the hype.[4] In the first place, Wikipedia in action is not some democratic libertarian paradise in cyberspace, but rather is predicated on a strict hierarchy, in which higher levels exist to frustrate and undo the activities of participants at lower levels.[5] The notion that "everyone can edit" is simply not true: many controversial pages would not even exist were interventions from those lower down in the hierarchy not blocked. But more to the point, by the criteria of the Wiki-workers themselves, 99.8 percent of all articles were neither deemed to merit "featured" nor "good" evaluations in 2006. The small proportion that was deemed superior often did not manage to maintain that ranking, however, since it is admitted that "featured" articles experience a 20 percent annual decay rate. In other words, high-quality articles tend to experience entropic degradation and backslide from the category as various Wiki-workers feel compelled to tinker with them. Although most Wikipedia activity is indeed volunteer work, the great bulk of that work is devoted to either (a) correcting ongoing vandalism, or (b) vicious infighting over the "correct" way to implement deletion policies. In other words, most Wiki-work is a huge Sisyphean waste of time, since the vandalism never stops, almost no entry converges to anything in particular (much less "truth"), and many "deleted" components have the vexing habit of recurring. As Scott (2006) puts it with poignant ruefulness, "There is no vacuum of politics. People who join Wikipedia because they are attracted to a space where it is uncouth to appeal to technicalities to lord over others and grab for power will then proceed to invoke technicalities and usurp power."[6]

Curiously enough, an important political lesson is to be learned here. From Schiff (2006) we discover that Jimmy Wales, the founder of Wikipedia, claims that he got the idea for the site from his reading of Friedrich Hayek's famous article on "The Use of Knowledge in Society," the ur-text of the Mont Pèlerin thought collective.[7] In other words, Wales subscribes to the precept that objective knowledge is a state rarely attained by any individual because his or her experience is subjective and idiosyncratic; that no individual is capable of understanding social processes as a whole; and that individual beliefs are frequently wonky beyond repair, but given appropriate (market-like) aggregation mechanisms for information, the system ends up arriving at the truth through "free" entry and exit. Furthermore, these aggregation systems themselves emerge willy-nilly through something resembling evolution, and not from the visions of some rational planner. Knowledge in this schema is frequently treated as though it were a disembodied "thing," and consequently human progress comes from the accumulation of information at various technological sites, which then serve to convey the relevant stuff to its decentralized user base.[8] In this version of liberalism, "Coercion is thus bad because it prevents a person from using his mental powers to the full."[9]

Wikipedia, says Wales, was intended to embody this epistemic orientation. Clearly, Wikipedia has been growing like gangbusters and is slowly sucking the lifeblood out of conventionally structured information sources like encyclopedias and newspapers; but in what sense is it actually a success? I cannot resist highlighting the irony that Wikipedia, the purported poster child of neoliberalism, cannot even manage to get its own internal entry on neoliberalism straight. But that irony is achieved at too low a price: after all, Wikipedia can't manage to get much of *anything* straight for very long (unless it is so arcane and dull that no precocious 12-year-old ever feels tempted to "edit" the entry). What it does manage to do is capture what passes for common knowledge of the median participant on the Internet at some specific point in time. The conviction that the truth "emerges" from random interactions of variously challenged participants in the precincts of Wiki-world (sometimes retailed in the popular press as "the wisdom of crowds") only holds water if we are allowed great latitude in the definition of "truth."[10] Neoliberals have great faith in the marketplace of ideas; and for them, the truth is validated as what sells.

The reader might object at this point: but Wikipedia is *not* a market and rejects advertising; that's what renders it so alluring to those inclined to rage against the machine! Here is where the political lesson comes home. One must start by inquiring how it is that Wikipedia has managed to displace so many other comparable websites that also attempt to aggregate information into bite-sized chunks for the masses. There are two fundamental considerations that interact to sustain and promote its growth, and both of them are indeed intimately related to neoliberal ideas. The first is: the secret to a successful website in the dawn of the twenty-first century is that it attract or expropriate *free information* and repackage it into formats that allow for capitalization and the creation of "derivatives" that can themselves be marketed. Sites like YouTube or Facebook or Twitter sucker people into providing free content, which can then be leveraged into something that can be retailed, such as advertising, personal information, marketing surveys, or surveillance. Wikipedia accomplishes this by appealing to the vanity of nonspecialists and autodidacts who are convinced their own lucubrations deserve as much attention as that accorded recognized intellectuals. But to tamp down the effulgent nonsense that emanates from those drawn to this narcissistic flame, Wikipedia then tries to banish all originality, insisting that everything be traced back to a "conventional" legitimate source, like encyclopedias, newspapers, or professional journals. This has been an inspired stipulation, since by construction everything that is legitimate on Wikipedia comes from somewhere else where someone else actually had to invest valuable time and resources into researching and vetting the results; Wikipedia gets it for free. The Wiki-workers who manage to extract or cut and paste this information in an era of ever-tightening intellectual property are themselves anonymous and slippery, so they can never be reined in or punished for their expropriations. The dynamic becomes more pyrrhic when one observes that the ease of access to Wikipedia has begun to destroy the subscriber base of those very same encyclopedias, journals, and newspapers. This practice still turns out to be central to the success of the modern neoliberal project in general, and not just in this specific instance.

The other important consideration involves the observation that access to Wikipedia is not sold for cash; or at least, not yet. But the success of Wikipedia is nonetheless traceable to how the site fits into the larger business plan of commodification of the Internet. In particular, the symbiosis of Google and Wikipedia goes quite the distance in explaining how it is that Wikipedia has been blessed with exponential growth. Google started out with a good search algorithm coupled to an essentially impossible goal: fast convenient access to everything on the Web. What Google needed for effective search was some other entity to preprocess the vast masses of dreck clogging the Web and cross-reference the refined results in such a way that it would show up early (usually on the first search page) on Google search results. (It was estimated in 2007 that Wikipedia entries show up in 95 to 97 percent of the top ten sites delivered in a Google search.) Conveniently, Wikipedia's policy of citing everything from other sources exactly meshed with Google's ranking algorithm. As in so many other instances, Google wanted access to such services for free. Thus Wikipedia materialized as a Godsend for Google's business plan. Moreover, the supposed Chinese Wall between Google and Wikipedia makes it possible for Wiki-workers to think they are squirreling away for the betterment of humankind, while Google positions itself to be the premier portal for information on the Web and the biggest corporate success story of the "New Information Economy."[11]

What are we to take away from this Wiki-interlude? First and foremost, neoliberalism masquerades as a radically populist philosophy, which begins with a set of philosophical theses about *knowledge* and its relationship to society. It seems to be a radical leveling philosophy, denigrating expertise and elite pretensions to hard-won knowledge, instead praising the "wisdom of crowds." It appeals to the vanity of every self-absorbed narcissist, who would be glad to ridicule intellectuals as "professional secondhand dealers in ideas."[12] In Hayekian language, it elevates a "cosmos"—a supposed spontaneous order that no one has intentionally designed or structured—over a "taxis"—rationally constructed orders designed to achieve intentional ends. But the second, and linked lesson, is that neoliberals are simultaneously elitists: they do not in fact practice what they preach. When it comes to actually organizing something, almost anything, from a Wiki to the Mont Pèlerin Society, suddenly the cosmos collapses to a taxis. In Wikipedia, what looks like a libertarian paradise is in fact a thinly disguised totalitarian hierarchy. In the spaces where spontaneous participation is permitted, knowledge in fact degrades rather than improves. But no matter, since the absolute validity of that knowledge is not the true motive or objective of the exercise, but rather subordination of the overall process to corporate strategic imperatives that provides the real justification of the format, as well as its economic foundation. It adds up to a "double truth" doctrine: one truth for the masses/participants and another for those at the top.[13] Something like the double truth doctrine also holds for neoliberal theories of democracy, as we shall shortly discover. It also holds for the notion of a "constructivist" approach to social reality.

One purpose of this book is to come to the aid of all those hapless Wikiworkers, and indeed, anyone else who seeks clarification for what we suggest has been the most important movement in political and economic thought in the second half of the twentieth century. As Plehwe explained in the Introduction, neoliberalism is not some figment of the fevered imagination of the left, but neither has it perdured as a canonical set of fixed doctrines (the right's mirror image of Mao's little red book). As editors, our own guiding heuristic has been that neoliberalism has not existed in the past as a settled or fixed state, but is better understood as a transnational movement requiring time and substantial effort in order to attain the modicum of coherence and power it has achieved today. It was not a conspiracy; rather, it was an intricately structured long-term philosophical and political project, or in our terminology, a "thought collective." The neoliberals were never parochial, so it seemed prudent for the collective represented by this volume to emulate their cosmopolitan stance. We have judged this necessary because neoliberalism remains a major ideology that is poorly understood but curiously, draws some of its prodigious strength from that obscurity.

In attempting to redress popular misrepresentations, my colleagues and I have provided chapters for an intellectual history in this book involving the careful study of some key people, key concepts, and key organizations, all of which have been of great importance for launching neoliberalism in different countries back in the 1930s and to eventually develop after World War II into the major rival of welfare state capitalism and socialist planning. Once identified, they then examined closely a selection of the debates the neoliberals organized in the course of the 1950s and 1960s to further develop and clarify their own understanding of proper approaches to philosophy, science, and knowledge.

In my view, it would be a mistake to regard neoliberalism as falling narrowly within the purview of the history of economics as such. The fallacy of identifying neoliberalism exclusively with economic theory[14] becomes apparent when we notice that the historical record teaches that the neoliberals themselves regarded such narrow exclusivity as a prescription for disaster. They engaged with a wide range of academic disciplines, without being card-carrying members of many of them, and they applied their preferred versions of social science to a substantial range of specific policy areas. Political theories of the state were also a major concern, especially in light of their familiarity with German and Italian doctrines unfamiliar in Anglophone circles. It is equally instructive to observe how the neoliberals rarely made a fetish of the distinction between theory and practice. In order to invoke some of the ways these debates were cashed out in political action, we conclude with some observations that shed light on the ways in which neoliberal knowledge has been mobilized in a few more recent decades to shape public discourse and policies at national and international levels, and thus to establish what is widely perceived nowadays as "simple common sense" in the realm of politics.

Perhaps I have been a bit too harsh on our Wiki-workers in this section; after all, they did ask one very good question: did the neoliberals ever use the term to refer to themselves? Contrary to the claims of our Wiki-workers, when the early MPS members cast about for a label to attach to the as-yet amorphous doctrine they had set out to construct, more often than not they did resort to the term *neoliberalism* in the early years of its existence.[15] In French, the term was being used by the circles around the participants in the Colloque Walter Lippmann in the 1930s.[16] Milton Friedman even used the term in the title of an early survey of the efforts of his comrades (1951). What has led so many subsequent commentators astray is the fact that most MPS members stopped using the term some time in the later 1950s. Indeed, at that juncture they ceased insisting that a rupture with the doctrines of classical liberalism was called for. This decision to support a public stance that the liberalism they championed was an effectively continuous political doctrine from the eighteenth century all the way through to their own revisionist meditations (such as endless paeans that it was all in Adam Smith) and therefore required no special neologism, turned out to be one of a number of precarious balancing acts performed in the course of constructing neoliberalism at the MPS. The historical fact that there nevertheless was a discernible rupture in doctrinal content over the course of roughly 1947–1980 is one of the reasons we have felt impelled to edit this volume. The outlines of that rupture are sketched in later in this chapter. The label "liberalism" has proven the bane of clarity of thought in political philosophy (Cerny 2008; Thorsen and Lie 2006). Nonetheless, we stand by the label of "neoliberalism" for the prognostications of the MPS thought collective throughout the later twentieth century because it is historically faithful to their own early behavior, and more to the point, it fits.

Mont Pèlerin as Criterion

It may seem that my co-authors have not yet confronted the Wiki-problem, since we have thus far neglected to "define" neoliberalism. This is because the premier point to be made about neoliberalism is that it cannot adequately be reduced to a set of Ten Commandments or six tenets or (N-1) key protagonists. First and foremost, it is better that it be approached as a "thought collective," a notion elaborated on below. Significantly, for being self-proclaimed champions of "individualism," neoliberals hardly ever tell their own story as though it were the narrative of one or two Nietzschean *Übermenschen*.[17] Instead of targeting just a few well-known neoliberal scholars (like Friedrich August von Hayek or Milton Friedman or Wilhelm Röpke or Jacques Rueff or James Buchanan) or high-profile neoliberal think tanks (like the Institute of Economic Affairs, the American Enterprise Institute, or the Heritage Foundation), we focus empirically on the central core membership that has conscientiously developed the neoliberal identity for more than sixty years now. If the target person or group bore any links to the Mont Pèlerin Society since 1947, directly or at one remove, then we count them as falling squarely within the purview of the neoliberal thought collective.

What do I mean by a "thought collective"? Clearly, here I am evoking the spirit of Ludwig Fleck's classic *The Genesis and Development of a Scientific Fact* (1979) and his notion of "a community of persons mutually exchanging ideas or maintaining intellectual interaction" (p. 39). Fleck gives a wonderful impression of the difficulty of a project such as this book, which is to provide a faithful historical account of the emergence of a novel intellectual formation: "It is as if we wanted to record in writing the natural course of an excited conversation among several persons all speaking simultaneously among themselves and each clamoring to make himself heard, yet nevertheless permitted a consensus to crystallize"

(p. 15). But rather than subscribing directly to his every tenet and definition, much less doggedly conforming to his "theory," I intend this homage to point toward the entire tradition of "science and technology studies," which treats epistemology as an ongoing social phenomenon rather than the static province of the isolated rational thinker. "A thought collective . . . is even more stable and consistent than the so-called individual, who always consists of contradictory drives" (p. 44). During his lifetime Fleck courageously resisted the German fascist regime, but more importantly, he provided inspiration for a whole range of postwar social theories of science from Thomas Kuhn to Bruno Latour. But the main reason to signal a science studies approach as germane to the problem of defining neoliberalism is that *they share a substantial amount of theoretical orientation in common.* For instance, Charles Thorpe has recently suggested that "the political concerns of science studies have pivoted around the formulation and criticism of liberalism" (2008, 63). Science and technology studies (STS) has been suspicious of liberal appeals to expertise to depoliticize politics and is skeptical of the temptation to reify the scientific community as an ideal model for the liberal order, just as the neoliberals have done. More to the point, both approaches adopt the position that perception and cognition are not directly determined as unique representations of an independently given objective world;[18] for instance, the impossibility of objective knowledge lies at the very heart of Hayek's notion of the market as the ultimate prosthesis for the process of the discovery of knowledge. Indeed, the dominant epistemic orientation of both science studies and neoliberalism could justly be called "constructivist," a commonality that will require further consideration shortly.

Consequently, in this volume we made use of the Mont Pèlerin Society network of organized neoliberal intellectuals and closely related roster of neoliberal partisan think tanks as our Rosetta Stone, a handy detection device to identify the relevant actors, and their linkages to other organizations and institutions.[19] At least until the 1980s—when the advance of neoliberal ideas led to a rapid multiplication of pretenders to the title of progenitors of neoliberalism—the MPS network can be safely used as cipher to decode with sufficient precision the neoliberal thought style in the era of its genesis. While arguably diminishing in importance over the last few decades, the MPS has nonetheless sustained an array of important functions that continue to shape the further development of neoliberalism, as well as related think tank networks.[20]

Mont Pèlerin should serve as our talisman primarily because it exists as part of a rather special structure of intellectual discourse, perhaps unprecedented

back in the 1940s, one we tend to think of as a "Russian Doll" approach to the
integration of research and *praxis* in the modern world. The neoliberal thought
collective was structured very differently from the other "invisible colleges"
that sought to change people's minds in the second half of the twentieth century. Unlike most intellectuals in the 1950s, the early protagonists of MPS did
not look to the universities or the academic "professions" or to interest group
mobilizations as the appropriate primary instruments to achieve their goals.
The early neoliberals felt (at that juncture with some justification) that they
were excluded from most high-profile intellectual venues in the West. Hence
the MPS was convened as a private members-only debating society whose participants were handpicked (originally primarily by Hayek, but later through a
closed nomination procedure) and who consciously sought to remain out of
the public eye. The purpose was to create a special space where people of like-
minded political ideals could gather together to debate the outlines of a future
movement diverging from classical liberalism, without having to suffer the in-
dignities of ridicule for their often blue-sky proposals, but also to evade the
Fifth Column reputation of a society closely aligned with powerful but dubious postwar interests. Even the name of the society was itself chosen to be relatively anodyne, signaling little in the way of substantive content to outsiders
(Hartwell 1995, 44). Many members would indeed hold academic posts in a
range of academic disciplines, but this was not a precondition of MPS membership. MPS could thus also be expanded to encompass various powerful capitalist agents. One then might regard specific academic departments where the
neoliberals came to dominate before 1980 (University of Chicago, the LSE,
L'Institut Universitaire des Hautes Etudes Internationales at Geneva, St. Andrews in Scotland, Freiburg, the Virginia School) as the next outer layer of the
Russian Doll, one emergent public face of the thought collective—although
one often never publicly linked to the MPS. Another shell of the Russian Doll
was fashioned as the special-purpose foundations for the education and promotion of neoliberal doctrines, such as the Volker Fund, the Relm Foundation,
the Lilly Endowment, and others (see Phillips-Fein, Chapter 8 in this volume).
These institutions were often set up as philanthropic or charitable units, if only
to protect their tax status and pretense of lack of bias.[21] The next shell would
consist of general-purpose "think tanks" (Institute of Economic Affairs, American Enterprise Institute, Schweizerisches Institut für Auslandforschung) that
sheltered neoliberals, who themselves might or might not also be members in
good standing of various academic disciplines. The think tanks then developed
their own next layer of protective shell, often in the guise of specialized satellite

think tanks poised to get quick and timely position papers out to friendly politicians or to provide talking heads for various news media and opinion periodicals.[22] Further outer shells have been innovated as we get closer to the present—for instance, "Astroturfed" organizations consisting of supposedly local grassroots members, frequently organized around religious or single-issue campaigns. Outsiders would rarely perceive the extent to which individual protagonists embedded in a particular shell served multiple roles, or the strength and pervasiveness of network ties, since they could never see beyond the immediate shell of the Russian Doll right before their noses. This also tended to foster the impression of those "spontaneous orders" so beloved by the neoliberals, although they were frequently nothing of the sort. Yet the loose coupling defeated most attempts to paint the thought collective as a strict conspiracy.[23] In any event, it soon became too large to qualify.

The MPS construction of neoliberalism was anchored by a variety of mainly European and American roots; encompassed a variety of economic, political, and social schools of thought; and maintained a floating transnational agora for debating solutions to perceived problems and a flexible canopy tailored with an eye to accommodating existing relations of power in academia, politics, and society at large. The unusual structure of the thought collective helps explain why neoliberalism cannot be easily defined on a set of 3 by 5 cards and needs to be understood as a pluralist organism striving to distinguish itself from its three primary foes: laissez-faire classical liberalism, social welfare liberalism, and socialism. Contrary to some parochial interests of some corporate captains (including some present in the Mont Pèlerin Society), neoliberal intellectuals understood this general goal to imply a comprehensive long-term reform effort at retatting the entire fabric of society, not excluding the corporate world. The relationship between the neoliberals and capitalists was not merely that of passive apologists or corporate shills.[24] Neoliberals aimed to develop a thoroughgoing reeducation effort for *all parties* to alter the tenor and meaning of political life: nothing more, nothing less.[25] Neoliberal intellectuals identified their targets, which, in Fabian tradition, had been described as elite civil society. Their efforts were aimed primarily at winning over intellectuals and opinion leaders of future generations, and their primary tool was redefining the place of knowledge in society, which also became the central theme in their theoretical tradition. As Hayek said in his address to the first meeting of the MPS:

> But what to the politicians are fixed limits of practicability imposed by public opinion must not be similar limits to us. Public opinion on these matters

is the work of men like ourselves . . . who have created the political climate in which the politicians of our time must move. . . . I am sure that the power of vested interests is vastly exaggerated compared with the gradual encroachment of ideas. (Quoted in Cockett 1995, 112)

One might have added, how much more powerful are ideas consciously forged with the vested interest firmly kept in mind! Not without admiration, we have to concede that neoliberal intellectuals struggled through to a deeper understanding of the political and organizational character of modern knowledge and science than did their opponents, and therefore present a worthy contemporary challenge to everyone interested in the history of science and the archaeology of knowledge.

Although the role of national institutions is indispensable in explaining the advance (or retardation) of specific doctrines across countries, as Peter Hall's (1989) book on Keynesianism has shown, the origins and the advance of neoliberalism cannot be explained without careful consideration of the transnational discourse community created by the founders of the Mont Pèlerin Society. Unlike previous histories of ideas, and taking a page from Hayek's playbook, we have offered an account that strives to understand the fortification of the power of ideas through integration of highly dispersed knowledge capacities within a neoliberal international academy. Whereas leading neoliberals denied any possibility of mere mortals outcompeting the market as processors of highly dispersed knowledge, their own efforts succeeded in constructing and deploying elaborate social machinery designed to collect, create, debate, disseminate, and mobilize neoliberal ideas. By doing so, they greatly advanced the understanding of a modern reengineered division of intellectual labor with proper roles assigned to academic and other professionals, in what amounts to a new technology of persuasion.

The Russian Doll of neoliberal organization was never intended to be transparent; the central core was not supposed to be visible from the think tank perimeter. The way it has evolved over half a century is not very easy to comprehend because neoliberal intellectuals guarded their privacy and prerogatives well. However, both an in-house history (Hartwell 1995) and a critical history (Walpen 2004) have unscrewed the multiple layers to some extent, providing a general overview with regard to the evolution of the neoliberal thought collective. Owing to the wide range of participants, countries, discourses and policy fields, controversies, questions, and battles to be tackled, many more detailed accounts will be required to fully understand its history. This book is the first sustained effort to dig deeper into some of the more important communities in countries frequently overlooked when it comes to neoliberalism (France, UK, and Germany). We aim to show that it is not enough to rest satisfied merely pointing at the seemingly potent generic political power of economic ideas, as did both John Maynard Keynes and Friedrich Hayek. The contributions to this book have been written to better understand the political and economic power of neoliberal ideas as they have played out in philosophy, economics, law, political science, history, sociology and many other disciplines.

A Neoliberal Primer

As the Introduction by Dieter Plehwe argued, no convenient or comprehensive Ten Commandments of neoliberalism ever issued from the bowels of the MPS. Even though the neoliberal thought collective persists in flexibly debating, incorporating, and rejecting new tenets and concepts, the reader has every right to expect some sort of summary statement of the doctrine, if only accompanied by the caveat that none of it is (or ever would be) inscribed in stone. Indeed, the purpose of this volume is to reveal the outlines of the construction of the doctrine in action, highlighting the ways in which various sectors and squadrons diverged from classical liberalism (and each other) in the course of their intellectual and political activities. Nevertheless, a half-century of experience has endowed us with sufficient distance to realize that there really is something distinctive that holds the neoliberal thought collective together other than mere expediency, and further, that it has enjoyed very real doctrinal purchase in the modern political arena. Many other scholars have struggled with this observation, and in our opinion, have written off the movement too quickly as a mere epiphenomenon of a certain type of economics. Two examples:

> Neoliberalism is perhaps most tellingly viewed as a sort of caricature of liberalism, where liberal concerns for individual liberty, political equality and human rights have been warped into a purely economic ideology whose concerns lie with the establishment of free markets and in keeping state intervention in such markets at bay. Neoliberalism thus understood is primarily a theory of how the economy ought to be organized, and not a political ideology in the same sense as political liberalism. (Thorsen and Lie 2006, 15)

Neoliberalism is commonly used in at least five different ways in the study of development—as a set of economic policies, a development model, an ideology, an academic paradigm, and an historical era. Moreover, beyond a shared emphasis on the free market and frequent connotations of radicalism and negativity, it is not immediately clear how these varied uses are interconnected. (Boas and Gans-Morse 2006, 38)

One advantage of approaching the thought collective through the MPS is that we immediately realize just how flawed any such definition must be. After all, as Hayek insisted in his opening address to the MPS in 1947, "a political philosophy can never be based exclusively on economics, or expressed mainly in economic terms" (1967, 150). Clearly, some of the less sophisticated MPS members might not have seemed to have faithfully adhered to that injunction—say, Milton Friedman, or Gary Becker—but keeping the entire thought collective in our sights acts as a protopaeduetic. Of course, there is no denying that the neoliberals have made their greatest inroads of all the professions into the field of economics.[26]

Nevertheless, the endeavor here is to provide a concise and necessarily incomplete characterization of the temporary configuration of doctrines that the thought collective had arrived at by roughly the 1980s. It transgresses disciplinary boundaries in precisely the ways the neoliberals have done. To circumvent questions of the extent of adherence or dissension from our telegraphed list, or indeed to renounce any attempt to bring them all up to date, we provide the tenets as bare statements, without much elaboration or full documentation. With apologies, this can be mitigated because we can direct the reader to the rest of this volume as partial elaboration of the individual tenets, as well as to the numerous works cited in the references in this volume.

1. The starting point of neoliberalism is the admission, contrary to classical liberal doctrine, that *their vision of the good society will triumph only if it becomes reconciled to the fact that the conditions for its existence must be* **constructed** and will not come about "naturally" in the absence of concerted political effort and organization. As Foucault presciently observed in 1978 (2004, 137), "Neoliberalism should not be confused with the slogan 'laissez-faire,' but on the contrary, should be regarded as a call to vigilance, to activism, to perpetual interventions" [our translation].[27] The injunction *to act* in the face of inadequate epistemic warrant is the very soul of "constructivism," an orientation shared (curiously enough) with the field of science studies. Classical liberalism and Burkean

conservatism, by contrast, disavowed this precept. The fact that during one phase of his career Hayek railed against something he called "constructivism" should not obscure this important fact. This becomes transmuted below into various arguments for the existence of a strong state as both producer and guarantor of a stable market society.

2. This assertion of a constructivist orientation raises the pressing issue of just what sort of ontological entity the neoliberal market is, or should be. While one wing (the Chicago School) has made its name attempting to reconcile one idiosyncratic version of neoclassical economic theory (which predates neoliberalism by more than a half-century) with this "nonnatural" orientation, other subsets of MPS have innovated entirely different characterizations of the market. The Misean wing of Austrian economics attempted to ground the market in a purely rationalist version of natural necessity. Perhaps the dominant version at MPS emanated from Hayek himself, wherein "*the market" is posited to be an information processor more powerful than any human brain, but essentially patterned on brain/computation metaphors.*[28] This version of the market is most intimately predicated on the epistemic doctrines covered above, which in the interim have become the philosophical position most closely associated with the neoliberal *Weltanschauung.*

From this perspective, prices in an efficient market "contain all relevant information" and therefore cannot be predicted by mere mortals. In this version, the *market always surpasses the state's ability to process information,* and this constitutes the kernel of the argument for the necessary failure of socialism. Another partially rival approach emanates from ordoliberalism, which argues that competition in a well-functioning market needs to be directly organized by the state. It is important to see that part of the function of MPS discussions was to explore whether these rather divergent visions of the market might nevertheless lead to more or less identical programs for state intervention in creating and sustaining a market society.

3. Even though the market is not treated as existing independently of the social and cultural framework, and there was no consensus on just what sort of animal the market "really" is, the neoliberals did agree that for purposes of public understanding and sloganeering, *market society must be treated as a "natural" and inexorable state of humankind.*

What this meant in practice is that natural science metaphors must be integrated into the neoliberal narrative. It is noteworthy that MPS members began to explore the portrayal of the market as an evolutionary phenomenon long before biology displaced physics as the premier science in the modern world-picture.[29] If the market was just an information processor, so too was the gene in its ecological niche. Because of this early commitment, neoliberalism was able to make appreciable inroads into such areas as evolutionary psychology, network sociology, ecology, animal ethology, linguistics, cybernetics, and even science studies.

4. A primary ambition of the neoliberal project is to *redefine the shape and functions of the state, not to destroy it.* Neoliberals thus maintain an uneasy and troubled alliance with their sometimes fellow travelers, the anarchists and libertarians. The contradiction that the neoliberals constantly struggle against is that a strong state can just as easily thwart their program as implement it; hence, they are inclined to explore new formats of techno-managerial governance that protect their ideal market from what they perceive as unwarranted political interference. Considerable efforts have been developed to disguise or otherwise condone in rhetoric and practice the importance of the strong state that neoliberals endorse in theory. One implication is that democracy, ambivalently endorsed as the appropriate state framework for an ideal market, must in any case be kept relatively impotent, so that citizen initiatives rarely change much of anything ("constrained" democracy instead of the allegedly existing "unconstrained democracy").[30] Hence, the neoliberals seek to restructure the state with numerous audit devices (under the sign of "accountability") or better yet, convert state services to be provided on a contractual basis. One should not confuse marketization of government functions with shrinking the state, however: if anything, bureaucracies become more unwieldy under neoliberal regimes.[31] In practice, "deregulation" cashes out as "re-regulation," only under a different set of ukases.

5. Skepticism about the lack of control of democracy is offset by the persistent need to provide a reliable source of popular legitimacy for the neoliberal market state. *Neoliberals seek to transcend the intolerable contradiction by treating politics as if it were a market and promoting an economic theory of democracy.* In its most advanced manifestation, there is

no separate content of the notion of citizenship other than as customer of state services.[32] This supports the application of neoclassical
economic models to previously political topics; but it also explains
why *the neoliberal movement must seek to consolidate political power by
operating from within the state.* (This is the topic of our final section.)
The spread of market relations is inevitably spearheaded by state actors. The abstract rule of law is frequently conflated with or subordinated to conformity to the neoliberal vision of an ideal market. The
"night-watchman" version of the state is thus comprehensively repudiated: there is no separate sphere of the market, fenced off, as it were,
from the sphere of civil society. Everything is fair game for marketization.

6. *Neoliberals extol freedom as trumping all other virtues; but the definition
   of freedom is recoded and heavily edited within their framework.* Some
   members of the neoliberal thought collective (e.g., Friedman) refuse
   to define it altogether, while others (Hayek) forge links to thesis 2. by
   motivating it as an epistemic virtue (Hayek 1960, 81). In practice,
   Freedom is not the realization of any political, human, or cultural *telos,* but rather is the positing of autonomous self-governed individuals,
   all coming naturally equipped with a neoclassical version of rationality
   and motives of ineffable self-interest, striving to improve their lot in
   life by engaging in market exchange.[33] Education is consequently a
   consumer good, not a life-transforming experience. Foucault is often
   strongest on the role of these "technologies of the self," which involve
   an elaborate revision in cultural concepts of human freedom and
   morality. This argument broke out within the MPS in the 1970s, with
   Irving Kristol accusing Friedman and Hayek of depending on a version of self-realization as the great empty void at the center of their
   economic doctrines.[34]

   Freedom can only be "negative" for neoliberals (in the sense of Isaiah
   Berlin) for one very important reason. Freedom cannot be extended
   from the use of knowledge *in* society to the use of knowledge *about* society, because self-examination concerning why one passively accepts
   local and incomplete knowledge leads to contemplation of how market
   signals create some forms of knowledge and squelch others. Knowledge
   then assumes global dimensions, and this undermines the key doctrine
   of the market as transcendental superior information processor.

7. Neoliberals begin with a presumption that *capital has a natural right to flow freely across national boundaries. (The free flow of labor enjoys no similar right.)* Since that entails persistent balance-of-payments problems in a nonautarkic world, neoliberals took the lead in inventing all manner of transnational devices for the economic and political discipline of nation-states.[35] They began by attempting to reintroduce pure market discipline (through flexible exchange rates, dismantling capital controls), but over the longer term learned to appreciate that suitably staffed international institutions like the World Trade Organization, the World Bank, and the IMF are better situated to impose neoliberal policies on recalcitrant nation-states. Initially strident neoliberal demands to abolish global financial institutions were tempered once the neoliberals used them primarily to influence staffing and policy decisions at those institutions, and thus to displace other internationalist agendas. Thus, it is substantially correct to observe an organic connection between such phenomena as the Washington Consensus and the spread of neoliberal hegemony (see Plehwe in the Introduction to this volume). This also helps address the neoliberal conundrum of how to both hem in and at the same time obscure the strong state identified in point 4 above.

8. *Neoliberals see pronounced inequality of economic resources and political rights not as an unfortunate by-product of capitalism, but as a necessary functional characteristic of their ideal market system.* Inequality is not only the natural state of market economies, but it is actually one of its strongest motor forces for progress. Hence the rich are not parasites, but (conveniently) a boon to humankind. People should be encouraged to envy and emulate the rich. Demands for equality are merely the sour grapes of the losers, or at minimum, the atavistic holdovers of old images of justice that must be extirpated from the modern mindset. As Hayek wrote, "the market order does not bring about any close correspondence between subjective merit or individual needs and rewards" (1967, 172). The vast worldwide trend toward concentration of incomes and wealth since the 1990s is therefore the playing out of a neoliberal script.

9. *Corporations can do no wrong, or at least they are not to be blamed if they do.* This is one of the strongest areas of divergence from classical liberalism, with its ingrained suspicion of joint-stock companies and

monopoly stretching from Adam Smith to Henry Simons. In the
1950s, the MPS set out entertaining suspicions of corporate power,
with the ordoliberals especially concerned with the promotion of a
strong antitrust capacity on the part of the state. But starting with the
Chicago law and economics movement (see Van Horn, Chapter 6 in
this volume) and then progressively spreading to treatments of entrepreneurs and the "markets for innovation," neoliberals began to argue
consistently that not only was monopoly not harmful to the operation
of the market, but in any event, it was an epiphenomenon attributable
to the misguided activities of the state and interest groups. The socialist
contention that capitalism bore within itself the seeds of its own arte-
riosclerosis (if not self-destruction) was baldly denied (Bair, Chapter 10
in this volume). By the 1970s, antitrust policies were generally repudiated in America. Neoliberals took the curious anomaly in American
case law, treating corporations as legal individuals (Nace 2003), and
tended to inflate it into a philosophical axiom. Indeed, if anything negative was ever said about the large corporation, it was that separation of
ownership from control might conceivably pose a problem, but this
was easily rectified by giving CEOs appropriate incentives (massive
stock options, golden handshakes, latitude beyond any oversight) and
instituting market-like evaluation systems within the corporate bureaucracy Thus the modern reengineering of the corporation (reduced vertical integration, outsourcing supply chains, outrageous recompense
for top officers) is itself an artifact of the neoliberal reconceptualization
of the corporation.

10. *The market (suitably reengineered and promoted) can always provide so-
    lutions to problems seemingly caused by the market in the first place.*
    This is the ultimate destination of the constructivist orientation
    within neoliberalism. Any problem, economic or otherwise, has a
    market solution, given sufficient ingenuity: pollution is abated by the
    trading of emissions permits; inadequate public education is rectified
    by vouchers; auctions can adequately structure communication chan-
    nels (Nik-Khah 2008); poverty-stricken sick people lacking access to
    healthcare can be incentivized to serve as guinea pigs for clinical drug
    trials; financial crisis can be rectified by the government auctioning
    off "toxic assets"; McCarthyism was thwarted by competition be-
    tween employers (Friedman 1962, 20); terrorism by disgruntled

disenfranchised foreigners can be offset by a "futures market in terrorist acts."[36] Ultimately, fortified intellectual property rights tended
to reify Hayek's utopia, if not his explicit vision: because the marketplace is deemed to be a superior information processor, all human
knowledge can only be used to its fullest if it is comprehensively
owned and priced.[37]

11. *The neoliberals have struggled from the outset to make their politi-
cal/economic theories do dual service as a moral code.* First and foremost,
the thought collective worshiped at the altar of a God without restraints: "individual freedom, which it is most appropriate to regard as
a moral principle of political action. Like all moral principles, it demands that it be accepted as a value in itself" (Hayek 1960, 68). However, Hayek in his original address to the first MPS meeting said, "I
am convinced that unless the breach between true liberal and religious
convictions can be healed, there is no hope for a revival of liberal
forces" (1967, 155). The very first MPS meeting held a session on "Liberalism and Christianity" (Hartwell 1995, 47). Yet the neoliberals were
often tone-deaf when it came to the transcendental, conflating it with
their epistemic doctrines concerning human frailty: "we must preserve
that indispensable matrix of the uncontrolled and non-rational which
is the only environment wherein reason can grow and operate effectively" (Hayek 1960, 69). It took a lot of effort, but the intellectual accommodation of the religious right and the theocons within the neoliberal framework has been an ongoing project at the MPS,[38] although
one fraught with contradictions that have dogged the liberal project
since the Enlightenment.

Freedom and the Double Truth of Neoliberalism

Like all really powerful political movements, neoliberalism attempts to reconcile any number of implacable antinomies by repeatedly squaring the circle.
This goes some distance in explaining why, by the late 1950s, the neoliberal
thought collective abruptly stopped asserting they were engaged in the construction of a "new liberalism" and subsequently suppressed all notions of a
rupture with previous classical liberal doctrines, contrary to all evidence. The
more perceptive commentators on the phenomenon of auto-validation had
come to realize that something novel was afoot, in particular by identifying

neoliberalism as an authoritarian variant of the liberal tradition. As early as 1955, Carl Friedrich noted that neoliberals "are fond of quoting Benjamin Constant: 'The government beyond its proper sphere ought not to have any power; within its sphere, it cannot have enough of it' " (1955, 513). Karl Polanyi, brother of the MPS member Michael Polanyi, deftly captured the dynamic:

> [T]he road to the free market was opened and kept open by an enormous increase in continuous, centrally organized and controlled interventionism. . . . Administrators had to be constantly on the watch to ensure the free working of the system. Thus even those who wished most ardently to free the state from all unnecessary duties, and whose whole philosophy demanded the restriction of state activities, could not but entrust the state with new powers, organs and instruments required for the establishment of *laissez faire*. (1957, 140)

By the later 1980s, when the MPS members began to smell the tang of victory, they felt free to *internally* discuss an irony that they could not freely admit out at the nether layers of their Russian Doll:

> Among our members, there are some who are able to imagine a viable society without a state. . . . For most of our members, however, social order without a state is not readily imagined, at least in any normatively preferred sense. . . . Of necessity, we must look at our relations with the state from several windows, to use the familiar Nietzschean metaphor. . . . Man is, and must remain, a slave to the state. But it is critically and vitally important to recognize that ten per cent slavery is different from fifty per cent slavery.[39]

Apparently, one could reconcile oneself to live in a world where quantitatively more state apparat abided with quantitatively less slavery (or serfdom), which should quell the rather naive hand-wringing one sometimes encounters, complaining that a quarter-century of neoliberal ascendancy has done little to reduce the size of the state, no matter how you choose to measure it (Prasad 2006, 7–12).

I would be remiss if I fostered the impression that *every* attempt to square the circle met with universal acclaim within the Mont Pèlerin Society. Perhaps the most fraught attempts to wave away contradiction have come with the persistent threat of schism over what might be called the Pragmatist vs. Romanticist wings of neoliberalism. Hayek himself admitted this in the mid-1980s, when he warned of "the constant danger that the Mont Pèlerin Society might split into a Friedmanite and Hayekian wing."[40] Mark Skousen (2005, 1)

POSTFACE

writes, "Anyone who has ever attended a Mont Pèlerin Society meeting will quickly attest that this international group of freedom-fighters are divided into two camps: followers of the Austrian School and followers of the Chicago School." There is a tendency to reduce the conflict to personalities or schools, but I believe the schism actually runs much deeper. It begins with what seems to be just another one of those impossible balancing acts so beloved by the thought collective: namely, to reject the mechanical image of how society works portrayed within neoclassical economic theory (e.g., Hayek, ordoliberals, Austrians) *while simultaneously* accepting jury-rigged versions of neoclassical economics that would dovetail with their own a priori policy preferences (e.g., Friedman, Becker, and Stigler). But this compromising position became more awkward with the passage of time: should the neoliberals make a pact with "orthodox" economic theory as substantially correct, bending it to their political ends, or should they plump for a wholesale revision of economic theory? Because an impressive phalanx of MPS members have managed to redirect orthodox neoclassical economic theory in a decidedly neoliberal direction since the 1980s, with innovations ranging from monetarism to human capital to efficient markets theory to public choice theory, it would seem that the Chicago Pragmatist strategy has carried the day; but that would be too hasty an assessment of the modern situation. The Chicago faction did indeed achieve early fame and success, but insiders often perceived that this happened because they were relatively shallow intellectually and that their approach to political action was insufficiently assertive and constructivist. Cultural differences were also factored into the equation, with Chicago being a little too "American" and "scientistic" for more refined European tastes. From an outsider's perspective, it does seem that over the longer haul the intellectual innovations of the Chicago wing have exhibited less staying power; many of the eleven tenets outlined in the previous section have fairly clear origins, if not thorough inspiration, in the Hayekian/Austrian wing instead.

Neoliberals tamed many of the contending contradictory conceptions by trying to have it both ways: to warn of the perils of expanding the purview of state activity *while simultaneously* imagining the strong state of their liking rendered harmless through some instrumentality of "natural" regulation; to posit the free market as an ideal generator and a conveyor belt of information *while simultaneously* prosecuting a "war of ideas" on the ground strenuously and ruthlessly (Blundell 2003); asserting that their program would lead to unfettered economic growth and enhanced human welfare *while simultaneously* suggesting that no human mind could ever really know any such thing, and therefore that it was illegitimate to justify their program by its consequences (Shearmur 1996); to portray the market as the *ne plus ultra* of all human institutions, *while simultaneously* suggesting that the market is in itself insufficient to attain and nourish the transeconomic values of a political, social, religious and cultural character (Megay 1970). "Neoliberal writings on allocation shift back and forth between libertarian and utilitarian vocabularies, with the two sometimes appearing interchangeably within a paper or chapter" (Oliver 1960).

Perhaps the greatest incongruity of the neoliberal thought collective has been that the avatars of freedom drew one of their most telling innovations from the critique of liberalism that had been mounted by totalitarian German and Italian political thinkers from the interwar period. Although a fair number of such writers were important for the European MPS members, the one that comes up time and again in their footnotes was the figure whom Hayek called, "Adolf Hitler's crown jurist Carl Schmitt, who consistently advocated the replacement of the 'normative' thinking of liberal law by a conception of law which regards as its purpose 'concrete order formation'" (1967, 169). It is a watchword among those familiar with the German literature (Christi 1984, 532; Scheuerman 1999, chapter 8) that Hayek reprises much of Schmitt's thesis that liberalism and democracy should be regarded as antithetical:

> Liberalism and democracy, although compatible, are not the same . . . the opposite of liberalism is totalitarianism, while the opposite of democracy is authoritarianism. In consequence, it is at least possible in principle that a democratic government may be totalitarian and that an authoritarian government may act on liberal principles . . . [in] demanding unlimited power of the majority, [democracies] become essentially anti-liberal (1967, 161).

Since the epistemic innovations covered in our first section informed the MPS thought collective that the masses will never understand the true architecture of social order, and intellectuals will continue to tempt them to intervene and otherwise muck up the market, they felt impelled to propound the central tenet of neoliberalism—that is, that a strong state was necessary to neutralize what he considered to be the pathologies of democracy. The notion of freedom as exercise of personal participation in political decisions was roundly denounced (Hayek 1960, 13): you cannot activate your species being by participation in the polis. Hayek insisted that his central epistemic doctrines about knowledge dictated that freedom must feel elusive for the common man: "Man in a complex society can have no choice but between adjusting himself to what to him must seem the blind forces of the social process and obeying the orders of a superior" (1972, 24). Paraphrasing Walter Benjamin, citizens must learn to forget about their "rights" and instead be given the opportunity to express themselves through the greatest information conveyance device known to humankind, the market.[41] This was not the night watchman state of the classical liberals; this was light-years from John Stuart Mill. The neoliberal thought collective, through the instrumentality of the strong state, sought to *define and institute* the types of markets that they (and not the citizenry) were convinced were the most advanced.[42] In this contention, they were merely echoing Schmitt's position that "only a strong state can preserve and enhance a free-market economy" and "only a strong state can generate genuine decentralization, [and] bring about free and autonomous domains" (quoted in Cristi 1998, 31, 34n7). This notion was echoed (without attribution) by Hayek: "If we proceeded on the assumption that only the exercises of freedom that the majority will practice are important, we would be certain to create a stagnant society with all the characteristics of unfreedom" (Hayek 1960, 32).

One can therefore only second the verdict of Cristi that, "In truth, Hayek owed much to Schmitt, more than he cared to recognize" (1998, 23). For Hayek and the neoliberals, the *Führer* was replaced by the figure of the entrepreneur, the embodiment of the will-to-power for the community, who must be permitted to act without being brought to rational account. While Hayek probably believed that he was personally defending liberalism from Schmitt's withering critique, his own political solution ended up resembling Schmitt's "total state" far more than he cared to admit. If it had been apparent to his audience that he was effectively advocating authoritarian reactionary despotism as a replacement for classical liberalism, it would certainly have not gone down smoothly in the West right after World War II. Furthermore, there was no immediate prospect of a strong authority taking over the American university system (by contrast with Germany in the 1930s) and sweeping the stables clean. In an interesting development that Schmitt did not anticipate, Hayek hit upon the brilliant notion of developing the "double truth" doctrine of neoliberalism—namely, an elite would be tutored to understand the deliciously transgressive Schmittian necessity of repressing democracy, while the masses would be regaled with ripping tales of "rolling back the nanny state" and being set "free to choose"—by convening a closed Leninist organization of counter-intellectuals. There would be no waiting around until some charismatic savior magically appeared to deliver the Word of Natural Order down from the Mont to the awestruck literati.

> This was sometimes admitted by members of Mont Pelerin in public, but only when they felt that their program was in the ascendant: Let's be clear, I don't believe in democracy in one sense. You don't believe in democracy. Nobody believes in democracy. You will find it hard to find anybody who will say that if, that is democracy interpreted as majority rule. You will find it hard to find anybody who will say that at 55% of the people believe the other 45% of the people should be shot. That's an appropriate exercise of democracy. . . . What I believe is not a democracy but an individual freedom in a society in which individuals cooperate with one another.[43]

Christian Arnsperger (2007) has captured the double truth doctrine nicely by insisting that Hayek had denied to others the very thing that gave his own life meaning: the imprimatur to theorize about society as a whole, to personally claim to understand the meaning and purpose of human evolution, and the capacity to impose his vision upon them through a political project verging on totalitarianism. It was, as Arnsperger puts it, a theory to end all theories; not so different from the end of history scenarios so beloved of his epigones. The doctrine of special dispensation for the Elect is a very powerful source of ongoing attraction of neoliberalism for a certain type of person, the feeling of having surrendered to the wisdom of the market by coming to know something most of the nattering crowd can't possibly glimpse: freedom itself must be as unequally distributed as the riches of the marketplace.

One notorious incarnation of the neoliberal double truth doctrine was the participation of numerous MPS members and affiliates in the coup that toppled the elected government of Salvador Allende in Chile in 1973. Milton Friedman spends a good chunk of his autobiography attempting to excuse and explain his actions away; afterward Hayek was also pilloried for his role. It was all just an unfortunate set of exceptional events, they intoned; it was not our fault. But Carl Schmitt taught that sovereignty is defined as the ability to determine the exceptions to the rule of law: "Sovereign is he who decides the state of emergency"; deploying the double truth doctrine in Chile showed that the neoliberals had arrogated sovereignty to themselves. Without recapitulating the fine-grained history of those events in Karin Fischer's article in this volume, our intention here is simply to point out how the neoliberals sought to reconcile their unconditional love of freedom with their support for a military dictatorship when called to account in public:

> LUCIA SANTA-CRUZ: "There is reference in your work to the apparent paradox of dictatorships that may be more liberal than a totalitarian democracy. But it is also true that dictatorships have other characteristics which contradict freedom, even if it is understood negatively as you do."
>
> HAYEK: "Evidently dictatorships pose grave dangers. But a dictatorship may limit itself *(se puede autolimitar),* and if self-limited it may be more liberal in its policies than a democratic assembly that knows of no limitations. I must admit that it is not very probable that this may happen, but even so, in a given moment, it may be the only hope. Not a sure hope because it may always depend on the good will of an individual and one can trust in very few individuals. But if it is the only opportunity in a given moment, it may be the best solution in spite of all. But only if the dictatorial government visibly leads to a limited democracy."

In the same interview, Hayek is reported to have said: "Democracy has a task which I call 'hygienic,' for it assures that political processes are conducted in a sanitary fashion. It is not an end in itself. It is a rule of procedure whose aim is to promote freedom. But in no way can it be seen in the same rank as freedom. Freedom requires democracy, but I would prefer temporarily to sacrifice, I repeat temporarily, democracy, before having to do without freedom, even if temporarily."—*El Mercurio* (unattributed translation) Sunday, April 19, 1981

Their readers in Chile may not have known it, but this was pure unadulterated Schmitt. If freedom becomes confused with the neoliberal utopia, then power necessarily devolves to an elite of "freedom fighters" who can decide when to invoke the "exception" to traditional mass notions of democracy, justice, and morality.

Notes

Many people contributed to this postface, especially the thought collective convened around this volume. I would particularly like to acknowledge the help of Dieter Plehwe and the referees for Harvard University Press in forcing me to clarify and hone the arguments. Valuable comments were provided by John O'Neill, John Davis, and audiences at Manchester, Oxford, Keele, and the Open University.

1. All primary source material from Mont Pèlerin meetings are quoted with permission from the Liberaal Archief, Ghent, Belgium, and will be cited in this chapter as LAMP, date. The handlist for this collection can be consulted at www.liberaalarchief.be/MPS2005.pdf.

2. These are excerpts from a website last visited October 23, 2006, and are very heavily edited down from a much larger and even more rambling set of texts. Some interesting discussion of the pros and cons of Wikipedia as a source of information are Read (2006); Poe (2006); Scott (2006); and Keen (2007).

3. But things are getting better of late. Naomi Klein (2007) manages to identify some of the key doctrines, especially when she quotes the German political theorist Carl Schmitt: "Sovereign is he who decides the state of emergency" (p. 131). For other sophisticated commentaries, see Apple (2006, 60–61); Ong (2006); Scheuerman (1999).

4. This section is based primarily on Poe (2006); Schiff (2006); and Scott (2006) and the entry "Criticisms of Wikipedia" in Wikipedia.

5. This was confirmed indirectly in a recent interview with Jimmy Wales, founder of Wikipedia, under the heading Greatest misconception about Wikipedia: "We aren't democratic. Our readers edit the entries, but we're actually quite snobby. The core community appreciates when someone is knowledgeable, and thinks some people are idiots and shouldn't be writing" (in Lewine 2007, 30). See also Bauwens (2008).

6. Just so we don't lose sight of Mont Pèlerin here, it is striking to observe that the German neoliberal Wilhelm Röpke made essentially the same observation about that organization forty-five years earlier: "To me, there is something so regrettable that verges on the crudely humorous, that a Society organized to further the search for the principles of a voluntary society of free men, should become rocked to its very roots by a contest for power" (quoted in Hartwell 1995, 123).

7. This paper, first published in 1945, is reprinted in Hayek (1972). Some good discussions on the epistemic principles of Hayek's philosophy are Burczak (2006); Caldwell (2004); O'Neill (2006); and Arnsperger (2007).

8. There is an important conceptual distinction to be made here, brought to my attention by John O'Neill. Hayek himself almost never treated knowledge as a "thing," but instead rather as tacit, local, and embodied—rather similar to the way in which Michael Polanyi described science. However, in order to render this proposition coherent with a number of other tenets later developed in the neoliberal thought collective, many subsequent neoliberals found it convenient to recast knowledge as more resembling a thing-like commodity, if only to have it resonate more closely with developments in the natural sciences and economics. For more on this, see Mirowski (2008).

9. Hayek (1960, 134). As with so much else in Hayek's oeuvre, Carl Schmitt got there first: "Thus the political concept of battle in liberal thought becomes competition in the domain of economics and discussion in the intellectual realm" (2007, 71). See also Scheuerman (1999).

10. "Yes, that means that if the community changes its [sic] mind and decides that two plus two equals five, then two plus two does equal five" (Poe 2006, 93).

11. Or to serve as preprocessor until such time as even Google became fed up with the fetid quality of Wikipedia entities. It is impossible in this brief section to keep up with fast-moving events, such as the launch of "Google Knol" in December 2007, as a version of Wikipedia that would depend to a greater degree on expert supervision of entry amendment. This in itself is a damning comment on the quality of Wikipedia.

12. Hayek (1967, 178). Attacks on "intellectuals" were a common refrain in the history of Mont Pèlerin and were not restricted to Hayek. See, for instance, Hartwell (1995, 161); Friedman (1962, 8). But of course the neoliberals don't renounce *all* expertise—just the stuff they don't like, as explained in this chapter, and in Mirowski (2007; Forthcoming b).

13. One example of the double truth doctrine is that Hayek does admit that "spontaneous order and organization will always coexist" (1973, 48). The codicil for the elect then comes with a rather tendentious rationalization concerning when and how organizations like Mont Pèlerin are legitimate within the doctrine concerning the evolution of natural orders, like, say, its mandate for the construction of market forms that do not already exist.

14. One of the more serious texts to recently commit this error is Thorsen and Lie (2006). James Buchanan clarified the place of economics within the MPS in his presidential address to the 1984 Cambridge meeting: "Professionally, economists have dominated the membership of the Society from its founding, but the whole thrust of the Society, as initially expressed in its founding documents, has been toward elaborating the philosophical ideas without which a free society cannot exist. That is to say, political philosophy is what this Society has been, is, and ought to be all about. And, as Max Hartwell will indicate to you in his paper this week, in the very founding of the Society, Hayek referred explicitly to his aim to set up an international academy of political philosophy" (Buchanan, Address to the 1984 MPS pp. 1–2, LAMP).

15. See, for instance, Hartwell (1995, 84, 93); and Walpen (2004, 1072, 1074).

16. For descriptions of early French precursors, see Laurent (2006, 131) and Denord (2001; 2007).

17. See, for instance, Cockett (1995); Hartwell (1995); Blundell (2003); and Skousen (2005).

18. For further on this similarity, see Burczak (2006); Smith (2005); and Shearmur (1996). "Reason, with a capital R, does not exist in the singular . . . but must be conceived as an interpersonal process in which anyone's contribution is tested and corrected by others" (Hayek 1972, 15).

19. This practice was first advocated in Plehwe and Walpen (2006). One should compare this device to other attempts to define neoliberalism, such as those found in Soederberg, Menz, and Cerny (2005); Cerny (2008); Robison (2006); Boas and Gans-Morse (2006); and Castree (2008) to see how it is necessary to go beyond the ineffectual observation that the neoliberals are "fractured" or otherwise diverse.

20. See, for instance, www.atlasusa.org, which describes how the Atlas Economic Research Foundation was founded in 1981 by Antony Fisher to assist others in establishing

neoliberal think tanks in their own geographic locations. It claims to have had a role in founding a third of all world "market-oriented" think tanks, including the Fraser Institute (Canada), the Center for the Dissemination of Economic Information (Venezuela), the Free Market Center (Belgrade), the Liberty Institute (Romania), and Unirule (Beijing). For more on the situation in the EU, see Corporate Europe Observatory (2005).

21. See the letter from Smedley to Antony Fisher dated June 25, 1956, quoted in Cockett (1995, 131): "[I]t is imperative we should give no indication in our literature that we are working to educate the Public along certain lines which might be interpreted as having political bias. . . . it might enable our enemies to question the charitableness of our motives."

22. Some important examples are the Heritage Foundation (USA), the Manhattan Institute (USA), the Fraser Institute (Canada), Stiftung Marktwirtschaft (Germany), and Center for a New Europe (Brussels). There are even specialized neoliberal think tanks devoted to science policy, such as the George Marshall Institute, the Annapolis Center, and the Ethics and Public Policy Center; note the anodyne names, hiding the political orientation.

23. See, for instance, the books by Stefancic and Delgado (1996); Sklair (2001); Ong (2006); and Saad-Filho and Johnston (2005). The necessity of distinguishing the building of a thought collective devoted to politics from a conspiracy theory is one major theme of this volume.

24. Some recent attempts to transcend the "echo chamber" account of neoliberalism are Phillips-Fein (2006); Nace (2003); Klein (2007); and Nik-Khah (2008).

25. Insistence on this point has been one of the great strengths of the Foucault-inspired tradition of analysis of neoliberalism, an argument made with great effect by Donzelot (2008).

26. "Despite the waste of . . . possibly one billion dollars in endowing chairs of free enterprise, we have been winning in economics for some time now. We have also done well in law, philosophy and political science. . . . History, moral philosophy and literature are a different matter" (Blundell 2003, 44).

27. See Burchell, Gordon, and Miller (1991); Barry, Osborne, and Rose (1996); and Lemke (2001). Hayek's constructivist struggles with scientism and naturalism are discussed further in Mirowski (2007).

28. This is discussed in greater detail in Caldwell (2004) and Mirowski (2002, 2007, 2008).

29. This is further discussed in Mirowski (forthcoming a). See also McKinnon (2005) and Castree (2008).

30. "Neoliberals tend to perceive democracy as desirable only insofar as democratic institutions encourage the development of the economic system they advocate" (Thorsen and Lie 2006, 20). See also Backhouse (2005) and Waligorski (1990). We elaborate on this tension in the next section.

31. On the modern trend toward privatized military functions, see Singer (2003) and Scahill (2007). The constant bewailing of the size of government as a win-win situation

for neoliberals: they complain about recent growth of government, which they have themselves fostered, use the outrage they fan to "privatize" more functions, which only leads to more spending and a more intrusive infrastructure of government operations.

32. In this regard, the nominally left-liberal tradition of social choice theory (Kenneth Arrow, Amartya Sen, John Rawls) by this criterion is just as neoliberal as the right-wing tradition of the public choice theory of Buchanan and Tullock and the Virginia School. See Amadae (2003) and Arnsperger (2007).

33. On negative rather than positive definitions of freedom, see Berlin [1958](1969) and Smith (1998). Even Berlin, not often considered a supporter of neoliberals, suggests that positive freedom leads inexorably to totalitarian systems. The neoliberal subject is not supposed to be free to meditate on the nature and limits of her own freedom—that is, the dreaded relativism that neoliberals uniformly denounce. On the neoliberal technologies of government of the self, see Rose (1999); Mirowski (2002); and Arnsperger (2007).

34. See Kristol, "Socialism, Capitalism, Nihilism," LAMP, Montreux meeting 1972: "And what if the 'self' that is 'realized' under the conditions of liberal capitalism is a self that despises liberal capitalism, and uses its liberty to subvert and abolish a free society? To this question, Hayek—like Friedman—has no answer."

35. See Helleiner (1994) and Thirkell-White (in Robison 2006).

36. On the ill-fated DARPA "Policy Analysis Market" project, see www.sfgate.com/cgi-bin/article.cgi?file=/c/a/2003/07/29/MN126930.DTL 2006; and Justin Wolfers and Eric Zitzowitz, "Prediction Markets in Theory and Practice," www.dartmouth.edu/~ericz/palgrave.pdf (accessed October 22, 2008).

37. This happened even though Hayek himself opposed strengthened intellectual property at various points in his career, and further, did not think all knowledge could be comprehensively articulated.

38. See, for instance, Long (2000); Linker (2006); Diamond (1995); and Eecke (1982). Hayek tipped his hand on his own approach: "Does liberalism presuppose some set of values which are commonly accepted as faith and in themselves not capable of rational demonstration?" [MPS archives, 1947 meeting] It seems clear from his later writings that he believed this was true about belief in the superiority of market organization itself.

39. James Buchanan, "Man and the State," MPS Presidential talk, August 31, 1986, 2, 11. LAMP, 1986 San Vincenzo, Italy, meeting records.

40. Hayek to Arthur Seldon, May 13, 1985, quoted in Hennecke (2000, 316).

41. Interestingly, here is where Hayek rejected the maximization of utility as the standard equilibrium concept in neoclassical economic theory. Markets don't maximize happiness; rather, "the use of the market mechanism brings more of the dispersed knowledge of society into play than by any other [method]" (1967, 174).

42. Hayek's frequent appeals to a "spontaneous order" often masked the fact that it was neoliberal theorists who were claiming the power to exercise the Schmittian "exception" (and hence constitute the sovereignty of the state) by defining things such as

property rights, the extent of the franchise, constitutional provisions that limit citizen initiatives. As Scheuerman (1999, 216) writes about the comparison to Hayek, "For Carl Schmitt, the real question is *who* intervenes, and *whose* interests are to be served by intervention."

43. Milton Friedman, in an interview transcript posted at www.thecorporation.com/media/Friedman.pdf (accessed October 22, 2008).

References

Amadae, S. M. 2003. *Rationalizing Capitalist Democracy.* Chicago: University of Chicago Press.

Apple, Michael. 2006. *Educating the Right Way.* 2nd ed. London: Routledge.

Arnsperger, Christian. 2007. *Critical Political Economy: Complexity, Rationality, and the Logic of Post-Orthodox Pluralism.* London: Routledge.

Aufderheide, Pat. 2007. "Is Wikipedia the New Town Hall?" *In These Times,* March 12: www.inthesetimes.com/article/3067/ (accessed May 2007).

Backhouse, Roger. 2005. "The Rise of Free Market Economics: Economists and the Role of the State since 1970." In P. Boettke and S. Medema, eds., *The Role of Government in the History of Economic Thought.* Durham, NC: Duke University Press.

Barry, Andrew, T. Osborne, and Nikolas Rose, eds. 1996. *Foucault and Political Reason— Liberalism, Neoliberalism and the Rationalities of Government.* London: UCL Press.

Bauwens, Michel. 2008. "Is Something Fundamentally Wrong with Wikipedia Governance Processes?" http://blog.p2foundation.net/ (accessed March 2008).

Berlin, Isaiah. [1958] 1969. "Two Concepts of Liberty." In *Four Essays on Liberty.* Oxford: Oxford University Press.

Blundell, John. 2003. *Waging the War of Ideas.* 2nd ed. London: Institute of Economic Affairs.

Boas, Taylor, and Jordan Gans-Morse. 2006. "From Rallying Cry to Whipping Boy: The Concept of Neoliberalism in the Study of Development." Paper presented at the Philadelphia meeting of the American Political Science Association.

Boltanski, Luc, and Eve Chiapello. 2005. *The New Spirit of Capitalism.* London: Verso.

Bourdieu, Pierre. 1998. "The Essence of Neoliberalism." *Le Monde Diplomatique,* December 8.

Burchell, Graham, Colin Gordon, and Peter Miller, eds. 1991. *The Foucault Effect.* Chicago: University of Chicago Press.

Burczak, Theodore. 2006. *Socialism after Hayek.* Ann Arbor: University of Michigan Press.

Burgin, Angus. 2007. "The Political Economy of the Early Mont Pèlerin Society." Paper presented at the History of Economics Society meeting, Fairfax, Virginia.

Burns, Jennifer. 2004. "In Retrospect: George Nash's *Conservative Intellectual Movement in America." Reviews in American History* 32(3): 447–462.

Caldwell, Bruce. 2004. *Hayek's Challenge.* Chicago: University of Chicago Press.

Castree, Noel. 2008. "Neoliberalizing Nature." *Environment and Planning A* 40: 131–173.

Cerny, Philip. 2008. "Embedding Neoliberalism: The Evolution of a Hegemonic Paradigm." *Journal of International Trade and Diplomacy* 2: 1–46.

Christi, F. R. 1984. "Hayek and Schmitt on the Rule of Law." *Canadian Journal of Political Science* 17: 521–535.

Cockett, Richard. 1995. *Thinking the Unthinkable: Think Tanks and the Economic Counter-revolution, 1931–83.* London: Fontana.

Corporate Europe Observatory. 2005. "Covert Industry Funding Fuels the Expansion of Radical Rightwing EU Think Tanks." www.corporateeurope.org/stockholmnetwork.html (accessed November 25, 2007).

Cristi, Renato. 1998. *Carl Schmitt and Authoritarian Liberalism.* Cardiff: University of Wales Press.

Cros, Jacques. 1950. *Le "néo-libéralisme" et la revision du libéralisme. Thèse droit.* Toulouse: Imprimerie Moderne.

De Long, J. Bradford. 1990. "In Defense of Henry Simons' Standing as a Classical Liberal." *Cato Journal* 9: 601–618.

Denord, François. 2001. "Aux Origines du neo-liberalism en France." *Le Mouvement Social* 195: 9–34.

Denord, François. 2007. *Neo-liberalisme version française.* Paris: Editions Démopolis.

Diamond, Sara. 1995. *Roads to Dominion.* New York: Guilford Press.

Donzelot, Jacques. 2008. "Michel Foucault and Liberal Intelligence." *Economy and Society* 37: 115–134.

Eecke, Wilfried Ver. 1982. "Ethics in Economics: From Classical Economics to Neoliberalism." *Philosophy and Social Criticism* 9: 145–168.

Fleck, Ludwik. 1979. *The Genesis and Development of a Fact.* Chicago: University of Chicago Press. (Reprint; original 1935).

Foucault, Michel. 2004. *Naissance de la biopolitique: cours au Collège de France, 1978–9.* Paris: Editions Gallimard.

Friedman, Milton. 1951. "Neo-liberalism and Its Prospects." *Farmand,* February 17: 89–93.

Friedman, Milton. 1953. *Essays in Positive Economics.* Chicago: University of Chicago Press.

Friedman, Milton. 1962. *Capitalism and Freedom.* Chicago: University of Chicago Press.

Friedrich, Carl. 1955. "Review: The Political Thought of Neo-liberalism." *American Political Science Review* 49: 509–525.

George, Susan. 1999. "A Short History of Neo-liberalism." www.zmag.org/CrisesCurEvts/Globalism/george.htm (accessed May 2007).

Hall, Peter, ed. 1989. *The Political Power of Economic Ideas: Keynesianism across Nations.* Princeton, NJ: Princeton University Press.

Hardt, Michael, and Antonio Negri. 2000. *Empire.* Cambridge, MA: Harvard University Press.

Hartwell, R. Max. 1995. *A History of the Mont Pèlerin Society.* Indianapolis, IN: Liberty Fund.

Harvey, David. 2005. *A Brief History of Neoliberalism.* New York: Oxford University Press.

Hayek, Friedrich. 1944. *The Road to Serfdom.* Chicago: University of Chicago Press.

Hayek, Friedrich. 1960. *The Constitution of Liberty.* Chicago: University of Chicago Press.

Hayek, Friedrich. 1967. *Studies in Philosophy, Politics and Economics.* New York: Simon & Schuster.

Hayek, Friedrich. 1972 [1948]. *Individualism and Economic Order.* Chicago: Regnery.

Hayek, Friedrich. 1973. *Law, Legislation and Liberty.* Vol. 1. Chicago: University of Chicago Press.

Helleiner, Eric. 1994. *States and the Re-emergence of Global Finance.* Ithaca, NY: Cornell University Press.

Hennecke, Hans Jorg. 2000. *Friedrich August von Hayek: Die tradition der Freiheit.* Düsseldorf: Verlagsgruppe Handelsblatt GmbH.

Hunold, Albert. 1955. "The Mont Pèlerin Society." *World Liberalism,* Spring.

Keen, Andrew. 2007. *The Cult of the Amateur.* New York: Doubleday.

Klein, Naomi. 2007. *The Shock Doctrine.* New York: Henry Holt and Co.

Knight, Frank. 1934. "Economic Theory and Nationalism." In his *Ethics of Competition.* London: Allen & Unwin.

Kristol, Irving. 1972. "Socialism, Capitalism, Nihilism." Unpublished paper presented to MPS.

Larner, Wendy. 2000. "Neoliberalism: Policy, Ideology, Governmentality." *Studies in Political Economy* 63: 5–25.

Laurent, Alain. 2006. *Le Libéralisme Américain.* Paris: Belles Lettres.

Lemke, Thomas. 2001. "The Birth of Bio-politics: Michel Foucault's Lecture at the Collège de France on Neo-liberal governmentality." *Economy and Society* 30: 190–207.

Leonhardt, David. 2002. "Scholarly Mentor to Bush's Team." *New York Times,* December 1.

Lewine, Edward. 2007. "The Encyclopedist's Lair." *New York Times Magazine,* November 18: 30–32.

Linker, Damon. 2006. *The Theocons.* New York: Doubleday.

Lippmann, Walter. 1937. *An Inquiry into the Principles of the Good Society.* Boston: Little, Brown.

Long, D. S. 2000. *Divine Economy: Theology and the Market.* New York: Routledge.

McCluskey, Martha. 2003. "Efficiency and Social Citizenship: Challenging the Neoliberal Attack on the Welfare State." *Indiana Law Journal* 78: 783–878.

McKinnon, Susan. 2005. *Neo-liberal Genetics.* Chicago: Prickly Paradigm Press.

Megay, Edward. 1970. "Anti-Pluralist Liberalism: The German Neoliberals." *Political Science Quarterly* 85: 422–442.

Mirowski, Philip. 2002. *Machine Dreams.* New York: Cambridge University Press.

Mirowski, Philip. 2005. "Sleights of the Invisible Hand: Economists Postwar Interventions in Political Theory." *Journal of the History of Economic Thought,* 27(March): 87–99.

Mirowski, Philip. 2007. "Naturalizing the Market on the Road to Revisionism." *Journal of Institutional Economics* 3: 351–372.

Mirowski, Philip. 2008. "Why There Is (as Yet) No Such Thing as an Economics of Knowledge." In Harold Kincaid, ed., *The Philosophical Foundations of Economic Science.* Oxford: Oxford University Press.

Mirowski, Philip. Forthcoming a. "On the Origins of Some Species of American Evolutionary Economics." Paper presented at the Conference on the Chicago School of Economics, Notre Dame, Indiana, September 2007.

Mirowski, Philip. Forthcoming b. *ScienceMart™: The New Economics of Science.* Cambridge, MA: Harvard University Press.

Nace, Ted. 2003. *Gangs of America.* San Francisco: Berrett-Koehler.

Nash, George. 1976 [1998]. *The Conservative Intellectual Movement in America since 1945.* Wilmington, DE: ISI.

Nicholls, A. J. 1994. *Freedom with Responsibility: The Social Market Economy in Germany.* Oxford: Oxford University Press.

Nik-Khah, Edward. 2008. "A Tale of Two Auctions." *Journal of Institutional Economics* 4: 73–97.

Oliver, Henry, Jr. 1960. "German Neoliberalism." *Quarterly Journal of Economics* 74: 117–149.

O'Neill, John. 2006. "Knowledge, Planning, and Markets." *Economics and Philosophy* 22: 55–78.

Ong, Aihwa. 2006. *Neoliberalism as Exception.* Durham, NC: Duke University Press.

Phillips-Fein, Kim. 2006. "Top-Down Revolution: Businessmen, Intellectuals and Politicians against the New Deal." *Enterprise and Society* 7: 686–694.

Plehwe, Dieter. 2005. "Neoliberal Hegemony." *European Journal of Sociology* 46(3): 559–562.

Plehwe, Dieter, and Bernhard Walpen. 2006. "Between Network and Complex Organization: The Making of Neoliberal Knowledge and Hegemony." In Dieter Plehwe, Bernhard Walpen, and Gisela Neunhöffer, eds., *Neoliberal Hegemony: A Global Critique.* London: Routledge.

Plehwe, Dieter, Bernhard Walpen, and Gisela Neunhöffer, eds. 2005. *Neoliberal Hegemony: A Global Critique.* London: Routledge.

Poe, Marshall. 2006. "The Hive." *Atlantic,* September, 86–94.

Polanyi, Karl. 1957. *The Great Transformation.* Boston: Beacon.

Prasad, Monica. 2006. *The Politics of Free Markets: The Rise of Neoliberal Economic Policies in Britain, France, Germany and the US.* Chicago: University of Chicago Press.

Read, Brock. 2006. "Can Wikipedia Ever Make the Grade?" *Chronicle of Higher Education,* October 27: A31–A36.

Robison, Richard, ed. 2006. *The Neo-liberal Revolution: Forging the Market State*. London: Palgrave.

Rose, Nikolas. 1999. *Powers of Freedom*. Cambridge: Cambridge University Press.

Saad-Filho, Alfredo, and Deborah Johnston, eds. 2005. *Neoliberalism: A Critical Reader*. London: Pluto Press.

Scahill, Jeremy. 2007. *Blackwater: The Rise of the World's Most Powerful Mercenary Army*. New York: Nation Books.

Scheuerman, William. 1999. *Carl Schmitt: The End of Law*. Lanham, MD: Rowman & Littlefield.

Schiff, Stacy. 2006. "Know It All: Can Wikipedia Conquer Expertise?" *New Yorker*, July 31.

Schmitt, Carl. 2007. *The Concept of the Political*. Trans. George Schwab. Chicago: University of Chicago Press.

Scott, Jason. 2006. "The Great Failure of Wikipedia." Speech delivered at Notacon 3, Cleveland, Ohio; available at www.cow.net/transcript.txt, last visited November 14, 2007.

Shearmur, Jeremy. 1996. *Hayek and After*. London: Routledge.

Singer, P. W. 2003. *Corporate Warriors*. Ithaca, NY: Cornell University Press.

Sklair, Leslie. 2001. *The Transnational Capitalist Class*. Oxford: Blackwell.

Skousen, Mark. 2005. *Chicago and Vienna*. Washington, DC: Capital Press.

Smith, Barbara Herrnstein. 2005. *Scandalous Knowledge: Science, Truth and the Human*. Durham, NC: Duke University Press.

Smith, Vardaman. 1998. "Friedman, Liberalism, and the Meaning of Negative Freedom." *Economics and Philosophy* 14: 75–94.

Soederberg, Susan, George Menz, and Philip Cerny, eds. 2005. *Internalizing Globalization: The Rise of Neoliberalism*. London: Palgrave.

Steel, Ronald. 1980. *Walter Lippmann and the American Century*. Boston: Little, Brown.

Stefancic, Jean, and Richard Delgado. 1996. *No Mercy: How Conservative Think Tanks and Foundations Changed America*. Philadelphia: Temple University Press.

Thorpe, Charles. 2008. "Political Theory in Science and Technology Studies." In Ed Hackett, Olga Amsterdamska, Michael Lynch, and Judy Wajcman, eds., *The Handbook of Science and Technology Studies*, 3rd ed. Cambridge, MA: MIT Press.

Thorsen, Dag, and Amund Lie. 2006. "What Is Neoliberalism?" University of Oslo Discussion Paper.

Waligorski, Conrad. 1990. *The Political Theory of the Conservative Economists*. Lawrence: University of Kansas Press.

Walpen, Bernhard, 2004. *Die offenen Feinde und ihre Gesellschaft*. Hamburg: VSA-Verlag.

Zmirak, John. 2001. *William Röpke*. Wilmington, DE: ISI Books.

Contributors

JENNIFER BAIR is Assistant Professor in the Department of Sociology at the University of Colorado.

FRANÇOIS DENORD is Chargé de Recherche at the Centre national de la recherche scientifique (CNRS)–Clersé, Paris France.

KARIN FISCHER is Lecturer at the Project on International Development, University of Vienna.

PHILIP MIROWSKI is Carl Koch Professor of Economics and Policy Studies and the History and Philosophy of Science at the University of Notre Dame.

TIMOTHY MITCHELL is Professor of Politics in the Department of Middle Eastern and Asian Languages and Cultures and the School of International and Public Affairs, Columbia University.

KIM PHILLIPS-FEIN is Assistant Professor of History in the Department of History at New York University.

DIETER PLEHWE is Scientist and Senior Fellow, Social Science Research Centre, Berlin, Department of Internationalization and Organization.

RALF PTAK is Senior Lecturer for Economics at the Institute of Comparative Educational Research and Social Science, University of Cologne (Germany).

YVES STEINER is a Ph.D. candidate in economics at the University of Lausanne (Switzerland), an independent researcher in the history of economic thought, and a journalist for the Swiss weekly *L'Hebdo*.

KEITH TRIBE is an independent scholar and Visiting Senior Research Fellow at the University of Sussex.

ROB VAN HORN is Assistant Professor of Economics at the University of Rhode Island.

Index